W9-BEF-425

Borderland Princess

Tonee
Words cannot
express my appreciation
for your contribution to
this book – Your cartoons are
terrific.
Always
Chuck
Campbell

View of El Paso (1885)

León Trousset (French, c. active 1838-1900)

(Courtesy of El Paso Museum of Art. Gift of Mr. And Mrs. J. Sam Moore, Jr. and family.)

THE BORDERLAND PRINCESS

Consort to Revolutionaries, Mercenaries, Criminals, and Patriots

C.E. Campbell

Historic Biographical Vignettes of the Famous, the Infamous, and the Unsung in El Paso and the Southwest

Green Street Publications

ISBN: 978-0-9904161-3-5

Green Street Publications
P. O. Box 953
Sunset Beach, CA 90742
www.greenstreetpublications.com

For Karen

Contents

Foreword

I will never forget the day I first met Chuck Campbell. I was working in the El Paso archives, reading documents about the Mexico-U.S. borderlands, when in popped a scholar from California, with sparkling eyes and a ready smile. Chuck was no ordinary researcher. A chemist by training, he had spent his career teaching public health science to university students and working with law enforcement officers investigating medical-legal fraud. Now retired, he was embarking on a different journey, one that would take him (among other places) into the El Paso County Historical Society and the University of Texas Special Collections Library, where much of El Paso's colorful four-hundred year history lies buried in drab folders and numbered boxes. His quest was a special one: he was searching for information about his El Paso grandfather, Charles M. Hendricks, MD (1877-1953), founder of the Hendricks-Law Sanatorium in 1909 and founding pioneer of the Sun Bowl (America's second oldest annual football bowl) in 1936.

Genealogy is a "gateway drug" to history and Chuck was soon hooked. Indeed, his publication rate has been nothing short of spectacular: *It's The* Journey (2012), Going the Extra Yard*: An Army Doctor's Odyss*ey (2013), Mines, Cattle, and Rebellion: The History of the Corralitos Ranch (2014), The Price Paid for Victory: A photographic Diary of an American Doctor in WWI. (2015), and now Borderland Princess: Consort to Revolutionaries, Mercenaries, Criminals, and Patriots (2017)—more books packed into a few short years than most historians manage to write in a lifetime. And none of these works are mere biographies or mini-histories. Mines, Cattle, and Rebellion is about the ranching-and-mining industries of northern Mexico and the American Southwest over nearly three centuries and their role as a catalyst for rebellion. Going the Extra Yard is about his grandfather's experience as a colonel and medical doctor in the American Expeditionary Force, but it is also a detailed account of the Western Front that adds to the canon of World War I literature. The same can be said for The Price Paid for Victory: it announces itself as a "photographic diary of an

American Doctor in World War I" but in fact it is a collection of stunning and rare photographs that reveal the totality of the Western Front experience during the years when American "Doughboys" dominated the Ardennes.

It has been my good fortune to keep in touch with Chuck over these past several years, as he continued to dig through historical records and compose his texts. Sometimes our paths would accidentally cross in the El Paso archives. Sometimes we would communicate via email, usually when one or the other of us was stumped by some historical question to which we hoped the other would know the answer. And sometimes we actually managed to set up a meeting in advance for an extended talk about our mutual research. I enjoyed these encounters enormously, not only because they allowed me to pick his brain about local El Paso history, but also because he has an easygoing style and an infectious laugh (not to mention a wonderful and well-informed spouse who often joined our discussions.) I also always had a covert mission to urge him to drop all his other projects and complete Borderland Princess as quickly as possible.

Now, at last, Borderland Princess has appeared and it is everything I hoped it would be! It is a biography of sorts, an intimate history of the magnificent Borderland Princess of downtown El Paso, which for decades played a larger-than-life role in the city's political and civic affairs before she faded from history in 1929. And also like his earlier works, this one is not just a life-and-times story writ small: it's a full-fledged history of early El Paso, from its pioneer days as a stagecoach stop to its emergence as an international railroad hub, gateway to Mexico, and center of intrigue during and after the Mexican Revolution (1910-1920). It's no rags-to-riches booster hurrah story either, but a sober assessment of a border town at a time of enormous growth and turmoil that brought out both the best and worst features of the city (it was no accident that he chose "Consort to Revolutionaries, Mercenaries, Criminals, and Patriots." as his sub-title). To paraphrase Bette Davis's character in All About Eve: "hold onto your armchairs, it's going to be a juicy read!"

Mark Cioc-Ortega, PhD
Professor and Chair of History
Stevenson Academic Services
University of California, Santa Cruz

Preface

Inspiration for a new book comes to the non-fiction writer from a myriad of places: events, emotional experiences, and challenges. Having just completed a six-year research venture that resulted in the publication of my book, Going the *Extra Yard: An Army Doctor's Odyssey,* I was faced with dozens of new potential topics. During the research phase of the earlier book, I had learned of a potential story about a glamorous, if not mythical ingénue, whose influence and escapades along the Mexico-United States border in 1900 was worthy of further exploration.

I met with Southwest historian and author, Leon Metz. Metz was not only the former archivist at the University of Texas at El Paso, but he had also written widely of the great Southwest of the late 1880s and the developing history of El Paso, Texas. Metz's ten books have contributed greatly to the popularization of Southwest history. Metz and I met at his home in August 2006. I presented my idea of exploring the story of the southwest ingénue, the "Borderland Princess." Metz concurred that it was a grand idea and one that was worthy of publication. He did, however, present a single caveat. "Don't do it," he warned, "there is nothing written and you'll waste time, money, and hit insurmountable roadblocks at every turn." "There are dozens of worthy historical issues with which to engage your efforts," he projected fatherly. With the gauntlet dramatically thrown at my feet, I winced under the challenge. As I returned to my home in California, I could not shake my desire to press on with my adventure to learn about the borderland princess.

I eagerly began searching every possible nook and cranny for verifiable and scholarly works that would lead me to success with this challenge. Seven years later, I had acquired more than five thousand books, articles, interviews, letters, and photographs about this elusive story. Out of this effort came the publication of my book, Mines, Cattle, and Rebellion in 2014. Cleary the story of the borderland princess was more than a single volume.

Metz was right. His prophetic warning of roadblocks, blind leads, and huge expenses in time and money surfaced almost immediately. During the first four and a half years I scoured newspaper morgues, university archives, county property records, cemetery documents, recorded oral histories, and libraries of every size and complexity for any reference to the Princess and her family. I also purchased and read more than 150 mostly rare and previously owned books. Many of the published works contained only slight reference to her, while others discussed various aspects of her role in history.

The quest to locate individuals who had a personal connection with her became a daunting challenge. Few people remain alive today who have memories of the Princess' social and political impact. Sadly, it became necessary to rely on secondary published sources that often contained misstatements, errors of fact, and journalistically manufactured comments to make some ancillary point. Author Eric Larson in his successful book, Dead Wake: The Last Crossing of the Lusitania, (New York: Crown, 2015: 541) warns: "One has to be very careful to sift and weigh the things that appear in books already published on the subject. There are falsehoods and false facts, and these, once dropped into the scholarly stream, appear over and over again, with footnotes always leading back to the same culprits." Understanding these pitfalls, extra care was made to corroborate information with multiple sources when possible.

A great deal of time was lost with my efforts at fact checking, validating, and corroborating the information that I discovered. I made serious efforts to locate and contact the living descendants of the Princess' family as well as those who had had either a working or intimate relationship with her. These efforts resulted in ventures to locales throughout Texas as well as New York, California, Florida, Michigan, and Westport Point, Massachusetts. I contacted one descendent in Geneva, Switzerland.

Many alternative sources of historical events were derived from extensive use of previously documented oral histories, memoirs, autobiographies and a series of personal interviews conducted by me over several years. These experiences were extremely valuable knowing the inherent limitations of fading memories and covert agendas, they still provided tremendous insight into life "back then" and add to the details and local color of the story.

By the spring of 2012, I had amassed a collection of nearly six thousand documents, photographs, government records, and interviews. At first glance, it looked like a huge jigsaw puzzle, with thousands of odd pieces scattered about. The task was daunting, yet its completion was clearly in view. It became obvious to me that it lacked first-hand input, information garnered directly from those who were there from the late 1880s to the Princess' horrific demise in 1929. The project needed the inclusion of the records of those whose actions, perceptions, and decisions led to her mystique.

In April 2012, I returned to El Paso to do one more review of documents at the El Paso Public Library and to retrieve copies of newly discovered "old" property records and deeds from the county clerk's office. My wife and research partner, Karen, found an article that we had previously missed that indicated that the Princess' parents were visiting from their home in Brooklyn and were staying at the home of Horace B. Stevens, a local realtor and property manager. Stevens was contracted by the Princess' parents to keep an eye on her comings and goings, to be there for her if things got out of hand, and to bail her out of trouble if she should need it.

We returned to the Special Collections Department of the library at the University of Texas at El Paso. With Karen's keen eye and the dedicated assistance of manuscript archivist Laura Hollingsed and department head Claudia A. Rivers, the personal and business papers of Horace B. Stevens were serendipitously discovered.

The Stevens Papers were a treasure trove of thousands of documents detailing his business ventures and personal reflections of the business community in and around El Paso. Included in the file were letters and correspondence that related to Stevens' overseeing and managing the affairs of the Princess as well as his activities with many of the early pioneers of El Paso including General Anson Mills. Stevens was extremely meticulous in his record keeping and was far from shy in expressing his personal feelings on social, business, and political activities of this bustling young town.

The survival of the Stevens Papers (MS 153) is a miracle in itself. Long after his death, his collected files found their way to the attic of the Mills Building in the heart of El Paso. Discovered at the time of a planned restoration of the building; the dust and bird-dropping covered records were subsequently donated to the Special Collections Department of the University of Texas at El Paso. These papers provide researchers with a magnificent window into the life and times of El Paso during its rise from a village outpost to major commercial center. These tender and fragile documents were carefully photographed, digitized, and cataloged. My pile of puzzle pieces had now almost doubled, but now the personal, first-hand records offered this book a completely new dimension.

At first glance, the reference citations and bibliography may seem exhaustive, but the sheer volume of material collected over the almost ten years of research, dictate their inclusion. The notes and references were placed at the end of each chapter to facilitate quick and easy access rather than trudge through a lengthy section containing all of the entries in one locale. Every effort was made to determine the source and provenance of each photograph and illustration; however, there were a few cases where the source could not be identified. Several of the photos were taken from the public domain, and that source was left blank. Other photographs were of very poor resolution, but their historical significance demanded their inclusion. Many of the historic photographs of El Paso are held in three prominent locations; the El Paso Public Library, the El Paso County Historical Society, and the Special Collections Department of the University of Texas at El Paso. Provenance was given to the individual location where I retrieved the photograph, even though many of the same photographs are held by all three depositories. Photographs and illustrations are placed throughout the book, except for most maps and color plates (Figures 111-125). They have been located at the back of the book just before the bibliography

A word about the Index—the original detailed index for this book of over 500 pages covering such diverse topics, events, places, and people required nearly thirty pages. Consequently, I decided to include a conservative version, highlighting only the major events and people, since the division of the chapters themselves will aid the reader in narrowing down searches.

This book focuses on the relationships between significant events and personages as the Borderland Princess evolved through history. Volumes have been written regarding each of these individuals and historic events. It is, to some degree, necessary to provide a brief background on these stories, but the true emphasis of this tome is the connection between these people and events and their direct relationship with the "Borderland Princess." Captured throughout are biographical vignettes of famous, as well as infamous, historical figures that were connected to the Princess during her glory days. To that end, I have organized this publication into a series of chapters, each focusing on specific events and people who shared some commonality in their relationship with the historical nature of the Borderland Princess as she evolved through the wild days of the close of the 1800s and the first thirty years of the twentieth century.

C.E. Campbell
June 2017
Huntington Beach, CA

Acknowledgements

A special word of appreciation and acknowledgement goes to the authors, contributors, and editors of the El Paso County Historical Society's (EPCHS) publication Password. Its contribution to the preservation of the history of the people, events, and places of this historically rich international region warrants appreciative praise. Most of the authors have done superb due diligence in the preparation of their contributions. Other writers present articles that are firsthand accounts and recollections of valued historical events. For the past sixty-one years, the society has enriched the potential success of all who take advantage of its immense archive of original documents and photographs. Successful completion of research projects at all levels are enhanced by the society's presence and cooperative spirit.

With enthusiasm and willingness to help, Pat Worthington, former EPCHS curator, and Richard Bussell, longtime volunteer archivist, have provided this author with countless hours of assistance over the past ten years. I am especially appreciative of Claudia Rivers, Laura Hollingsed, and Abbie Weiser archivists, of the C.L. Sonnichsen Special Collections Department of the University of Texas at El Paso, who have given so many hours of research assistance, whether in person or by internet communication, during this very protracted research project. This project was further aided by the cooperative assistance of the Archives and Special Collection Department of New Mexico State University, the Arizona State Historical Society, Historical Society of Washington, D.C., the Brooklyn Historical Society, and most significantly by Mr. Danny Gonzalez of the Border Heritage Center of the El Paso Public Library.

The search for the Princess' lineage proved both complicated and time consuming. Following the trail to Massachusetts, Florida, and Switzerland, I am most grateful to Shirley Davenport and Carol Curley, great-granddaughters of Lucius and Harriett Sheldon, who raised and heralded the Princess' early life. I especially appreciate Shirley's effort as she provided me with insight into the family's history and furnished me precious family photographs of her great-grandparents. I am equally appreciative of the contribution made to this writing by Charles and Tony Russell, great-grandsons of Henry King Sheldon. Their recollection of interaction with the Sheldon family added a special dimension to this story. Tony's artistic contribution has added a bit of humor to this project.

I want to express my appreciation to my illustrators and artists whose contribution to this book helped to bring it to life. Specific recognition goes to Jim Cole of Chatham, Massachusetts, and Faina Danielian and Stefani Thomas of Burbank, California for their artistic interpretation of the Borderland Princess. I am deeply indebted to cartographer Michael Shensky of the California State University Long Beach, for his map making skill and I am in awe of Mary Velgos, graphic designer, who so masterfully interpreted my ideas for the cover of this endeavor. To Max Grossman, Joel Guzman, and Bernie Sargent of El Paso, special thanks for responding to my desperate emails regarding confusion over details and issues of historic El Paso photographs. Words cannot express my excitement of Landon Berg's photographic contribution, a young man with a clear and concise eye for architecture and it's photography.

A project as immense as this could only have been concluded with the tireless help of many other university archivists, documentarians, librarians, countless interviewees, and my friends and family who tolerated my repeated withdrawal into my document-encased catacomb.

Dr. Mark Cioc-Ortega and educator Dave Kemp; provided kind and constant encouragement during some of the bleakest days of this effort and for their tireless effort at reviewing the manuscript, I am ever so grateful. Mardee de Wetter, author, poet, nonagenarian extraordinaire and dear friend; her kindness, wit, wisdom, memories, and guidance will be part of me forever. Documentarian Don Ray has constantly provided me with input that always improves the quality of my efforts at telling historical stories. I am ever so indebted to Paul Foster and his magical executive assistant, Teresa Guerra, for helping to bring closure to this fascinating and engrossing adventure. A project of this magnitude survives only because of the hard work and dedication of those on the sidelines.

It is to historian Dr. Gary Shumway that I owe immense gratitude. Gary guided his red pencil through every word and line of this effort, smoothing and challenging my writing so to raise it to its highest level of historical accuracy and presentation.

Finally, a very special word of acknowledgement and heartfelt wishes to author and historian Mr. Leon Metz, for planting the seed that grew into this effort of sharing and bringing to light this magical piece of American history.

Introduction

I honestly beleave it iz better tew know nothing than tew know what ain't so. Henry W. Shaw, 1874[1]

Who is this borderland princess? What was her mystique? How could she manipulate the peoples and governments of two nations so significantly as to alter their infrastructure, patriotism, and finances; bring them to the brink of war and cost one of them a whole generation of their citizens? Was she real or simply Southwest folklore conjured by weary "locals" or journalists to offer solace to a confused populace? Lured by the discovery of gold in California and the promise of riches beyond imagination, a desperate volume of Americans and international immigrants grew anxious for an all-weather transcontinental route from the east. They forged west in huge numbers to find the nirvana promised by the shining cache found in the hills of Sacramento. So intense was the western migration that Congress began in earnest to find a new path to the west. As the dreamers, entrepreneurs, hucksters, and the desperate, trekked west, they founded and formed new communities from Missouri to the Pacific Ocean.

The barons of Wall Street, flushed with European investment funds following the Civil War, looked to the west and its potential, to meet the needs of their growing capitalism. Investments in railroads, mining, and ranching soared. Powerful New York, Boston, and St. Louis families became the driving forces extracting the riches and resources from the new frontier to drive the industrialization of the antebellum era.

Out of the chaos and corruption of war-wracked Mexico, emerged a new and ruthless leader who would ride to power on a theme of promised "non-reelectionism." He was driven to bring his backward and poverty-stricken "new" republic into the modern age, to enter it into the community of world nations as an equal. As his reign continued, Porfirio Diaz became the despotic ruler that not only opened the doors to foreign investment from the United States and Western Europe, but he did so at the expense of the Mexican people. His 37-year reign not only expropriated his country's natural resources, enriched his small and powerful inner circle, the cientificos, but he masterfully sowed the seeds of rebellion and revolution that would drive him into exile and nearly destroy his country as severely as if it had been invaded by a foreign enemy.

Conceived from the collision of these three seemingly unrelated phenomena in the latter part of the nineteenth century: the gold rush, fresh European capital, and an investment-hungry third world country; and sired by capital greed and nurtured by entrepreneurialism fostered by Edison's light bulb and its sudden demand for copper and other ores, a Princess was born.

Groomed by the westward migration of the iron horse and encouraged by the open door policy of a dictator's misguided perception of what was best for his country—the Princess grew from infancy. Her impact far exceeded local history. As she continued to mature, her role in national and international history and intrigue expanded beyond rational expectations. The citizens of Mexico and the United States would never be the same. She was, to say the least, to be reckoned with.

This mature Princess entertained or provided a bed for some of the most famous and infamous men of history. Historically significant characters as: Presidents William McKinley, William Howard, Taft, and Teddy Roosevelt; Mexican President Francisco Madero; American Army General John Pershing and rebel outlaw Pancho Villa were among the hundreds who fell under her mystical spell. The world of photojournalism and news reporting from the scenes of war matured into adulthood under her watchful eye. She even had an extensive relationship with one of the first female war correspondents writing for the American press. These presidents and generals; spies and soldiers of fortune; politicians and industrialists; criminals and lawmen; and writers and journalists were only the individuals she courted. She also left her imprint on the planning, execution, and curtailment of the Mexican Revolution of 1910-1920, the origination of the U.S. Border Patrol and the early formation of the FBI and its efforts at focusing on domestic espionage.

El Paso was a rough and tough "wide-open" town filled with racial diversity, with Anglos and Mexicans working side-by-side with sophisticated souls whose cunning was designed to fleece them of all they owned. Shadows of the legends of Wyatt Earp, John Selman, Billy the Kid, and Jeff Milton lurked in alleys of this dusty West-Texas town. In the early 1880s, four great railroads laid tracks towards El Paso's bars, gaming houses, and bordellos. This was a wicked place, and the Princess was right in the middle of it all.

Was she real or a myth? Is her story apocryphal or the stuff of urban legend? She certainly was real. She was born in El Paso, Texas in 1888 to Lucius and Harriet Sheldon. Lucius was the scion of a wealthy New York investment banking family whose permanent home was Brooklyn, New York. Just as she became a teenager, in 1900, the Princess turned her interest to entertaining and providing services to men, and some women, from all walks of life. She succumbed in a flaming inferno in 1929, at the age of 41. She was born on historic ground and lived a unique and significantly important life, albeit, way too short.

She had become the center of civic and social life of El Paso during most of her life; as the little village on the east side of the Rio Grande grew into a major and significant community of cattle, copper, cotton, and climate, as well as a major railroad hub at the commercial portal into Mexico. El Paso today is the largest city on the Mexican and U.S. border, and the site of the largest American military installation in the United States.

Just who was the Borderland Princess? She was the Sheldon Hotel, Block 5 Lot 28 in the center of El Paso, Texas; in the heart of the great historic American Southwest.

Figure 1. The Sheldon Hotel. El Paso, Texas. 1906
(Author's Collection)

The story of the Sheldon Hotel is inexorably tied to the history of the million-plus-acre Corralitos Ranch and Candelaria Mines of Chihuahua, Mexico. The Corralitos' New York syndicate owners and the calculated activities of Wall Street barons and industrialists as J.P. Morgan and his cousins; the mining families of Stokes, Phelps, Towne, and Guggenheims; and the Jay Gould—C. P. Huntington railroad empires, have left a major imprint on not only the history of El Paso, but also on turn-of-the-century American history.

This is not a simple story, but one, which offers the reader insight into a fascinating view of early turn-of-the-century American history. There are individuals, intrigues, and intricacies that make the study of the Mexican Revolution and its associated events not only interesting, but also highly significant in light of the current era of corruption and today's drug-based civil war.

One can only imagine standing in the doorway of the west entrance of the Sheldon Hotel looking out onto Pioneer Plaza. Although it is informally referred to as the Little Plaza, it could just as easily been called Southwest's History Plaza. From this vantage point, one could see the "Newspaper Tree" where the Camino del Norte Hotel (formerly the Hotel Paso del Norte now stands). Looking slightly south on El Paso Street could be seen El Paso's first mayor, Ben Dowell's saloon, and gaming hall, which became the village's center of social and political activity.

The plaza was host to Wyatt Earp's wanderings, where Marshal Dallas Stoudenmire killed four men in seconds, where President McKinley addressed an adoring crowd, and where Presidents Díaz and Taft rode elegantly in horse-drawn gilded carriages, parading through town marking the 1909 historic event of the "Two Republics." General Pershing formed and paraded his troops upon their return from the Punitive Expedition in the plaza. Through the plaza's portals previously passed the leaders, schemers, and arms smugglers of the Mexican Revolution; the prohibition profiteers; and some of the greatest war correspondents and journalists the world has ever seen. The Sheldon Hotel's shadow fell upon the plaza as the spies and secret service agents; the early Border Patrol Officers, the Texas Rangers, and the new to be formed FBI agents met and shared tales and information to protect our country's new frontier.

The story begins with the infusion of Wall Street money and influence into the peaceful countryside of northern Mexico. Haciendas, ranches, and rich mines soon became the property of the cunning capitalists in New York's vast financial kingdom. The Sheldon Hotel in El Paso, Texas is one of the outgrowths of that capitalism. The hotel's impact on American history is profound; her impact on the Southwest is epochal.

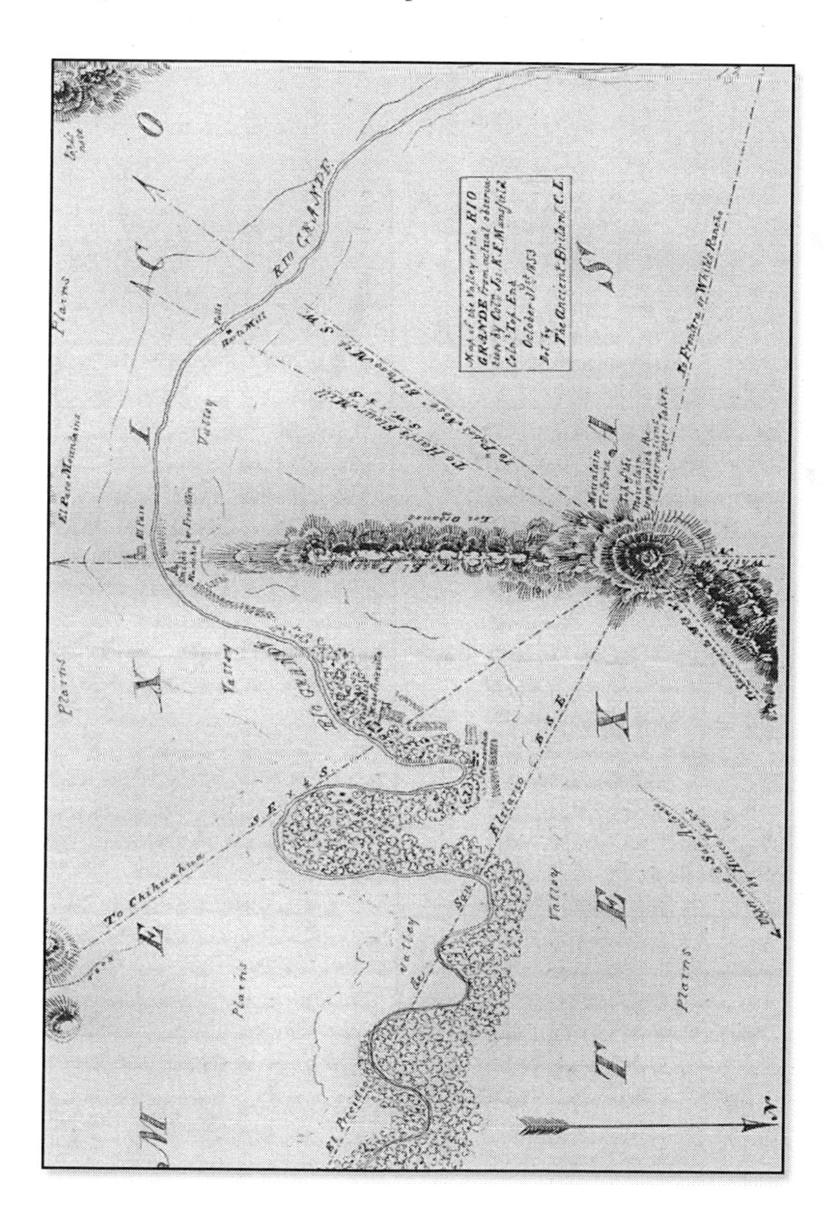

Figure 2. The Mansfield Map - 1853. Looking down on Mt. Franklin to the bend in the Rio Grande separating the two villages of Franklin (Smith's Rancho formerly Ponce de Leon Rancho) and Ciudad Juarez. NOTE: Map is oriented to the south. (From Strickland's El Sabio Sembrador El Paso in 1854)

Chapter One

El Paso del Norte

Rising from the topography of North America, mountain ranges tend to traverse the continent from north to south with wide valleys and plains separating the ranges. These open plains generally provided unobstructed passage, yet the ranges created huge obstacles for passage from east to west as the history of the westward migration of North America has recorded.[1] Topography governs the migration of man and beast as well as the flow of rivers and streams. A great natural pass exists through the Rocky Mountains as the range descends into the great Chihuahuan Desert to become the Sierra Madres. These paths and trails were first followed by wild animals and savage men. Evidence supports that man has occupied the El Paso del Norte region, in quest of food, water, and shelter for the past 11,000 years.[2]

When the Spanish explorers arrived in the 16th century, they found the great river, the Rio Grande emerging from the arroyo between the two ranges. They named the site El Paso del Norte (the Pass of the North). As the Rio Grande streamed south from its headwaters in the Colorado Mountains, it rounded the bend below the pass and began to flow eastward. This formed a natural ford, where travelers, adventurers, merchants, cowboys, outlaws, gold-seekers, and the gaming crowd all collided over the ensuing four hundred years to become Ciudad Juárez on the west bank in Mexico and El Paso, Texas on the east bank. Today the passage has evolved into a major thoroughfare of man, machine, and commerce, Interstate 10.

The early 1800s was a period of immense growth among the little villages on the west side of the Rio Grande; its population was approaching 8,000.[3] The Mexican Constitution of 1824 permitted and encouraged these local settlements to develop some role of self-governance. As a result, the landowning and mercantile aristocracy took over political control, usually to their own financial advantage. Castes formed the lives and life-styles of the Spanish descendants, the Indians, and the Mestizo. El Paso del Norte was the largest and most successful of the villages.

El Paso del Norte's growth was facilitated by its role as an outfitting base for north-south excursions and expeditions. Mexican Independence and the establishment, defeat, and subsequent re-establishment of the Mexican Republic, and the creation of the Republic of Texas from 1836 to 1846; had little effect on these Chihuahuan and New Mexico settlements. These settlements "were separated by too great a distance from the center of disturbance to become involved in any of the bloodshed and conflicts of the period and simply accepted the new conditions as they were imposed upon them."[4]

During this period, there were no English-speaking setters and no settlements on the American side of the Rio Grande even though the river became the dividing line between Mexico and the newly formed Republic of Texas. It was, as Owen White describes, "…some years after Texas had acquired her independence, in fact not until after her annexation by the United States that the territory in which [the City of] El Paso is situated, began to be looked upon by Texans and Americans in general as a desirable locality."[5]

The economic success of many of the Mexican merchants in El Paso del Norte by the 1800s was startling. Juan Azcárate and his wife, Eugenia, owned and operated several large cattle ranches and silver mines on their land grant that covered the Casas Grande, Janos, and Corralitos locales in Chihuahua. With the wealth and success of their mines and ranches, they moved from El Paso del Norte to the center of their ranching and mining empire. They built a hacienda and named it "Casa Grande del Amo" (Large house of the owner) in the middle of an old Spanish village that had been established in 1740 on the east bank of the Casa Grande River called the Corralitos Ranch.

Prior to Azcárate's death in 1851, his son-in-law, American merchant Hugh Stephenson, took over operation of the ranch and mines. Stephenson along with fellow merchant, James W. Magoffin, were considered early pioneers and operators of the American settlements that now comprise the modern city of El Paso. The Corralitos was sold to the infamously powerful Zuloaga family whose legacy is surrounded with atrocities against Indians and political corruption.[6] The Corralitos ranch and mines, in years to come, would play a major role in the pathway to the gold rush in Sacramento and after it was acquired by New York investors, the million-acre property became the center of hostilities in the Mexican Revolution of 1910.[7] (See figure 111)

Another powerful El Paso del Norte merchant was Don Juan Maria Ponce de León. Ponce de León was a cousin of Eugenia Azcárate and a descendant of the Spanish explorer and conquistador of the early 1500s. Don Juan Maria Ponce de León was a wealthy freighter, farmer, rancher, flour miller, and merchant. His ranching and farming activities became so large that he expanded to unutilized land across the Rio Grande opposite El Paso del Norte. In order to legalize these activities, he petitioned the municipal council (ayuntamiento) for a grant and the title to the lands north of the Rio Grande. Following a survey of the lands, the ayuntamiento granted Ponce de León approximately 106 acres of land upon which he continued his thriving farming and ranching enterprise. He paid the municipality eighty dollars.[8] He built a small single story adobe house for use by his employees. The adobe house (located at what is now the intersection of El Paso St. and Paisano Dr.) was destroyed by the flood of 1830.

In May of that year, the ayuntamiento granted Ponce de León a second grant whereupon he built a second ranch house, two stories high with adjoining facilities to house over a hundred workers who were cultivating his farm and caring for his livestock. He constructed an irrigation ditch to deliver Rio Grande water, planted wheat, corn, and grapes. This second grant doubled the size of the Ponce de León grant to over 200 acres. The Ponce Rancho subsequently became the center of downtown El Paso, Texas.[9]

Many great historical events are the direct result of the confluence of several equally significant historical occurrences. The capture of a lost and wandering American Army officer and his expedition, the southern march of Missouri volunteers that resulted in the Battle of Brazito, and the discovery of gold in California; all added to the attention given to the little Mexican village on the west side of the Rio Grande and its subsequent growth.

Coinciding with the Lewis and Clark Expedition of 1804 of the northwest, Lieutenant Zebulon Pike led an expedition through present-day Colorado. While in the vast mountains of Colorado, Pike became disoriented as to his location and his party became lost. They were rescued and eventually arrested for illegal entry by the Spanish into whose territory they had wondered. The Spanish took their prisoners to Chihuahua where they were held until 1807. Following some political negotiations, they were released at the Louisiana border. Pike and his men began recounting their adventures in Mexico and the El Paso valley. Pike reportedly said, "The settlement is by far the most flourishing town we have been in and as finely cultivated fields of wheat and other small grain as I ever saw, and also numerous vineyards from which were produced the finest wine ever drank."[10] As Pike's descriptions spread, particularly to merchants, trappers, and freighters in Missouri; new migration began to the southwest and El Paso del Norte in particular.

During the Mexican-American War of 1846General Stephen W. Kearny captured the New Mexico capital at Santa Fe without a single shot being fired or drop of blood spilled. On September 25, General Kearny, preparing an expedition to California, left Colonel Alexander Doniphan temporarily in charge of Santa Fe. Upon the arrival of General S. Price, Doniphan was to lead an expedition of the Second Missouri Mounted Volunteers down the trail into Chihuahua by way of El Paso del Norte.

Doniphan engaged the Mexican army in what became known as the Battle of El Brazito on the river bank of the Rio Grande on land obtained by Hugh Stephenson from a Spanish land grant, about forty miles north of the present site of El Paso.[11] On Christmas day, 1846, Doniphan defeated the Mexican army against huge odds, losing only one soldier and eleven wounded compared to the Mexican loss of over 300 dead and almost 600 wounded. The account of this significant confrontation and the influence of other El Paso pioneers is worthy of review.[12]

From his successes at Brazito, Doniphan's expedition entered El Paso del Norte peaceably. The soldiers were soon able to capture the Chihuahua City. The significance of these events, besides the obvious, was the fact the Missouri volunteers were so impressed with the friendliness of the residents of El Paso del Norte and surrounding area, that after returning home, many of the former soldiers returned to the area and became settlers along this portion of the Rio Grande.

The Treaty of Guadalupe Hidalgo, signed on February 2, 1848, marked the end of the Mexican-American War in favor of the United States. The treaty added an additional 525,000 square miles to United States territory, including the land that makes up all or parts of present-day Arizona, California, Colorado, Nevada, New Mexico, Utah, and Wyoming. In addition, Mexico ceded all claims to Texas and recognized the Rio Grande as America's southern boundary.

From its headwaters in south central Colorado, the Rio Grande (Rio Bravo del Norte) meanders south into New Mexico and Chihuahua separating El Paso del Norte into what eventually became two distinct settlements. The river frequently changed course, moving east or west depending on the river's response to natural geological processes and frequent spring flooding on its eventual 1900-mile journey to the Gulf of Mexico. The location of the Rio Grande southeast of Stephenson's Concordia property was significantly east of its present location before 1829. Historic Concordia Cemetery part of Stephenson's El Rancho de la Concordia, is located under the I-10 and US 54 freeway interchange slightly over three miles from the site of Ponce's Rancho in downtown El Paso.

Following the Treaty of Guadalupe Hidalgo in 1848, the river became the primary boundary between the United States and Mexico.[13] A relatively short portion of the river functions as the boundary between the states of Texas and New Mexico. Because of the constant changing of the course of the river, using the Rio Grande as a boundary separating two sovereign republics became a major social and political problem. (Several boundary commissions were established to resolve these issues; among them were the Mexican-United States Boundary Commission in 1850 and the International Boundary and Water Commission in 1889. Final resolution of these issues didn't occur until the Chamizal National Memorial was established in 1974.)

The Treaty of Guadalupe Hidalgo extended the boundary from the Gulf of Mexico to a location several miles north of the city of El Paso and then west to the first branch of the Gila River. The boundary line was diplomatically drawn using a map prepared by cartographer J. Disturnell of New York. When the American government attempted to verify the exact boundary with an on-site survey, it was discovered that the Disturnell map was in error. The city of El Paso was actually located 40 miles north of the Disturnell map and that the Rio Grande was actually 130 miles to the west. Under pressure from railroad barons to establish a southern transcontinental route along the Mexican-U.S. border, the American government entered into a negotiation with Mexico. The result was the purchase of the disputed land for ten million dollars. In 1853, the Gadsden Purchase was consummated. The rich Mesilla Valley became part of the United States and the railroad plan moved forward.[14]

Crossing over the Rio Grande from El Paso del Norte to the settlements on the north bank (Note: the City of El Paso is both east and north of the Rio Grande depending on the exact spot of the crossing. See the next chapter, The Changing Rio Grande.) was, except when the river was dry, a most formidable task. As the river altered its course from east to west, freighters and emigrants searched for a spot where the current was slow and the water shallow enough to allow the travelers to ford the river without much difficulty. As the river curves around Mule Driver's Mountain, a crossing provided such a ford. (The mountain was renamed Mount Cristo Rey. A forty-foot limestone statue of Christ was erected in 1939.)

A successful American merchant and trader named T. Frank White built a trading post (White's Rancho) at the crossing in August of 1848 and named the crossing Frontera, Spanish for border, since the crossing was near the border of Texas, New Mexico, and Chihuahua.[15] Frontera became the first American settlement on the east bank of the Rio Grande.[16] By mid-1849 there were more than four thousand emigrants camped along the river's edge.[17] White's Rancho became the most popular of the early American El Paso settlements. Additional settlements appeared at Simeon Hart's mill, Ponce Rancho near the irrigation ditch (acequia) built by Juan Maria Ponce de León to operate his flour mill, James W. Magoffin's Magoffinville just east of the Ponce Rancho, and Hugh Stephenson's Concordia settlement further east.

The discovery of gold in California by James W. Marshall at Sutter's Mill was an unexpected boon to El Paso del Norte in 1849. Gold seekers from the east would travel by steamer to New Orleans and then by wagon or horseback through Texas, following the southern portion of the Rio Grande to El Paso del Norte. They would re-supply in El Paso for the final trek across the Chihuahuan and Gila desert to the area of San Diego and then north to the gold fields. This great adventure was captured in journals and accounts as part of the Parker H. French Expedition.[18] While the north-south emigrant trade supported significant growth to the size and economy of El Paso del Norte, the new east-west trade seemed to enhance the significance of the El Paso area, on both sides of the river. While the travel and supply trade prospered, the region's "isolation, lawlessness, and regular attacks by Indians, discouraged prospective settlers from moving into the region."[19]

The military governor of New Mexico appointed Frank White local magistrate and collector of customs even though Frontera was located in Texas.[20] It wasn't long before the distant and isolated El Paso area was overrun by unsavory and criminal individuals who turned a peaceful village into a rough and violent place. Con men, gamblers, women of questionable reputation, and criminals trying to escape the grasp of American justice; co-mingled with the rough and desperate miners and vaqueros from the desolate mountains and ranges of northern Chihuahua. The United States government was beginning to consider the significance of sending troops to protect these American settlements and the many travelers who passed through the area from the continuing Apache incursions. White's Rancho was being considered a potential military post.[21] As the popularity of the other American settlements increased, many travelers choose to ford the river at the lower crossings, which allowed easier access to the other four settlements. In addition, the military chose to establish its new post at the lower site and activity at Frontera began to diminish. Eventually, the trading post was abandoned.[22] Today the site of White's Frontera can be found just west of the intersection of Doniphan Drive and Frontera Road and east of both the Rio Grande and the New Mexico state boundary. The Mexican-United States Boundary Commission placed a historical marker at the site of Frontera settlement. The marker is reportedly buried on Frontera Road alongside the railroad tracks at the intersection in the shadow of Mount Cristo del Rey.[23]

By 1850, most of the business activity of El Paso del Norte (Juárez) was in the hands of a handful of American merchants and freighters. Despite stiff tariffs imposed by the central Mexican government, the economy was American driven. Combined with the long periods of inactivity between passing wagon-trains and the growing political unrest throughout the rest of Mexico, the local economy began to wane. American public interest was soon focusing on the emerging conflict of the Confederacy and the potential of civil war.

In the early-1860s, under the direction of Napoleon III, France invaded Mexico. Napoleon installed Maximilian I, the brother of the emperor of Austria in April of 1864, and with the aid of conservative Mexican monarchists, France controlled most of the Republic of Mexico. Mexican opposition led by Benito Juárez remained active until Maximilian forces were eventually defeated in 1867. Mexican President Benito Juárez frequently used El Paso del Norte and the city of Chihuahua as his government-in-exile. Following the end of the American Civil War in 1865, President Andrew Johnson attempted to help Juárez in his battle against the French; for he ordered General Philip Sheridan to supply Juárez's troops with tens of thousands of surplus rifles and pistols. Sheridan later wrote, "We left at convenient places on our side of the river to fall into their hands."[24] In 1867, the final French forces were defeated, Maximilian was executed, and President Juárez returned to Mexico City. El Paso del Norte changed its name to Ciudad Juárez in honor of President Juárez on September 16, 1888.

Over the subsequent years, Ciudad Juárez became a political haven for Mexican revolutionaries and anti-government rebels including Francisco Madero, Pancho Villa, and others during the period of the Mexican Revolution of 1910-1920. It became a smuggling center and an American tourist destination during prohibition. Once a city of great wealth and peaceful prosperity, Ciudad Juárez, a city of a million and a half, eventually devolved into a drug-centric cartel crime zone, just a stone throw from America's largest border city, El Paso, Texas.

Notes and References

[1]"The Southwest Border Area." http://countrystudies.us/united-states/geography-19.htm

[2] Timmons, W.H. *Four Centuries at the Pass: A new history of El Paso on its 400th Birthday.* (El Paso: City of El Paso Arts Resources Department, 1980.), 1.

[3]Timmons, W.H. *El Paso: A Borderlands History*. (El Paso: Texas Western Press, 1990.), 74.

[4] White, Owen P. *Out of the Desert: The Historical Romance of El Paso*. (El Paso: The McMath Company, 1923.), 22.

[5] Ibid: 24. "Americans were rather slow in taking the hint, and for several reasons, and quite a number of years after 1836 there was no settlement on the northern bank of the Rio Grande. The principal one of these reasons probably was that the Republic of Texas never extended its executive functions this far west. Under the treaty, which established the boundary between Texas and Mexico, everything east and north of the Rio Grande was recognized as belonging to the Republic of Texas. This immense domain, which included the eastern half of the present state of New Mexico, in which nearly all of the Mexican or Spanish settlements were located, was too large for Texas, in her then embryonic condition to administer properly. Legislatively Texas undoubtedly claimed that she owned all of the territory alluded to–in fact she kept on legislatively claiming it long after she had ceased to own it—but judicially and executively she may be said to have failed utterly to bring it under her sovereignty. The result was that, although it was legally a part of Texas, the territory to the north and for many miles to the east of El Paso was, during the entire period of Texas Independence, without any government whatever except such as Mexico still continued to exercise." (White)

[6] Campbell, C.E. *Mines, Cattle, and Rebellion.* (Sunset Beach: Green Street Publications, 2014.), 25-30.

[7] Ibid, 24.

[8] Bowden, J.J. *Spanish and Mexican Land Grants in the Chihuahuan Acquisition*. (El Paso: Texas Western Press, 1971.), 104. Bowden refers to the purchase price in pesos not U.S. dollars, as is reported by other historians.

[9] Metz, Leon. *City at the Pass*. (El Paso: Mangan Books, 1980.), 19.

[10] Sonnichsen, C. L. *Pass of the North: Four Centuries on the Rio Grande.* (El Paso: Texas Western Press, 1968.), 101.

[11] Hugh Stephenson purchased from the Azcárate family, a 900-acre tract of the land grant and established the Concordia Rancho around 1840. The rancho was east of downtown El Paso in the area of today's Concordia Cemetery. In addition, Stephenson obtained from the Mexican government the Brazito Grant, a critical piece of borderland real estate of some 23,000 acres a few miles south of old Mesilla

[12] See Owen P. White's Out *of the Desert: The Historical Romance of El Paso*. (El Paso: The McMath Company, 1923.), 24-38.

[13] Depending upon the techniques used, the river is the fourth or fifth longest river system in North America. With the building of the Elephant Butte dam in 1916, the spring flooding was contained and the direction of the river became somewhat stabilized.

[14] *Bulletin of the American Geographical and Statistical Society.* (New York: The Society, 1852.), 103. "The History of Mesilla: The Gadsden Purchase." *Viva Mesilla!* (Mesilla, NM: Mesilla Town Government.) Accessed 18 July 2016.

[15] Reyes, Daniel, et.al. (2003). "Frontera settlement." *Historical Markers Project.* (El Paso: EPPC Libraries. Accessed 10 March 2012.

[16] Strickland, Rex W. *Six Who Came to El Paso: Pioneers of the 1840s.* (El Paso: Texas Western Press, 1963.), 10.

[17] Ibid.

[18] Campbell (2014): 40-50.

[19] Martinez, Oscar. *Border Boom Town: Ciudad Juárez since 1848l.* (Austin: University of Texas, 1978.), 11.

[20] Reyes (2003). Timmons, W.H. *El Paso: A Borderlands History*. (El Paso: Texas Western Press, 1990.), 105.

[21] Ibid, l06.

[22] Reyes (2003).

[23] Ibid.

[24] Kelly, Patrick J. "Lincoln Looks South of the Border." November 22, 2013. *The Opinion Pages (The New York Times.)*. Accessed 16 March 2015.

Figure 3. ***The Great Western*, Sarah Borginnis Davis Bowman, Heroine of Mexican-American War. Early El Paso innkeeper, restaurateur, and madam. 1849**
(By Tony Russell, Author's collection)

Chapter Two

Early El Paso

Summarizing El Paso's rich four-hundred year history is a daunting task at best. War and peace, prosperity and famine, cultural immersion and rebellion, and the influx of the moral and immoral presents a fascinating read, but remains beyond the intent of this book. Should the reader want to explore these experiences, many well-written tomes are available that will satisfy both the academic and history novice. Owen P. White's classic 1923 Out of the Desert: The Historical Romance of El Paso is written with such flare and honesty as to provide an enthralled first-hand experience. Equally as significant is White's humorous 1942 opus, The Autobiography of a Durable Sinner, where he shares his perception of El Paso as seen through the eyes of one of its native sons. C.L. Sonnichsen's Pass of the North, W.H. Timmons' A Borderland History, Oscar J. Martinez' Border Boom Town and any number of books by León Metz will satisfy even the most severe thirst for history of the area. The focus of this book remains on the development of El Paso as it relates to the history surrounding the Borderland Princess, the Sheldon Hotel. As a result, the fascinating story of many of these pioneers will not be included. (See figure mike map)

The Changing Rio Grande

From just about anywhere in El Paso with elevation, El Paso del Norte (Juárez) can be viewed across the Rio Grande, however, there is inconsistency as to referencing whether the Mexican city is on the west side or south side of the river. Conversely, is the city of El Paso located on the east side or north side of the Rio Grande? Because of the meandering of the river and depending on one's location in El Paso, the answer is both. In the flow south, the river begins a slight movement east just below the campus of the University of Texas at El Paso, then abruptly turns east at the Santa Fe St. International Bridge where Santa Fe St. and El Paso St converge. (See figure 112)

The river continues east to where South Yarbrough Dr. connects to the U.S.-Mexico border and them turns to continue its southward movement. To facilitate the reader's understanding, the present author has chosen to refer to the two cities as being across from each other as the river travels from its northern headwaters to the south eventually empting into the Gulf of Mexico. Readers will facilitate their comprehension by referring to a map.

Sparsely used as farmlands, the east side of the Rio Grande didn't really see significant develop as an agricultural domain until Juan Maria Ponce de León received his land grant from the municipal leaders of El Paso del Norte in 1827. While he continued to live in El Paso del Norte, he filled the lands with orchards, vineyards, and fields of wheat.

Juan Maria Ponce de León re-built his rancho on the east side of the Rio Grande following the Flood of 1830 and the destruction of his original adobe house. He constructed his new hacienda on higher ground, on what is now the northwest corner of El Paso Street and Mills Ave. (formerly St. Louis St.) roughly in the block where the current Plaza Theater is located on Pioneer Plaza While Ponce de León maintained his residency in El Paso del Norte, he visited the rancho on a regular basis and built it into a thriving settlement.

Once the territory east of the Rio Grande was securely under the control of the United States government, the appearance of Army troops became more than a rumor and the value of the land in the El Paso valley, up to and including Mesilla and Las Cruces, began to increase. Land speculators like Simeon Hart, Hugh Stephenson, and James W. Magoffin acquired deeds and land certificates and subsequently became land barons.

Benjamin Franklin Coons

In the summer of 1849, Don Juan Maria Ponce de León sold his Ponce Rancho to a Benjamin Franklin Coons, a "businessman" from St. Louis who had had some success in Santa Fe. Benjamin Coons was described as a "sometime" Santa Fe trader, freight contractor for the United States Army, commission merchant, and the first business failure of El Paso.[1] Coons casually referred to his new property as Coons Rancho, but later began to refer to it as Franklin. The settlement at Franklin had acquired significant attention as a stage station that it became desirable to have a post-master. Since Coons was the only applicant, he was appointed and subsequently named the settlement Franklin, after himself.[2] The name stuck until 1859.

European immigrants fled to the American east coast to escape the growing militarism of their homelands and the multi-national revolutions that spread across the continent in 1848.[3] Filled with the desire to find the Promised Land, many headed to the southwest frontier. When gold was discovered in California in 1849, the swell of migration brought 90,000 new arrivals. By 1855, it was estimated that as many as 300,000 gold-seekers had passed through.[4] The little village across from El Paso del Norte became a frequent stopping point for those heading to the "golden hills" of Sacramento. Many of the caravans heading west traveled the "Donner" route over the Sierra Nevada, others traveled by steamship around Florida to New Orleans or various gulf cities of Texas. From there they traveled overland up through routes that followed either the Rio Grande or the El Camino Real from Mexico City. Franklin's location at an easy ford in the Rio Grande made it a perfect destination before heading on through the New Mexico and California deserts.

In the run-up of the "Americanization" of the river's eastside village, the early American businessmen married the daughters of upper-class Mexican families (Hart, Stephenson, and Magoffin) and established their new homesteads on the lands that would soon become El Paso.

Ben Coons had previously arranged with Maj. Jeffery Van Horne to move his troops from the presidio at San Elizario to Franklin. Coons had enlarged the property with storehouses, corrals, and a store to accommodate his freight business. Van Horne took advantage of these improvements and leased the rancho for $250 a month, and the rancho became the first military post in the area. The military establishment was called The Post Opposite El Paso, Mexico. The tenure of the military's presence at the Coons ranch was short lived. Coons had experienced one business failure after another; much of it resulted in supply problems for the Army. After two-year tenure, the military moved the troops north 40 miles to Fort Fillmore in July of 1851.[5]

Much has been written that the city of El Paso sprang forth from the old Ponce ranch house at the head of El Paso St. where it intersects with Mills Ave. [St. Louis St.] There exists a bit of historical embellishment that has supported this belief. In actuality, Ponce de León built a small two-or three-room mud choza [hut or shack] as a lodging place for some of his farm workers, the vaqueros and goat herders.[6] The large commodious adobe ranch house that has often been identified as the Ponce Rancho was built by Ben Coons in his effort to make the facility acceptable to the military around 1849. The Ponce ranch house was first the Coons' Ranch and later the Smith's ranch house in the middle

1850s. [7]It was this structure that eventually developed into the first phase of the historic old Central Hotel.

As a point of disambiguation, the site of the Central Hotel was located on the north side of the Pioneer Plaza where the current Plaza Theater is located. It was located on the site of the former White House department store at San Francisco St. The Central Hotel burned down on July 4, 1896. Adjacent to the Central Hotel, was the Grand Central Hotel located on the corner of St. Louis St. (Mills Ave.) and Oregon St. the current site of the recently renovated twelve-story Mills Building. The elegant Grand Central Hotel, built by Mills and Crosby, burned down February 11, 1892. The Sheldon Hotel was located directly opposite the Central and the Grand Central Hotels on the east side of Pioneer Plaza (aka Little Plaza) where St. Louis St. (Mills Ave.) and Oregon St. intersect.

A young German immigrant, Anton B. Rohman [Rohmann], who had established his business acumen in El Paso del Norte (Juárez), crossed the river and opened an eating establishment in the adobe building that Coons had built for the military. In 1854, there were no hotels or lodging facilities in Franklin. Rohman with his wife and daughter converted the establishment into a boarding house, becoming the first hotel in Franklin (El Paso). An English-born trader and freighter, Frederick Augustus Percy, arrived in El Paso and was hired by Coons as a wagon train manager. After working at several various positions, he began writing a newsletter in 1854, which became the first newspaper in American El Paso. His handwritten and artfully illustrated paper, El Sabio Sembrador [The Wise Sower (disseminator or broadcaster)], appeared in three issues. In the only copy preserved, he wrote of the Rohman boarding house and eatery:

> A new hotel has opened at Franklin under the auspices of that "Prince of Cooks" A.B. Rohman; his boarders have nothing to do but laugh and grow fat.[8]

Rohman was not only known as the first hotelier in El Paso's history, he was also known by his lack of language skills:

> Rohman's role as a restaurateur was noted often by visitors… [he was described by visitors] he has forgotten half of his German; his English learned in the United States is slipping away; he retains little of his French which he seems once to have known well; his Spanish which he

has learned in the past few years consists only of tags and scraps; so, strictly speaking, he is unable to speak any language.[9]

Rohman and his wife, Emily, had the distinction of being the first residents and entrepreneurs to install a cooking stove, wooden floors and the first carpeted floors in Franklin.[10] In addition to his early hotel and restaurant, Rohman extended his business acumen to additional activities including a mercantile store, and became the agent in charge of the Pacific Express Company's El Paso office that he operated out of a store front at 41 El Paso St. just below the Little Plaza.[11] Rohman also maintained a contract to provide the Army with corn and other staples.

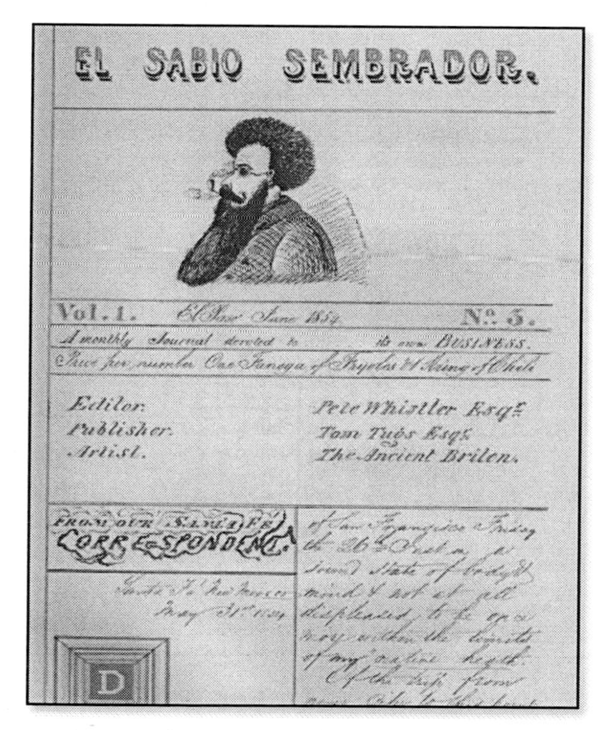

EL SABIO SEMBRADOR.

Vol. 1. No. 3.

A monthly Journal devoted to its own BUSINESS.

Editor: Pete Whistler Esqr.
Publisher: Tom Tugs Esqr.
Artist. The Ancient Briten.

CORRESPONDENT.

Figure 4. Masthead of Frederick Augustus Percy' newsletter known as the first newspaper in American El Paso. (From Strickland's *El Paso in 1884.*)

The masthead of Volume 1, Number 3, of El Sabio Sembrador indicates that there were three individuals working on its publication and Percy's name is not listed anywhere. The three names, "Peter Whistler, Esq." "Tom Tugs," and "the Ancient Briton" listed were all incarnations of Percy's creations. Percy's historical relationship with early El Paso continued when he married Leonore Stephenson, daughter of early pioneer Hugh Stephenson and lived at the Concordia Rancho where he died in 1870.[12]

The Great Western

At this juncture, it is important to note that historical research has identified a predecessor to the Rohman's mantle of being the first boarding house or hotel operator in El Paso. Sarah Bowman (aka Sarah Knight Borginnis Bowman), a multi-married character who had a habit of taking a husband in a gather-ye-rosebuds-while-ye-may manner and often dispensed with bothersome formalities like marriage certificates and divorce decrees,[13] was an Amazonian-sized Anglo. Sarah Bowman at 6ft.2in, 200 pounds, with blazing red hair was born circa 1813. She had a historic past that dates back to the Mexican-American War and General Zachery Taylor. Her role with the U.S. Army expanded her presence beyond that of soldier's wife, laundress, cook, and nurse. She became known as "The Heroine of Fort Brown" because of her aggressive courage in battle while serving with General Taylor.[14] Her sobriquet, "The Great Western," is in reference to the unforgettable SS Great Western, the first successful trans-Atlantic steamer and the largest steamship (twin steam-driven paddle wheels on both sides of her 235-foot-long hull in the world, which crossed the ocean in 1838.)[15] She was known to be proud of her nickname.

In Robert Johannsen's book about the Mexican-American War (1846-1848)[16], "'The Big Western' had attracted attention before General Taylor reached the Rio Grande. Women employed by the Army as cooks and laundresses were generally taken by sea from Corpus Christi to Point Isabel, which was the Army's staging area. Sarah, showing her strong nerves and physical power, insisted that she travel overland with the men, driving her own donkey-cart laden with cooking utensils and supplies, and displaying qualities which the best teamster in the train might have envied."[17]

Author Brian Sandwich writes that three momentous events occurred in 1848 that would change the complexion of the United States, and the West in particular. The discovery of gold in California in January 1848 caused a tidal wave of easterners and Europeans to cross the difficult, mountainous, and often barren plains. The southern route through El Paso offered an all-weather passage to the northern California land of riches and dreams. One week following the discovery of gold by James Marshall at Sutter's Creek, the Treaty of Guadeloupe Hidalgo ended the Mexican-American War and drew an international boundary, which resulted in El Paso becoming an American village. The issuance of General Orders 58 by the U.S. Army created the third significant event. This declaration ordered federal troops to El Paso to protect the westward migrating citizens in search of their dreams.[18] (The true and accurate portrait of the California Gold Rush days was that riches came to only a handful and most of the East coast and European immigrant dreamers returned home, desolate, discouraged and heavily in debt. Few were able to stay and etch out a living by other means.

After the war, eyeing the new potential in El Paso, Sarah Bowman found her way to Mexico where she operated a variety of businesses, including restaurants, hotels, and brothels. In 1849, she made her way across the Rio Grande to El Paso. There she joined forces with Ben Franklin Coons, and erected a small hotel and restaurant at his post on the Ponce de León rancho.[19] Frost writes, "While no direct reference has been encountered, it is highly probable that Sarah's "hotel" was also a brothel, since she had run the American House in Saltillo and would later have such places in Yuma and Patagonia, Arizona."[20] Her business ventures in El Paso catered to the flood of "Forty-niners" who descended upon this little dusty village while on their way to the gold fields of California. This clearly establishes Sarah as the first Anglo female resident of El Paso.[21]

In writing his biography of adventurer and Union General Isaac H. Duval, author Dillon recaptures some of Duval's notes and journal entries:

> Late the next day, we started up our bank of the Rio Grande toward El Paso. Late in the afternoon, we reached a point opposite the town. In this town [El Paso/Magoffinville/Coons' Rancho] we found an American woman keeping a ranch or hacienda who was, without doubt, the largest woman whom I had ever seen who had retained her activity. She called herself "The Great Western," and I think she was entitled to all the glory there was in the name. She was the queen of her people, as she was the only American woman there. She claimed that she was the widow of an American sergeant of the U.S. Army who had been killed

> in the Mexican War. She was a great favorite with the Mexican women, and certainly had the confidence of all. I was able to rent from her a room for my small party, and a corral for the animals.[22]

An early Texas Ranger, John Rip Ford said, "she had to be approached in a polite—if not humble—manner since she had the reputation of being something of the roughest fighter on the Rio Grande." [23] Reports of Sarah's kindness can also be found. Writing in his diary of 1849, Cox states, "Among the residents of this place is 'The Great Western,' a female of notorious in the late war," but continues with describing another's letter, 'We found the far-famed Great Western at this place on our side of the river. She was celebrated in the Mexican War and did good service in a number of battles. She is six feet one inch in height and well proportioned. She treated us with much kindness.'"[24]

Sarah's tenure in El Paso was brief. In 1850, with a new husband in tow, she headed to Fort Yuma where she again operated restaurants and "hotels."[25] A Fort Yuma soldier said at the time, "She has been with the Army twenty years and was brought up here where she keeps the officer's mess. Among her other good qualities she is an admirable 'pimp'. She used to be a splendid-looking woman and has done good service but is too old for that now."[26]

Sarah was described as having an aura that "protected her from the hazards of frontier life. Indians and outlaws alike were awed into a respectful distance by her epic proportions and sexuality, not to mention her apparent willingness to use the guns she carried. She made do with the erratic availability of provisions and consistently gave an impression of kindness to Anglo travelers who stayed with her. Even her customers approached her in a 'polite, if not humble manner.'"[27]

Sarah died in 1866 at 53, reportedly from a spider bite.[28] She was buried with full military honors at the Fort Yuma cemetery. Following the decommissioning of Fort Yuma in 1883, she was re-buried at the National Cemetery at the Presidio in San Francisco.[29] Historians have used a lot of words including generous, loyal, devoted, aggressive, and brave to describe Sarah Bowman, "The Great Western." The community of Yuma, Arizona, however, paid her its greatest compliment. Folks there proudly called Sarah Bowman their First Citizen. However, as one observer stated, "because of her habit of adopting a number of Mexican and Indian children as well as packing two pistols, and she shore could use em." He went on to say admiringly, "She was hell of a good woman. Sarah was 'The Greatest' whore in the West."[30]

The Central Hotel, the Newspaper Tree, and Mrs. Gillock

While Sarah and the Rohmans may have shared the same physical locale at the old Ponce adobe at Coons' ranch, the Rohmans clearly operated the first "real" boarding house or hotel in El Paso that remained in operation over a durable time-period. The Rohmans were clearly "first" in many categories, but Sarah Knight Borginnis Bowman must also be remembered as the first Anglo woman and the first of a long list of "madams" to grace the history and streets of old El Paso.

Rohman's daughter, Amelia, soon married Vincent St. Vrain one of the original founders of the El Paso Company and the St. Vrains began a successful quest in acquiring many of the central lots shown on the 1859 Mills Plat. After St. Vrain died, Amelia married John B. Tays, the commander of Company C of the Texas Rangers stationed in El Paso on May 3, 1878. Tays was the younger brother of Pastor Joseph W. Tays who founded St. Clements Episcopal Church, the first protestant church in El Paso.[31] John B. Tays served as El Paso's postmaster and the city's first marshal; however, Tays was more successful in his private ventures than in his duties as a civil servant. He acquired a fortune in cattle raising, railroad construction and extensive El Paso real estate.[32] Not long after the El Paso Company organized the village, the Rohman family turned over the operation of their hotel to a third party in a lessor/lessee arrangement. Mr. Rohman died in El Paso, possibly in the 1870s. Eventually, Mrs. Rohman and her daughter, Amelia Tays moved to Ontario, California where they lived out their lives comfortably.

Over the years, the Rohmans leased their property to a variety of lessees. Among them was John Dougher in 1881.[33] Dougher's success with the Central eventually landed him the job of managing the Grand Central Hotel when Mills and Crosby opened February 13, 1884.[34] In 1893, George W. Newell and his wife obtained the lease on the Central Hotel. They ran it for about nine years until the property was eventually sold.[35]

The various parties to lease the Rohman hotel included one of El Paso's most colorful characters, specifically Elizabeth Gillock and her husband, Major Braxton Gillock. The Gillocks arrived in El Paso sometime in the mid-1850s from San Antonio where he worked as a government contractor driving freight trains to the Army base in El Paso and served as a postmaster.[36] Braxton Gillock was most likely urged to move to El Paso by his friend Ben Dowell. Gillock and Dowell, who began to acquire multiple parcels of downtown El Paso property, operated a saloon, gaming house, post office and a freighting business. Over the years, Braxton Gillock was selected "justice of the peace." By the early 1860s, Judge Gillock slowly began to develop into an ardent secessionist, along with Dowell and most of the local businessmen of El Paso. This put him at political odds with the two Mills brothers (Anson and W. W. Mills.)

In 1860, the townspeople of El Paso formed a vigilance committee and planned a public election to go on the record to support the secessionist movement of the Confederacy. The town fathers told the public that they were expected to cast a unanimous vote and "dark hints were let fall as to what was likely to happen to anyone who interfered with the plan."[37] Mills writes:

> I was notified by the same committee that the vote of the county must be unanimous for secession, and that I would imperil my life if I voted against it. Phil Herbert, a violent secessionist and personal friend of mine, came to my house on election day and said, "Mills, are you going to vote?" I said that I was. "Well," he said, "I know how you are going to vote. I am going to vote for secession, but I would like to go with you. If there is trouble, I will defend you." He had a pistol and advised me to carry one, and we went together to the polling place. This was in a large gambling house, in which was Ben Dowell's post office. The judge of the election was Judge Gillock recently from Connecticut, [Mills apparently was in error, Judge Gillock was recently from San Antonio.] a violent secessionist.
>
> Herbert and I entered, arm in arm, and Herbert first presented his ballot, which Gillock received and cast into the ballot box near the door. I drew from my pocket a sheet of foolscap paper on which was written, "No separation – Anson Mills," in large letters, and unfolding it, I held it up to the sight of half a dozen army officers and others playing billiards, faro and other gambling games, saying, "Gentlemen, some of you may be curious to know how I am going to vote. This is my ballot." Gillock refused to receive it, but Herbert said, peremptorily, "That is a legal vote. Place it in the box." And Gillock did so. We left the room unmolested.
>
> My vote was one of the two cast against secession in El Paso County, when there were over nine hundred cast for secession. Some were legal, but the majority, cast by Mexican citizens from the other side of the river, was not. My friends, particularly Herbert, felt it would be

> foolhardy to remain longer. Herbert went to Richmond, joined the Confederacy, and was killed in the Battle of Mansfield, LA., at the head of his regiment. I decided to go to Washington and join the federal forces.[38]

Owen White[39] reminds us that although there were only two votes against secession, "This, however, cannot be taken as an indication that there were only two Union men in the county. In fact, there were quite a number, but they either did not vote at all in the election, or else they cast ballots which were against the principles that they believed in.

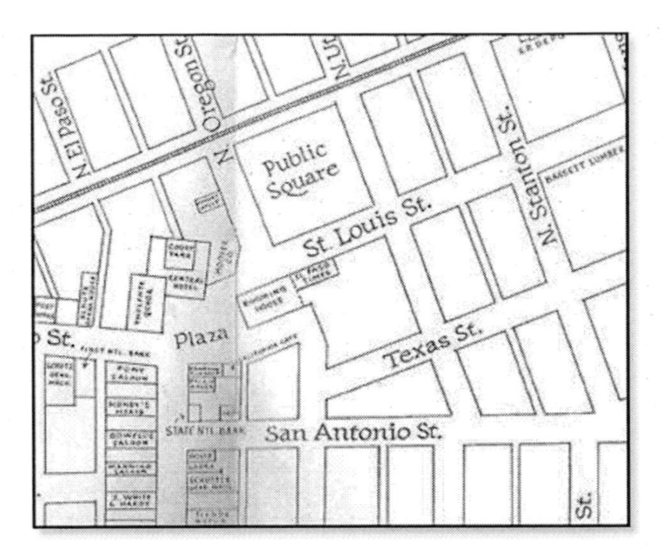

Figure 5. "Hell's Half-acre" From an adaptation of real estate agent Thomas H. Conklin fire insurance map drawn in 1881. (Special Collections Department, University of Texas at El Paso Library.)

Figure 6. Central Hotel at the head of El Paso St. 1880.
(El Paso Public Library, Francis Parker Collection)

Mrs. Gillock showed a firm hand in taking over the management of the Rohman property and was successful in accommodating the many gold-seeking travelers who passed through El Paso on their way to California. At this time, the Rohman property had taken on the name of the Gillock House. Mrs. Gillock ruled her empire with an iron fist. When travelers failed to pay their bills, Gillock frequently strolled out into the Little Plaza and posted the names of those travelers who were behind in their rent as a way of publicly shaming them. Running through the Little Plaza was the main acequia (irrigation canal) and along its banks was a stand of very large cottonwood trees. These trees provided the much needed shade in the plaza. Among the cottonwood trees was an ash. Gillock, and others, tacked notices of all kinds on the tree, and it soon came to be known as the newspaper tree. This became the public bulletin board and served as the political, social, and moral voice of early El Paso. The original tree has long since passed to the great beyond, but a small replica of the tree and a bronze plaque remain on the east side of the plaza, adjacent to where the Sheldon Hotel once stood.[40]

Elizabeth Gillock's role in the history of the Sheldon hotel cannot be overstated. When the 1859 Mills plat was drawn, she was noted as owning the eastern half of Block 5 (soon to be part of the Sheldon's land holdings) as well as the eastern corner of Oregon and St. Louis (Mills Ave.) streets, opposite the San Jacinto Plaza and the exact spot where Anson Mills and Josiah Crosby built their Grand Central Hotel. Her sale of the property to Mills and Crosby was essential to build the Grand Central.[41]

The burning of the Grand Central is also paramount to the creation of the Sheldon Hotel. Before the Grand Central was built, that small piece of property, used as a corral by the residents of the Central Hotel, was known locally as the "Hell's Half Acre."[42]

Mrs. Gillock's acerbic persona has been documented by some of El Paso's leading citizens who knew her or who were her tenants in the boarding house she ran. James P. Hague, local attorney and civic leader, wrote a letter to his wife of his impressions of his first arrival to El Paso in 1871:

> As I write you with this poor quill in the month of May, in a cold damp room on the ground floor, with one window and one door, a place meant for insects such as those that devoured me last night, and it didn't seem fair treatment after the stagecoach experience, which left me with some spots all over my body. It feels like I have been

> transplanted and carried away against my own will when I had really planned it all; and as an excursion or a dream of a kingdom like Don Quijote (sic) created, and destroyed. People are needed badly here. At present, there is no one around but Mrs. Gillock, a creature that resembles a crocodile even as to a long tail that sweeps the ground when she walks. Mrs. Gillock is a species that never goes near the water and never undressed in her life. She is the owner [lessee] of the Rohman house where I am living at present.[43]

Another account of Mrs. Gillock is contained in the history of the pioneer Coldwell family's arrival in El Paso in 1873:

> At that time El Paso had only about half a dozen families. It was an official station for the Customs House and my Father was there to be the Collector. As I remember, the residents were Joe Magoffin, his wife and son. Mr. and Mrs. Slade.(sic) Mr. Slade was the Deputy Collector. Mr. Hague and his family, Mr. Blacker, his wife and two daughters and old Mrs. Gillock, who had been there with her husband, long since dead, and had kept a kind of hotel at the time 49ers were making their way west, gold-seeking.[44] She was a most interesting old woman, whom it was much more prudent to have as a friend than as a foe—kind-hearted until she got "mad," and then nothing could stop her. We used to go there every day of our lives and she would tell us stories. Every day at the dinner table Father would fix up a big tray of everything we had on our table, our man would then take it to Mrs. Gillock. Her house was hard (sic) by the Customs House where we lived. She owned her hotel and the land around it. Her trade was gone with the 49ers, so she lived in the old rambling hotel all alone, it was of adobe and almost in ruins. We would sit there in her living room in rainy weather and we would hear a splash when the rain would finally wash through the adobe roof of some distant unoccupied room, and would pour down with the mud and the straw, and she would hardly move. She was accustomed to hearing that. Finally, when the railroads did come out there, years later, she sold all her property for $17,000 so that made her old age comfortable. She finally died in El Paso.[45]

The Central or the Grand Central Hotel?

By 1880, the Rohman owned (St. Vrain-Tays family) Gillock boarding house had become the Central Hotel and the St. Vrain-Tays family continued to hold it and a great deal of other property in downtown El Paso until the early 1900s.[46] The old Central Hotel, remained a two-story adobe style structure with Spanish portals for most of its life, then, possibly after a devastating fire in 1884, it was rebuilt and enlarged. The old Central Hotel is considered the first hotel built in El Paso, facing down El Paso Street it was located where the Plaza Theater is located and where the White House Department store and the McCoy Hotel (above the department store) remained for so many years.[47] Today it has been completely rebuilt and is known as the Centre Building, which is attached to the current Mills Building and is owned by billionaire Paul L. Foster. The Central Hotel was, in its latter days, used as a cheap lodging house with business offices on the ground floor. It remained somewhat successful until the building and the opening of Mills and Crosby's Grand Central Hotel right next door. The Central Hotel continued to survive even though the city council tried to pass regulations and resolutions to put it out of existence.[48] The Central Hotel burned down in 1896, four years after the elegant Grand Central was destroyed by fire in 1892.

The impact that the Rohman hotel enterprise, which evolved into the Central Hotel and Mills' and Crosby's Grand Central Hotel, had in the history of the Sheldon Hotel should not be understated. One consistent difficulty arises regarding these early hotels. Many history writers seem to have mixed up their actual locations in the downtown plaza area. The works of Sonnichsen, Strickland, White, Hamilton, Jones, Cool, and El Paso Times journalist Chapman, will leave the reader a bit confused.

The story of the Gillock House and its actual location is a major part of the confusion that surrounds the history of the Central Hotel and its next-door neighbor, the Grand Central Hotel. Many references in the local newspapers get the two hotels mixed up, even today. When reviewing the history of these seminal El Paso landmarks, it is important to check the dates and location. In an article in the El Paso Herald, May 8, 1894:

> The Central Hotel property has been an eyesore long enough, and now that Col. Mills and Crosby have agreed on the partition, two attractive business structures are to go up on the site. Col. Mills will erect a two-story brick block to the north corner, and Crosby will build a one-story brick block to the south.[49]

Clearly, the article was referring to the Grand Central Hotel, as the Central hadn't burned until July, 1896. These are far from isolated examples of the confusion.[50]

There is no more respected Southwest historian and author than C. L. Sonnichsen. His voluminous and ambitious writing of local history is the spine of Southwest history. Yet, he has fallen victim to this confusion. His writing suggests that the Central Hotel and the Rohman Hotel were two different buildings and that the Gillocks operated a hotel across the street where the Sheldon Hotel would soon rise [Now the Plaza Hotel]. Writing in his book, The State National Since 1881: The Pioneer Bank of El Paso (1971):

> It was a one-street community. A town had been platted (sic) in 1859 but nothing much had happened to any thoroughfare but El Paso Street, so called because its extension through the sand hills took one by a meandering route to the river, where he could ford or ferry. At the head of this street was the Plaza, the spot we now call Pioneer Plaza or Little Plaza to distinguish it from San Jacinto Plaza a block to the east. Through this little sun-soaked square, the village irrigation ditch ran, and people with something to sell gathered to display their wares. San Francisco Street entered the square from the west, and a few business houses, notably those belonging to the Schultz brothers, were functioning there. The Central Hotel looked directly south down El Paso Street. The White House department store occupies the site now. Where the Mills Building stands, Mrs. Rohman had her hotel, and directly across the way, about where the Plaza Motor Hotel [Sheldon Hotel] rises now, Major and Mrs. Braxton Gillock ran another hostelry.[51]

In an interview with Mr. Richard Bussell, of the El Paso County Historical Society in 2010, another piece of confusion was added to the mix. Mr. Bussell was considered the most significant individual in El Paso regarding the history of local hotels and boarding houses. He had amassed a very large collection of data which is available at the society's office. Bussell told the writer, "In 1859, when William "Uncle Billy" Smith was selling off his property to the original founders of El Paso, the ranch which he had purchased from Juan Ponce de León's heirs (Mrs. Ponce and daughter), the property which came to be the 1884 Grand Central Hotel and then the 1911 Mills Building, was sold to Mr.

and Mrs. Braxton Gillock. The Gillocks operated a boarding house from the adobe building, which, incidentally, was also next to Mrs. Rohmans' boarding house which later became the Central Hotel."[52]

In order to aid in the clarification of this confusion, the writer reviewed the hand-drawn maps prepared by T.H. Conklin, local El Paso realtor and insurance agent, in 1881 and 1882. These maps show the existence of the Central Hotel at the head of El Paso Street and the property soon to contain the Grand Central as vacant or a storage yard. The maps further show details of the George Giddings operated San Antonio-San Diego Mail Line's corral on the future site of the Sheldon building at Block 5, Lot 28. (See Appendix II) Following this map review, the writer conducted an exhaustive search of the El Paso Sanborn Fire Insurance Maps. The names and placement of the Central and the Grand Central Hotels were further confused by these documents.[53]

Notwithstanding the evidence that Mrs. Gillock owned property in Block 5 (Lots 32 and 33) and Block 17, and despite the confusion that has surfaced regarding Gillock and the two "Center" hotels; the writer has concluded that Mrs. Gillock and her husband arrived in El Paso around 1857. She was the power manager of the early years of the Rohman's Central Hotel located at the head of El Paso Street at the Little Plaza and she did not operate a separate and distinct boarding house. Her impact on the city of El Paso was immense with her role in the Newspaper Tree and her selling of property to facilitate the building of the Grand Central Hotel by Crosby and Mills.

The Post Opposite El Paso, Mexico, returned to El Paso in 1853 under orders of then Secretary of War, Jefferson Davis and was relocated at Magoffinville, slightly east of the former location at Coon's Ranch. The following year the post was renamed Fort Bliss in honor of Lt. Colonel William W. Bliss, who had been the military adjutant to President Zachary Taylor who had died in 1850. [President Taylor died after 16 months in office in July 1850 from a gastrointestinal infection thought to be cholera.]

Following the spring flood of the Rio Grande in 1867, the Fort Bliss post was moved further from downtown El Paso; to the region of the Stephenson Concordia Rancho adjacent to what is now Concordia Cemetery. The post moved again in 1878 to a permanent post near Simeon Hart's mill on river's edge near what has become the campus of the University of Texas at El Paso. Then in 1893, with the political and financial influence of the town leaders and shakers, the Army again relocated the post to its present site on the Lenoria Mesa about four miles from El Paso civic center. Fort Bliss, with its addition of the White

Sands Missile Range in New Mexico is now the largest military installation in the United States.

Uncle Billy Smith

Coupled with huge business losses in his freighting company and the loss of income from the Army, Coons was unable to continue with the payments on the property. Title to the property reverted to Ponce de León just before the Don's death in 1852. After Ponce's death, his wife and daughter sold the repossessed property to a Kentucky trader named William T. Smith in 1854[54] for $10,000.[55]

Smith's often described as a "white-haired, boyish-faced almost illiterate Kentuckian, who made up for his ignorance of letters by an extra measure of the milk of human kindness."[56] The local residents of Franklin called him "Uncle Billy" probably based on his most affable personality and his affinity for being an "easy touch." After Smith acquired the Ponce land grant as well as an additional 640 acres of nearby land, he would sell or give pieces of the property to just about anyone who would ask.[57] Because of his piece meal manner of distributing his property, the village of Franklin became a zigzag pattern of alleys, roads, and property lines. In addressing this issue, historian Mark Cioc-Ortega wrote of the difficulties of laying out the city plan:

> Neither Coons [Benjamin Franklin Coons] nor Smith ["Uncle Billy"] had the geometric mentality of a town planner… Smith parceled off small plots of land in a helter skelter manner, paying little attention to the dictates of grid design….the houses had been built at random, without a survey, on plots given by Mr. Smith, the few streets were neither parallel nor at right angles.[58]

This issue became extremely pronounced when a city plat was prepared in 1859 and the confusion remains today in the central downtown district of El Paso. [It was the custom of the time to name principal streets and roadways with the names of the destination of the various stage routes. (San Francisco, St. Louis, Santa Fe, Kansas, and San Antonio.) Many other streets were named after prominent pioneers and landowners. (Magoffin, Mills, and St. Vrain.) [For a detailed explanation of the perplexity of the lay-out of the city see the Cioc-Ortega article.]

Uncle Billy demonstrated his generosity in his relationship with one of the most significant of the town's early pioneers, Judge Josiah Crosby. When the widowed Crosby married his second wife, Josephine Bremond, in 1856, Smith "felt that he must express his admiration of her [the new bride] in concrete terms. Three acres of land in the downtown section conveyed his sentiments adequately."[59]

Judge Crosby's role in the early growth and development of El Paso in general and the Sheldon Hotel in particular is of regnant importance. Josiah F. Crosby, born in South Carolina in 1829, moved to Texas to live with his uncle. There Crosby studied law under a well-known jurist and future Texas Attorney General, James Willie and a group of private tutors, including soon to be jurist Joel Ankrim. In 1848, a special act of the legislature, because of his young age, was passed and Crosby was admitted to the state bar and appointed district attorney of the Third Judicial District (Corsicana, in Navarro County, southeast of Dallas). In 1850, Crosby married his first wife but she died after two years. Crosby's health began to deteriorate with respiratory issues and he resigned his position.

In the spring of 1852, Crosby's friend, Judge Joel Ankrim, convinced him to move to a different climate to improve his health. Crosby and Ankrim joined one of "Uncle Billy" Smith's wagon trains at San Antonio and headed west toward El Paso. Two years later, Crosby was elected district attorney to the Eleventh Judicial District (El Paso County) and at the same time became an attorney for freighter "Uncle Billy" Smith. After his marriage to Josephine and the gift of three acres, the Crosbys had eight children. In 1859, the Crosbys announced the birth of their first child, William. William Crosby became El Paso's first native-born American.[60] The birth of young Crosby brought the total male American population of El Paso, in these pre-civil war days, to forty-four.[61] "Of course, there were always present in the town quite a number of floaters—travelers who came and went without asking or being asked questions. These individuals left behind no permanent records of their visits with the exception, now and then, of an individual or two who remained to take up his permanent abode in the cemetery, which was located in what is now Sunset Heights [later to become El Paso's most expensive and desirous location]."[62]

Shortly thereafter, Smith wanted to sell the remainder of his "Ponce" property and concentrate on building up his freighting business. Crosby convinced Smith to join with several other local businessmen and form a property syndicate to purchase the vast Smith ranch. Joining Crosby and Smith in The El Paso Company venture were Vincent St. Vrain, W. J. Morton, and local goat farmers John and Henry Gillett.[63]

The Mills Plat of 1859

The El Paso Company, under Crosby's leadership, hired Anson Mills. Mills, a former Army surveyor, who had recently arrived in El Paso to build the Butterfield stage station on what would become El Paso St. and Overland Avenue. The new stage station was across the street from an adobe building that housed Ben Dowell's gaming saloon, bar, store and post-office. It was the center of the town's social activities. [Currently the site of the Paso del Norte Hotel.] In his history of El Paso, journalist Owen White wrote:

> The population at the time was about 300, mostly Mexicans, there were twenty professional gamblers. No body (sic) worked…that is, nobody except Mexicans worked regularly. The 'white men' in the community did practically nothing for the very simple reason that there was nothing to do and that Uncle Ben Dowell's saloon sheltered the entire American male population of the town for the greater part of every day and for nearly all of every night.[64]

Mills was to prepare a plat of the property the company had acquired from Smith and to attempt to adjust the street layout to correct the hap hazard nature of the town as a result of Smith's "generosity." In early 1859 Mills submitted his plat to the El Paso Company and received $100 and four lots valued at fifty dollars each(Block 26, Lots 116 and 117; Block 30, Lot 134 and Block 27, Lot 137),[65] currently the site of the El Paso Convention & Performing Arts Center. Writing of his submission of the plat of Franklin to the El Paso Company, Mills stated:

> Franklin Coontz (sic) turned out an undesirable citizen, and it was suggested that I rename the city. As this was not only the north and south path of the Rio Grande through the Rocky Mountains but also the only feasible route from east to west crossing that river, for hundreds of miles, I suggested that El Paso would indicate the importance of the location. It was decided to so name.[66]

In reviewing the Mills plat of 1859, it becomes very clear that Vincent St. Vrain appeared to acquire many very prized lots, particularly those that surrounded both the Little Plaza (Pioneer) and the San Jacinto Plaza. St. Vrain's in-laws, A.B. Rohman and wife, operated their previously described adobe boarding house in Block 17 Lot 176, which eventually became the Central Hotel on the site just east of the current Plaza Theater. Among other St. Vrain's El Paso property, as shown on the Mills Plat, was the eastern half of Block 6, bounded by Oregon, San Antonio, San Francisco and El Paso streets. This property was used by Mrs. A. B. Rohman as her garden. Mrs. Rohman sold her garden for $5,000 and just eighteen months later, El Paso businessman, T.H. Conklin, purchased it for $20,000 in 1883.

El Paso was on the threshold of a boom.[67] Block 6 was later known as the Bronson Block and had a multiple of businesses located there. Among them was the Coney Island Saloon. The Coney Island's main entrance was at 111 North Oregon St., adjacent to the alley that ran behind the future Sheldon Hotel. The Coney Island, owned by Tom Powers was a wild and bawdy place. A historical site filled with gaming, assaults, murder[68], and the attempted assassination of Sen. Albert B. Fall,[69] whose own scandalous life punctuated the history of the Sheldon Hotel. Today, the Coney Island Saloon has been replaced by the fine dining Cafe Central, and the Bronson Block is now the 15-story, aptly named One Texas Tower, that replaced the long-standing 7-story First National Bank.[70]

The Rohman's Central Hotel was originally located in one of the adobe buildings that Coons built on the Ponce rancho facing El Paso St. on property that was identified as being owned by St. Vrain on the Mills plat. Adjacent to the Central Hotel was a piece of property own by the Braxton Gillock and his wife that rounded the corner from St. Louis St. (Mills Ave.) to Oregon St. facing San Jacinto Plaza.

The Gillock's also, according to the 1859 Plat, owned property across St. Louis St. between Oregon and Utah St. (Mesa Ave.). Adjacent to the boarding house was a corral and stage station utilized by George H. Giddings and his San Antonio-San Diego mail and stage line (discussed later). Eventually, Mrs. Gillock sold her property next to the Central Hotel to Mills and Crosby for their Grand Central Hotel. Later, her heirs sold her Block 5 lots to a property syndicate controlled by a Boston banker, railroad man, and co-owner of the Corralitos Ranch in Chihuahua, Mexico, Thomas Wentworth Peirce, Jr. Mr. Peirce obtained ownership to the land owned by the estate of George Giddings. Mr. Peirce then sold the Giddings property (Block 5 Lot 28) to Lucius M. Sheldon who built the Sheldon Block office building. The city of El Paso, wanting to open up Oregon St., traded a portion of the Little Plaza that resulted in the bulk of the Sheldon Block jutting out into the plaza.

The completion of the 1859 Mills plat was only the beginning of Anson Mills' interaction with El Paso and Judge Crosby. As the Civil War loomed, the majority of landowners and civic pioneers were Confederate sympathizers. It seemed that the only two outspoken pro-Unionists were Anson Mills and his brother W.W. Mills. When the war broke out, El Paso became depopulated of American inhabitants. "Nearly every one of the forty-four went into either one army or the other, and although quite a few of them returned after the war to take up once more the building of their city, the greater part of them passed on quietly out of the history of the town."[71] Anson Mills left immediately for Washington, D.C. and rejoined the Union Army and his brother went to New Mexico to work for the Union commander.

After service in the Union Army, Brig. General Mills began to focus on improving the army's cartridge belt in 1866. He modified and developed a process to weave the whole belt in one piece without sewing, which would eliminate the problem of corrosion on the brass cartridges held in leather belts. He built a power-weaving loom and opened his factory in Worcester, Massachusetts in 1893. Soon after the death of his son, Anson Cassels Mills in 1894, Mills purchased a large eloquent row house at 2 DuPont Circle in Washington, D.C. By 1905, the Mills belt factory was producing a thousand belts a day. He sold his interest in the company and made a fortune. His belts were soon used by military forces around the world and modifications of it are still being used.

Mills returned to El Paso following the successful establishment of his belt company on the East coast and continued his acquisition downtown El Paso property. That culminated when he joined forces with local lawyer and landowner, Judge Josiah Crosby. In 1883, Crosby and Mills built the Grand Central Hotel on the property at the corner of Oregon St. and Mills Ave. just east and adjacent to the Central Hotel including the sliver of corner property owned by the Gillocks. When the hotel opened for business in 1884, it was the largest hotel in Texas.[72] Their partnership was rift with issues. When their Grand Central Hotel burned down in 1892, their partnership erupted into conflict that resulted in Mills refusing to rebuild the Grand Central or any hotel for that matter in El Paso. The Sheldon Block office building was located across the street and was damaged by the Grand Central's fire. When Mills decided to erect an office building, the owners of the Sheldon decided to convert their property into a hotel.

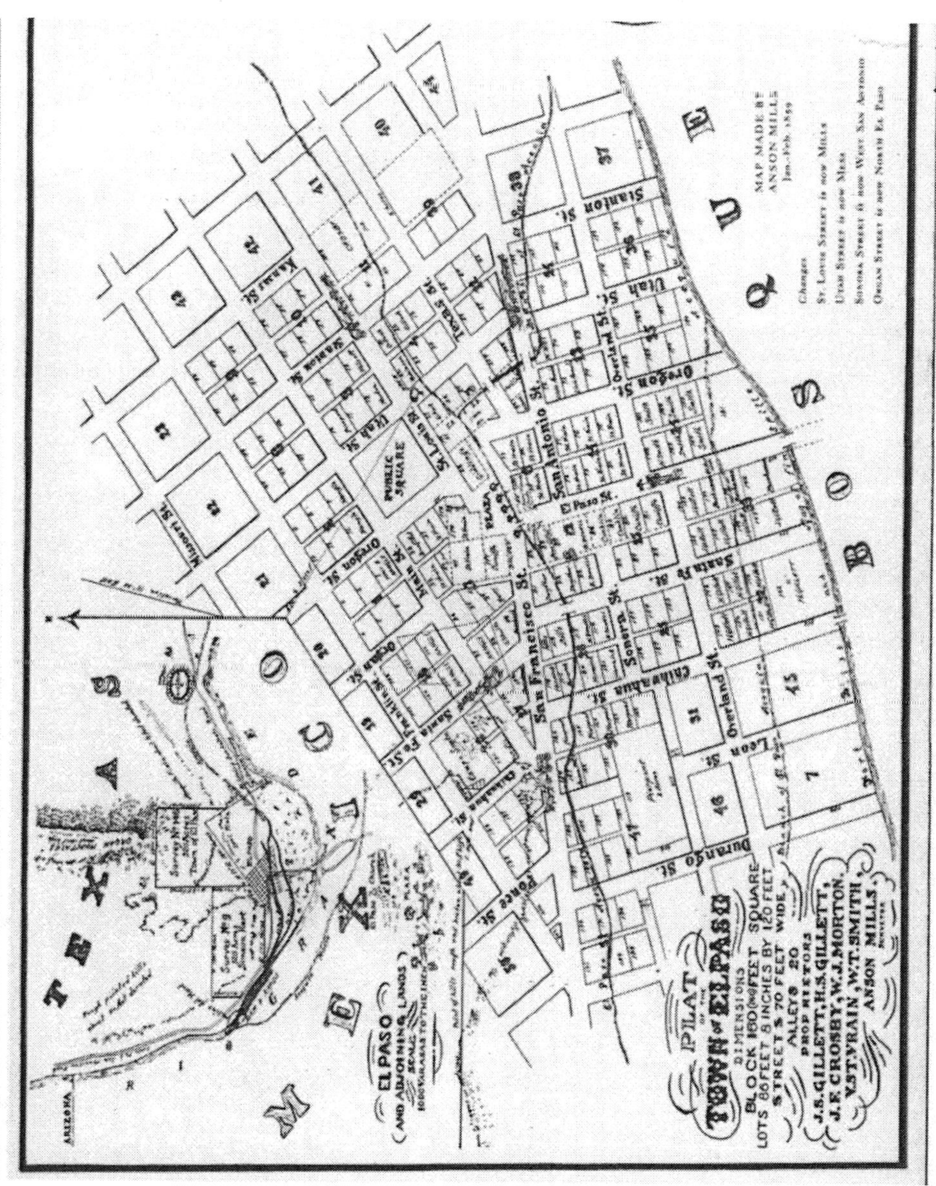

Figure 7. The Mills Plat of 1859. (El Paso Public Library)

**Figure 8. Judge Josiah F. Crosby
1839-1904**
(Special Collections, Masonic Collection, University of Texas at El Paso)

**Figure 9. General Anson Mills
1834-1924**

Figure 10. Mills Building, Washington, D.C. One block west of the White House. Eight story general office building. ca. 1940. Rebuilt and enlarged in 1966.
(Historical Society of Washington D.C.)

Figure 11. The Mills cartridge belt. The source of Gen. Mills' fortune.

In 1912, Mills rebuilt his two-story office building into a 12-story property, which became the tallest building in El Paso when it was completed. Eventually, Mills left El Paso and returned to live out his later life at 2 DuPont Circle in Washington D.C. to watch over his office building at 1700 Pennsylvania, one block west of the White House. Mills built that building prior to the building of the Mills 12-story El Paso enterprise. Mills wanted his El Paso building to be exactly like his Washington edifice.[73] The current Mills Building in Washington was re-built in 1966 and is still reportedly still controlled by Mills descendants.

Judge Crosby's intransigence over the re-construction of the Grand Central acted as a catalyst to convert the Sheldon Block into a hotel in 1900. However, Crosby's role in the Sheldon activity in El Paso far predates the Grand Central fiasco. In 1880, Crosby and his friend from Austin, Texas, George B Zimpelman purchased the huge Corralitos Ranch and mines from its long time owners, the heirs of the infamous Zuloaga family. Zimpelman was a former Confederate officer, sheriff, and land speculator. It was their intent to sell the ranch to a syndicate of Wall Street capitalists. E.D. Morgan (a cousin of J.P. Morgan) and a group of New York and Boston investors and railroad entrepreneurs headed the Corralitos Company. Crosby and Zimpelman retained a small percentage of ownership and Zimpelman was employed as ranch manager. When the syndicate took control, they hired as one of their mining engineers, Gardner Sheldon, the son of a wealthy New York investor and friend of E.D. Morgan, Lucius M. Sheldon. During the next several years, Gardner Sheldon made numerous trips to El Paso and became convinced of its real estate investing potential. Over the next several years, Gardner continued to urge his father to invest in El Paso.

In 1879, El Paso began a slow but steady evolution as four great railroads began their capitalist race for access to not only the commercial portal to Mexico, but also the southern route of the much anticipated southern route transcontinental railway linking the east coast to the gold fields of California. White writes in his autobiography:

> In the year in which I was born El Paso began to undergo a change of life. In that year, four great railroads began laying their tracks in the direction of its barrooms and gaming resorts, the result being that the town at once began to fill up with border parasites coming in to prey upon the railroad payrolls. For the first six or eight months these men,

> and the few women who were with them, came in a trickle, by the end of another six, with the railheads drawing nearer and nearer, they arrived in a flood. They came in buckboards, buggies, wagons, stages, on foot, and on horseback. They ate what they could forage, drank anything, slept with anybody; worked feverishly during the day erecting shacks to live in, and caroused vigorously throughout the night. This was a wicked period in the life of El Paso. Everything was under control: under control of gals and gunmen, to the end that in one year more killings took place in El Paso than had ever taken place in the entire career of any of the so-called really tough towns of the frontier. But what of it? These killings were unimportant. No one, not even the relatives of the deceased, gave a damn about them. No one had time to, because everyone's attention was centered on the race between the Santa Fe and the Southern Pacific, which were, each one, trying to beat the other into the town.
>
> The Southern Pacific won: it brought its first train in on May 13, 1881 and immediately El Paso underwent a series of changes that were quick and startling.[74]

The Coming of Age

Not only was 1881 the year that the major railroads arrived in El Paso, it was also the year that Gardner Sheldon's father, Lucius M. Sheldon, purchased Block 5 Lot 28 in the heart of El Paso from the group of investors that included Thomas Wentworth Peirce, Jr., one of the major Eastern stockholders of the Corralitos Ranch. Lucius Sheldon began to develop portions of the property into retail establishments along St. Louis Street incorporating Lot 31 to the corner of Utah Street (Mesa Ave.)[75] At Gardner's urging, Lucius Sheldon intended to build a four-story office building at El Paso Streets and St. Louis eventually purchasing the property that formerly housed the George B. Giddings's San Antonio-San Diego Stage Line that corners the two plazas, across the street from what would become the Grand Central Hotel. In 1886, Lucius Sheldon began construction of a four-story office and commercial building that opened for business in 1888 and was known as the Sheldon Block. In 1900, the office building was converted to what became, at that time, the most significant hotel in the southwest, the Sheldon Hotel. [The Corralitos Ranch and early Sheldon investment in El Paso is the subject of the author's 2014 book, Mines, Cattle, and Rebellion.]

In a letter dated July 25, 1882, Gardner wrote his father about further investing in El Paso:

> I have been looking around town to see what other investments there were in case you wanted to put any more money yourself in El Paso real estate. I only saw two desirable properties both of which they ask a good price for but I have sufficient faith in El Paso to believe that any investment in El Paso at anything like reasonable rates is a good one. One property is situated corner El Paso and Overland Street being that occupied by M. Rothschild Jewelers and by the Lone Star Newspaper office consisting of two lots, 22' on El Paso St. x 76' deep on Overland Street and the other adjoining Overland 38' x 43'. I don't know what it is renting for now but ought to rent for $200 per month. It can be bought for $8000. The best is Schuster's property on El Paso St. fronting on said Street 72 feet by hundred [sic] and 20 feet deep and consisting of three stories, which would not be without tenants at $100 per month each. One is rented at that figure and in case of sale Schuster reserves right to remain in his two stores until June 1 for $250 per month making $250 per month for the three to June 1 at which I am sure the three could be rented for $300 per month if not more. It can be bought for $15,000. It is the best investment in town.[76]

As the old cantankerous Judge Crosby continued to dominate property development in El Paso his catalytic role in Lucius M. Sheldon's entrance into El Paso property is, partly responsible for the vast holdings that Sheldon acquired, that made him, according to tax records, the largest property tax payer of the era.

Following the Union victory in 1865, a judge in New Mexico ordered the seizure of all property belonging to confederate sympathizers in El Paso including Crosby, Dowell, Hart, Magoffin, and Stephenson among others. Saloon owner and eventual El Paso mayor Ben Dowell was exempt from the New Mexico ruling. Apparently, Dowell sent his Masonic Lodge brother, W.W. Mills, an ardent Unionist, a letter asking for help regarding the confiscation order. From his exile in El Paso del Norte, he wrote, "He was tired of living a "dog's life," asking Mills' forgiveness for any difference, and seeking his intervention with the military to enable the Dowell family to return home." Mills complied and soon entered into a business venture with Dowell involving horse racing down Overland Street, a few blocks from Dowell's saloon which he reopened when his property was restored.[77]

Crosby, along with Magoffin and Stephenson, argued successfully before the New Mexico Supreme Court that the jurisdiction of the New Mexico courts did not extend to El Paso, Texas. The United States Supreme Court heard the appeal and the New Mexico Supreme Court decision was upheld. Full recovery of their property was protracted.[78]

By 1878 the politicians of Washington D.C. and the powerbrokers of New York and Boston, eyed El Paso and the early stage routes that led through the little dusty town as the portal of the southern route of a transcontinental rail system connecting east with west, without the encumbrances of fickle and threatening weather changes. Simultaneously construction was launched for the Atchison, Topeka & Santa Fe, the Southern Pacific, the Texas & Pacific, and the Galveston, Harrisburg & San Antonio railways. C.K. Holiday, T.G. Phelps and C. P. Huntington, J. Gould, and T.W. Peirce, Sr. bounded into the race with ample amounts of money and chicanery pushed their roads in the direction of El Paso. In the end the only real winners were Huntington and of course El Paso. It wasn't long before the Mexican Central railroad began to have a major presence and the little dusty village on the banks of the Rio Grande became a major focus of worldwide attention. El Paso became America's portal for retail and wholesale trade into Mexico.[79]

The city had extensive cattle-raising, mining, smelting, and cigar-manufacturing interests. Scattered among its streets were the Federal Building, county courthouse, city hall, post office, high school, hospital, and of course, the Sheldon Hotel.[80] One of El Paso's Forty-Four, James Gillett, local peace officer, described El Paso of that day, "Real estate dealers, cattlemen, miners, railroad men, gamblers, saloon keepers, and sporting people flocked to town. At night there was no room for people on the sidewalks and they filled the streets."[81]

Owen White describes the local men in their anticipation of the arrival of their long held dreams:

> Most of the men who made their homes in El Paso before the advent of the railroads, and many who came afterwards, yielded to the temptations offered by the freedom of the times. They drank immoderately, gambled recklessly, lived lavishly, loosely, and indiscriminately with women of easy virtue, and in the end either died as the result of dissipation or were suddenly snuffed out in a gun fight originating over some trivial and unworthy cause.

> El Paso's fathers, those who lived through the earliest American period and saw the fulfillment of their hopes, did not do these things. They were typically men who could be in but not of the dissipations of the times. As we have already said, they associated humanly with all classes of men. They consumed their share of the liquor of the day; they "sat in" at poker, monte, and faro-bank, in all probability, they patronized dance halls. But these things they always and invariably did as leaders of the men with whom they associated and never as victims of the vices which were consuming their fellows.
>
> Throughout the long period of time that these men had waited for their dreams to come true, they maintained their ascendency in the community in which they lived by dealing fairly and honestly with all comers, and by insisting that all comers deal fairly and honestly with them. It may have been chance, it may have been foresight, or it may have been the natural desire which men have to associate with their kind that caused the Americans to congregate in El Paso and made El Paso become an American town. But no matter what the cause, results were obtained which have since proved to be of incalculable benefit to the Southwest.[82]

The growth and evolution of El Paso derived from the arrival of the railroads in El Paso can be traced back to the brief but poignant success of one particular member of the Forty-four; George H. Giddings. This credit lays at the doorway of an old adobe store and corral, just diagonally east of the old Ponce Rancho and the Rohman hotel, on the Little Plaza at Block 5 Lot 28 of the Mills plat of 1859.

Notes and References

---

[1] Strickland, Rex W. *Six Who Came to El Paso*. (El Paso: Texas Western Press, 1963.), 12.

[2] White, Owen P. *Out of the Desert: The Historical Romance of El Paso*. (El Paso: The McMath Company, 1923.), 43.

[3] Brands, H.W. *The Age of Gold: the California Gold Rush and the New American Dream.* New York: Anchor, 2003.), 93-103.

[4] Starr, Kevin, and Richard Orsi (eds.) *Rooted in Barbarous Soil: People, Culture, andCommunity in Gold Rush California*. (Berkeley: University of Califiorina Press,2000.), 57-61.

---

[5] Timmons, W.H. *El Paso: A Borderlands History*. (El Paso: Texas Western Press, 1990.), 110-112.
[6] Strickland (1963), 9-10.
[7] Ibid.
[8] Percy, Frederick A. *El Sabio Sembrador*. (El Paso: the author, 1854.), 12. In Strickland (1969).
[9] Strickland, Rex W. *El Paso in 1854*. (El Paso: Texas Western Press, 1969.), 34n.
[10] Cool, Paul. *Salt Warriors: Insurgency on the Rio Grande.* (College Station: Texas A&M University Press, 2008.), 25.
[11] Sonnichsen, C. L., and M.G. McKinney. *The State National Bank of El Paso Since 1881: The Pioneer Bank of El Paso.* (El Paso: Texas Western Press, 1971.), 61.
[12] In a publication by James Magoffin Dwyer Jr. entitled "Hugh Stephenson" published in the *New Mexico Historical Journal* dated January 1954, Vol. 29 No. 1, 3-4. A list of the Stephenson/Azcárate children presented by the author. Horace, Marguerite, Hugh Jr., Adelaide, and Benicia. The name Leonore is not mentioned. Unless that is one of the daughter's middle name, the Dwyer article is in error. Percy's wife, Leonore was verified by U.S. Federal Census of 1850.
[13] Ledbetter, Suzann. *Shady Ladies: Nineteen Surprising and Rebellious American Women.* (New York: A Forge Book, 2006.), 72.
[14] Ibid: 72-77. A humorous and literate recounting of Sarah's path to become the "Heroine of Fort Brown."
[15] Sandwich, Brian. *The Great Western: Legendary Lady of the Southwest.* Southwestern Studies No. 94. (El Paso: Texas Western Press, 1991.)
[16] Johannsen, Robert W. *To The Halls of Montezuma: The Mexican War in the American Imagination.* (New York: Oxford University Press, 1985.)
[17] Ibid, 139.
[18] Sandwich, 23.
[19] Ibid, 22-27.
[20] Frost, H. Gordon. *The Gentleman's Club: The Story of Prostitution in El Paso.* (El Paso: Mangan Books, 1983.), 16-17.
[21] Sonnichsen, C.L. *Pass of the North: Four Centuries on the Rio Grande.* (El Paso: Texas Western Press, 1968.), 126.
[22] Dillon, Richard H. *Texas Argonauts: Isaac H. Duval and the California Gold Rush.* (San Francisco: Book Club of California, 1987.), 76.
[23] Ibid, 187n (65).

[24] Cox, C.C. "From Texas to California in 1849: The Diary of C.C. Cox." *Southwestern Historical Quarterly*. Vol. 29 No.2. (October, 1925), 132.
[25] Sandwich, 26.
[26] Ledbetter, 78.
[27] Anderson, Greta. *More Than Petticoats: Remarkable Texas Women*. (Guilford, CT: Morris Book Publishing, 2013.), 16.
[28] In the epilogue of the Brian Sandwich book, *The Great Western: The Legendary Lady of the Southwest.*(1991), 62. He writes, "Edward Tuttle is the only source as to her cause of death. His memory of dates and facts were occasionally clouded. He said in his remembrances that Sarah built and run (sic) the first hotel in the town Yuma in 1866, and died there the following year from a bite of a Tarantula spider.' He refers to her death as being from a 'poisonous spider' and a venomous Tarantula or spider in the same story. A Tarantula bite would not normally be fatal, though some other poisonous creature would certainly be a possible cause of death.
[29] Blevins, Don. *A Priest, a Prostitute, and Some Other Early Texans*. (Guilford, CT: Globe Pequot, 2008.), 24. In the book, *More Than Petticoats: Remarkable Texas Women* written by Greta Anderson, the author on page 18, without notation, states," In 1980 her body was removed, along with the buried remains of soldiers, to be interned in the presidio in San Francisco." Based on information from the National Cemetery at San Francisco, Anderson's reference appears to be a typographical error. In August of 1890 the US Army exhumed the 159 bodies buried at Fort Yuma and moved them to the presidio at the San Francisco National Cemetery.
[30] Aker, Andrea. "The Story of Sarah Bowman: Yuma's First Citizen Left a Lasting Impression." *Arizona Oddities*. January 21, 2011. Accessed 9 September 2015.
[31] Cool, Paul. "J.A. Tays: The Frontier Battalion's Forgotten Officer." *The Texas Ranger Dispatch.* Issue 7, summer 2002. (Waco, TX: The Texas Ranger Hall of Fame and Museum, 2002.) Accessed 8 September 2015.
[32] Ibid, 18.
[33] *El Paso Times* March 2, 1881.
[34] *El Paso Herald* February 15, 1890. 4:2.
[35] Chapman, Bob. "Old Central Hotel built on site of Ponce de León's Ranch House." *El Paso Times.* March 9, 1952.
[36] 1850 Federal Census records showing their residency and Mr. Gillock's occupation as a government contractor in San Antonio. The 1860 Census indicates that the Gillocks had moved to El Paso where his occupation was described as hotel keeper.
[37] White (1923), 61.
[38] Ibid.

[39] Ibid.
[40] Cioc-Ortega, M. "What's in a name? A homage to the original Newspaper Tree." *newspapertree.com* July 4, 2007. Accessed 27 March 2015.
[41] El Paso County Book of Deeds, Book 2, p. 596. Elizabeth Gillock sold her share of lot 36, Block 17 and fractional lots lying between lots 36 and 37 to Anson Mills and Josiah F. Crosby for $6,000 on May 20, 1882.
[42] Mills, W.W. *Forty Years at El Paso 1858 - 1898: Recollections of War, Politics, Adventure,Events, Narratives, Sketches, Etc.* (Washington: Library of Congress, 1901.), 34.
[43] Corcoran, Lillian Hague. "He brought the railroad to El Paso – The story of James P. Hague." *Password.* Vol. 1, No. 2 (May, 1956), 49. In 1873, Hague and W.W. Mills (Gen. Anson Mills' brother) deeded land that they owned to the Southern Pacific Railroad for a depot in downtown El Paso.
[44] Braxton and Elizabeth Gillock did not arrive in El Paso until 1857, so the reference to the 49ers is clearly in error. Data derived from either the written or oral histories are frequently filled with errors caused by fading memories. This is certainly the case in this family history of the Coldwell as told by one of the daughters, Mrs. McCain. The editor, Eugene O. Porter has made every effort to highlight these errors.
[45] Porter, Eugene O. "From Austin to El Paso in 1873: A Saga of the Coldwell Family." *Password.* Vol. IX, No.2, summer 1964, 60.
[46] Cool, 259.
[47] A narrative found on page 94 of a written note book that contains the record of the oral history of El Paso pioneer attorney Richard Burgess. It appears that it was not written by Mr. Burgess, but is included with his papers. Located in MS 262 Box 25, even though it contains a cover sheet indicating Acc. 977 Box 6, Book 1. Special Collections, University of Texas at El Paso.
[48] *El Paso Herald.* January 9, 1892, 4:2.
[49] *El Paso Herald*, May 8, 1894, 1:6.
[50] *El Paso Daily Times*, March 5, 1890, 7:5; *El Paso Herald,* January 14, 1921, 1:4; *El Paso Times*, April 22, 1940, 4:2; among others.
[51] Sonnichsen and McKinney (1971), 1, 14.
[52] Bussell, Richard. Personal interview, El Paso, 20 August 2010.
[53] The writer spent many hours reviewing hundreds of maps including the Sanborn maps dated 1883-1927. The Sanborn maps of 1883-2 clearly show the position of the Central Hotel in relation to the Grand Central during the Grand Central's construction on the east side of the Central Hotel at the corner of Oregon and St. Louis Streets. This map adds to the confusion by labeling the Grand Central as simply the Central Hotel. Then in

the 1885 map, following the construction, Sanborn labeled both hotels under the banner of the Grand Central Hotel. In this 1885 map and subsequently in the 1888 map, a bridge is shown connecting the two hotels at the second floor. This map introduces the presence of a third hotel, the Center Block Hotel on the old Ochoa site at El Paso and San Francisco Streets. The 1893 map shows the ruins of the Grand Central Hotel following the devastating fire in February 1892, but shows the Central Hotel at the site of the future White House department store and the Plaza Theater. However, Sanborn labels this hotel as the Grand Central rather than the Central Hotel. This map continues to refer to the Center Block Hotel at the northwest corner of where San Francisco and El Paso Streets intersect. In the 1900 Sanborn map, the Grand Central site now houses the first Mills Building (two-story) and the Central Hotel site is now referred to as the Plaza Block. The Center Block Hotel is still located at San Francisco and El Paso Streets. The Conklin and Sanborn Maps are housed in the special collections department at the University of Texas at El Paso. In addition, the Sanborn collection is available online from the Perry-Castañeda Map Collection at the University of Texas at Austin. While this does not specifically offer an explanation for the confusion of the two adjacent and similarly named hotels, it does show how this historic confusion has been fostered.

[54] Bowden, J.J. *The Ascárate Grant*, Master's thesis, 35.

[55] Ibid.

[56] Sonnichsen (1968), 143.

[57] Bowden, 35.

[58] Cioc-Ortega, M. "Anson Mills and the Platting of El Paso, 1858-1859." (*Password.* Vol. 58.), 53-59.

[59] Sonnichsen (1968), 143.

[60] White (1923), 59.

[61] The pre-war forty-four referred to are listed by name on page 65 of Owen P. White's *Out of the Desert: The Historical Romance of El Paso.* El Paso's Forty-Four: J.F. Crosby, Simeon Hart, Henry J. Cuniffe, H.S. Gillett, J.S. Gillett, Phil Herbert, Jams Magoffin, Joseph Magoffin, Samuel Magoffin, Anson Mills, W.W. Mills, Emmett Mills, Samuel Schutz, Joseph Schutz, George H. Giddings, H.C. Hall, Henry Skillman, Brad Dally, Hugh Stephenson, William Smith, Vincent St. Vrain, A.B. O'Bannon, William Morton, Charles Merritt, Henry C. Cook, B.S. Dowell, Nim Dowell, Fred Percy, Rufus Doane, Billy Watts, Emilio Deusechesne, Rus Howard, A.B. Rohman, H.L. Robertson, Dr. Nangle, Charles Richardson, B.W. Gillock, J.B. Terry, Charles Music, Andrew Hornick, H. McWard, Bill Conklin, Mr. Tibbetts, and Tom Miller

[62] Ibid, 60.

[63] The El Paso County Historical Society provides a brief but most accurate summary of El Paso history on their website.
[64] White (1923), 52.
[65] Mills, Anson. *My Story*. (Washington: Press of Byron S. Adams, 1918.), 54.
[66] Ibid.
[67] Lone Star Newspaper, Vol. VIII, No. 45 February 14, 1883.
[68] Jackson, Ken. "Joe Brown's murder trial." *El Paso Bar Journal.* October/November 2012, 11-14. Historical accounts of the murderous activities of the Coney Island can be reviewed among the writings of numerous Southwest historians, including Metz, Sonnichsen, White, and others. The Jackson article is of significance because it is concise, detailed, and brief as well as not being labored with legalese.
[69] Selcer, Richard et.al. *Legendary Watering Holes: The Saloons That Made Texas Famous.* (College Station: Texas A & M University Press, 2004.), 149.
[70] The First National Bank merged with American National Bank in 1914.
[71] White (1923), 63
[72] Kohout, Martin D. "Josiah Frazier Crosby." (The Handbook of Texas Online. March 4, 2011. Accessed 21 March 2013.
[73] Letter from Anson Mills, November 23, 1906 to Horace B. Stevens. UTEP MS 153 box 82. Digital retrieval number 901.
[74] White, Owen P. *Autobiography of a Durable Sinner.* (New York: G.P. Putman's Sons, 1942.), 41-42.
[75] These Sheldon stores can be observed by reviewing various Sanborn maps of this time frame.
[76] Campbell, C.E. *Mines, Cattle, and Rebellion.* (Sunset Beach: Green Street Publications, 2014.), 77-81.
[77] Hamilton, Nancy. "Tribute to Ben Dowell." (*Password*. Vol. 28 1992):16-20.
[78] Timmons (1990), 149-151.
[79] "El Paso". *Monthly Business Review.* Vol.36, No. 7. (Dallas: Federal Reserve Bank of Dallas), 90.
[80] "El Paso." *The New International Encyclopaedia* Editors: Gilman, Daniel, et.al. Vol. VII. (New York: Dodd, Mead and Company, 1905.), 11.
[81] Goetting, Charles A. (Mrs.). "A tribute to James P. Hague." (*Password*. Vol. xx, 1973), 148-150.
[82] White (1923), 127.

Figure 12. Pioneer Plaza (Little Plaza) looking east to the Vendome Hotel (later the Orndorff). Central Hotel on left and Sheldon building site center right. ca. 1885.

(Courtesy of Joel Guzman)

Figure 13. Pioneer Plaza in front of Central Hotel, ca. 1890.

(El Paso County Historical Society.)

Chapter Three

Block 5 Lot 28

The store, stage office, and corral sitting on the Little Plaza's east side where St. Louis Street joins El Paso Street across from San Jacinto Plaza was right in the middle of the town's social activity. "Old Dad" Atkins and his young German apprentice, Fred, usually spent the night at the store and this tended to dissuade the local criminal element from pilfering the store's stock. One evening in 1859, Atkins was called away and Fred remained alone in the store's sleeping quarters. The next morning upon his return, Atkins discovered that a window on the south side of the adobe building had been dug out. Fred's lifeless body was discovered in his bed, having been slain by fourteen stab wounds. Large amounts of money and merchandise had been taken. Several days later, after the window had been replaced, the early morning was announced by the crack of a shotgun. Apparently, the same or new robbers were denied entrance through the same window by the sound of a poorly aimed shotgun by "Old Dad" Atkins. El Paso was changing.[1]

George H. Giddings

The store had belonged to the C.J. Cook Company, a San Antonio dry goods and freighting company. In 1846, Pennsylvania native, George H. Giddings had traveled to San Antonio and had become a clerk in the Cook Company store. Two years after George's arrival, the two owners of the business announced their retirement. From his savings, Giddings purchased the business, including its satellite store in El Paso for $12,500.[2] During his time operating the business he purchased the operation of the San Antonio-Santa Fe mail line from David Wasson. Giddings operated the 1,100-mile route to Santa Fe with major losses from Indian raids and the failure of the government to increase its financial support, the San Antonio-Santa Fe mail line barely stayed in business. In 1857, the federal government issued a mail contract to James E. Birch to run the San

Antonio-San Diego (SA-SD) Mail Line and some of the Birch route overlapped with Giddings' line. Birch named Giddings to be his operator on the SA-SD line, from San Antonio to El Paso.[3] By 1859, Giddings San Antonio Mail Line had its headquarters on the lot where the Sheldon building would soon appear.[4] Giddings had been accepted as one of the local "Forty-four."

With the growth in the Anglo population following the California Gold Rush of 1849, a major need developed to provide improved modes of transportation and communication. Stage lines became an alternative to the lengthy and dangerous voyages around Cape Horn by ship. The first regular monthly mail service from San Antonio to Santa Fe was carried by Captain Henry Skillman on horseback in 1849.[5] Skillman would become a spectacular character in the history of the stage lines in the Southwest. During the Civil War, he would resurface as a spy for the Confederacy while he worked for the Union Army. Two years later, "Big Foot" Wallace provided the horseback service to El Paso.[6]

In 1854, the first coach mail contract had been issued to Wasson, who shortly thereafter transferred the contract to the San Antonio freighter; Giddings operated the line to Santa Fe from 1854 to 1858.[7] If successful these stagecoach and mail lines would be the precursor to the southern route of the transcontinental railroad. The clamor for improved transportation and communication between the Atlantic and Pacific Coast was stirring in Washington. In the second session of the 32nd Congress in 1852-1853 the Senate paid more attention to the subject. It was commonly held that "where the mail stage lead, the railroads would follow," and the discussion of one always led to the discussion of the other.[8]

While Giddings operated the San Antonio-Santa Fe Mail line and he became a perfect partner to James E. Birch, the 21-year old New England based entrepreneur. Rather than test fate with his future, Birch chose to purchase a team and wagon and provide transportation and supplies to the mining camps. It was not long before James E. Birch had established the California Stage Company and made his fortune and returned to the east. Birch heard that Congress had passed the Postal Route Bill establishing the San Antonio to San Diego via El Paso route, without appropriation, in August 1856. Birch seized the opportunity, knowing that the appropriation would soon follow, purchased control of the existing San Antonio-San Diego Line of George Giddings.

Following a fierce competitive battle, Birch was awarded the federal mail route from St. Louis to San Francisco, thus creating the first transcontinental overland mail route. The SA-SD line acted as a "political pilot-fish for a huge political shark." It became a political wedge for a strictly Southern enterprise looking forward to a Southern railroad.[9]

After Giddings acquired the Cook and Company firm in El Paso, he got title to the firm's property at Lot 28 and Lot 31 in Block 5. This included land that soon became the Sheldon and Hilton hotels, the Kress Building where the old Federal Building once stood, and the piece of Oregon Street between the two buildings and a strip south from St. Louis Street (Mills Ave.) across Texas Street to San Antonio Street.[10]

The stage station was a low rambling adobe building with a corral adjoining it to the east on Lot 31 Block 5. The property extended the whole length of the block between St. Louis (Mills Ave) and Texas Street. Using the Mills plat as a reference, this corral was adjacent to Lot 27 Block 5 then owned by Elizabeth Gillock, just one-half block from her property at Lot 20 and 21 of Block 4, at the intersection of Stanton and St. Louis.[11] Across the way from the corral, Giddings operated his store on the property that juts out into the Little Plaza that soon became the site of the Sheldon.[12]

The Jackass Mail

The oft-repeated and compellingly brief history of Giddings' San Antonio-San Diego Mail Line and the origin of its "Jackass Mail" nickname has been told from a wide variety of points of view. Philatelists, western stagecoach buffs, National Parks rangers, serious journalists, and southwest amateur and professional historians have all covered this history. Popular magazines, newspapers, and professional journals have presented this story so well that there has sprung from these roots several associations and annual gatherings to celebrate the early success of the 150-year old mail line. The writer believes that among all the available treatises, that written by Robert N. Mullin's, Stagecoach Pioneers of the Southwest, is the most engaging and well referenced.[13]

The Post Office invited bids for the route in April 1857:

> One bidder was H.F. Cook, who offered semi-monthly service over the 1410-mile route between San Antonio and San Diego for a mail subsidy of $149,800 a year from July 1, 1857 to June 30, 1861. Before the contract award was made, Birch acquired, by assignment, Cook's rights, and obligations under the Cook bid. ...On June 22, 1857, it was

announced that James Birch had been awarded the San Antonio-San Diego mail contract. On July 9, 1857, just eighteen days after Birch was awarded the contract, the first assignment of mail left San Antonio for San Diego.[14]

Just as the Birch line was beginning, the political climate in Washington, D.C. changed. The newly elected President James Buchanan appointed a new postmaster general, who in turn awarded a major mail contract, from Memphis/St. Louis to San Francisco to John Butterfield, a close friend of President Buchanan, and the businessman behind the Wells Fargo and American Express companies. This new route would overlap the Birch route on the San Antonio to San Diego leg. Birch had already hired Isaiah C. Woods as general superintendent and George Giddings as supervisor of the route. There would be a delay of sometime in order for Butterfield to get up to speed and actually begin his line. Birch felt that the delay would give him a chance to go to Washington and resolve things and regain his contract. The first mail from San Antonio left for San Diego and arrived August 31, fifty-three days after its start from San Antonio.[15]

Hurrying back to Washington, Birch left San Francisco by the side-wheel steamer, Central America, but on the night of September 12, 1857, a violent storm hit the Atlantic south of Cape Hatteras and the steam ship was lost:

> Four hundred passengers and crew went down with the ship; three escaped in a lifeboat and one other, Birch, managed to reach a floating raft. After nine days without food or fresh water…and 428 miles from where the steamer sank, the men in the lifeboat were finally sighted and picked up by a passing vessel…Birch had been swept off by a wave and carried away by the sea.[16]

With Birch dead, his widow attempted to keep the San Antonio-San Diego line operating. Things deteriorated upon her appointment of a family relative to run the business. Giddings appealed to the postmaster general, and the contract was then transferred to Giddings. The line continued, however, its profitability remained in doubt because of the mounting depredations from the Indians who roamed along the "emigrant trail" between El Paso and Yuma. The stagecoaches were pulled by mules along the northern portion of the trip, but when the coaches turned to the west to cross the great Colorado Desert, the 180 miles to San Diego, the coaches could not travel in the soft sand. As a result, the passengers and cargo would have to transfer the backs of mules. This is frequently identified as the source of the nickname, "The Jackass Mail." It is espoused by two of the Giddings descendants[17] that the name was first employed in 1857 by an editor in a San Francisco newspaper who referred to the San Antonio to San Diego stages as being pulled by "jackasses." The editor of the San Diego Herald rather abruptly pointed out that his "colleague" in San Francisco could not tell the difference between a mule and a jackass and the name the Jackass Mail Line remains a footnote in history when referring to Mail Route number 8076.[18] (See figure 113)

With his political connection to President Buchanan and astute business experience as the third founder of both Wells, Fargo & Company and American Express, Butterfield's Overland Mail route from St. Louis to San Francisco grew enormously and the government continued to reduce Giddings' portion of the mail route.

Lincoln enlists Giddings

In late 1860, just prior to the closure of the SA-SD line, Giddings went to Washington D.C. to lobby his case for federal reimbursement for the losses he encountered from both the loss of the mail contract and the continuing Indian depredations.[19] While in meetings with the newly appointed Postmaster General Montgomery Blair (who was a friend of Giddings, Blair informed Giddings that he would receive $80,000 in back post office payments, which had been entrapped in bureaucratic red tape. Blair had been responsible for getting the Giddings' mail contract extended anther four years.[20] Congress and the rest of the Washington establishment were less interested in his request for reparations than they were clearly concerned about an impending secession movement from the southern states and the potential for civil war. In an unpublished thesis, Steven Giddings Thorn wrote:

> On the night he was to return to Texas, George called on Blair to offer again his gratitude. Blair informed him that he should stay put in Washington, [President] Lincoln wished to speak to him. At approximately 8 p.m. that same evening, Blair led an astonished George past White House security and into a large conference hall where Lincoln was meeting with his cabinet. The President gestured for

George to sit in the chair next to him. In his memoirs, George recalls that Lincoln said:

> Mr. Giddings you have been highly recommended to me by Postmaster General Blair and my old friend Calusha A. Grow of Pennsylvania as a prominent businessman of Texas and a thoroughly reliable man.

After questioning George on his background as a businessman in Texas, Lincoln got to the point:

> I have sent for you with an object. I wish an important secret message delivered to Governor Houston of Texas. Before reading and confiding in you, I must first swear you in as a member of my Cabinet, all of whom are sworn to secrecy and not to divulge anything taking place at this meeting. This I must do before entrusting you with this message. Hold up your right hand.

George knew that Lincoln's "propensity for joking" was one of his strengths that got the Illinois politician into the White House. But George waited for the punch line that never came. Lincoln was deadly serious. George recited the oath and became a member of the cabinet.

The message George was to deliver to Houston informed the governor that Lincoln had appointed him to the rank of a major general. War had not yet broken out between the North and South but storm clouds were gathering. Houston was asked to organize a volunteer army of 100,000 men and to control all U.S. property in Texas. If Houston chose to comply with the order, Lincoln promised adequate support from the U.S. Army and Navy.

The President and George shared differences on how the message was to be conveyed to Houston. George said:

> This is an important document. I would suggest, for that reason, that you send it by some officer of the regular United States Army.

To which he [Lincoln] answered:

> If those Texans caught a regular United States Army Officer with that document in his possession, they would surely hang him.

George continued:

> If they should catch me with it, they would hang me just as quickly as they would an Army officer or anyone else.

Lincoln replied:

> In that event, I will not insist on your taking that message, as I do not desire to subject you to such peril.

After several minutes of the ping-pong conversation, Giddings agreed to deliver the message. Whether it was due to patriotic guilt on George's part or Lincoln's famous gift of persuasion will never be known.[21]

George left for Texas that night, full of uncertainty about the future of America. With high hopes for a resolution, he had arrived in Austin too late. Texas had just seceded.[22] Giddings then returned to his business operations in El Paso. On April 12, 1861, Giddings learned that his SA-SD mail line had been attacked by Indians and the crew massacred at Steins Pass at the Arizona-New Mexico border and that his brother J.D. Giddings was one of the victims. Later that afternoon, he learned that the Confederate Army had fired upon Fort Sumter and the unthinkable Civil War had begun.[23]

San Antonio Mail Line Abandoned

In May 1861, the Butterfield station property at Overland and El Paso Streets, originally built by Anson Mills, was sold to Giddings by Owen T. Tuller, the acting agent for the Overland Mail Company. At that time, Giddings claimed to be the sole owner of the San Antonio-San Diego mail line. After the conclusion of the Civil War, Giddings lost possession of all of his El Paso property because of his sympathy to the southern cause. After protracted post-war legal issues were resolved, ownership of the Giddings property in Block 5 returned to Giddings and his family.

The Overland property was re-possessed in a trust of the Overland Mail Company in June 1868 by a D.N. Barney[24]. In the ensuing years, the Overland Mail office property became a residence of note, housing many of El Paso elite families and notorious characters.[25] The Giddings' San Antonio-San Diego Mail line was abandoned because of the war and Giddings returned to Austin and organized and financed a company of cavalry. Col. Giddings and his soldiers engaged Union troops at Brownsville, Texas, the last engagement of the war fought after Lee's surrender at Appomattox.[26] Poor communication was the evil slayer.

After the war, Giddings returned to Austin and began to practice law, engage in mining developments in Mexico, and write his memoirs. He then returned to Washington, D.C. to continue his plea for reparations from the Indian attacks on his business despite the ruling of the Court of Claims in 1861. His claim for the $231,720 was denied by the U.S. government.[27]

Title to the Giddings properties along St. Louis Street was returned to the Giddings family who leased it out for a variety of purposes. In 1868, the property became a way-station for Benjamin F. Ficklin. After the Civil War, Ficklin received a government contract for weekly mail service throughout Texas even though he had briefly been arrested for suspicion of complicity in Lincoln's assassination. He provided weekly mail and express service from Arkansas to San Antonio with a branch line to El Paso. Aptly enough, he named his mail and stage-line the San Antonio-El Paso Line.[28] Ficklin's antebellum accomplishments are worthy of review. Ficklin was one of the early developers of the Pony Express, where in January 1860; he was appointed the general superintendent of the newly formed mail courier line that ran from St. Joseph, Missouri to Sacramento, California.

Also in 1860, Ficklin was instrumental in the formation of the Pacific Telegraph Company which eventually was absorbed into the Western Union Telegraph Company, which was the first transcontinental telegraph operation that provided a method of near-instantaneous communication between the east and west coasts during the 1860s.[29] (A detailed time-line of Birch, Giddings, and the San Antonio Mail Line is presented in the appendix of Wayne Austerman's book, Sharp Rifles and Spanish Mules: The San Antonio-El Paso Mail, 1851-1881.)[30]

Battlefield surgeon, Confederate cavalry officer, mail and stage-line entrepreneur, lawyer, real estate developer, and presidential secret agent; George H. Giddings died at the age of 80 while visiting his daughter in Mexico City in 1902 and is buried in a local Mexico City cemetery. His burial at American military cemeteries was prohibited by law because of his service in the Confederate Army.

The coming of the railroads to El Paso was clearly the hallmark of the growth and evolution of this little dusty town. It was specifically, the arrival of

Gould's Texas and Pacific Railroad that delivered the coup de grâce to the San Antonio-San Diego Mail Line. On January 1, 1882, she was put out of business, for good.[31]

The true story of the San Antonio Mail Line and the Butterfield Overland Mail route has suffered historical distortion as journalists and some historians rewrite history. When one today travels east on Interstate 10 through Texas and New Mexico or on Interstate 8 linking California and Arizona, many historical landmarks tout the route as the trail of the Butterfield Stage Line. As Thorn writes, "not one historical monument mentions the accomplishments of the man who was the predecessor to the Butterfield Route. His name was George H. Giddings and his life and accomplishments were every bit as noteworthy as his more celebrated successor, John Butterfield."[32]

The El Paso Federal Building

The Giddings heirs continued to hold the property until they sold it to the syndicate controlled by the estate of Thomas Wentworth Peirce, Sr. and his son Thomas Wentworth Peirce, Jr. with other family members, as well as Charles Balbridge and R.S. Spofford. The sale, along with Lot 28, also included lot 31, the parcel that had contained the SA-SD corral. (See figure 114)

The actual title and completion of the sale of the Giddings property was met with confusion and litigation. In March of 1884, the Peirce syndicate entered into a 'Deed of Exchange' with the City of El Paso to open up Lot 28 and to extend Oregon Street to pass through to St. Louis Street, thus separating Lot 28 from Lot 31.[33] In late 1888, the Peirce group sold the northern half of lot 31 to the federal government for $5,000 as a future site for the El Paso Federal Building, which would include the U.S. Customs House.[34] This transaction was not without major complications that involved a lawsuit brought by the Giddings heirs against the Peirce group.

Before construction could begin on the Federal Building, it was necessary for the citizens of El Paso to raise, by subscription, $2,000 to pay off the issues regarding the title and the Giddings' lawsuit.[35] The protracted agony for the citizens of El Paso was abated when the U.S. Attorney General approved the title clearance and released the $150,000 that had been appropriated for the construction.[36] The building was constructed in 1892 and was an imposing edifice that fit right in with the other four story buildings on St. Louis Street including the Sheldon Block and the Grand Central Hotel. The El Paso post office was one of the first government agencies to move into the building on the first floor and remained until 1920, when it moved to its own facility. The customs office occupied the second floor and the federal court was on the third floor. The Weather Bureau occupied the base of the imposing tower that rose above the third floor. The Federal Building was one of the first all brick buildings built in El Paso, the first having been built in 1886 at Second and El Paso Streets.[37] Prior to the building of the Federal Building, the old Giddings site was home to the Airdrome Outdoor Theater.[38]

The Federal Building site previously had a collection of Chinese centered businesses (laundries and restaurants) and was referred to as "Chinatown." It was row after row of shacks mixed among well-established buildings on the surface on the southeast corner of St. Louis St. (now Mills Ave.), between Utah St. (now Mesa St.) and Stanton St. and below the street level, a dank honey-comb of opium dens and passage ways, twisting and turning in all different directions .[39]

The Federal Building at Oregon and St. Louis Streets (Mills Ave.) would remain an imposing structure for 46 years. Many locals were unhappy with the thought of the demolition of the building. Some wanted the building turned over to other government agencies and still others wanted it to become a museum. The government abandoned the building because of space, not the condition of the building. The building was sold to S. H. Kress & Company[40] for $235,000 who immediately razed it.

While being destroyed, the strength of its "bones" was revealed, the mortar used in the brick structure was made of limestone, rather than cement and this added to the difficulty in tearing the structure down. The Oregon Street entrances with its eminent portals were a city landmark. El Paso Judge Coldwell purchased the portal for $80 and installed them at his farm in Socorro, Texas. He wanted them for sentimental value.[41]

Former El Paso Mayor, Tom Lea, wrote in 1937 an editorial about the loss of the old Federal Building and its portals, "They (the portals) have seen the city grow from a little adobe town in which it was the crowning arch of glory to an imperial little city. The have seen the streets change from dust and mud to the smooth blocks of paving. They have seen the skyline change from the flat tops of mud buildings to the spires and lights that now mark the sky."[42]

The Kress retail company built the architecturally significant building that remains at the site today.[43] The Federal Office and Court House building was then relocated in 1936 to the triangular property between Myrtle and San Antonio at 511 E. San Antonio into a rectilinear Neo-Classical Revival style building with Art Deco influences that remains today, even though the Federal Building and

Courts moved several blocks east. The 1936 Federal Building was built on the site (Block 44) of the old El Paso City Hall building which was sold to the City of El Paso by Lucius M. Sheldon in January 1899.[44]

The Peirce Syndicate Sells

The senior Peirce was a Boston-based capitalist who concentrated in brokering Texas products on the eastern seaboard. He was the primary backer of the Galveston, Harrisburg, and San Antonio Railway Company, one of the four roads that were racing toward El Paso in the early 1880s. The G.H. & S A began as the Buffalo, Bayou, Brazos, and Colorado Railroad in 1850.

Peirce purchased BBB&C railroad out of bankruptcy in 1873 and with the aid of a grant from the City of San Antonio, changed its name to Galveston, Harrisburg, and San Antonio Railroad. The rail race to El Paso ended when Colis P. Huntington and his Southern Pacific railroad arrived in El Paso on May 19, 1881.[45] Huntington's Southern Pacific then strategically joined the westbound effort of Peirce's G.H. & S.A. in January 1883, at location near the Pecos River, three miles west of Langtry, Texas. Langtry was where "Judge" Roy Bean had his saloon and law practice, the "Law West of the Pecos." This combining of assets, gave Huntington virtual control of the second transcontinental railroad in the United States. At the time of Peirce's death in 1885, he owned more than 700,000 acres throughout Texas as well as a major stake in the ownership, with his son, of the million-acre Corralitos ranch and mines in Chihuahua, Mexico.

The Peirce syndicate sold Lot 28 Block 5 to Brooklyn capitalist Lucius M. Sheldon for $15,000. The deed to the property was formally documented in El Paso County on June 9, 1886,[46] and construction began on a four-story office building later that year. The Sheldon Block office building with 140 offices and 11 stores opened in 1888. In January 1891, the Giddings heirs were ordered by a district court judgment in response to a suit filed by them to challenge the original sale to the Peirce syndicate. The Giddings heirs were to issue a quit-claim to Sheldon regarding Lot 28 and were to release Lot 31 (site of the San Antonio-San Diego Mail line corral) to the Peirce syndicate for $5,000, Lots 159-164 in Block 34, and to pay all court costs.[47]

Figure 14. Fire Department training for high rise fires on the Sheldon Block. ca. 1889.
(Courtesy El Paso Fire Department.)

Over the years, journalists and want-to-be historians have taken a great deal of liberty in relating the storied history of Block 5 Lot 28 and the soon to be built Sheldon Hotel and its developer, Lucius M. Sheldon. Because the Sheldon Hotel was at the center of the Mexican Revolution and sat on the site of Conrad Hilton's first high-rise hotel, scribes from many genres have made comments. I have selected just two as examples. It has been described that Dr. Lucius Sheldon was visiting El Paso with his sickly son, when he had an epiphany that there was a great future in El Paso from an investor's point of view.[48] In a photograph of the El Paso Fire Department practicing with their new hook and ladder equipment on the Sheldon Block office building in the late 1880s, the caption reads:

> The ground floor of the Sheldon Building housed a number of railroad, real estate, and express offices. This building had the second passenger elevator in El Paso; the first elevator was in the Grand Central Hotel. Lucius Sheldon of Brooklyn erected this building as an investment after he brought his son to El Paso for lung trouble. The son died in El Paso as the result of his ailment. The building was erected in 1887, and was the first office building with a passenger elevator.[49]

Another writer, while relating the Sheldon to the Hilton Plaza hotel stated, "The history of the Plaza Hotel begins when the Sheldon Hotel was built but burned down one year later by un-known causes."[50]

Not true. Lucius Sheldon was not a doctor of any kind and records show he only attended college briefly,[51] and his son was a mining engineer working at the Corralitos Ranch and Mines in Chihuahua, Mexico. Sheldon was a shrewd and successful venture capitalist who had business ventures in many states. He was the scion of a powerful New York financial family and was a close associate of some of the biggest banking moguls and railroad men in the United States. None of Sheldon's five sons died in El Paso. The Sheldon Hotel did not burn down a year after it was built...far from it, the Sheldon Building and Hotel remained in operation for 41 history-packed years.

Notes and References

[1] Mills, W.W. *Forty Years at El Paso 1858-1898: Recollections of War, Politics, Adventure, Events, Narratives, Sketches, Etc.* (Washington, D.C.: Library of Congress, 1901), 35-36.

[2] Mullin, Robert N. *Stagecoach Pioneers of the Southwest*. Southwestern Studies Monograph No. 71. (El Paso: Texas Western Press, 1976.), 9.

[3] Schneider, Beth. "Giddings, George Henry." *Handbook of Texas Online.* Accessed 16 November 2015.

[4] Mullin, 9.

[5] *New York Herald.* November 11, 1858.

[6] Bartlett, John R. *Personal Narrative of Explorations and Incidents in Texas, New Mexico, California, Sonora, and Chihuahua, Connected with the United States and Mexican Boundary Commission, during the years 1850, 51, 52, and 53.* Vol. II. (New York: D. Appleton & Company, 1854.), 397.

[7] Conkling, Roscoe F., and Margaret B. Conkling. *The Butterfield Overland Mail: 1857-1869: Its Organization and Operation Over the Southern Route to 1861; Subsequent over the Central Route to 1866; and under Wells, Fargo and Company in 1869.* Volume I (Glendale, CA: The Arthur H. Clark Company, 1947.), 90-91.

[8] Johnson, M.M. *The San Antonio-San Diego Mail Line.* Unpublished Master's Thesis (History). (Los Angeles: University of Southern California, 1938.), 2.

[9] Banning, William, George H. Banning. *Six Horses.* (New York: The Century Company, 1930.), 111.

[10] "Pioneer's Descendants Make Home in El Paso." *El Paso Times*. July 10, 1957.

[11] Conkling, 62. Plat of the Town of El Paso, 1859.
[12] El Paso Plat
[13] Mullin, 9
[14] Ibid, 11.
[15] Ibid, 14.
[16] Ibid.
[17] Giddings, Emily Chase, and Emmie Wheatley Mahon. "The Jackass Trail." *Password*. Vol. II, No. 3 (August 1957): 91. Thorn, Steven Giddings. *Col. George H. Giddings: The San Antonio–San Diego Stagecoach Line and other adventures in the great southwest.* Unpublished Master's Thesis - History. (University of San Diego, 1994.), 26.
[18] Mules are a cross between a female horse and a male donkey, known as a "jack." They are very similar in appearance to horses, but generally have greater intelligence than their parents. Mules are large, sure-footed, sterile, and temperamental. Donkeys are an entirely different species and tend to be small and exceedingly more stubborn than mules, even though they are intelligent. They are cautious, friendly, and because of their size, are often used as a form of power in agriculture, particularly where space is limited or restricted.
[19] Giddings, George H. *The Case of George H. Giddings, Contractor on the Overland Mail Route from San Antonio to San Diego.* (Washington, D.C.: H. Polkinhorn Publishers, 1860.),
[20]Thorn, 60-62.
[21] Ibid, 62.
[22] *El Paso Herald Post*. September 30, 1935, 6:3.
[23] *El Paso Times*. July 10, 1957.
[24] Conkling, 62.
[25] Ibid. Conklin noted that Judge Gaylord J. Clarke; Albert J. Fountain I, father of the murdered A.J. Fountain, a local attorney who was at the center of many famous southwest trials; the J.P Hague family; and Judge Newcomb all resided at the old Overland/Butterfield station.
[26] *El Paso Herald Post* (1935).
[27] *El Paso Times*, (1957).
[28] Miles, Susan, and Mary B. Spence, "Ficklin, Benjamin Franklin," Handbook of Texas Online. Accessed 16 November 2015.
[29] Austerman, Wayne R. *Sharps Rifles and Spanish Mules: The San Antonio – El Paso Mail, 1851-1881.* (College Station: Texas A & M University Press, 1985.), pp.315-323.
[29] Ibid, 206.
[30] Ibid, 315-323.

---

[31] Ibid, 323.
[32] Thorn, 2.
[33] El Paso Deed Book No. 5, 415.
[34] *El Paso Times*. January 26, 1936, 18:6.
[35] *El Paso Times*. May 5, 1888, 5:4.
[36] *El Paso Times*. May 28, 1888
[37] *El Paso Herald Post*. September 22, 1932.
[38] Leibson, Art. "1946: Know El Paso – City stole county seat." *El Paso Times*, August 31, 1946. Additional reference to the Airdrome is made on the henrytrost.org internet side and references photographs that show the Airdrome that are in the Aultman Collection at the El Paso Public Library, A5000, A5511, and A5615.
[39] *El Paso Herald Post.* July 13, 1929. Dickey, Gretchen. "Downtown Opium Dens Attracted Many." *Borderlands*. (EPPC Libraries. Vol 21, 2002.) Accessed 11 Dec. 2010.
[40] The S.H. Kress Company should not be confused with S.S. Kresge Company, which was the predecessor to K Mart Corporation (Sears Holdings).
[41] *El Paso Times.* March 1, 1937.
[42] El Paso Times, February 27, 1937.
[43] *El Paso Times*. December 12, 1936.
[44] *Sheldon Family Papers, 1854-1899*. (M-3116.7, 1995). University of Michigan. These papers contain copies of the agreement of sale between Sheldon and El Paso's Mayor Joseph Magoffin as well as blue prints that relate to the transfer of title.
[45] The El Paso County Historical Society uses May 12, 1881 as the official day of the arrival of Huntington's Southern Pacific Railroad as when a construction locomotive arrived. The EPCHS makes no mention of May 19, 1881, however, noted historians Sonnichsen and Timmons only refer to the May 19 date.
[46] El Paso Deed Book No. 8, pp.509-510. Special Collections, University of Texas at El Paso.
[47] El Paso County Clerk's Office Book 23, 209-211.
[48] "The Storied History of the Sheldon Hotel." *El Paso Times*, February 3, 1952. This article has been repeatedly re-posted over the years. "1973: Sheldon bought plaza block for $15,000 in 1881; constructs office building." *El Paso Times*. May 31, 1973, reprinted again in the *EPT* on December 9, 2011 as part of the *Tales from the Morgue* series.
[49] "Hotels: Sheldon Hotel." Vertical File, Border Heritage Center, El Paso Public Library. This photograph may be from the Aultman collection for it has the number B260 that is vaguely visible. A copy of the photo with the caption was obtained in 2007.
[50] http://at-the-plaza.com/history.html

---

[51] *Williams College General Catalogue of Non-Graduates*. Williamstown, MA: the College, 1910. No other collegiate records could be found.

Chapter Four

The Sheldons of Brooklyn

When Isaac Newton Phelps, a New York City dry goods merchant, joined forces in 1834 with merchant James Sheldon to form Sheldon, Phelps & Company; there was no doubt that the pair's ambition and tenacity would develop their little wholesale and import hardware and cutlery shop into one of the nation's largest and most successful hardware and arms businesses. Within a couple of years, their business had grown to cover almost the entire city block at South Williams and Stones streets in Manhattan's Lower East Side, adjacent to the booming financial district and just three blocks west of the East River.[1] As their business grew, both Phelps and Sheldon retired early and turned their business over to the three Sheldon sons.

Isaac Newton Phelps

While Phelps and Sheldon each went their separate ways in mid-century, they both transferred their business acumen into the banking, real estate, and the insurance business. While each rose to head large institutions and serve on many boards of directors of large successful concerns, it is hard to imagine that each could foresee the enormity of their success and the reach of their lineage in American history. Isaac's cousin, Anson G. Phelps became highly successful in cattle, railroads and, of course, copper. Anson G. Phelps founded the Phelps Dodge Company with his sons-in law, William E. Dodge and Daniel James. The copper mining behemoth controlled and developed the Copper Queen Mine in Bisbee, Arizona.[2] Through the growth of the copper mining industry, special rail lines ran to smelter operations in El Paso, Texas. Today, the Phelps Dodge Company is part of the world leader in copper mining, Freeport, McMoran Copper & Gold Inc. Through a series of marriages between the descendants of both Isaac and Anson Phelps, the Phelps dynasty has become associated with the well-known Stokes family of New York.

Central to El Paso's economic survival was the El Paso Smelter operations that eventually became ASARCO[3] and part of the Phelps Dodge Mining Empire. Right in the middle of the growth of the El Paso's copper industry stood the Sheldon Hotel. The Sheldon Block and eventually the Sheldon Hotel, was the site of the early offices of the copper ore industry. Lucius M. Sheldon, the son of Isaac Newton Phelps' partner, James Sheldon, built the Sheldon Block and Hotel. The Phelps-Sheldon partnership had come full circle.

Isaac Newton Phelps' (1802-1888) financial success led him to build one of the most magnificent mansions in New York City at 231 Madison Ave. in 1854. By 1888, J.P. Morgan had purchased the mansion. At the time, Morgan was residing at an adjoining residence previously owned by a Phelps relative. The mansion remains today as the main building of the J.P. Morgan Library, a New York City landmark.[4]

James P. Sheldon

James P. Sheldon's (1798-1852) lineage is equally significant to American history. While it is difficult to top the financial magnitude of Phelps Dodge, the three Sheldon sons became part of the social registry of New York and Brooklyn and left their footprints in yachting, railroads, streetcars, animal husbandry, farming, real estate, banking, and insurance. Just like the Phelps, the long arm of the Sheldons reached across the country and into Mexico. One Sheldon descendant was responsible for part of the development of the National Cathedral in Washington, D.C. as we know it today.

Sheldon and his wife, Ann (nee Owen) were both of old and well known New England families and James was a direct descendant of the Archbishop Sheldon of Oxford England.[5] In 1828, the Sheldons moved from Windsor, CT to Brooklyn Heights and established their home near the foot of the Brooklyn Bridge. It was a convenient location for it provided easy access to the Manhattan location of his business. Eventually, the family settled in a five-story brownstone at 86 Pierpont Street on the corner of Henry Street. The Sheldons had three sons, James O. Sheldon (b.1823), Henry K. Sheldon (b.1826), and Lucius M. Sheldon. (b.1829). James P. Sheldon had become a prominent figure in financial activities in and around New York City. He was one of the original investors who built the Erie and Delaware, Lackawanna & Western railroad.[6] He had turned the hardware business over to Henry and spent most of his time in retirement in the banking and investing business. James died in 1852 while traveling with his family in Marseilles, France. (See figure 115)

It was customary for the successful and wealthy of New York to obtain property to establish summer homes to escape the wilting heat of the city. Mrs. Ann Sheldon, in 1866, purchased over 100 acres of land adjacent to and including one-half of the shoreline of Silver Lake, in the mountains of Susquehanna County, in north-central Pennsylvania, 160 miles from Brooklyn. (The significance of this purchase will come later.)

James O. Sheldon

James Owen was the eldest child of James and Ann Sheldon and during his adult lifetime, he lived in Manhattan rather than Brooklyn, as did his two brothers and parents. James O. entered the family hardware business at the age of 21. As his success and wealth evolved, he entered the banking and investment business at the age of 26 and left the hardware company in the capable hands of his younger brothers. It was not long before James was a primary investor and board member of the New York, New Haven and Hartford Railroad, Fulton Elevated Railroad of Brooklyn,[7] Boston, Hoosac Tunnel and Western Railroad Company,[8] Brooklyn Elevated Railroad (Kings County Elevated Railroad), New York Post-Graduate Hospital and Medical School (NYU), Metropolitan Fire Insurance Company,[9] and the Manhattan Trust Company.[10]

James and his wife Jane (nee Terry) had four children, only two daughters and a son lived to adulthood. James left the confines of Manhattan in 1855 and moved into retirement to a rural farm in Geneva, New York. He purchased the 450-acre White Spring Farm and began to raise cattle. He paid $3000 for an imported English prized Shorthorn bull by the name of the "4th Duke of Geneva." From that auspicious beginning, James built a valuable herd of shorthorn cattle that only added to his fortune.[11] The Sheldon breeding operation became the most celebrated Shorthorn Durham (A breed suitable for dairy and beef.) herd in the world.[12] (The farm is currently part of the Belhurst Castle-White Springs high-end hotel operation that is adjacent to Hobart and William Smith Colleges in Geneva.)

After sixteen years in the cattle business, James moved back to his home at 12 East 40th Street between Fifth and Madison Ave. in Manhattan in 1878, and remained active in social and philanthropic activities until his death at his home at the age of 84 in April 1907.

Henry K. Sheldon

Henry Sheldon was the second of James and Ann Sheldon's three sons and the most visible in both social and financial circles. He attended public schools and subsequently attended the University of the City of New York (CUNY).[13] Henry worked for his father in the hardware business but was extremely unhappy in the family business and he soon traveled to Germany, Austria, and Italy to study art and music.[14] By the time Henry's father died in 1852, he was called home to take over the operation of the Sheldon-Phelps Company, which he did reluctantly. He changed the name of the firm to Sheldon, Hoyt and Co. and ran it until 1870, when he sold it just before the Depression of 1872. With a sizable fortune from the sale of the hardware business, Henry began a new career in banking, railroads, mining, insurance, and real estate. By the time of his death in 1902, he had substantial ownership and management duties in the American Exchange National Bank, the Brooklyn Savings Bank, the Fidelity & Causality Co., the American District Telegraph Co., the Brooklyn Trust Co., the

Figure 15. Sheldon Building New York City 1940. (Demolished)
(New York Public Library)

Figure 16. Henry K. Sheldon
(Courtesy of Tony Russell)

Brooklyn Savings Bank, and the Texas and New Orleans Railroad.[15] The city of Sheldon, Texas (18 miles northeast of Houston.) and Sheldon Lake were named after him because of his activity with the T & NO railroad and his acquisition of large amounts of surrounding land.[16]

Henry's real estate holdings were vast, in New York, Pennsylvania, Texas, and Mexico. One piece of property is of special interest, the Sheldon Building in the financial district of lower Manhattan. Construction of the 12-story commercial building was completed in 1896 at 68-70 Nassau Street / 32-34 John Street.[17] The building was adjacent to the still standing John Street United Methodist Church. The church, located at 44 John Street, is the oldest Methodist congregation in North America and was established in 1766.[18] The Sheldon Building was demolished around 1970 and replaced in the 1980s by a large high-rise office building that today serves as the Federal Reserve Bank of New York Annex. The annex is located a short block north of the main Federal Reserve Bank of New York building at 33 Liberty Street.

Henry's non-business interest included his yacht, the Myeera at the New York Yacht Club[19] and rare book collecting. He left a private library of more than 4000 volumes, many of which are remarkable, and nearly every one notable for binding, rarity, or antiquity.[20] However, his primary interest was the arts and music. Both he and his wife were accomplished musicians and major supporters of the Philharmonic Society of Brooklyn that was established in 1857. He was also the president of the Brooklyn Academy of Music.

The year after Henry's mother purchased the land around Silver Lake, in the mountains of Pennsylvania between the Blue Ridge and Catskill Mountains, Henry purchased the property from her. In 1884 and 1893, Henry added a great deal more acreage around the lake and used the unpretentious Victorian country house as a summer cottage. He named his mountain retreat, Sheldoncroft and summered there for over 30 years.

Henry married Anne (nee Embury) in 1853 and they had two children. Their son, Henry J. Sheldon died as an infant and their daughter, Anna (b. 1859) married an Episcopal Priest, James Townsend Russell. At the time of the engagement between Anna and James Townsend Russell, her father had some hesitancy in allowing his daughter to marry a stage actor. Her father soon devised an elaborate plan to determine if James T. Russell was the proper man to marry his precious daughter. Adelina Russell Bolwell, James' younger sister related the incident (paraphrased):

Because of this disapproval, young James Townsend immediately changed careers and entered a seminary to become a cleric. Henry still hadn't given his blessing on the upcoming marriage as he felt he needed to make doubly sure the Russell family was of acceptable stock. Henry who was an extremely wealthy and highly visible "Wall Streeter," grew a mustache, donned a non-typical wardrobe, and traveled to Lima, Ohio, to investigate the Russell family. When he arrived in Lima, he went to the Lima House Hotel to ask about the Russell family. The desk clerk indicated that the senior Mr. Russell was in fact sitting out on the hotel's front porch, conversing with a group of oil men. Henry, in full disguise, went to the porch and eavesdropped on Russell's conversation.

Knowing Mr. Russell was engaged in conversation at the hotel, Henry went to the Russell residence which was just a few blocks from the hotel. Instead of knocking on the front door, Henry went to the side door and knocked. Mrs. Russell, busily performing kitchen duties, let Henry in. Henry asked of Mr. Russell's presence, knowing where he was. Mrs. Russell told him that her husband was at the Lima House Hotel. After looking around the house and chatting for about fifteen minutes, Henry indicated that he would go to the Lima House and meet with Mr. Russell. Then Henry, abruptly left the house and headed for the train station. Mrs. Russell, turned to her young daughter and said that Mr. Sheldon had just been there. She told her daughter that she just knew it was Mr. Sheldon because, "there is nobody here that looks like a New Yorker." Mrs. Russell immediately wrote her son that Henry Sheldon had just made an unannounced visit. Sheldon couldn't fool her, she knew perfectly who he was.

Years later, long after Henry had given Anna and James his blessing, Mrs. Russell met again with Henry saying, "I don't know why it is, but you don't look like you did when I saw you before." He said, "Oh, when did you see me before?" Mrs.

Russell replied, "Why in Lima." Nothing more was ever said about Henry's investigative roguery. [21]

The Sheldon's daughter, Anna, lived with her parents at their Brooklyn home at 220 Columbia Heights, with a spectacular view of the East River and the skyline of lower Manhattan. (The 1860 brownstone is still there, only the Manhattan skyline has changed. The Sheldon's six-story 9,000 sq. ft. residence is now a five-unit coop apartment with each unit valued at around $3 million.) Anna continued to live with her parents in Brooklyn and at the summer retreat at Sheldoncroft after she married until she and her husband moved to Washington D.C.

Henry's health had been in decline as he celebrated his 76th birthday on February 14. Although he had been an invalid for some time, there was no warning that things would take a turn for the worse. A week after his birthday celebration, he came down with a cold, which expanded to pneumonia.[22]

After Henry's death on March 2, 1902,[23] his daughter Anna Sheldon Russell and her husband the Rev. James T. Russell demolished the old country Victorian cottage and built a spacious 18-room nine-bedroom mansion with accompanying boathouse, barns, dairy farm, and stables on the 450 acres fronting Silver Lake.[24] "This was Sheldoncroft*'s* physical structure, impressive for the size, wealth, and beauty that it represented. The asking price was $75,000 for the entire property when the Russells put it up for sale in 1939. In 1940, the Scranton Diocese of the Catholic Church purchased the majority of the property as a rest home for priests. In 1970, the Diocese sold the land and the buildings. The buildings were demolished and the property further sub-divided. No trace of Sheldoncroft now exists."[25]

Figure 17. Sheldoncroft, H.K. Sheldon's summer home in Susquehanna County, PA. (Courtesy of Tony Russell)

The Rev. James Townsend Russell served as the Rector of the Washington National Cathedral (Cathedral Church of Saint Peter and Saint Paul in the City and Diocese of Washington) from 1918-1929. Adjacent to the large grounds of the Cathedral (Completed in 1990 after 83 years of construction.) was a private home known as the Beauvoir Mansion. In 1918, the Russells purchased the Beauvoir estate as their private residence. In 1922, the Russells indirectly provided for the development of the Cathedral Elementary School. They bequeathed their house, the Beauvoir Mansion (3500 Woodley Rd NW.) and its 13 ½ acres to the National Cathedral. The Cathedral trustees determined, following Canon Russell's death in 1929, that the Beauvoir, with its sprawling grounds and oak grove, would be the perfect space for a new elementary school, and in 1933, the National Cathedral Elementary School was born. Canon Russell and his wife are both buried in the Cathedral. [26]

Lucius Marcus Sheldon

Lucius was the youngest of the three Sheldon sons and the most reclusive of the family. Relatives described him as being extravagantly generous to his nieces and nephews during holidays, and he showed genuine compassion for strangers who were in need. He generally remained somewhat withdrawn and a bit aloof with a keen eye for a good business deal. He was remembered as a portly gentleman, who was constantly fiddling with his gold watch and chain, and incessantly smoking cigars.[27] Lucius M. Sheldon and his family are at the heart of this story.

Figure 18. Lucius M. Sheldon
(Courtesy of Shirley Davenport)

Lucius's parents arranged to send him to Williams College in 1847. Williams College was a private liberal arts men's college in Williamstown, MA that catered to wealthy families.[28] College records indicate that he was a freshman in the 1847-48 class and may have only attended for one year.[29] It appears that he returned to Brooklyn and the family business following his one year at college.

Lucius married in the mid-1850s and continued to work at the family's hardware and arms wholesale and manufacturing business. Following his father's death in 1852, he moved to 123 Montague St. to an ornate brownstone only a block from his family home on Pierpont St. in Brooklyn Heights. The Montague St. home was also only three blocks from his brother's (Henry) home at 220 Columbia Heights on the East River. Lucius and his wife, Harriet (nee Hutchinson) had five sons, Lucius M. Jr. (b. 1858), Gardner H. (b. 1860), Warren O. (b. 1861), Clarence W. (b. 1864), and Henry K., Jr. (b. 1870).

Detailed records of Lucius' business activities are sketchy at best. In the 1860s, Lucius moved his family to the Seneca-Geneva area of New York where he became an active farmer while still maintaining some ties to the mercantile dry goods trade with his half-ownership of the Blake, Fairchild & Fanshawe Dry Goods Co.[30]

While living with his family in Geneva, his youngest son, Warren Owen, died of scarlet fever at the age of 18 months on March 2, 1863, just two months after the death of his brother James' three year-old daughter, Jane McCall, of the same illness, also in Geneva.[31]

On May 24, 1864, another son was born to Lucius and Harriet Sheldon, Clarence Wellington. In 1865, the Sheldons returned to their Montague Street townhouse in Brooklyn. By 1870, they had moved temporarily to their farm in Ramsey, Minnesota[32] (32 miles northwest of St. Paul) and then returned to Brooklyn soon thereafter. Following his early education in the local public schools, Clarence entered Yale University's Sheffield Scientific School and graduated in 1884 with a degree in biology.[33] The following year, Clarence entered the College of Physicians and Surgeons in New York City, graduating with his medical degree in 1887.

Dr. Clarence Sheldon completed two years residency at New York Hospital before pursuing additional studies at the University of Vienna. He married in 1890 and established a medical practice specializing in pathology in Brooklyn. In less than a year, his health began to fail and he had to abandon his practice of medicine. He spent the next year traveling Europe and North Africa (Algiers) in search of solutions for his degrading health status. He died on October 19, 1894 of general sclerosis of the brain [Multiple Sclerosis] at the age of 30. He left his widow Marion and a young son, Bruce Smith Sheldon.[34]

Unlike his brothers who invested in high profile business ventures, Lucius concentrated primarily on real estate even though he had significant investments in the Mutual Reserve Fund Life Association of New York and was a director and investor in the Nassau Fire Insurance Company of Brooklyn and eventually, the El Paso Street Railway.[35]

Lucius' investment portfolio included mines in Montana,[36] the Arizona Territory, and Mexico.[37] In Wisconsin, Lucius would frequently purchase property from Civil War Union veterans who had received the post-war patents of government land as part of the Homestead Act of 1862.[38] He owned a large parcel of property in the mining area near Lynn, Wisconsin[39] as well as nine large parcels in Hendren Township, Wisconsin.[40] In manuscript files at the University of Michigan, there are documents that substantiate Lucius Sheldon's land holdings equaling 15,724 acres located in Illinois, Iowa, Minnesota, and Missouri.[41]

Real estate broker Horace B. Stevens, who was Lucius' management agent in El Paso, stated that Lucius concentrated on buying distressed properties, tax foreclosures, and vendor's liens. In many instances, he helped finance some of El Paso's leading businesses and real estate enterprises. (In the hundreds of letters contained in the Stevens Papers, Stevens often referred to Sheldon as the largest property tax payer in the county.)[42]

Lucius and Harriet Sheldon maintained a moderate social life within the 'proper' social registries that occupied the wealthy in the New York and Brooklyn communities. Lucius (as well as his namesake elder son) was a member of the Thirteen Club of New York.[43] This was a men's social club that was dedicated to debunk the superstition that it was unlucky to have 13 people seated together at a table. It was "believed that one of the 13 would die within a year." It was the custom of the club to host dinners on the 13th of the month with 13 people at a table. By 1887, the Thirteen Club had 400 members including Presidents Arthur, Cleveland, Harrison, McKinley, and Theodore Roosevelt. [The "13 at a table" superstition had its origin from The Last Supper wherein Jesus and his twelve disciples dined and Jesus died soon after.][44] The Sheldons were ardent art collectors. They collected ancient and modern paintings and 177 were sold at auction following Lucius' death in 1908 and netted a substantial amount of money.[45]

Lucius' second son, Gardner, stimulated his father's investing interest in El Paso, Texas. In 1879, Gardner graduated from the School of Mines at Columbia University, the first mining and metallurgy school in the United States. At the age of 20, fresh from college, the young mining engineer, as was often typical of children of privilege, delayed immediate employment for an opportunity to spread his wings and see the country. Then, with three of his newly minted mining friends, they headed for parts west. The four young men headed to the western territories, with their backpacks and rifles, in search of excitement and adventure before they returned to the routine of carving out a career and satisfying the dreams that their parents often had expressed. After a year of driving mail coaches and managing stagecoach line-stations, Gardner accepted a job as a mining engineer and facilities manager at the Corralitos Ranch and mines in Chihuahua, Mexico. The Corralitos Company based in New York City and operated by banker E.D. Morgan. Morgan, a cousin of J.P. Morgan, was a contemporary and close friend to both Lucius and Henry Sheldon. He formed a syndicate that included John T. Terry and Thomas Wentworth Peirce, Jr. and others. They owned the million-plus acre cattle ranch, which included multiple mixed ore mines.[46]

The ore (silver, gold, copper, and zinc) taken from the San Pedro Mines was transferred by special company owned trains (Mexican Northwestern Railroad- Ferrocarril Noroeste de México) to El Paso and Juárez for smelting and processing. The connection between the ranch and rapidly growing El Paso was clear. Gardner, watching the growth of El Paso, in letter after letter, tried to convince his father to invest in the potential of the American border town. Gardner began his own investment in El Paso with the purchase of a house and adjacent land located at what is now the northeast corner of Campbell and San Antonio Streets.[47]

Taking the lead from his son, Lucius began to purchase property in downtown El Paso, including a row of commercial buildings running along St. Louis Street (Mills Ave.), including numbers 108, 208, and 210. In 1886, he purchased Block 5 Lot 28 as previously described from the Thomas Wentworth Peirce Jr. syndicate who were also owners of the Corralitos ranch and mines. Following the advice and inspiration from his son, Lucius built a most successful El Paso financial enterprise in addition to the Sheldon Block and Hotel (Block 5, Lot 28.) Gardner in his frequent letters to his mother and father proclaimed repeatedly that he would not return to the East, that he had found where he belonged.[48] Then suddenly, Gardner died at the Corralitos Ranch.

Over the next twenty years, Lucius' land holdings in El Paso became immense. At one time or another, he either owned or held the notes on many key properties that are part of El Paso's history. They include but are not limited to:

- El Paso Convention Center (30 lots at Santa Fe and Sonora Streets.).
- Old El Paso City Hall (Triangle Block 44 at San Antonio St. and Myrtle.).
- El Paso County Courthouse (San Antonio, Campbell, Kansas, and Overland).
- Richard C. White Federal Building. 111 S. Florence St. (Corner of Florence and San Antonio).
- The Toltec Building (717 San Antonio St.).
- Block 218 lots 14-20 (San Antonio, Kansas, and Campbell Streets).
- Park at Campbell & Magoffin (Adjacent to Immaculate Conception Catholic Church).
- South El Paso Street commercial buildings (115, 324-326, 417, 419, 511, 515, 519, and 521.)
- Block 292 – Peirce/Findley Addition. 30 residential lots (California, River, Octavia, and Ange Streets.).
- Block 133, lots 4 & 5 (El Paso Street at 3rd).
- Block 6, lots 2 & 3 Franklin Heights (Now I-10).
- Block 265, lots 9 & 10 (Montana, Kansas, and Stanton).[49]

Lucius and Harriet Sheldon were no strangers to the tragedy and grief of losing a child. Twenty-six years earlier, they had lost their youngest son, Warren, at the age of 18 months. Losing Gardner was unusually difficult because he had resided in Mexico the last ten years of his life and only saw the family sporadically. Gardner's sudden death at the age of 30 surely was a surprise. The letter from the Corralitos management indicated that the details of his death would be forthcoming. Thorough research has not discovered those documents. His death, most likely, was the result of an injury or sudden illness. His parents were but a week's train ride from the ranch. Had his health's deterioration been protracted, his family would have had time to reach him.

The family ordered a casket to be waiting for Gardner's remains when they arrived in El Paso by train from the Corralitos. However, the train from the ranch returned Gardner to Brooklyn via Laredo, Texas, and did not pass through El Paso. The casket remained there unused. Mr. Foucar, a friend and business associate of Gardner, had the coffin placed in storage in a vacant room in the southeast corner of the Sheldon Block building. The family held Gardner's funeral at their home on Montague Street in Brooklyn. The Sheldon family plot at Green-Wood Cemetery in Brooklyn gained a new resident.

Six months after Gardner's death, his older brother, Lucius M. Sheldon, Jr. moved to El Paso from Brooklyn to manage his father's investment activities in El Paso and Mexico and to serve as a general agent for the Mutual Reserve Fund Life Association, one of the Sheldon family's enterprises. Lucius, Jr., in September, 1889, opened an office in the Sheldon Block office building that his father had just built and had commented in December to the family friend, Mr. Foucar, that the stored coffin purchased for Gardner should be sold, as it was a piece of furniture that would not be needed for years to come.

On a weekend hunting trip 10 days after the coffin comment at the resort at Samalayuca, just a few miles south of Juárez, Mexico, Lucius Jr. was walking with a group of fellow hunters, including his friend Foucar. Lucius Jr. suddenly stopped and said to his friends that he didn't feel well and staggered forward. Caught by his friend Foucar, he pushed Foucar's aid aside and said, "I'm alright, I think I'll take a smoke." He then sat down and lit a cigarette. After a couple of puffs, he threw the cigarette aside and said, "Foucar, I feel curious. I believe I'm sick and you had better call the other boys." His friends moved Lucius Jr. to a bed and had him lay down, he protested that he would be all right in a few minutes, but he never spoke again, only nodded his head when he was spoken to by his friends. Not thinking that there was anything seriously wrong, his friends retired to dinner. The friends became concerned over his extreme passiveness. The group of friends rubbed Lucius Jr.'s body with whisky to increase circulation and telegraphed that a doctor be sent immediately. By the time the doctor arrived, Lucius Jr. had died from heart disease and complications of a ruptured blood vessel that had caused internal hemorrhage.[50] Lucius Jr.'s friends returned his body to El Paso and the coffin of his younger brother finally was used. Lucius M. Sheldon, Jr., was returned to 123 Montague Street for his funeral and his final resting place at Brooklyn's Green-Wood Cemetery. Lucius Jr. died at the age of 31, nine months following the death of his little brother.

Five years later, Clarence W. Sheldon MD, the eldest of the two surviving sons, died from complications of multiple sclerosis following a prolonged illness, at 30 years of age. The remaining son, Henry K. Sheldon, Jr., picked up the mantle and began to manage the family's affairs from their base in Brooklyn. The shock of losing three adult children in their early thirties in such a short span of time must have been devastating to both Lucius and Harriet.

Henry K. Sheldon, Jr. was the youngest of Lucius and Harriet Sheldon's sons and was born in Brooklyn in 1870. The Sheldons named their son after Lucius' brother, banker, and investor Henry King Sheldon. This was probably done to honor Henry because Henry's own son had died in infancy. Henry Jr. was educated in the private schools of Brooklyn and spent the summers in Westport

Point, Massachusetts where his family had a home. Over the years, as Henry Jr. aged, he and his father, Lucius, began to purchase additional property in the Westport Point area northwest of Martha's Vineyard and just east of Newport, Rhode Island overlooking Buzzard's Bay.

Henry Jr. attended Yale University, graduating in 1891, and immediately entered law school at Columbia University School of Law. He transferred to New York Law School and graduated in 1893. He opened his law practice at 68 Nassau St. New York, in his uncle Henry's building and maintained a practice in Westport Point. On April 4, 1908, he and Alice (nee Wing) were married in Washington D.C. and they had a daughter, Gladys who married into the Henry Plante family of Westport Point. As the years progressed, he spent the majority of his time assisting his father, Lucius, in the management of the family's financial assets. During the El Paso investment period of Lucius, Henry's role would increase, until by 1900 he was essentially handling all of it. He and his family continued to live with his parents at 123 Montague and in Westport Point.

In Westport Point, the Sheldons had a home on a sloping piece of property that provided magnificent views of the bay and they imported a large number of beech trees on the vast lawn-covered estate. Henry expanded the family's holdings to include the regal Valentine house at 1991 Main Rd. This property became the Sheldon family home until he sold it to his mother in 1907. The house was a commanding structure (Empire with Italianate features) with a view of the river and expansive lawns and gardens and remains today as one of the most beautiful in the area.

Figure 19. L.M. Sheldon's summer home, Westport Point, MA.
(Westport Historical Society)

The Westport Historical Society has stated that today the property is a rooming house for students who attend the University of Massachusetts at Dartmouth, Massachusetts about 12 miles away. Following the death of his father, Henry expanded real estate holdings by buying up several additional houses, vacant land, and depressed farms. He founded a local railroad company with the intention to provide transportation down to the shoreline. However, little track was laid. With the Crash of 1929, Henry lost everything. So dire were the circumstances that Henry's wife, Alice, had to become a housekeeper.[51] Henry managed to survive until October 26, 1942, when he succumbed to a heart attack.[52]

On November 25, 1908, Lucius M. Sheldon died at his home in Westport Point of complications surrounding his three-year battle with senility. Harriet died seven years later from a cerebral hemorrhage at her Westport Point home.[53] The multi-generational Sheldon resting place is Sheldon Knoll at Green-Wood Cemetery in Brooklyn. The Sheldon family site is section 66 and lot 981 and contains the three Sheldon brothers, James O, Henry K, and Lucius M. and their respective families. (See figure 116)

Notes and References

---

[1] *Sheldon & Co.'s. Business or Advertising Directory; Containing the Cards, Circulars, and Advertisements of the Principal firm of the cities of New York, Boston, Philadelphia, Baltimore, etc. etc. A book of Reference.* (New York: John F. Trow & Company, 1845.), 109.

[2] The size and magnitude of the Phelps Dodge copper operations is staggering. Carlos A. Schwantes' *Vision & Enterprise: Exploring the History of the Phelps Dodge Corporation* beautifully presents the history of the company and its growth into today's business culture. See bibliography for details.

[3] American Smelting and Refining Company.

[4] Three interconnected families, Isaac Newton Phelps, John Jay Phelps, and William Dodge built three enormous mansions next to each other on Madison Ave. between 36th and 37th Street. Isaac Newton Phelps owned No. 231, the northern-most of the houses. Unlike his copper mining neighbors, his wealth, estimated at about $5 million (today $130 million) was made in hardware, banking, and real estate. By 1882, J. P.

Morgan purchased the J.J. Phelps house. When William Dodge died in 1903, Morgan purchased the property and immediately had it demolished to make way for a garden. When the Isaac Newton Phelps heir died, J. P. Morgan purchased the forty-five room No. 231 house for his son. In 1928 No. 231 became the last remaining house on the block when the J. P. Morgan Sr.'s house was demolished to provide for the expansion of the J. P. Morgan Library. (http://daytoninmanhattan.blogspot.com/2011/09/1854-phelps-morgan-mansion-n0-231.html)

[5] Randall, Charles, and Debra Adelman. *Reminiscences: The Russell Estate at Silver Lake*. (Susquehanna County, PA: Charles Randall, 2007.), 17.

[6] "Henry K. Sheldon." *Biographical Record of Northeastern Pennsylvania including the counties of Susquehanna, Wayne, Pike, and Monroe.* (Chicago: J.H. Beers & Co., 1900.), 521-522.

[7] *New York Times*, July 8, 1888.

[8] *New York Times*, August 19, 1886.

[9] *New York Times*, July 18, 1859.

[10] *New York Times*, April 25, 1907. Hall, Henry. *America's Successful Men of Affairs: An Encyclopedia of Contemporaneous Biography. Vol. II.* New York: New York Tribune, 1895.), 588-589.

[11] Cutter, William R. *New England Families: Genealogical and Memorial; A Record of the Achievements of Her People in the Making of Commonwealths and the Founding of a Nation. Vol. III.* (New York: Lewis Historical Publishing Company, 1913.), 1168.

[12] White Springs Manor History brochure. Accessed 25 August 2009.

[13] Ross, Peter, and William Smith Pelletreau. *History of Long Island: from its earliest settlement to the present time.* (New York: Lewis Publishing Company, 1903.), 852

[14] Interview with Anthony Russell, Henry K. Sheldon's great-grandson. 13-15 January 2011.

[15] The Texas and New Orleans Railroad connected New Orleans to Houston, Texas. During the Civil War the T&NO was used as a Confederate supply line and was guarded by Confederate soldiers. After a series of acquisitions and reorganizations, the railroad's president was John T. Terry, who also happened to be a major stockholder in the Corralitos Ranch and a close friend of both Henry K. and Lucius Sheldon. In 1881, C.P. Huntington purchased the T&NO and rolled it into the Southern Pacific Railroad Company. As a result, the T&NO became a major part of the new transcontinental route.

[16] Ibid.

[17]"Sheldon Building." *Emporis*. Accessed 12 December 2013.

[18] Jason Radmacher, Pastor, interview John St. Methodist Church, February 13 2013.

[19] *New York Times*, May 4, 1902.

[20] Ross and Pelletreau. *History of Long Island: from its earliest settlement to the present time.* (New York: Lewis Publishing Company, 1903.): 852-854.

[21] This account of the Henry K. Sheldon's attempt to vet his future son-in-law was provided in the interview of Anthony Russell, Feb.17, 2016 and was written by Adelina Russell Bolwell in the 1950s.

[22] *Brooklyn Eagle.* March 3, 1902.

[23] Ibid.

[24] Randall, 15.

[25] Ibid, 16.

[26] Russell, interview. There is a plaque in the Cathedral that reads, "To the Glory of God and in grateful memory of James Townsend Russell, Canon of the Cathedral Church of St. Peter and St. Paul from 1918 to 1929. And of his wife Anna Sheldon Russell Presbyterian daughter of a New England Puritan whose joint gift of Beauvoir and of the adjoining Oak Grove has helped to make the Cathedral Close a site of unsurpassed beauty."

[27] Russell, interview.

[28] Williams College today is a co-educational liberal arts college located on a 450-acre campus in Williamstown, MA. The college was founded in 1793. The fees today near $70,000 per year and currently has around 2,000 students with 330 academic staff.

[29] *Williams College General Catalogue of Non-Graduates.* (Williamstown, MA: the College, 1910.), 24. The Archivist at Williams College confirmed by telephone that Lucius attended only his freshman year. October 13, 2010.

[30] *New York Daily Times*. Feb.8, 1855

[31] *Geneva Gazette.* "Early Marriages and Death Notices – Ontario, County, New York For 1863." Accessed 12 March 2010.

[32] United States Federal Census 1870.

[33] *Obituary Record of Graduates of Yale University* (New Haven, CT: Yale University, June 1895.), 341.

[34] *The Brooklyn Medical Journal*. June 1895, Vol. 9, No. 6., 378-379.

[35] *Horace B. Stevens Papers*. (MS 153).

[36] "Montana Mining Notes." *The Engineering and Mining Journal* Vol. 28, No. 15. (New York: The Scientific Publishing Company, 1879.), 260.

[37] Stevens Papers.

[38] Grant Township, Clark County, WI.

[39] Block 12, lot 17, Oneida County, WI.

[40] Plat map Hendren Township, 26N, Range 3W 1860-1880 blocks15, 22, 26, 17, 28, and 31 and 320 acres of farmland.

[41] *Sheldon Family Papers, 1854-1899*. [M-3116.7, 1995]. (Ann Arbor: University of Michigan, 1995.)

[42] Stevens Papers.

[43] *New York Times*. May 9, 1888.

[44]See Nathaniel Lachenmeyer's *13: The Story of the World's Most Popular Superstition*. (Philadelphia: Running Press, 2004.)

[45] *New York Times*. Jan. 24, 1914.

[46] The history and the backstory of the Corralitos Company and its Chihuahua ranch and mining operations and its subsequent impact on El Paso and the Mexican Revolution is the subject of the author's 2014 book, *Mines, Cattle, and Rebellion.*

[47] *Sheldon Family Papers, 1880-1899*. (MS 402) Letter from Gardner to father, July 25, 1882.

[47]There are many more properties scattered through the El Paso downtown area. All the properties listed have been confirmed through property records, including deeds on file with the El Paso County clerk's office and documents in old deed record books held in the Special Collections Department at the University of Texas at El Paso. These documents have been copied and are in the author's possession.

[48] Campbell, C.E. *Mines, Cattle, and Rebellion: The History of the Corralitos Ranch.* (Sunset Beach, CA.: Green Street Publications, 2015.): 67. The 275-year history of the 1.5 million-acre Corralitos ranch and mining empire involved the last days of the bloody Mexican-Indian wars. This rich history further served as an example of foreign capital intrusion into Mexico as a possible catalyst to the Mexican Revolution of 1910. One of the earliest ventures of the anti-Díaz and anti-American revolt was ignited on the lands of the Corralitos Ranch. The ranch was an active center of the battles between the Federals and the Rebels. As General John J. Pershing, with the American Punitive Expedition in 1916, searched for Pancho Villa after Villa's invasion of Columbus, New Mexico, the Corralitos Ranch was at the forefront of this early failure of the American military forces. The Corralitos' Candelaria Mining Company became one of the largest and most profitable mining operations in northern Mexico. The Corralitos Ranch was an early impetus to the building of the Mexican Northwestern Railroad that brought the newly captured ore into the emerging smelter center and transportation hub of El Paso, Texas. Underestimating the ability of the Mexican people to band together and renew "Mexico for the Mexicans" was a difficult lesson for the Corralitos Company to learn. The Corralitos Ranch was in the middle of it all.

[49]*El Paso Times* December 31, 1889.

[50]Shirley Sheldon Davenport, Interview.

[51] *Bulletin of Yale University, Obituary Record*. January 1944. No.1.

[52] Death Certificates No. 16 and 438 Westport, MA. Commonwealth of Massachusetts, and *New York Times*, November 13, 1915.
[53] Davenport, interview.

Chapter Five

The Sheldon Block: Building for Business

El Paso turned the corner in its evolving history in 1881 as the railroads brought the schemers, the con men, the ne'er-do-wells, and a whole litany of souls looking for a new life or thrilling adventures. Bordellos, gaming halls, saloons, brew houses, and gunslingers filled just about all the available space in town. As the rails of the Southern Pacific; Texas & Pacific; the Atchison, Topeka and Santa Fe; the Galveston, Harrisburg and San Antonio (G.H. & S.A.); and the Mexican Central were completed by in 1884, a new and more sophisticated visitor began to arrive. These were the American businessmen: bankers, investors, mining entrepreneurs, and cattlemen, as well as a full range of European immigrants.

Among the most significant of the European immigrants who found their way to El Paso during this booming westward migration were the Jews from Germany and Austria-Hungary. Blumenthal, Freudenthal, Kohlberg, Krakauer, Krupp, Mathias, Schuster, and others left their mark on local business history.[1] They came attempting to escape "the militaristic regimes of their European homelands, coupled with the promise of rich rewards and opportunities on the Southwest frontier."[2] With new migrants came the abundance of new wealth and the demand for greater and more elaborate entertainment, office venues, and hostelries.[3] Into this climate, Lucius M. Sheldon, at the constant urging of his son, purchased the history-laden for $15,000 Block 5 Lot 28 from the Boston capitalist Thomas W. Peirce et.al.[4]

At the time of Sheldon's acquisition, there were several lack-luster hotels, the Vendome (on the east side of the big plaza) and the Pierson (St. Louis St. and Kansas St.). Opened in 1876, the Vendome ruled supreme as the most elegant hotel in the region, with an efficient bell ringing system to aid the residents' comfort. Guests could summon a porter with a single ring, request ice water with two rings, three rings meant a fire was needed (to warm the room), and four rings would bring the porter with hot water.[5] By the time the railroads arrived, the hotel's luster had begun to tarnish. In 1899, Mrs. Charles DeGroff ("Mama De") of Tucson, [nee Mrs. Lee H. Orndorff], purchased the Vendome Hotel for $41,000, remodeled the hotel, added a fourth story, and renamed it the Orndorff Hotel. Years later, in 1926, Mrs. DeGroff completed a ground-up 1.5 million dollar rebuild.[6] Mama De died a month before the opening of her new nine-story grand hotel. Two years later, the Orndorff family added two additional floors. After a series of ownership changes, the hotel became known as Hotel Cortez and is steeped in its own fascinating history. The hotel ceased operation as a hotel in 1970 and today, after extensive remodeling, the Cortez [office] Building remains one of the crown jewels of the downtown historic preservation project that includes the Mills Building and the Centre Block.

Hearing rumors of the impending arrival of the Southern Pacific Railroad, local resident, William M. Pierson, had visions of the growth that would soon overtake El Paso. In 1881, he opened an impressive three-story 40-room[7] brick structure that had wide verandas surrounding the second and third floors. While the public areas were large and welcoming, the rooms lacked running water and other amenities, although there was a public bath at the end of the hallway on each floor.[8] With a change in management and some remodeling, the "New" Pierson Hotel was re-opened on February 5, 1885.[9]A fire on February 13, 1891 destroyed the second and third floor of the hotel. The owners remodeled the second floor and left the first floor intact. The hotel was minus its entire third floor and continued to operate until 1929, when a new structure housing the local newspapers was built on its site.[10]

The aging Central Hotel (on the west side of the big plaza and north of the little plaza.), along with a menagerie of rooming and boarding houses, was a staple among the local and transient populations. It became Sheldon's intent to build office space for the booming economy and thus become a major player in the growth of this new import/export international trading portal rising in the Southwest.[11] The Sheldon Block, the four-story red brick office building with the first elevator in an office building in town, opened for business in 1888.[12] The Sheldon Building soon provided rental space to doctors, lawyers, architects, mining companies, real estate entrepreneurs, the Federal Post Office, and the U.S. Weather Service as well as retail space for local merchants. As the venerable Vendome and Pierson hotels became less inviting to the new clientele of capitalists and "doers," it became clear that El Paso was in need of a large first-class hotel.

Early El Paso pioneers, J.F. Crosby and Anson Mills, who already owned various properties surrounding the two plazas,[13] began to acquire additional land from some of the other powerful landowners including the St. Vrains, Tays, Gillock, and others in order to erect a large and fashionable hotel. The Grand Central Hotel opened in 1884 and was touted as the largest and most elegant hotel in the Southwest. It quickly became the social center of the city as well as attracting notables from all over the world to its elegantly furnished rooms and vivid gaming rooms. Journalist Owen P. White, describing the Grand Central Hotel wrote:

> Whether the statement of the owners in regard to the size of their hotel was true or false we are not prepared to say. To us it seems that it carries with it a very strong flavor of advertising propaganda. But there is one thing that they could have said that would have admitted of no contradiction; regardless of the size of the hotel it was pre-eminent in one of its features. It was equipped with the finest bar-room in the West and it was a boast of the town that at its gambling tables all that a man had to do was establish a credit and the bridle would be taken off the games so that he could bet with no limit at all between him and the high and beautiful north star.[14]

After only eight years of operation, on February 11, 1892, a fire roared through the structure for eleven hours, leveling the once elegant hotel to a pile of ash and scorched timbers. The hotel's destruction openly demonstrated to the city leaders that El Paso's fire department was not only poorly staffed, but also very unequipped to protect the growing city. After prolonged debates, the El Paso City Council provided the fire department with a few pieces of new equipment and 1,000 feet of hose. However, in the end, only 100 feet of hose was actually supplied.[15]

The Crosby and Mills Grand Central Hotel and its subsequent destruction played a pivotal role in the emergence of the Sheldon Hotel. The relationship between Crosby and Mills had been deteriorating over the years that the Grand Central operated, so when it was time to agree as to whether to rebuild the hotel or develop the property in some other manner, conflicts arose and a significant stalemate ensued. The city wanted the hotel rebuilt, but the discord between Crosby and Mills made it most complicated. Many local leaders tried to entice St.

Louis investors to enter the city with subscription schemes to rebuild the hotel. In the end, Mills took a significant stand and indicated that he would not rebuild a hotel on his property, but instead, would develop the property as a site for retail stores and professional offices.

Having acquired Block 5 Lot 28 in 1886, Lucius M. Sheldon, accompanied by his son Gardner's friend and business partner, E.L. Foucar, obtained a building permit for a four-story brick office structure containing 140 offices and 11 stores on March 19, 1887. The plans for the structure were made available for review at the office of architect Edward Kneezell.[16] The preliminary plans indicated that the building would be an unbroken block with three sides of the building showing an ornamental style with glazed brick and terra cotta trim. The fourth side, facing the alley, was to remain plain. The proposed building would front roughly 76 feet on St. Louise St. (Mills Ave.), 129 feet on Little Plaza, 120 ft. on San Francisco St., and 156 ft. on Oregon St.[17] The building would contain offices that averaged a width of 25 feet and a depth of 40 feet. Several of the corner offices would be considerably larger. Of the 140 offices, 75 would have outside light. A large triangular atrium/skylight would be in the center of the building.[18] It is presumed that Kneezell was the architect. However, no official records regarding the building remain, even though; the Historic Preservation Office in El Paso confirmed him as the architect.[19] Kneezell moved his offices into the Sheldon building as soon as it opened. (Whether Kneezell was the actual architect or just the local architect working as liaison for the Brooklyn based Parfitt Brothers firm is not clearly confirmed by a review of the records. Some documents indicate that Foucar discharged Kneezell from all supervision responsibilities before the building was completed.)[20]

There was clearly a Brooklyn connection between Sheldon and fellow Brooklynite, architect Walter E. Parfitt and his Parfitt Brothers firm. How much influence the Parfitt firm had on the building of thc original building is open to speculation. Sheldon did contract the Parfitt Bros. firm when he expanded the Sheldon Block into the Sheldon Hotel in 1899.

Sheldon arranged to have El Paso real estate broker and property manager, H.B. Stevens, be his El Paso representative and to manage the building and eventual operation of his new venture. Stevens also maintained a similar role with the business affairs of Gen. Anson Mills while Mills resided in Washington, D.C. (See figure 118)

Figure 20. The Sheldon Block shortly after the four-story office building was completed in 1888. (El Paso County Historical Society)

Figure 21. Five-story Sheldon Hotel 1905.
(El Paso Public Library, Aultman Collection)

When the Sheldon Block opened for business in 1888 (See figure 117), there was not a lack of willing tenants. The building filled rapidly. According to the city directory of the time, the following table lists the businesses that were among the first to occupy the building during its first decade. (See figure 22) The list is certainly not complete and many tenants were somewhat transitory, but its review allows for a general feel of the business activities that were evolving in the growing city.

As the years progressed, many of the business tenants began actually living in their business suites and the number of El Paso residents who took rooms in the building's upper floors for residential purposes also increased as the population of El Paso expanded and the availability of rooming and boarding houses decreased. Just about all the doctors, dentists, and lawyers had their offices in the Sheldon, but the building was huge and many of the rooms on the upper two floors were converted into housekeeping rooms. There were even rumors that some of the rooms became "business suites" for working young women.[21]

It is of historical significance that among the physicians who had offices or who maintained a residence in the Sheldon Office building during this time, six were among the founders of the El Paso County Medical Society: Drs. Justice, Yandell, Race, Higgins, Wedgeworth, and Schuster.[22]

A great many of the business tenants and residents of both the Sheldon office building and later the Sheldon Hotel played a significant role in southwest history and will be pivotal in future chapters. From the list of tenants in the following table, three are singled out for a brief review.

The Oracle of Ore

Nothing has been more iconic than the 800-foot smokestack of the old ASARCO smelter adjacent to the U.S. and Mexican border on the west side of El Paso. The structure and its predecessors loomed over the evolving city for more than 125 years, reminding the entire enormous legacy that the early smelting operation had on the economic growth of the border region. It also was a symbol of environmental degradation and the impact that the resulting health hazards would have on the thousands of smelter employees and residents that resulted in a multi- billion dollar cleanup attempt. The demolition of these towering icons on April 13, 2013 was witnessed with mixed emotions.[23]

Writing on the history of gold, silver, copper, and lead smelting, author Isaac Marcosson states:

> The story of mankind is the narrative of persistent search for health, wealth, or happiness. Around each of these age-old objectives has evolved a graphic story of frustrated hope and triumphant consummation. In none of them is there such spirit of romantic adventure, or such manifestation of the vagaries of the Goddess Chance, as there is in the hunt for treasure embedded in the bosom of Mother Earth. The various metals, created by time and by cataclysmic upheavals of Nature, have contributed to the social and economic advancement of the human race and likewise to a far-flung utility that touches the life of every human being the world over. Civilization has marched with mining. As an eminent historian of mining has pointed out, "Trade follows the flag, but the flag follows the pick." Mining has founded financial dynasties, colonized immense domains, and opened up vast agricultural and industrial empires. Whether delved by hand in the great open spaces or gashed by giant machinery out of mountainsides, the mine has been the outpost of progress.[24]

Into this quest came a young highly focused mining engineer and entrepreneur, recently graduated from the Ohio State University in 1881. Robert Safford Towne arrived in El Paso following his survey of Mexican mines in Chihuahua and he was convinced that with the arrival of the railroads, El Paso would be the perfect location to process the ore from the Mexican and American Southwest mines and then transport the metals to the industrial Midwest and East. By 1883, Towne had established the Mexican Ore Company, which assayed and graded the ore from the Mexican mines. In 1887, with the financial backing of the Kansas City Consolidated Smelting and Refining Company he established the El Paso Smelter Company on 1,156 acres along the Rio Grande. With an initial workforce of 250 and a 100-foot high smokestack, the smelter processed over 12,000 tons of lead bullion the first year and was, for more than thirty-years, considered the most important smelting operation in the Southwest.[25]

When the Sheldon Block opened for business in 1888, Towne set up his two companies as separate entities in the new office building. The smelter facilities were built on the west side of town and Towne soon became active in the Mexican Northern Railroad operations that brought the ore into the smelters.

In 1899, the El Paso Smelter, part of the Kansas City Smelter Company, was reorganized into the American Smelting and Refining Company. By the turn of the century, ASARCO had built multiple lead furnaces and the first copper smelter in El Paso to become one of the major employers in the region along with the railroads and the military.[26]

In tandem with the intricate and interwoven tracks of both large and small railroads and the presence of American troops, Towne's mining and smelter operations helped make El Paso the largest and most important city between Denver and Mexico City and between San Antonio and Los Angeles.[27]

El Paso was the perfect site for such operations, as it was at the crossroads where "American ore moved east and Mexican ore moved north" and was surrounded by a large prevalence of cheap labor. In clear violation of immigration laws, the company hired hundreds of Mexican nationals to the smelter's labor force.[28] The smelter's Mexican employees began to build what came to be known as Smeltertown, a shantytown beset with massive poverty and a serious potential for lead poisoning of the "indentured" employees and their families. As the workforce grew, Smeltertown grew into a company town that included churches, markets, schools, and a post office. Payroll records from 1895 indicate that the Mexican employees earned about $3 a day ($86 per day in 2013 dollars.) and some made only $1.20 per day, yet also had funds deducted by the company to pay for the hospital, housing, and what they purchased from the company store.[29]

Dr. Smokestack

The influence of Towne's smelter on the history of El Paso is undeniable. One of the early physicians who had offices in the Sheldon Block building was Michael P. Schuster, MD., who was closely allied with the smelter and its operation as well as the founding of the El Paso County Medical Society. Little did Dr. Schuster imagine, while looking out his Sheldon Block office widow up Oregon Street, that over the next 100 years, the hospital that he founded in 1902 would grow into the massive medical complex known today as The Hospitals of Providence located adjacent to the University of Texas at El Paso campus.

Dr. Schuster graduated from the University of Vienna in 1889 specializing in diseases of the eye, ear, nose, and throat; gaining prominence as an eye surgeon. Schuster came to the United States in 1891, settling in Kansas City. It was in Kansas City that he met Robert S. Towne and accepted his offer to develop a hospital and become the company surgeon at Towne's El Paso Smelter. In 1894, Schuster, along with Towne's nephew, Dr. Henry Towne Safford, established the small company hospital situated on a hill next to the smelter's operation.[30] The company hospital remained in continuous operation until it closed in 1966.[31] In addition to his duties as general surgeon at the smelter, Schuster established a private practice in downtown El Paso at the Sheldon Block building.

Once ensconced in his office at the Sheldon, he quickly recognized the need for more hospital beds in the city. He developed plans to give El Paso another much-needed hospital in addition to Hotel Dieu (House of God, run by the Sisters of Charity and named after Hotel Dieu de Paris, the oldest hospital in Paris.). Local citizens thought this was providential, thus derived the name for the new hospital.[32] Schuster formed the Providence Hospital Association along with his wife, Eugenia, Dr. Henry Safford, and a few others. The Association purchased the first hospital building, a two-story Congregational church school (Rio Grande Congregational Training School) building at North Santa Fe St. and Upson Ave. (now the I-10). After adding a third-story to the building, the 40-bed hospital opened in 1902. Schuster remained very active in the medical community of El Paso, particularly during the Mexican Revolution of 1911. Schuster died in 1918, and the Providence Hospital remained controlled by the Schuster's wife, Eugenia and their two daughters until 1946. The two Schuster sons both became local physicians.

In addition to her administrative acumen, Eugenia, daughter of a Hungarian aristocrat, was an accomplished pianist who had studied with Franz Liszt. She was active in the founding of the Woman's Club of El Paso, which had close ties with Sheldon Block building in the development of the first kindergarten in Texas and the founding of the El Paso Public Library. She was also responsible for bringing international opera singers to local venues. In 1953, the hospital moved to its present location on Oregon St. where it has grown into a massive medical campus, Sierra Providence, now owned by the Tenet Healthcare Corporation.

The Physician-Priest

As a young child of fourteen in his native England, George H. Higgins knew that he wanted to be a church [Episcopal] missionary. With that focus, Higgins finalized his English education with a medical degree in London. Shortly thereafter, he moved to Canada to complete his religious education culminating in being ordained an Episcopal Priest at St. Paul's Cathedral in 1874. Higgins migrated to the United States and served the church in several different locations before leading a congregation in Colorado City, Texas; 380 miles east of El Paso.

Judge Josiah F. Crosby led the movement to change the local Episcopal Church in El Paso from its mission status, to a full-fledged parish in 1877. The bishop selected the Rev. Dr. George H. Higgins to join the new parish as its priest. Higgins became the third priest to lead the El Paso congregation, but the first identified as its "rector." The physician-priest had extreme difficulty in raising his family of five children in the small four-room parsonage and with an annual salary of $1,500. As a result, he began to augment his income by starting a part-time medical practice. The St. Clement's congregation, which included some of the most influential families of early El Paso (Mundy, Tays, Mills, Conklin, Hague, Gillock, Pierson, Dowell, Rohman, Gillette, Fountain, Crosby, Clarke, Slade, Cole, Payne, McCutcheon, among others.),[33] believed that all of his time should be given to the church. The church leaders soon reduced his salary to $1,200. The rector's salary was not always paid in full and oftentimes was more than a month behind.[34]

Not long after his reduction in salary and the ultimatum by the church leaders, Higgins and his wife suffered the loss of their two little sons within a few days of each other. Higgins, with no alternative than to resign, entered medical practice full-time. At this time, Higgins opened his medical office in the Sheldon Block building. Higgins was described by the St. Clements Church historian, MacCallum as, "Dr. Higgins was universally and deservedly popular and much beloved during his ministry…he is a man ripe in spiritual living and experience, and his teaching and preaching is a veritable benediction. The present congregation of St. Clement's asks no greater pleasure than to see him in his robes with snowy white hair, occupying the pulpit, which he has been called on to do many times by the rectors and vestries of every ministry since his retirement in 1891."[35]

Over the ensuing years, Higgins continued to assist St. Clement's Church in providing sermons when requested. In 1922, he faithfully provided leadership until a new rector arrived to replace the Rev. Fuller Swift who had been driven from St. Clement's for adultery. He continued to assist the leadership of the church until his death in 1927 at the age of 81.[36] There may have been other issues regarding his relationship as the rector of St. Clement's Church, as it was oft reported that the physician-priest had a sincere drinking problem.[37]

The Sheldon Block building continued to be a significant fixture in downtown El Paso, fronting on the two major plazas and opposite the beautiful Grand Central Hotel of Crosby and Mills. The Grand Central opened in 1884, first as a three-story hotel with a fourth-story added the following year. The

$80,000 hotel had 200 rooms with hot and cold running water and baths on each floor and several suites with complete baths. There was a hydraulic elevator and on the ground floor a bar, dining room, a billiard parlor, and a barber shop.[38]

There was an increased flurry of new tenants coming and going as the city grew in population and economic significance. The availability of housing was putting pressure on local activity, resulting in many of the tenants using the rooms of the Sheldon Block as residences. Stovepipes protruding from some of the widows of the upper stories were evidence of the changing status of the office building. Through it all, the Grand Central Hotel and the Sheldon office building maintained a close and successful symbiotic relationship, each providing an essential element to the expansion of the community's economic growth.

In the early hours of February 11, 1892, a fire erupted on the fourth floor of the Grand Central Hotel and by seven o'clock, the once magnificent hotel was reduced to ash and charred timbers. "Like an angry demon, the fiery element of destruction leaped upward and reached out across the street to gather its deadly embrace the handsome Sheldon Block. The angry elements were working in unison. A perfect gale spring up to fan the devouring flames into increased activity. Thousands of spectators stood in the two plazas, watching with painful anxiety which way the battle would go. The city's water pressure was a failure."[39] With the Sheldon's proximately to the fiery disaster, it's a miracle that the Sheldon survived with only slight and repairable damage.[40]

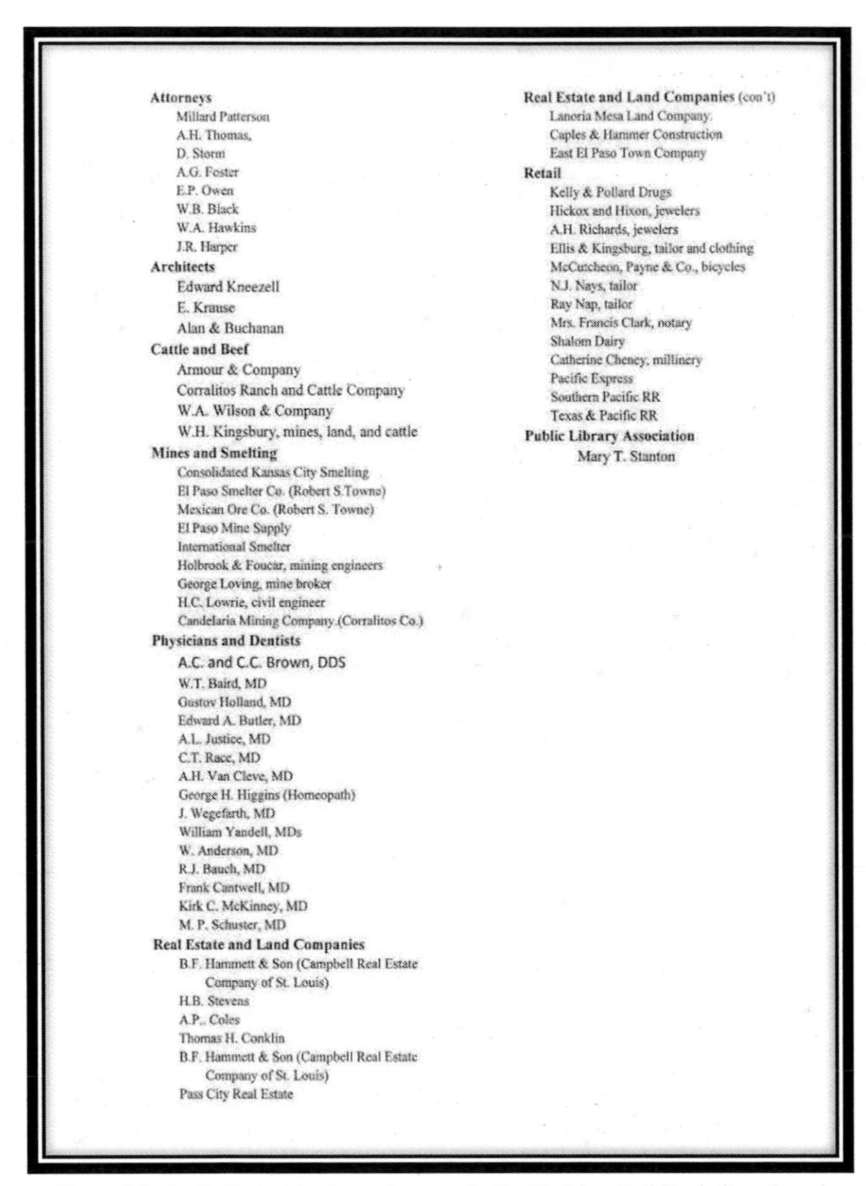

Attorneys
- Millard Patterson
- A.H. Thomas,
- D. Storm
- A.G. Foster
- E.P. Owen
- W.B. Black
- W.A. Hawkins
- J.R. Harper

Architects
- Edward Kneezell
- E. Krause
- Alan & Buchanan

Cattle and Beef
- Armour & Company
- Corralitos Ranch and Cattle Company
- W.A. Wilson & Company
- W.H. Kingsbury, mines, land, and cattle

Mines and Smelting
- Consolidated Kansas City Smelting
- El Paso Smelter Co. (Robert S.Towne)
- Mexican Ore Co. (Robert S. Towne)
- El Paso Mine Supply
- International Smelter
- Holbrook & Foucar, mining engineers
- George Loving, mine broker
- H.C. Lowrie, civil engineer
- Candelaria Mining Company.(Corralitos Co.)

Physicians and Dentists
- A.C. and C.C. Brown, DDS
- W.T. Baird, MD
- Gustov Holland, MD
- Edward A. Butler, MD
- A.L. Justice, MD
- C.T. Race, MD
- A.H. Van Cleve, MD
- George H. Higgins (Homeopath)
- J. Wegefarth, MD
- William Yandell, MDs
- W. Anderson, MD
- R.J. Bauch, MD
- Frank Cantwell, MD
- Kirk C. McKinney, MD
- M. P. Schuster, MD

Real Estate and Land Companies
- B.F. Hammett & Son (Campbell Real Estate Company of St. Louis)
- H.B. Stevens
- A.P., Coles
- Thomas H. Conklin
- B.F. Hammett & Son (Campbell Real Estate Company of St. Louis)
- Pass City Real Estate

Real Estate and Land Companies (con't)
- Lanoria Mesa Land Company.
- Caples & Hammer Construction
- East El Paso Town Company

Retail
- Kelly & Pollard Drugs
- Hickox and Hixon, jewelers
- A.H. Richards, jewelers
- Ellis & Kingsburg, tailor and clothing
- McCutcheon, Payne & Co., bicycles
- N.J. Nays, tailor
- Ray Nap, tailor
- Mrs. Francis Clark, notary
- Shalom Dairy
- Catherine Cheney, millinery
- Pacific Express
- Southern Pacific RR
- Texas & Pacific RR

Public Library Association
- Mary T. Stanton

Figure 22. Partial list of business tenants in the Sheldon Building's first decade. Tenancy based on a review of El Paso City Directories and Sanford Fire Insurance Maps.

Notes and References

---

[1] This Jewish enclave of businessmen and entrepreneurs played an enormous role in the developing history of El Paso and its involvement in the Mexican Revolution
[2] Timmons, W.H. *El Paso: A Borderlands History*. (El Paso: Texas Western Press, 1990.), 190.
[3] White, Owen P. Out of the Desert: The Historical Romance of El Paso. (El Paso: The McMath Company, 1923.), 160.
[4] *El Paso Times*, May 31, 1973.
[5] *El Paso Herald Post*, "Old Vendome Hotel was elegant." Jan. 1, 1936.
[6] *El Paso Times*, June 13, 1954.
[7] *El Paso Times*, Feb. 3, 1980, described the hotel as having 73 rooms.
[8] *El Paso Times*, Jan. 27, 1952.
[9] *El Paso Daily Times*, February 6, 1885.
[10] *El Paso Times*, Aug. 9, 1965.
[11] *El Paso Times*, Feb. 3, 1952.
[12] The first elevator in El Paso was in the Crosby-Mills Grand Central Hotel.
[13] A review of the Mills plat of 1852 identifies clearly who the landowners were in the two-plaza area.
[14] White (1923), 160
[15] Murphy, James R. *Images of America: El Paso 1850-1950*. (San Francisco: Arcadia Publishing Co., 2009.), 23.
[16] *El Paso Times*, Sep. 7, 1886.
[17] *El Paso Times*, Mar. 3, 1887.
[18] Ibid.
[19] De La Cruz, Tony. Personal interview.
[20] LMS, letter to HBS, 26 Jan. 1893.
[21] "Hotel Sheldon, Landmark for 40 Years, Comes Down." *El Paso Herald- Post.* August 28, 1929.
[22] Funkhouser, Barbara. *The Caregivers: El Paso's Medical History, 1898 – 1998.* (El Paso: Sundance Press, 1999.), 81.
[23] "El Paso Says Goodbye to Landmark." *The Wall Street Journal.* Apr. 14. 2013.
[24] Marcosson, Isaac F. *Metal Magic: The Story of the American Smelting and Refining Company*. (New York: Farrar, Straus and Company, 1949.), 1.
[25] Perales, Monica. *Smeltertown: Making and Remembering a Southwest Border Community*. (Chapel Hill: The University of North Carolina Press, 2010.), 33.

[26]Metz, León. *El Paso Chronicles: A Record of Historical Events in El Paso, Texas*. 3rd. (El Paso: Mangan Books, 1993.), 103.
[27] Perales, 29.
[28] Garcia, Mario T. *Desert Immigrants: The Mexicans of El Paso, 1880-1920.* (New Haven: Yale University Press, 1981.), 52.
[29] Rivers, Claudia, interview
[30] de Wetter, Mardee B. interview.
[31] "Asarco: A History Timeline of the Smokestack in El Paso!" accessed 16 Nov. 2015.
[32] *El Paso Times*. Jan. 10, 1952.
[33] de Wetter, Mardee B. *Watchtower on the Rio Grande: St. Clement's Church, El Paso, Texas 1870- 2008.* (Mesilla Park, NM: The Institute of Historical Survey Foundation, 2012.), 34.
[34] Ibid, 60
[35] MacCallum, Esther D. *The History of St. Clement's Church, El Paso: 1870-1925*. (El Paso: The McMath Company, 1925.) Wayne, Melanie K. *Whose House We Are.* (Bloomington, IN: WestBow Press, 2014.), 74.
[36] Ibid.
[37] White, Owen P. *The Autobiography of a Durable Sinner*. (New York: G.P. Putnam's Sons, 1942.), 45.
[38] Ward, Dorothy. "Tourist Attractions in El Paso (1885): An Excerpt from the Mexican Guide." *Password*. Vol. XXXI (1986), 90.
[39]Chapman, Bob. "Magnificent Grand Central Hotel consumed by 'Fire Demon' in 1892." *El Paso Times.* Mar. 2, 1952.
[40] Horace B. Stevens, letter to Lucius M. Sheldon, 11 Feb. 1892. (UTEP-MS 153.)

Chapter Six

Scorched: A Change in Direction

Sitting in eloquence, the cupola on top of the fourth floor of the Grand Central was a mark of the luxuriousness of this stately hotel that had garnered a wide international reputation as the grandest in the southwest. Sadly, this architectural beacon was also the source of the devastating fire that soon leveled the auberge. Dutifully assigned, the early morning bellboy was sent to the recently added fourth floor, to the room of a Mr. Donahue at 4:30 a.m. to wake him so he could report to his job by 5:30 a.m. as the conductor on the Silver City-bound Santa Fe Railroad. Upon returning to the ground floor office, the bellboy reported that he had smelled smoke on the fourth floor. The exact origin of the fire in the cupola was never determined.[1]

Figure 23. The Grand Central Hotel of Mills and Crosby adjacent to the Central Hotel on the left. ca. 1890.
(From an old print in the author's collection.)

At the same time, the night man at the Vendome Hotel, across the plaza, had noticed a small fire in the Grand Central's cupola. A local beat cop, Officer Delfrais, who was passing the Vendome at the time, was notified and he immediately sounded an alarm. (The city's great alarm system would not work unless initiated by a police officer.)[2] Confusion reigned, as patrons were awakened and attempted to evacuate the building. Many just left their belongings unaware of the seriousness of the situation and holding the mistaken belief that they would return later to gather their possessions. Many of the patrons lost everything, a few lost extremely valuable trappings, and jewelry.

As the sorrowfully ill-equipped fire department attempted to wage war upon the spreading flames by pouring water on the blaze, the torrid winds, generated by the fire, blew against the streaming flow of water, delaying the Firemen's heroic if futile effort. Following the total collapse of the building, the local newspapers began to call attention to the fact that the hotel did not have any fire escapes and that alone could have resulted in a serious loss of life. In front-page editorials, the newspapers berated the city leaders:

> The lack of fire escapes in the building might have caused a serious loss of lives. This terrible occurrence should make the city officers more vigilant in exacting the requirements of the law. All large buildings should be provided with ample fire escapes. The law requires it and there is no reason for exception. Besides, the Fire Department wants additional conveniences to secure a water pressure that will reach the high buildings of the City.[3]

As the flames shot across the street to the Sheldon Block, pushed feverishly by the strong hot fire-generated winds from the northwest blowing right on the building with intense heat, the Sheldon's night watchman ran to the Sheldon's roof and turned the building's hose loose to keep the flying embers from igniting. As the fire roared across the street, the commotion awakened the Sheldon's resident staff. Everyone joined in the effort to keep the building thoroughly wetted down, and they rushed to close all of the windows to keep the sparks from entering and kindling. All seven of the large plate glass windows on the ground floor facing the Grand Central were broken. Many of the windows on the upper floors were also blown out, the paint on the front and west side of the building was severely scorched, and most of the upper window awnings were burned beyond repair. By the quick action of its employees, the Sheldon Block survived and no one was injured beyond the night watchman who suffered superficial burns around the face and neck.[4]

Figure 24. Grand Central Hotel following the fire in 1892.
(El Paso County Historical Society)

The new Federal Building just east of the Sheldon Block caught on fire several times, but the action of the fire department extinguished those threats without damage. Amazingly, the Central Hotel adjacent to the Grand Central, sustained only minor damage. The loss to the Grand Central Hotel was approximately $115,000, most of it covered by insurance.[5]

The fear of building fires spread through the community primarily because of the inadequate equipment controlled by the fire department, the lack of fire escapes, and poor water pressure throughout the city. About a year following the fire at the Grand Central, on April 10, 1893, the Sheldon Block building experienced a second, albeit small, fire of its own. Around four o'clock in the morning, the night watchman smelled smoke and finally discovered the blaze was in a storage closet on the second floor. As soon as he opened the door to the closet, the smoke and flames roared out. With the aid of a policeman who was across the street, the hotel staff used the building's fire apparatus and hose to extinguish the fire in a few minutes. The city fire department responded to the fire alarm, but was not needed. The hose system and water pressure worked fine.

The fire burned into adjoining closets and through the floor to a closet on the main floor. Everything was charred and blackened and a great deal of water damage occurred to both the Texas & Pacific Railroad office and the pharmacy located on the ground floor. While the actual cause of the blaze remained unknown, the building manager theorized that someone, intending to discard a cigar stub, opened the closet door and tossed the stub toward a bucket in the closet. The stub missed the bucket and landed on the floor next to a broom. Unaware of the mistake, the individual closed the closet door depriving the closet of a draft and the stub simply smoldered for several hours until the combustion occurred.[6]

While the actual loss was around $500, the main issue was the fear that the fire generated among the tenants, many of whom evacuated the building in their nightclothes. Soon after the fire, Sheldon ordered the establishment of regular fire drills and periodic safety checks of the fire apparatus. In addition, all closets and the basement storage areas were cleared out and organized to reduce fire potentials. Building vacancies increased as many people became prejudiced about a building that had had recent fire alarm activity.[7]

The loss of the Grand Central Hotel had a direct effect on several of the ground floor businesses in the Sheldon Block. The pharmacy located directly opposite the hotel and the Hixson jewelry store lost a great deal of trade business with the hotel gone, and would probably move out of the building if the Grand Central was not rebuilt.[8]

Many factors drove a wedge between the relationships of the Grand Central's owners. Judge Crosby, while remaining in El Paso, continued his extensive real estate activities and legal career, and General Mills returned to Washington, D.C. where he focused on his military and non-military endeavors. With the fire at the Grand Central Hotel, local business leaders pushed the two investors to again join forces and rebuild the grand hostelry.

As an absentee landlord, Mills had developed a business relationship with Horace B. Stevens to represent his interests in El Paso. Mr. Stevens had a similar relationship with Lucius M. Sheldon, the absentee owner of the Sheldon Block. Several days following the fire, Mills, through Stevens, discussed the rebuilding of the Grand Central with Sheldon. He indicated that he knew that Sheldon understood the problems with Judge Crosby and that he understood that Sheldon would not want to enter into business with him. It had become general knowledge that Judge Crosby had begun to lose his head for business and often got drunk at the last moment that resulted in an air of unreliability.[9]

Mills suggested that Sheldon buy out Crosby's interest in the now vacant Grand Central land and enter into an arrangement with him to rebuild the Grand Central. To attempt to sway Sheldon toward this arrangement, Mills reiterated that the future of the Sheldon Block would be bleak if the hotel were not rebuilt. Mills stated, "That the burning of the Grand Central would detract a good deal from the Sheldon [Block] as many of the offices were located at the north end and because of the close proximity of the hotel, and should anyone erect a hotel at another part of the city, it would detract from that part near the Sheldon." [10]

Within a couple of months of the fire, financial interests from Kansas City were exploring ways to build a replacement hotel in downtown El Paso. These financiers had obtained an option to purchase the old Custom House lot at the corner of San Antonio and Utah (now Mesa) Streets for building a $200,000 "elite" hotel. While a large hotel anywhere in the city would be a good thing for the city, building on the old Custom House lot would have an adverse effect on the Sheldon Block. Several groups, including the Kansas City bankers and a group of local investors were willing to consider the vacant Grand Central property and form a subscription syndicate to raise the needed funds to rebuild the hotel, but Mills' participation was paramount.[11]

Timing is the key and the Panic of 1893 threw a huge roadblock in the decisions regarding the future of a new hotel for El Paso. Availability of European capital began to shrink and foreign investors began a run on U.S. Treasury gold. Bank runs spread across the country, major railroads, including the Northern Pacific Railway, the Union Pacific Railroad, and the Atchison, Topeka & Santa Fe Railroad failed. Bankruptcies spread, companies and banks failed, unemployment soared, and prices collapsed. Newly elected President Grover Cleveland was forced by these circumstances to borrow huge sums of gold from J.P. Morgan and the eminent Rothschild banking family of England.

Talk of the possibility of building the Rio Grande Project, which included the Elephant Butte dam in New Mexico, gave hope to the people of the southwest. (The project stalled under the pressure of the Panic of 1893, but construction began on the Rio Grande in 1905 and the dam opened in 1911.)

In correspondence with Stevens regarding the creation of a hotel syndicate for the rebuilding of the hotel, Lucius M. Sheldon wrote:

> I am willing to give $100 as you suggest, but do not feel that I could advance more. If times are hard in El Paso, it is a lithe to what they are

> here [New York]. I have never known such uncertainty and stringency. One Bank president, upon being approached by investors, declared they were down so low they were going around picking pins up off the floor. While the above may be a slight exaggeration, still all is unrest and uncertainty, so $100 is all I feel I ought to advance. I sincerely hope the project may be successful, and trust you will keep me posted as to its progress.[12]

The financial circumstances of 1893 were hurting Sheldon. Writing to Stevens, he stated, "I can now use money here to great advantage, and it has occurred to me that it would be a good time to draw down some. I dislike to draw down my balance very low, but would be very much pleased to have now some twenty-five hundred to three thousand dollars…remit as much as you can spare, that is leaving enough in the bank to meet your expenses and a small balance besides." [13] Sheldon had repeatedly entertained the idea of converting the Sheldon Block into a hotel, but because of the financial circumstances, such action was not feasible and he continued to refuse to enter into a deal with Crosby and Mills. In order to raise the capital for either venture, Sheldon would have to sell seven per cent securities and that would not be wise under the existing situation. Sheldon could not spare a single cent.[14]

If the hotel could be rebuilt, with the government building on the east and the hotel on the west, the position of the Sheldon Block would forever be fixed. Stevens, sensing that Sheldon's financial situation had improved, urged him to begin to buy up property in the downtown area, as the individuals who owned the property appeared extremely hard up and would be willing to sell cheaply:[15]

> We are practically without hotel accommodations now, and as illustration of how it is hurting us, I would say that last winter the town was full and this winter season hardly any have come in, from the fact that [word] has gotten out that no accommodations are to be had; so many people went away last winter because they could not be taken care of. Mills stands ready to join in any enterprise towards building a hotel, but will not go in with Crosby, now if he [Crosby] could be bought out and the Tays property bought [the Central Hotel], a stock company could be organized…and properly managed, then if the dam is built, it will be a bonanza.[16]

For some time, Sheldon had some very serious concerns about the state of the Sheldon Block and that it had not "come up" to his investment expectations, as rent receipts were dropping and room vacancies were expanding. By years end, he was beginning to think of an alternate plan for the Sheldon Block:

> I have realized since erecting it, that the city is not ripe yet for such a large office building and the situation now shows clearly that affairs are drifting from bad to worse. What El Paso does need and which would pay handsomely as everyone agrees is a hotel, one first class and managed well that would secure the tourist and other transient patronage of the southwest. This is certainly true and that a good hotel could pay in El Paso is beyond question. Now it has seemed to me especially with the building in the state it is now, and with the prospect getting worse, certainly none of it getting any better, that I ought to change its character and turn it into a first class hotel.[17]

Over the next year and a half, a stream of schemers and would-be entrepreneurs flowed through the city with scores of subscription plans for the rebuilding of the Grand Central. The city leaders were growing impatient, as was Gen. Mills. By March 1894, Mills and Crosby had reached an agreement to separate their joint property, with Crosby taking the corner with 65 feet fronting the Sheldon and running back to the first store of the old Central Hotel and plans to build one-story stores. Mills indicated that he might do the same, except to build his with walls strong enough to take multiple stories if needed.[18] Crosby began a multi-year effort; it seemed to Stevens and Mills, to retard every enterprise, which would in any way benefit El Paso.[19]

When Gen. Mills returned to El Paso in April of 1894 after the property separation had been finalized, he made it very clear that he would not become involved in any future hotel projects, whether on his share of the property or any other site. He was severely depressed over the death of his young son, Anson Cassel Mills, from appendicitis on February 25, 1894. Mills had expressed that he no longer had a male heir to leave his property to and he wanted to make life as simple as possible for his wife and two daughters. Gen. Mills wrote to Stevens regarding the new two-story office building on the old Grand Central site:

> In order to instruct my daughter, Constance Lydia, in business methods, I have made an agreement with her that if she will attend to

> the collection of the rents from those two-stories, through you, the same as I have been doing, that I will give her five per cent of the collections, so that you will hear only from her in that matter hereafter, and make
> checks payable to her. I will be obliged to you if you would take a little special pain in your correspondence with her to get her rightly started, as she is only fifteen years old.[20]

Over the years, Constance Lydia increased her business acumen and eventually was in charge of most of the General's business affairs. After Constance Lydia Overton died, she left the properties to her husband Winfield. Upon his death, the Overton's two daughters and their families assumed control. One of the daughters, Mabel Overton Cotter bought out the other heirs and retained sole ownership of the properties, which included the El Paso Mills Building. Mable and her husband Ralph Evans Cotter sold the building to the Mills Building Ltd., for $350,000 in October 1965.

In September 1974 Donald Feretel, general partner of Mills Building Ltd., sold the building to the Mills Tower Financial Corp for $3,000,000.[21] This note was financed by the Jefferson Federal Savings and Loan Association of Meriden, CT. Soon thereafter, Lawrence M. Bower became involved in the Mills Tower Financial Corp, by investing $75,000 in January 1976. His exact role in this phase of the transaction is not clear. In the mid-1970s, the Westcap Corp. (Northwestern Life Insurance Company of Austin) began purchasing the mortgage notes. In June 1987, the real estate arm of the El Paso Electric Company, Franklin Land and Resources, Inc., purchased the building for its headquarters, from James R. Foutch, the trustee of the Northwestern Life Insurance Company for $5,000,000.[22]

Mills met with local architects to develop plans for a two-story building with two stores on the inside 44 feet of the hotel property, to be built out of the debris from the burned Grand Central.[23] These plans were not immediately begun. Mills appeared to have recovered a bit from his family tragedy and that opened the door to further pressure to rejoin the idea of rebuilding the Grand Central on the old site.

As the years progressed, El Paso became accessible from all parts of the U.S. and Mexico as seven railroad lines traversed the city, as it became a point of distribution for Arizona, New Mexico, West Texas, and Mexico. The Southern Pacific from California; the Galveston, Harrisburg & San Antonio from New Orleans; the Atchison, Topeka & Santa Fe from Kansas City; the Texas & Pacific from St. Louis were the main lines. They were joined by the Mexican Central from Mexico City; the Rio Grande, Sierra Madre & Pacific that extended into Northern Chihuahua, and the El Paso & Northeastern, commonly known as the White Oaks Line, which connected to the Chicago, Rock Island & Pacific Railroad. These railroad lines, when fully operational, stimulated the local commerce beyond expectation.[24]

Nearly all excursions stopped in El Paso. El Paso being so close to the Mexican Republic, soon became an attractive departure point for international tourists. El Paso was equal distant, 1200 miles, from Mexico City, San Francisco, New Orleans, and St. Louis. The American and European medical communities were beginning to see El Paso as a recovery potential for tubercular patients, because of its climate and elevation. The one thing lacking was a first-class hotel. There was but one open at the time, the Pierson, which existed with only 60 rooms and actually, couldn't even be considered a good second-class hotel.[25] The only other hotel was the Vendome, which was closed because of an ownership dispute. These facts were not ignored, either by the local town leaders or by Gen. Mills himself.

Mills, entrenched in his steadfast rejection of rebuilding the hotel, continued with his plans to build an office building with a campaign to poach some of the major tenants from the Sheldon building. He approached the Texas & Pacific Railroad that he would build them an office just exactly to suit them and contacted the Pacific Express Company with the same offer if they agreed to leave the Sheldon. This surprising conduct certainly did not ingratiate himself with Lucius Sheldon, who had previously been on very friendly terms.[26]

Regardless of Mills' stubborn position, the money people from Kansas City and St. Louis presented multiple schemes to form hotel syndicates. One plan was to build a new hotel at the Overland Block, south of the two plazas. The possibility of success of the Overland Block plan created urgency on the part of those who wanted the hotel on the old Grand Central site. Opposition to this plan was primarily because it would decentralize the business and downtown area. The Overland backers had plenty of money and the opposition had to create a stock company and sell subscriptions.[27] Wanting to build on the old Grand Central site, the local leaders even turned to notorious robber baron Jay Gould, operator of the Texas & Pacific Railroad, for financial help.[28]

With plans for stores and offices on the old Grand Central site set in his mind, Mills continued to show signs in 1895 of his willingness to sell his property to a hotel stock company if he could get the right price and that the hotel would be capitalized at $200,000.[29] This venture would also require the purchase of the Crosby property (that had previously been separated) as well as the Tays property where the recently burned (1894) Central Hotel had been located.

The Central Hotel, often and most confusingly was referred to as the old Grand Central. The Central, originally the Ponce de León ranch house, was first established in 1827 and operated by a series of different proprietors including the previously mentioned Rohman and Gillock families. The one-story adobe was modified in later years, with a second story added when the Southern Pacific Railroad arrived in 1881. The second story was built of California redwoods.[30]

Under the guidance and direction of Horace B. Stevens, Lucius Sheldon found himself as lead proponent of this plan. Mills stated that he would accept $8000 for his half of the land for a new hotel, or would be willing to give the land up if he were permitted to retain the four stores that he had built. Sheldon rejected the proposal as being too high, "If we have to pay so much for the land [including the high asking price for the Crosby property], it will bring the whole amount to be raised entirely too high. They [Mills] ought to throw the land in as stock, and help the people of El Paso along. It seems to me too much, considering the present condition of El Paso."[31]

The haggling and stalling continued to October 1897. The Overland Block deal fell through and El Paso remained without a first-class hotel. False starts and frustrations continued regarding the formation of a stock company to build on the old Grand Central site. Sheldon finally was able to get 90-day options on the Crosby and Tays portion of the property [Block 17] that was needed to build the new hotel. Sheldon, through H. B. Stevens, submitted an option request to Gen. Mills:

> [Sheldon] must know exactly what the site will cost. I have already obtained options form the Crosby and Tays people. Complying with Mr. Sheldon's desire, I enclose herewith an option for 90 days leaving the amount blank. Will you kindly fill in the amount of cash you are willing to take for the property for such an enterprise, and forward the option to Mr. Sheldon? If Mr. Sheldon succeeds in getting a satisfactory price on this piece of property, I feel quite confident of his ability to push the matter to a finish, and give us a hotel, which will be

> an ornament to El Paso. He proposes to spend not less than $250,000 in the hotel building, and $40,000 in furnishings.[32]

Mills returns the option request to Sheldon with his new price for the property. Stevens immediately contacts Mills:

> Upon my return from Mexico, I found a letter from Mr. Sheldon in which he states that he had received your letter enclosing [the] option on your property in Block 17. I was a little surprised to find that your price on 90 days option was $26,000, for I remembered your letter relative to my going before the Board of Equalization last July or August, at which time I made the arrangement that you were willing to take $14,000 for the property previous to building the last building [two-story office], allowing that this had cost $4000, would bring the property up to $18,000, and I could not understand what had accounted to increase the value of this property to $26,000. In the beginning, I assured Mr. Sheldon that the full Block could be purchased for $50,000. In making these figures, I based my opinion upon what people had been asking for the property. It will probably surprise you now when you know that the price asked for the Block is over $76,000. From my letter of October 4, I tried to make it plain that the property was not desired for speculative purposes, but to be used for building a hotel that would be an ornament to El Paso and would help to increase other values. I am very much afraid that Mr. Sheldon will have to give up the project on account of the high price asked, unless those who own the property are willing to take what would be a reasonable figure.[33]

This sudden change in Mills' approach to the hotel project mystified both Stevens and Sheldon. Not long before the request for the 90-day option was submitted, Mills had authorized Stevens to sell all of Mill's El Paso property, including his portion of Block 17, his shares in the El Paso Street Railway, and several other pieces of downtown property for a total of $20,000.[34]

In early 1899, Mills purchased the corner property across from the Sheldon Building from Judge Crosby. That corner piece had been retained by Crosby since the separation of the old Grand Hotel site. Six months later, Mills let a contract to build a two-story building (The first El Paso Mills Building.) on the site that would cost $22,800 to complete with plans to add two additional stories if needed. The first floor would contain stores and offices and the upper floor would have "Lodge and Club rooms."[35] The old Vendome Hotel was sold to Alzina (Mama De.) Orndorff DeGroff and her husband Charles, inn-keepers from Tucson. The DeGroffs renamed their hotel, the Orndorff and began an extensive renovation in order to turn it into a first class venue. The building would still remain fairly small and not fulfill the current needs of a large first-class hotel for El Paso.[36]

As Sheldon revisited his 1894 idea of converting the Sheldon Office building into a first-class hotel he began early contact with the Brooklyn architects. He also arranged to sell his majority share of Block 44 to the City of El Paso for the new city hall. Judge Crosby and local realtor and future mayor, B.F. Hammett, also agreed to the sale. On November 17, 1898, the city purchased Block 44 for five dollars (and other considerations) and a new city hall was planned for the triangular property at Myrtle and San Antonio Streets.[37] Sheldon agreed to the sale only if the city would build the municipal structure without a fire department and jail. Crosby agreed also only if a portion of the property was established with a park.[38] At the apex of the property, the city agreed to establish a small park to consummate the sale. Today, the Aztec Calendar Park is located on the site. The old City Hall was demolished in 1960 and replaced by a Federal Court building at 511 E. San Antonio across from the El Paso County complex.

At the end of April 1898, the head housekeeper of the Sheldon Building, Mrs. Lucy Barbee, died suddenly. Her death brought attention to the fact that the Sheldon Building had been a key fixture in the life of one of the most significant and controversial individuals in American social and political history, a true American renaissance man.

Notes and References

---

[1] Chapman, Bob. “Magnificent Grand Central Hotel consumed by ‘Fire Demon’ in 1892.” *El Paso Times.* Mar.2, 1952.

[2] Beard, Jan. “Fire levels luxurious Grand Central Hotel.” *El Paso Times*, July 19, 1965.

[3] Ibid.

[4] Horace B. Stevens (HBS), letter to Lucius M. Sheldon (LMS), 11 Feb. 1892. Box 24, 121. (UTEP-MS 153.)

[5] Kohlberg Family Papers. (University of Texas at El Paso, Special Collections MS 369.Box 2, file 10.

[6] HBS, letter to HKS (Lucius Sheldon’s son.) 10 Apr. 1893. Box 26.

[7] LMS, letter to HBS, 15 May. 1893.

[8] HBS, letter to LMS, 4 Mar. 1892. Box 24, 130.
[9] HBS, letter to LMS, 5 April. 1894. Box 26, 107.
[10] HBS, letter to LMS, 17 Feb. 1892. Box 24, 127.
[11] HBS, letter to LMS, 16 Mar. 1892. Box 24, 153.
[12] LMS, letter to HBS, 17 Oct. 1893. Box 24.
[13] LMS, letter to HBS, 26 Jan. 1893.
[14] HSK, letter to HBS, 27 Dec. 1893.
[15] HBS, letter to LMS, 2 Dec. 1893. Box 26, 61.
[16] Ibid.
[17] LMS, letter to HBS, 21 Dec. 1893. Box 26.
[18] HBS, letter to LMS, 6 Mar. 1894. Box 26, 61.
[19] HBS, letter to Mills, 6 Mar. 1895.
[20] Anson Mills, letter to HBS, 8 Feb. 1897.
[21] In September 1974, Donald Fertel, general partner of Mills Building Ltd., sold the building to the Mills Tower Financial Corp for $3,000,000. This note was financed by the Jefferson Federal Savings and Loan Association of Meriden, CT. Soon thereafter, Lawrence M. Bower became involved in the Mills Tower Financial Corp, by investing $75,000 in January 1976. His exact role in this phase of the transactions is not clear. In the mid-1970s, the Westcap Corp. (Northwestern Life Insurance Company of Austin began purchasing the mortgage notes. In June 1987, the Franklin Land and Resources, Inc., the real estate arm of the El Paso Electric Company, purchased the building from James R. Foutch, the trustee of the Northwestern Life Insurance Company for $5,000,000. (Book 162, page 34 and Book 87, page 478.El Paso County Clerk's Office). The entire scandal surrounding the purchases of the Mills Building and the Blue Flame building by convicted felon, Bob Jones is worth significant historical review.

[23] HBS, letter to LMS, 5 April. 1894. Box 26, 107.
[24] The El Paso Northeastern was eventually purchased by the Phelps Dodge Company and merged into the El Paso Southwestern Railroad.
[25] HBS, letter to LMS, 9 Feb. 1899. Box 28, 32.
[26] HBS, letter to LMS, 17 April. 1894. Box 26, 107.
[27] LMS, letter to HBS, 13 Mar. 1895.
[28] LMS, letter to HBS, 14 Feb. 1895. Box 26.
[29] HBS, letter to Mills, 22 Feb. 1895.
[30] Kohlberg papers.
[31] LMS, letter to HBS, 9 Mar. 1895.
[32] HBS, letter to Mills, 17 Oct. 1897. Box 27, 45.
[33] HBS, letter to Mills, 5 Nov. 1897. Box 27, 60.

---

[34] HBS, letter to LMS, 30 Oct. 1897. Box 27, 60.
[35] HBS, letter to LMS, 16 Jun. 1899. Box 26, 86.
[36] Ibid.
[37] Latham, W.I. "Remarks." *Password*. Vol. XXII, 182.
[38] HBS, letter to LMS, 24 Aug. 1898. Box 28, 121.

Chapter Seven

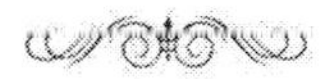

The Renaissance Man of the Southwest

There is no doubt that the early 1880s punctuated El Paso's four-hundred-year history with the arrival of the railroads. From that event, the tiny dusty village on the far West Texas border began its influence upon America's westward migration and economic entrance into the world's economy with its base in cotton, cattle, copper, and climate. Also arriving in this Texas hamlet was the iconic and controversial character, Lieutenant Henry O. Flipper, fresh from his headline grabbing Army court-martial and subsequent dismissal from military service. He was just one of a long list of fascinating men and women who affected El Paso with their association with the Sheldon Block and subsequent hotel. Henry Flipper was a renaissance man in the truest sense and has today become a hero of Black America.

In 1878, shortly after graduating from West Point, Flipper penned his autobiography, The Colored Cadet at West Point, recounting his experiences as the first African American to graduate from the military academy. Thirty-eight years later, he authored his second autobiography, Black Frontiersman: The Memoirs of Henry O. Flipper, which chronicled his life on the western frontier up to 1916.

Born a slave in 1856 to parents who themselves, through persistence and enterprise, sloughed off the shackles of indenture. Henry's father rose to success as a much sought after saddle maker and leather craftsman. Flipper's parents became part of the South's elite black gentry and with the aid of the American Mission Society's schools for black youths in Atlanta, Henry and his siblings received an enormous educational privilege.[1]

Henry, admitted to West Point in 1873, was the first African American to graduate and receive a commission as a Second Lieutenant in the U.S. Army.

Assigned to the all-black 10th Cavalry, Henry O. Flipper headed to the remote West to aid in the Indian Wars and engaged his skill as a civil engineer for the Army. Henry's military star was on the rise when he successfully devised what became known as Flipper*'s Ditch*. Established as a National Historic Landmark in 1977, the Flipper designed and constructed draining system (1878) at Fort Sill, Oklahoma, prevented a potential malaria outbreak and remained in use for over 100 years.[2]

In 1881, the Army transferred his unit was to Fort Davis, Texas, and it was there that his reputation and character was challenged and tarnished. Part of Flipper's duties was to maintain control of the fort's commissary funds. Through a series of unfortunate events, Flipper was charged and court-martialed for embezzling military funds and conduct unbecoming an officer and a gentleman. Acquitted of the embezzlement charge, the court convicted him of lying to his commanding officer regarding the mishandling of the government funds. The story of Flipper's life as a cadet and his subsequent problems at Fort Davis are chronicled in several well-documented and historic biographies. The books by Robinson, Johnson, Eppinga, and Flipper himself, go a long way to provide detailed accounts of these trying experiences of America's first Negro graduate of the military academy at West Point. (See bibliography)

Figure 25. Lieutenant Henry O. Flipper
A Renaissance Man

What sets Flipper's life apart from so many others who have been subdued by the military justice system, was the magnitude of his post-court martial professional and personal accomplishments and the forty-year commitment he made in his lifelong attempt to clear his name and regain his military standing.

Six feet one inch tall, Flipper was bi-racial with light copper colored skin and weighed around 170 pounds. He believed himself intellectually superior to most Americans of the era regardless of their racial background, and he exhibited the manners of a southern military aristocrat.[3] He was introspective, almost stoic-like and guarded against revealing his emotions to others. Despite his unfortunate experiences with the Army, he was extremely nationalistic. Although genuinely cordial toward individual Mexicans, he shared the view that as a people, they were essentially inferior.[4]

Following his dismissal from the Army, Flipper managed a long and remarkable career as a civil engineer, mining engineer, oil engineer, inventor, cartographer, and interpreter. In addition, he was a newspaper editor, historian, author, Mexican land and mining law expert; as well as a special agent for the Justice Department, aide to the Senate Committee on Foreign Relations, assistant to the Secretary of the Interior, and an executive for an international oil company. If that were not enough, he was also an expert linguist, not only fluent in Spanish, French, German, but in the Athapascan language of the Apaches.[5]

As a private citizen, in 1898, Flipper would begin his long and complicated journey to right what he believed to be the injustice of his dismissal from the Army. From 1898 until 1924, he had nine unsuccessful bills introduced in the Senate and the House of Representatives to support his reinstatement. Despite his extraordinary post-military professional successes and accomplishments by a man of any race, Henry Flipper never achieved in his lifetime his dream of re-instatement. He succumbed to a heart attack at the age of 84 on May 3, 1940, essentially penniless, unsung, lonely, and all but ignored by his fellow Americans and the media of the day. While his adventures were full of dangers and hardships as he ventured deep into the wildest reaches of the Indian territories, the American Southwest, Mexico, and South America, he survived with loneliness as a constant adversary.[6] He was buried in a plain wooden coffin and without any reference to his government service.

Regarding Flipper's immersion in the turmoil of racism, black historian Quintard Taylor[7] wrote that Flipper, "was no racial crusader and thus did not generate the support or acclaim from much of the African American leadership that accompanied those of far more modest accomplishments. Flipper remained estranged from the national black intelligentsia because he refused to transform his personal difficulties into a racial cause celebre."[8]

Thirty-six years after his death, the Military Board of Corrections would eventually change (November 17, 1976) the status of his dismissal and reburied Flipper with full military honors on February 11, 1978.[9] The Board rejected any criminality, ruled that Flipper's dismissal was too severe a punishment, and changed the records to reflect an honorable discharge. It should be noted, that contrary to many accounts of Flipper's life, his dismissal in 1882 was not a dishonorable discharge. The Army simply discharged him without comment, stating that his services as a soldier were neither needed nor desired.[10] Furthermore, the vote of the Board was not unanimous. There was one dissenting vote. That board member stated, based on Flipper's own record of false reports and statements, "[Flipper's actions] clearly represents misconduct of a very serious nature and should not be taken lightly. Even though Flipper was acquitted of embezzlement, it appears that he was guilty of misappropriation of some of the funds in question and the sentence should be allowed to stand."[11]

In 1999, President Bill Clinton issued a full presidential pardon to Henry Flipper posthumously erasing the imputation that he had carried for most of his life. Some accounts of the pardon stated, "that the pardon exonerates Flipper of charges that he tried to cover up losses to a quartermaster account at Fort Davis—charges that the Army agreed were false more than 20 years ago."[12] This comment was just not factual.

Figure 26. Flipper memorial bust at Fort Leavenworth, KY.

Not all historians believe that the Army Board of Corrections of Military Records and the President's actions were completely justified. These issues are clearly discussed in detail in Robinson's 2008 book and the privately printed book by Johnson.[13] Those issues—congressional and presidential—and the belief that Flipper was clearly guilty of conduct unbecoming an officer and a gentleman, but was subjected to unreasonably harsh punishment—the dismissal—remains today as controversial as ever. Eppinga summarizes, "there can be no doubt that racial prejudice played a part in his court-martial and subsequent dismissal from the military. Nevertheless, it cannot be denied that Flipper was careless with Army finances or that he deserved discipline for his actions. However, the punishment of dismissal did not fit the crime."[14]

The issue of racial prejudice has haunted the Flipper affair for years. Robinson writes: "if one considers the possibility of racism in the failure to reinstate Flipper, one must also consider the possibility that the sixteen-year wait [the delay between his dismissal and his first attempt at reinstatement], together with the allegations against officers now dead and the overall tone of the petition, may have worked against him. Flipper claimed that his arrest and subsequent court-martial was all part of actions by the military because he had had a relationship with a white woman while at Fort Davis. He tried to blame it all on race, making his claim long after the witnesses were no longer available. One therefore may conclude that Flipper's case became a racial issue only when it was resurrected in the 1960s, a time in which the so-called race card became the wild card that could tilt a hand."[15]

Robinson reached a different conclusion in his 2008 book from that in his earlier work regarding the Flipper affair:

> I came to the unpleasant realization that I had been wrong. Flipper, it now seemed to me, was the author of his own problems. I was not alone in this conclusion...Over the past thirty years a whole body of mythology has grown up around the Flipper affair, and the mythology has received official sanction from the Federal Government. Flipper's many adherents will no more question the myth of his victimization than the devotees of St. Christopher will question the myth of a giant bearing the infant Christ across a river...So it is with the Flipper affair. An army officer, who happened to be black, was convicted on proper evidence, in a more than fair trial, and dismissed as he deserved to be. A legend has developed that because he was black he was railroaded. The legend, however, serves to illustrate the underlying truth of genuine cases of racism in the army of the period. Unfortunately, it also has served to obscure those cases.
>
> Because of the great social upheavals of the second half of the twentieth century, the Flipper affair has assumed a political and social significance that is entirely out of proportion to the historical reality. Although the case had been resolved decades earlier, it had to be re-resolved, regardless of the facts. For his family, this is understandable. For politicians and social activist, it is an imperative. The efforts culminated with a pardon issued to Flipper by President William J. Clinton on February 19, 1999. Clinton's speech at the pardoning ceremony was standard political fare. He perpetuated the myth of a dishonorable discharge and said, "Today's ceremony is about a moment in 1882, when our government did not do all it could do to

> protect an individual American's freedom. It is about a moment in 1999 when we correct the error and resolve to do even better in the future."
> He added that a "later Army review board suggested he had been singled out for his race" but did not mention that this army review board convened more than ninety years after the fact, nor that its suggestions (as opposed to conclusions) were not unanimous." ... In view of his subsequent achievements, a pardon for an offense committed as a young man is entirely appropriate. Nevertheless, it must be remembered that a pardon is not exoneration. The very use of the word "pardon" establishes that an offense was committed for which the government extends forgiveness. The record is not expunged.[16]

Should Flipper be singled out as an example of pride for black America? Absolutely, but his enormous contributions were that of not just an African American, but of a truly gifted, talented and persistent American. The foregoing clearly establishes that Henry Flipper was not only a most accomplished individual, but also, even today, highly controversial. His relationship with the housekeeper of the Sheldon Building plays out in a life full of adventures and involvements with an array of characters, interestingly, mostly women. One issue that surfaces rather consistently when reading the volumes of books and published articles about Flipper is the fact that he never married, that he remained somewhat of an enigma, that he was a loner, as well as an elitist. Some writers called him a snob. Some slight references appear regarding a love affair that ended sadly because of racist and archaic state miscegenation laws.[17] Other accounts suggest that Flipper was in fact married and sired a family during his time in Mexico City.[18]

In April 1892, Flipper wrote to his brothers, Joseph and Festus, and said that he was still a bachelor and would most likely always remain one:

> I shall certainly not marry any one I have ever seen out here. There is a nice lady in El Paso that would make a fine wife for any one, but she is now married to a splendid gentleman, and—"Thou shalt no covet thy neighbor's wife"—I have never seen any other woman out this way, colored, white or Mexican, that I would give a fin for as a wife. All the nice girls are back east where you are.[19]

From these writings, assumptions of his personal life are drawn, but evidence clearly shows that these remarks were not terribly accurate descriptions of Flipper's behavior or his true feelings. Based on his prior experiences and behavior with several other women, those remarks may have been just 'thoughts' that he presented to his family for their consumption and were his attempt to protect his true beliefs and behavior. Theodore Harris, editor of the second Flipper autobiography, explained that his research on Flipper revealed that he didn't discuss the women in his life, with very few exceptions, because he was just too private a person, guided by strict puritanical Christian beliefs regarding sexual and romantic issues. As a result, Flipper's writings are devoid of much discussion about his personal life and exploits with women.[20]

To clarify Flipper's involvement with the Sheldon Building's Lucy Barbee, a full chronicle of Flipper's life and his romantic relationships begins back in the days before his admission to West Point.

The Anna White Affair

Flipper met Anna P. White during their college years in 1872 while they both attended Atlanta University. Their relationship continued even after he left Atlanta to attend West Point. Their engagement was announced in 1876 prior to his graduation.[21] After his graduation in 1877 and on the advice of Flipper's brother, the Rev. Joseph Flipper, and Anna's own parents, she broke off the engagement and returned the engagement ring to Flipper. She had succumbed to the pressure from her and Flipper's family that his future was going to be in fighting Indians and they did not believe that Anna could endure the hardships and deprivations required with relocating to the untamed Southwest.[22] Flipper joined the 10th Cavalry and soon found himself in the wild and woolly west, knee-deep in the Indian Wars and frontier military life at Fort Sill, Oklahoma. Anna soon married Augustus Shaw of Brunswick, Georgia and had children and a comfortable life until her husband's death in 1914. Anna returned to Atlanta and four years later, she and Flipper resumed their correspondence.[23]

The Mollie Dwyer Affair

While stationed at Fort Sill, Oklahoma, Flipper's widowed Captain Nicolas Nolan had recently remarried a younger woman. Capt. Nolan brought his new wife and her sister, Mollie Dwyer, to his post at Fort Sill. Capt. Nolan's new wife soon invited Flipper to join them on a regular basis for meals at their quarters. As a result, Nolan's sister-in-law developed a platonic relationship with Flipper and the two of them spent considerable time together. On Sundays, Flipper and other officers and their women, used to chase coyotes and jackrabbits on horseback out on the plains.[24] When Flipper's cavalry company transferred to Fort Davis in Texas, Nolan and family, including Mollie, joined them at the fort in Texas. The social relationship between Flipper and Mollie continued. In the meantime, the company's First Lieutenant, Charles E. Nordstrom, began to show some serious interest in Mollie and the relationship with Flipper began to wane.

The public interracial friendship between Flipper and eligible Mollie was certainly a serious issue at the isolated frontier outpost. Resentment began to become an issue. Shortly thereafter, in 1881, Flipper's problem at Fort Davis began to escalate, eventually culminating in his court-martial and eventual dismissal from the Army. In Flipper's second autobiography, he attempted to convey that these recreational horse rides were more than casual and hinted he may have been in love with her. Yet aside from Flipper's 1916 memoir, there seem to be no letters or diary entries from anyone on the matter. Flipper apparently fabricated the story to blame his downfall on rivalry over Mollie's affections between himself and Lt. Nordstrom.[25] Thus, the implied relationship with Mollie and its subsequent animus as a cause for Flipper's troubles never existed.[26] Robinson concludes:

> Such a relationship would have been extremely awkward in the context of the 1880s. As a group, white women in the West viewed African Americans with the same disdain as their Eastern sisters, the old prejudices simply moved along with them from one region to the other. Black people were considered inferior because of race, color, and their status as former slaves. Physical features, also, were used to parody them or to describe them simply as "hideous." Even if Mollie Dwyer did not share these prejudices, as the daughter of a country judge whose duties would have included enforcing Texas' anti-miscegenation laws, she would have been more than slightly aware of the awesome social and legal barrier between herself and Flipper.[27]

Yet, despite the fact that well documented research material supports that Flipper's relationship with Mollie Dwyer was strictly platonic and that it never developed into anything romantic before her marriage to Lieutenant Nordstrom, there exists a body of literature that continues to promote the contrary. Goss wrote that Flipper: "had a torrid love affair with a white woman, Molly Dwyer. Molly and Henry's love was doomed because of the taboo of interracial marriage and the fact that Henry's archenemy, Nordstrom, was obsessed with Molly. Nordstrom's hatred for Henry drove him to frame him for embezzlement by stealing $3000 from his locker…After his acquittal he was unfairly given a dishonorable discharge for 'actions unbecoming an officer.'"[28] In addition, Lee reports, "Although he was court-martialed and dismissed from the Army—most likely because of a smear campaign following his marriage to Anne Eleanor Dwyer (A Caucasian)—he was finally pardoned by President Bill Clinton in 1999."[29] (There was no marriage, in fact, the name Anne Eleanor Dwyer was that of Capt. Nolan's wife, Mollie's sister.)

The Lucy E. Smith Affair

Steeped in mystery and intrigue, Flipper's relationship with Lucy Smith is rooted deeply in his court-martial at Fort Davis in 1881. Flipper, as was commonly practice among Cavalry officers of the time, employed a black servant, Lucy, to do housekeeping and cooking chores. According to the consensus of those in the Fort Davis community and those who were involved in the court-martial proceedings, she was also his mistress.

During the court-martial, both the judge advocate and defense counsel referred to her as Lucy Flipper, albeit they immediately corrected their comments.[30] Flipper and Lucy's obvious "living together" challenged the wildly held Victorian values that required that such relationships, if they existed, were to be discreet. As such, neither the judge advocate nor the defense counsel made this an issue. Officers at these far-flung outposts were expected to contain their social lives to each other or with individuals in civilian life who were of equal status and they were certainly not to become involved with enlisted personnel or the 'servant class.' The relationship between Flipper and Lucy Smith, and his previous activities involving Mollie Dwyer, clearly violated this social convention and most certainly put him on a collision course with his fellow officers.[31]

Flipper was a trained civil engineer, but his assignment at Fort Davis required bookkeeping and accounting expertise which he completely lacked. He had failed to make timely deposits on behalf of the commissary accounts and subsequently told his commanding officer that he had in fact made the deposits. He had placed the funds in his personal trunk inside his quarters. It appears that this failure to divulge his inept organization and bookkeeping skills and lying about it to his commander, was the final issue of the charges against him as there was no actual loss of funds.

During the investigation following Flipper's arrest and confinement to the guardhouse, his commanding officer, Colonel Shafter, had Lucy taken to his office and they discovered nearly $3000 in cash and checks hidden on Lucy Smith's person. Shafter concluded that Lucy was Flipper's mistress and co-conspirator in a scheme to steal government funds.[32] He had Lucy arrested and taken to the Presidio County jail. Local citizens hired an attorney and when the lawyer pointed out that, the unendorsed checks were of no material value to Lucy, the local authorities released her on own recognizance.[33] "Yet, Lucy," writes Robinson, "of all people, had the most access to the money in Flipper's trunk. If anyone stole the government funds, it was Lucy, either alone or together with any of the other shadowy figures who apparently had access to Flipper's quarters."[34]

Secretary of War, Robert Todd Lincoln, and General of the Army William Tecumseh Sherman soon cited Flipper's confinement to the six-and-one-half by four-and-one-half foot cell in the guardhouse as an act of humiliation to an officer. They concluded that racial prejudice accounted for Flipper's extraordinarily harsh treatment and ordered Colonel Shafter to transfer Flipper to house arrest at his quarters.[35] This issue would later play a significant part in the reversal of the consequences of Flipper's dismissal from the Army. The Flipper court-martial affair captured national attention because of his celebrity as the first African American graduate of West Point. Public attention soon dissipated, however, from the nation's press when the murder trial of President James A. Garfield's assassin, Charles Guiteau, began in Washington, D.C. on November 14, 1881.

During the court-martial proceedings, both the defense and the Army counted on Lucy's testimony to bolster their respective arguments. Lucy Smith portrayed herself, "as a naïve, dim, easily intimidated servant, playing to the stereotypes of the era. In doing so," Taylor writes of her inconclusive testimony, "she succeeded in removing herself from culpability."[36] Johnson wrote that Flipper could not, "publicly admit that the blind trust which he had reposed in his housekeeper, and probable mistress, had been so ruinously betrayed. He probably never admitted this even to himself."[37] While he rarely mentions Lucy Smith in his writings, Flipper maintained his belief in her innocence for the rest of her life. He always insisted that she was innocent of any wrongdoing.

Practically nothing was known of Lucy Smith's background. She just rather appeared along the San Antonio-El Paso Road. Her upbringing, marital status, and early life remain unconfirmed; she just seemed to be a fixture around Fort Stockton and Fort Davis. Following the Flipper court-martial, no one ever determined what happened to young Lucy. Where did she go? Was she one of the "rootless wanderers who populated the western frontier and disappears from history?" On the other hand, did she reappear again to be part of Flipper's life as he emerged from his cloud of dishonor and took up residency in El Paso? Whether Lucy Smith of Fort Davis and Lucy Barbee of the Sheldon Building had any more in common than first names is total speculation. Research has uncovered very little about Lucy Barbee's history before her appearance in El Paso. That history remains as much a mystery as Lucy Smith's suddenly disappearance.

The 'Lady Flo' Affair

Following his dismissal from the Army, humiliated and disgraced, former Lieutenant Henry O. Flipper arrived in El Paso hoping to begin a new career as a civil engineer on July 3, 1882. Flipper chose not to return to the East with its rigid racial segregation but to remain in the ethnically diverse southwest.[38] While he may have arrived in El Paso disheartened, he didn't arrive alone. His companion was reportedly an extremely intelligent and beautiful black woman named Florida J. Wolf, who in her own right, would become a significant character in El Paso's early history.[39]

Flipper's relationship with Wolf ended suddenly when he deserted her shortly after their arrival. Wolf eventually became the "common law" wife of Lord Delaval Beresford, a wealthy English nobleman. After years of operating cattle ranches in Texas and Mexico (a neighboring ranch to the El Paso influencing Corralitos Ranch in Chihuahua) and battling the Beresford family over her inheritance following Beresford's tragic death, Wolf remained in El Paso. There is little doubt that Lady Flo, because of her activities, had some degree of interaction with the Sheldon Hotel, as Sheldon served as the center of civic activity in downtown El Paso. She became known as 'Lady Flo' and continued her social life as a grand party-giver and charitable benefactor.[40]

The Mexico City Affair

In the late 1880s, Flipper was busy surveying northern Mexico and working for the Luis Terrazas family operated Banco Minero and various American oil and land companies controlled by Col. William Greene and Albert B. Fall. He traveled extensively throughout Mexico and in 1887, frequently traveled to Mexico City on business. In his article about Flipper's marriage and Mexican family, Eckhardt reported that, after Flipper's death his family insisted that he had been a bachelor his entire life and had never been married, yet there was evidence that there was a Flipper family living in Mexico City. This family, Eckhardt continued, exhibited distinctive African-mixed facial features, and claimed to trace its descent from an Enrique [Henry] Flipper. The American Flipper family would have to disavow this marriage because Flipper would have to have married in the Catholic faith and that would have been an affront to the staunch Georgia Baptist family. Furthermore, the scandal would have cast some pale over the efforts to reverse his dishonorable discharge.[41]

Believing this Mexican tale to be preposterous, I contacted and interviewed Theodore Harris, the editor of Flipper's second autobiography. Harris said, "It is plausible, especially considering that Flipper was in Mexico City at that time and that he consistently withheld elements of his personal life from his family. Flipper's interest in exotic women was well known among his contemporaries. While it is plausible, I doubt its authenticity without seeing legitimate primary source documents."[42]

Searching for primary source documents, I subsequently contacted Charles Eckhardt and asked him for the specific source that he used to support his assertion that Flipper had sired a family in Mexico City. Eckhardt said, he didn't have any real documentation to speak of, but that he had been told by a friend that they had seen several people in Mexico City who were of mixed race, claimed to have Flipper as a surname, and looked similar to the photos of Henry Flipper. So much for plausible.[43]

The Luisa Montoya Affair

In 1883, Flipper began his professional career as a civil engineer and surveyor working for various entities in throughout Mexico. Over the next several years, his adventures took him throughout the southwest, often returning to his residence in El Paso.

Capitalizing on his experience in northern Mexico and his Spanish language skills, he developed knowledge regarding Spanish and Mexican land grant laws. As a result, he began to spend a great deal of time in the late 1880s in and around Nogales, Arizona. By the 1890s, he had established his business in Nogales specializing in mineral, mine, and land surveying as well as working on land claims for the Justice Department as a special agent with the Court of Private Land Claims.[44] As his career forged ahead, he began to reduce his constant traveling and decided to settle down in Nogales in 1888, where he had purchased some property and briefly became the editor or the local newspaper. The early residents of Nogales have bestowed upon Flipper the mantle of

"Savior" because of his work in the Court of Private Land Claims, where his laborious effort resulted in resolving major landowner issues over problematic land grants. Eppinga in an article in the Journal of Arizona History details Flipper's efforts in the resolution of the Los Nogales de Elias land grant.[45]

During this period, he began a relationship with a Mexican woman by the name of Luisa Montoya. By 1891 they had decided to marry, but were denied by Arizona Territory miscegenation laws that prevented individuals of different races to marry. (The law was finally repealed in Arizona on January 15, 1962 and Mexicans were legally considered Caucasians.)[46] Not dissuaded by these unjust laws, in 1891, he and Montoya chose to enter a legal contract. The sheer fact that Flipper would pursue such a legal recourse to a common-law marriage is clear evidence of his feelings and commitment to Montoya to want to provide her with as close a relationship to marriage that he could arrange.[47] Signed on September 10, 1891 by Flipper and Montoya and the witnesses present, the contract reads:

> That the full name of said part of the first part is Henry Ossian Flipper...That the full name of said second party is Louisa (sic) Montoya...That first and second parties do hereby jointly make this their declaration of marriage...That said parties do hereby agree to take each other as husband and wife and to live together as such from the date hereof...That their marriage has not been solemnized, but this declaration of marriage is made in lieu of such Solemnization.[48]

Having overcome the legal barrier of marriage, the happy couple remained together for less than a year.[49] It was following this experience that Flipper sent his eloquent letter in April 1892 to his brothers disavowing his interest in women and marriage in. In 1897, Flipper moved from Nogales to Santa Fe and maintained a home there until his duties with the Court of Private Land Claims ended in 1901. Sometime in the middle 1890s, he began frequent trips to El Paso where he began a new relationship.

The Lucy Barbee Affair.

Exactly when Flipper met Lucy Barbee is lost to history. Were Lucy Barbee and Lucy Smith the same? This question was posed to Harris, the historian who edited Flipper's second autobiography. Harris said that he felt that it was a real possibility, considering Flipper's almost blind support of Lucy Smith's innocence, yet, there is a complete lack of substantiation.[50]

Lucy Barbee arrived in Texas in the late 1880s from Bloomington, Illinois, following her divorce from a man named Henderson. Anxious to start a new life, she left a house that she owned in Bloomington[51] to her two sisters, Mrs. Ed (Caroline) Brewer of Champaign/Urbana, IL, and Mrs. J. E. Jackson of Cairo, IL.

Lucy, who was bi-racial, took a job as housekeeper at the newly opened Sheldon Building in the heart of downtown El Paso. Stevens, the local real estate and insurance agent who managed the property for Sheldon and who also maintained an office in the building, hired her. Over the years, Lucy and Stevens' family became extremely close, as was the case with many of the other residents and tenants. There existed a sense of fellowship and brotherhood between black and white, similar to that that sometimes existed during slavery days in the South. It was in this manner, that all who met Lucy held her in high esteem. Lucy lived in rooms 65 and 67 of the Sheldon during the nine years that she worked there.[52]

As their romance grew, Flipper gave her an engagement ring and they developed plans to marry. Flipper deposited money into a special bank account in her name to use to purchase a house on Leon Street. Contrary to subsequent Flipper writings [53] and other accounts of Flipper's attitude toward marriage and his dealings with people that he believed were beneath his intellectual stature, he said, "that his whole soul was devoted to her, and I had hoped to soon make her my wife."[54] In 1898, with their romance in full swing and with his pursuit of his career as an engineer and expert on Spanish and Mexican land law, he traveled to Washington, D.C. on business. While in Washington, he began his campaign with the House Committee on Military Affairs to reverse his dismissal from the Army.

In early April, Lucy became ill and found it necessary to have a medical procedure to remove a tumorous growth. She apparently recovered sufficiently during the next several days to get up and move about. Then she suddenly relapsed and her condition deteriorated over the next two weeks. Mr. Stevens and some other of Lucy's friends arranged to have her moved from her residence in the Sheldon Building to Sister's Hospital (Hotel Dieu). Her condition remained grave; she experienced chills and an extremely high fever. Stevens arranged for a new team of physicians and she was diagnosed with a severe case of peritonitis. Then on Tuesday, the 26th she rallied and began to show signs of improvement, her pulse became regular and strong, her condition steadily improved, although she remained extremely sick.[55] On Wednesday, April 27, Stevens arranged to have Lucy prepare a legal Will and Testament, naming her sister, Mrs. J.E. Jackson, as executor, just in case things did not improve.[56] And they did not.

Stevens wired Flipper of the tragedy, Stevens followed up his wire to Flipper writing:

> Dear Sir:
> It is with deep sorrow I write you confirming my dispatch of Lucie's death. I know how deeply you will feel the blow, and feel that in times like this, words are idle. We all loved and cherished Lucie for all her true worth. There was no truer, or better woman in the word. She was thought very much of by everybody she [was] in contact with, and especially those she has ministered in sickness. Out of her abundance of health, she gave freely. Her funeral will take place today at 3 o'clock. She will be laid to rest in my family lot in Evergreen Cemetery. My telegrams sent from time to time, will tell you how much in doubt we were in her recovery, but she seemed so much better Monday, Tuesday, and Wednesday, that we entertained very strong hopes that of her recovery. Thursday forenoon, he pulse was very irregular and her condition that the poison was effecting her nerves. She died very peacefully and for the last few days did not suffer much. Everything that was possible to do was done for her. I have wired both of her sisters, and have response from one of them. After consulting with friends here, we have thought it best to bury her here. Her funeral will be largely attended, for she was a universal favorite. Among her effects, I find a certificate of deposit for $489, which she told me was money given her by you to purchase property which I had been negotiating for her, and which could not be closed on account of defective title. From your telegram, I take it that you wish this money to be used defraying the expenses of her illness and death. She left a will giving all her real and personal property, to her sister in Cairo, Ill.,, Mrs. J.E. Jackson, except her diamond ring and bracelet which she desired to be given to you, as your property. I have written her sisters fully of the situation. Advising them of the money here in the bank, and that it belonged to you. Mr. Patterson, who has advised Lucie in legal matters, tells me that the money cannot be used without first obtaining Mrs. Jackson's consent. I have guaranteed the payment of all expenses here and there need to be no undue haste in the matter. I will have everything together by the time I receive your letter so I will know how to act.
>
> In sorrow, I am sincerely yours, HBS[57]

Flipper remained in Washington, D.C. attempting to resolve his issues with the Army, as he could not return to El Paso in time for the service. A very large crowd of El Pasoans attended the funeral held at the A.M.E. Church and at Evergreen Cemetery.[58] Lucy's Will was very clear and straightforward. She directed that in the event of her death, all expenses and debts be paid and all of her real estate (in Illinois) and personal property be given to her sister, Mrs. J.E. Jackson of Cairo, Ill. whom she appointed as executor. She stated that her diamond engagement ring and bracelet be returned to Henry Flipper as his property. Supported by information from the bank and other witnesses, the $489 certificate of deposit in the El Paso bank actually belonged to Flipper and was to be returned to him since the purchase of the Leon Street property had been delayed because of problems in obtaining a clear title.

If losing his soul-mate and the love of his life wasn't tragic enough, Flipper would find himself embroiled in conflict with Lucy's sister and heir, Mrs. J.E. Jackson for months to come. When notified of Lucy's death, her sister began to demand of Stevens that he immediately return all of Lucy's personal property, including the engagement ring and bracelet and the certificate of deposit. It is not clear why Lucy selected Mrs. Jackson over her other sister, Caroline Brewer to receive all of the property. It may have been that Mrs. Brewer was financially stable and that Mrs. Jackson needed the financial support.

Henry Flipper had absolutely no use for Lucy's sister, Mrs. Jackson and her preacher husband. In response to being notified of Lucy's death, Flipper wrote to Stevens the following:

> Your telegram announcing the sad death of Miss Lucie Barbee just received...Please secure all of her property and please allow no one, especially no colored person in El Paso to have access to or control over it. I will write to her sister, Mrs. Ed Brewer, in Champaign, Illinois, and ask her to go to El Paso and take the property, after such debts as Lucie may have not have been paid. There was some $500 to $600 in the bank in her name, but which belonged to me. If necessary, use that toward paying her debts. If not necessary, return what remains of it to me. Her engagement ring might be held for me.[59]

As the conflict over Lucy's property escalated, Flipper again asked Stevens to intervene:

> Mrs. Brewer writes me from Urbana, Ill.,(sic) that J.E. Jackson, the husband of Mrs. Jackson, Lucie's sister, they have written to you and to the bank directing that the $489 of my money be sent to him at once. I wrote you to use this money, all of it or as much as necessary, to pay Lucie's debts in El Paso. While I am still willing that that should be done, I am unwilling that any of it should go to a negro (sic) preacher of the greed and caliber of J.E. Jackson. I am unwilling that he should have any of Lucie's things. I know that cannot be avoided under the terms of her will. I do not know what the laws in Texas are in such cases, but I presume they provide for the probate of wills. If they do, can't you have yourself appointed administrator of the estate with power to settle the estate, pay all the debts, etc.? I would like to have you buy in such things as you know I gave Lucie, buy them in as cheaply as possible, paying for them out of the $489 and send them to Mrs. Brewer. The piano, furniture, pictures, sewing machine ought to bring enough to pay Lucie's debts, counting what I pay for to save them and keep Jackson from getting them. The money I gave her for the lots was over $600.00. She gave $20.00 of this amount to bind the deal and used $82 to pay for repairs on her house at Bloomington, Ill. …I have no purpose in all this other than to see that Lu's good name is kept (unintelligible) from all clouds…and to see that a worthless negro like Jackson does not rob me…I leave the whole matter in your hands confident that you have my feelings about Lu's good name and that you will do what is right in the matter.[60]

After a series of some innocuous letters to Stevens, Mrs. Jackson letters took a vile turn, first writing, "I received your letter dated June 14 and contents considered. I have no disposition to take one penny of any one's earnings and mislead the most illiterate of earth's creatures [Flipper] but wanted to thoroughly be satisfied in my mind that this money belonged to Lieutenant Flipper. Dear Sir and friend, send the goods early to my address 614-21 St."[61]

Soon after, Mrs. Jackson attacks Stevens in a series of letters presumably written for her by her preacher husband[62]:

> Dear Sir:
> We are in receipt of box of Jewelry. Bill of lading and your letter. The goods have not reached here as yet. H.O. Flipper has his money which he contended for but that toilet set and bicycle are mine by Will and

> law. I have no arrangements to make with Flipper. He wrote me an insulting letter about the money. I gave him the money so he should not dictate the disposition of my sister's things over which he has no control. Dear Sir, I am somewhat disappointed in your holding back a part of the things for Flipper to say who shall have them. You said repeatedly that the money was his and could be proved by several witnesses. You promised to send receipts of all the bills of Lucy's sickness etc. You said nothing about the trunk of clothes in the Bill of Lading. You promised me that you would protect my interest there but it seems as if you are somewhat inclined to protect Flipper's. He has his money since that is true he has no more to do about the personal and real estate than a man that never saw Lucy. You told me in your letters that you would act according to my instructions. If you will be so kind to do it then, please send those things to my address at once.[63]

In the end, by October 1898, the battle over Lucy's estate seemed to resolve itself, Lucy's debts were paid, Flipper got the ring and the bracelet, and Mrs. Jackson received a trunk of dresses, a minor collection of jewelry, and a $4000 house in Bloomington with a mortgage at seven percent…and Mrs. Brewer got nothing. "I am sure," wrote Flipper, "her [Mrs. Jackson] conscience can rest easy, and I am sure mine can and will."[64]

Flipper returned to his adventurers and exploits in and around Santa Fe, New Mexico and Nogales, Arizona. Lucy's final resting place, in the end, was not in the Stevens family plot, whether she was moved from the Stevens' plot or never actually buried there is not known. Lucy is at Evergreen Cemetery; in front of George Huffman, to the right of Floyd and Alice Whitney and to the left of Perry Dunn; in an unmarked and unremarkable grave. As remembered by W.M. Yandell, M.D. following her death, "Her blood was a mingling of the white and black races; she inherited the good qualities of both—the bad qualities of neither—and she was an honor to our common humanity."[65]

The Anna P. White Affair…again.

Anna White, Flipper's former fiancée from his West Point days, had married Augustus Shaw of Brunswick, Georgia and settled down to a fairly typical family life while Flipper was adventuring throughout the West. Following the death of Augustus Shaw in 1914, Anna White Shaw's son, William, an Atlanta lawyer, said that his mother renewed communication with Flipper in 1918 during the time that Flipper returned to live in El Paso.[66]

Flipper became an El Paso resident again during the years 1912-1919 and as such there is little doubt that he frequented the Sheldon Hotel, for the lobby, dining room, and bar were major social gathering places. Not only did he resume his engineering duties when he became employed by oil development entities controlled by Col. Greene and Albert Fall. He also engaged in historical research and journalism.[67] Impressed with the intellectual skill that Flipper possessed, Senator Albert Fall hired Flipper in 1919 and took him to Washington, D.C. to work as a translator and interpreter for the Senate Committee on Foreign Relations, then investigating political affairs in post-revolutionary Mexico. During his employment with Senator Fall, Flipper returned to his involvement with the Sheldon Hotel. When the Senate Foreign Relations Subcommittee held hearings on Mexican Affairs in 1919, Flipper served the subcommittee as translator and interpreter.

Flipper continued to work for the Senator Fall until 1921 when Fall was appointed Secretary of the Interior by President Harding. Fall then selected Flipper to become the assistant to the Secretary of the Interior and sent him to the Alaskan Engineering Commission.[68] During Flipper's time in Washington, D.C., in the 1920s, he and Anna White Shaw, now a grandmother became re-engaged.[69] Flipper continued to work for the Department of the Interior until 1923, when Secretary Fall was disgraced by the infamous Teapot Dome Scandal. Flipper soon accepted a job as an oil engineer for the Pantepec Petroleum Company of William F. Buckley, Sr. and headed to Venezuela.

Anna and Flipper discussed her moving to Venezuela with him but ultimately decided against it because she was responsible for her two grandchildren and had some doubts about whether Flipper's new salary with the oil company could support this new family. Flipper moved to Venezuela without Anna until the Crash of 1929, when the oil exploration industry collapsed. Flipper returned to Atlanta in 1931 virtually penniless. He took up residency with his brother Joseph, and spent the last ten years of his life struggling to clear his name with the Army. He and Anna White Shaw lived very near each other, but did not resume their relationship. He died in 1940.

The Mysterious Mrs. Brown.

Henry O. Flipper's second autobiography about his life in the western frontier up to 1916, certainly gives interesting insight into his version of what transpired during his life. The first chapter of the book compiled and edited by Theodore Harris, is a collection of letters that Flipper's family discovered that he had written to Anna White Shaw. Some historians refer to Flipper dedicating this autobiographical work to a Mrs. Brown of Augusta. When I asked Harris about this confusion and the role that Mrs. Brown played in Flipper's life, he said, "Mrs. Brown was definitely Mrs. Anna P. White Shaw. Where the name Brown came from is anybody's guess." He (Harris) may have inadvertently used the Brown name instead of White-Shaw's. Harris also stated that the error could have been made by a copy editor and was never caught. "There was no Mrs. Brown," Harris replied, "It was Mrs. Shaw."[70]

Notes and References

[1] Flipper, Henry O. *Black Frontiersman: The Memoirs of Henry OL Flipper.* Compiled and edited by Theodore D. Harris. (Fort Worth: Texas Christian University Press, 1997.), 3-4.
[2] Ibid, 4-5.
[3] Eppinga, Jane. *Henry Ossian Flipper: West Point's First Black Graduate.* (Plano, TX: Republic of Texas Press, 1996.), 25.
[4] Taylor, Quintard Jr. Introduction to Flipper's first autobiography, *The Colored Cadet at West Point,* (Lincoln: University of Nebraska Press, 1998.), xvii.
[5] Eckhardt, E.C. "The Lost Epic: Henry O. Flipper, 10th Cavalry." *Texas Escapes.* July 30, 2912.
[6] Harris, Theodore, interview
[7] Dr. Quintard Taylor is professor of history at the University of Washington and an expert in African-American history in the American West. He has authored six books.
[8] Taylor (1998), vii-xiii.
[9] Robinson, Charles M. III. *The Fall of a Black Army Officer: The Racism and the Myth of Henry O. Flipper. (*Norman, OK: University of Oklahoma Press, 2008.), 159.
[10] Ibid, 7-8.
[11] Ibid, 158.
[12] Specht, Jim. "Clinton issues pardon 117 years overdue." *El Paso Herald*, February 20, 1999.
[13] Johnson, Barry C. *Flipper's Dismissal: The Ruin OF Lt. Henry O. Flipper, U.S.A. First Coloured Graduate of West Point.* 1980.
[14] Eppinga (1996), v.
[15] Robinson, 4.
[16] Ibid, 10.

---

[17] Miscegenation refers to the marriage or cohabitation of people of different racial groups, as in the marriage between a white and black or as often interpreted in the Southwest, as between a white and a Mexican. In 1967, the U.S. Supreme Court ruled that all states laws prohibiting miscegenation were unconstitutional. *Loving v. Virginia.*

[18] Eckhardt, interview.

[19] Eppinga (1996), 170.

[20] Harris, interview.

[21] Taylor (1998), xxii.

[22] Ibid.

[23] Ibid.

[24] Flipper, (1997), 18-19.

[25] Robinson, 35.

[26] Ibid, 150.

[27] Ibid, 34.

[28] Goss, Herbert C. "The Color of Courage" The website is presented because it is difficult to find. (https://sites.google.com/site/herbertgoss/home/writing-samples). 20 Sep. 2010.

[29] Lee, Oliver. "June 15, 1877: First African American Graduates from West Point." *Takepart.com* (June 14, 2010). *http://www.takepart.com/search/June%2015%2C1877%20First%20african%20american%20graduates%20from%20west%20point* Accessed 3 Aug 2012.

[30] Johnson, 19.

[31] Knight, Oliver. *Life and Manners in the Frontier Army.* (Norman: University of Oklahoma, 1978.), 4-6.

[32] Taylor, xxx.

[33] Eppinga (1996), 90-91.

[34] Robinson, 151.

[35] Taylor, xxix.

[36] Ibid, xxxi.

[37] Johnson, 22.

[38] Flipper (1997), 7.

[39] Eppinga (1996), 133.

[40] Porter, Eugene O. Lord Beresford and Lady Flo. Southwestern Studies Monograph No. 25. (El Paso: Texas Western Press, 1970.), 9-11.

[41] Eckhardt, interview.

[42] Harris interview.

[43] Eckhardt, interview.

[44] Flipper (1997), 7.
[45] Eppinga, Jane "Henry O. Flipper in the Court of Private Land Claims: The Arizona Career of West Point's First Black Graduate." (*The Journal of Arizona History*. vol. 36, spring 1995.), 33-54.
[46] Devine, Dave. "Respect and Esteem: A Look back at Henry O. FlipperA Tucsonan and West Point's first African American graduate." *Tucson Weekly.* February 16, 2006.
[47] Eppinga (1996), 168-170.
[48] Ibid.
[49] Taylor, xli.
[50] Harris interview.
[51] Henry Flipper, letter to HBS, 8 May 1898.
[52] El Paso City Directory, 1889-1890, 89
[53] Eppinga(1996), 170.
[54] Flipper, letter to HBS, 28 April 1898.
[55] HBS, letter to Mrs. LMS, 27 April 1898.
[56] "Last Will and Testament of Lucy Barbee. Executed on April 27, 1898 at El Paso, Texas." Probate Will Records 1838-1940. vol. 9, page 616. McLean County, Illinois. (Accession number 3/0096/01.) Illinois Regional Archives Depository (IRAD), Illinois State University, Normal, IL.
[57] HBS, letter to Flipper, 29 April 1898.
[58] "Lucy Barbee Funeral." *El Paso Herald* April 29, 1898.
[59] Flipper, letter to HBS, 28 April 1898.
[60] Flipper letter to HBS, 19 June, 1898.
[61] Jackson, letter to HBS, 21 July 1898.
[62] HBS, letter to Flipper, 30 September 1898.
[63] Jackson, letter to HBS, 2 August 1898.
[64] Flipper, letter to HBS, 23 October 1898.
[65] "Lucy Barbee: In Memorium" *El Paso Herald.* April 30, 1898.
[66] Harris Interview.
[67] Eppinga (1996), 196.
[68] Taylor, xxxvii.
[69] Robinson, 156.
[70] Harris, interview.

Figure 27. View of San Jacinto Plaza, from the left, the two-tower Banner Building, the Federal Building, Sheldon Hotel, and the 12-story Mills Building on the right during a parade. ca. 1920s. (El Paso Public Library, Aultman Collection)

Chapter Eight

4th Floor, Room 127

The efforts of the early adventurers, investors, entrepreneurs, along with the huge immigrant class from central Europe, stimulated and nursed the growth and evolution of this far-west city. The railroads brought west the wild, the wicked, and the worthy; and slowly tamed the "Six-shooter Capital" into a broad-based economic success story. However, it was the women who brought culture, education, and created a social life that would soon flourish and strike a blow at the vice-oriented lawless community. The wives of Hague, Mills, Magoffin, Sheldon, Kohlberg, Schuster, Morehead, and others, created the environment into which their children could be raised to overcome the obstacles that were inherit in the isolated frontier region of the Southwest, to turn it into the largest and most important American city on the Mexican border.

Writing on the impact that women had in the later years of the nineteenth century, journalist Owen White said:

> All at once quiet, educated, and refined women who had been reared in Christian and civilized influence, found themselves suddenly transplanted into an atmosphere which literally reeked with the odor of the world, the flesh and the devil.
>
> Instantly with that intuitive, God-given instinct that good women have, they saw the path of duty that lay before them, and straightway and courageously they set out to follow it.
>
> El Paso with its wild, uncouth, uncivilized, and un-Christian ways was not a place in which those women dared to rear and educate their children. What the town needed, and what it received from these mothers was the touch of a woman's hand; and the story of their

> accomplishment is one that every mother in El Paso—even the mothers of today—should read with a feeling of gratitude and appreciation.[1]

The wives of the arriving central European Jewish merchants and tradesmen had as much of an impact on the development of the new cultural, educational, and religious renaissance that was overtaking the city as did the Christian women. In 1898, the Jewish community built the first Reformed synagogue, Temple Mt. Sinai, and remains today as the centerpiece of the Semitic activities in the area. The Sheldon office building became the locus of the pioneering women's activism during the last decade of nineteenth century.

The El Paso Public Library

The founder of the El Paso Public Library purportedly, the oldest public library in Texas,[2] arrived in the southwest in 1884, the year after graduating from college in Plainville, Georgia. Mary I. Stanton moved west to join her older brother who was an El Paso attorney. Mary soon was teaching third grade at El Paso's first public school, Central School, located on the northeast corner of Campbell and Myrtle Streets. (Across the street from property owned by the Sheldon family.) After teaching just one year, she left to do graduate study in Indiana and then returned to Central School a year and half later to begin a twenty-eight year career in the local schools.

Stanton's passion was her collection of 600 books brought with her from Georgia. After a few years of teaching, Stanton noticed the difficulty that some of the male high school students were having reading and she decided to establish in 1894, a reading club for the boys using her personal collection. During her time as a local teacher, she began to socialize with several of the local women who had established a Child Culture Study Circle. This group had among its members, Mrs. Olga Kohlberg, Mrs. W.W. Mills, and frequently, Mrs. Harriett Sheldon, when she visited from Brooklyn with her husband, Lucius M. Sheldon. The group eventually changed its name to the Current Topics Club.[3] As the number of books increased, as well as the size of the boy's reading club, the group soon outgrew Stanton's own room in the Sheldon. Lucius and Harriett Sheldon offered Stanton a larger room, room 127, on the fourth floor to store her books, hold her club meetings, and from which she would loan the books to the boys who then numbered about twenty. Stanton recalled, "Such interest and generosity were sincerely appreciated, and most encouraging to members of the club." [4]

Mary Stanton described in her own words her effort:

> I first organized a Reading Club for boys of high school age, and its members used my personal library of six or eight hundred volumes that I had placed in a room on the fourth floor of what was then the Sheldon Office Building.
>
> Each member of the club contributed either some periodical to our reading table each month, or fifty cents, as a membership fee. In my absence, the key to the reading room was hung in the elevator, so that members could have access to the room. Books taken out were recorded in a blank book, with the date and name of the borrower; and, such was the integrity of the club, no book was ever lost![5]

The room was opened two hours a day, three days a week and was staffed by volunteers. By June 1895, the reading club became so popular, that many adults wanted the "privilege" of using room 127. Membership was no longer limited to boys and but became open to all who paid a fee of "fifty cents per month, or half that sum and one monthly periodical."[6] The active members of the Current Topics Club formed the first library association to manage the business affairs of the library, the Sheldons stopped charging rent for the room, and Mary Stanton became the first librarian

As the library grew, it became obvious that a larger facility was going to be needed for the library. Local activists requested that the El Paso mayor provide space in the new city hall that was then under construction, but would not be completed for an additional seven months. As the Sheldon building was preparing to under its conversion, Stevens writes to Sheldon:

> I have just been called upon by a committee of ladies from the public library, who state that they have arranged with the city to give them two rooms in the new City Hall for their library, but that this will not be completed until about the middle of next September. They have now about 1100 volumes and find that they have not space enough in Room 119 (sic) which they have been occupying. They state that they have monthly subscriptions amounting to $25 per month which they can afford to pay for a suitable room, and they desire me to write you ascertaining if you will rent them the offices formerly occupied by the Texas & Pacific Railroad for $25 per month until the rooms in the new

> City Hall are ready. They of course consider that this is much below the regular rental of the offices, but would consider the difference as a donation from you. They hope, by getting on the ground floor in a prominent place, to arouse such interest that they can build up a very fine library when located in the City Hall. Will you kindly advise me of your wishes in the matter?[7]

Shortly after Sheldon accepts the offer from the library association, Stevens informs Sheldon that he had just received word from one of the members of the library association's board, that the library "will not take the Texas & Pacific." [8] No explanation for the change was offered.

In December 1899, the library moved into two rooms in the new city hall and the library association expanded its membership to include some of the most notable of El Paso's citizenry, among them local doctors, lawyers, and bankers.[9] With the expanded and influential board, contact was made with the Carnegie Corporation[10] and a library grant of $35,000 was received on January 14, 1902. The new Carnegie library opened with 4,000 volumes on April 25, 1904 at 500 North Oregon Street (Across the street from the current main library building.) and was one of thirty-four Carnegie funded libraries in Texas between 1898 and 1917. (The Carnegie Library was demolished in 1968.) The Carnegie Corporation established 1689 libraries in the United States with grants equaling over 46 million dollars.

Figure 28. Mary I. Stanton 1862-1946
(El Paso Public Library)

The *Woman's Club*

Continuing to use Stanton's library in room 127 of the Sheldon Building these women, under the guidance and leadership of Mrs. Ernst Kohlberg and

Mrs. W.W, Mills, the Current Topics Club would evolve into the Woman's Club of El Paso. Holding their meetings in the Sheldon Building was a great asset to the activities of these women, as the Sheldon was the center of the social and business life in town.[11] The history of the El Paso Public Library and the Woman's Club are both buried deep within the history of the Sheldon Building. In 1896, the library in the Sheldon Building was cramped and busy all of the time, so the Current Topics Club chose to move back to the home of the then president, Mrs. W.W. Mills. About a year later, Mr. Mills was appointed United States Consul at Chihuahua and the Club lost their meeting place. Stanton offered the use of the library room in the Sheldon and the Club returned.[12]

One of the outcomes of the Current Topics Club was the creation of the Kindergarten Association and the establishment of a private, tuition based kindergarten in 1892. The Kindergarten Association set as a goal, the establishment of a kindergarten to be "free" and located in the public schools. As a way of inducing the local school board to undertake such a project, the association offered the equipment, material, and teacher if the Board would establish the kindergarten in the public school system. The first public kindergarten in Texas was established in 1893 in El Paso and was located at the Central School. Over the years, the Woman's Club moved from one location to another. In 1899, the Sheldon Building was preparing for its conversion to a hotel, and the library had moved to the city hall. The Woman's Club created a multitude of projects and organizations, all with the intent to improve the quality of the community.

The Woman's Club worked tirelessly to clean up the streets, sidewalks, streetcars, restaurants and organized to assist the many tubercular patients who came to recover in El Paso's sunshine. They were instrumental in cleaning up the drinking water, having the city switch to well water instead of the contaminated water from the Rio Grande. The role that the Sheldon Building played in the history of the Woman's Club is inseparable from the positive contributions the Club made to life in El Paso. The club eventually built its current facility on North Mesa St. in 1916. [A detailed history of the Woman's Club is carefully documented in Cunningham's *The Woman's Club of El Paso*: The First Thirty Years (1978).]

The Weather Bureau

The U.S. Army Signal Corps transferred the management of the Weather Bureau to the Department of Agriculture in 1890 and opened its first station and office in El Paso under the supervision of Nathan D. Lane, a 20-year veteran of the Signal Corps as a telegraph operator. Lane had served the Army during the Indian Wars throughout the New Mexico and Arizona territories. When the bureau opened its new El Paso observation station, it was located in the Sheldon Block Office building in rooms 122 and 124.[13]

Lane worked the Sheldon office for 16 years, getting on the job by 6 a.m. and continuing for 10 to 15 hours a day, every day, rain or shine. Finally, he requested a leave of absence, Lane told a local journalist:

> I have been here for 15 years in this tower, watching El Paso, and probably love the place and take as much interest in its progress as anybody. I have not been in the best of health, however, and the exacting duties of the office made it necessary for me to take a rest. At the end of my leave I do not know where I will be assigned. I have watched El Paso grow from practically a village to her present position as a city, from this little tower here, and it will seem odd to say the least, not to be able to look out over the town every day, as I have done many times each day, for the past 15 years.[14]

Just about everyone in El Paso knew Lane and his daily wanderings throughout the town, particularly the Federal Building and the Sheldon Office building. Lane died January 23, 1920 at 69.

In August of 1894, the weather office was moved to the new Federal Building with its unique tower. Just about the time that Mary Stanton moved her book collection and boy's reading room into the Sheldon. It moved several more times, finally locating in the 12-story Mills Building in 1925 where it remained for 10 years.

Figure 29. Vintage newspaper photograph of the U.S. Weather Service office in the Sheldon Block office building prior to moving to the Federal Building across the street in 1892. (U.S. Weather Service)

The Post Office

It had been widely reported that El Paso's post office was located in the Sheldon Building before it moved to its own building at Myrtle and San Antonio Streets. In a series of letters between Lucius Sheldon and his son, Gardner Sheldon, a mining engineer at the Corralitos Ranch in Chihuahua owned by New York banking interests, the son writes his father about the plans for a new Post Office building to be built across the street from the son's El Paso home at Myrtle and San Antonio:

> ...going to put up a two-story stone building and move the Post Office there. You may not be particularly pleased to hear this as it will take the P.O. out of your building, but will improve my property and after all may be just as well for you, as Mrs. Porter [Postmaster] paid you a ridiculously small rent for the space she occupied and was all the time kicking about one thing or other and wanting something done–just like a woman. (Don't let Mother see that). The trouble is a woman can kick and grovel and make such trouble and you can't say anything at all in return. A man, you can damn up and down—if you want to, of course–tell him if he don't like it to lump it, but a woman—no.[15]

It turns out that the 1882 letter regarding the Post Office location in the Sheldon Building pre-dated the actual building of the Sheldon Office building. The El Paso Post Office did move to the Myrtle and San Antonio address in 1883. The reference in the letter of a Sheldon building in 1881 was referring to Sheldon's earlier investment in a block of adobe buildings in the Chinese area along St. Louis St. at the southeast corner of Utah St. (now Mesa) just east of the original El Paso Times building.[16] The Sheldon Stores consisted of five individual stores. This location is the current site of the Robert-Banner Building.[17] The exact locale of the post office is murky at best, for it moved on a regular basis until a permanent building was established in 1883. An article in the 1881 El Paso Times indicated that the post office was on Overland St. before it moved to the Utah St. location.[18] In early 1906, the government contacted Sheldon and expressed interest in purchasing the lots adjacent to and north of the Post Office building owned by Sheldon. The present postal property had been completely built upon and it would be necessary to buy part or all of Sheldon's property. The demand for expanding the Post Office was clear testimony of the city's growth and significance.[19]

Notes and References

---

[1] White, Owen P., *Out of the Desert: The Historical Romance of El Paso.* (El Paso: The McMath Company, 1923.), 162.

[2] Murphy, James R. *Images of America: El Paso 1850-1950.* (San Francisco: Arcadia Publishing Co., 2009.), 61. This claim by Murphy is challenged by research that has determined that the Rosenberg Library of Galveston, Texas, through a gift from Henry Rosenberg, in 1893, established a local "free" public library and this library traces its lineage to the Galveston Mercantile Library that opened in 1871. Clearly predating the El Paso Public Library. (See the Handbook of Texas Libraries, 34-38.)

[3] Cunningham, Mary S. *The Woman's Club of El Paso: Its First Thirty Years*. (El Paso: Texas Western Press, 1978.), 2, 8.

[4] Ibid,13.

[5] Ibid, 12.

[6] *Handbook of Texas Libraries.* (Austin: Texas State Library Association, 1904.), 26-29.

[7] HBS, letter to LMS. 11 Feb. 1899.

[8] HBS, letter to LMS. 10 Mar. 1899.

[9] *Handbook of Texas Libraries* (1904), 27.

[10] The Carnegie Corporation was the vehicle that Andrew Carnegie created in 1911 to consolidate the five entities that he previously used to donate monies to over 2500 public libraries worldwide between 1883 and 1929. Not bad use of the money that Carnegie received from the sale of the U.S. Steel Company.

[11] Cunningham, 7.

[12] Ibid, 17.

[13] "*Meteorological Summary for 1889*." Timeline and History of the Weather Organization in El Paso. (National Weather Service. NOAA.) Accessed 19 November 2014.

[14] *El Paso Times*. May 2, 1954.

[15] Gardner Sheldon, letter to LMS. 25 July 1882. Handwritten letter contained in the Sheldon Family Papers, MS 402, UTEP Special Collections.

[16] Insurance Fire Map drawn by Thomas H. Conklin from Sonnichsen and McKinney. The State National Since 1881: The Pioneer Bank of El Paso. (El Paso: Texas Western Press, 1971.)

[17] *El Paso Herald*. February 12, 1910.

[18] *El Paso Times*, April 2, 1881.

[19] HBS, letter to LMS via Henry K. Sheldon, Jr. 2 Mar. 1906.

Chapter Nine

A First-Class Hotel...finally

As El Paso approached the turn to the Twentieth Century, it was dealing with enormous growth, building, and political issues that seemed to center on the city's thriving "vice" industry of booze, gambling, and prostitution. If that were not enough, wild and scary stories about life in El Paso spread from coast-to-coast. For example, the yellow fever scare was hard to correct when the city leaders finally identified its cause. Mexico had been dealing with yellow fever issues in the 1890s and when symptoms began to surface in El Paso near panic broke out. Saloonkeepers would place empty kegs of beer outside their establishments every morning to be collected. Scavengers from across the border would drain off the dregs into another container and scurry off for free guzzles of brew. Located next to many of the saloons were bootblack stands. The saloonkeepers told the bootblacks to wash off their brushes at closing and the water ran into the empty beer kegs standing next to them. Along came the scavengers and they drained off the blacken ruminants of beer. The police picked up the sleeping men and hauled off them to quarantine because they were throwing up a black mixture that caused many to think it was black vomit, an early sign of yellow fever. It was not until several days later that the owner of the kegs noticed the black residue in the kegs was from black shoe polish. However, the stories had already hit the wire and a new dimension was added to El Paso's reputation.[1]

After almost seven years and with nothing having emerged as a satisfactory solution for El Paso's lacking a first-rate hotel to replace the "lost" Grand Central, Lucius M. Sheldon began to put in play his long-delayed plans to convert his four-story office building into a stately grand hotel.

Horace Stevens had been Sheldon's agent since the opening of the Sheldon Block. As Sheldon's agent, confidant, and friend, he was suddenly surprised when he heard from intermediaries that Sheldon had made arrangements with John Fisher, then the proprietor of the Pierson Hotel, to become the manager and leasee of the soon to be built remodel of Sheldon Block into the Sheldon Hotel. Clearly upset by this sudden news, Stevens wrote Sheldon:

> The fact that as soon as I returned I found that Mr. Fisher had reported that he has all arrangements made to lease the entire building both the upstairs and the lower floor for $15,000 per annum. He has spoken to [some local prominent] businessmen here, and has been soliciting subscriptions for the payment of the first years rent. I do not quite understand the situation, and several people who have been solicited have spoken to me to know if there was anything in Mr. Fisher's representations, and if he had rented the building. To these queries, I of course replied that I knew nothing of your business with Mr. Fisher but I hardly thought it possible that you would make these arrangements without letting me know. Of course, I do not wish to interfere in any way, and if you can get a good tenant at the rate of $15,000 per year, I think you will be making an extra good trade and you want to make it by all means, provided you can satisfy yourself of the renter's ability to meet such a rental. I would, however, question the advisability of giving up the lower floor to a man like Fisher. If you have made the trade with Mr. Fisher it would be a personal favor to me if you would advise me as early as convenient on account of my office location. I might be out of an office at a time of the year when it would be hard to get a suitable location. If I knew it early enough I could probably make arrangements with Gen. Mills to take one of the offices in his new building and would then not be inconvenienced very much. Of course you understand why I speak as I do about the first floor renters if from the fact that you might receive these direct and thus would be sure of a very large part of the rents from the building, rather than to let the value get into anybody else's hands and losing your chances of the rent being paid.[2]

Sheldon responds to Stevens by telling him that no deal was finalized between himself and Fisher and that he really did not take the offer seriously. "You may be very sure Mr. Stevens," Sheldon adds, "I would have done nothing definite without consulting you; for I have a very strong personal regard for you and value your friendship highly in addition to a confidence in your good judgment in business affairs. I had no serious idea of anything when you paid us a visit nor is anything settled now by any means."[3]

Sheldon explained that Fisher had requested that he [Sheldon] keep the proposition a secret for business reasons, probably that he wanted to sell his current lease of the Pierson or get someone else to take it off his hands, before it became known that there was a prospect of there being another hotel. "I knew," writes Sheldon, "that Mr. Fisher had never kept a first class house and his experience lay in and his ability was probably adapted to such a hotel as the Pierson, but I thought he might grow into the business."[4]

With the continuing advice of Stevens and Sheldon's Brooklyn architect, Walter E. Parfitt, Sheldon finally reached a lease agreement with Fisher. The following letter from Stevens to Sheldon provides some early insight as to the potential conflicts that would arise between Stevens, Fisher, and Parfitt:

> It has given me more pleasure than any letter I have ever received. I thank you very much for the kindly words and expressions of confidence contained therein, and you may rest assured that your confidence is not misplaced, and that I shall, no matter what comes, zealously work for your interest. Of course I had no reason to expect to know anything about the hotel project unless you saw fit to tell me; that you did not see fit and that I was in no way apprised of it naturally humiliated me, from the fact that my position here as your agent had given me a standing in the community and the people to whom I have rented places in the building for many years were looking to me to protect them.
>
> From the time of the first rumor in the newspapers of the proposed change I was besieged from day to day by your tenants who desired to know the exact truth of the statements made and the situation. I could only advise them that I know nothing but felt sure that your past relations with me and the long intimate business acquaintance would prompt you to tell me everything at the proper time, Upon Mr. Parfitt's arrival here I took it for granted that he was sent as your architect, and endeavored to show him every courtesy possible, I spent nearly the entire day of his arrival with him, visiting the different business people, and took him to lunch at the Orndorff, and showed him every courtesy possible, offering him your rooms in the building, in order that it might perhaps save you some expense. He stated that he preferred to speak

with Mr. Fisher at the Pierson, as he could then judge better of his capabilities as a hotel man.
As I wrote you in the letter sent at Mr. Parfitt's suggestion not one of

the people we visited thought Mr. Fisher [was] the man for the position. I have been thoroughly convinced of this from the beginning, but want you to understand that it was through no ill feeling or prejudice against Mr. Fisher. Our relations have always been of the pleasantest character, but I feel towards the man just as I spoke to you when I saw you last. I am, however, and have been all along thoroughly convinced that he is not the proper man to run a first class hotel. Since his first visit, Mr. Parfitt has never seen fit to give me information or in any way consult me concerning your plans. This of course was his privilege and I have no right to complain if he did not see fit to take me into his confidence, but I naturally felt that in my position as your agent I ought to know something about it and I felt that I could be of material assistance to him.

My long acquaintance here in connection with your building would in a measure warrant me in stating that I could probably assist him. All of the matters in connection with the leasing of the building I have only learned through the newspapers to whom Mr. Parfitt seems very kind, and seems to have a desire that his name should appear often in print. Mr. Parfitt, accompanied by Mr. Fisher, went pretty thoroughly through the building, examining the rooms and calling on the different tenants and advising some of them that they would probably have to vacate within 30 days. I was not asked by Mr. Parfitt to accompany him on his trip, in fact, the whole matter was taken out of my hands, and I had no connection with it.

Yesterday Mr. Parfitt in company with Judge Buckler [one of Sheldon's lawyers] requested that I go with them to arrange to have the tenants vacate; this I declined to do, and told Mr. Parfitt that I did not know that he had any authority to act in such matters for you. I told him in emphatic terms that I did not think his treatment of me was at all courteous and that I declined to turn the matter over to him until I heard from you. I advised both he and Judge Buckler that I thought they ought to hear from you before having the building vacated, for, in event of the trade falling through you would be left with a lot of vacancies and might thereby lose considerable rent. In this Judge Buckler agreed with me, and agreed that nothing should be done until I hear from you, therefore I wired you as follows, "Parfitt has signed agreement with Fisher. Wants the building vacated. Shall I turn your business over to him?" to which you replied that I was to remain as your agent and protect your interests, and you may rest assured, Mr. Sheldon, that I will do this to the best of my ability.[5]

Stevens addressed a major issue with Sheldon, that because of the way that Parfitt has laid out the ground floor, available store space for additional income will be reduced and a great deal of rentable space would be converted to non-income hotel use. He details how he would alter the architect's plans to utilize the available space to increase the level of building income beyond what is generated by the hotel lease.[6] Stevens writes:

Of Mr. Fisher's financial ability, I know nothing. I presume you will be able to satisfy yourself on this point. I understand that he has $8,000 or $9,000 in the bank here. The subscription he proposes to raise is not being taken kindly, and I do not think he will be able to get $8,000 [more], if that. I trust I have not annoyed you by writing such a long letter, but I felt that my sense of duty towards you from the kind treatment that I have always received at your hands and the kind regard in which I hold you and your family must prompt me to give you the exact situation as I see it, however mistaken I might be.

After the conversation today with Mr. Parfitt he stated that in his contract with Mr. Fisher you would require a local manager to look after things, and that he could not recommend me for that position as owing to my prejudice against Mr. Fisher, I would not be fair minded. I think this was said more in the nature of a threat that he might be able to put me in position that would perhaps keep me from saying too much. You know me too well to know that such things would have any influences, and that whether I was your agent or not our past relations and your uniform kind treatment of me would not permit me to stand idly by and see your interest suffer in the least. You also know me well enough to know that with business matters I am fair and just, and that I will never allow prejudice to interfere with business matters.

Mr. Parfitt also took occasion to remark today on the filthy condition of the building. For your information I would state that the building is now very much the same as it was the last couple of times you visited it, hardly up to the standard that Lucy used to keep it, but you of course

> fully realize that I have done it for the past year at a great deal less expense, but without Lucy's valuable assistance I have not been able to keep things as neat and as clean as I would like.
> I sincerely trust that these matters will yet come out all right, and that Mr. Fisher may make a success and model hotel man. I however think that your interests at stake are too great to take any chances, and if he does not make a success of it in a year or two you would be left with your building so cut up that it will be of no use as anything but for hotel purposes, and a lot of useless furniture.[7]

As Stevens prepares for the actual construction to commence, he reviews the plans as submitted by the architect, Mr. Parfitt. He notices that of the 118 rooms in the building, only 78 will actually be available for use as a hotel. The other 40 rooms will be non-revenue as bathrooms, hotel offices, and closets. If the hotel is a success, as he states repeatedly, it will need additional rooms. He writes to Gen. Mills and proposes to build a bridge across from the upper floor of the Sheldon to the third or fourth floor of the Mills Building and rent the space for hotel purposes should Mills add two more floors to his building.[8]

Mills responded positively to the idea of adding a third and fourth floor to his building and the connection of one or two glass-enclosed bridges by indicating that the contractors that were working on his present two-story building (Buchanan and Powers) would add the two additional floors for $24,000. If Sheldon would pay $250 per month for 76 rooms for hotel purposes in those two upper stories and allow him to draw the steam heat from the Sheldon to heat his entire building and sell the old Sheldon Building steel elevator, the deal might be able to be completed.[9] In conversations with Mills, Sheldon remained non-committal even though he knew that he did not have enough rooms for a successful hotel. Sheldon did not want to build additional stories on his building if he could avoid it, even though he had had his building constructed in such a manner that he could add additional floors in the future.[10]

Several days later, Mills and Sheldon met to discuss the closure of the additional floors and the bridge deal, when Sheldon tells Mills that he will sell him the old elevator and provide steam for his building, however, that he does not have any real use for additional rooms at present. Mills immediately wires Stevens and tells him to get the contractors to complete the building as originally contracted and to forget the additional stories.[11]

The issue of the additional stories on the Mills Building came up again in April of 1900 when he indicated to Stevens that he would not consider additional stories until all of the current leases expired in about two and a half years and instructed Stevens not to initiate any additional leases beyond that time.[12] Then a few months later, Mills stated that his contractors were planning to build a four-story building on the lot north of his building (where the St. Regis Hotel was eventually developed) with a 100 feet fronting on Oregon Street and a two story addition on his present building for $80,000.

Ernest Kohlberg was the owner of the lot and Mills offered him $15,000 to purchase it.[13] Kohlberg, the owner of the first cigar company in the Southwest, the International Cigar Factory at 115 South El Paso St. (now the Camino del Norte Hotel), rejected the offer and eventually built the St. Regis Hotel on the site. Kohlberg also owned the St. Charles Hotel (the Merrick Bldg.) at 301 S. El Paso St., the El Paso Electric Light Company, and the Southern Hotel at 423 South El Paso St. Kohlberg was murdered by the Southern Hotel proprietor, John Leech, on July 17, 1910. Leech rented the 50-room Southern Hotel from

Figure 30. Old photo of the two-story Mills office building on the site of the former Grand Central Hotel across the street from the Sheldon decorated for the Taft-Diaz parade in 1909. (El Paso County Historical Society)

]

ohlberg for $300 per month. Because of his gambling issues, Leech fell six months past due ($1150). During a confrontation with Kohlberg, Leech shot him in the back.[14] After a scandalous trial, Leech was sentenced to life in prison, but

was pardoned after serving less than eight years by the unscrupulous Texas governor "Pa" Ferguson in 1918.[15]

Mills never did add the additional two floors on his building.[16] He did however, raze the building in 1911 and began construction of a twelve-story office tower that opened in 1912 and remains today.

The idea of joining separate buildings by a bridge was not new. Stevens had suggested to Sheldon back in 1894 when Sheldon first considered converting his office building into a hotel, that they connect the Sheldon with the Lane Building that was immediately behind the Sheldon. The Lane building was the site of a saloon, restaurant, china store and a barbershop. It would be possible to connect the second floor of the building to the Sheldon and the space leased or rented and used as a location for the hotel's kitchen. The idea of connecting the two buildings collapsed when the owner of the property would only agree to a lease of fifteen years and would not present a reasonable offer for purchase.[17]

The Architect

While there is some doubt as to the exact role that architect Walter E. Parfitt may have played in the building of the Sheldon Block Office Building in the late 1880s, there is little doubt as to Parfitt's participation as lead architect in the conversion of the office building into a hotel in 1899. A review of records indicate that local El Paso architect Edward Kneezell worked on the office building, but whether he was the lead architect or just a local contact person for the Parfitt Brothers' firm in Brooklyn is clouded by the dust of time. Most sources indicate that the Parfitt firm conceived and remodeled the building into the hotel and that Kneezell was responsible for just the addition of the fifth floor in 1901.

The Brooklyn architect was a close acquaintance of Sheldon; in fact, Parfitt was the architect in 1885 of the eight-story classic London Queen Anne-style Montague, Berkeley, and Grosvenor apartment buildings just a few doors from Sheldon's stately home at 123 Montague Street. Parfitt also designed the John S. James house at 9 Pierpont St. just across the street from Sheldon's brother Henry K. Sheldon's home at 220 Columbia Heights St.[18] The Parfitt and Sheldon connection is multi-faceted and covers many years. At the time, Montague Street had earned the title of Wall Street of Brooklyn. Today Montague Street area is known as the Brooklyn Heights Historic District. Walter E. Parfitt was the first of three architect brothers to arrive in the United States from England. They first began designing typical brownstone row houses in the

Italianate and Neo-Greek style and then moved into picturesque brick and terra cotta designs in the Queen Anne style.

The Parfitt Brothers excelled in the Queen Anne and Renaissance Revival styles of architecture. The brothers were widely acclaimed throughout New York City and Brooklyn, building hundreds of residential buildings and a significant number of public buildings, most notably a landmark fire house in Bushwick, Engine Company 52 (now Engine Company 252. Six members of this company were lost on 9/11.). They also designed eighteen Brooklyn churches including St. Augustine Catholic Church, Grace Methodist Episcopal Church, and Mt. Lebanon Baptist Church. Their rise to prominence during the final two decades of the nineteenth century and the early years of the twentieth century was heavily accented by their work on major institutional projects. Walter Parfitt may have been responsible for the eventual conversion of the Montague building into a hotel shortly after completing the Sheldon conversion after the turn of the century. The 1920 census reported 103 households living in the converted hotel at 105 Montague Street.[19]

The brothers were also renowned for the commissions that they almost got but lost. They came in second for designing the municipal building across from City Hall, the Brooklyn Museum, and the Brooklyn Historical Society building at 128 Pierpont St.[20]

Not only were the Parfitt Brothers a successful and prominent design firm, they also excelled in land speculation. At one point, they owned 133 lots in what is now the Crown Heights area of central Brooklyn, encompassing over one square mile of property just southwest of the historic 225-acre The Evergreens Cemetery, not to be confused with Green-Wood Cemetery a few blocks southwest also in Brooklyn. The Parfitt Brothers will go down in Brooklyn history as owning more property than any other individuals, except the infamous Litchfield family of the Long Island Railroad.[21]

Walter Parfitt and his wife had six daughters and one son, William A. Parfitt. Walter eventually brought William into the Parfitt Brothers firm to serve as an on-site superintendent representing the firm. It was in this capacity that William Parfitt affiliated with the Sheldon Hotel conversion project and became a major player in the dysfunction that occurred between the architects, the builders, and Horace B. Stevens, Sheldon's El Paso representative. After Walter Parfitt retired, William continued the firm.[22]

The animosity between Stevens and Parfitt was obvious right from the beginning of the early development of the $35,000 hotel project. Finally, when

Parfitt brought his son into the picture as an on-site superintendent, the contention escalated.

The Reconstruction Plans

Against Stevens' hesitation about Parfitt's costs projections and the competency of the new leasee of the hotel, John Fisher, Sheldon initiated the project when he formally announced the deal with Fisher on September 18, 1899 and sent his architect to El Paso to let the bids for the construction. Parfitt announced that:

> We are making good progress to a satisfactory conclusion on the matter. Everything between Mr. Fisher and myself (sic) is still embryo, and no definite line of action has been decided on. I am working on the plans aided by suggestions offered by Mr. Fisher, and, in a few days I hope to have completed a statement which will explain everything in detail to the El Paso public. I could not tell you what changes will be made, when they will begin or about when the work would be completed.[23]

Fisher held a grand gala as the proprietor of the Pierson Hotel and proprietor-elect of the new Sheldon Hotel at the Pierson on September 23, 1899. All the local civic figures gathered to toast the finality of El Paso's quest for a first-class hotel and that the new hotel would mark the beginning of a new era for the bustling community.[24] On the day of the gala, the El Paso Herald released the latest version of the plans.[25]

The main entrance to the new hotel would front St. Louis Street (now Mills Ave.) opposite the San Jacinto Plaza. The entrance would consist of a highly decorated passage hall, a vestibule, twenty-feet wide, and forty-feet deep, leading to a wide registration area directly under a skylight with highly decorated glass and a huge fireplace off to the right. To the left of the main entrance, as was the custom of the day, would be a ladies entrance, with its own small reception room that would face Oregon Street. At the far end of this ladies reception room would be an electric elevator reaching to the fourth floor in less than three seconds. To the left of the registration area would be located a seventeen by thirty-four foot reading/writing room, illuminated by the skylight and large windows facing Oregon Street. A ten-square foot check-room would be adjacent to the reading room.

Located to the right of the main entrance, a thirty-six by eighty-foot dining room with a two-hundred-person capacity would look out through a large floor-to-ceiling plate glass window onto the Little Plaza. The dining room would include a musician's gallery and a large open fireplace similar to the one located in the registration office area. To the rear of the dining room, a large silver or serving room would be adjacent to the entrance into the twenty-six by thirty-four foot kitchen equipped with ranges, broilers, and steam tables with widows looking out to the alley and San Francisco Street. Beneath the kitchen, a refrigeration room and storeroom would be located in a twenty-eight by fifty-four foot open space. Just in front of the kitchen would be an entrance thru to the registration office, a restroom, and an always-open small café.

Just off the main vestibule a wide stairway would lead down to a thirty-two foot wide and one hundred-twenty foot long bar and billiard room beneath the dining room. Two bowling alleys would be located next to the ornate forty-foot bar. Because of the declining elevation of the west side of the building, a street level entrance would lead out to the Little Plaza. Opposite the bar and billiard room, under the store located at St. Louis and Oregon Streets, would be the barbershop.

Around the perimeter of the remaining ground floor, there would be six stores, one each occupying the face corners of the building and the remaining stores fronting Oregon Street opposite the Federal Building would be rented.

Above the main floor, one hundred large living and sleeping rooms would be arranged in suites, so some guests could connect several rooms with a bath. The average size of the rooms would be fourteen by sixteen, with the largest nineteen by twenty. Each room had one to three windows, looking out to either the streets or the interior skylight-well. A large ladies parlor was to be located on the second floor and the hotel was to have more than fifty bathrooms, with ten extra bathrooms in private rooms. Each room would be steam heated and contain closet space and be connected to the registration desk by telephone.[26]

Not long after the contracts were sent to bid, Sheldon and Parfitt chose to reject all of the incoming bids. By way of explanation, Parfitt stated that, "owing to the complexity of the project the bids were not specific enough. That general contract for specific parts of the build would be issued with Rattenbury and Davis receiving the carpentry and iron work, foundation and plaster work to Sorenson and Morgan, the plumbing to the Chicago firm of Baggot & Company, and the electrical issues to Tucker Electrical of New York City. The cost of construction would range between $17,000 and $38,000 and take up to three months to complete."[27] Sheldon also had Parfitt utilize used material from the demolition on his construction of a series of one-story store rooms on San Antonio Street and the building of a New York style six-unit two-story row house on Myrtle Ave. just east of the new city hall (Block 44).[28]

The existing tenants of the Sheldon Building were given until December 15 to vacate, as the construction was slated to begin then. Parfitt announced that he planned to strengthen the existing building's foundation, "so that we shall be able to add three stories to the present height if necessary."[29]

Once the actual construction began, problems developed. Issues of a plumber's strike in Chicago would have a delaying effect on the work in El Paso, as would difficulties of out-of-the-area fabrication material not arriving on schedule. Parfitt, wanting to introduce his son, William A. Parfitt, to the architect and construction industry, arranged with Sheldon to hire the son for $30 per week to act as the on-site superintendent. The inexperienced William had enormous difficulty dealing with the local trades and they continually complained to Stevens about his obnoxiousness. Young Mr. Parfitt would on a routine basis, take extended trips across the border during weekends, making his supervision sporadic at best.

Aside from the typical problems that surround a major construction project, the personality conflicts rose to a major level. The senior Parfitt continued to complain to Sheldon about Stevens' role in representing Sheldon's El Paso interests. The problem became so severe that Stevens wrote to Parfitt directly:

> You are an unmitigated liar. After you have digested that, allow me to say that I am acquainted with your attempt to besmirch my character to Mr. and Mrs. Sheldon. These lies written by you, you know to be false in every particular. I ask you to write, <u>at once</u> a letter of retraction such as I can show to Mr. and Mrs. Sheldon, admitting that you lied and had no information for the statements made by you to them concerning my character. Failing to do this, I shall know you for the cowardly, hypocritical [bastard] I have always taken you to be. I first think [in] considerable time if I do not receive <u>your retraction</u> I shall commence both civil and criminal proceedings against you in which my presence in New York with the Sheldons as my witnesses, supported by <u>hundreds</u> of affidavits from people here. Don't you think the whole affair will make interesting reading for your church & Sunday school

> class? If I am compelled to go on before I get through with you, most of Brooklyn will know what a lying hypocrite you are.[30]

Stevens' letter ignited a firestorm of activity between El Paso and Brooklyn. Sheldon had become quite ill and was slowly recovering, when he received Stevens' letter. Sheldon's lawyer son, Henry K. Sheldon, Jr. responded to Stevens and requested that he withdraw the Parfitt letter as it was severely upsetting both of his parents:

> I have wired you today to write no more letters or take no further action regarding our friend. I did so because the receipt of your letter had agitated both Father and Mother very much, a result I know would be the last thing you would wish. He [Parfitt] has stated to Father that there was no truth in this alleged statements and neither Father nor Mother for one moment believe a word, not a breath derogatory to your moral character. Now Mr. Stevens I ask you as a personal favor, on my parent's account to kindly drop this matter. He made the statement yesterday to Father, as I said above, and any further agitation will only distress us, your friends. Not for ten thousand dollars would I have either Father or Mother dragged into any suit. Even this little threat has agitated Father considerably and he is not in good health. So kindly, to please us, write no more letters or send any further word to our friend, nor take any further action in the matter. Even if he writes you, kindly throw his letter in the wastebasket without reading it. On no account, answer him further. He may threaten to turn your letter over to the Postal authorities, but he won't. Please wire me. Believe me there is need for this haste. Very Sincerely Yours, Henry K. Sheldon, Jr.[31]

It was the custom at that time, to request that a letter (the original) be returned to sender when there was an issue of error or retraction. As a means of resolving this controversy Henry Sheldon asked Stevens to return Parfait's letter and that Parfitt would return the letter that Stevens wrote. Henry writes to Stevens:

> Mr. Parfitt has virtually intimated he would sue Father unless we found your letter. Father is at present quite ill, he has an abscess on his chest, which the doctor is watching and is very nervous. His hands tremble all the time and this excitement has laid him pretty well on his back. I have assured him however; it will turn out all right and thought it best to return Parfitt your letter. Mr. Parfitt says he will return this letter to you

> if you will simply say you were misinformed and desire its return. Now I know it is a great deal to ask.
>
> For a very good reason, namely he can't! [Return the Stevens letter] He sent your letter around to me and "I lost it." He can never see it again. You had better remove the copy from your letter-book [files]. It can serve no purpose there. It can serve no purpose there as the original is "lost."[32]

Several days later, Henry wrote Stevens some additional advice on the matter:

> I am very busy today but have sent you a telegram not to send any letter to Parfitt but to let the matter drop. I drafted the letter [previous shown] hastily but upon reflection would not have you send such a letter or any letter for any consideration. He has retracted fully and denies everything so you should be satisfied. Father is better now, but very mad and I assure you that any further agitation of this unfortunate matter appears as the most blow you could give him. Therefore, please let the matter drop. I do not for a moment believe you intended such a result from your letter, but had I known you intended taking action which might drag Father and Mother in as witnesses I should certainly have sought to dissuade you. After the statement, I made to the Herald as to Father's regard for you; I hardly believe you would question it.[33]

Stevens attempted to put closure on the entire matter by writing to Henry Sheldon to dismiss the entire matter and that he still had a score to settle with Parfitt when the proper time comes and that he was advised by his attorney not to include anything in the letter that would have violated Postal laws. He clarifies that the issue of the house lease to Fisher was a more important problem, than letters to Parfitt that would certainly never see the light of day in a public forum.[34]

As the construction continued, new problems of William Parfitt's supervision began to immerge. He failed to detail the exact purpose of payments that he made to local contractors, rather he simply said that so much was paid to whom for whatever. Stevens became suspicious of the possibilities of impropriety existing in the billing process and began to question whether the junior Parfitt was informing his father of his salary, leaving open the possibility that the senior Parfitt could deny that his son had been properly paid his $30 per week.[35] Stevens informed the Sheldons that William Parfitt's extensive trips away from the site was causing problems. He writes to Sheldon, "Mr. Parfitt Jr. went to Chihuahua last Sunday, and every Sunday he takes a trip to some point near El Paso. I presume the old man is making such a good thing out of the Sheldon that he can afford these extra expenses."[36] (Clearly Stevens is totally unaware of the extent of the Parfitt land holdings and wealth.)

Stevens issues a warning to Sheldon that there might be some secret dealings between Parfitt and Fisher. He asserts Fisher's and Parfitt's calculations to not get into the building before the middle of September is so that Fisher won't have to pay rent during the dull season when revenue will be slight, suggesting collusion between the two to Fisher's advantage. "It appears to anyone who takes any notice of the affairs that you have been getting the worst of this deal from the very beginning, for which I feel very sorry, but of course I have been powerless to help you to any extent."[37]

The Sheldon Hotel was formally handed over to Mr. Fisher on August 25. Stevens and Judge Buckler, a Sheldon attorney, went carefully over the building with Fisher. Fisher contends that many things were left unfinished and the job could be described as just plain sloppy. Stevens agrees with Fisher's assessment in most things. "The painting is one of the poorest pieces of work I have ever seen. I doubt very much if there is 50 pounds of white lead in the entire work," writes Stevens, "neither young Parfitt nor anybody else could fail to see this." [38]The touchup painting should have been referred by Parfitt to the original contractor, but was not and the repainting cost was sent directly to Sheldon. Fisher pointed out that, among other things, the elevator was not correctly installed. On this issue, Stevens reports being told by the elevator people:

> Mr. Parfitt was in such a hurry to get away from here that he came to our place and ordered some weights and said he would hang them himself; he did and did it entirely wrong and the elevator came near going through the roof on one occasion, and on another occasion went through the cellar. It was absolutely necessary to do the entire work over, which necessitated a great deal of carpenter work as well as machine work.[39]

That the conversion was completed in any shape at all and on any time frame is a testament of sheer will. The project was scheduled to be completed in two or three months, but it was ten months later, that the Sheldon Hotel, finally opened its doors to the public at 2 o'clock on the afternoon of September 9, 1900. Until late that evening, the hotel was visited by many hundreds of people. At six o'clock the doors to the dining room were thrown open and two hundred of El Paso's most notable citizens enjoyed a most fanciful feast. Bands played and banners waved. The hardwood floors shined and the lobby and writing room were elegantly furnished with rich leather chairs and individual writing desks. There were over a hundred rooms, each elegantly furnished with a brass bed, and forty rooms had private baths. El Paso now, after seven years, could boast of having a "hotel equal to any in the state, and by a long way the best in the Southwest.[40]

As previously stated, Gen. Mills' attitude toward Judge Crosby and his own continued reluctance to rebuild the Grand Central went a long way to convince Lucius Sheldon to convert his office building into a first-class hotel. Mills, even though he moved his residence to Washington, D. C. and shifted his attention to things military and financial, continued to remain connected to the Sheldon Hotel. Whenever he returned to visit his investments in El Paso, he stayed at the new Sheldon Hotel. On one such occasion, his experience with the Sheldon led to some cleaver intrigue and skullduggery. The exact date of this episode is not clearly defined in Mills' autobiography, My Story, but occurred within a couple of years of the Sheldon Hotel's opening.

Mills returned to El Paso on business and was promptly sued for $11,000 for liens on some of his local holdings. Prior to the trial, Mills received two anonymous notes urging him to bribe the jury in order to win the case. He immediately notified Judge Wilcox of the potential misconduct. While Mills and his attorneys were in the Judge's chambers, a message was delivered to him telling him that a man wished to meet him. Suspecting that this was a message from the individual that had sent the bribery notes to him, Mills received permission from the Judge to set a trap. He met with a Mr. Compton, who was identified as the "end man" on the jury. Mr. Compton told Mills to pay him $3000 for a favorable judgment, adding that the he had surveyed the jury and a majority had agreed. Mills told Compton that, "As a business man I could not part with so large a sum on the guarantee of one man. I asked to see them all privately, two at a time, after 9:00 p.m. in my room at the Sheldon Hotel.[41]

With the Judge's approval, Mills enlisted Deputy Sheriff Will J. Ten Eyck and the Court Reporter McKelligon to meet him at the Sheldon at 8:45 p.m. Mills had the two get behind a folding bed in the corner of the room and observe the activities that were developing. When Mr. Compton entered, he began to search the room. Mills writes:

> If he wanted to do business with me to sit down and do it, asking peremptorily where the second man was. He was downstairs, and when Compton brought him up I asked them to state plainly what they could do. Hunt, the other man handed me a paper with the names of all the jurors with the sums a majority had agreed to receive, some as low as $50. I placed the paper in my pocket and after a little further talk to make sure they had been well heard, told Compton to bring up the next man. But he never returned.[42]

All of Mills' compatriots agreed to keep the episode a secret until the next day in court. When the Judge convened the trial there was no standing room available.

The Judge said:

> Gentlemen of the Jury: Since last session the defendant in this case has handed me certain letters which I desire to read to you. The first appears to have been filed in the post office, El Paso, on the 20th day of June of the present year, and is as follows: 'Mr. Mills, if you want to win your case you must fix the jurymen in this case liberally or you will lose. A friend.'
>
> The second is as follows: 'Mr. Mills if you are going to do anything, do it quick and have the money and nothing else. Go to the man at the west end of the jury box. It must be money or you will lose. A friend.'[43]

The Judge asked each juryman if he knew anything about the notes. All denied any knowledge, the end men most particularly. Mills was then called to the stand to tell his story omitting the part about the deputy sheriff and the court reporter. As he read the amounts that each were willing to take in the bribe, one of the jurymen cried out, "For God's Sake, Judge, stop; this! My parents are respectable people, and when they read this it will break their hearts!" As Mills continued with his account of what happened, Mr. Compton violently yelled, "You are a God damned liar." as the sheriff forced him back into his seat.[44] Compton and Hunt denied all of Mills' contention. Soon the sheriff and the court reporter corroborated Mills' comments that they heard while they were concealed behind the bed. Compton and Hunt hung their heads. The Judge announced a mistrial, discharged the jury, all except Compton and Hunt. Both jurymen were arrested, convicted, and sent to prison.[45]

A Fifth Floor is added

It soon became evident that the number of rooms in the four-story Sheldon was insufficient to meet the demands. While many had expressed doubt as to the ability of the hotel's proprietor to make the hotel succeed, the demand was obvious that a fifth or sixth floor would need to be added. Fisher began negotiations with the Sheldons expressing that he has had to turn away patrons on a regular basis.[46]

Henry K. Sheldon, Jr., in May 1902, indicated his family's intention to add a fifth floor to the building. The addition would provide thirty-seven new rooms. The new wooden addition would be designed by Edward Kneezell and built by Rattenbury and Davis, the original contractors for the hotel conversion project.[47] The fifth floor project was completed and occupied by January 1903.[48]

Figure 31. San Jacinto Plaza with the Federal Building and the Sheldon Hotel in the background. Note the two-story Mills Building on the right, across from the Sheldon. ca. 1905. (El Paso Public Library, Aultman Collection)

As the hotel gained in popularity, events and episodes occurred that clarified the new position that the Sheldon Hotel had in the Southwest, as it was without a doubt the center of social and civic activities of El Paso and far west Texas for years to come. (See figures 119 and 120) The El Paso Times reported:

> Eyes of old-timers light up and then with subdued softness, they recall the old Sheldon Hotel, because in the early days the city's social, cultural, and business life revolved in and about this hostelry. Also, the hotel was the headquarters for mining and cattle men. In a time when there were revolutions in Mexico and ammunition was being smuggled

across the border, the lobby was crowded with picturesque figures, such as the Mexican leaders of uprisings, soldiers of fortune, big name newspaper correspondents, and photographers, which doesn't mean that any one of them ever negotiated a transaction which was not strictly legal. Before the Sheldon, the old county courthouse was standing in those days and the elite of the city, in tails and evening gowns, held regular exclusive dancing parties in one of the district court rooms. All that changed when the hotel was operating.[49]

Notes and References

[1] *El Paso Herald*. July 13, 1929.
[2] HBS, letter to LMS. 9 Sep, 1899.
[3] LMS, letter to HBS. 15 Sep. 1899.
[4] LMS, letter to HBS. 19 Sep. 1899.
[5] HBS, letter to LMS. 21 Sep. 1899
[6] Ibid.
[7] Ibid.
[8] HBS, letter to Mills. 6 Nov. 1899.
[9] Mills, letter to HBS. 11 Dec. 1899.
[10] Mills, letter to HBS. 16 Dec. 1899.
[11] Mills, letter to HBS. 21 Dec. 1899.
[12] Mills, letter to HBS. 25 Apr. 1900.
[13] Mills, letter to HBS. 13 Aug. 1900.
[14] Cioc-Ortega, Mark and Evelina Ortega. "The Leech Trial of 1910: The Hardest Fought Legal Battle in the History of the El Paso Courts." *El Paso Bar Journal*. Part I Dec. 2011-Jan.2012, 9-11.
[15] Ibid, Part II Feb.-Mar. 2012, 11.
[16] The search of the Mills and Stevens letters clearly demonstrate his vacillation regarding adding the additional floors, but no definitive statements support the fact that he actually did not build the extension. However, a review of the photos of the 1909 visit to El Paso by Presidents Taft and Díaz clearly shows the Mills building as a two-story office building next to the four-story St. Regis Hotel owned by Kohlberg.
[17] HBS, letter to LMS. 7 Feb. 1894. HBS, letter to LMS. 11 Feb. 1894. HBS, letter to LMS. 16 Feb. 1894.
[18] *Save the Slope Blog*. 22 Jan. 2002.
[19] *New York Times*. Nov. 17, 2002.

[20] Morris, Montrose. . "Walkabout: The Parfitt Brothers, part 2. *Brownstoner: Brooklyn Inside and Out.* 28 Oct. 2010. Accessed 14 Feb. 2011.
[21] Spellen, Suzanne. "Walkabout: Parfitt Brothers, Architects." *Brownstoner: Brooklyn Inside and Out.* 26 Oct. 2010. Accessed 12 Dec 2012.
[22] *Brooklyn Eagle.* December, 1918.
[23] *El Paso Herald.* September 19, 1899.
[24] *El Paso Herald*. September 25, 1899.
[25] *El Paso Herald*. September 23, 1899.
[26] This description was based upon the design plans as presented in the *El Paso Herald* article, the plans changed somewhat during the construction, but the letters between Sheldon and Stevens suggested that the changes were not significant. The author made every effort to secure copies of the submitted plans to the city of El Paso of both the 1888 original Sheldon Block and the conversion to the Sheldon Hotel. This effort was met continually by either bureaucratic stalling or shuffling that included: "their destroyed." "they must be misfiled," "their lost," and in one case, "why?"
[27] *El Paso Herald*. December 11, 1899.
[28] Ibid.
[29] *El Paso Herald*. November 28, 1899.
[30] HBS, letter to LMS. 27 Feb. 1900.
[31] HKS, letter to HBS. 6 Mar. 1900.
[32] HKS, letter to HBS. 7 Mar. 1900.
[33] HKS, letter to HBS. 10 Mar. 1900.
[34] HBS, letter to HKS. 11 Apr. 1900.
[35] HKS, letter to HBS. 18 Jun. 1900.
[36] HBS, letter to LMS. 7 Jul. 1900.
[37] HBS, letter to LMS. 30 Jul. 1900.
[38] HBS, letter to LMS. 25 Aug. 1900.
[39] HBS, letter to LMS. 27 Dec. 1900.The letter was actually written by Stevens' brother, Charlie as Stevens was on vacation in Mexico.
[40] *El Paso Herald*. September 10, 1900.
[41] Mills, Anson. *My Story*. (Washington: Press of Byron S. Adams, 1918.), 255.
[42] Ibid.
[43] Ibid.
[44] Ibid, 256.
[45] Ibid.
[46] *El Paso Herald*, January 2, 1901.
[47] HKS, letter to HBS, 5 May, 1902.

[48] HBS, letter to HKS, 19 Jan. 1903.
[49] *El Paso Times*, August 25, 1946.

Figure 32. The Sheldon cigar and newsstand in the lobby of the hotel. R.N. Settle, proprietor. 1911. (Courtesy of Carl. C. Williams)

Figure 33. Sheldon Hotel room with a bath and a view. 1911. (El Paso Public Library, Aultman Collection)

Figure 34. El Paso Bank and Trust in the Sheldon Hotel at Oregon St. and St. Louis St. (El Paso Public Library, Aultman Collection)

Chapter Ten

Residents and Tenants

The history of the Sheldon Hotel intersects with the history of antebellum recovery, the Mexican Revolution, the westward migration, the expansion of the railroads, the burgeoning of Wall Street as it expands into the cattle and mining industries, the build up to WWI, the corruption of national politics, and the era of prohibition. One can only imagine standing in the doorway of the west entrance of the Sheldon Hotel and looking out on the Little Plaza, it doesn't take much to realize that, although it is called Pioneer Plaza, it could have just as easily been called History Plaza. From this vantage point, one could see the old Newspaper Tree where the Camino Real (Hotel Paso del Norte) now stands and looking slightly south on El Paso Street to old Ben Dowell*'s Saloon* and Post Office. Imagine the image of Wyatt Earp resolutely looking for confrontation while wondering around the plaza. It's where Marshal Dallas Stoudenmire killed Four Men in Five Seconds and U.S. President McKinley addressed an adoring crowd in the plaza from the steps of the Sheldon. American President Taft and Mexico's President Díaz rode elegantly in gilded horse drawn carriages through town, parading to mark the historic event of the two Republics meeting on both sides of the border, and where General Pershing formed his troops upon their return from the Punitive Expedition of 1916.

Through the portals of the Sheldon's west entrance passed the leaders and schemers of the Mexican Revolution, Mexican and American military officers, arms smugglers, the prohibition profiteers, and some of the greatest war correspondents and journalist the world has seen. Where the spies and secret service agents of Mexico and the United States, the Border Patrol officers, the Texas Rangers, and the newly formed FBI agents met and shared intelligence, told stories, and toasted their drinks to the protection of our country's new frontier.[1] (See figures 121 and 122)

The Sheldon Hotel opened for business in early September 1900, under the management of John W. Fisher. Many locals doubted the success of his tutelage. Despite these naysayers, including realtor H.B. Stevens, the hotel was almost an instant success. Indeed, it was so successful that the addition of a fifth floor was undertaken almost immediately (completed in 1902) at a cost of $35,000. "Thirty-seven rooms, some with baths, will substantially increase the hotel's capacity."[2] From all accounts, the hotel became the civic, political, and social center of turn-of-the-century El Paso. Set among the bathhouses, bars, and bordellos of El Paso Street, the Sheldon attracted a more "elite," "genteel," and ambitious lot. The Sheldon became the meeting hub for professional associations, social clubs, and politically ambitious "rings" of moneyed citizens who wanted to clean-up the remnants of the wild and woolly west. Cattlemen, mine owners, and cotton brokers made enormous deals in hotel's lobby, bars, and dining rooms. The women of El Paso dragged their men to the banquet rooms for their dances and major social gatherings.[3]

As the swanky social affairs increased and with the visitation of powerful banking and railroad barons, men in business suits, often in formal attire with "tails," arrived. Soon civic and business leaders joined forces to develop a private exclusive "male only" club. The Toltec Club was established so they could provide visiting dignitaries with lavish "entertainment," far from the seedy and bawdy dens of sin along South El Paso and Utah (Mesa) Streets. In 1910, the club moved into their elaborate five-story building on land previously owned by Lucius M. Sheldon at 602 Magoffin Ave.[4] Journalist and longtime El Paso resident Owen White writes:

> The Toltec Club, where the town's leading males now did most of their drinking and gambling and reminiscing over their lost manhood, was one of the best institutions of its kind west of the Mississippi River. I loafed there and thus came in daily contact with visitors from all over the country who were noted for their brilliancy, and who never left El Paso without carrying away fond memories of what the Toltec Club had either done to or for them.
>
> No prominent stranger was immune to Toltec hospitality, with the result, as far as I was concerned, that my friends were once again unable to decide whether I was a halfwit or genius. The proponents of the halfwit theory finally won. I knew it when the Toltec Club's entertainment committee, headed by W.H. Burgess, who to this day is a splendid orator, asked me to make the speech of the evening at a banquet to be tendered to four visiting United States Senators.[5]

As the hotel attracted the "good" people of El Paso, it also attracted a large and somewhat heterogeneous group of criminals, gamblers, and thieves; many times, it was difficult to distinguish them from the local lawmen and politicians. Corruption was rampant, certainly not unlike other urban cities throughout the country at the time.

Businessmen and tourists from around the world began to flock to the border city. Most notably were the "lungers." This cavalcade of tubercular patients descended upon El Paso like locusts to take advantage of the medicinal value of the climate and the large tuberculosis recovery industry that was growing at an astonishing rate. Tubercular sanatoriums and medical specialists made this a significant part of the growing economy and clearly boosted the Sheldon Hotel's occupancy.[6] It was estimated that between the arrival of the railroads in 1881 and 1920, 25,000 sick individuals came to El Paso "chasing the cure." El Paso was considered an ideal recovery locale because of the altitude, the sunshine, and the climate. Many international physicians, themselves suffering from pulmonary illnesses, came themselves and stayed on as members of the growing El Paso medical community.[7]

While the Sheldon's role in the formation of the U.S. Border Patrol and the evolution of the Bureau of Investigation into the FBI and the bureau's domestic law enforcement activity is important, the seminal event surrounding the Sheldon was its participation in the Mexican Revolution (1910-1920).

These events became observable in the later years of the decade. Writing from Juárez, William G. Shepherd, internationally renowned and the most well-known journalist and war correspondent of the time, described in detail some of the real, and sadly, some imaginary exploits of the revolution from his place at the Sheldon bar. Shepherd's reputation was dramatically reported with his eyewitness account of the tragic Triangle Waist Company fire in New York in March 1911.[8]

The hotel's stores and lobby filled with new merchants including Kelly and Pollard Drugs, the International Exchange Bank, a cigar shop and news stand (J. Murtha), a barber shop (C. Newsom), a tailor shop (N. Ray), several real estate offices, railroad ticket and freight offices (Texas and Pacific), and the Sheldon Bar and Sheldon Cafe located in the basement.

The International Exchange Bank

The International Exchange Bank is of particular interest. Enrique C. Creel, the primary owner of the Banco Minero (which became the fourth largest bank in Mexico at that time) became the president of the bank and located it in the lobby of the Sheldon Hotel in the early 1900s. The bank transacted general banking business and the buying and selling of Mexican currency.[9] At the same time, Creel, founded the Banco Central Mexicano that by 1910, had become the second largest bank in Mexico.[10] Creel was a primary actor in the financial and political history of Mexico. Because of the notoriously unscrupulous history of the Creel business practices, some historians have labeled the International Exchange Bank as possibly being involved in money laundering and smuggling schemes. Kentucky born Creel became the son-in law of General Luis Terrazas in 1880. Terrazas was the political boss throughout Chihuahua, Mexico.

Don Terrazas developed the largest land and cattle empire in the Western hemisphere, consisting of over ten million acres of land in Chihuahua and 500,000 head of cattle.[11] Terrazas would often correct people who inquired whether he was from Chihuahua by repeating "No soy de Chihuahua, Chihuahua es mío" ("I'm not from Chihuahua, Chihuahua is mine").

Creel managed the Terrazas banking assets throughout Mexico and the multiple industrial operations developed by the Terrazas family. Historians refer to Creel as the J. P. Morgan of Mexico.[12] The political and financial machine of the Terrazas-Creel families controlled Chihuahua with an iron fist, and when the revolution exploded in Chihuahua, they were the primary force behind President Díaz and his attempt to quell the rebellion. Eventually, the Terrazas-Creel families fled Mexico following the outbreak of the revolution, but returned shortly thereafter and re-established their control. Enrique Creel then established the Guaranty Trust and Bank a few blocks from the Sheldon with a large component of local El Paso investors, including Max Krakauer, Ben Degetau, and Britton Davis all of whom played a role in arms dealing with both sides of the conflict.[13] The Guaranty Bank eventually built a five-story building at Stanton and San Antonio Streets. The Guaranty Bank building was originally opened in 1903.

In 1928, the Guaranty building was remodeled by Trost and Trost architects into the 110-room Gateway Hotel. In 2011, the building was the center piece in a human smuggling and gambling operation. The building's owner was convicted of conspiracy, money laundering, and lying to the IRS. In 2014, the hotel was forced to close by order of the fire marshal.[14]

Creel's career exceeded beyond financial institutions, as he partnered with Terrazas in many land development and began to make a name for himself in Mexican politics. He served as the official interpreter during the Taft-Díaz historic meeting at the border in 1909, as governor of Chihuahua just as the revolution erupted, as the head of President Diaz's Mexican secret service along the American border, and as the Mexican ambassador to the United States.[15]

El Paso Bank and Trust

When Creel closed the International Exchange Bank to concentrate on the Guaranty Bank operation in 1916, its place in the Sheldon Hotel was taken over by the El Paso Bank and Trust, a locally operated and controlled financial institution. While many El Paso merchants altered their consumer business to include major arms dealing during the revolution and the resulting arms smuggling, such as the firm of Krakauer, Zork, and Moye;[16]so it was with the laundering of money. The El Paso Bank and Trust from its offices in the Sheldon Hotel facilitated the funding of a major portion of the various phases of the revolution. Historians Harris and Sadler in their book The Secret War in El Paso, report that according to an FBI[17] agent:

> The bank's vice president, Alfred H. Kerr, stated confidentially that he was doing a good business changing pesos at a discount for dollars to be used by the rebels to purchase munitions—one transaction involving $80,000—were also being deposited for the same purpose. Kerr said that those putting up the money included General Luis Terrazas, who was currently staying at the Sheldon, where he had rented a whole floor; ex-president Díaz; and Enrique Creel, sometime foreign secretary, and Terrazas' son-in-law. Kerr also said that Krakauer, Zork, and Moye were the principal purveyors of armament to the Orozco rebels.[18]

El Paso banking institutions reported, during 1914-1920, as much as an 88 percent increase in deposits.[19] Beginning in 1910 and throughout the years of the Mexican Revolution, El Paso became the financial center of the revolutionary enterprise. It could almost be called the headquarters of revolutionary Mexico and the Sheldon Hotel its capital building.[20]

The El Paso Bank and Trust, through a series of acquisitions and a merger with the Rio Grande Bank and Trust soon became part of the City National Bank, which would close its doors in 1924. The banking business of the

City National was then taken over by the State National Bank that been established by Charles R. Morehead, a major player in the early growth of El Paso's evolution to big cityhood.[21] The State National Bank in El Paso eventually became part of the Compass Bank. In 2007, the Compass Bank merged with BBVA (Banco Bilbao Vizcaya Argentaria), a multinational Spanish corporation, to become BBVA Compass. BBVA also owns Bancomer, Mexico's largest financial institution. The Compass Bank thrives in the economic structure of today's El Paso. (See fig. 32)

While the El Paso Bank and Trust was operating out of the Sheldon Hotel, it became unwittingly involved in a drug smuggling operation. The president and vice-president of the bank routinely had lunch in Juárez during the middle of the week. The customs officers were having difficulty trying to determine how a known addict was able to smuggle his stash into El Paso. It was later determined, that the suspect was secreting his contraband in the fenders of the bank president's car.[22]

Among the permanent residents in the hotel were the future mayors of El Paso: realtor B.F. Hammett (1901-1903); druggist Charles E "Uncle Henry" Kelly and the U.S. Collector of Customs, former sheriff Pat Garrett, the lawman who killed the notorious Billy the Kid. Mayor Kelly was nicknamed "Uncle Henry" by Dr. A.J. Justice, one of El Paso's pioneer physicians. In Kelly's early days while clerking at the Campbell Drug store located in the northwest corner of the Sheldon Office Building, Dr. Justice who had an office in the building, would frequent the drug store. Justice, who was notoriously famous for forgetting people's names, persisted in calling Clerk Kelly, Henry. The name soon caught on and everyone called him Uncle Henry through the years."[23] Kelly had arrived in El Paso from Mississippi as a 19-year old "lunger" seeking the cure for tuberculosis in 1883. He resided his early days at the Sheldon Block after its completion, until his commercial success afforded him the ability to purchase a home. He remained at the Sheldon for his business operations for many years.

Charles E. Kelly

Kelly was the founder of the Kelly and Pollard Retail and Wholesale Drug house that maintained its operation in a storefront on the northwest corner of the Sheldon Hotel. Prior to its flourishing financial success, the Kelly and Pollard Drug store was located at the southeast corner of the hotel, fronting at 210 N. Oregon Street. The store was just a few steps away (across the alley) from the historically "bawdy and wild" Coney Island Saloon. Kelly and Pollard also operated People's Drugstore located in a one-story adobe building at the site of the Capes Building, just south of the Sheldon.[24]

During his term as mayor, he frequently boasted that he "could be elected as Mayor for life."[25] By 1915, Kelly became the powerful Democratic political boss of the area and was the leader of the political powerhouse known as the Ring that dominated the political environment of El Paso for years. In 1902, Kelly was elected county treasurer, to which he was re-elected three times. In 1910, he was appointed mayor after the sudden and somewhat mysterious death of then Mayor Robinson at a local construction site.

On August 14, 1910, a fire broke out at Calisher's Dry Goods Store located in the three-story Buckler Building located just south of the Sheldon Hotel on the northwest corner of Texas Ave. and Mesa Street. Mayor Robinson arrived at the fire and was attempting to warn the engaged firemen of impending danger, when he and a fireman were killed as a wall collapsed on them.[26] The Buckler Bldg. was rebuilt in 1910 into a two-story Trost designed structure that became the home of the Elite Confectionary, a favorite hangout of Pancho Villa and his rebels. In 2012, the building was restored to its original state and is currently a CVS pharmacy.

Figure 35. Charles "Uncle Henry" Kelly 1863-1932
(El Paso County Historical Society)

After completing Robinson's unexpired term, Kelly was elected mayor in April of 1911. The election of Kelly in this pre-Mexican Revolution time period proved beneficial to the city. El Paso needed a strong and powerful political leader, and in Kelly, that is what they got—and more.

There is little doubt that pistol-packing Kelly[27], as a political dictator with the backing of the Ring, controlled El Paso during a tumultuous time. The Ring and its leader were frequently described as "responsible, resourceful, ruthless, and unbeatable."[28] Evidence of Kelly being involved in any expressly illegal activities never really surfaced. However, political machines like the Ring cannot exist without cash, and Kelly was adept at finding it. It was reported that:

> Old-time city employees will tell you that they kicked back part of their salaries to finance operations (we would say now that they contributed to the campaign fund) and expected to do so when they accepted their jobs. Kelly himself was not interested in either wealth or the trappings of office. What he wanted was power, and he preferred to exercise it quietly and effectively from behind the scene. When you ask an old timer if Kelly was ever to his knowledge unethical, he is apt to reply, "No, he wasn't crooked. He was practical—just practical. … He ran his show his own way and he believed in controlling rather than suppressing vice."[29]

The El Paso Herald wrote, "While he has selected heads of his various departments, he makes the appointments and conducts those departments according to his own fancy without going through the formality of consulting the chiefs of departments, and thereby hangs the principal bone of contention. And now Mayor Kelly is going fishing. He will be gone for 30 days and perhaps when he returns he will have a conflict on his hands, which require all the reserve energy he can store up while he is back in Mississippi."[30]

Kelly's contribution to El Paso and the state of Texas far outweighed any of the negative issues that may have surfaced during his dictatorial reign. He organized the Taft-Díaz presidential meeting in 1909; obtained the privately held water company (waterworks) for city ownership;[31] he enlivened the University of Texas Board Of Regents, and brought the Texas School of Mines (now UTEP) to the rolling hills of Sunset Heights. During his seven years on the board of the University of Texas, he led the opposition that defeated a proposal to sell the oil rich lands of the University of Texas, thus enabling the University to collect millions upon millions of dollars in revenue to this day.[32]

Kelly wrote an insightful letter to President Taft on behalf of his community and the depredations that were occurring on the border in March 1911. Kelly and his administration were faced with the issue of keeping El Paso and her citizens neutral in the exploding Mexican Revolution and found themselves confused by the U.S. government's interpretation and enforcement of neutrality laws. The Neutrality Act of 1794 makes it illegal for an American to wage war against any country at peace with the United States. (This first

American neutrality act was later re-codified by the Hague Convention of 1907.) The Act declares:

> If any person shall within the territory or jurisdiction of the United States begin or set on foot or provide or prepare the means for any military expedition or enterprise...against the territory or dominions of any foreign prince or state of whom the United States was at peace that person would be guilty of a misdemeanor.

Kelly, responding to the kidnapping and the demand for ransom of an American Catholic priest by the Juárez based rebels, wrote to President Taft to inform him of this and numerous other hostile exploits. He clearly indicated that he would no longer remain neutral as required by the U.S. neutrality laws:

> You are doubtless by this time informed as to the deplorable state of affairs now existing in the City of El Paso in consequence of the continued anarchy in the City of Juárez just across the international boundary, and the wanton outrages daily perpetrated on our people, who to their misfortune are compelled to cross the line into Juárez, by the orders and sometimes by the hands of the host of military chieftains who rule and ravage the frontier opposite this City. You doubtless have not been informed of one instance, however, which came under my personal observation. It was such an example of combined meanness, brutality and contempt for the United States, its citizens and its officials, that I think it is my duty to lay it specifically before you. ....
>
> Mr. President, this is not the only and is far from being the greatest outrage perpetrated upon unoffending Americans in the town just across the river. I respectfully ask how long this will be suffered to continue. From an attentive observation of the situation during the last fifteen months, it is my deliberate opinion that so far, the chief effect of the presences of the United States troops on this border is to prevent American citizens from defending themselves; but for the presence of the American soldiery it is not conceivable that the people of this city would have quietly submitted to the bloody outrages of May or have failed to avenge the daily outrages permitted in Juárez, and to prevent their repetition by the same means which three generations ago when resorted to by a smaller number, were sufficient to scatter the organized

forces of Mexico and establish the independence of the Republic of Texas.

Mr. President, your patience has long been tried by events across the river; it is probably equal to further trials. Your fellow citizens here who look to you for protection, who it is your duty to protect, have themselves exhibited a moderation that under the circumstances may be called amazing, but their patience will probably be exhausted before that of the administration. The government of the United States is doing everything to avoid irritating the susceptibilities of our Mexican neighbors, the time has now come to do something, to prevent the American people on this frontier from having just cause to manifest by their acts that they will the help that they will immediately receive from their fellow citizens of the State, are more than sufficient to protect this town and for that matter to maintain order all along the adjacent border.

You doubly have been informed by the military commanders at this place that I have heartily co-operated with them in all their efforts to maintain the neutrality of the United States, etc. These Gentlemen are restrained by your orders, there are no restraints upon me, except such as are imposed by positive law. I have legal advice to the effect that my powers are sufficient to prevent any destruction of life and property within this City, even if the cause thereof originates in a foreign territory, and that the agents of the United States who may attempt to interfere with me in the discharge of this duty will themselves be violators of law. Mr. President, I shall use that power in case of necessity. Do not misunderstand me Mr. President, I do not purpose (sic) to maintain order in the City of Juárez, Mexico, but I do intend to protect life and property in the corporate limits of El Paso, Texas.
Very respectfully,
Charles E. Kelly
Mayor of the City of El Paso[33]

Mayor Kelly's letter was responded to by the assistant secretary of state, Huntington Wilson, acting on behalf of Secretary of State Philander C. Knox. It was not surprising that Kelly did not receive a direct response from President Taft. Secretary Wilson wrote on March 20, 1912:

In reply, I am glad to be able to inform you that the President and the various Departments of this Government concerned are constantly doing their utmost to afford protection to Americans and American interests, not only in El Paso but [also] in at all other places along the Mexican border and throughout Mexico.

You will, however, of course understand that in acting up on its very great solicitude for the lives and property of El Paso citizens, the fate and welfare of other Americans, some of whom are exposed to great danger, must not be lost sight of; and this Government in adopting the course it has deemed necessary to follow has, in compliance with what is believed to be the imperative necessities and equities of the whole situation, been guided by the interests of all American citizens affected and of this entire country.

There is not, I beg to assure you, any disposition whatsoever on the part of this Department not to admit that the circumstances set forth and the situation outlined in your letter are deplorable, but it ventures to observe that during the present unrest in Ciudad Juárez, it would appear to be the part of greatest prudence for citizens of El Paso to remain on American soil and not to cross the boundary into Juárez and thus risk creating a serious international situation by subjecting themselves to the dangers with which, as you so clearly point out, their presence in Juárez might be attended.

This Department quite agrees that as Mayor of El Paso you have not only a right but a positive duty to secure adequate protection for life and property in that city in accordance with the laws of the state of Texas and with the municipal laws of El Paso, but it feels, nevertheless, that it may with propriety, in view of certain intimations contained in your letter, suggest as proper to have in mind in adopting measures to this end, the last paragraph of Section 10 of Article 1 of the Constitution of the United States, reading as follows:

> "No state shall, without the consent of Congress, lay any duty of tonnage, keep troops, or ships of war in times of peace, enter into any agreement of compact with another state, or with a foreign power, or engage in war, unless actually invaded, or in such imminent danger as will not admit of delay."

I am, Sir, Your obedient servant, Huntington Wilson, Acting Secretary of State[34]

As was Kelly's style in all things political and commercial, he was wont to have the last word. In response to Secretary Wilson's letter, he responded on March 26, 1912 with:

> In answer to your letter I have the honor to inform you that I have at all times borne in mind the manifold and often conflicting duties devolved upon the United States by the disturbed condition of Mexico, and so bearing in mind, to the best of my ability, in all things cooperated with the officers of the United States at this point, although in some instances I was of the opinion that a different course was preferable to the one adopted by them. An examination of my letter will disclose the manifest fact that at the time of the writing thereof I did keep in mind the Section and Article of the Constitution to which you refer. Whatever may be its interpretation by the Department (and our cemeteries contain evidence as to what that interpretation is), I am of the opinion that the firing of shots from a foreign territory into American streets and American homes is an actual invasion and to the extent of my power I will treat it as such whenever the City of El Paso is the point invaded. Furthermore, it is my duty to safeguard to the extent of my power, life and property in said City and no resistance under my direction to any unlawful act can possibly be a violation of the Constitution of the United States.
>
> Very respectfully,
> Charles E. Kelly
> Mayor of the City of El Paso[35]

What the exact effect that Kelly's letters had on the problems facing El Paso's citizenry is not fully known, but the government did increase its show of force and the level of border depredations involving Americans seemed to level off.[36] Colonel Edgar Z. Steever ordered all the troops from Fort Bliss to the city and El Paso took on the appearance of an armed encampment. Members of the Texas National Guard, a sheriff's posse, and eleven Texas Rangers joined the soldiers. The Taft administration declared an arms embargo in March 2012.[37]

"Uncle Henry" Kelly's bellicosity, dictatorial demeanor, and attention getting behavior could have been spurred on by his somewhat small physical stature.[38] A familiar story was frequently repeated about Kelly and his frustration when he wasn't recognized. When Kelly rode with Presidents Díaz and Taft in the celebratory parade through downtown El Paso in 1909, a political foe of

Kelly remarked, "Twenty years ago he was washing bottles here." When he heard of the remark, Kelly is reported to have said, "Yes, but I washed 'em well!". He was further described as one who knows no odds, "As quiet and diffident as a school mouse, when that mallet-like jaw shoots out and the pale blue eyes come to a point, El Paso or that part of it which is within range, ducks for the cyclone cellar."[39]

Acting on behalf of Mayor Robinson, prior to becoming mayor himself Kelly had been visiting rebel leader Madero's encampment and was intending to return to El Paso by way of the footbridge near the site of the old El Paso Brick Company. Noticing that the footbridge was extremely crowded; Kelly removed his coat and shoes and decided to wade across the Rio Grande in frigid winter weather. Upon reaching the American side, the American troops detained him and asked what he was doing? Kelly mentioned his name and business, but the Fort Bliss stationed troops did not recognize him and refused to allow him to enter the United States. He returned to the Mexican side, but was met with rejection by the Mexican troops who refused his admittance. Kelly appeared to be a man without a country. After several frustrating hours, Kelly made a second attempt to cross the river to the American side, this time the troops notified their commanding officer, Col. Edwin Glenn, who finally was able to identify himself and allow him to return to El Paso.[40]

Kelly's relationship with the Sheldon Hotel extended far beyond that of tenant and resident, for he gained an international reputation for interceding in a threatening confrontation between Pancho Villa and Soldier of Fortune, Col. Giuseppe Garibaldi, in the days following the fall of Ciudad Juárez in 1911.[41] Following the Revolution and Villa's retirement from active "soldiering," Kelly and Villa remained great friends and often met for "socializing" in the kitchen at Kelly's ranch house in the south valley near Socorro and Fabens.[42] One of the issues discussed between them was Villa's desire to become president of Mexico, but he had reconciled that it was never going to happen because he couldn't read and would never know what he was signing.[43]

By election time in 1915, the "anti-ring," "anti-vice," and reformist movement was in full swing and lawyer Tom Lea, Jr. defeated Mayor Kelly with an overwhelming majority. The opposition to Kelly seemed to be a result of the influx into the city of a new generation of lawyers and politicians.

Mayor Kelly wasn't the only political boss who maintained regular ties with the Sheldon Hotel. Governor George W. P. Hunt of Arizona was a frequent guest of the hotel and a close friend of the subsequent owner of the Sheldon,

Mama "D" DeGroff. Governor Hunt, the primary author of the Arizona State Constitution, was the first Governor of Arizona, serving seven terms as well as being appointed the U.S. Ambassador to Siam by President Woodrow Wilson. His burial site is a massive pyramid that sits atop a hill in Papago Park in Phoenix.[44]

Many nationally known performers, of all genres, routinely visited El Paso to give concerts and performances in the local theaters and opera house on El Paso Street. Artist Frederick Remington was a regular patron of the Sheldon, in fact he wrote in his journal his disfavor when he arrived and the Sheldon was booked full and was very lucky to find lodging at the St. Regis.[45]

Senator Albert B. Fall

Local lawyer, Albert B. Fall maintained a room in the hotel with his El Paso office across the plaza. Fall would eventually build his El Paso mansion just east of downtown and would gain notoriety as a U.S. Senator and Secretary of the Interior. Senator Fall's presence in Congress also had a profound effect on the outcome of WWI.

Republican Senator Albert B. Fall of New Mexico was an ardent isolationist and was repeatedly on the Democratic Party's hit list. So important was his senatorial defeat in 1918 that it would have created a Democratic-Republican tie in the Senate, and with Wilson's Democratic vice president's (Thomas R. Marshall) tie breaking vote, the Democrats would have control of the Senate and the Republicans would have lost the chairmanship of the important Foreign Relations Committee.

During the campaign of 1918, President Wilson had leveled severe personal attacks against Senator Fall, who was, at the time, still grieving from the loss of his only son and one of his daughters to the rampant Spanish Flu pandemic. This political tactic completely backfired against President Woodrow Wilson. Senator Fall had garnered a great deal of sympathy from his constituents and won the election by a margin of 2,000 votes. This shifted the senate to the Republicans, and the senate chose Henry Cabot Lodge as chairman of the critical Foreign Relations Committee. The Republicans then opposed anything that Wilson wanted, including the Treaty of Versailles, which contain the blue print for the League of Nation, which the Republicans opposed. In March 1920, the U.S. Senate finally killed the treaty. The United States never ratified the Treaty of Versailles and United States did not join the League of Nations. This failure plagued President Wilson until his death in 1924.

Fall became the central figure in the political scandal known as the Tea Pot Dome Affair that would eventually send him to prison. The Tea Pot Dome scandal had been considered the most significant and outrageous political scandal in American political history until the Watergate scandal that led to the resignation of President Nixon in August of 1974. Fall was convicted of accepting a bribe from oil barons Edward Doheny and Harry Sinclair in 1929, despite the fact that both and Sinclair were acquitted of bribing Secretary Fall. Sinclair did spend several months in prison for contempt of court and contempt of congress. Doheny and Sinclair remained wealthy and powerful oil magnates for the rest of their lives.[46]

Fall's relationship with the hotel continued long after he moved into his El Paso home (1725 Arizona Ave.) and to his Three Rivers Ranch just south of Carrizozo, near Alamogordo, NM. Fall frequently stayed as a guest at the hotel and was regular patron of the Sheldon's bar and gaming tables. It was, however, his complicated and intertwined relationship with another Sheldon resident, Pat Garrett, which animates history's interest. (See below) Fall an ardent democrat, switched his party allegiance to the Republican Party in 1904. Eight years later, he became one of the first two United States Senators from New Mexico following its admittance as the forty-seventh state in the union. He served in the senate until March 4 1921, when President Warren G. Harding appointed him secretary of the interior.

Figure 36. Sen. Albert B. Fall 1861-1944

Before Senator Fall's fall from grace, he had another significant relationship with the Sheldon Hotel. Commencing on February 11, 1920, Fall, as chairman of the Subcommittee of the Committee on Foreign Relations of the United States Senate conducted an extensive hearings. These hearings, held in room 30 of the Sheldon Hotel, were a follow up to similar hearings that he held in 1913, to investigate the matter of outrages on citizens of the United States in Mexico.[47]

Pat Garrett

As the elite and refined masses migrated west, the towns and cities found it was to their advantage to tame the "wild and open" nature of their communities. It became necessary for city leaders to find men who were as rough and tough as those that needed containment. As a result, the city marshals, sheriffs, and even the Texas Rangers and U.S. Marshals, were men who were often the "worst of the worst"; men whose sullied reputations were so bad as to not be challenged by the 'bad guys.' Law enforcement was tended by the likes of Dallas Stoudenmire, John Selman, Wyatt Earp, Doc Holiday, and Bob Olinger,[48] the killer with a badge. Even John Wesley Hardin, the West's most notorious gunman, walked both sides of the streets of El Paso, vacillating between being a lawyer, lawman, and murderer.

Out of such a mold was Pat Garrett. Garrett had arrived in New Mexico as a buffalo hunter at the time when the great herds were being decimated by both the Indians and greedy white traders. He moved to Lincoln County in 1878, just as the Lincoln County War, the economic turf battles between rival gangs, was ending. Wild range killers and outlaws, including Billy the Kid, were in total rampage. The Kid, born William Henry McCarty Jr., frequently used his step-father's name, Henry Antrim as well as the name William H. Bonney.

In a gun battle with the Lincoln County posse, Billy the Kid killed William Brady, the sheriff. The New Mexico Territorial Governor, Republican Lew Wallace, (author of the book, Ben Hur) put a bounty of five hundred dollars on the Kid. Soon thereafter, Garrett was elected sheriff of Lincoln County and set about a campaign to find Billy the Kid. In 1880, Garrett captured the Kid at his hideout at Sinking Springs, NM and returned him to Mesilla via Santa Fe to stand trial for the murder of Sheriff Brady. The court of Judge Warren Bristol appointed Albert J. Fountain, a well-known El Paso and Mesilla lawyer as defense counsel. Fountain, while highly regarded, was a significant personal, legal, and political foe of Albert B. Fall.[49]

Figure 37. Sheriff Pat Garrett 1850-1908

On April 10, the jury convicted the Kid in the murder of Sheriff Brady. Judge Bristol said, "On May 13, 1881, William H. Bonney, alias the Kid, alias William Antrim, be hanged by the neck until his body be dead."[50] Garrett and two of his deputies, the outrageous Bob Olinger and James Bell were ordered to transport the Kid back to Fort Sumner for the sentence to be carried out. Because the local jailhouse was inadequate, Garrett arranged to have Bonney and other prisoners shackled to the floor in the courthouse. When Garrett was away on sheriff duties, Bonney managed to escape from custody, killing Olinger and Bell in the process.

It took Garrett three months to track Bonney down at the Fort Sumner home of Bonney's friend, Pete Maxwell. Bonney was not at the house when Garrett entered, but was expected to return shortly. Garrett hid in Maxwell's bedroom. Bonney entered the room with the exclamation "¿Quién es? ¿Quién es?" (Who is it?). Bonney drew his gun, but not before Garrett fired twice and killed Billy the Kid.[51] It was the bullet that immortalized Garrett in the annals of American history. As newspapers and writers tried to capitalize on the incident, Garrett set out to write his own account of the shooting. Ghost written by his friend Ash Upson, he released The Authentic Life of Billy the Kid in 1882 to a somewhat lacking public response.

For whatever reason, the $500 reward was not paid to Garrett and in 1884; he failed in his election for the state senate. Disenchanted with the way things were developing in New Mexico he resigned as sheriff and moved to Texas, where he was promptly appointed a lieutenant in the Texas Rangers. Again, disillusionment set in within the year and Garrett returned to his New Mexico ranch and later ran for sheriff of Chavez County in the Roswell area, this time he lost the election and moved to Uvalde, Texas, southwest of San Antonio, to raise horses.

While Garrett was falling on a string of hard and disappointing times, Albert Fall had become involved in a personal and professional battle with fellow lawyer Albert J. Fountain (Billy the Kids' defense counsel). Fountain was active in the Republican Party and was prosecuting relentlessly the unchecked cattle rustling that was ravaging southwest New Mexico in the 1890s. Fall, was serving as counsel to various mining companies and cattle thieves. Fountain was able to procure an indictment against rancher Oliver Lee and the "Tularosa Gang," [52] who was a close friend and neighbor of powerful and ruthless democrat Fall. Fall made no secret of his opposition to Fountain's rigorous actions against the thieves.

On February 1, 1896, Fountain and his eight-year-old son disappeared on a desert road near the White Sands dune fields. Their bodies have never been found. Even to the most naïve, it seemed that Fall and Oliver Lee were somehow implicated in this heinous crime. (Further details of the Fountain and Fall conflict can be found in Owen's book, The Two Alberts.)

The territory governor of New Mexico democrat William T. Thornton, remembering Garrett's dogged pursuit of Billy the Kid, contacted him and installed him as sheriff in Las Cruces in 1896, the seat of Doña Ana County, New Mexico. After two years, Garrett had garnered enough evidence to charge Oliver Lee, Jim Gilliland and 2 others in the murder of the Fountains. None other, than Albert B. Fall, represented Lee and the others during the trial, which in short order, acquitted the defendants, and stoked the animus between Fall and Garrett, the two former Sheldon residents. Garrett remained the sheriff of Doña Ana County two additional terms.

Garrett had become somewhat of a hero in the eyes of many, including "Rough Rider" President Theodore Roosevelt. President Roosevelt appointed the six-foot-five father of eight[53], U.S. Collector of Customs for El Paso in December 1901.[54] Despite strong opposition, the senate confirmed the appointment on January 2, 1902.[55] During his brief tenure at the Federal Building, Garrett lived in the Sheldon Hotel, directly across Oregon Street from his office in the Federal Building. Things did not go well for Garrett in his official duties, complaints began to flood into the Treasury Department regarding Garrett's incompetency. His contentious attitude toward the large cattle and mining companies, especially the Corralitos Cattle Company, resulted in repeated reprimands from Leslie Shaw, secretary of the treasury.[56] During the same time, Garrett had become increasingly quarrelsome and violent as his personal economic fortunes continued to decline.[57]

In 1905, President Roosevelt, in an attempt to smooth the roughness of Garrett's reputation, invited him to attend a "Rough Riders" convention in San Antonio. What made a questionable situation worse was that Garrett invited his best friend, Tom Powers, to accompany him. Powers was the one-eyed, hard-drinking, gun-toting, professional gambler who owned the Coney Island saloon that was just out the back door of the Sheldon Hotel. While at the convention, photographs were taken of the President with Garrett and Powers. The press immediately picked up and published the photographs and the White House became significantly embarrassed that the President had been photographed with Powers, a man of such questionable reputation. Roosevelt, believing that Garrett had lied about Power's true persona, chose not to re-appoint Garrett to his government position.[58]

Garrett had introduced Powers to the president as a prominent Texas cattleman. Roosevelt in expressing his displeasure over the entire incident said that to have Garrett, "bring up as his intimate friend a man who…was well known as a professional gambler, and then have myself, Garrett and the gambler taken in a photograph together…not a happy incident."[59] Even though the President arranged to have the secret service collect and destroy the negatives, Garrett's life took a turn from which he would never fully recover. When asked by a reporter about his future, Garrett responded, "I have a ranch in New Mexico and I will go there for a time. Just what my future plans will be I do not know. However, I am going to do something and don't expect to be idle. I have no complaint to make against anyone for my removal. I simply take my medicine."[60] Disillusioned and nearly destitute, Garrett returned to the Las Cruces area and put his run-downed Bear Canyon ranch up for sale. The isolated ranch, heavily mortgaged to wealthy neighbor, W.W. Cox, was equally encumbered by a grazing lease to a local cowboy named Wayne Brazel, who worked for Cox. Garrett was also delinquent in county taxes. The ranch was located near the site of the Fountain murders.[61] Garrett was now back in the shadows of the nemeses that had targeted him in the Fountain murder investigation.

As Garrett continued to struggle in his attempt to sell his ranch, his major issues of conflict seemed to be with Cox and Brazel. A James B. Miller approached Garrett, with a sales deal if details could be reached with Brazel's lease on the ranch. Miller had intimated that he wanted to move a huge herd to the Garrett ranch. Miller's partner, Carl Adamson, went to the Garrett ranch to take Garrett to a meeting with Miller in Las Cruces. On February 29, 1908, Adamson stopped his wagon for Garrett to relieve himself just as Brazel approached them on horseback. As he was standing alongside the wagon, he was shot and killed. Adamson and Brazel left Garrett's body and headed for Las Cruces where Brazel admitted to the assassination stating that Adamson had witnessed the self-defense shooting. Brazel went on trial for the murder and was acquitted on May 4, 1909, defended by none other than Albert B. Fall and his associates.[62]

Exactly who killed Pat Garrett became an enormous mystery. James B. Miller didn't have a herd of cattle and was a known professional assassin by the name of *Killin' Jim Miller* who was associated with the El Paso gang of Mannie Clements and Clements' second cousin John Wesley Hardin. Very few historians believe that Brazel actually killed Garrett. Historians everywhere have all speculated the Garrett was in fact killed by either Adamson, Cox, Print Rhode, or Miller. All of whom were clients, neighbors, and associates of Albert B. Fall. [63]

James Madison Hervey was the attorney general for New Mexico at the time of the Garrett murder. To put the entire mystery in perspective, he wrote the results of his investigation into the murder with the stipulation that it not be published until eight years after his death. The Hervey report is somewhat lengthy, but it pulls together issues surrounding Garrett and Fall and one of the most iconic murder mysteries in the southwest. In 1961, his assessment of the incident was released and published. Excerpts shed a greater focus:

> Practically all of Garrett's time and thought [as sheriff of Doña Ana County] was devoted to apprehending the murderers of Colonel Fountain. He had various clues, and at one time took a posse and arrested a man upon whom his suspicious centered, but apparently, he was wrong, as the man was tried and acquitted, and thereafter Garrett continued the search. This he did long after his term as sheriff had expired. In the country east of Las Cruces, there was a cattle baron by the name of Cox. He had been operating a ranch in that country for a long time. With these preliminaries, I shall note what was said about Garrett's death at the time it happened and what I afterwards found out.
>
> I was attorney general of New Mexico from 1907 to 1909. Garrett was killed in February 1908, on the highway just east of Las Cruces. There was a man with him at the time by the name of Carl Adamson, whom I once defended on a charge of smuggling Chinamen into the United States. The report was brought to Las Cruces that a young man by the

name of Wayne Brazel had killed Garrett in an altercation over a ranch. Apparently the only disinterested witness was Adamson.

New Mexico was a territory at that time and the attorney general was an appointee of the Federal Government. George Curry was the governor and a personal friend of mine. He came to me soon after the news of Garrett's murder was out, and said that he would go down to Las Cruces the next day to the funeral and suggested that I go along, as the talk was running pretty high among Garrett's friends and there might be trouble. It had gotten out that Albert B. Fall (later U.S. Senator) had been retained to defend Brazel and that the [local] district attorney was a pretty close friend of Fall's. He thought there should be an independent investigation.

I went to Las Cruces, and while the Governor was attending the funeral, I saw Carl Adamson and asked him to go with me and show me the exact place where Garrett was killed and how it happened. We took Fred Fornoff from Santa Fe along with us. He was a noted peace officer and captain of the State Mounted Police. Adamson said he had met Garrett in El Paso and had indicated that he wanted to buy a ranch and Garrett said that he had one east of Las Cruces that he would like to sell. He and Adamson had gone to the ranch, looked it over, and were returning to Las Cruces in a buckboard. Brazel caught up with them on horseback, Adamson saw that Brazel had a Winchester strapped to his saddle but didn't see any other arms. Garrett had a sawed off shotgun leaning against the dashboard in the front of the buckboard. This he always carried in that place.

Brazel said to Garrett, "understand you're trying to sell the ranch," and Garrett said he was, that he was trying to sell it to the man he had there with him. Brazel said, "You leased me that ranch and you can't sell it." Garrett replied either that he had not leased it to him, that it was subject to sale. They talked along rather heatedly for a while and then Garrett reached for the shotgun and said, "If I can't get you off of it one way, I will another." Brazel, instead of reaching for his Winchester, pulled a six-shooter and shot Garrett twice. … While Fred Fornoff and Adamson were talking (we had stopped our buckboard at the same place where he said Garrett had stopped), I walked back some thirty or forty feet to where Adamson said he had stood and at that place I happened to spy a new Winchester rifle shell on the ground.

Garrett was shot in the back of the head and once in the front of his body. The place where I was told that he was found was not in his buckboard but on the side of the road. In this particular locality on the south side of the road there are high sand hills and on the north side the black brush was pretty thick. A few days later I read Brazel's story about this and the whole thing looked suspicious to me—Garrett being found not in the buckboard but on the side of the road. The finding of the shell also was a strange development. Brazel had never been considered a dangerous man. A number of other things aroused my suspicion. We returned to Santa Fe that night and the next day I told Captain Fornoff that there was something wrong about the story. He said he thought so too, but that we had no money to try to find out anything.

A month or so later I had business in El Paso, where Garrett had spent a good deal of time and found out who some of his friends were. One was Tom Powers, the owner of the Coney Island Saloon and pretty well-to-do; another was a Dr. Culinan. I took a personal interest in this matter because Garrett had been a friend of my father and if he had been murdered I thought the guilty parties should be prosecuted. … I went to Chicago some six or eight months after Garrett's death and contacted [newspaper man Emerson] Hough. I knew that he was friendly with Garrett because Garrett had obtained for him the material for [Saturday Evening Post] "The Wasteful West" stories, and told him this entire story and asked him if he, alone or with some other friends, would make up a thousand dollars or so to try to find out who killed Garrett, but he said Garrett owed him considerable money and that he was pretty pushed for money anyway and he couldn't do it.

Then he made this remark: "Jimmie, I know that outfit around the Organ Mountains and Garrett got killed for trying to find out who killed Fountain and you will get killed trying to find out who killed Garrett. I would advise you to let it alone." After this admonition, I decided not to be so active but I never lost interest in trying to find out whether my suspicious were well founded. After my return to El Paso, I told Captain Fornoff that he had an expense account and that he might try to get up some kind of business in El Paso and see what he could find out. There were a bunch of tough characters still around El Paso, not the least of whom was Tom Powers himself. Another was [John Wesley Hardin's cousin] Manning Clements, the brother-in law of Carl Adamson, the sole witness in the killing. Fornoff made the trip to El

Paso and came back and said he had made a real discovery but he did not know whether he would ever be able to prove it. …

Fornoff had learned that a wealthy ranchman near El Paso had hired Miller to kill Garrett, whom the rancher despised, and had paid Miller $1,500 to do the job. The money had been handed over to Miller in the office of some lawyer in El Paso by Manning Clements. Part of the deal was that the ranchman would furnish a man who would say he killed Garrett in self-defense, and the rancher was also to furnish one witness who would corroborate the statement. The trouble was that Fornoff had no proof. Brazel was the man who was to say he killed Garrett in self-defense, with Adamson, Manning Clements brother-in-law, as the witness.

The story must be true because it corroborates not only what Fornoff found out in El Paso but it also corroborates the general circumstances of the case as above related: the suspicion that Garrett was shot in the back of the head, the killing occurred at a place where a man could easily hide and do the shooting; the finding of the Winchester shell some fifty feet off the road; and the unlikelihood that Brazel would have killed Garrett or that Garrett would make such a fool play.

In my own mind I am satisfied that the above is the way Garrett met his death and that it grew out of his constant desire to find out who killed Fountain. Nearly everybody connected with the case is now (in 1953) dead. Brazel, a big strapping fellow, died suddenly of a heart attack. The ranchman died recently. Adamson died of typhoid fever. Somebody killed Manning Clements in El Paso, and Miller was hanged in Oklahoma by a mob for murdering a former United States marshal.[64]

The Fountain murder case tied the two Sheldon Hotel residents together somewhat diabolically. While there exists no patent proof that Fall was directly involved in either the Fountain or Garrett murders, he was nevertheless clearly in the shadows of both of these events that typifies the nature of the untamed Southwest during the turn of the century. Yet, the Sheldon Hotel continued to play a role in the lives of some of the actors involved.

Notes and References

[1] Timmons, W.H. *El Paso: A Borderlands History*. (El Paso: Texas Western Press, 1990.), 221; 335n, 7.
[2] *El Paso Herald*, September 18, 1902.
[3] Among the plethora of activities held at the Sheldon Hotel during its first decade were the first annual meeting of the newly formed El Paso County Medical Society, regular meetings of the First Christian Science Church, the West Texas Cattlemen's Association, regular meetings of the Women's Club planning of the Mid-Winter Carnival, the International Boundary Commission, the 12th National Irrigation Congress, elaborate receptions for international performers who appeared at the Myar's Opera House, the World Series of Cafe Roping, and the beginning of a long tradition of very formal and elegant dances held in the spacious hotel's banquet room.
[4] *El Paso Times*, June 23, 1952, 32.
[5] White, Owen P. *The Autobiography of a Durable Sinner*. (New York: Putman's Sons, 1942.), 100.
[6] Spier, Wener, et. al. "Tuberculosis: The beginnings of El Paso as a medical center." *Password.* XLII (1997), 107-119. Funkhouser, Barbara. *The Caregivers: El Paso's Medical History, 1898-1998.* (El Paso: Sundance Press, 1999.)
[7] Ibid, 107.
[8] Shepherd, W.G. "Eyewitness at the Triangle." *New York World*, March 26, 1911 in Allon Schoener's *Portal to America: The Lower East Side, 1870-1925.* (New York: Henry Holt Co., 1967.)
[9] Worley's *Directory of the City of El Paso, 1901*, 37.
[10] Prendergast, Simon. "Personnel of El Banco Commercial." *Paper Money of Chihuahua*. Accessed 17 Feb. 2016.
[11] Wasserman, Mark. "Enrique C. Creel: Business and Politics in Mexico, 1880-1930." *Business History Review*, Vol. 59 No. 4 (1985), 648.
[12] Ibid.
[13] Ibid, 651.
[14] "Gateway Hotel Remodeling." henrytrost.org. Accessed 17 Feb. 2016.
[15] Ibid, 645.
[16] Harris and Sadler (2009), 71.
[17] America didn't have a national police force, so on March 16, 1906 (some sources give July 26, 1908), Attorney General Bonaparte and President Theodore Roosevelt created the BOI (Bureau of Investigation)
[18] Ibid, 71-72.
[19] Arredondo, Jaime, et.al. (ed.) *Open Borders to a Revolution*. (Washington, D.C.:

Smithsonian Institution Scholarly Press, 2013.): 160.

[20] Sonnichsen, C.L. *Pass of the North: Four Centuries on the Rio Grande.* (El Paso: Texas Western Press, 1968.), 389.

[21] Sonnichsen, C .L., and M.G. McKinney. *The State National Since 1881: The Pioneer Bank of El Paso.* (El Paso: Texas Western Press, 1971.), 86.

[22] Perkins, Clifford Alan, and C. L. Sonnichsen. *Border Patrol: With the U.S. Immigration Service on the Mexican Boundary 1910-1954.* (El Paso: Texas Western Press, 1978.), 47.

[23] *El Paso Herald*, September 13, 1910.

[24] Oral history of the three Kelly daughters. (El Paso: Digital Commons@UTEP. Interview no. 87.1. 26 Mar 1973.), 2.

[25] Freudenthal, Samuel J. *El Paso Merchant and Civic Leader: from the 1880's through the Mexican Revolution.* Southwestern Studies No. 11 (El Paso: Texas Western Press, 1965.), 23.

[26] Oral History Interview No. 87.1.: 1.

[27] Ibid, 6.

[28] *El Paso Times*, April 23, 1989.

[29] Sonnichsen, C.L. (*1968)*, 371.

[30] *El Paso Herald*. June 8, 1911.

[31] Oral History No. 87.1.

[32] C.E. Kelly, CVF. (El Paso Public Library, Border Heritage Department.)

[33] Charles E. Kelly Letter to President William H. Taft. 11 Mar. 1912. (El Paso Public Library, C.E. Kelly, CVF.)

[34] Huntington Wilson Letter to Charles E. Kelly, 20 Mar. 1912. (El Paso Public Library, C.E. Kelly, CVF.)

[35] Charles E. Kelly Letter to Huntington Wilson, 26 Mar. 1912. (El Paso Public Library,C.E. Kelly, CVF.) No record of additional correspondence was located on this topic.

[36] Hartmann, Clinton. "Charles Edgar Kelly." *Handbook of Texas Online*. Accessed 17 Dec 2010.

[37] Timmons, 215.

[38] Sonnichsen (1968): 370.

[39]*El Paso Times*, July 26, 1959.

[40] Chambers, Kathy. "A Man Without a Country." *Password.* Vol. XIV., 84-85.

[41] *New York Times*. May 18, 1911,

[42] Oral Interview No. 87.1.

[43] Ibid.

[44] A personal postcard written to his wife Helen from El Paso with the handwritten message, "am leaving for St. Louis confirmed Governor Hunt's relationship with the

Sheldon Hotel. "This hotel is filled up fine and is well-furnished throughout. Our friends the DeGroffs are well—Love G.W.P.H. February 17, 1911. The George Hunt Collection, Arizona State University, Spec. Coll. HD39.9.

[45] Remington's Journal, April 6, 1097. www.frederickremmington.org. Accessed 26 Mar. 2009.

[46] *Sinclair v. United States, 279 U.S. 263 (1929).*

[47] United States Senate. *Revolutions in Mexico: A Hearing before a subcommittee of the Committee on Foreign Relations, Sixty-Second Congress, second session Pursuant to S. Res. 335 (1913) and S.Res. 106* (*1920.*)Washington, DC: GPO, 1913 and 1920.

[48] Weiser, Kathy. "Robert Olinger—Killer with a Badge." *Legends of America.com*. August 2015. Accessed 21 Feb. 2016.

[49] Metz, Leon C. *Pat Garrett: The Story of a Western Lawman*. (Norman: University of Oklahoma Press. 1974.), 169.

[50] Ibid, 88.

[51] Ibid, 117.

[52] Suhler, R.A. "Ben Williams, Lawman." *Password.* Vol.XXVII (1992), 23.

[53] It is interesting to note that Elizabeth Garrett, one of Pat Garrett's eight children became blind, it is commonly believed, shortly after birth as a result of the misuse of a medication for an eye infection. In her adult life, she became a music and voice teacher and was known as the "Songbird of the Southwest" and history will remember her as the songwriter of the New Mexico's state song, *O Fair New Mexico.* She was a close friend of Helen Keller and died after a fall in Roswell, NM in 1947. The *Find a Grave* site reports that her service dog was guiding her out of her house during a thunderstorm and she tripped and struck her head on a curb. The youngest of Pat Garrett's children, Jarvis P. Garrett, died in 1991, leaving a large family that stills resides in New Mexico.

[54] *El Paso Herald*, December 16, 1901.

[55] *El Paso Herald*, January 2, 1902,

[56] Metz, (1974), 246-247.

[57] Hurst, James W. "The Death of Pat Garrett." (*southernnewmexico.com* July 17, 2003.) Accessed 1 June 2009.

[58] Metz, (1974): 252-253.

[59] Ibid, 254.

[60] Gardner, Mark L. *To Hell on Fast Horse: Billy the Kid, Pat Garrett, and the Epic Chase To Justice in the Old West.* (New York: William Morrow, 2010.), 224-225.

[61] Ibid, 278.

[62] Ibid, 292-295.

[63] Ibid, 292. Shirley, Glenn. *Shotgun for Hire: The Story of "Deacon" Jim Miller, Killer of Pat Garrett.* (Norman: University of Oklahoma Press, 1970.)

[64] Hervey, James M. "The Assassination of Pat Garrett." (*True West Magazine*. March-April 1961.), 17; 40-42.

Chapter Eleven

Diamonds, Nuts, and Murder at the Backdoor

Almost from its opening day, the Sheldon Hotel attempted to attract the most successful and elite of residents and guests. Its lobby, dining rooms, and banquet halls were designed and operated to meet the needs as El Paso's center of social and civic activities. Located to the west, south, and east of the Sheldon, was an enormous array of bars, bordellos, and gaming houses to meet the needs of the less sophisticated. Those riotous dens were the centerpiece of the anti-vice and reformist's movement that was moving through the community as the new century dawned. El Paso had been a refuge for outlaws and gunslingers turned lawmen such as Dallas Stoudenmire, John Wesley Hardin, and John Selman, and by the turn of the century they had found their way to a timely justice at boot hill. Lesser-known gunmen, such as Mannie Clements, "spent their time shaking down prostitutes and bullying meeker citizens. Clements drifted to El Paso around 1894 and for the next fourteen years wore a badge as a deputy constable, constable, deputy sheriff, and an El Paso police officer. It didn't take long for Clements to become a professional hit man, an inexpensive assassin-for-hire.

While it appeared that there were saloons in every block, several remain icons in the history of old El Paso. The Gem Saloon and the Manning Brother's Coliseum were both across the little plaza from the Sheldon's west entrance at 110 S. El Paso Street where the Hotel Paso del Norte / El Camino Real, is now located. Just a short block south of the Sheldon were the Wigwam Saloon at the southwest corner of Oregon Street and San Antonio Ave., where the State National Bank was erected and the Acme Saloon at the northwest corner of Mesa Street (Utah) and San Antonio Ave., across the street from the Poplar Department Store site. These were the venues of some of the most famous and notorious murders and shoot-outs in Southwest history. The killing of John Wesley Hardin, the fastest gun in the west with upward to 50 kills, the Constable John Selman murder at the hands of U.S. Marshall George Scarborough and their most remarkable trials and subsequent acquittals are fodder for Old West aficionados.[1]

Among the most acclaimed of these entertainment establishments was the Coney Island Saloon co-owned by Pat Garrett's close friend, Tom Powers.[2] The Coney Island was located in the shadow of the Sheldon Hotel and adjacent to "Uncle Henry" Kelly's drug store on Oregon Street, sitting just 12 feet across the alley and facing the new Federal Building. In addition to the Coney Island, gambling boss, Tom Powers obtained ownership of the Wigwam Saloon and converted it into El Paso's first movie theater when his drinking and gambling establishments began to suffer under the pressure of the ever increasing movement of the anti-vice and reform activists.[3]

Volumes can be written about the large numbers of murders that occurred at the Coney Island Saloon, it was however, the murder of Mannie Clements, Jr., at the Coney Island Saloon in 1909 that inextricably connects the enigmatic history of the Sheldon Hotel to two of its most ill-famed residents: Senator Albert B. Fall and Sheriff Pat Garrett.

The saga began with a secret meeting at the St. Regis Hotel (across the San Jacinto Plaza from the Sheldon Hotel) attended by a group of well know Pat Garrett haters, among others: ranchers Oliver Lee and W.W. Cox, Carl Adamson (known to be married to Clements' wife's cousin), Wayne Brazel, Mannie Clements, Jr., Killin' Jim Miller (Clements' son-in-law and related by marriage to the infamous John Wesley Hardin), and of course, Albert B. Fall. The purpose of the meeting instigated by Pat Garrett's neighbor Cox, according to León Metz,[4] was to plan the killing of Garrett so that Cox could obtain Garrett's land (especially the water) as he feared that Garrett was getting too close to solving the Colonel Fountain mystery and that would implicate most of those attending the meeting. Without rejecting the veracity of the meeting, Metz raises the question about the sketchily documented sources used by the various historians and writers who discuss this episode.[5] A key member of this clandestine council was Mannie Clements, who eventually was identified as thc bagman in the payment of funds to Killin' Jim Miller,[6] the identified killer of Garrett at the office of a lawyer, assumed to be Albert B. Fall.[7] Miller, also ``known as "Deacon Jim has often been considered the worst of the worst, an outlaw whose evil reputation surpassed John Wesley Hardin. He was the most notorious assassin-for-hire in the Old West.

Although Clements and Fall may have been complicit in the planning and execution of the Garrett murder in February 1908, they were not at all friendly. Clements harbored significant ill will towards Fall who had managed to get an acquittal for John Selman who killed Clements' cousin, John Wesley Hardin. Clements made repeated public pronouncements about his hatred for Fall, especially when he had been drinking, which for all practical purposes was all the time. On two occasions, he actually made attempts to assassinate the future senator. The first attempt was made at the Coney Island. Fall had been in the "wine room" drinking by himself. The wine room was to the back of the bar and was somewhat cordoned off from the rest of the bar so as to permit the presences of female patrons. Clements walked up to Fall and stuck a gun in his face, he stood there just holding the gun without shooting. At that moment, the local justice of the peace, Charles Pollock stepped in and Clements retired from the confrontation. Journalist Owen White offers an interesting perspective on the attempted assassination:

> Had he done so what a difference it would have made in American history! Carl Magee of Albuquerque, and Bug Speers of the New York Times, would never have gone on trial of the little black bag [the bribe]; Teapot Dome would never have been leased to Harry Sinclair, Harry himself would never have gone to jail in Washington; the administration of Warren G Harding would not today be as a stench in the nostrils of Christian historians, and Albert B. Fall would not have come into the autumn of his life in a disgraced and debilitated state.
>
> The killers' next effort was again in the Coney Island, Fall was drinking at the bar with some friends when Clements, who was a bit drunk, walked in, pulled his gun, and got no further. In El Paso a man had to be quick to get by with a killing and Clements was probably too tight to be as fast as necessary. Somebody slapped his gun up in the air, two or three men threw him out into the street, and once again was Fall deprived of the privilege of dying an honored citizen.[8]

Following Clements latest attempt at killing Fall, he had gotten involved in the armed robbery of a wealthy out-of-towner named Sam Van Rooyen. Van

Rooyen identified Clements as being part of the gang that robbed him of his jewelry. During the trial, Clements was observed glaring down the jurors with threatening stares. He was quickly acquitted, but lost his constable job. Desperately out of funds, he went to the Coney Island to seek contacts for his services as a hired gun.[9] Clements entered the Coney Island Saloon around 6 p.m. on December 29, 1908 and ordered a drink. Immediately upon being served, while speaking to several others at the bar, he was shot in the back of the head.[10]

"Mannie Clements just committed suicide," was the howl heard emanating from the front door of the saloon. What is most astonishing is that the barroom was full of patrons, even to the point of overcrowding, and no one, absolutely no one saw anything or could offer any insight.[11] No one could agree as to who fired the shot, some of the witnesses said that they had seen a man in a long coat and hat rush out of the back door, but nothing conclusive.[12] Burt "Cap" Mossman, the first Arizona Ranger,[13] and Captain John R. Hughes, of the Texas Rangers,[14] were among the throng in the Coney Island at the time of the shooting. They were reported to have said when a fellow member of the crowd stood up to look at the Clements body, "Sit down, we don't want to get mixed up in this."[15]

Many years later, historian Sonnichsen reported that one of the individuals in the bar that night told him that Tom Powers repeatedly stated that, "Clements has committed suicide."[16] Jubilation appeared to be the word of the day and Albert Fall was so moved that he called the county sheriff and prosecuting county attorneys that no one was to be arrested for the murder.[17]

Eventually, one of the Coney Island's bartenders, Joe Brown, was arrested and taken to trial for the murder of Clement. According to witnesses, Brown, holding a gun in a bar towel, shot Clements and then dropped the gun in a sink of soapy water. When all the facts were in, the jury acquitted Brown in less than an hour.[18] El Paso journalist Owen White writes of the Brown trail, "Joe Brown's trial created more perjurers than El Paso ever had before. It was astonishing. One after another some two dozen El Pasoans, all of whom had been standing within 20 feet of Mannie Clements when he was shot, swore they didn't know who did it. It was clearly a miracle: a bullet from Heaven."[19]

During the one-hour deliberation, the jury took six ballots before coming to agreement on a verdict. The first three ballots yielded four votes for acquittal and eight guilty. On the fourth ballot, three jurors changed their vote to acquittal. During the sixth ballot, the lone holdout surrendered for a unanimous vote of acquittal. In explaining the acquittal one of the jurors, focusing on the prosecution's last minute surprise witness, Mr. Randall, said:

> The only two credible witnesses the state had to connect Brown with the crime were Walter B. Randall and Fred Mueller. We did not know Randall, and so many shady characters were brought forward as witnesses that we were afraid of him. His story was straight enough and he looked like an honest, respectable man. But Fred Mueller testified that he ran into the saloon immediately after the shot was fired and met Brown coming out in his shirt sleeves. The time was too short for him to get his coat off, and Randall testified that the man he saw had on a coat.[20]

Another juror said he was influenced by the fact that if Brown had wanted to kill Clements he could have done so when Clements entered the saloon, and in front of everybody, because Clements had previously threatened to kill Brown.[21]

The verdict was a complete surprise to both sides. When the news of the acquittal reached the Coney Island and the other El Paso watering holes, there was a wild scene of rejoicing and wine flowed like water. It was reported that, "It is among the probabilities that more champagne was drunk last night over the acquittal of Brown than was ever drunk in one evening in the history of El Paso."[22] Chief of police Ben. F. Jenkins, (former Collector of Customs in El Paso) commenting on the outcome of the trail stated:

> I have nothing to say regarding the outcome of the prosecution of Joe Brown. As the public will remember, when I was made chief of police I received the hunting down of the murderer of Manen (sic) Clements as a legacy from my predecessor in office. I tried faithfully as an officer of the law to find Clements' slayer. I am not prepared to say whether or not mistakes were made or in what measure the police department fell short in its duty. A jury of Mr. Brown's peers has found him innocent of the crime of which he was accused, and as an officer of the law I cannot go behind that finding. I have no word of reproach, no fault to find with the results.[23]

The testimonies and strategies of this historic trial was presented in the El Paso Times (May 15, 1909) and makes for fascinating reading, almost like a script from an old Perry Mason television episode.

Journalist Owen White, an active El Pasoans at the time of the Clements murder and the Brown trial, reportedly stated that he believed Albert B. Fall hired one of the Coney Island bartenders to kill Clements for reasons relating to the assassination attempts. The bartender, he believed, fired a pistol though a dishcloth, muffling the sound, and then dropped the gun into a sink. The chief prosecutor in the case, Walter Howe, has stated that he thought that Brown did kill Clements, but in a 1946 interview, he stated that he had changed his mind, and said, "Tom Powers killed Mannie Clements."[24]

Tom Powers, whose tarnished reputation brought such disfavor from the president of the United States and drove Pat Garrett back into New Mexico to face his inevitable demise, became a wealthy and somewhat "respected" local businessman until the El Paso reform movement doused his financial and political standing. He found his final peace just a short distance from the burial site of Mannie Clements with its peculiar headstone at Evergreen Alameda Cemetery, both in the shadow of the disgraced Senator Albert B. Fall.

Four months after Clements' murder, his son-in-law and co-conspirator in the Garrett murder, Killin' Jim Miller, killed Deputy U.S. Marshal Gus Bobbitt in Ada, Oklahoma. About three weeks after that murder, an angry mob stormed the local jail and lynched Miller on April 19, 1909. He is buried at Oakwood Cemetery in Fort Worth, Texas.

"These people were relics of another age," historian C.L. Sonnichsen lamented, "trapped in an atmosphere of change, and gradually being ground under as they failed to adjust to a new era.[25]

Not all of the Sheldon's tenants and residents experienced such dark and somewhat dismal lives; many became significant pioneers in the growth of El Paso's economic, social, educational, and political future. Others left their mark with institutions that are part of today's El Paso. Ike Gettagno and Shibley Abdou Azar were two such successful entrepreneurs.

Ike Gettagno

The relationship of the Sheldon Hotel with local diamond and jewelry merchants goes back to the days when Lucius Sheldon first opened the Sheldon Block as an office building. George W. Hickox and William T. Hixson established their diamond and jewelry business at the southwest corner of the Sheldon Block building, just south of the west entrance facing the Little Plaza. Hixson maintained living quarters on the upper floors of the building.[26] Hickox and Hixon Jewelry later moved to 111 San Antonio Ave.[27] In 1898, A.H. Richards established his jewelry store on the east side of the Sheldon Block, next door to the Kelly Drug store[28] and remained there until the hotel conversion in 1900 when Richards moved to 103 S. El Paso Street.[29]

Young Turkish immigrant, Ike Gettagno, with his wife and two daughters, headed west after arriving in New York. Ike had the *immigrant's* dream of finding a new and exciting life. They boarded the California-bound train and headed for their future. As was the custom, trains routinely made overnight stops in El Paso on their way to the coast. When Ike got off the train to stretch his legs he walked around the downtown area. When he saw the Sheldon Hotel, he fell in love with the hotel and the city. He got his family off the train and began to build his new life in the border city and the Sheldon Jewelry was born.

In July 2006, the author interviewed Sidney Kligman, who with his son Greg, were the current owners of Sheldon Jewelry in an attempt to gain insight into the relationship between the Sheldon Hotel and Kligman's business. Kligman related the story of Ike (Isaac) Gettagno's early arrival in El Paso and shared the history of the Sheldon Jewelry operation as best as he could remember it. Ike Gettagno and his wife, Miriam operated the store for many years at the hotel, employing one of their daughters, Bea, to assist them when the physical demands on them became a problem. Bea was handicapped with a major leg issue and she even had difficulty running the store.

In 1920, the Sheldon Jewelry store moved from one location in the Sheldon Hotel to the southeast corner of the hotel at Oregon and Mills, the former location of the El Paso Bank and Trust. Gettagno, in announcing his move, placed the following ad in the El Paso Herald:

> Monday, July 19th, the Sheldon Jewelry Company opens the finest Jewelry Store in the Southwest. No expense has been spared to make the new store the most complete and beautiful in El Paso. Ample floor space, special lighting fixtures, and interior fittings have been brought to this city from the makers of the finest equipment in the country. The location is at the most important street corner in the shopping district, and therefore, accessible to shoppers. The stock displayed is without a rival anywhere. You are invited to visit us and to see for yourselves this latest and most modern jewelry house, which compares favorably with the Fifth Avenue shops, from which I have brought to you many of the specialties I recently acquired in the East. A cordial invitation is extended to attend on opening day, which will be a red letter day in the shopping history of El Paso. I. Gettago[30]

When Ike Gettagno died, at 91 in 1970 the year following Miriam's death at 87, they left the store in the hands of Bea. The other daughter, Irene had long since moved to California and had no relationship with the store.

Bea ran the store the best that she could, but with her parents gone she needed more assistance. She hired an experienced jewelry man from Ohio to assist in the management of the business, but for whatever reason, the relationship soon soured and Bea sold a portion of the business to Bernie Lauterbach and David Sanders in the 1950s. They were the proprietors of another jewelry store with several locations in El Paso. Employed as a store manager at the Lauterbach and Sanders firm, Sidney Kligman was transferred to the Sheldon Jewelry store to assist Bea Gettagno. Kligman indicated how impressed he was with Bea's jewelry knowledge, but was particularly impressed with her Juárez connections with rich Mexican consumers, who would become a significant base of the Sheldon's financial success.

With the financial help of Bob Brown, the owner of the Wholesome Dairy Company, Kligman took full control of the Sheldon Jewelry Company, and several years later bought out his silent partner in 1962. With the demise of the Sheldon in 1929, Kligman moved the store a block to the Trost designed Muir building on the southeast corner of Mills and Mesa. Kligman grew the company into three stores before consolidating the entire operation to their last location at 5446 N. Mesa in the late 1990s.[31]

For more than 100 years the Sheldon Jewelry Company had maintained its stellar reputation in the Southwest, so there was some melancholy when Kligman's son Greg, now the sole owner of the store, announced in December 2015, that the fabled institution was closing its doors forever, young Kligman just wanted to retire. He said, "I'm done, I'm ready to retire."[32]

Shibley Abdou Azar

Shibley Azar, a 20 year-old Syrian immigrant, arrived in El Paso around 1907 and opened a little hard candy shop in what is now downtown El Paso. When asked why he picked El Paso, he replied, "I came just for the glamor."[33] Five years later, he expanded his business to include nuts as well as candy and opened a shop with his brothers, George and Elias, in the Sheldon Hotel at 203 N. Oregon Street. The Azar Brothers Confection took over the space previously used by the Charles McCullough Confection shop. As his business grew, he expanded to a pecan shelling and packaging business and established an off-site factory. Shibley and his Syrian born young wife had, over the next several years, five children: daughter Aneica, Shibley Jr., twins Edward and Philipp, and daughter Nini. Shibley was 33 years old when he married his 15-year-old bride.[34] In 1921 Shibley, George, and Elias dissolved their partnership. Shibley continued with the Azar Nut Company moving from the Sheldon to 520 San Francisco Street,[35] while George moved to San Antonio and Elias headed for Los Angeles. The business continued to expand moving to larger facilities at 1620 Bassett Ave. and finally to a large factory located in the 1900 block of Mills Ave., becoming the fourth largest nut processing company in the United States by 1973.[36]

Shibley was getting most of his pecans from Texas growers in east Texas, south of San Antonio, but availability was becoming as problem as Texas grown pecans were considered the best. In 1926, he urged local farmers to establish pecan groves, "I think pecans could be grown in this [the upper Mesilla and lower Mesilla] valley."[37]

Taking his lead from Shibley, cotton farmer Deane Stahmann, who owned enormous acreage in both the upper and lower valleys, decided to beautify his home on the 4,000-acre cotton farm with the planting of pecan trees. Mardee de Wetter, poet, author, and former El Paso first lady, remembers the planting of the first pecan tree in front of the Stahmann's magnificent home when she was a young teenager in the mid-1930s.[38] By the time Stahmann had finished planting, he had planted 95,000 trees on his property along Highway 28, the Oñate Trail, just south of Mesilla, New Mexico.[39]

Shibley retired in 1948 and turned the business over to his three sons, Shibley Jr., and twins Ed and Phillip. The business grew enormously and the family sold the business to the Sara Lee Division of Consolidated Foods Company of Chicago in 1970. Through a series of mergers and acquisitions, the Azar Nut Company became a minor subsidiary of a growing conglomerate. Still highly profitable, the Azar brothers bought back their business from Consolidated Foods in 1973.[40]

Over the succeeding years, under Ed and Phillip's control, the Azar Nut Company became the third largest nut processing and packaging company in the United States. With its hard candy subsidiary, Sunshine Confections, and their institutional food service company, the company is now part of Mount Franklin Foods of El Paso. Mount Franklin Foods is itself a subsidiary of the Elamex Corporation a Mexican diversified manufacturing and real estate holding company that produces metal and plastic parts for the appliance and automotive industries, and food items related to its candy manufacturing and nut packaging business.

There is little doubt that many former tenants and residents of the Sheldon Hotel made a significant impact on both the positive and the negative aspect of life in the southwest. During the lifetime of the Sheldon Hotel, the first two decades of the twentieth century, El Paso had become a primary point of interest worldwide as was evidenced by the both the number and political significance of its national and international visitors. As world leaders, political and military, descended upon the "little village at the pass of the north," the Sheldon Hotel was in the middle of it all.

Notes and References

---

[1] There are hundreds of books and articles that chronicle these fascinating cases, particularly those by Metz, Sonnichsen, Gardner Selcer, and Owen White.

[2] The money man behind Michael Thomas "Tom" Powers was W.E. Truesdell. Powers died in January 1931 and is interred at Evergreen Alameda Cemetery.

[3] Trevizo, Jacqueline."1880s Brought First Theaters to Town." *Borderlands*. (EPPC Libraries.) Vol. 19, 2000, 2.

[4] Metz, (1974), 298.

[5] Ibid.

[6] Hervey, James M. "The Assassination of Pat Garrett." (*True West Magazine*. March-April 1961.), 42.

[7] No specific proof exists liking Fall to either the secret meeting or the actual killing of either Fountain or Garrett, it all remains circumstantial; interestingly so.

[8] White, Owen P. *The Autobiography of a Durable Sinner*. (New York: G.P. Putnam's Son, 1942.), 102-103.

[9] Jackson, Ken. "Joe Brown's murder trail." *El Paso Bar Journal*, October/November 2012, 11.

[10] Owen White writes that Clements was shot in the heart, but most other sources, including Sonnichsen support the back of the head shot.

[11] White, (1942), 103.

[12] "Mannie Clements: Keeping with the Family Tradition – Gunfighter." *The Tombstone Epitaph.* February 2002.

---

[13] Hunt, Frazier. *Cap Mossman: Last of the Great Cowmen.* (New York: Hastings House, 1951.)
[14] Martin, Jack. *Border Boss: Captain John R. Hughes – Texas Ranger.* (Austin: State House Press, 1990.)
[15] Boardman, Mark. "The Curious Murder of Manny Clements." True West Magazine. April 22, 2014.
[16] Jackson, (2012), 12.
[17] White, (1942), 103.
[18] *El Paso Times*. May 15, 1909.
[19] Jackson, (2012), 13.
[20] *El Paso Times,* May 15, 1909.
[21] Ibid.
[22] Ibid.
[23] Ibid.
[24] Jackson, (2012), 14.
[25] Ibid.
[26] *El Paso City Directory*, 1889.: 67. Sanborn Maps of Texas. (Austin: University of Texas, Perry-Castañeda Library Map Collection, El Paso 1888.), no. 2.
[27] *El Paso City Directory*, 1901, 190.
[28] Sanborn Maps of Texas. (Austin: University of Texas, Perry-Castañeda Library Map Collection, El Paso 1898.), no. 7.
[29] *El Paso City Directory*, (1888), 8.
[30] *El Paso Herald*, July 17, 1920.
[31] Sidney Kligman, Personal interview.
[32] "Shake up in the jewelry biz." *El Paso Inc.*, posted 11 Jan. 2016.
[33] *El Paso Herald*, November 23, 1967.
[34]1920 Census Record. Accessed 20 Dec. 2015.
[35] *El Paso Herald*, October 7, 1921.
[36] Ibid, January 26, 1973.
[37] Ibid, March 16, 1926.
[38] Mardee de Wetter, Personal interview. El Paso, August 15, 2012.
[39] *El Paso Herald*, April 4, 1953.
[40] Ibid, December, 18, 1973.

Chapter Twelve

Presidential Visitations

Over the years, many American presidents have visited El Paso, mostly having to do with issues of the border or the military at Fort Bliss. During the period of the Sheldon's life span, three sitting presidents and one former president visited El Paso and nestled into a relationship with the Sheldon. Presidents Benjamin Harrison, William McKinley, William H. Taft with the Mexican President Porfirio Díaz, and former President Teddy Roosevelt all came and left significant historical footprints. In the succeeding years, long after the passing of the Sheldon, El Paso has continued to be a political destination for the White House tending to issues surrounding immigration and international trade.

Benjamin Harrison

The twenty-third president of the United States, Benjamin Harrison, was the grandson of the ninth President, William Henry Harrison. Benjamin Harrison was the first sitting president to visit El Paso during his whirlwind train tour through the south beginning April 14, 1891. The month-long trip took him through major cities of the south and the Pacific Coast, with a multitude of stops as the tour returned in May to Washington, D.C. By traveling out into the country by train, whistle-stop presidential tours were a way for presidents to gauge public opinion and determine how the populace truly felt about existing political policies and to test the public's reaction about impending initiatives.[1] The White House billed the trip as a patriotic endeavor, not a political one. Harrison's attempt to travel 10,000 miles and deliver 140 impromptu speeches within the limit of 30 days was a remarkable achievement.[2]

Clearly, there is no direct relation between Harrison's visit to El Paso and the Sheldon Hotel, as the hotel didn't open for almost ten more years in 1900. Standing tall and casting a long shadow from its towering Queen Anne cupola on the train tracks but a hundred yards away, the Sheldon Block office building witnessed the presidential parade move through downtown to the El Paso Courthouse. The courthouse, opened in 1888, was an imposing structure sitting on the block bounded by Campbell, San Antonio, Kansas, and Overland streets. (The current site of the El Paso County Court and office building.) The parade of horse drawn carriages carried the official party as well as an invited party of dignitaries from Mexico through the parade route. President Díaz of Mexico was invited but chose not to attend and sent official stand-ins.[3]

President Harrison arrived in El Paso at 10:00 am on April 21, 1891[4], with a Mexican band playing, but that changed to Hail to the Chief when the cannon at the railroad depot boomed out its salute.[5] Harrison did the obligatory meet and greet, rode in the parade, and delivered a speech and was gone within two hours. The local newspapers headlined their stories of the presidential visit with, "All Hail! He has come. He has gone, and El Paso has every reason to feel more than proud." Ten years following President McKinley's visit, the paper again led the story of that visit with, "McKinley has come and gone."[6]

The Grand Central hotel became the scene of the visiting journalists who reported this major international affair throughout the world. The indirect relationship to the Sheldon and El Paso was that the presidential visit drew attention to the town and would set the stage for the next several presidential visits that would directly affect the Sheldon Hotel. President Harrison's mode of transportation and his speech provides some insight into the closing days of the 19th Century. There appeared to be some prohibition against the president traveling across the American boundary into Mexico, without permission, but the first lady had no such restrictions and traveled across the border and interacted with the citizens of Ciudad Juárez.[7]

The Pullman Palace Car Company of railroad entrepreneur George Pullman magnificently outfitted the presidential train in order to provide a self-contained transport since it was a whistle-stop process across the country that did not afford the time to stop and stay-over at various cities along the route. The train was composed of five cars behind the engine and tender. The first car contained both a generator for train lighting and pressure pumps; and a 141-gallon potable water storage tank. Also contained in this first car, named the Aztlan, was a library and smoking car outfitted with special ventilation to deal with the cigar smoke. The second car was the dining car named the Coronado that was composed of lots of silver ornamentation and plush red, white, and green upholstery. The president's car, the New Zealand was next. The New

Zealand had a double-drawing room and two private sleeping apartments. Behind the president's car was the Ideal, with a large drawing room and six adjacent smaller drawing rooms for the staff and guests. Bringing up the rear was the Vacuna, a library-observation car with 16 heavily upholstered chairs. The back end of the Vacuna had a seven by nine foot open speaking platform. Gilbert Gia has beautifully described details of the train in his article Presidential Visits to Bakersfield, 1880 and 1891.[8]

No sooner had the trip been announced, than the Boston Globe reported:

> These cars that are bearing Caesar Harrison and his presidential fortunes could buy a first-class farm in Kansas...He and his party of 14 are therefore expending at least $1,500 a day of somebody's money, for no one has any idea that Mr. Harrison will pay a solitary dime for all the splendor and luxury…A direct appropriation from the treasury for the purpose, it's plain, will never be made, but 'my Postmaster General' as Mr. Harrison calls Mr. Wanamaker has a vast discretion in the making of mail contracts, and how can he fail to deal generously during the next two years with the presidents of the great lines who have entertained him, and his master, as men were never [before] entertained by railroad princesses and potentates?[9]

It can only be assumed that in the subsequent train visitations to El Paso by Presidents McKinley and Taft, their accommodations were magnificently grander.

Harrison, speaking from in front of the El Paso County Courthouse delivered, yet again, another speech, something he was doing four and five times a day on his tour:

> My fellow citizens—I have been journeying for several days throughout the great state of Texas. We are now about to leave her territory and receive from you this parting salutation. Our entrance into the State was with every demonstration of respect and enthusiasm. This is a fitting close to the magnificent expression, which the people of this State have given to us. I am glad to stand at this gateway of trade with the great republic of Mexico. I am glad to know that it is not only a gateway of commerce, but a gateway of friendship; that not only do these hurrying vehicles of commerce bear the products of the fields and mines in mutual exchange, but that they have facilitated those personal

relations which have promoted and must yet more promote the friendliness of two independent liberty-loving peoples.

I receive with great satisfaction these tributes of respect which have been brought to me by the Governor of Chihuahua and the representatives of the army of Mexico. I desire to return to them and through them to the people of Mexico and to that illustrious and progressive statesman who presides over her destinies not only my sincere personal regard, but an assurance of the friendliness and respect of the American Government and the American people. [Political lathering of praise on the ruthless dictator Porfirio Díaz—political lathering hasn't changed a bit, only refined.] I look forward with interest to a larger development of our trade; to the opening of new lines of commerce and new avenues of friendship. We have passed that era in our history, I hope, when we were aggressive and unpleasant neighbors. We do not covet the territory of any other people, but do covet their friendship and those trade exchanges which are mutually profitable.

All commerce and trade rest upon the foundation of social order. You cannot attract an increased citizenship except as you give to the world a reputation for social order, in which crime is suppressed, in which the rights of the humble are respected, and where the courts stand as the safe bulwark of the personal and public rights of every citizen, however poor. I trust that as your city grows you will see that these foundations are carefully and broadly laid, and then you may hope that the superstructure, magnificent in its dimensions, perfect in its security and grace, shall rise in your midst.[10]

The second paragraph above is most prophetic in relation to the issues to surface at the turn of the century involving the border and the Mexican Revolution; and the third paragraph is significantly relevant to the issues facing us today. The presidential train departed El Paso after about two hours and headed west to Deming, New Mexico and on to the Pacific Coast. Among the multitude of stops was one in Bakersfield, California on April 25, to an enthusiastic crowd from the speaking platform of the observation car, the president said:

My friends, I am very much obliged to you for your friendly greeting and for these bouquets. You will excuse me if I seem a little shy of the

> bouquets. I received one in my eye the other day, which gave me a good deal of trouble…It has been a very long journey and has been accompanied with some fatigue of travel, but we feel this morning, in this exhilarating air and this sweet sunshine refreshed with your kind greeting, as bright and more happy than when we left the National Capital. We are one people absolutely; the government at Washington…is dependent upon no man. It is lodged safely in the affections of the people, and has its impregnable defense and assured perpetually in their love and veneration for law.[11]

From Harrison's speeches it is clear that political hyperbole and pandering to the crowd is certainly not new, just a bit more intense today. It has been recorded that Harrison was an intrinsically quiet man, but very outspoken regarding the openness of the White House. Years later he said of living in the White House:

> It is an office and a home combined—an evil combination. It is open to visitors from 10 am to 2 p.m.—without card of introduction. There is not a square foot of ground, not a bench, nor a shade tree that the President or his family can use in privacy. Until screens were placed in the windows of the private dining room, it was not an unusual incident for a carriage to stop in front of them while the occupants took a gratified view of the President and his family at their breakfast or lunch.[12]

Historians, as a rule, discount the success of the Harrison administration, except for his attempt at dealing with racial and civil rights issues, the passage of the Sherman Anti-trust Act, and the creation of National Forests. Some presidential firsts have been ascribed to Harrison. He had electric lighting installed in the White House and had the first lighted White House Christmas tree, and he was the first president to make a sound recording. Harrison had a fairly active post-presidential life, but succumbed to pneumonia on March 13, 1901 at the age of 67.

William McKinley

In April 1901, the twenty-fifth president of the United States, William McKinley, embarked on a cross-country train tour, similar to the one established by Benjamin Harrison. This would differ in two very specific ways. President Harrison's trip was purportedly non-political, while McKinley's venture was decidedly political. McKinley's travels would take two months rather than the whirlwind month-long trip by Harrison. While both presidents would travel through the South and on to the Pacific Coast, McKinley would include a northern route through New England, to include a stop at the Pan American Exposition to be held in Buffalo, New York. McKinley and his vice-President Teddy Roosevelt had achieved a decided victory over the Democratic candidate, William Jennings Bryan in the election of 1900.

McKinley had dealt with the Spanish-American War, post-Civil War sectionalism, and corporate trusts' issues. His success with these major obstacles aided his reelection. Now free of such major concerns and not dealing with reelection to a third term, he established a political agenda that would require enormous congressional backing from the Democrats and support from the general population. The president was hoping that his visits to the Southern states, including Texas, Southwest territories, and up the West Coast, would garner the public support he was seeking in order to influence each state's congressmen, in order to further advance his political agenda, especially from a Republican president from a northern state. He was full of confidence that the trip would ease the resentment of the post-Reconstruction South.

On April 29, he left Washington, D.C. on the special train in the special presidential palace car, the Olympia, accompanied by a large cadre of cabinet members and politicians. The number fluctuated throughout the trip, depending on each specific destination. Also along on the trip were the typical support staff and his wife Ida. As it turned out, having his wife along created enormous problems with his itinerary.

Ida S. McKinley was, sadly, extremely prone to major mood swings and other issues related to her chronic depression and epilepsy. Her depression seemed to magnify itself following the sudden death of the McKinley's second-born daughter, five-month-old Ida. Her mental health deteriorated even further with the death two years later of their first-born daughter, three-year-old Katie, from typhoid fever. Ida McKinley drifted into a world of morosity and invalidism.[13] She struggled bravely to keep up with her responsibilities as First Lady, but her decline was making even the simplest of efforts difficult.

The New York Times described the Pullman Palace car and the train that would take the president and his cabinet on their transcontinental tour as "a marvel of luxury. The president will sleep in the magnificent Pullman, the Olympia. A description of this car would fill an Oriental Prince with wonder apartments fit for monarchs are provided for the servants. Silk, satin, plush, and velvet are lavishly used in furniture decorations."[14] The 70-foot long car had accommodations for nine passengers.

The seven-car train consisted of the Atlantic, a combination baggage and smoking car, with a 21-foot lounge fitted with upholstered chairs, writing tables, and a library. The dining car, the St. James was connected to two compartment cars, each with seven staterooms and two drawing rooms. Two 12-section drawing room sleeper cars for the guests and cabinet members preceded the President's Olympia. The presidential car had a private dining room at one end that opened to an exterior speaker's platform. All the private rooms contained a toilet and were lavishly appointed in marble and onyx. All the cars, accented in hues of tomato red vermillion, with appropriate wainscoting and flooring stunned the press with its opulence.[15] The train was pulled by Engine 926 which was rotated with Engine 905, both painted and decorated with national symbols and flags. Before entering an expected stop, the engines were draped with floral decorations. Floral covered and gilded horse drawn carriages were previously arranged at the arrival destinations where street travel or parades were planned.

As experienced by President Harrison, President McKinley was the recipient of vicious attacks from political adversaries, critics, and the press regarding the opulence of the caravan of private cars. While presidential benefactors donated the expenses of the train, critics estimated that the cost of the train was in excess of $50,000, an enormously large sum in 1901. The press described, "The seven car train drawn by two locomotive engines, extravagant, frivolous, palatial and that it lacked not one thing to make luxury superlative."[16] The Pullman Company provided all the cars except the Olympia, while twenty-seven different railroad lines provided other services along the route. The criticism centered on the idea that the corporate and business elite had bought the president and that resulted in the possible public appearance that presidential favors were for sale.[17] These criticisms are a relevant commentary even in today's political arena.

The presidential train arrived in El Paso around 9:00 a.m. on Sunday, May 5, 1901 en route from San Antonio. Long before the arrival of the train, the depot and surrounding grounds were filled with spectators from both El Paso and Ciudad Juárez seeking to get a glance at the American president. When the train pulled into the depot, it traveled past the station to the extreme western end of the siding between Campbell and Kansas streets. There it would remain until it left on its trip westward at noon on Monday, May 6.

McKinley had requested that there be no celebrations on Sunday, as he preferred to spend a quiet day going to church and taking a leisurely carriage ride around El Paso even though there were extravagant goings on in Juárez celebrating Cinco de Mayo. Following a brief meeting with the Sheldon Hotel's manager, John Fisher, who was the chairman of the organizing committee and some city dignitaries on the rail siding, McKinley and his wife retired to the *Olympia's* private dining room for breakfast, in full view of the growing crowd. The organizing committee had arranged for the president and his party to attend the Methodist Church on Stanton Street, but the president changed to the Trinity Methodist Church because its pastor, Rev. W. Leftwich was an old friend.

The El Paso Times reprinted a previously published story regarding the presidential visit of 1901, it which it stated that the, "hotel gained notoriety in 1901 when President William McKinley spent the night there with three other members of his staff."[18] Actually, President and Mrs. McKinley, and the majority of the members of his traveling party spent the night on the train, despite the gracious invitation by Mr. Fisher on behalf of the Sheldon Hotel.

On the evening of May 5, the Sheldon Hotel and the city hosted a major banquet in honor of the news correspondents and other distinguished visitors. According to newspaper accounts:

> It was the most successful entertainment of the kind ever given in El Paso. The guests were unanimous and hearty in their expressions of appreciation, and as each guest was made to feel that, he was the especial object of attention bestowed, so each seemed to feel that he had a direct part in making the occasion such a conspicuous success. The menu was an elaborate one, and well served. The decorations of the dining room were marvelous for their abundance and originality. Special guest was Charles E. Smith, the Postmaster General and editor of the Philadelphia press.[19]

On the western portico of the Sheldon Hotel, a massive grandstand had been erected looking out into Pioneer Plaza (Little Plaza). The grandstand was covered with a large tent-like structure. The Sheldon was the largest building in town and was decked with flags and bunting all festooned with the colors of both the United States and Mexico.

Figure 38. President McKinley addresses crowd in Pioneer Plaza from Sheldon Hotel. 1901

Figure 39. President William McKinley (1843 – 1901)

There were 15-16 thousand people filling the plaza awaiting the arrival of the presidential party.[20] A flower bedecked parade of carriages and several marching bands arrived around 10:00 a.m. The president and his wife took their seats as the parade of brief welcoming speeches was delivered. President Porfirio Díaz did not attend as he was in the middle of a Congressional meeting in Mexico City, but his political and military representatives presented various greetings.

Seated adjacent to and around the president were the members of his cabinet, while to the left of the president was a specially built platform upon which many school children were standing, each bearing a small American flag. The children serenaded the crowd with singing America, the president was the first in the grandstand to stand. As the children sang the national anthem, the president could be seen with his lips following the words and his fingers beat time on the rim of his hat.[21]

McKinley reviewed the parade composed of companies of Mexican soldiers, three Mexican bands, marching members of benevolent and fraternal societies, veterans, and platoons of El Paso police and firemen. But by far the most engaging aspect of the parade was the 1200 school children lead by 150 local kindergarten children each dressed alike and carrying an American flag. Because of her health, Mrs. McKinley viewed the parade from a carriage.[22]

A significantly observed issue was the lack of presidential security. In the newspaper published later in the day:

> One thing that seems queer to the vast majority of citizens is the fact that the president goes from place to place entirely unattended and unguarded. Should an assassin desire to take his life it would be comparatively easy matter for him to carry out his designs and escape. Yesterday when the president drove to the church, there was not a policeman or other officer in sight. It is customary for the president to have no bodyguard, but to many people it seems strange that sensible precautions are not taken to protect the ruler of a great nation. It seems that common prudence would dictate such a course. However, republican simplicity abhors all the customs of European courts, and the president must take the same chances as any other man, although history bears evidence of the bloody work of assassins in this country. In reality the presidents stands little chance of losing his life, but to the monarchs of Europe his utter disregard of danger must appear ludicrous.[23]

In light of what happened to McKinley in the near future, this was a most foreboding editorial.

Following the reading of greetings from President Díaz, McKinley arose, stepped forward to thundering applause and cheers delivered what has often been referred to as a brilliant and significant speech:

> Mr. Mayor, General Hernandez, Governor Ahumada, and my fellow citizens. For the hospitality of the people of El Paso, which has been as delicate and considerable as it has been sumptuous, I beg to return my most sincere thanks. I am glad to be in this cosmopolitan city. I am glad to know that assembled here within your gates are the men of all races,

all nationalities and all creeds, but under one flag, the glorious Stars and Stripes. Acknowledging allegiance to no other Government but the United States of America, and giving willing sacrifice at any time, the country may call for the honor of our Nation and the glory of our republic I am glad to know that this city believes in expansion. That it has been doing a great deal of itself in the last four years. That it has more than doubled its population in the last half of the recent decade and given promise of still greater advancement and prosperity in the decade now at hand. You have here, my fellow citizens, the true national spirit, the spirit of enterprise, of development of progress, of building the structure of liberty and free Government on the broad and deep foundations of intelligence, virtue, morality and religion. …

My fellow citizens, if there was ever any doubt about ours being a united people, if you could have traveled with me 2800 miles from the capital at Washington to the city of El Paso, that doubt would have been completely dispelled. There was never such unity in the United States as there is at this hour. There was never so much for a Nation of 75,000,000 people to be proud of as at this hour. We have sent our army and our navy to distant seas and they have only added glory in our flag. They have brought no shame upon the American names. We sent them to China to rescue our beleaguered representatives and they did the work and did it magnificently with the approval of the civilized world.

But it is not in the art of war that we take our greatest pride. We are not a war-like people. We are not a military people. We never go to war unless we have to make peace. Our pride is in the art of peace, in material and intellectual development, in the growth of our country, in the advancement of our people in civilization, in the arts, in the sciences and in manufactures. This is the great pride of the American people. Here we are on the border line between the United States and another great republic and on this side of the line we have 35 American soldiers, and on that side of the line there are less than 150 Mexican soldiers. So that we are dwelling in peace and amity and causing "peace on earth and good will to men."

We want to settle our differences if we ever have any with the powers of the world by arbitration. We want to exhaust every peaceable means for settlement before we go to war, and while we have authority to raise 100,000 troops, the necessity does not exist for that number and

> we do not propose to raise but 55,000. So don't be alarmed about militarism or imperialism. We know no imperialism in the United States except the imperialism of a sovereign people.
>
> Having said this much, I only want to again express the pleasure which all of us feel at having been received so cordially and hospitably by this people and to thank you for having given us on Sunday as quiet and reposeful a time as though we had spent it at home.[24]

At the conclusion of the speech, McKinley had indicated that he wanted to look over into Mexico. The presidential entourage, including the Mexican officials, left the grandstand at the Sheldon Hotel and headed for the international boundary. At the United States Customs Office at the foot of the international bridge, both American and Mexican officials pointed out the 300-year-old Guadeloupe Church, the Spanish prison, and other Juárez landmarks. From his vantage point, he could see the Sierra Madre Mountains in the distance. Unlike President Harrison, who went halfway across the bridge to the boundary line, McKinley did not step on the bridge. Shortly after viewing Juárez, the McKinley party returned to the railroad siding area and the presidential train that was building up its steam. As the train pulled away from the depot, the demonstration of four bands and huge throngs of well-wishers made for an adoring gesture from an appreciative city. Local police had to clear the tracks so that the locomotive might start its next leg of the journey west. McKinley waved from the rear platform as the train picked up speed.

Notwithstanding Mrs. McKinley's serious health issues, she somehow developed an infection in one of her fingers early in the trip. After the trip doctor attempted to lance it, the infection grew worse after leaving Los Angeles. The infection had spread to her heart. This condition became life-threatening and after several days in San Francisco, even though she showed some improvement, the decision was made to cancel the remainder of the trip and return to their home in Canton, Ohio for an extended rest.[25]

Because of Mrs. McKinley's illness and the cancellation of the remaining half of the presidential tour, the June 13 visit to the Pan-American Exposition in Buffalo, New York, was rescheduled to September 6. Because of recent assassinations of world leaders in Europe by anarchists[26], George B. Cortelyou, McKinley's chief of staff, arranged for additional security to attend the president when he went to the exposition.

McKinley delivered his speech at the Temple of Music at the fairgrounds concluding:

> [The American Spirit] cannot be stopped. These buildings will disappear; this creation of art and beauty and industry will perish from sight, but their influence will remain to 'make it live beyond its too short living, with praises and thanksgiving.' Who can tell the new thoughts that have been awakened, the ambitions fired and the high achievements that will be wrought through this Exposition? Gentlemen, let us ever remember that our interest is in accord, not conflict, and that our real eminence rests in the victories of peace, not those of war. We hope that all who are represented here may be moved to high and nobler effort for their own and the world's good, and that out of this city may come, not only greater commerce and trade for us all, but, more essential than these, relations of mutual respect, confidence, and friendship which will deepen and endure. Our earnest prayer is that God will graciously vouchsafe prosperity, happiness, and peace to all our neighbors, and like blessings to all the peoples and powers of earth.[27]

In a cheerful mood following his speech around 4:00 p.m., McKinley moved to the steps outside of the Temple of Music and was accepting congratulations from individuals. Standing to his left was his chief of staff Cortelyou, when a medium-sized ordinary looking man approached as if to greet the President. The man's right hand was bandaged and he managed to get two feet in front of the President. When McKinley smiled and extended his hand, there rang out two sharp cracks. McKinley stood with a look of bewilderment and then collapsed having been shot in the abdomen. The gun was instantly knocked from the man's hand and he was thrown to the ground by two secret service agents, and "blows rained upon him by the infuriated detectives and soldiers."[28] The President was rushed to the nearby residence of John G. Milburn, the Exposition's president. After being attended to by all available doctors, the President succumbed to gangrene and infection 12 days later. It was reported that his last words were, "Good-bye all, good-bye. It is God's way. His will be done."[29]

McKinley's assassin was 29-year-old self-described anarchist, Leon Czolgosz, who it appeared, was a disciple of Emma Goldman. Goldman was the political activist who is credited with spreading anarchist philosophy throughout

North American and Europe. Czolgosz was tried for the murder of the President on September 23 in an eight-hour trial.[30] The court sentenced him to death by electric chair three days later. The sentence was carried out on October 29, 1901.

The Sheldon Hotel, host to the McKinley El Paso appearance, the site of the clear and sudden awareness of the absolute vulnerability of the president of the United States. The Sheldon was the thread that connected the cross-country trip to its tragic end at the Temple of Music, with the crack of two gunshots.

On September 14, Teddy Roosevelt assumed the presidency following the death of McKinley. Roosevelt became the first vice president to be elected to a full presidential term on his own. During his elected term, he shifted his political point of view and began to challenge big business and support labor unions. In this way, he was able to assure that his friend William Howard Taft would replace him in 1909.

William Howard Taft.

As the furtive winds of disconnect and despair began to spread over Mexico, it was becoming clear, even to the aged Porfirio Díaz himself that his 35-year-reign as dictator was fading. Díaz, over the broken backs of most of her citizens, brought impoverished and backward Mexico into the new century. Mexico was rich in resources and abundant with cheap labor, but lacked the financial backing to establish a robust industry and bountiful agriculture; he felt he needed to attract American and European capitalists with open arms. He took land and other assets from the poor to provide huge land grants to his cronies for their support in making the political climate accessible to the moneyed foreign investors, particularly from the United States.

During the extended reign of Díaz, some level of stability and order existed in Mexico, however, only at the cost of human liberty. Díaz pounded his will upon the masses as it suited him and his elite inner circle. While he served each term in an elected position, there existed no democratic government in Mexico where "due process" was a basic tenant and elections were equally free. Díaz was accustomed to the liquidation of his political enemies "like the petty criminals caught stealing foodstuffs or almost anything no matter how trivial, were shot, sometimes with a kangaroo court trial, frequently with none at all."[31] Díaz tolerated absolutely no opposition. He would dispatch his emissaries to seek out all who opposed him with orders to "Catch in the act, kill on the spot. 'Pan o Palo: bread for the hungry, to keep them quiet; a club for the recalcitrant, to keep them in line.'"[32]

Díaz's reign saw the exploitation of Mexico's natural resources through secret and preferential treatment of American investors like of J.P. Morgan, the Guggenheims, Rockefeller, Greene, Hearst, and They built the railroads, dug the mines, extracted the oil, and ran vast million-acre cattle ranches; all on the backs of the poor and disenfranchised millions of Mexicans. As the first decade of the twentieth century was ending, the Mexican elite, the cientificos and the American/European industrialists were controlling eighty percent of the economy—while the rest of Mexico was falling further into poverty. Díaz managed to lift political corruption to the highest level seen in the Western Hemisphere.

The hue and cries of land reform, political purge, and "Mexico for Mexicans" was getting louder. The seeds of rebellion were sown, particularly along the United States-Mexican border. El Paso became a haven for the growing anti-Díaz movement, with its easy access, weapon availability, and a most sympathetic population of Mexican exiles and, lest we forget, a greedy hoard of merchants.

It would therefore be to Díaz's advantage to show some American support and alliance with the United States, as well as to encourage the American political base to maintain its official stance of neutrality. Such a connection would, he thought, shore up his failing political position at home and help him etch out one more term as president. Consequently, through a series of back-channel efforts, he hoped to set-up a political summit with the American president, William Howard Taft. Díaz utilized Taft's very close friend, Judge L. R Wilfrey, who was in Mexico City involved in a legal case, to communicate to Taft about setting the summit.[33]

Taft also felt that such a meeting would help him politically. He had planned a cross-country tour to gain political capital following his support of the Payne-Aldrich Tariff Act that angered his fellow republicans. He was under immense attack from his fellow Republicans and the media for his Aldrich position, that to avoid criticism he needed to get away. He indicated to reporters, "that he was anxious to get as far away from Washington as he could. He would have gone to Alaska had it not been for Mrs. Taft's illness, and he had not given up hope of going to Hawaii soon. The proper way to gain an understanding of the country he claimed, was 'to go to the four corners and the places between.'"[34] Knowing that American business ventures had more than two billion dollars invested in Mexico, attending the summit became a valued act for him to undertake.

The invitations were sent:

The President of the United States to the President of Mexico.

June 25, 1909
My Dear Mr. President:
I have your courteous note of June 16th, sent me thru Judge Wilfley and thank you sincerely for your kindly attitude. I sincerely hope that in the course of a trip I hope to take in September and October in the Southwest I may have the pleasure of meeting you at El Paso or some convenient station at the border. It would gratify me very much to meet one in the flesh who had done so much to establish order and create prosperity in his own country and in so doing has won the admiration of the entire world.
Sincerely yours,
Wm H. Taft.

The President of Mexico to the President of the United States.

July 6, 1909
My esteemed Mr. President:

I have received your courteous letter of the 25th of last month, in which you have been pleased to very graciously and amicably invite me to meet you at El Paso or other station of our frontier, during the trip which you propose to make in the Southwest of your country in the months of September and October. I shall be most pleased to know personally the illustrious citizen who has deserved the votes of his compatriots for first magistrate of your great nation, neighbor, and friend of Mexico. I accept by this your courteous invitation, provided that our meeting can be arranged for some days after the opening of the Mexican Congress, which takes place on the 16th of September.
With most cordial expressions of friendship,
I remain, etc.
Porfirio Diaz [35]

The two governments agreed on July 9 that the summit meeting would be held October 16, 1909 at El Paso. There was some immediate resistance from El Paso because of a previously arranged civic event, so the meeting place was tentatively moved to San Antonio. After a security assessment was made of San

Antonio, the locale was shifted back to El Paso and the city would have to reschedule their other event. It was determined that San Antonio had a large population of Mexican exiles that could have created demonstrations protesting Díaz's presence.[36]

On September 14, 1909, the 27th President, eventually the 10th Chief Justice of the United States, and the president credited with instituting the income tax, left by train on his political tour of southern and western states. This majestic train was pulled by two engines and consisting of two Pullman sleeper cars, two additional cars for officials, a dining car, and the Pullman presidential car, the Mayflower. A pilot train for security purposes preceded the presidential special by fifteen minutes.[37] The train would arrive in El Paso on the morning of October 16 for what the press called the Most Eventful Diplomatic Event in the History of the Two Nations.[38] It would be the first meeting in history between a sitting president of the United States and the president of Mexico. In fact, it would be the first time that a sitting American president would travel to Mexico.

The Presidential Pullman: The Mayflower

The Pullman Company had elaborately decorated the Mayflower for its previous user, W.C. Greene, the copper magnate and founder of the Consolidated Copper Company associated with the riot-driven Cananea Mines strike in Sonora, Mexico in 1906. The presidential use of the Mayflower extended beyond Taft. Three years after Taft used the car to travel to El Paso, former president Theodore Roosevelt used it to campaign against Taft for another run at the presidency in 1912. The Mayflower had taken him to Milwaukee on October 14, 1912 for a speech. Roosevelt, coming out of his hotel, was approached by John Schrank who stuck a .38 revolver in Roosevelt's chest and fired point blank. Roosevelt had been wearing his Army overcoat and had his 50-page speech folded up in his breast pocket. The assassin was immediately taken away and Roosevelt demanded to be taken to the site of his speech. He delivered his speech with a dime-size hole in his chest. During his speech for the Progressive Party, (nicknamed the Bull Moose Party) as candidate for president, he told the audience: "Friends, I shall ask you to be as quiet as possible. I don't know whether you fully understand that I have just been shot—but it takes more than that to kill a Bull Moose. But fortunately I had my manuscript, so you see I was going to make a long speech, and there is the bullet—there is where the bullet went through—it probably saved me from it going into my heart. The bullet is in me now, so that I cannot make a very long speech, but I will try my best."[39] The would-be assassin was soon committed to a Wisconsin state mental hospital where he died from natural causes 29 years later.

Figure 40. The St. Regis Hotel, El Paso citizens and dignitaries awaiting arrival of President Taft prior to his meeting with Diaz at the Chamber of Commerce. 1909 (El Paso County Historical Society)

The Taft Arrival in El Paso

The presidential train pulled into the El Paso depot around 9:00 a.m. on October 16, 1909 and proceeded slowly west on the tracts to the intersection of North Oregon Street and Main, just half a block from the Sheldon Hotel, but only a few steps from the St. Regis Hotel on the west side of San Jacinto Plaza. President Taft stepped off the Mayflower's rear platform into one of the most tightly woven, scripted, and choreographed diplomatic ventures the State Department had detailed. Every movement and wording of the presidential comments and toasts were specifically outlined. Each of the invited dignitaries, in top hat and tails, stood in a receiving line on the sidewalk as the President moved inside to the St. Regis. The hotel's elaborately festooned dining room was the site of a breakfast with state and city dignitaries. The surrounding area was crowded with El Paso and Juarez citizens hoping to get a glace as the President moved through the crowd.

As the crowd crushed against itself, 14-year-old Noll Morgan got into a fight with 16-year-old Lawrence Wimlier as they attempted to see the presidential party. Morgan pulled a knife and stabbed his schoolmate. The numbers of people and the chaotic nature of the scene prevented an ambulance from attending to Wimlier before he died just yards from the hotel entrance and the breakfasting President. Someone was thoughtful enough to tear down two American flags and draped them across the youngster's lifeless body. The heartbroken Morgan was immediately arrested and taken to jail. The orchestrated event hardly missed a beat.[40]

As the President emerged from the breakfast, he entered a waiting carriage and rode around the plaza to witness some 4000 schoolchildren waving flags and singing, My Country Tis of Thee. As the caravan of carriages and their escorts left the plaza area, they went to the newly opened Trost designed Chamber of Commerce building at 310 San Francisco Street, where the President would meet with President Díaz for a brief meeting. The Chamber building was about three blocks west of the Sheldon Hotel, behind where the current Convention Center and Southwest Field are located.[41]

With the Grand Central Hotel lost in ashes, the only two significant hotels at the time were the cigar king Ernst Kohlberg-owned St. Regis and the Sheldon Hotel. The role played by the St. Regis was quite dramatic with the arrival of the President and the official breakfast. The Sheldon and the St. Regis were both hosts to the large numbers of newspaper men, Texas Rangers, special deputies, and the secret service agents from both countries. More significantly, the Sheldon actually hosted the President.

The Sheldon's proprietor, John Fisher, was the leasee of the hotel operations, while the building and the land was managed by H.B. Stevens who represented the Brooklyn-based owner, Lucius M. Sheldon. Fisher was fond of saying when speaking about the success of the Sheldon Hotel, that President Taft was a guest when he came to El Paso to meet with the Mexican President.[42] This is not completely accurate. The President was in El Paso for only 11 hours for the entire event. He used the Presidential Suite at the Sheldon for several hours to rest between his Chamber of Commerce meeting, speedy trip across into Juárez to greet Díaz on Mexican soil, his return trip to review the military parade, and to make a few comments at Cleveland Square Park where the current El Paso Museum of History and the main El Paso Public Library are located. He then retired to the Sheldon to rest before he returned to Juárez that evening for the fancy banquet held in his honor by President Díaz at the Juárez Custom House. After that, he returned to the Mayflower and the train left El Paso.

The Historic Event: Taft-Diaz Meeting

The Taft-Diaz Meeting was heavily scripted, the President traveled by carriage from the St. Regis, around the San Jacinto Plaza to the Chamber of Commerce building, where he would await the arrival of President Díaz. In all his glory, bedecked in a flashy military uniform, the Mexican president arrived about 11:00 a.m. in a stately gilded carriage, often described as being "among the most elaborate in the world."[43] A large contingent of American soldiers escorted Díaz. As Díaz crossed the international border, he was asked by an Associated Press reporter about his impressions of the United States. Díaz responded with full political flair: "The high and well-understood citizenship of this virile people, who have succeeded in interpreting the propositions of government promulgated by the immortal Washington and his illustrious compatriots, has made practical in their country the best of all governments—the government of the people by the people. My impression is most pleasing."[44]

Figure 41. El Paso Chamber of Commerce Building, site of the Taft-Diaz meeting on the American side of the border. 1909

(El Paso Public Library, Aultman Collection)

The two Presidents exchanged greetings and entered the Chamber's main room. The two heads of state retired to a private room, with only Enrique Creel and a bottle of champagne in attendance for a fifteen-minute private meeting. (Creel, the notorious banker, was also the Mexican Ambassador to the United States.) There were no interpreters, as both men were bilingual and Creel could provide any necessary language assistance if necessary.

Whether the topic of the Chamizal[45] dispute was discussed was never determined, however, there had been previous agreement between the two governments that no national flags of either country would fly over this section of land, through which ran the road to and from the border bridge and the area in south El Paso was declared a neutral territory. Following the brief meeting, Díaz and his party left the Chamber building and returned to Juárez. Within the hour, President Taft and his party left for the Santa Fe Street international bridge and arrived at the middle of the bridge at high noon. Taft changed into a waiting Mexican carriage and was driven to the Juárez Customs House escorted by Mexican police and military bands for a brief ceremonial visit with Díaz.

Figure 42. Pomp and circumstance of the Taft-Diaz meeting in Juarez and El Paso. 1909. (El Paso County Historical Society)

After a few minutes with Diaz, Taft returned to the center of the bridge, got into the American carriage and was escorted by a large contingent of soldiers and escorted to a reviewing stand at Cleveland Square. From his place in the reviewing stand, the President watched a robust military parade that lasted over an hour, with marching units and veteran's groups. At the closure of the parade, the President delivered his only official address of the visit to El Paso:

> For the first time in history, except once, and that was when Theodore Roosevelt stepped over the border in Panama [1906], when we were so

> mixed up on the Zone with Panama that it did not seem to be quite stepping out of the country, a president of the United States has stepped upon foreign soil and enjoyed the hospitality of a foreign government. … The prosperity of the United States is largely dependent upon the prosperity of Mexico, and Mexico's prosperity depended upon ours, at least, in this part of the country. …An event like this that marks the undying friendship of the two countries is one in which any who takes part may well have pride.[46]

Figure 43. Parade in front of the Sheldon Hotel celebrating the Taft-Diaz meeting, 1909.
(El Paso Public Library, Aultman Collection.)

Figure 44. President William Howard Taft (1857-1931)

At the conclusion of the parade, Taft left the podium and retired to the Presidential Suite at the Sheldon Hotel, where he would rest until he was escorted ceremoniously back to the Juárez Customs house for an elaborate state banquet. Details of the banquet, the menu, the attendees, the decorated surroundings and all the pomp of the event, can be read about in Crawford's[47] and Crippen's,[48] and any national newspaper of October 16 or 17, 1909. The two presidents were each presented with a solid gold goblet and made the predictable political toasts. President Díaz was the first to raise his goblet:

> I raise my glass to the everlasting enjoyment by the country of the immortal Washington of all the happiness and prosperity, which justly belong to the intelligent industry and eminent civisms that are the characteristics of the mannerly and cultured American people and to the enduring glory of its historic founders. I raise my glass to the personal happiness of its illustrious president who has come to honor us with his presence and friendship.

President Taft's response, in part:

> I rise to express in the name and on behalf of the people of the United States their profound admiration and high esteem for the great, illustrious, and patriotic president of the Republic of Mexico... The people of the United States respect and honor the Mexicans for their patriotic devotion, their will, and for their steady advance in industrial development and moral happiness. ...I drink to my friend, the president of this great republic, to his continued long life and happiness and to the never-ending bond of mutual sympathy between Mexico and the United States.[49]

At the conclusion of the festivities, President Taft returned to El Paso in the same manner that he had done previously that afternoon. This time, however, it was under the cover of darkness except for the illumination provided by the extra lighting that had been set up along the streets leading to downtown El Paso. The Presidential procession, preceded by a cavalry escort, got lost on their way back to The Mayflower at Oregon and Main streets. The president's entourage lost fifteen or twenty minutes wandering the dark streets of El Paso, until a local and somewhat startled citizen noticed the parade was meandering up a dark street in the opposite direction of the waiting train. Eventually, the president and his party found the train, and departed El Paso around 8:00 p.m. for his brother's ranch near San Antonio for several days of rest.[50]

All the while, a steaming cauldron of rebellion and unrest was brewing throughout Mexico, particularly in the northern Mexican states. The future of the Díaz government was clearly in doubt as was the concern about the fortunes of the American capitalists, who had so much to lose with their huge investments in Mexico. Everything would change in the next year. So tenuous was the political climate that the American military moved over three thousand soldiers from Fort

Sam Houston near San Antonio, into the El Paso area. Large numbers of elite Mexican troops filled the streets and alleys of Juárez.[51] El Paso police augmented their ranks with over a hundred specialized deputies to add to the soldiers, Texas Rangers, and various federal agents. The climate, outside the Custom House and the Chamber of Commerce building was foreboding and tense.

As Taft headed to San Antonio, he dictated a letter to his wife and expressed his impressions of the meeting with Díaz. The letter, on White House stationary and dated October 17, 1909, reads in part:

> Reaching El Paso about nine o'clock, we had a ceremonious breakfast, at which no speeches were made. Then wearing a light gray tie and light gray gloves, I proceeded with my body guard to the Chamber of Commerce building, which had been decorated with a view to the reception of President Díaz. We had here congrated (sic) a full regiment of Infantry, two squadrons of Cavalry, and two batteries of Artillery, under the command of a Brigadier-General. The town of El Paso has a population of about forty thousand, of whom perhaps six or seven thousand are Mexicans. It is a very enterprising place, and while in Texas, is really more connected with New Mexico than it is with Texas, and as it is the crossing place for the business between Mexico and the United States by rail, its business is assuming large proportions. The Chamber of Commerce is a very enterprising body. They took charge of our side of the reception.
>
> Díaz arrived with his suite and with a small escort of his mountain guards who were gorgeously clad in helmets and feathers, and he himself had a uniform with decorations emblazoning his appearance, which quite outshone your husband's civil garb. The old man, who is said to be about eighty years old, is really most remarkable in point of agility, quickness of perception and dignity of carriage. There is great fear, and I am afraid a well-founded fear, that should he die, there will be a revolution growing out of the selection of his successor, as Americans have about $2,000,000 [error: meant two billion] of capital invested in the country, it is inevitable that in case of a revolution or internecine strife we should interfere, and I sincerely hope that the old man's official life will extend beyond mine, for that trouble would present a problem of the utmost difficulty. I am not quite sure at whose instance the meeting was had, but I do know that I received a communication, perhaps directly from the old man, of an informal character, saying how glad he would be to have such a meeting brought

about. He thinks, and I believe rightly, that the knowledge throughout his country of the friendship of the United States for him and his government will strengthen him with his own people, and tend to discourage revolutionists' efforts to establish a different government.

I had a private conversation with the old man through Mr. Creel, formerly Ambassador to the United States, who speaks English beautifully, and who is part American at any rate, and who was complimented at my suggestion that he act as interpreter in our confidential interview. ... I returned the visit within twenty minutes or more, and was received in the Custom House of the city of Juárez on the other side of the Rio Grande.

I experienced no particular emotions in crossing from our territory into that of a foreign government and certainly encountered no danger. Reports of the presence of cranks, socialists, and revolutionary people were rife, but Wilkie, the head of the Secret Service, was here with a number of agents, and everything was done which ought to have been done to protect us. Indeed I think there was probably more than enough, but all is well that ends well.

Returning from the visit, we had a military review of the United States troops and some of the state troops and civic bodies, and then I made a speech to an audience of perhaps five or six thousand people who had gathered in the park. Then I went back to the hotel [Sheldon] and had a little lunch and went to bed and got one and a half hours sleep or more. Then I saw some Yale men and some Ohio people, The Ohio people gave me a sombrero of Mexican manufacture, which will hang upon the wall and form one of a number of reminders of this trip.
Then having put on evening dress, I went across the river again, and was received by President Díaz in the same place, but they had fitted up in the patios of the Custom House a most beautiful banquet hall, ornamented in admirable taste and having every appearance of a State salon. The President sat in a big chair on one side of the table, and I sat in a big chair just opposite him. ...Wilfley [close friend and confidant of Taft's] was here and tired me. He is as conceited and as bumptious as ever, and was very anxious to have me say a good word for him to Díaz, in order to facilitate his bringing of a claim for a mine which he hopes will be successful. I don't know anything of the justice of his claim, and I did not say anything to Díaz about it and don't intend to. Wilfley pressed himself forward when General Díaz and I withdrew

after the dinner for a little private conversation, hoping that I might say something to Díaz about it, but I was blind and did not see him, or at least affected not to see his desire to have me present him to Díaz. He has the cheek of a government mule. I am getting really quite disgusted with him. ...

I think the Mexican Government must have gone to great expense in preparation for the welcome, and certainly they manifested every possible pleasure at my coming. I am glad to have taken part in this event, which is unique in the history of any country in connection with this. I am quite sure that the meeting will make for good in the relations between Mexico and ourselves, and in the strengthening of the power of the existing government there. ...

We left El Paso last night about nine o'clock and we are now riding through the most God-forsaken part of Texas, hoping to reach San Antonio about half past seven tonight. ... It is now the 17th which leaves but fourteen days remaining of this month, and ten days in November, which will bring me to the White House and to you. I believe the trip has been a success. It may be that I am not a good judge. It may be that it has not accomplished the purposes which I started out to accomplish. One can hardly tell in respect to this until some little time has elapsed. But whatever happens, it will be a delight to be with you again and to settle down more or less quietly under the roof of The White House

With lots of love for Eleanor and Johnny and a great deal for yourself,
Your loving Will[52]

Presidential Security Issues: Assassination Attempt

The international fervor of anarchism had continued to grow which resulted in significant changes in presidential security. When Taft was informed that special precautions had been taken in regards to his safety, he roared with laughter, inquiring, "Why should you have worried? If anyone wanted to get me, he couldn't very well have missed such an easy target."[53] He indicated that security precautions had so improved that he believed no assassin could again walk up to a president with a revolver under his handkerchief, as happened to McKinley. He expressed that having a constant guard was a great burden to the president, adding, "It is a little difficult to get away from the feeling that one is under surveillance himself rather than being protected from somebody else. If a person is determined to kill a president, and he is willing to give up his life for it, no such protection will save him. The worst danger is from those who have lost part or all of their reason and whom the presence in the community excites."[54]

On October 15, a Chicago newspaper released a story about the discovery of a plan to assassinate both President Taft and President Díaz in El Paso. The story related that Chief Wilkie, head of the Secret Service, had sent several agents, disguised as laborers, to infiltrate anarchist and socialists organizations to identify the men who were planning the attack. Responding to the story, Wilkie said that the story about assassinating the two presidents was "rot." Wilkie added, "A large number of Mexicans had been arrested as suspects, but no importance attaches to their arrest. If there was any danger to either of the presidents, they would not be brought to El Paso or Juárez."[55]

Notwithstanding Chief Wilkie's denial of a potential plot, John Hays Hammond, a wealthy friend, and travel companion of Taft, arranged to hire a well-respected private bodyguard, Frederic Russell Burnham, to join the presidential train and put together a special protection detail to bolster the president's protection in El Paso. The President had a huge cadre of protectors from all types of specialized fields. A reporter for a New York newspaper wrote:

> There have been secret service men, militia, regulars, cowboys, police and rangers, and Chief Wilkie to meet them in El Paso, but with Major Frederick Russell Burnham along, the necessity for Chief Wilkie's presence is not apparent. The Major is so well known along the border that it is said the fact that he is seen in the crowd will ensure the departure of all troublemakers. There is a superstition down here that he has eyes in the back of his head, and that he can produce a gun from the air, if necessary. ...He is the most modest and the quietest blue-eyed 5 foot 4 inch man yet encountered on the Presidential tour, though he has the record here and in South Africa of having killed at least twenty men, either in self-defense or in the line of duty as an officer.[56]

As it turned out, Hammond's intuition about hiring Burnham was correct. On patrol outside of the El Paso Chamber of Commerce building, Burnham and a Texas Ranger, Charles R. Moore, were looking for anything suspicious. They spotted an individual who appeared to be writing in a notebook, but something just didn't look right. Burnham and Moore moved closer to the man. Moore grabbed his arm as Burnham took his wrist. They discovered a small "pencil gun" often referred to as a "palm pistol" concealed in his right hand, just a few feet from Presidents Taft and Díaz.[57] The man was held briefly and released following the end of the meetings. The incident was conducted so quietly and smoothly that it didn't arouse any attention.[58]

During the security patrol of the downtown area, more than a hundred guns and knives were temporarily confiscated by the agents, probably from just ordinary Texans not potential assassins.[59]

Notes and References

---

[1] Frantz, Edward. "A March of Triumph? Benjamin Harrison's Southern Tour and the Limits of Racial and Regional Reconciliation." *Indiana Magazine of History*. Vol. 100 No. 4. (2004), 293-320.
[2] Hedges, Charles. *Speeches of Benjamin Harrison*. (New York: John Lovell Co.,1892.), 290.
[3] *El Paso Herald*. June 5, 1963.
[4] In an article published by the *El Paso Times*, August 26, 2010, reprinted from an article originally published June 6, 1963, columnist Art Leibson stated that the Harrison train arrived at 7 am. This contradicts all other records of the president's visit to El Paso.
[5] *El Paso Times*. August 26, 2010.
[6] Ibid.
[7] Ibid.
[8] Gia, Gilbert P. "Presidential Visits to Bakersfield, 1880 and 1891." *Historic Bakersfield and Kern County* www.gilbertgia.com , 6-8.
[9] Ibid, 8-9.
[10] Hedges, 334-335.
[11] Gia, 11. It is interesting to note that while Gia sources this quote to the *Kern County Californian* (predecessor to the *Bakersfield Californian*), May 2, 1891, the speech is completely left out of the Hedges book of Harrison Speeches.
[12] Harrison, Benjamin. *This Country of Ours.* (New York: Charles Scribner, 1897.), 177-178.
[13] Gould, Lewis L. *American First Ladies: Their Lives and Their Legacy.* (New York: Garland Publishing, 1996.), 281-282.
[14] *New York Times*. April 5, 1901.
[15] Ibid.; Jandura, Greg. "The Pan-American Exposition 1901. Chapter 1, McKinley and Prosperity" http://trainweb.org/wnyrhs/panam1901.htm
[16] "About the McKinley Excursion," Hereford Reporter (Texas) May 10, 1901.

[17] Klaess, William. "The President of the Whole People: William McKinley's Visit to Texas in 1901." Thesis: Texas Christian University.
[18] *El Paso Times*, March 10, 2010.
[19] *El Paso Herald*. May 6, 1901.
[20] Clarence Harper Oral History.
[21] *El Paso Herald*: May 6, 1901.
[22] *San Francisco Call*, May 7, 1901.
[23] Ibid.
[24] Ibid.
[25] Gould, 291.
[26] "Against all authority." Anarchism is the political philosophy that disavows any form of government. All societies and their institutions should be self-governed.
[27] McClure, Alexander K. *The Authentic Life of William McKinley: Our Third Martyr*. (Washington, D.C.: W.E. Scull, 1901.), 310.
[28] Ibid, 316.
[29] Ibid, 333.
[30] Ibid, 452.
[31] Smith, Cornelius C., Jr. *Emilio Kosterlitzky: Eagle of Sonora and the Southwest Border.* (Glendale, CA: The Arthur H. Clark Company, 1970.), 154.
[32] Ibid, 156.
[33] Harris and Sadler (2009), 1.
[34] Anderson, Judith. *William Howard Taft: An Intimate History*. (New York: W.W. Norton, 1981.), 175.
[35] Library of Congress, Accessed 7 Mar. 2016.
[36] Harris and Sadler (2009), 3.
[37] Milliorn, Mark. "The Other Presidential Car." *Random Thoughts by Mark Milliorn.* 5 May 2015. markmilliorn.blogspot.com Accessed 6 March 2016.
[38] *El Paso Herald*, October 16, 1909.
[39] O'Toole, Patricia. "The Speech That Saved Teddy Roosevelt's Life." Smithsonian.com November 2012. Accessed 7 March 2016.
[40] *New York Times*, October 17, 1909.
[41] Dawson, Ron. "William Howard Taft's Trip to El Paso to meet Mexico's President Porfirio Díaz in 1909." *El Paso & Southwestern Flyer*. (Historical Railway and Locomotive Society, n.d.)
[42] Sheldon Remodeling documents from the Henry Trost Historical organization. http://www.henrytroast.org Accessed 5 March 2010.
[43] *El Paso Times*, October 17, 1909.

[44] *Los Angeles Herald*, October 17, 1909.

[45] The Chamizal Dispute was a conflict involving about 600 acres of land between El Paso and Ciudad Juárez caused by the natural shift in the Rio Grande, which had been previously determined to be the international boundary. The area was once the only pathway between the two border cities and tensions were very high, especially during the Taft-Díaz Meeting in 1909. The issue was finally resolved on September 25, 1964 between American President Lyndon B. Johnson and the Mexican President Adolfo Mateos.

[46] Crawford, Charlotte. "The Border Meeting of Presidents Taft and Díaz." *Password* (1958) Vol. 3, 86-96

[47] Ibid.

[48] Crippen, Robert B. "Celebration on the Border: The Taft-Díaz Meeting, 1909." *Password*, (Fall 1984), 115-123.

[49] *El Paso Herald*, October 17, 1909.

[50] *New York Times*, October 17, 1909.

[51] *New York Times*, October 13, 1909.

[52] William Howard Taft, Library of Congress.

[53] Ross, Ishbel. *An American Family: The Tafts, 1678 to 1964*. (Cleveland: World Publishing Company, 1964.), 231.

[54] Ibid.

[55] *The Chicago Journal*, October 15, 1909.

[56] Kemper, Steve. *A Splendid Savage: The Restless Life of Frederick Russell Burnham*. (New York: W.W. Norton, 2016.), 325-326.

[57] Ibid. and Harris and Sadler (2009), 213

[58] Ibid, 214.

[59] Kemper, 325-326.

Chapter Thirteen

Change of Ownership

The Taft-Díaz meeting in Juárez and El Paso did little to quell the fervor of discontent and unrest; it seemed to feed the growing resentment against the dictator. No area of Mexico was more attuned to this than the sister-cities along the Rio Grande. During the early run-up to the revolution, the Sheldon Hotel was attracting many different kinds of people who were more than willing to violate the United States' position on the maintenance of neutrality in the growing conflict. The Sheldon Hotel was becoming the epicenter of revolutionary activity in El Paso.[1] Along with these activists were the hundreds of corporate sales representatives from the East Coast and Midwest industrial centers who were trying to sell their goods and services to the burgeoning community and to participate in getting a piece of the action of the smuggling enterprise that was thriving in the border town. They too, became residents at the Sheldon Hotel

Federal agents descended upon El Paso in a major attempt to deal with the time-honored tradition of the smuggling, which was only experiencing a change in the nature of goods and the direction that they were going. Arms and barbed wire to Mexico replaced the smuggling of Chinese into the United States. The consensus among El Pasoans was that smuggling was not a criminal enterprise; it was just the financial life of El Paso. These agents became a regular part of the activity that was taking place at the Sheldon Hotel.

The rich and powerful political bosses and land barons used the Sheldon Hotel as a way station on their way to the financial havens in New York and the political center of Washington, D.C. Enrique Creel rented the entire second floor of the Sheldon for his family as they were traveling to Washington where he would be based and serve as the Mexican Ambassador.[2] Creel's father-in-law, General Don Luis Terrazas, Governor of Chihuahua frequently would rent entire floors of the Sheldon for a variety of purposes.[3] Terrazas and Creel together owned over 14 million acres of Mexican land, mostly in Chihuahua. Less than one percent of the families of Mexico owned 85 percent of the nation.[4]

The growing success of the reform movement to rid or curtail the vice activities in El Paso, only encouraged the growth and movement of vice to Juárez. Tourists from the East on their way to California would stop off for a few days in El Paso which would result in day trips across the border for a wild good time, Juárez became El Paso's greatest asset, as many of these tourists would become customers of the Sheldon Hotel. This only increased as the United States moved into the Prohibition era.[5] The County Medical Society, the Rotary and Kiwanis organizations, among a host of other social and fraternal groups, used the hotel for meetings and events on a regular basis.[6]

All this activity began to wear on the Sheldon Hotel and it was becoming apparent that before long, she would be in need of serious maintenance and remodeling. Lucius Sheldon was growing weary of the contentious relationship that he was having with his leasee, John Fisher, the proprietor and manager of the hotel operation. [7] At the same time, Mr. Sheldon was experiencing some serious health issues and turned the Sheldon Hotel's affairs over to his lawyer son, Henry K. Sheldon, Jr. Henry Jr. acted on Lucius' behalf with H.B. Stevens, the Sheldon family's business manager in El Paso.[8] By 1905, Lucius Sheldon, at 76, was suffering from, what doctors described as, senility. Over the next three years, he removed himself from all matters of business, relying on his son to handle everything. Henry K. Sheldon, Jr. began to sell off Sheldon properties in El Paso and elsewhere.[9] It is important now to stress that it is customary for the land and buildings of hotels to be owned by one entity and the hotel branding, operation, and management is done under a lease to different entity. This was certainly the case of the Sheldon Hotel and it remains the generalized business model today, although some hotel companies own the property and operate the hotel as a single facility. As a result, following the line of succession of the Sheldon's ownership becomes, at times, confusing and complicated.

On November 25, 1908, Lucius M. Sheldon died at the age of 79 from complications associated with senility at his retreat home in Westport Point, Massachusetts. He was buried at Green-Wood Cemetery in Brooklyn in the family plot on Sheldon Knoll.[10] Harriet survived her husband for eight years and was also laid to rest at Green-Wood.

On March 12 1907, Henry K. Sheldon, Jr. with the aid of H.B. Stevens arranged to sell his father's building to Mr. and Mrs. Charles DeGroff for approximately $340,000.[11] The Sheldon Hotel had recently been assessed by the county clerk's office as having a value of $148,000.[12] The DeGroffs were then the owners of the Orndorff Hotel (formerly the Vendome Hotel) that was half a block away on the east side of San Jacinto Plaza. They operated the two hotels as the Sheldon Hotel Company, composed of the Charles DeGroff, Alzina Orndorff DeGroff, her son Burt Orndorff, and a silent partner named Bradford Hardie. The purchase of the Sheldon by the DeGroffs was pronounced by the local newspapers as the largest property deal in the history of El Paso.[13]

The DeGroffs

The DeGroffs planned to spend upwards of $100,000 to upgrade the aging Borderland Princess. [14] When the DeGroffs took control of the property, they did not renew the operating lease to John Fisher and installed Mrs. De Goff's son, Burt Orndorff as manager.[15] The Fisher lease expired on August 1, 1910, and soon thereafter, they entered into a plan to remodel the "Sheldon into a pretentious structure."[16] Charles DeGroff told reporters, "The city has enough hotels at present and it is not my plan to have a new one erected. The Sheldon can be made into a first-class hotel. We will make that a first-class structure in every particular."[17]

The Sheldon Hotel closed on August 25, 1910 and a major construction program began under the supervision of the architecture firm of Trost and Trost. The DeGroffs replaced all building's plumbing and added 25 new bathrooms throughout the building. They replaced the elevators and shifted the main entrance from the Mills Avenue location back to the Pioneer Plaza side on the west and lining it with marble. They remodeled the lobby, the stairways leading from the lobby to the second floor and to the basement and rebuilt the retail offices on the main level. Marble finishes were added to the exterior and the beautiful exterior brick and terra cotta that had been unceremoniously painted over by Fisher were restored.[18] Following an extended furniture buying trip to the East, they installed new, modern furniture throughout.[19]

With the remodeling of the Sheldon, a local institution was going to fade away, an institution that was a downtown mainstay to all who passed by, particularly non-guests of the hotel. The El Paso Herald ran an editorial lamenting this major municipal loss. The editorial gives immense insight into the daily life of downtown:

> No one is refused a drink at this substitute for the town pump. There is but one place downtown where the public knows that a cool drink of

ice water may be had without even the asking. That is at the Sheldon. When the water from the alligator pool hydrants is lukewarm in the summer and impossible to drink, the old copper cooler in the arcade off the Sheldon lobby is perspiring under its load of trapped thirst quenchers. Many thirsty ones attracted during the hot summer afternoons, an almost steady stream of the thirsty may be seen drifting through the front entrance of the hotel and up to the spigot where their thirsts are quenched with the free ice water.

For the past 10 years, the big rectangular cooler has been filled regularly with ice water. Presumably for the guests of the hotel, the water cooler is in reality a public benefaction. Not one of 100 of the drinkers is a guests or ever would be guests at the hotel. They are the people who come downtown to shop, plaza loungers, streetcar men and others who know of no other available source of supply. It requires a total of 500 pounds of ice to keep the water in the old cooler at a point where it will produce the pleasant slaking feeling as it floats down the parched throat of the thirsty. The cooler holds 20 gallons of water and it is often filled as many as five times during the day, making a total of 100 gallons of water that is consumed by the passing throng.

This is provided without cost by the hotel management and to date no one has ever been known to express an appreciation of the accommodation by so much as a "thank you." As an actual test of the cooler's popularity, an account was kept of those whose thirst was satisfied. For 30 minutes a count was made of the persons, and during that time, from 3:30 to four 'clock Thursday afternoon, there were exactly 28 persons. Although it was an off-hour for the ice water business, according to the hotel men, the cooler was doing business at the rate of almost a thirst a minute, and Thursday was not a particularly hot day. Sunday is the best day of the week at the cooler and a line may be seen in front of the spigot resembling the line in front of a theater box office. Of the 28 persons who drank at the Sheldon cooler, 12 were business men, five streetcar motormen and conductors, six were kids, including three Herald newsboys, two were women, one a small girl, one Mexican, and one negro, who by the way was the only one who drank from his own glass which he had brought with him from a barber shop. Of the total number, but one was a guest of the hotel, and according to chief clerk Cole, the guest who drinks at the cooler is the exception.

> The quantity of ice water consumed at this semi-public drinking place during a year's time is truly enormous and the ice used in cooling it sufficient to build a respectable ice palace? In the plaza if the sun would stand for it. Where these patrons of manager John Fisher's free ice water fountain will go for their thirst quenchers in the future is not known. There is no other drinking place where ice water may be had by everyone. The old adage that one does not miss the water until the well goes dry, applies to the Sheldon cooler, for there will be many persons carrying thirst around with them, after the Sheldon closes with the old cooler, as dry as a death valley drought.[20]

The Sheldon Hotel Company opened the hotel for occupancy on November 1, 1910. The Sheldon Hotel Company with Charles DeGroff as president and his step-son, Burt Orndorff as secretary, leased the hotel operations to the newly formed Orndorff Hotel Company.

The Orndorff Hotel Company was composed of Burt Orndorff, as manager, and Lee Orndorff, sons of Mrs. Alzina Orndorff DeGroff, operated the Sheldon independently of their mother's hotel, the Orndorff Hotel. Her third son, Seth became a local sheriff. The lease arrangements would require that the Orndorff Hotel Company (the lessee) would pay the Sheldon Hotel Company (the lessor) $30,000 a year, payable at $2500 at the first of each month. The Orndorff boys would pay all the utilities, taxes, and maintenance of the interior and exterior of the Sheldon Hotel. Furthermore, they were expected to furnish the hotel as would be expected in a first-class and they would not be permitted to allow public gambling except for billiard and pool. If they failed at any of these tenets, the lease would be immediately terminated and all property would become the property of the Sheldon Hotel Company, which in reality was operated by their mother.[21] With the Sheldon restoration completed, the hotel had a couple of top-rated years, entertaining the full range of patrons that found their way to El Paso.

In 1912, the grandeur of the Sheldon began to fade, as Zach T. White, wealthy El Paso developer and entrepreneur opened his Trost and Trost designed $1.5 million Hotel Paso del Norte. Among the elaborate furnishings was a magnificent large Tiffany stained glass dome over the lobby. The elite visitors and wealthy Mexican businessmen began to favor the Paso del Norte Hotel over the Sheldon. While the Sheldon continued to operate, it no longer was the "grandest hotel" in the Southwest.

Figure 45. Hotel Paso del Norte just prior to its opening in 1912.

While Charles DeGroff tended to a real estate business, Mrs. Alzina DeGroff, known to family and friends as "Mama De" was characterized as "forceful character, character that comes from integrity, courage, self-assurance, and "force" that derives from intelligence, vision, will power, daring, and skill."[22] She hit El Paso by storm in 1899 as a successful hotelier, eventually acquiring, in addition to two hotels, enormous commercial property along Texas Ave. and a ranch of several thousand acres south of El Paso.

"Mama De" DeGroff

Allie (Alzina) Allis, was born in Louisiana in 1859 She moved to Moundville, Missouri and married a young railroad man named Lee H. Orndorff at the age of 19 in 1878. Soon after the birth of their second child, Seth, they moved to Tucson, Arizona in 1886. Lee was killed a year later in a train yard accident when he was trapped between two train cars. Widowed with three young children (Burt, Seth, and Lee Jr.) she moved into a small house and rented out one of the rooms to help support the family.[23] Later, she moved to a 16-room house, then to a two-story adobe hotel in 1894, which had the distinction of being Tucson's first operating hotel. She finally converted her property to a 60-room two-story hotel with screened-in sleeping porches. This became the largest and leading hotel in the Tucson.[24]

Figure 46. Mrs. Alzina (Mama De) Orndorff DeGroff. 1858-1926
(El Paso Historical Society)

Figure 47. Tucson Orndorff Hotel after remodel. 1910.
(Tucson Historical Society)

Figure 48. Tucson Orndorff, formerly the Cosmopolitan. 1890
(Courtesy Tucson Historical Society)

Originally built by Robert Phillips in the 1850s as the Phillips House, it was acquired by Hiram Stevens, a Tucson businessman, who remodeled it and opened it as the Hotel Cosmopolitan in 1874.[25] After marrying the Tucson postmaster, Charles DeGroff, in 1890 Alzina, and her new husband converted the Cosmopolitan into the Orndorff Hotel and ran it for eight years with great success at the corner of N. Main Ave. and Pennington Street. The old Orndorff Hotel, was incorporated into a portion of the Old Presidio wall. In the early 1930s the building was purchased by the City of Tucson and used as a police annex and is the site of the current Tucson City Hall. The Orndorff building was demolished in 1935.[26]

Desiring to expand her hotel operations, Alzina, in 1898 learned that the Vendome Hotel on the San Jacinto Plaza in El Paso was for sale. After seeing the potential of the Vendome, she eventually convinced her hesitating husband to make the move. Not having quite enough money for the down payment, she managed to get a loan from a friend in California, Francis J. Heney, former Arizona Attorney General, and purchased the old hotel for $41,000.

After arriving in El Paso, she showed her newly acquired property off to some reporters and said:

> The entire building is in a fearfully filthy condition. In Tucson, the city health officer would have condemned a house containing so much filth as a nuisance and a menace to public health. Some of the bedrooms resemble pigpens as far as the dirt is concerned. The bedding in some of them [rooms] is not fit to ornament the hovel of poverty. First of all, we are going to get rid of this dirt and burn some of the bedding.
>
> Then we are going to have the new part of the building repaired, repapered, and refurnished throughout, including new carpets in the rooms and halls. The dining room will be repapered and the office remodeled to make it roomier. As soon as we get the new part of the building, the dining room, and the office in proper condition, we will open the house for business and then turn our attention to the old portion of the building and proceed to make it habitable.
>
> We will have to spend ten or twelve thousand dollars putting the building in shape for business and after this is done we will give our attention to the matter of enlarging the hotel. People who come here from the north to spend the winter want as much of El Paso's genial sunshine as they can get, and for that reason we will want to add

> another story to the old part of the building as soon as possible, so as to have that many more sunny rooms during the forenoon, and also increase our number of sunny rooms in the afternoon.[27]

So successful was the Orndorff, that the DeGroffs began buying up land along Texas Ave. and eventually built their large home, called The Ranchita on an acre of land at 2103 Texas Ave. The house is still there, although it is difficult to see from the street as it is now surrounded by a large auto parts store. As the commercial success of Texas Ave. grew, it appeared that El Paso was moving to the east and crowding their special retreat. Then, they moved their retreat down the valley to The Big Ranch about 17 miles south, just beyond Ysleta.[28]

Now with the Sheldon gone, Mama De turned her attention to rebuilding the Orndorff Hotel. After more than twenty-five years of operating the Orndorff Hotel, in 1924, she borrowed $825,000 and had the firm of Trost and Trost design an eleven-story $1.5 million dollar deluxe hotel building to be erected on the site of the former Orndorff Hotel at 310 N. Mesa Street. The new hotel was to be designed as homage to the early Spanish conquistadores. Just a few weeks before the scheduled formal opening of the new hotel, Mama De visited the constructed site and inspected the steam-heating system and apparently became ill, possibly because of the massive temperature change she experienced. She was quickly diagnosed with pneumonia and died on March 9, 1926.[29] The 300-room hotel formally opened to the public in September 1926.[30] Through the years, the ownership and name of the new Orndorff had changed to the Hussmann Hotel and later The Cortez Hotel. Now it is an office building that has seen a variety of owners including public utilities, government agencies, and private investors.

The Syndicate

With the purchase of the Sheldon and with the Orndorff Hotel doing so well, the DeGroffs, while Burt served as manager of the Sheldon, The DeGroffs turned their attention to their new enterprise, The Cortez Hotel. Then in February 1916, the DeGroffs sold the Sheldon to a group of El Paso businessmen for $400,000. The new owner's syndicate included Felix Martinez, Julius and Robert Krakauer, James McNary, J. Mundy, Richard Burges, and Burt Orndorff. The purchase included the land, the building, and the Orndorff Hotel Company, the hotel operating company that ran the hotel with Burt Orndorff as general manager. Part of the deal included a five-year sunset on the deal with the operating company, and the plans were to raze the building and erect a modern building in its place.[31]

Figure 49. El Paso Orndorff Hotel 1920.
(El Paso Library, Aultman Collection)

Figure 50. Hotel Cortez built by the DeGroffs on the site of the El Paso Orndorff Hotel in 1926. (El Paso Public Library, Aultman Collection)

Figure 51. Artist rendering of downtown El Paso. Sheldon center right across from the Mills Building circa 1920. The Rio Grande appears as the white ribbon running horizontally through the upper portion. The mountains of Mexico in the background.
(El Paso Public Library.)

Albert Mathias

In 1920, successful dry goods wholesaler and land developer, Albert Mathias, purchased the Sheldon Hotel from the Sheldon Company syndicate composed of the Krakauers, McNary, Martinez, and others for $500,000. Most of the transaction was in cash and some real estate owned by Mathias. This was, according to the local newspapers, the largest cash real estate deal ever made in El Paso.[32] Soon after the transaction, Mathias extended the lease to the Sheldon Operating Company for five more years with an annual fee of $38,000. The Sheldon Operating Company, under the management of Burt Orndorff and the Krakauer estate, had been operating the hotel for the syndicate before the sale to Mathias.

Connected to the Sheldon Operating Company in an interesting way was Joe Goodell, president of Citizens Financial Company of El Paso and his good friend and client, Conrad Hilton, who operated other Texas hotels.[33] When the Sheldon Operating Company, under the Mathias' lease, was restructured after Burt Orndorff left, Goodell was elected president in 1923. Goodell had assisted Hilton in financing his first two hotels. Goodell and Hilton's name began appearing on stationary connected to the Sheldon Operating Company.[34] Joe Goodell and Conrad Hilton were close friends and drinking buddies from New Mexico. Goodell operated the Albuquerque Business College and Hilton ran a small adobe hotel and store in San Antonio, New Mexico, 80 miles south of Albuquerque. In 1922, Goodell sold the business college and moved to El Paso and bought a finance company.

In conversations with Dr. Phil Goodell a professor of geochemistry at the University of Texas at El Paso and Joe Goodell's son, he told the author that his father carefully filtered information about his relationship with Hilton because he was angry at Hilton for not helping his old friends when they needed the help after they had assisted Hilton in the rebuilding of the Hilton Hotel Company after its near collapse in dealings with Mathias. He felt that Hilton should have put Joe on the Hilton board of directors or had him associated with the company in some way.[35] For unclear reasons, in 1927, Mathias issued the operating company lease to a Paxton C. Steele.

In the middle of the great depression, it was Mathias who entered into a 99-year lease contract to allow Conrad Hilton to build his first, from the ground up, high-rise Hilton Hotel.

Notes and References

---

[1] Harris and Sadler (2009), 31.
[2] Ibid, 22.
[3] Ibid, 72.
[4] Johnson, William W. *Heroic Mexico: The Violent Emergence of a Modern Nation.* (Garden City, New York: Doubleday and Company, 1968.), 29.
[5] Timmons (1990), 227.
[6] *El Paso Times*, August 25, 1946.
[7] HBS, letter to LMS. 25 Oct. 1901.
[8] HBS, letter to HKS. 5 May. 1905.
[9] HBS, letter to HKS. 31 Jan. 1907.
[10] Death Certificate, Commonwealth of Massachusetts.
[11] *El Paso Times*, August 25, 1946. In a subsequent article, the *EPT* reported the amount of the sale as $200,000.
[12] HBS, letter to HKS. 14 Mar. 1907. Tax receipt No. 1814.
[13] *El Paso Herald*, February 23, 1957.
[14] El Paso County Clerk's office. "Sheldon Hotel Remodel." Henrytrost.org/buildings Accessed 3 March 2015.
[15] *El Paso Times*, May 31, 1973.
[16] *El Paso Herald*, November 23, 1909.
[17] Ibid.
[18] *El Paso Herald*, August 6, 1910. These were the descriptions presented before the renovations, but all indications are that they were carried out to the letter.
[19] *El Paso Times*, July 14, 1910.
[20] *El Paso Herald*, August 6, 1910.
[21] Lease agreement executed and filed on October 5, 1910. El Paso County Clerk's Office.
[22] Pierce, Burtram Orndorff, and Alzina Orndorff Gay. "Mama De: Tower Builder." *Password*, Vol. XVIII (1973), 6-13.
[23] *El Paso Times*, November 4, 2010; *El Paso Post*, August 11, 1926.
[24] *Portrait and Biographical Record of Arizona: Commemorating the Achievements of Citizens Who Have Contributed to the Progress of Arizona and the Development of its Resources.* (Chicago: Chap.m.an Publishing Company, 1901.): 736-737.
[25] Thiel, J. Homer. "In Search of *El Presidio de Tucson*" Official Website of the City of Tucson. Accessed 11 Mar. 2016.
[26] Orndorff, J. "Orndorff Hotel, Tucson, AZ." Genealogywise.com (Topic: 352328) Accessed 14 Mar. 2016.

[27] "The Hotel Deal is consummated." *The El Paso International Daily Times*, Vol. 19, No. 95, April 23, 1899. The Portal to Texas History. Accessed 11 Mar. 2016.
[28] Pierce, 10.
[29] *El Paso Herald*, March 11, 1926.
[30] Metz, León. *El Paso Chronicles: A Record of Historical Events in El Paso, Texas.* (El Paso: Mangan Books, 1993.), 211.
[31] *El Paso Herald*, February 5, 1916.
[32] *El Paso Herald,* May 5, 1920.
[33] Phillip and Grace Goodell, children of Joe Goodell. Personal Interview. El Paso, Texas, August 5, 2011.
[34] *El Paso Herald*, August 8, 1962. (Side Bar Remarks by Pooley)
[35] Ibid.

Chapter Fourteen

Madero Builds a Rebellion

Countless scholars, researchers, journalists, and historians have written and published, both recently and in years past, well-documented volumes containing accounts of the events and characters of the Mexican Revolution. It was a convoluted and complicated story between 1910 and 1920. A story that took over a million lives and lasted over five years before the most violent phase of the revolution finally ended. "Political and military leaders came and went like the seasons; lives and careers flamed and ended in meteoric fashion."[1] The central list of political and military characters included: Díaz, Madero, Villa, Orozco, Zapata, Huerta, Carranza, and Obregón; and they were all schemers one way or another. They were the leaders of multiple coups *d'état* that led them to the presidency of Mexico and to the assassin's revenge. All except Díaz, who died in exile in France, following his resignation, Díaz fled Mexico for Paris aboard the German steamship, Ipiranga on May 25, 1911, just 14 days after the fall of Ciudad Juárez.[2] The bloodshed, violence, and intrigue that surrounded the rebels' defeat at Casas Grande, Díaz's defeat at the Battle of Juárez of 1911, the La Decena Trágica (The Ten Tragic Days) in 1913, and the Villa invasion of the United States at Columbus, New Mexico in 1916; all deserve review by even the casual reader. These particular chapters are not a review of those aspects of the revolution, but of the events of that were directly related to the Sheldon Hotel and its role in the rebellion.

As 1910 drew to a close, the storm of rebellion was growing like a windswept range fire, growing and moving in a multitude of directions with each passing day. In 1908, Díaz granted an interview to an American journalist, James Creelman, at the Chapultepec Castle in Mexico City. That interview became the catalyst that ignited the Mexican Revolution. Creelman published the interview in the March issue of *Pearson's Magazine*.[3] Díaz, however, was unaware of the American edition and gave the interview believing that his words were for a foreign audience and would never be translated or published in America or Mexico.[4] This decision proved to be a fatal error in judgment. Creelman's interview was entitled President Díaz: Hero of the Americas. Creelman wrote:

> There is not a more romantic or heroic figure in all the world, nor one more intensely watched by both the friends and foes of democracy, than the soldier-statesman, whose adventurous youth pales the pages of Dumas, and whose iron rule has converted the warring, ignorant, superstitious, and impoverished masses of Mexico, oppressed by centuries of Spanish cruelty and greed, into a strong, steady, peaceful, debt-paying, and progressive nation....For twenty-seven years, he has governed the Mexican Republic with such power that national elections have become mere formalities. He might easily have set a crown upon his head.
>
> It is something to come from the money-mad gambling congeries [assemblage] of Wall Street and in the same week to stand on the rock of Chapultepec, in surroundings of almost unreal grandeur and loveliness, beside one who is said to have transformed a republic into an autocracy by the absolute compulsion of courage and character, and to hear him speak of democracy as the hope of mankind.

Creelman quotes Díaz as saying:

> It is a mistake to suppose that the future of democracy in Mexico has been endangered by the long continuance in office of one President, I can say sincerely that office has not corrupted my political ideals and that I believe democracy to be the one true, just principle of government, although in practice it is possible only to highly developed peoples. ...I can lay down the Presidency of Mexico without a pang of regret, but I cannot cease to serve this country while I live.
>
> Yes, yes, I know, it is a natural sentiment of democratic peoples that their officials should be often changed. I agree with that sentiment. ... I have waited patiently for the day when the people of the Mexican Republic would be prepared to choose and change their government at every election without danger of armed revolutions and without injury to the national credit or interference with national progress. I believe that day has come.[5]

The early seeds of the revolution began in 1908 with the Creelman interview, when President Díaz asserted that Mexico was now ready for democracy and a free election. Díaz announced in 1909 that the government would hold a free election in 1910 and new candidates needed to prepare for the election. Díaz had repeatedly stated that he would not run for reelection, but as the Election Day approached, he changed his mind. He would run for re-election at the age of 80. Other historians claim that the revolution actually began on the early morning of June 1, 1906 with the walkout and strike of the discontented miners employed by the Cananea Consolidated Copper Company controlled by New Yorker W.C. Greene in Sonora.[6]

The powerful grip that Díaz had over the republic began to weaken, collapsing under enormous internal corruption, and the regime became vulnerable.[7] The poor became poorer and more than half of the rural population was bound to debt slavery. The focus of discontent centered on the state of Chihuahua and Ciudad Juárez. Into this fray entered the well-education idealist from a wealthy land-owning family, Francisco I. Madero, Jr. Madero challenged Díaz and he gained widespread support, particularly in the north, for the 1910 election. Running on his self-funded progressive party, his successful campaigning caused Díaz to realize that he might not have control of this election as he had had in his previous seven elections.

Figure 52. Francisco Madero, leader of the Mexican Revolution, 1911.(1873-1913)
(Author's Collection)

The Mexican and international press called Madero's revolutionary movement the "No-Re-Electionist Party" that was based on a platform of land reform and effective suffrage. Madero began to draw large crowds of supporters in the months prior to the election. Díaz became gravely concerned over Madero's ability to draw crowds of 25,000 or more people. Díaz's thugs and operatives disrupted Madero's speeches, destroyed his campaign literature, and shut down the Madero newspaper. Just prior to Election Day, Madero went to see President Díaz and made an offer in order to keep the peace. Madero offered to withdraw from the election if Díaz would appoint him as vice-president and negotiate some of the changes that Madero had in mind. The aging President rejected the Madero offer and had him arrested and jailed. On Election Day, the official results indicated that Díaz had been re-elected almost unanimously. This undisputable case of massive electoral fraud aroused widespread anger and only intensified Madero's popularity. Fresh from the rigged election, Díaz proclaimed himself Mexico's leader for the next six years.

Shortly after his incarceration, Madero escaped from Díaz's jail. Disguised as a railroad worker or a priest, depending on your source, he crossed back into the United States and headed north. Stopping in San Antonio for financial support from his family's American bank accounts, he continued on to El Paso and eventually crossed back into Ciudad Juárez. Surrounded by supporters and fellow revolutionaries, Madero chose to redress the Díaz election through violence.

On November 20, 1910, Francisco Madero declared himself "provisional president" and issued a call-to-arms, The Plan of San Luís Potosí that called for the nullification of the 1910 election and for all Mexicans to take up arms. That date marks the start of the Mexican Revolution. Mexico engulfed itself in a civil war, as opposing political groups fought each other for the control of the country and the unseating of the Díaz regime. Fighting broke out all over Mexico, but primarily in the northern mineral rich state of Chihuahua. The fighting was at first scattered and each skirmish would fall to a different victor. Díaz became more and more concerned about the rebel activity in Ciudad Juárez. This alone seemed to energize Madero.[8]

The Mexican Revolution up to 1916 referred to the broad and extensive revolt against tyrannical leadership. The rebellion occurred in four phases. The **Díaz Phase** was the Madero Revolution in northern Mexico during November 1910 and May 1911. The **Madero Phase** was composed of the Reyes Rebellion in November 1911; the Orozco Rebellion, February to May 1912; the Felix Díaz Rebellion, October 1912; and the Mexico City Revolt of February 1913, (Tragic Ten Days). This was followed by the **Huerta Phase,** The Constitutionalist Civil War, from February 1913 to August 1914. The fourth was the **Carranza Phase,** the Villa-Zapata Revolt, August 1914-1916.[9]

The Ten Tragic Days ("La Decena Trágica") of February 9 through February 19, 1913 was stimulated by the absence of Diaz, who had been the common enemy. The Mexican Revolution spun out of control which culminated in Huerta's coup d'état and the murder of Madero. This event ignited the most violent four years of the revolution.

The rebellion continued with the Villa invasion at Columbus, New Mexico in March 1916 and with a string of military battles and skirmishes that did not begin to wane until 1920. Through it all, the Sheldon Hotel remained the group home of the correspondents who telegraphed their version of the depredations around the world. The hotel's featured role and the residence of choice of the major actors, lessened when the Paso del Norte Hotel opened and attracted the more significant decision makers in 1912. Yet, the Sheldon remained active, particularly in the smuggling of arms while the strategy making activities moved across the street.[10]

Madero's large and wealthy family made their way to El Paso, Texas. In the rooms and lobbies of the Sheldon Hotel, in the heart of downtown El Paso, revolutionary supporters and the Madero family "met, planned, plotted, and prepared to go to war against the federal government of Mexico and the Díaz legions."[11] The Madero family was one of the richest in Mexico and while Catholic, its roots were Portuguese-Jewish. The family's wealth came from large land holdings, cotton farms, mines, banks, rubber factories, and a wine and spirit business.

The Madero clan was composed of the Francisco I. Madero, Sr. who brought access to the family fortune. The three Madero brothers[12] were Francisco Jr., who at 37 was a five-foot-two-inch, black-bearded, dreamy-eyed idealist, the most unlikely looking of the three Madero brothers to become the face of the insurrection. He was of slight build, a vegetarian, a spiritualist, and had a shrill voice when he was excited. Francisco was the eldest of 14 children (including one half-brother).[13] Raúl Madero a vigorous field soldier who appeared to enjoy military action, but lacked the understanding of the consequences of war. (Raúl was the second child in the Madero family with the name Raúl. The first, Raúl died early in his life, and Francisco Jr. believed that this brother's spirit would guide him in his efforts to rid Mexico of Díaz. When another son was born following the death of Raúl, that child was then named after him.) Raúl was slender but physically extremely strong and not at all as temperamental as his brother. Raúl was less of a dreamer than Francisco.[14]

The third brother, Gustavo A. Madero, was in charge of finances and the recruitment of the revolutionary army. Following the death of Francisco Jr. Gustavo during La Decena Trágica, Raúl briefly became the Governor of the state of Nuevo León in 1915. Then in 1957 was elected Governor of the state of

Coahuila and served until 1963. Raúl died in 1982 at the age of 94.[15] Following the defeat of Díaz, and Francisco's assumption of the Mexican presidency, Gustavo was appointed minister of finance. He died in the coup d'état that toppled the Madero government in February 1913.

While continuing to work out of their rooms at the Sheldon Hotel, in January 1911, the Madero family also established a business office to facilitate the recruitment aspect of the rebellion. This office was under the management of Abraham Gonzalez, an equally zealous revolutionary. The Gonzalez office was located in two rooms on the fifth floor of the Caples Building, just south of the Sheldon Hotel at 300-306 E. San Antonio Avenue. Gonzalez, with Gustavo Madero's financial connections, focused on securing outside financing for the ongoing revolution as well as luring mercenaries to augment the struggling rebel army. While concentrating their activities in the northern region of Mexico, particularly the Juárez—El Paso area because of easy access to smuggled arms, it was unlikely that sufficient capital existed in the region to support their cause. This has led historians to suggest the possibility of external financial support from American enterprises such as Standard Oil.[16] There was some evidence that the Madero family alone financed upwards of one million dollars of the Madero phase of the revolution.[17]

Abraham Gonzalez was equally successful in putting together a group of nearly 100 soldiers of fortune. Many were actively recruited, but others found their way to El Paso on their own, in search of excitement, riches, and a place to hide from American authorities, as they were wanted criminals from every possible type of crime. They came from everywhere; many were professional mercenaries with extensive experiences in selling their services in civil rebellions world-wide. While most were Americans, several were internationally known mercenaries, who had captured headlines and public interest around the world, and when this battle was won, would move on to the next revolutionary crisis. A few were idealists, in search of the opportunity to bring democracy to a noble cause, "the rescue of the downtrodden poor of Mexico." They formed what was called El Falange de los Estranjeros, the "Foreign Legion," under the command of Italian mercenary Col. Giuseppe (Peppino or Jose) Garibaldi II.

Garibaldi, the grandson of the great Italian liberator and namesake, who history has credited with uniting Italy in the 1880s, maintained a room at the Sheldon Hotel during his stay in the Juárez region during the revolutionary battles in the northern region around Ciudad Juárez. He was handsome, blond, polished, and European in temperament and fastidiousness. While the Madero brothers were educated in Mexico City and the United States, Garibaldi, at age 31, had been in four wars and was a product of the world and from a large family of international mercenaries. When he presented himself to Madero and his rebel officers to volunteer his services he said, "Señor, we Garibaldi's do not believe in tyranny."[18] He made multiple trips back and forth from the Madero camp along the Rio Grande and the battle fields to his room at the Sheldon.

The Sheldon Hotel was the social and civic center of activity of this major mining, agricultural, transportation, and export hub of the southwest. The hotel's profile and location made it a mecca for revolutionaries, mercenaries, newspaper correspondents, and secret service and federal agents from both the United States and Mexico. This was just the beginning of the Sheldon's role in connecting El Paso to the Mexican Fiesta of Death.[19]

Madero put ex-mule driver Pascual Orozco and the bandit Pancho Villa in charge of his ragtag army of landless peasants and angry merchants and farmers, who lacked uniforms, weapons, and military experience, but were committed fierce pro-democracy freedom fighters. One historian described the Madero army as:

> The rebel armies were not armies, but neither were they merely peasant mobs. There were peones, to be sure, but in addition, servants, shopkeepers, mechanics, beggars, miners, federal army deserters, lawyers, United States soldiers of fortune, young and old, bandits and idealists, students and teachers, engineers and day laborers, the bored and the overworked, the aggrieved and the adventuresome, all constituted the rank and file. Some were attracted by commitment to the cause and some by the promise of spoils, some joined impulsively, and others with careful forethought.[20]

The state of the Mexican army wasn't much better at that time. Díaz's army was top-heavy with officers, some nine thousand commanding about eighteen thousand troops. Most of the officers were corrupt cronies of Díaz and too old to physically lead troops into battle. In addition, Díaz had the habit of changing commanders on a whim and that would disrupt troop loyalty to their commanders. The enlisted men, for the most part, did not enlist. They were conscripted out of prisons or from the agricultural fields under pressure from government gangs.[21]

Col. Garibaldi's team of international mercenaries augmented the generals' troops. Following their humiliating defeat at Casas Grande, the ranks of the Madero army swelled and the acquisition of arms and materiel prepared them for their assault on Juárez in May.

For those living in El Paso, the ongoing saga of the Mexican Revolution had been someone else's war. It was Mexico's war. However, the fighting was so close to them that violence in Ciudad Juárez could easily be watched from the rooftops of El Paso buildings and homes. The Mexicans, the rebels and the loyalists, were firing cannons at each other in the streets. When the projectiles exploded on their targets, the Sheldon, and the other major buildings in downtown El Paso shook as if in an earthquake.

Figure 53. Vintage postcards editorializing and reporting on events was the Facebook, Instagram, and Twitter of the time. (Author's Collection)

The battle rattled the nerves of all of the citizens of El Paso. They were confident that the battlefront would never cross the river into the United States. The people on the ground in El Paso quickly learned that stray bullets did not recognize political boundaries. At least two people on the American side of the border died and many others were wounded from gunfire that came from across the river. It is probably important to keep in mind that El Pasoans did not view the leaders of both sides of the revolution as bigger-than-ever or anything; they were just interesting outsiders who were preoccupied with concerns that didn't affect the day–to-day lives of the local Americans. That is not to say that their concerns were not important to them or, for that matter, interesting to hear about —but their problems were foreign problems. As the rebellion widened and accelerated, many El Pasoans began to sympathize with the insurrectos and were willing to help them, even if there wasn't any profit in doing so.[22]

With the constant looting and routing by the revolutionary rebels, the disruption of train service across the border, and the destruction of local industries, many Americans in Mexico and panic-stricken Mexican citizens rushed across the river into El Paso, bringing the threats and fears with them causing a major impact on the citizens of El Paso. It was no longer a foreign problem. As the rebellion grew, foreign companies that had made major investments in Mexico began to complain to Washington, D.C. Before long, more federal agents, Texas Rangers, and military personnel joined the legions of newspaper correspondents who descended upon El Paso in general and the Sheldon Hotel in particular. The Sheldon was now the residence of some of the mercenaries, the Madero family, Mexican and American secret service agents, Mexico's would-be leaders, deposed leaders, and the military leaders of the rebels, the federals, and the tense American military leaders.

Figure 54. Iconic photo of El Pasoans watching the revolution in Juarez from the roof top of the Hotel del Norte. ca. 1912.
(El Paso County Historical Society)

The lobby and bar of the Sheldon made for a most fascinating venue. Unpredictably, there was considerable cross-communication between the various factions. The clamor for U.S. intervention was rampant.[23] Not long after Madero and his forces began their follow up activity after their defeat at Casas Grande, a devastating fire occurred in Manhattan in New York, the Triangle Factory Fire that garnered international attention. A witness to the tragedy was a young United Press reporter, William G. Shepherd, who phoned in details of the unfolding tragedy to a reporter who telegraphed the minute-by-minute account of the blaze that saw 146 women killed in fifteen minutes. His reporting propelled him into the high ranks of newspaper reporters.[24] He soon became a recognized war correspondent, whose career would take him around the world to report on war's ugly progress. One such confrontation was the Mexican Revolution.

In May 1911, Shepherd had arrived in El Paso, checked into the Sheldon Hotel, and surrounded himself with the hordes of other world-renowned newspapermen who congregated at the Sheldon. His accounting of the activities in the Sheldon's lobby paints a clear picture of the hotels interaction with the revolution as it was expanding:

> Most of the big things in the insurrecto war have happened in the lobby of the marble Sheldon Hotel at El Paso. Most of the heroes live there. All of them plot there, standing about en masse or sitting in the lobby chairs, looking much like talkative drummers. Evening is the proper time for the war conservations in the lobby. In a rocking chair sits Colonel Steever of our own Fourth cavalry. If there is intervention at this point, he is the man who will start it. Yet he is gossiping with Judge Carbajal, personal representative of Díaz.
>
> A bevy of laughing women, dressed in black, pass through the corridor. Among [them] is Mrs. Madero, wife of the liberator, and two of his younger sisters. They are on their way to the café for a merry dinner. An elderly man, with dark whiskers, carrying an umbrella, and wearing an alpaca coat—an old-fashioned business man—gets a batch of telegrams from the hotel clerk and takes the elevator for his room. He is Francisco Madero, father of the insurrecto leader. Here stands Michael Brenan, the roofing salesman of Birmingham, Alabama, who took his vacation at this time to get into the fight with the insurrectos. He used to sharp shoot every day and at night sneak through the federal lines to the river, cross to El Paso, where he could get a good night's sleep at the Sheldon Hotel and then hurry back, early in the morning, before the battle was renewed, sneak through the lines again, at the risk of his life, get his gun and start to work again.

Here's a lank young Englishman of thirty. They call him Forbes. His clothes are magnificently cut and new, but torn. Everybody knows his name isn't Forbes. He has the best suites in the hotel. During the battle of Juárez he hired a livery horse, rode over late [to] the insurrecto trenches, and got permission to fight with them. He had a rifle, which was the wonder of the entire army. It cost $500, and he said he had killed elephants and tigers in India with it. They put him to sharp shooting, and the insurrectos will tell that this mysterious Englishmen must have killed at least thirty men with his deadly aim during the three-day battle.

You'll see ragged Americans in the lobby crowd. They were [among] the insurrectos, but, because of the stories of American looting during the fight, they have been dismissed from the Madero army. They complain to everyone who will listen, particularly to the newspaper men, that Madero hasn't treated them fairly. Most of them are jobless adventurers, but say Mexican insurrectos will tell you that these fellows led the attack on Juárez and fought best of all. They won't tell you their right names.

Passing in and out among the groups are the newspaper correspondents from various corners of the world. Chances for American intervention appear to have created an interest in the Mexican situation in all civilized countries. Mysterious suave little Japs stand about. Mysterious Germans, mysterious Italians, mysterious Englishmen, listening and talking, but telling no one they are here. Half a dozen United States secret service men chat in a corner. Through the lobby passes Mayor Kelly of El Paso, who does not seem to be able to recover from the astonishment which arose when El Paso suddenly became a center of world interest. With him is the chief of police, who has twenty men. In Texas fashion they pass out to the barroom.

Men in khaki—fierce looking men—Orozco, Blanco, and Villa—insurrecto generals, clank through the corridor to the stairway, scorning the elevator. They are going to see Madero, the elder. Here in this lobby they gather—representatives of all the clashing interests, men from both sides, and men who may be on sides that have not as yet developed. Some of them, before this is through, may be deadly enemies.

> But tonight they chat and gossip and exchange salutations, just as if they were merely guests of some summer resort hotel. Over here at Juárez, the insurrecto camp is quiet. The evening fires are dying, though it is only 9 o'clock. Most of these insurrectos are farmers. The life of a soldier is strange to them. Many of them are afraid of their own guns. But in them has been stirred the same liberty fires that caused the Yankee farmers to "fire the shot heard around the world" in 1776. Here in Juárez is the fighting machine—over there at El Paso are its engineers.[25]

After the fall of the Díaz regime, Shepherd was one of the correspondents who traveled with Madero to Mexico City to take his place at the Presidential Palace.[26] He authored a book in 1917 entitled Confessions of a War Correspondent while covering WWI, in which he lamented the pain of war when he and a fellow writer had met a former soldier on the street:

> The moral and mental disintegration that is caused by military service in individual cases is shocking. This applies to all armies that I have seen. "That fellow would be better dead." Said a friend of mine, as an Englishman we had known in peace times walked away from us after a chance meeting. "Everything that was good in him is dead already."
>
> "I've quit writing," he said, with a weak grin that displayed the absence of two front teeth. "Something's happened to me. I can't even try to do it. Anyhow, what's the use? It's all war." That man that he had been a year before would have killed himself with his own gun rather than become the man we saw and talked with that afternoon. His was only a typical case.
>
> Every mother, sister, and wife in Europe has seen some change of this sort take place among the men-folk she knows. Sometimes it is less, but sometimes death would be better than the upheaving conversion to baseness which war produces. "No more books or music and no more women. I'm simply rotting mentally."
> I have had officers make this confession to me in five different languages in seven different armies, "I'm rotting, and I can't help it." Not all the bad things of war happen to human bodies.[27]

Owen P. White, journalist and author, and chronicler of El Paso history described his experience at the Sheldon Hotel during the run-up to the Battle of

Juárez in a witty and humorous manner. The Chamber of Commerce, in their attempt to maintain a positive image with all the visiting newspapermen, provided a huge banquet at the Sheldon Hotel in their honor. White commented on the sudden presence of so many newspapermen:

> Madero, at the head of 1,500 of the most raggedest (sic) soldiers the world ever saw, armed with everything from bows and arrows up to one two-inch cannon made from a freight-car axle, appeared on the opposite side of the Rio Grande to lay siege to the city of Juárez. This being the only war at the time El Paso was soon even more cluttered up with high-power news sleuths than it had been for Dan Stuart's Fistic Carnival.[28] These war correspondents, however, were more than mere news getters. They were news makers. They were geniuses who could magnify a friendly gunfight, or a personal cutting affray between Mexicans, into a major engagement of opposing armies, and once they even went so far as to cable columns around the world when three poor peons, who to them were federal spies, were taken in for smuggling mescal. It was all nonsense, every dispatch, the boys sent out bore an El Paso date line.
>
> The Chamber of Commerce, out of sheer gratitude to these gentlemen of the press for the gaudy lies they were telling about the war on the town's doorstep, decided to tender them a banquet. From what I had seen of these fourth-estaters, especially in Tug Wilson's place, were Bill Shepherd and David Lawrence in just one session [they] cooked up a battle and wired descriptions of it to their papers. I couldn't understand why they needed a banquet. They already knew how to drink anyhow.
>
> Furthermore as they had no senatorial dignity to preserve, and as some of them even wore signs on their brows, "Dangerous If Aroused." …I decided to duck any party given in their honor. But I couldn't. I also wore a label. I was El Paso's most notorious halfwit, and so once again, an entertainment committee put it up to me to tell our distinguished visitors just who and what they were. I did it, and as every distinguished guest present, except Alfred Henry Lewis, whose liver was not in working order, was already very tight when I arose to speak, and hence easy to insult, it was one of the softest assignments I ever tackled. … Also with us that night, as representatives of the real hostilities of the Mexican Revolution, were a number of genuine

> Mexican heroes. Raul Madero, dreamy-eyed, tight, and weepy. Gustavo Madero, tight but not weepy, who later ran away with the Mexican Treasury, ...and Garibaldi. He also was there, and although he was full as a tick he was very dignified about it and very quiet. ...He was so handsome, so distinguished-looking, wore such a lovely uniform, and had such a grand pedigree![29]

The activities occurring in the Sheldon Hotel during the planning and prosecution of the Mexican Revolution were wide and varied, but they had one major thing in common. The warring actors mingled and shared information, camaraderie, and intrigue in the safe-haven marbled walls of the Sheldon. All of this taking place under the watchful eyes of the Mexican and American agents and the international press. This cemented the Sheldon's role in the battle for "Mexico for Mexicans."

Notes and References

---

[1] Tanner, E. C. (1970). *The Texas Border and the Mexican Revolution.* (Unpublished Master's Thesis, Texas Tech University.), 1.

[2] Lansford, William Douglas. *Pancho Villa*. (Los Angeles: Sherbourne Press, 1965.), p. 90.

[3] *Pearson's Magazine* was an influential monthly periodical in New York with roots that date back to 1896 in England.

[4] "Distant Neighbors: The U.S. and the Mexican Revolution." Library of Congress. www.loc.gov/rr/hispanic/mexico/creelman.html Accessed 14 March 2016.

[5] Creelman, James. "President Díaz: Hero of the Americas." *Pearson's Magazine.* Vol. XIX No. 3 (March 1908), 232-235.

[6] Sonnichsen, C.L. *Colonel Greene and the Copper Skyrocket.* (Tucson: University of Arizona Press, 1976.), 177.

[7] Tanner, 2.

[8] Gonzales, Michael J. The Mexican Revolution: 1910-1940. (Albuquerque: University of New Mexico Press, 2002.), 73.

[9] Tanner, 102.

[10] Scott, Hugh L. *Some Memories of a Soldier.* (New York: The Century Co., 1928.), 526.

[11] Katz, Friedrich. *The Life & Times of Pancho Villa*. (Palo Alto: Stanford University Press, 1998.), 670.

[12] The three Madero brothers added their mother's maiden name, González, to theirs, a common Latin tradition.
[13] Emerson, Edwin. "Madero of Mexico." New Outlook (New York, 1911.), 616.
[14] Lansford, 63.
[15] *New York Times*, October 10, 1982.
[16] Greib, Kenneth J. "Standard Oil and the Financing of the Mexican Revolution." *California Historical Quarterly*. Vol. XLX (March, 1971) No. 1, 59-71.
[17] Emerson, 616.
[18] Lansford, 63.
[19] Tarleton, John. "The Mexican Revolution." *John Tarleton's Brief, Irreverent History of Mexico* (1997). Accessed 20 Feb 2007.
[20] Meyer, Michael C., and William L. Sherman. *The Course of Mexican History.* Seventh Edition. (New York: Oxford University Press, 2003.), 480.
[21] Scheina, Robert L. *Villa: Soldier of the Mexican Revolution*. (Dulles, VA: Brassey's Inc., 2004.), 6.
[22] "El Paso Center of Revolution." *The Junior Historian*. Vol. 15, No. 1. September 1954. Texas State Historical Association. Accessed 5 March 2016.
[23] Garibaldi, Giuseppe. *A Toast to Rebellion.* (New York: Bobbs-Merrill, 1935.), 268.
[24] Shepherd, William G. "Eyewitness at the Triangle." *Milwaukee Journal*, March 27, 1911.
[25] Shepherd, William G. "Friend and Foe – and Mysterious Observers in Touch Elbows in Hotel Lobby—Real Heart of Mexican War." *Logansport Daily Reporter*, June 5, 1911.
[26] *El Paso Times*, November 3, 1911.
[27] Shepherd, William G. *Confessions of a War Correspondent.* (New York: Harper & Brothers Publishers, 1917.), 210-211.
[28] Dan Stuart was the boxing promoter who was responsible for the Fitzsimmons-Maher prizefight fiasco held along the Rio Grande in 1895. See Leo N. Miletich's book *Dan Stuart's Fistic Carnival* (Texas A&M Press, 1994.)
[29] White, Owen P. *The Autobiography of a Durable Sinner*. (New York: G.P. Putnam' Son, 1942), 113-114.

Figure 55. Gen. Giuseppe Garibaldi II. Mercenary Extraordinaire. (El Paso County Historical Society)

Figure 56. Col. Emilio Kosterlitzky. The Eagle of Sonora, feared chief of Mexican Secret Police and American spy.

Chapter Fifteen

The Fall of Juárez

The rebels stole or purchased the war materiel with Madero money and smuggled it across the border. Madero's troops only had two pieces of artillery with which to conduct their war. One, the Blue Whistler cannon that had been stolen from its memorial mooring in front of the El Paso City Hall by sympathetic El Pasoans under the directions of Dr. Ira Bush, and a homemade cannon made from a train axle by Col. Garibaldi in a train shop in Mexico. Both saw very limited action as they easily imploded within the first couple of firing attempts. One of the earliest connections of the Sheldon Hotel with the brewing rebellion across the Rio Grande was the relationship that the hotel had with the million-acre Corralitos Ranch in Chihuahua. The ranch was a perfect example of American investment into Mexico by Díaz invitation and a source of anger and violence by the Mexican people. Lucius Sheldon's son worked as a mining engineer for the Corralitos and while there, convinced his father to invest in El Paso property, which eventually led to the building of the Sheldon Block.

In testimony before Senator Fall's United States Senate sub-committee hearings at the Sheldon Hotel in 1913, the Corralitos' mining manager, George Laird, stated that the Mexican Revolution of 1910 actually began at the Corralitos Ranch. He stated that he was aware of the coming of the revolution three months before it actually began. He reported that José Inés Salazar, along with Pascual Orozco and Pancho Villa had demanded supplies from the Corralitos to supply their army as they moved in support of the Madero Revolution. The rebels took arms, dynamite and fuses as well as horses, mules and saddles from the Hacienda de Corralitos. Four days later, the killing began in Janos, the small community adjacent to the large ranch and moved on to the Mexican city of Casas Grande.

Madero had divided his volunteer army into two columns, sending one toward the capital city of Chihuahua City under the leadership of Orozco and

Madero, with absolutely no military experience, led the remaining group of about 600, including eighty of the foreign legion, toward the Chihuahua city of Casas Grande. After a horrendous battle, during which the Mexican garrison received 500 reinforcements, the rebels were seriously defeated. It didn't take long for Madero, who had been wounded in the right arm, to realize that he needed to leave the actual military engagements in the hands of those who were experienced fighters.[1] The Maderistas retreated and regrouped to battle another day. Their next attempt would be Ciudad Juárez in May 1911.[2] Madero was well aware that, strategically, whoever controlled Ciudad Juárez would ultimately control Northern Mexico. El Paso and its sister city at the border, Juárez, were the railroad hubs that not only connected the north to Mexico City, but also the American city was the source of equipment and munitions.

Madero had established his Mexican headquarters on the river's edge in a small adobe house with red, white, and green awnings south of the American Eagle Brick Company's factory and the white obelisk Boundary Marker One. (The marker identified the border between the United States and Mexico, just across the river from the former site of the ASARCO smelter works.)

Figure 57. Madero's revolution headquarters on the Mexican bank of the Rio Grande across from the El Paso smelter operations. (up arrow). The U.S. - Mexico Boundary Marker. (rt. arrow)

(Rio Grande Collection, Special Collections and Archives, New Mexico State University)

The adobe house was scattered among a half dozen other adobe buildings on a flat 100 acre area. Attached to it on the north side was a low dirt-roof hut that probably served as quarters for Madero's servants.[3] The building was situated such that Madero could see the roads leading into and out of Juárez, and

Figure 58. Madero in white suit in the doorway of his Mexican headquarters, *Las Casita Gris*, (The Gray House). 1911
(El Paso County Historical Society)

Figure 59. Madero and wife at *Las Casita Gris*. She actually resided with the rest of the Madero family at the Sheldon during this time period.
(El Paso County Historical Society)

Figure 60. Two unidentified men standing on the American side of the U.S. boundary next to boundary marker #1, just yards from Madero's headquarters, *Las Casita Gris* in Mexico. (El Paso Public Library, Aultman Collection)

Figure 61. Both photos show the two monuments to the Mexican Revolution. ca. 1930. In the TOP photo the monument on the left is the U.S. Boundary Marker #1 identifying the U.S. and Mexico's official border. The monument on the right is dedicated to the Madero headquarters, *Las Casitas Gris.* The LOWER photo shows the Smelter across the river in El Paso. Today, both the *Las Casitas* monument and the Smelter smokestack are gone and access to the border marker is highly restricted.

(El Paso Public Library, Southwest Collection)

the adobe house had an "easy escape" path to the footbridge crossing the Rio Grande in case he needed to get to a safer location in the U.S. The press nicknamed the headquarters Las Casita Gris (The Gray House).[4] Routinely Madero would cross back over the Rio Grande at night and go to his rooms at the Sheldon Hotel where he could bathe and change into civilian clothes.[5]

The story of the Battle of Juárez is an interesting review of early guerilla warfare and the consequences of the rebel army's leaders directly violating the order from their commander-in-chief to not attack the city. Nevertheless, the rebels did attack and took the city, captured the garrison, and relieved the federal commander of his sword. The battle was a complex and horrendous event that left the blood of rebel and federal soldiers and innocent bystanders flowing through the streets of a nearly decimated city.

It should be pointed out that there were multiple Battles of Juárez during the decade of revolution. The May 1911 battle was the event that cascaded the rebellion into high gear. Juárez was again the target of revolution on November 12, 1913. Pancho Villa failed to capture the city and fled when the federal troops received 11 trains full of reinforcements. The third battle was waged on June 15, 1919 when Villa, as he was invading Juárez, antagonized the large contingent of American soldiers who were guarding El Paso, causing them to cross the border and chase him out of town. In defeat, Villa left for Durango, but there, Villa suffered a humiliating defeat at the hands of the federals. Following the debacle at Durango, he retired to his ranch in Canutillo, near Parral, Chihuahua, and President Carranza issued Villa a full pardon.

In early April, Madero was secretly meeting with Díaz's representatives at the Sheldon Hotel. Although the effort lasted several days, nothing came of it. Minor battles continued, especially south of Juárez. Then Madero announced that he was going to attack Juárez at 6 p.m. on April 20 unless the Juárez garrison surrendered. Six p.m. came and went, Madero postponed his attack as he was short on ammunition and was being pressured to negotiate a peace because of the existing fear of American intervention. While the rebels waited, their leaders, Madero, Orozco, Garibaldi, and at times Villa, would cross over the river to the Sheldon Hotel. Garibaldi kept his room there through the campaign, as did the Madero family, but Orozco went to the hotel and registered for a room.[6] The American secret service, as well as its Mexican counterpart, roamed around the two plazas and the sidewalks next to the Sheldon, in this case, they checked the hotel's register and noticed Orozco's name. After consulting with Mayor Kelly, the chief of police, the U.S. Marshal, and the secret service agents, Mayor Kelly decided that it would be best for El Paso that Orozco be immediately returned to Mexico. The mayor had Orozco driven to a spot near the smelter, and was told to wade back across the Rio Grande to the Madero camp.[7]

The peace negotiations continued, with the mandate that Díaz resign being the major obstacle. On May 7, still hopeful for a deal, it was then that Madero ordered his troops to not attack Juárez. He then left the camp without telling anyone to lead a four-man peace commission in case the government changed its mind. The Madero peace commission met again at the Sheldon Hotel. Composed of Madero, his father Francisco Sr., Pino Suárez (soon to be his vice president), and Dr. Vazquez Gomez and Francisco Carbajal representing Díaz. They traveled to a grove of cottonwoods on the west bank of the Rio Grande now referred to as the Peace Grove near Hart's Mill a mile and a half from Juárez.

Figure 62. Conference that resulted in the *Treaty of Ciudad Juarez* and end to the first phase of the Mexican Revolution. From the left: Francisco S. Carvajal, Dr. Francisco Vazquez Gómez, Francisco I. Madero, Sr., and José Maria Pino Suárez. (Library of Congress)

While preparing to storm Juárez, the rebels and the soldiers of fortune sat idle, bored and anxious, chaffing to get to the city; and for some, to gather the spoils and bounty and run. While Madero was incognito, Orozco and Villa decided to attack Juárez when they noticed that the federals were slightly pulling back. The fighting was fierce and ugly. Timothy G. Turner, a reporter for the El Paso Herald—whose subsequent career resulted in the publication of a seminal work about the Mexican Revolution, Bullets, Bottles, and Gardenias and a journalistic career with the New York Herald and the Los Angeles Times—reported that Madero reaffirmed that there would be no attack on Juárez just as the fighting commenced. "Madero lost all control," reported Turner.[8] Madero returned to camp, and somewhat unwillingly, accepted the advance on Ciudad Juárez.

Figure 63. The rebel leaders who disobeyed Madero's orders to not attack Ciudad Juarez. They led the Battle of Juarez. From the left, Pascual Orozco, Oscar Braniff, Pancho Villa, and Giuseppe Garibaldi. May 8, 1911.
(From: Garibaldi's *A Toast to Rebellion*)

At the same time, General Juan Navarro, the federal commander was encouraging his 500 troops to stay the course. As he prepared to address his troops, he held his breath with effort, pulling down on his trim beautifully tailored grey blouse. His riding breeches were immaculate and tucked into tight riding boots. His white hair and neat beard were perfectly barbered. Juan Navarro was a very good soldier and very loyal to Díaz. "I want the patrols doubled—tripled! Get me Villa. Locate Madero's band of traitors. Find me that swine Orozco, and that meddling foreigner, Garibaldi. I have a wall to stand them all up against. Bring them to me!"[9]

Journalist William Lansford painted a picture of how El Paso was swelling with excitement as the revolutionary fever was spreading and the real possibility of a major battle, just a stone's throw from downtown El Paso, was going to begin. Lansford writes:

> The impending "Battle of Juárez" had received so much publicity in American newspapers, and drawn so many sightseers to the border city of El Paso that one writer described it as "a glorified Barnum and Bailey circus." Tourists with box cameras, college girls, newspaper correspondents, movie cameramen, salesmen, self-styled soldiers-of-fortune (most of them bums who ran at the first shot), and little old ladies from Peoria – all bent on a peek at "those Mexican bandidos!" – flocked to the streets of Juárez, daily, hoping for that ultimate thrill…a "real" battle.[10]

Garibaldi, who was in charge of the two-piece artillery, used the homemade cannon that he had made from train parts at Madera, named Long Tom, and fired three shots at the Juárez garrison. The second shot destroyed the water tower, and the third shot caused the self-destruction of the cannon.

Figure 64. The rebels manufacture cannon at train yards in Madera, Chihuahua.
(El Paso Public Library, Aultman Collection.)

Figure 65. Following the destruction of the water tower and the self-destruction of the homemade cannon. (El Paso Public Library, Aultman Collection)

It wasn't long after that, that General Juan Navarro, the commander of the federal forces, surrendered at 2:30 p.m. on May 10 after two days of battle. As he handed his sword over to Garibaldi, Villa and Orozco called for his execution. There had been bad blood between Orozco and Navarro since early days in the rebellion, when Navarro was responsible for killing many of Orozco's men. Madero, respecting Navarro, allowed him to cross the river to freedom and set in motion the brewing conflict between himself and his general. Villa, having never cared for Garibaldi, was angered that it was Garibaldi and not himself who accepted the sword of surrender. Despite the huge objections of Orozco and Villa, Madero allowed General Navarro to leave and cross the river to El Paso unmolested. Madero appointed Garibaldi provisional mayor of Juárez and head of his personal bodyguard.[11]

Villa, somewhat unrepentant, said, "We contrived to launch our attack by Military logic, circumventing Sr. Madero, who was no military man. ... Sometimes a civilian chief is unable to see what is plain to the eyes of his military subordinate. If the success of a campaign or a revolution is at stake, that subordinate must be guided by his own judgment."[12]

Figure 66. General Navarro surrenders to Garibaldi May 10, 1911.
(Jimmy Hare photograph from Garibaldi's *A Toast to Rebellion.*)

Figure 67. Navarro and Madero following the surrender.
(Jimmy Hare photograph from Garibaldi's *A Toast to Rebellion.*)

Figure 68. Vintage postcard of the damage along a Juarez street following the Battle of Juarez, 1911. (Author's Collection)

Figure 69. Iconic photograph of the victors of the Mexican Revolution, many were ultimately assassinated. Note: Second row left Pancho Villa and Garibaldi fourth from left.
(El Paso County Historical Society)

Angry, Orozco returned to his room at the Sheldon[13], but was met by Oscar Braniff (an influential banker) and Esquivel Obregón (who would later become Minister of Finance under President Victoriano Huerta), two of the envoys from the Díaz government who had been trying to extend peace talks with Madero. Braniff and Obregón, trying to divide the various rebel leaders, stoked Orozco's anger and encouraged him to return to the Madero headquarters and confront Madero regarding the handling of General Navarro's release.[14] In addition to his anger with Madero over the Navarro issue, he was not happy that Madero had appointed General Venustiano Carranza to be his Minister of War, even though Madero had promoted him to brigadier general.

Garnering support from Villa, Orozco went to see Madero at the Juárez customhouse. While Villa waited with his soldiers outside, Orozco confronted Madero in an act of mutiny, with a gun in his hand, he demanded that Navarro be executed and at that, he, Madero, should be arrested. Reacting forcefully, the diminutive Madero jumped into the towering Orozco's face and shouted "I will die first! You're dismissed." and exited the customhouse and addressed the waiting forces of Villa and Garibaldi he reiterated that he was the president.[15] At the end of his remarks to the assembled rebels, Madero says, "But these gentlemen and I have discussed General Navarro's fate at length, and we feel common decency demands that we parole him. It would be uncivilized for me to decree his execution. I have therefore given the general my personal assurances of safe conduct across the American border. I cannot go back on my word." [16] On the surface, Madero seemed to forgive Orozco for his insubordination. The clandestine meeting at the Sheldon Hotel between a disgruntled Orozco and the smooth Díaz operatives eventually bore fruit, when Orozco rebelled against the Madero presidency in 1912.

President Díaz resigned and went into exile. Madero had acquired the keys to the presidential palace and Mexico would be at peace. That did not happen. The rebellion then went into high gear and for almost the next decade, the revolution continued as the major actors in the cause for reform, turned the civil war onto themselves.

Madero's first official act after returning to the Sheldon Hotel on May 10 following the fall of Juárez, was to delegate to his father the task of issuing passports to those wishing to enter Juárez. One historian related how the process worked:

> To get to Papa Madero it was necessary to enter a swell American hotel and experience the horrors of an American elevator and the none too indulgent favors of haughty American hotel employees. For the American curiosity hounds who wished to smell the dead bodies stinking in the streets of Juárez it was a simple task to seek out Papa Madero and get their little slip of paper. They came in droves and they cluttered up the streets of Juárez and got in the road of men trying to clear up the debris. Sheer rage was in the hearts of Orozco and Villa by this time. Orozco issued an order that the Mexican end of the international bridge be closed and nobody be allowed to pass. Papa Madero himself, with a party of friends, was refused admittance.[17]

Madero proclaimed his position as the leader of Mexico and, ensconced in his Sheldon room, organized his presidential cabinet and developed his outline for the treaty. The Treaty of Ciudad Juarez concluded the initial phase of the Mexican Revolution. Historian C.L. Sonnichsen, writing on the events of May 1911 wrote:

> The fall of Juárez was the beginning of triumph and tragedy for Madero. After a great formal ball in the customhouse, attended by many Americans, he assembled his troops on May 20 for a farewell speech and departed for Mexico City to gain the presidency and lose his life. That was the end of the first phase of the Revolution. Nothing as bad as that three-day battle happened again to the border cities, but the excitement and danger were by no means over. In fact, for several years it was one scare after another as no less than ten revolutionary parties in Mexico split off, realigned, and jockeyed for position. A counter-revolution started in January 1912, when Madero's former friend and supporter Emilio Vázquez Gómez assumed the provisional presidency, but Orozco managed the matter so that there was no bloodshed. General Jose Ines Salazar occupied Juárez with 400 vasquistas on February 23, again with no fighting. A month later Orozco turned against Madero, supporting Vázquez Gómez and declaring Juárez the capital of the Republic. In August, it was all over with Orozco, and again El Paso was full of refugees, intrigue, and suspicion.[18]

On the evening of May 21, Madero's father, Francisco I. Madero, Sr., and Dr. Vazquez Gomez met with the Díaz representative, Francisco Carbajal at the Sheldon Hotel. Pino Suarez was unavailable for unspecified reasons and the others drove to the Juárez customhouse to sign the Treaty of Ciudad Juárez. The group thought that Suarez would join them, but when he didn't show, they decided to return to the Sheldon and look for him in his room and at the "soda fountain. Not locating Suarez, they returned to the customhouse. When they arrived, they found the building locked. A local Mexican newspaper reporter held his notebook as a table and Carbajal was the first to sign the document by the light of matches held by the others. Soon, someone complained about their fingers being burnt by the matches. It was then necessary to align the cars so that the headlights shown onto the steps of the customhouse as the other three fixed their signatures to the treaty document.[19] Pino Suarez signed the document the following day.[20]

The treaty specified that Díaz and his vice president, Ramon Corral, were to resign and Francisco de la Barra would serve as interim president until elections could be held. In addition, Madero had the right to name provisional state governors and approve de la Barra's cabinet.

Several weeks after the Treaty of Ciudad Juárez was signed and Madero was off to Mexico City and the poor of Mexico continued in fear, poverty, and frustration; the El Paso Times published an article that shed some light on the devastating results of the fighting. The paper reported that during the Battle of Juárez the reason that the rebels sustained very light casualties while inflicting terrible losses on the defending federal troops, was that the federal ammunition plant had been putting an insufficient amount of powder in its cartridges, causing the bullets to have reduced accuracy and shortened travel.[21]

While writing his reminiscences of the revolution, Patrick O'Hea, the chairman of the British Chamber of Commerce in Mexico had been living in Mexico attempting to keep tabs on British investments. He was witness to the realities of the rebellion as it wound through various parts of Mexico. As a non-American foreigner, he had a different perspective of what was happening around him. He concluded, "Like such a tempest came the Revolution, with fitful impulse at first, then gathering strength as the dreaded autocrat was seen to be sinking on his feet of clay. Like the destruction of the storm was the wrack that the Revolution left in its wake, a sad sight of sorrow and loss, yet inevitable and ultimately destined to reinvigorate and revive where first it had destroyed. With it, unhappily, passed forever many precious customs. The heritage of a past that will not live again, and perhaps to which time will tend to lend an unrealistic gloss."[22]

Pancho Villa v. Giuseppe Garibaldi

One of the most noteworthy events regarding the Sheldon Hotel and the Mexican Revolution became newspaper fodder around the world. There in the lobby of the Sheldon Hotel, Pancho Villa had come to kill his former compatriot, Col. Giuseppe Garibaldi. Bloodshed was avoided by the instincts of El Paso Mayor "Uncle Henry" Kelly.

The Washington Times published the following article about the insurrection in Juárez; this was most typical of the press coverage outside of the southwest. See the italicized portion for insight into one of the reasons that Villa became so upset at the press coverage in that Garibaldi, though not through any effort of his part, became the revolution's hero and darling, often brushing aside Villa and Orozco:

> The provisional president expects to go south himself in a few days to Mexico City, and he does not expect again to meet his army in the field. In the presence of the army today, he commissioned as general, Giuseppe Garibaldi, the Italian "soldier of fortune," who commanded

> and planned the attack on Juárez. The soldiers under Orozco and Villa left today for Casas Grandes and vicinity, ostensibly to be ready for an assault on Chihuahua [City] if necessary, but more particularly to get them out of Juárez, where such a large band of vile men is considered far from safe. Then, too, they will have better pasturage for their horses, and most of the men are accustomed to living in that region and will feel more at home.[23]

To brand Villa a bigot would be an understatement. Because most of the hacienda owners (Haciendados) were foreigners, either American or to a greater extent Spaniards (who were only part-time residents,) Villa developed a long standing hatred for the "high-strutting Spanish-European image. Garibaldi, with his European manners, accent, and dress was, in Villa's mind, cut from the same cloth. Villa hated the Chinese almost with the same vigor, as they were the merchants, storekeepers of Mexico, and moneylenders, yet he was not anti-Semitic.[24]

Pancho Villa didn't drink, didn't smoke, and could not read, yet was able to communicate well and establish a well-oiled public relations program. Villa was known as a man with a volcanic temper and an insatiable appetite for ice cream, peanut brittle, and women; probably in that order. He had a deadly fear of the unknown and the unexpected and was suspicious of everything and everyone, often suddenly changing his sleeping arrangements several times and at the last second.[25]

Born in a small village of Rio Grande in the State of Durango on June 5, 1878, José Doroteo Arango Arámbula was the oldest of five children. By the time, he was a young teenager; he became the head of the family and was responsible for taking care of his mother and two brothers and two sisters. When he was 16, he attempted to defend his sister from sexual assault by the landowner, Augustin Lopez Negrete. (or his son, the story varies according to the source) Doroteo killed the rapist, fled the oppressive environment, and hid in the mountains, spending six years on the run. While there, he joined a group of fugitives and became a bandit. Legend has it that Doroteo changed his name to Francisco "Pancho" Villa, in honor of a famous bandit that had been killed in the mountains of Durango.

Newspaper correspondents were enthralled by Villa's bawdy and attention- getting disposition; he was great copy, his obscenities uproarious, and his activity was the substance of bylines all over the world.[26] Journalist and author, John Reed was a favorite of Villa and spent a great amount of time traveling with him throughout Mexico. Reed, whose writings of Villa turned him into an international hero, described him as:

> The most natural human being he'd ever seen natural in the sense of being a wild animal. He says almost nothing and seems so quiet as to be almost diffident. If he isn't smiling he's looking gentle. All except his eyes, which are never still and full of energy and brutality. They are as intelligent as hell and as merciless. The movements of his feet are awkward-he always rode a horse – but those of his hands and arms are extraordinarily simple, graceful and direct. They're like a wolf's. He's a terrible man."[27]

> One hears a great many stories of Villa's violating women. I asked him if that were true. He pulled his mustache and stared at me for a minute with an inscrutable expression, "I never take the trouble to deny such stories," he said. "They say I am a bandit, too. Well, you know my history. But tell me have you ever met a husband, father, or brother of any woman that I have violated?" He paused: "Or even a witness?"[28]

Villa has been described as being one of the most "mythologized military-political leaders in Latin American history, standing alongside such independence era greats as Bolivar and O'Higgins, Benito Juárez, and Emiliano Zapata. Yet in revolutionary status quo, Villa wasn't admitted to the pantheon of the Mexican Revolution until former Villaistas and leftists pushed it through the Mexican Congress in 1966. At that time, a leftist deputy gave Villa his perfect epitaph: "A Revolution has never been made with flowers. In fact, the Villa's power continued beyond his assassination in 1923; three years later enemies entered his crypt and stole away his head. 'There. Now we're sure he's gone."[29]

El Paso Herald reporter Tim Turner, who had interviewed and traveled with all the major revolutionary characters, both federal and rebel, from the beginning of the Madero action through the Carranza presidency, described Villa:

> Morally, Villa was neither a good nor a bad man, as near as I could get at his nature from my own acquaintance with him and what people told me who had observed him throughout the revolution. He was merely a primitive man with some pro-social instincts, sometimes apparently a desire to do the right thing, but such ignorance of the world and such a violent emotional nature that he usually did the wrong thing. Then, too,

> Villa no doubt had that hypocrisy common to bandits about robbing the rich to help the poor. They always see to it that they give the poor only enough to arouse a gratitude that aids them in times of stress, keeping for themselves the lion's share until they themselves become rich men.
>
> Villa, they said, was not a sadistic killer; he killed in anger, when from his viewpoint he was morally right, but with a viewpoint too often wrong. ...Perhaps in such cases a leader likes to have handy somebody worse than he so by comparison he himself may not appear so bad. But from a practical standpoint the classical type of bandit chieftains and leaders like Villa in rough-and-tumble Mexican revolutionary politics actually need somebody handy who will kill without asking questions.[30]

American Army Chief of Staff General Hugh Scott described Villa: "He was as unmoral as a wolf; nevertheless he had some fine qualities if you could reach them... He never violated his compacts with me...Villa was a great sinner but had been greatly sinned against. He had the germs of greatness in him and the capacity of higher things under happier circumstances." General John J. Pershing, commander of Fort Bliss who would in a few years, chase Villa into Mexico after the Columbus invasion said, "He was taciturn and restless, his eyes were shifty, his attitude one of suspicion."[31]

Villa was still seething from the release of federal commander Navarro and the fact that the commander surrendered his sword to Garibaldi rather than to himself. Villa actually never liked Garibaldi from the very first day, and throughout the entire conflict, their relationship was abrasive. When he learned that Madero had accepted Garibaldi into the rebel force, Villa complained vehemently to Madero that Garibaldi was not only a foreigner but also an incompetent. Madero responded to this assault on his authority and judgment by the bandit Villa by declaring, "The deed is sanctioned by history. Every time a people have fought for its liberty, numerous foreigners have fought in the ranks of the liberators." Reminding Villa that the grandfather and father of Garibaldi "always have placed their sword at the service of the oppressed, Señor Garibaldi has given proofs of modesty and subordination which I have not found in all those who surround me."[32] Madero had accepted a variety of foreigners to help augment his rebel army besides Garibaldi, he accepted General B.J. Viljoen, a veteran of the Boer War; Sam Dreben, "the fighting Jew;" "Dynamite" Oscar

Creighton, a stockbroker who found Wall Street too tame and became expert at blowing up federal trains; and purportedly, Hollywood movie star, Tom Mix.[33]

Villa's boiling point appeared already to have been reached, but then Madero appointed Garibaldi a brigadier general on May 12 passing up Villa with the appointment.[34] Also Madero did nothing to stop the Italian soldier of fortune from commenting that Villa and Orozco were both cowards and had not actually participated in the hand-to-hand battle in Juárez and that Garibaldi alone had been the victor.[35] By this time, Villa lost all control and with two of his men in tow and two pistols in his belt, headed for the international bridge to confront Garibaldi at the Sheldon Hotel, proclaiming, "I'm going to kill that Italian bastard."[36]

When he arrived at the Sheldon about 1:30 p.m. his actions, nervous wandering about as if looking for someone, attracted the attention of the secret service agents that seemed to be ever-present in and around the Sheldon. Not finding Garibaldi, Villa did see Roque Gonzalez Garza seated in the corner of the Sheldon bar. Garza had been appointed by Madero as the official historian of the Battle of Juárez. Villa immediately approached Garza to make sure that he had the Villa version of the battle and knew that he had better write it correctly and downplay Garibaldi's role. Seated opposite them was one of the secret service agents who not only saw the pistols but also was aware that Villa was on the hunt for Garibaldi.

Garibaldi was an idealist beyond question, but also a man with a high affinity for adventure, was not at the hotel at that moment, as he was out with his camera taking pictures. When he returned to the lobby of the hotel, the agent warned Garibaldi that the rustler, horse thief, bandit, butcher, rebel general, and murderer was looking for him. Garibaldi appeared somewhat unphased by the potential danger and approached a group of friends in the middle of the lobby. Just then Villa, who was an adept horseman, but somewhat clumsy in his gait as he moved his stocky frame around, was accompanied by Gustavo Madero. They entered the lobby and the moment Villa saw Garibaldi, he flew into a rage and headed for this young tall blond Italian who was wearing his first mustache. At the same time, three secret service agents came between the two hostile warriors. Knowing that something needed to be done, Gustavo Madero ushered Villa quickly into the elevator and they went up to the Madero suite. During the five minutes that Villa and Madero were upstairs, the secret service agents had contacted Mayor Kelly, Col. Steever of the Fourth Cavalry, and Chief of Police

Jenkins. The secret service agents with Mayor Kelly's contingent and Col. Steever confronted Villa as he reentered the lobby.

When Villa saw Garibaldi, his face was purple with rage. Mayor Kelly had contemplated arresting Villa, but upon discussing the situation with the others, decided that an arrest might cause greater harm to all. Kelly felt that Villa's men in Juárez, most of who were extremely desperate characters, might get revenge against innocent and defenseless Americans in Juárez, so the decision was to disarm him rather than arresting him. Kelly and Chief Jenkins took Villa into the Kelly and Pollard Drug store, which was just off the hotel lobby and personally disarmed him saying, "Villa, I have made up my mind to lock you up, but for good and sufficient reasons I have determined to send you back to Juárez. I have issued orders that you shall not be allowed to cross over the river again if you are armed. If you do, I will put you in jail and the American courts will do the rest. Now you are going back to Juárez. Come on."[37]

With that, the little diminutive blue-eyed Irish politician had corralled and disarmed the thuggish heavy-set pistol-packing bandito. The agents escorted Villa to a waiting carriage and drove him to the borderline in the middle of the international bridge. The furious Villa got out and headed across the bridge into Juárez.

Garibaldi, according to the New York Times report on the significant de-escalation of what could have been a critical American-Mexican crisis, said:

> Before coming to the hotel, I was told that Villa was in town and wanted to see me. I was perfectly willing to see him, for I realize that he is not entirely to blame in this matter. I do not know whether Villa was here to assassinate me or not, but if he was it was due to his wild and uncontrollable temper. Persons who know his disposition and how easily he can be worked into a fury have gotten hold of him and they not he, in my opinion, are responsible for his actions today. They are the persons who are trying to create dissension in the insurrecto army, and a person of Villa's temperament is exactly suited to their business. The United States Secret Service is a fine institution.[38]

With a lobby, restaurant, and bar full of newspaper correspondents, soldiers, and mercenaries; magazines, papers, and books around the world have digested multiple accounts of the incident. Most are full of various versions that are clearly different. Yet, the tenor and the significance of the outcome of the incident remain in same.

Garibaldi, in his 1935 autobiography A Toast to Rebellion provided a slightly different version of the incident. While details differ, his version provides some clarity regarding the motivations for Villa's tirade as well as the state of the new Madero regime. Following the Navarro surrender, the active leaders of the junta, Madero, Orozco, Villa, and Garibaldi met at the little adobe headquarters adjacent to the border monument:

> In the meantime, I was sent into El Paso to negotiate with the American authorities regarding our relations to the bridges. I was poorly equipped for a mission of this sort for I had; like the rest of us, only my fighting gear that was not over-clean despite the efforts of my orderly. We discussed this problem in Madero's headquarters, and everyone present including the President, emptied his pockets. Thus with the total capital of the revolution – seventy-four dollars and sixty cents – I crossed the bridge.
>
> On the far side I was caught up on the shoulders of a cheering crowd and carried to my destination, the Hotel Sheldon. The owner [Burt Orndorff], a friend of mine, gave me his best room and promised to provide me with fresh clothes. While I was luxuriating in a needed bath, there was a rap on the door.
>
> "Who is it?" I called.
>
> "Earl Harding of the New York World." Came the answer. "My paper wants a front-page story of the Battle of Juárez."
>
> This gave me the idea of trying to recoup the slender resources of the revolution.
>
> "How much?" And no doubt Harding thought me very mercenary.
>
> "My editor has authorized me to pay you five hundred dollars."

Figure 70. Garibaldi hounded by the press in the Sheldon after the Battle of Juárez.
(By Tony Russell: Author's Collection)

"All right. Get a typewriter."

Harding returned in no time at all, and while soaping myself over and over, I dictated the story. And when I finally emerged from my bath, there on the dresser was a check for five hundred dollars. But I never saw Harding himself until later on.

With clean clothes, money in my pocket, and a drink on the table, I felt a new man and faced the officers at Fort Bliss with equanimity. Then I returned to Juárez and reported to Madero, who smiled at the dandy I had so suddenly become. Perhaps a faint trace of feminine perfume had intruded itself into my mission.

I went back to El Paso again to complete the arrangements and made my headquarters for several days at the Sheldon. …

Passing between Juárez and El Paso in the in the course of my duties, I heard that most of the American volunteers were in El Paso celebrating the victory and I did not blame them for that. But somehow Orozco's and Villa's followers started the rumor that these men had sacked the Chinese colony in Juárez and had retired across the border with their ill-gotten gains. There was, of course, no truth to this story. But the American volunteers retaliated by saying that Villa was a coward because he had not shown up during the battle.

Pancho Villa crossed at once to El Paso, but, as he did not know where these men were, he went to the Sheldon to get their addresses from me. Not finding me there, he waited in a state of fury.

I was out taking pictures with a camera Earl Harding had given me, and when I returned to the hotel, my friend the Chief of Police met me and told me not to enter because Villa was inside threatening to shoot me on sight. But I was not going to be frightened out of entering my own hotel.

I walked into the lobby, and there was Villa, leaning over the desk and talking to the room clerk. A short distance away were two detectives watching him and guarding the entrance.

I stepped toward him, and a few paces away, I stopped and pulled out my camera, focusing it on him.

"Ho, Pancho!" I called.

> He wheeled like lightning, his hands on his guns. When he saw who it was, he dropped his hands and said, "I was only going to ask you for the names of the Americans who called me a coward."
>
> Before I had a chance to answer, the Police Chief came up with the two detectives and carted Villa off to a private room where they disarmed him. Then they took him to the border and told him not to come back.[39]

As the years of the revolution continued amidst horrific loss of life and property, the Sheldon Hotel remained a continued presence in the middle of the planning, congregating, and smuggling that fed into the flames that continued to sweep Mexico. The names of the winners, the losers, and the profiteers changed as frequently as the presidency of the Mexican republic. The Orndorff family that owned the Sheldon during these times was steadfast in their attempt to remain neutral, but that proved to be a most difficult task. A new breed of sleuths from Germany joined mercenaries, military leaders, secret agents of both the United States and Mexico. Newspaper correspondents continued to fill the rooms and bars of the Sheldon cranking out battle scenes and human interests stories for international consumption, often without ever leaving their seat or putting down their drink.

Two regulars were almost fixtures in the halls and lobby of the Sheldon. Pancho Villa continued to make his presence noticed when he was in the El Paso and Juárez area. His love of ice cream led to the Elite Confectionary, down Oregon Street, on a regular basis and he used those visits as an excuse to cruise through the hotel and meet friends and make sure that the journalists, who were holding court in the Sheldon bar, were maintaining his public image as he wanted. Villa also frequently visited his pulmonologist, Dr. Charles M. Hendricks, who had an office in the Mills Building directly across the street from the Sheldon.[40] Villa is not known to have stayed overnight in the hotel, as he preferred to reside in his own El Paso house with his first wife, Luz Corral, on Prospect Street or at the Roma Hotel on South El Paso Street.

General John "Black Jack" Pershing, commander at Fort Bliss, was a regular at teatime in the Sheldon Hotel lobby.[41] He would sit and observe the carryings on between the heterogeneous mixes of international characters as an intelligence gathering exercise. He frequently was joined for personal chats by various newsmen and by his friend and neighbor, Dr. Hendricks.[42]

There occurred in 1916 an interesting episode in the history of the Sheldon that connected it to the newly opened Paso del Norte Hotel across the plaza.

The General Scott Affair

Following the March 9, 1916, invasion of Columbus, New Mexico by the rebel Pancho Villa, and the American incursion into Mexico by the Punitive Expedition under the command of General Pershing to find Villa, the governments of Mexican President Carranza and President Wilson of the United States came to a stalemate. In early May, President Wilson ordered Generals Funston and Scott to meet with Carranza's representative to resolve the issue. General Hugh Scott was a perfect choice for this mission, as the old Indian fighter was not only the Army Chief of Staff, but was fluent in Spanish and expert in the affairs of border life. President Carranza sent his Minister of War General Alvaro Obregón. The first meetings were held in Juárez and accomplished little, both sides appearing intransigent. The American generals invited Obregón to dine in the Army train car parked on a siding in the El Paso train yards. This meeting also went badly. General Funston was so frustrated by the Mexican attitude that he refused to participate in any further meetings.[43]

Several days later, Scott received a secret note from Obregón to meet him clandestinely in a suite at the Paso del Norte Hotel across the street from the Sheldon on May 3. The Sheldon Hotel was chosen not to be used because of the swarm of newsmen roaming all around the hotel seeking a scoop. Scott who was being watched intently by the newsmen, had to develop a scheme to get across the plaza without being followed. Scott writes:

> There were about thirty press correspondents in town watching events with a camera constantly near each end of our [train] car. Our departure from the car was telephoned all over town and our every movement watched. I wanted to get into Obregón's room at the hotel without the knowledge of anybody else for delicate negotiations cannot be successful in a crowd. I walked around town making small purchases here and there for about an hour until I thought all suspicion allayed, then stopped a covered laundry wagon, got in it and asked to be put down at the service entrance of the hotel and was taken up on the baggage elevator to the proper floor.[44]

After a twelve-hour marathon meeting, Obregón who had steadfastly stuck to the demand that the Punitive Expedition forces must be immediately withdrawn from Mexico, relented. The agreement was that the American forces would gradually withdraw and the Mexican government would increase its effort to capture Villa. When the document was sent to Carranza, he rejected it unless the Americans set a time certain for the withdrawal of Pershing's troops. President Wilson refused and the meeting ended. It was reported that Funston and Scott said following the collapse of the meeting, "We evidently came to discuss one question, Obregón another."[45]

The Punitive Expedition continued its search for Villa until February 5, 1917 when the Pershing troops re-crossed the border empty-handed. While they did not capture Villa, they did disrupt his military organization and learned some very strategic lessons that would become of paramount significance a year later as the United States joined the Allies in World War I.

As the revolution continued into less violent episodes, the Sheldon remained significant in its relationship to the rebellion, although the hotel began to share that role more and more with the Paso del Norte Hotel. While El Paso continued in the smuggling of arms, the community's attention was shifting to El Paso's Fort Bliss and its sudden and growing involvement in the European conflict between the Allies and the threats of Kaiser Wilhelm of Germany. New European military personalities began to arrive in the Southwest and at the Sheldon in particular.

Notes and References

[1] Harris and Sadler (2009), 40-41.

[2] Senate Subcommittee Hearings: *Revolutions in Mexico*. Held in El Paso at the Sheldon Hotel on September 7, 1912. United States Congress, Senate. Committee on Foreign Relations. Senate. 62d Congress. 1913. (Washington, D.C.: Government Printing Office, 1913.)

[3] Monaghan, Jay. *Schoolboy, Cowboy, Mexican Spy.* (Berkeley: University of California Press, 1977.), 139. And Romo, David D. *Ringside Seat to a Revolution: An Underground Cultural History of El Paso and Juárez 1893-1913.* (El Paso: Cinco Puntos Press, 2005.), 86. See photography.

[4] Shapleigh, Ballard C. "¡Viva Los Licenciados!" *El Paso Bar Journal*.(October/November

2010. Part I.), 17. Las Casita Gris, the Gray House is often referred to as the White House by some historians and journalists. The actual translation is The Gray House.
[5] Johnson, William W. *Heroic Mexico: The Violent Emergence of a Modern Nation.* (Garden City, New York: Doubleday & Company, 1968.), 57.
[6] Sonnichsen, C. L. *Pass of the North: Four Centuries on the Rio Grande.* (El Paso: Texas Western Press, 1968.), 396.
[7] Shapleigh, Ballard C. "¡Viva Los Licenciados!" *El Paso Bar Journal*. October/November 2010, 18.
[8] Atkin, Ronald. *Revolution! Mexico: 1910-1920.* (New York: J. Day Co., 1969.), 67.
[9] Lansford, William Douglas. *Pancho Villa*. (Los Angeles: Sherbourne Press, 1965.), 59.
[10] Ibid, 75.
[11] Ibid, 87.
[12] Atkin, 67.
[13] After having been escorted from the Sheldon Hotel by Mayor Kelly, Orozco managed to return and secure a room surreptitiously.
[14] Ross, Stanley R. *Francisco I. Madero: Apostle of Mexican Democracy*. (New York: Columbia University Press, 1955.), 167.
[15] Sonnichsen (1968), 401.
[16] Lansford, 89.
[17] Crichton, Kyle S. *Law and Order Ltd.: The Rousing Life of Elfego Baca of New Mexico*. (Santa Fe: New Mexican Publishing Corporation, 1928.), 118.
[18] Ibid, 402-403.
[19] *El Paso Herald,* May 22, 1911.
[20] Ross (1955), 169.
[21] *El Paso Times*, June 15, 1911.
[22] O'Hea, Patrick. *Reminiscences of the Mexican Revolution.* (Mexico, D.F.: Centro Anglo-Mexicano Del Libro, 1966.), 12.
[23] *The Washington Times*, May 21, 1911.
[24] Lansford, 75.
[25] Atkin (1969.), 146.
[26] Harris and Sadler (2009), 42.
[27] Krauze, Enrique. *Mexico: Biography of Power, A History of Modern Mexico, 1810-1996.* Translated by Hank Heifetz. (New York: Harper-Collins, 1997.), 316.
[28] Reed, John. *Insurgent Mexico.* (New York: International Publishers, 1914.): 130-131.
[29] Milholland, David. "John Reed in Mexico & Latin America." *Oregon Cultural Heritage Commission.* Accessed 12 April 2016.

[30] Turner, Timothy G. *Bullets, Bottles and Gardenias.* (Dallas: South-West Press, 1935.), 167-169.
[31] Scheina, Robert L. *Villa: Soldier of the Mexican Revolution*. (Dulles, VA: Brassey's Inc., 2004.), 98-99.
[32] Ross (1955), 144.
[33] Johnson, David N. *Madero in Texas.* (San Antonio: Corona Publishing Company, 2001.), 106.
[34] *El Paso Times*, July 27, 1932.
[35] Katz, Friedrich. *The Life and Times of Pancho Villa.* (Palo Alto: Stanford University Press, 1998.), 118.
[36] Meed, Donald V. *Soldier of Fortune: Adventuring in Latin America and Mexico with Emil Lewis Holmdahl.* (Houston: Halcyon Press, Ltd., 2003.), 108.
[37] *New York Times*, May 18, 1911.
[38] Ibid.
[39] Garibaldi, Giuseppe. *A Toast to Rebellion*. (New York: Bobbs-Merrill Company, 1935.): 296-297, 301-302.
[40] Charles M. Hendricks Personal interview.
[41] Perry, John. Pershing: Commander of the Great War. (Nashville: Thomas Nelson, 2011.), 99.
[42] Campbell, C.E. *Going the Extra Yard: An Army Doctor's Odyssey*. (Burbank: Endangered History Project, 2013.), 61.
[43] Scott, Hugh L. *Some Memories of a Soldier.* (New York: The Century Co. 1928.), 525-526.
[44] Ibid.
[45] Metz, León C. *Borderland: The U.S. Mexico Line*. (El Paso: Mangan Books, 1989.), 226.

Chapter Sixteen

Mercenaries: Idealists or Looters?

The mere mention of the word mercenary brings to the modern reader thoughts of the Blackwater Group, the private army used by the American government to augment its military operations in Iraq and Afghanistan, to provide security for Department of State personnel, and possibly carryout missions that may have been beyond the accepted range of "rules." Retired navy seals established the Blackwater Group in the late 1990s. They soon changed their name to Academi in 2011 following some adverse press. The mercenary organization continues to operate in secretive and clandestine operations for a price. There doesn't appear to be any real consensus as to the use of the terms Mercenary and Soldier of Fortune. Most writers use the terms interchangeably, yet some declare a significant difference between the two. A mercenary is one who fights for a nation or a political leader, other than his home state or nation, motivated solely by financial gain; often including free access to the remnants and booty of the vanquished. On the other hand, the use of the term Soldier of Fortune is frequently used to indicate a mercenary who is motivated by the ideals and principles of the conflict.[1] In the present text, these terms are used synonymously as foreign volunteers who fought alongside Mexican nationals for either side of the conflict; men fighting to escape a dark past, fighting for pay, fighting for the love of adventure and/or for the "hell of it."

"I saw few soldiers of fortune except one—and he was a dry-as-dust scientist studying the action of high explosives in field guns—who would not have been tramps in their own country," wrote journalist John Reed in his well-respected book, Insurgent Mexico.[2] Lawrence Taylor, in his analysis of the role of the mercenary in the Mexican Revolution counters Reeds comments: "In contrast to Reed, and as another example of the image of the adventurer in the public mind, there are the numerous novels and films that portray the mercenary in the Revolution as a romantic hero. Yet, apart from the excellent and exciting narrative left by Reed [in 1914] and the stereotype conjured up by Hollywood, there exists a great deal of documentation concerning the participation of the

Figure 71. The American Soldiers of Fortune with its commander, Garibaldi second row, third from the left. 1911.
(El Paso County Historical Society)

Figure 72. Vintage postcard of Garibaldi and his soldiers of fortune.
(Author's Collection)

foreign soldier in the Mexican Revolution. This material reveals that such men did not, as Reed asserts, represent the worst of their countrymen nor did they win the war single-handedly. Although relatively small in numbers, they made a substantial contribution in terms of affecting the course and outcome of the military struggle."[3]

The enlistment of foreign mercenaries for war can be traced back to the mid-Fourth Century B.C. when the king of Persia (Xerxes I) used hired Greek soldiers to invade Greece. The practice of using these hired fighters became so common in 17th and 18th Century that among the European states, only Switzerland never employed foreigners.[4]

Many of the mercenaries who enlisted in the Madero cause had just served in various African and South American rebellions, had unique experiences, but the majority of the volunteers lacked specific skills other than to fill the ranks of the rebel infantry. Among the El Falange De Los Extranjeros [The Phalanx of Aliens, loosely translated means a tight group of foreign officers or fighters.] or American Legion, were a group of 60 to 80 under the command of Garibaldi.

Most of the mercenary activity took place 1910 to 1915. The relationship between the Mexican rebels and the mercenaries was diaphanous at best. Jealousies and misunderstandings were rampant, "many Mexican commanders were offended by the presence of foreigners in their ranks due to a mixture of patriotic sentiment and fear of the newcomers, whom they referred to as 'gringo spies.' They criticized foreign volunteers for being filibusteros Extranjeros — who would desert to the opposite camp for better offers of pay."[5] Historians would later indicate that the mercenaries were no more prone to switch sides than was the average Mexican officer or enlisted man whose sense of loyalty was apt to change depending on the changing fortunes of war. "Dislike and distrust of the mercenaries was fairly common throughout the Revolution and Mexican attitudes towards the mercenaries often reflected biases or prejudices towards the nations from which they came."[6]

Following the Battle of Juárez, the group somewhat disbanded, many leaving to fight in new rebellions, while others just tried to rebuild their lives upon returning to the United States. The El Paso Herald reported in 1911:

> The "American Legion" of the insurgents is not going to be part of the command much longer. They are quitting the service fast and are now practically out of it, according to all reports. Charges of looting by the

> Americans were made in Juárez to Col. G. Garibaldi. A Chinaman in particular made a charge that some of them had taken money from him. Garibaldi asked Lt. Linderfelt to investigate the charges but it is said that nothing was done. … Then it was noticed that at least some of the Americans admitted that they are quitting, but declare that they are piqued because they did not receive credit or glory for what they did.
>
> While most of the Americans fought well in Casas Grandes and Ciudad Juárez, the company collectively had caused more trouble than any other group. Of the 35 original members of "the American Legion" only a few remain. Since the attack, scores of Americans have taken arms and are strutting around Juárez as if they were real heroes. It is doubtful if ever again an American company will be formed on an organized basis. Those Americans who have some military service, either in the regular army or filibustering in South America, have proved themselves of value as fighting men. But in all, the Americans have made more trouble than all the other foreigners—Italians, Germans, Swiss, and Spanish—put together, and if any are kept in the service, it will be as individuals in Mexican command.[7]

There was extreme competition among the gathered newspapermen, and it is somewhat difficult to measure the veracity of the above article, for it may be more of an opinion piece rather than a true report, and it was published within a couple of days after the Juárez battle.

As the Revolution continued and moved through its various phases, new faces, new volunteers, new soldiers of fortune slowly replaced Garibaldi's group; but they continued to congregate in and around the Sheldon Hotel.

There existed great resistance to accepting foreign volunteers. The Díaz government, fearful of international complications and embarrassments, rejected almost all of those volunteers who were willing to side with the dictator. One of the notable exceptions was the Moscow-born Russian sailor who deserted his country to become one of the most feared of Díaz's agents, Col. Emilio Kosterlitzky. Díaz appointed Kosterlitzky as chief of the Mexican border patrol, the Rurales, as well as had him serve in a multitude of military roles and as an expert linguist, speaking fluently nine languages (English, French, Spanish, German, Russian, Italian, Polish, Danish, and Swedish).

One of the flashiest and most romantic characters of the Madero foreign legion was, Col. Giuseppe (Peppino) Garibaldi II, the Italian Soldier of Fortune, and grandson of the Italian unifier General Giuseppe Garibaldi I. He is often referred to by his nickname Peppino, to prevent confusion in history with his namesake, General Giuseppe Garibaldi I (1807-1882). In the pages that follow are brief summaries of the most high-profile mercenaries that were active during the various phases of the Revolution. More space is devoted to Garibaldi than the others, partly because his role in the Madero rebellion was so significant, partly because he was a man of ideals and principles, but also because his affiliation with the Sheldon Hotel was so public.

While Garibaldi maintained a residence in the Sheldon Hotel, Col. Kosterlitzky was a frequent visitor and would occasionally keep a room at the Sheldon and at the Orndorff Hotel in El Paso.[8] Garibaldi authored his autobiography in 1935, A Toast to Rebellion[9], which remains one of the most fascinating tomes of the Mexican Revolution, as well as his storied adventures around the world earning him the recognition as one of the greatest soldiers of fortune of all time. Kosterlitzky's biography, Emilio Kosterlitzky...Eagle of Sonora and the Southwest Border[10] written by C.C. Smith, Jr. was published in 1970. This book tells of the Kosterlitzky saga in the Mexican army and his role in defending Díaz during the Mexican Revolution, his arrest in Arizona in 1913, and his eventual employment as a spy for the American government. Smith's father was a contemporary of Kosterlitzky and provided rare insight into his subject not afforded to other authors.

Col. Giuseppe (Peppino) Garibaldi, II

Born in Melbourne, Australia, in 1879, the son of General Ricciotti Garibaldi, a globetrotting soldier of fortune, Peppino channeled his entire life to the military service of the oppressed and downtrodden peoples around the world. As a young adult, Peppino, the eldest of six sons carried on the Garibaldi tradition established by his grandfather, the great Italian liberator, Giuseppe Garibaldi I. (Some historians, mostly international, refer to him as José rather than Peppino.) The senior Garibaldi's successful career as a military leader and his skill at bringing the common people of the various independent states of Italy together into one nation in the 1860s; led to the unification of the nation. The unification of Italy, following the Franco-Prussian War, established Garibaldi as a national hero.

Peppino would frequently join his father and five brothers and other volunteers in the Garibaldi Legion. The Garibaldi Legion was a small but forceful Italian unit of the French Foreign Legion, often referred to as the "Red Shirts," as they engaged in revolutions and rebellions around the world.

In his autobiography, Garibaldi relates how in 1897, at the age of 17, he climbed out the window of the Technical College at Fermo, Italy, where he was studying engineering, to join his father in the Greek war with the Turks:

Figure 73. Col. Giuseppe Garibaldi II, 1911. 1879-1950

(Author's Collection)

> After completing my meal, I hastened to join my comrades outside, and to my surprise, instead of noisy groups playing or arguing, I found the whole school of about three hundred students, silently waiting my arrival. Without a word, a friend handed me a newspaper with the headline, ITALIAN VOLUNTEERS UNDER GENERAL GARIBALDI SAIL FOR GRECO-TURKISH WAR. As soon as I overcame my surprise and understood the full impact of the news, I was filled with pride.
>
> "I will join my father," I declared, "I'll go to Greece too, and you are going to help me." I was immediately the hero of the moment. Excited students crowded around shouting advice and offering help and insisting that they would accompany me to war. Then, catching sight of a professor approaching, we agreed in whispers to meet again late that night.
>
> Mingled with my excitement over my impulsive decision was a feeling of resentment. My father had always promised to take me along the next time he went to war. I had wanted to go to a military school so as to follow our family tradition properly equipped, and had only been persuaded to go instead to an engineering college by the assurance that

> I would be allowed to learn the art of war on battlefields instead of in barracks. That too, was the Tradition.
>
> The afternoon classes and study hours seemed endless. Mathematical problems were confused with railroad timetables, and chemical formulas were crowded out of my mind by thoughts of cheering crowds and flags and night marches and charging troops. The very air was fierce and light, and intoxicating like a strange gas. And the food that evening was unlike anything I had tasted before. After an interminable wait on our dormitory beds, we heard the bell of a near-by church solemnly toll midnight. We rose and along pitch-black corridors and up winding stairs we stole to our prearranged meeting under the roof. A few candles were lighted and sheltered cautiously in the darkness.
>
> When the whole student body was gathered. I mounted a box and addressed the meeting with youthfully sententious but deeply felt oratory. I spoke of my gratitude and devotion to the college and of my loyalty to all the assembled students. I told them what I knew of the Turkish oppression of the Greeks in Macedonia and Crete and of the direct causes of the war. ...Then rather lamely, I ended with a request for a rope made of sheets that would reach the ground from a window on the floor below, and also for funds to take me home.
>
> I was immediately supplied with more than enough money and sheets to reach to Inferno. Several of my friends insisted that they would accompany me, but I told them that my only chance was to go alone. One end of the long white rope was tied securely to an iron ring near the window, and the other with my traveling bag was lowered to the ground. In the darkness of the dormitory good-byes were whispered, I swung out of the window and lowered myself on the knotted rope. Hands from the upper windows waved me a silent farewell. I knew all my fellow students envied me, but at that moment, I was feeling far from brave.[11]

After a brief visit with his mother where he told her, "As the eldest son, the decision [to join his father] was mine to make. Father must not be left alone so far away and in the midst of danger." Still his mother resisted his decision to go and would not do anything to help him. "Then I'm going without your consent. I have enough money to take me to Rome on the night train, and I shall manage somehow to get on from there." His mother smiled tenderly and said, "Take care of Father and come back to me."[12]

Garibaldi made his way to Athens where his father was assembling a band of Italian volunteers to fight in the Greek war against the Turks. It was there, in the Garibaldi tradition, "he donned the Garibaldi's traditional red shirt, because a man in a red shirt can neither hide nor retreat."[13] Garibaldi joined up with other Italian volunteers and was met by his father at the Athens train station. A group of his officers and a welcoming cheering crowd surrounded his father. He put both hands on his son's shoulders and said, "I would never have lifted a finger to get you here, son, but I'm glad you've come. I'll need you."[14]

Following his initiation into the world of mercenaries, he was frequently quoted as stating that he resented being called a soldier of fortune, he said that the only time he ever fought against his ideals and moral convictions was in the Boer War where Britain fought for control of South Africa, when he joined a mounted column under Lord Kitchener. While serving with the Red Shirts (Garibaldi Legion) in Uruguay, he wrote:

> I was surprised one day to receive a cable from my father in Italy, ordering me to go to South Africa to join the English forces fighting against the Boers. … The Boer War had now been going on for over a year. After their early reverses, the British had driven the Boer commandos before them and were occupying the Orange Free State and the Transvaal, relieving the isolated garrisons that had managed to hold out during the days of Boer supremacy. My father's cable left me in a quandary, for my sympathies were with the Boers. According to the general opinion held throughout the world, the two tiny Boer republics were fighting valiantly for their independence against the might of the vast British Empire.[15]

By the time Garibaldi was 23, he was a veteran warrior of the Boer War and was leading 3000 rebel Venezuelans against their dictator Cipriano Castro. Not everything went well in Venezuela and Castro captured Garibaldi. Castro placed Garibaldi aboard the ship Zamora and had him taken to the prison at the Fortress of Puerto Cabello about 140 miles west of Caracas. Garibaldi wrote, "We lost all sense of time on board the Zamora, but since eternal damnation is reserved for hell, that voyage ended at last. The rolling of the ship ceased, the engines stopped, and we heard the clank and rattle of the anchor chain. Above us loomed the sinister walls of the fortress of Puerto Cabello."[16]

Days turned into weeks, weeks into months. Garibaldi kept a record of the passing days on the wall of his cell, "My jailers would not answer any questions, even as harmless as one as the date. Their silence was maddening, and I began talking to myself to hear the sound of a human voice. But this proved a dangerous habit, for from innocuous topics I turned to discussing the injustice of my treatment and worked myself into frenzy. I was slipping, I suppose, into madness."[17] With the help of a fellow inmate and his stealth at scavenging miscellaneous items, he escaped the prison and swam to safety through waters thick with sharks.[18] Once free, he contacted the Italian Consul at Puerto Cabello who told him that Castro would allow him to leave Venezuela. The consul arranged for his departure. As he was preparing to leave, he wrote:

> I noticed that despite the casualness of my departure several secret agents had boarded the train after me. I was accompanied to La Guairá by a friend who owned copper mines with an office near the pier from which my ship was to leave. We entered the building without so much as a glance of interest at the tall steamer across the street, but saw that Castro's agents had stationed themselves at the head of the pier. When the time came for the ship to sail, I strolled innocently across the street examining with studied interest some samples of ore which I held in my hands. Reaching the pier head, I made a sudden dash for the gangplank and gained the deck closely followed by two detectives. But the captain of the ship had received his instructions from the Italian Minister, and as soon as I was on board, he stepped quickly across the gangplank with an Italian flag in his hands. He defied the protesting agents to board the ship and told them that he would not give me up without a written order from the Italian Minister.
>
> The whistle sounded, hawsers were cast off, and the gangplank hauled in. As the screw commenced to turn and open water appeared between the ship and the pier, I felt safe at last. And in the stern, I watched the peaks of Naiguata sink slowly into the sea, while many memories crowded my mind: Petare, El Guapo, Ciudad Bolivar—and the tragic ending of our hopes in the fortress of Puerto Cabello. As I went to the bow and turned my eyes in the direction of far-off Italy, I knew that I had left my youth behind on the battlefields and in the prisons of Venezuela.

> On my trip home to Italy I could not help being concerned about the accounting I should have to give my father. By joining the Venezuela rebellion, I had carried the Tradition to a new part of the world without so much as consulting him; and instead of victory, our campaign had ended miserably in defeat and imprisonment. What is more, the cause, however gallant in its inception, had been marred by the stigma of flagrant treachery. I could expect no easy judgment from General Ricciotti Garibaldi.[19]

Following a trip to Panama at the request of the Italian Minister of Foreign Affairs, Garibaldi eventually found his way to California where he worked as an engineer in oil fields and on railway construction. Soon he felt the sirens call of Mexico. Arriving in 1910, he wrote, "Since 1876, when he overthrew Benito Juárez in a barrack revolution, Mexico had been under the iron domination of the dictator Porfirio Díaz. Peonage still flourished, and most of the land was in the hands of the Church and large landowners. Oppression was the rule. Ever since Cortez had landed at Vera Cruz and marched on the Aztec Empire, Mexico's history had been written in blood, and tyrant had succeeded tyrant."[20]

After his participation in the Revolution and escorting Francisco Madero to Mexico City to assume the leadership of Mexico, Garibaldi left Mexico and went to Boston in the fall of 1912. It was in Boston that he attempted to transfer his mining and oil lands to an American syndicate. Suddenly, he received a cable from his father who was in Athens. "Come at once," his father, pleaded. Just days before Greece, Serbia, Montenegro, and Bulgaria had attacked Turkey and the Balkan War had begun. Garibaldi left immediately to continue the Garibaldi Tradition. He described this new adventure:

> I arrived [in New York] at six and at noon I was aboard the Patria, which was carrying home eight hundred Greek volunteers to fight against the Turks. We landed at the Piraeus and I reached Athens to find my father on the point of leaving that same evening by train for the front. The Red Shirt volunteers had already gone on ahead. At the hotel my mother was awaiting me with my uniform ready. I was greatly saddened by my father's appearance. His once vigorous frame now rested on crutches, which he was compelled to rely on in all his movements. But his spirit was as indomitable as in the past: he was still the custodian of the Tradition.

> Fifteen years before I had come as a schoolboy of seventeen to fight for Greece against the same enemy, innocent of war and the world. Now I had returned, this time a major general in the Greek Army, surrounded by the same flaming Red Shirts of our volunteers, for the same Tradition and the same ideal. From the beloved hands of my father and mother, I received my uniform, my sword, and my rank.[21]

As 1914 approached, the Garibaldis, fearing the unrest that was rumbling through Europe, contacted the British government and volunteered their Garibaldi Legion to serve in the British army. The British government rejected the offer on nationalistic issues. When the calamity of the Sarajevo assassination of Archduke Ferdinand occurred, Garibaldi prepared to go to France and join their army. He read in the French papers that his father had offered to raise an Italian legion of Red Shirt volunteers to serve the beleaguered French nation. Garibaldi's father at the Battle of Dijon had captured the only flag the Germans lost in the Franco-Prussian War. "It was a bitter disappointment to him, lame and in his sixty-eighth year that the French War Office decided that I, a younger man, should assume command of the Red Shirts in 1914. And, from China, Egypt, Cuba, the United States, and Italy came seven Garibaldis, his sons, to follow his lead and offer their swords to France. Two gave their lives. Such is the Tradition."[22]

The German government feared the Garibaldis as soldiers, it was reported that the Germans had placed a $10,000 price on the head of Giuseppe Garibaldi, dead or alive. Although the Germans issued an immediate denial, the Garibaldi supporters indicated that they had significant evidence that the report was correct.[23]

The Garibaldi Red Shirts[24] were fighting in the Argonne region in March 1915, when word came that the Italian government was planning to join the Allies in the fight against the Central Powers. The French government then released the Italian soldiers to return to their native homeland and mobilize on behalf of Italy. Garibaldi and his four surviving brothers, with a group of other Italian volunteers, left the French service and joined the Italian fighting force in the Alpine Brigade on the Italian front. The brigade moved to the Cadore region on Italy's border with Austria. The Garibaldi Legion had taken an oath to defeat the Austrians or die in the attempt.[25]

After the war, Garibaldi made an attempt to live a quiet life. This was one of the few failures in his diverse and adventuresome life. He became an ardent anti-Fascist and vocal opponent of Mussolini. When Mussolini seized power of Italy in 1922, Garibaldi move to France where he remained and continued his anti-Fascist activity. In a cleaver act by the Fascist regime of Mussolini, rumors were spread that, in fact, Garibaldi was actually a Mussolini spy stirring up demonstrations and revolts in order that the ringleaders were discovered and destroyed. No matter how untrue, Garibaldi was arrested and convicted, ultimately serving two months in prison.[26] His brother, Ricciotti Jr., was also arrested and sentenced to a lengthy prison term.[27]

His anti-Fascist activity led to a confrontation with a group of Fascist militiamen when he called the militia "a gang in the pay of the Government," while leading a group of Italian veterans in an Armistice Day celebration. General Varini, the Fascist militia commander, then challenged him to a duel. Garibaldi ignored the challenged, but stated that he would accept a duel with Premier Benito Mussolini himself. The Italian dictator ignored the counter-challenge and Garibaldi returned to France.[28]

In 1924, he moved to the United States and lived there until 1940.[29] During his time in the United States, Garibaldi continued with a high-profile life continuing to travel around the country on speaking tours on subjects regarding his adventures, his seven wars, and the defense of his wrongly imprisoned brother. He also became a radio personality on WCDA (1250 AM). This was an Italian language radio station in Manhattan supported by the Italian Historical Society of America and many other Italian businesses whose mission was to assist and prepare Italian immigrants to becoming American citizens. (The WCDA stood for *Corriere d'America* and was dissolved in 1933.)[30]

In February 1926, Garibaldi married divorcee Mrs. Madalyn Nichols Taylor of New Orleans. However, because of some rather questionable issues surrounding her Mexican divorce from her previous husband, Garibaldi arranged for an annulment which was secretly granted by the court in Nyack, New York on March 9, 1929. They remarried after the technicalities were resolved.[31]

Garibaldi returned to Italy in 1940 and in 1943, the occupying Germans arrested him and sent him to prison at Regina Coeli. (Rome's best-known prison and jail built in 1654.) After the end of the war, he and his wife maintained a very private life in Rome, where he died at the age of 70 in May 19, 1950.

Throughout Giuseppe Garibaldi's life, he espoused the belief that traditions of a country are its strength and without traditions, it is no country. In 1932, while living in New York, he wrote the dedication to Boechieshis' book about his grandfather, Garibaldi: In the Light of History. It clearly and succinctly summarizes the principles and ideals of Garibaldi:

> The awakening spirit of redemption, leading Italy out of the darkness of the Middle Ages, engraved upon history the names of the men who fulfilled her unification. As the shepherd in the high peaks of our Alps, as dawn sees the gradual rising of the sun repulsing all darkness and dispelling all fogs, so the people in spirit and body met and received the coming of the flaming Red Shirt. From the chains of foreign dominators, to the infamous prisons of the Liparian Islands, to the horrors of the inquisition of the Popes, blended in sorrow and misery but tempered by steel, in thousands, the martyred patriots rose to destiny and answered the roll call. Leading them to victory was one patriot, one hero in the midst of man —GARIBALDI—The reader of these pages will realize that overcoming all prejudices, surrounded by mistrust and jealously, with treason and implacable enemies waiting for him at every turn of the endless road to liberty, my grandfather will always remain the true symbol for the Italian people.
>
> Giuseppe Garibaldi
> New York, June 2, 1932[32]

Col. Emilio Kosterlitzky

History leaves little doubt that Emilio Kosterlitzky was one of, if not, the most brutal and barbaric of all of the military leaders of the Mexican Revolution, whether rebel or federal. Known as the Iron Fist of Dictator Porfirio Díaz,[33] Kosterlitzky with his band of ruthless Guardia Rural, the rurales, prowled the Mexican-U.S. border in search of Díaz's political opponents and their followers. Organized similarly to the Texas Rangers of the time, they built a reputation of equal disgust. The cutthroat rurales were primarily composed of "reformed" bandits, hardened criminals, and conscripted felons from Mexican prisons. These rurales were so nicknamed because they were always patrolling the countryside and never in garrisons or major encampments. Under the leadership of Kosterlitzky, Mexicans of all strata of society feared the rurales and Col. Kosterlitzky. The colonel was answerable only to President Díaz whose philosophy of maintaining order was "Catch in the act, kill on the spot."[34]

Kosterlitzky, a tall and erect figure with dark flashing eyes, a bristled full mustache, and never without his Cossack's sword, immediately gave the impression of being an aristocrat. He was an expert equestrian in his wild pursuit of fugitives along the border and "was followed by tales of ruthless discipline of his own men, of captives who dug and died in their own graves, and of frequent resort to El ley del fuga—the law for those who died while trying to 'escape'." [35] Kosterlitzky was often called Juez de Cordada which meant "Judge of the roped ones," Suggesting that the name grew out of the rurales affinity for hanging suspects when they couldn't convince their captives to "escape."

Figure 74. Emilio Kosterlitzky Chief of Mexican Secret Police, *Rurales,* and later an American spy. 1853-1928

Emil Kosterlitzky was born in Moscow in 1853. His father was a Russian Cossack cavalry officer and his mother was German. While he became a unique linguist, his passion was to follow his father's example as a mounted military officer. Yet he ended up as a young teenager in the Russian navy. He deserted his post on a Russian man-of-war ship in Venezuela in 1872 and eventually made his way north to Mexico, where he changed his name to Emilio, and joined the Mexican cavalry in May 1873. Kosterlitzky became a Mexican citizen by his marriage to Francisca Lopez (1877-1940) and quickly rose through the ranks of the Mexican military. As a Mexican soldier, he engaged in battles with the Apaches, Yaquis, and Maya Indian warriors in the 1880s.

With the success in the Apache Wars, Díaz now had access to the northern portion of Mexico, mineral rich Chihuahua, and Sonora, and used that to induce more American investment into his nation that eventually led to the Mexican Revolution. Kosterlitzky had been recognized as a major contributor to Mexico's success against the Indians. Díaz promoted Kosterlitzky and assigned him as an officer in the gendarmería fiscal, the mounted state patrol, or rurales to the state of Sonora in 1885. There he managed the people, merchandise, and capital that crossed the border and worked closely with the Arizona Rangers to control border crossing and maintain the confidence of foreign investors.

Things began to change for Díaz around 1900, and he formed a new military force, the Guardia Rural, with Kosterlitzky as its commander of nearly 1200 rurales.[36] In 1906, Kosterlitzky and his rurales were sent to Cananea, a mining town in Sonora where nearly 5,000 Mexican mine workers had gone on strike. The Mexican workers, averaged three and a half pesos a day compared to the five pesos that the American workers were making. The strike against the Cananea Consolidated Copper Company owned by the infamous New York copper magnate William C. Greene, is one of the most significant events in Southwest history. The rurales were to back up the enforcement activities of the volunteers who had come from Bisbee, Arizona to help Greene's local enforcers.

Historian Sonnichsen wrote of the press reports of the strike and indicated that there may have been some real bias shown by such American journalists as socialist John Kenneth Turner, who described the strike in his 1910 book Barbarous Mexico, although he had never been to the mining town.[37] Turner had written that the strikers were never aggressive against the company, even though several company employees had been killed, and that Kosterlitzky had behaved with complete barbarity. "Miners were taken from the jail and hanged. Miners were taken to the cemetery, made to dig their own graves and were shot. Several hundred of them were marched away to Hermosillo, where they were impressed into the Mexican army. Others were sent away to the penal colony on the island of Tres Marias."[38]

Another account of Kosterlitzky activity at the strike states, "Late in the day a detachment of rurales arrived under the command of Colonel Emilio Kosterlitzky. 'Justice' was quick for those workers Kosterlitzky considered ringleaders: they were rounded up, escorted out of town, and hanged from trees. The strike was broken, and the workers, threatened with induction into the army, returned to their jobs."[39] Whether the details of Kosterlitzky's actions are accurate, the reports and innuendos went a long way to solidify Kosterlitzky as a heinous terror along the Mexican border.

Kosterlitzky was identified by Americans as a, "mythical icon not unlike the U.S. cowboy. The fact the he rode the Mexican countryside, not the Russian steppe, made him only more romantic. If the violence of the frontier made Kosterlitzky a citizen of a foreign land, the fantasy of the frontier ensured his rise as a local hero. His white skin—and white horse—set him apart from his brown-skinned neighbors, whom white Americans equated with banditry, not heroism. In popular accounts, he was a picturesque leader, whereas his colleagues were considered rough characters."[40]

As a commander of a military force, Kosterlitzky was dedicated to the principle of loyalty to the constituted authority, so with the fall of Díaz, he continued to serve under the newly elected president, Francisco Madero. The nepotism and continued dalliance of Madero was a cause of alarm among many of his previous supporters. In particular, General Alvaro Obregón, who was in command of the Sonora state forces and was in direct opposition to Madero and his subsequent replacement Victoriano Huerta after Huerta had Madero assassinated. Huerta's savagery was severe and Obregón then aligned himself with the rebels. Thus began the Huerta Phase of the Mexican Revolution, the Constitutionalist Civil War under the leadership of future president, Venustiano Carranza. Kosterlitzky never liked either Madero or Huerta, but remained loyal to the Federal Government.

Early in 1913, Kosterlitzky, seeking medical treatment for an eye wound, returned to El Paso.[41] Subsequently he granted an interview with the El Paso Herald regarding his involvement in the rebel activity in Sonora:

> Wait till I get back there, I'll make those fellows sorry, I am a defender of the established government, whatever it may be, and I always have been. These men are invaders. They will find little sympathy but much lead when they come to Sonora. Rojas – bah! He's the one I want to get. I cannot see more than 50 yards now, but I will lead my men blind after that fellow! When I return, the invaders will see what the federal Rurale can do. He is the greatest fighter I have ever known. With my men to lead, I will want nothing more to complete my career than to drive this horde from the state.[42]

Carranza had enlisted Pancho Villa and Alvaro Obregón as his chief officers. Obregón chased Kosterlitzky into Nogales, Sonora. Obregón and his force of 1500 had Kosterlitzky and his 285 rurales penned up against the border at Nogales, Arizona. The battle at Nogales was very one sided from the beginning, as the 2000 federal reinforcements had not arrived and Kosterlitzky made the public pronouncement that, "things look pretty bad." All movable valuables, including safes, were taken to the American side from the Mexican customs house, and Nogales banks began to transfer funds to the American side of the border.[43]

Knowing that capture by the rebels would be certain death, Kosterlitzky moved his troops across the border into the United States and surrendered to Captain Cornelius C. Smith on March 13, 1913. Kosterlitzky presented his

Cossack sword to Captain Smith as he surrendered.[44] (See the endnote regarding the return of the sword to the Kosterlitzky family.) While it is true, "that Obregón personally would not have harmed Kosterlitzky or his men, his followers almost certainly would have, or made a try. The Rurales were respected and admired by the property owners, but feared and hated by the peon—and Obregón's army was made up of peons. He simply demanded unconditional surrender, and that spelled death to Kosterlitzky's people. Kosterlitzky did the only thing he could have done. He fought, hoping for victory, and when further resistance proved futile, he surrendered his men to American forces that they might live."[45]

Following six months in jail in Nogales, Arizona, Kosterlitzky, and his men were moved to an internment camp at Fort Rosecrans in San Diego where he lived in a small framed house with his family just inside the Fort's main entrance. He remained at Fort Rosecrans until October 1914. The Mexican government declared a general amnesty and many of the rurales returned to Mexico that October, Kosterlitzky however, while he retained his Mexican citizenship, chose not to return.[46] While in American custody, Kosterlitzky was promoted to brigadier general by Mexican President Huerta. Kosterlitzky refused the promotion because he viewed the act as purely honorary and meaningless. He never used the title, and referred to himself as Colonel until his death.[47]

Local FBI agent E.P. Webster[48] contacted the interned Kosterlitzky and asked him if he would arrange to have some of his fellow Mexican internees go to downtown San Diego and mingle with locals and see if they could learn anything about revolutionary activities that might be going on near the border. Kosterlitzky acted as the translator for the information when it was collected.[49]

His relationship with Webster would prove significant when he moved to Los Angeles in October 1914. He bought a house, a small bungalow at 2170 W. 31st. Street, in downtown Los Angeles, just a few blocks west of the University of Southern California.[50] It was there that he led the life of a translator for the U.S. Postal Service. That, however, was subterfuge; he was in fact, because of his previous experience with agent Webster, hired by the Department of Justice and worked as spy for the FBI (A counter-espionage agent against the German spies working in the Los Angeles area.) beginning on March 26, 1917. He lived incognito, his mission was to mingle within the German community and loiter around Pershing Square (Pershing Square is a public park in downtown Los Angeles, California, one square block in size, bounded by 5th Street to the north, 6th Street to the south, Hill Street to the east, and Olive Street to the west.)

During the last year of WWI, Kosterlitzky, wearing dark glasses and casual dress, moved from one bench to another at Pershing Square. He acted as if "reading the paper," but eavesdropped on anyone speaking in a foreign language. He would snoop around the alleys leading off the park in search of suspicious-looking objects that might be "drops." He passed himself off as a German doctor and through social interaction and eavesdropping German immigrants; he gathered intelligence that was helpful as the United States was moving closer to entering WWI.

Amid the post-war years, he continued his work with the FBI and helped the agency apprehend bootleggers and rumrunners. "From today's condescending viewpoint, the techniques of undercover agents of the 1920s seem to smack of comic opera bouffe, filled with cloak and dagger arrests, thin disguises, hot-chases through city streets with guns blazing, and all the rest. Indeed many of Kosterlitzky's arrests were made in just such manner, but it is to his everlasting credit that he and his associates were able so frequently to get their men."[51]

After nine years as a counter-espionage agent, Kosterlitzky retired on September 4, 1926 because of failing health. On March 2, 1928, at his home he rallied his children to his side and said, "I am going to die, I can leave you nothing except the most wonderful fortune in the world, your mother, a jewel beyond price, and a name you can be proud to bear."[52]

The Los Angeles Times published the following notice of Kosterlitzky's death. Sadly, they referred to him as "General" rather than "Colonel" as was his wish:

> General Emilio Kosterlitzky rugged old soldier of one hundred battles late yesterday answered his last command. Death summoned him in his residence at 2170 W, 31St. Street, and soldier-like, he was in full marching order and ready to go. He went as he had lived, fearless, self-confident, and competent. A faint attempt at a battle yell that had terrorized Yaquis in the dim long ago...this was the general's last earthly act as he stepped through the portals into the final enlistment.[53]

In remembering Kosterlitzky, author and former El Paso Herald reporter, Tim Turner wrote an account of the Mexican Revolution in his memorable book, Bullets, Bottles, and Gardenias, He shared his contact with Kosterlitzky in the Sheldon Hotel:

One day I heard that Col. Emilio Kosterlitzky the noted rurale chief of the Diaz regime, was in town and I found him in the Hotel Sheldon lobby. He had remained loyal to the old regime and gotten out by the skin of his teeth. He was a Russian, son of a Cossack officer. He had come to American, served as a trooper in the US army, and, going over into Mexico, became a colonel of Rurales in Sonora. Kosterlitzky is said to have been the man who actually caught Geronimo, the Apache chieftain, but that is a controversial subject to be shunned like the devil. Col. Kosterlitzky was a soldierly-looking man, tall and straight. He was then well along in years, but straight and active. In the Sheldon lobby they had a long row of comfortable upholstered arm chairs, some rockers, and some not. When Kosterlitzky and I sat down to talk he happened to pick a rocking chair – they all looked alike – and he was no sooner seated than he jumped up white as a sheet and I could see he really was afraid of something. "I must get another chair," he exclaimed. "I wouldn't sit in one of those damned rocking chairs for anything. Do you know, young man, there is nothing as dangerous as a rocking chair?" It seemed that Kosterlitzky himself had never been injured by a rocking chair, but he had once known a man who had fallen over backward in one and broken his neck.

Years later I saw much of Kosterlitzky in Los Angeles, where he lived with his family in a bungalow in a long row of other bungalows occupied by retired Middle West farmers. A few years before he died he was troubled by a lump in his back, and went to see a physician about it. The doctor said it felt like some hard body that had lodged in the muscles of his back.

"Have you ever been wounded by a bullet?" he asked. Kosterlitzky said he had been wounded in ten or fifteen places. The doctor said that if it was a bullet it could easily be cut out. The old rurale chief, however, flatly refused to go to a hospital. "You come out to my house tomorrow and cut it out without damned monkey business," he said, "and don't bring along any chloroform or morphine, I don't like dope." Protesting, the doctor did it. The patient grappled hold of the foot a bed while the surgeon cut away.

Kosterlitzky was the most eloquent swearer I ever knew, an expert in both English and Spanish. As the doctor cut he spewed up a steady stream of this, adding Russian oaths he had forgotten since his early youth. Sweat streamed from Kosterlitzky's face but he never budged an

> inch until finally the surgeon had it out. "My God!" exclaimed the doctor, "why this is a slug as big as a Ford bub nut. What in the world is it?"
>
> "Oh," said Kosterlitzky looking around, "that's what I thought. That's a .60 caliber ball from one of those old Confederate rifles the Apaches had. I remember when it hit me. It knocked me plumb off my horse and down into the arroyo."[54]

Cornelius Smith, Jr., the son of the army captain that accepted Kosterlitzky's Cossack sword at Nogales, concluded his biography of the old Eagle of Sonora:

> Like any country, Mexico has had its share of military heroes. Some are enshrined in Mexican literature and some live in the equestrian statues of Mexican parks and plazas, or look grandly down from oil paintings at the visitors in Chapultepec Castle. There are no songs about Emilio Kosterlitzky and his straight figure rides no bronze horses in the plazas of Sonoran towns. But he was one of the best soldiers Mexico ever had. Adios Coronel, y vaya con Dios.[55]

Loathed and feared by the common man, respected by the military man, and appreciated by the Americans in whose service he gave so much, he rests with his family, just inside the gates of Calvary Cemetery, in East Los Angeles.

Who were the other mercenaries who were members of Garibaldi's Foreign Legion? In expressing his concern about these foreign fighters, Pancho Villa reportedly said, "Are they so stupid, and so blind, that they'd die for freedom over there—and leave slavery right across the line? I have several gringos with me, as dynamiters and machine gunners. A fat little Jew named Samuel Dreben, and a big bastard named Tracy Richardson. They chew nails and spit bullets. Garibaldi has a redheaded loco dynamiter named Creighton, with balls like a stallion. Why are they here?"[56]

A whole cadre of unusual characters filled the ranks of Garibaldi's fighters, some truly heroic men with honorable histories of fighting for their ideals; others were just ragtag losers who were trying to hide from their past failed adventures or the strong arm of the law. Some, like Dreben[57] and Richardson are easily traced to the Sheldon Hotel. Most of the others were members of the contingent of fighters that frequented the Sheldon's lobby, bar, and gaming rooms and documentation is a bit sketchy. Yet their identities and exploits became well known as a result of their friendships and drinking relationships with the large contingent of newspapermen and authors who were at their side in the lobbies and bars of the Sheldon during the Mexican Revolution. Unlike books written about New York's iconic hotels and elite apartments, the Pierre, the Plaza, the Dakota, and the Waldorf-Astoria, there are no registration ledgers or registered leases to document the tenants and visitors to the Sheldon.

Following are a few profiles of some of these extraordinary mercenaries who became historic heroes and fodder for the glamorization of the American Foreign Legion by the international press.

Sam Dreben, the Fighting Jew

Along with Tracy Richardson, Sam Dreben was clearly a professional soldier, an expert machine gunner, and a major asset to the rebel army during the Mexican Revolution. He had become a very good friend of Burt Orndorff, the owner and manager of the Sheldon Hotel. Orndorff had made a long-standing offer of free lodging to any of the known mercenaries who came through El Paso during the multi-phases of the revolution, particularly if they had a "story to tell." [58] Whether Orndorff was genuinely generous or a shrewd businessman, who wanted to "stack" his lobby and bars with interesting characters willing to tell of their adventures which would in turn attract locals and tourists to his enterprise, is just conjecture, nevertheless, Dreben was considered one of the best and most popular of the guests to frequent the hotel. Dreben lived at the Sheldon for an extended period, until he purchased a small home in El Paso. Richardson and Dreben, who met while serving under the mercenary Lee Christmas in Nicaragua, were complete opposites in both looks and demeanor. Richardson was tall and slender, but tough, quiet, and deliberate in his actions. Dreben was short and stocky with a humorous, yet aggressive personality who was impulsive and a bit of a lady's man.[59]

Figure 75. Sam Dreben 1878-1925 Soldier of Fortune

During their adventures in the revolution, the Mexican army captured both Richardson and Dreben and forced them to face a firing squad. Clearly they were spared. Richardson looked more like a fierce heroic soldier of fortune than his dumpy companion, did remained extremely close to Dreben. Richardson described him: "Sam Dreben, the fighting Jew. There was a character. All Latin America was ringing with stories of his wild doings, his soldierly qualities, and his happy-go-lucky disposition. He didn't look the part at all. He was the last man you would pick out of a crowd to be a soldier. Short, heavy set, with a large comedy nose, a stomach always straining at the belt, he was a walking vaudeville act. Always kidding, always carefree and happy, he could make a bunch of men laugh when they were ragged, starving, and facing violent death."[60] "He never learned what it meant to be afraid. Like Gunga Din, he just never seemed to know the need of fear."[61]

Samuel Dreben was born in Poltava, Russia, in 1878 and his mother raised him to be a rabbi, but he wanted to be a soldier. When he turned eighteen, he left home and managed to work his way first to New York and then to Philadelphia. Unable to find a job, he enlisted in the U.S. Army and was sent to the war front in the Philippines in 1899. Not long after seeing action there, the Army sent his infantry unit to rescue the diplomatic legation in China during the Boxer Rebellion in 1900. His military actions in the Philippine insurrection, the Boxer Rebellion in China, and the Honduran revolt during the La Guardia campaign were unremarkable and ordinary.[62] That was because he had yet to get behind the power of the machine gun. From that time forward, his fierceness as a deadly soldier became apparent and acclaimed.

When his enlistment ended, he got a job as a municipal rat catcher in San Francisco. It didn't take him long to recognize that that wasn't his kind of job, so he re-enlisted in the Army. When his second enlistment ended, he found himself, after one night of gambling, flat broke in the Panama Canal Zone and without a job.[63] The next day, Lee Christmas, a well-known soldier of fortune, recruited Dreben and he entered the Guatemalan and Nicaraguan revolutions. Christmas had been a high profile character in and around New Orleans and had recruited most of his band of mercenaries from former soldiers and he trained them extensively in guerilla warfare. It was during this action that Dreben met his fellow machine gunner, Tracy Richardson. According to one account:

> Dreben became involved in a Central American revolution, which seemed to be going nowhere, both sides fighting aimlessly and listlessly. Sam picked the likeliest-looking side and got a job organizing its army. He drilled, cussed, fed, and paid his troops, but got

> no appreciable results. They still lacked spirit. Thinking it over, he hit upon a brilliant scheme. Appealing to their love of glory and finery, he promoted every man in the army. The lieutenants became captains, the captains became colonels, the colonels became generals, the generals became field marshals, and the buck privates became second lieutenants. There were no enlisted men. He then outfitted them all in splendid uniforms trimmed with gold braid, the whole army looking like the male chorus of the Strauss operetta The Student Prince. Now the bedizened officers fought like devils.[64]

Dreben left Central America and headed to the rebellion underway in Mexico. He used his machine gun skills on behalf of Madero's attempt against Díaz. "Mexico quickly became a textbook case of the corruptibility of power. No sooner was an idealist seated in the presidential palace, than he himself became a tyrant. Dreben was so busy fighting for Huerta, Orozco, Carranza, Salazar, and Pancho Villa on their way to the palace and then fighting against them once they got there, that he took up residence in El Paso [Sheldon Hotel], the first place he called home since he left Russia, and an easy commute to whichever revolution was currently playing across the Rio Grande."[65]

In addition to his machine gun activity, he served as Villa's purchasing agent (gun running) in the acquisition of arms and ammunition. From offices in the Sheldon Hotel, Dreben would acquire and orchestrate the movement of weapons and ammunition across the Rio Grande. He was well aware of the embargo on the export of any arms to Mexico that had been established by President Taft, and the possibility of jail time and losing his American citizenship.[66] He continued to work the arms business with Felix Summerfeld, who was not only associated with Villa, but also was a known German agent. It was suspected that Dreben and Summerfeld acted as the conduit between Villa and German espionage activities to draw the United States into a war with Mexico and therefore making the American allegiance with the Allies very difficult.[67]

When Carranza and Villa broke their alliance, he switched sides and remained loyal to Carranza. When Villa attacked Columbus, New Mexico in 1916, Dreben's allegiance to the United States, his adopted country, surfaced and he joined General Pershing's Punitive Expeditionary Force to chase Villa serving Pershing as a scout.[68] Dreben only spent a month with Pershing. General Pershing dismissed Dreben when evidence surfaced that Dreben was gambling as well as cheating the American troops. Dreben returned to El Paso and entered the real estate and insurance business in his office in the Sheldon Hotel.[69]

By the time, he was forty years old, he had married Helen Spence, a beautiful nineteen-year-old and purchased a house at 2416 Montana Ave. and had a newborn daughter. However, following the death of his child, Dreben became extremely depressed and his focus on his business ventures began to wane. As the European war fever spread throughout the country and it was becoming obvious that the United States was going to become involved, Dreben began to channel his energy toward the war bond effort. When the United States entered into WWI, a special company of El Pasoans was formed, and Dreben was one of the first to enlist.

Dreben told his friend, Burt Orndorff why he was enlisting, "Burt, I can never pay back the debt I owe Uncle Sam. He is the greatest uncle I ever had and he can have everything I've got. He can have my arm, my leg, or my life. I came to this country a poor Russian immigrant twenty years ago, without even a penny, and look what Uncle has done for me."[70] At a banquet held in his honor by some of El Paso's leading citizens the night before he was to report, an English gentleman rose and urged the gathering to buy war bonds and the audience donated $25,000. Dreben rose from his seat and addressed the crowd:

> You gentlemen cannot know how proud I am to fight for my country, you are nearly all Americans by birth. I am a citizen because America was kind to me when I was homeless and running away from persecution. You don't know what it is to live under an autocratic government, to be always afraid of tomorrow, always living in the shadows. ... Tonight you have bought $25,000 in bonds for a man who is a stranger to all of you. You all know me, every one of you. I am no stranger. I am asking that you do as much for Sam Dreben as you just did for this stranger.[71]

He sat down, and the crowd purchased an additional $30,000 in bonds. The next day he left El Paso for his next tour as an American soldier. The Army soon promoted him to first sergeant and he engaged in several major offensives in France, including the Meuse Argonne and the Champagne offensives, again serving under his friend, General John J. Pershing. He distinguished himself on a multiple of occasions saving the lives of his commander and several of his men, as well as capturing machine gun emplacements near St. Etienne and killing twenty-three of the forty Germans single-handedly.[72]

For his exemplary heroic military actions, he was awarded the highest French honor given an enlisted man—the Medaille Militaire—and the Croix de Guerre with Palm. The Italian government awarded him the Italian War Cross and the United States bestowed the Distinguished Service Cross.[73] The DSC was awarded to Dreben for his actions on Oct 8, 1918 in the No-*Man's Land* battle near St. Etienne as a machine gunner in Company A, 141st Infantry, 36th Division. The American citation read:

> He discovered a party of German troops going to the support of a machine-gun nest, situated in a pocket near where the French and American lines joined. He called for volunteers and, with the aid of about 30 men, rushed the German positions, captured four machine guns, killed more than 40 of the enemy, captured two and returned to our lines without the loss of a man.[74]

After the war, he returned to El Paso and resumed his real estate and insurance business. While Dreben was proud of his medals, a war correspondent friend of Dreben said, "Sam's two most cherished possessions were his Jewish ancestry and his American citizenship."[75]

Returning to El Paso Dreben found that not all was good for him. While he was in France, his wife had become the talk of the town with her infidelities. Helen Dreben had become well known in El Paso as the first woman in El Paso to dye her hair red. That was a "daring thing when even bobbed hair marked a girl as something of a wanton."[76] He was granted an uncontested divorce on June 9, 1919 after charging that she had committed adultery in El Paso, New Orleans, and other places. In addition, he had never been very accepting of the cause of the death of his four-month-old daughter, which the doctors declared was gastroenteritis. He had always believed it was due to neglect.[77]

In the years that followed, he filled his time with business and did extensive traveling and granting "war hero" interviews around the country. General Pershing announced that Dreben and Sergeant Alvin York and several other war heroes, would be the honor guards at the third annual Armistice Day celebration on November 11, 1921. On one of his interview trips, he met and married Mrs. Meada Andrews in 1923, a widow who went by the name of Cleo.

When one of his business ventures failed, a mine in New Mexico and many investors lost sizable amounts of money, Dreben immediately set about to restore his investor's losses and that act of responsibility gained him enormous respect, but left him flat broke. Reporter and playwright Damon Runyon wrote: "He was a lusty, gusty chap when we first met him. He loved to laugh, sing, eat, drink, and gamble. He loved to spend his money entertaining his friends. He liked expensive clothes and jewelry. He made a lot of money at one time out of a mining venture on New Mexico, but we heard he broke himself giving back their dough to stock purchasers when the mine turned out to be a bust. That was the kind of man Sam was."[78]

Writing about the remarkable true-life adventures of Samuel Dreben, Meister wrote: "

> His new wife, sensing the baggage that came along with life in El Paso, urged Sam to forget Texas and get a fresh start in California. Sam agreed. By years end he closed his office [in the Sheldon Hotel[79]] in El Paso, packed his bags, shook everyone's hand, kissed no one good-bye and was on a train heading west, eager to start a new life in California. Sam hit the ground running when he got to the coast. Somehow, he sensed that L.A. was his last chance to lead a 'normal' life. In double-quick time, the affable war hero became a special agent for the West Coast Life Insurance Company, joined the usual assortment of Veterans' groups, and made a score of new friends. By 1925, he was so totally immersed in the here and now lifestyle of California that the memory of past battles and roads not taken soon dimmed. Samuel Dreben was finally just a regular, every day kind of guy.[80]

However, business ventures and failing health were becoming a major issue in Dreben's life. Things continued in a downward spiral and on May 9, 1925, Cleo wrote to a family friend:

> Things have gone from bad to worse for us the past year. Sam got into some trouble here over gambling, left here (Los Angeles), and went to San Francisco. After a few months there and no business, we came back here. Still Sam acted queer – always threatening to kill himself or leave me and drinking, gambling or something. I was near distraction, for I did love Sam and wanted to try and help him find himself. Along in December he commenced to have terrible headaches, he would go nearly wild, and his speech got bad. He commenced to wobble and stumble, so he went to see three different doctors and no one could find anything wrong with him physically. One suggested a blood test. … The specialist said that he could cure him. He gradually grew worse.

> He used a cane and reeled like a drunken man, and he was so embarrassed. People looked at him and friends kidded him, and he being so proud and sensitive, bless his wonderful heart. ...It nearly grieved him to death. ...The past six months Sam had changed so – he was so companionable, so humble, so leaning on me for everything We worked so hard to cure him and I prayed so hard.[81]

On March 14, 1925, Cleo dropped him off at his doctor's office for his usual injection on her way to work. The doctor's nurse filled the syringe with the wrong medication and the doctor, in error, injected the lethal dose into his neck at the base of the brain. Dreben collapsed and was taken to the hospital where he died after several hours without gaining consciousness at the young age of 47. The coroner stated that Dreben "died of medicine erroneously administered at the office of Dr. Walter W. Brem when a non-graduate nurse became confused as to dosage." [82] The nurse had injected Dreben with an arsenic solution and the coroner indicated that no one was criminally responsible.[83] In June following the death of her husband, Cloe sued Dr. Brem for $70,000. An undisclosed settlement was reached.[84]

In speaking of Dreben's death, Tracy Richardson wrote: "Old soldiers never die? Old soldiers of fortune always die broke. After eight years of fighting, I think that part of the definition, which pertains to luck, is about all that applies to the soldier of fortune. He needs a lot of luck all through the game. And though I have known scores of soldiers of fortune, camped and rode and slept and ate and fought beside them. I never knew one yet who, if he played the game straight, as I have tried to, ever had any fortune bestowed on him as long as he was a soldier of that fickle dame."[85] Richardson described his dear friend and comrade, "Back of that vaudeville exterior was a cool, calculating brain, a courage that nothing daunted. He seemed to take thousands of wild chances with death and emerge by fool bull luck. But when you knew him, you learned how carefully he planned every detail and how little he left to chance."[86]

As an example of how history is modified by the inaccuracy of the pen, O'Hea in his 1966 book, Reminiscences of the Mexican Revolution, wrote, "It was a surprise therefore, somewhere in the middle ninetten-fifties, I think, by chance to read in an El Paso newspaper the announcement of the peaceful death in a hospital of that Texas border-town of his birth, of Samuel Drebbin (sic), popularly known as the 'Fighting Jew.' "[87] He was not born in El Paso and died in Los Angeles....

In tribute to his old friend and Sheldon Hotel ally, author and newsman Damon Runyon wrote:

> Sam Dreben was the bravest, the gentlest, and the courtliest man I ever knew. They called him "The Fighting Jew." You looked at him, a short, dark, chunky, almost pudgy man of self-effacing manner, and you wondered why. He struck you as anything but a fighter. He was almost painfully polite, always apparently greatly abashed. His voice was soft and low. But beneath the velvet of his demeanor was the iron of a warrior soul. Through his veins poured the red, red blood of a passionate soldier. He had one great tremendous love, and that was love of his adopted country and his country's flag. It was his religion, I have known many thousands of men who have worn the uniform of the American Army, but I have never known a man who held it in such absolutely devout love as Sam Dreben. He certainly had no fear of death. He had contempt for anyone who did fear death. He looked on that fear as something in the nature of cowardice and Sam couldn't forgive cowardice. Perhaps that is because he didn't understand it. He was one of those men who are born without fear.
>
> I write of him in sadness. He was my friend. You read in Proverbs: "There is that sticketh closer than a brother. That was my friend, Sam Dreben. He was a friend that wouldn't fail in his friendship, a friend that couldn't fail. If I had a mission, or a secret, that I felt I couldn't trust to any other living soul, if I had been in trouble, in distress, I would have turned to Sam Dreben in serene confidence, knowing that hell and high water couldn't hold him back. Do you know that kind of friend? If I were asked to write his epitaph I would put it in a very few words, I would simply grave in the granite shaft above his day: "Sam Dreben—ALL MAN!"[88]

He is buried at Grandview Memorial Park, Glendale, California.

Hail Dreben!

There's a story in that paper

I just tossed upon the floor

That speaks of prejudice against the Jews;

There's a photo on the table
That's a memory of the war
And a man who never figured in the news.
There's a cross upon his breast —
That's the D.S.C. (distinguished Service Cross)
The Croix de Guerre, the Militaire,
– These, too.
And there's a heart beneath the medals
That beats loyal, brave and true —
That's Dreben,
A Jew!
Now whenever I read articles
That breathe of racial hate,
Or hear arguments that hold his kind to scorn,
I always see that photo
With the cap upon his pate
And the nose the size of Bugler Dugan's horn.
I see upon his breast
The D.S.C.,
The Croix de Guerre, the Militaire —
These, too.
And I think, Thank God Almighty
We have more than a few
Like Dreben,
A Jew!

Damon Runyon

– 1942

Tracy Richardson, Machine Gunner

Ten miles outside of Managua, Nicaragua, American soldiers of fortune camped with the rebels waiting for scouting reports to assist them as they advanced on to the capital. One of the Americans became restless waiting and chose to take a horseback ride through the countryside. After three hours, he decided to return to camp. He was on an unfamiliar road, which he thought would take him back to the rebel stronghold. Suddenly he found himself in the middle of the capital city of Managua. Crowds of locals looked upon him with distrust; he was an armed and ragged American riding through their streets. Continuing his pensive ride, he heard, in English, someone hailing him. "If you are one of Estrada's supporters, you better hide. Here come into my house," the stranger said. While in refuge, he and the stranger were accosted by two of the federal officers.

Figure 76. Tracy Richardson 1892-1949

Being alone and without many options, the soldier of fortune grabbed his pistol and threatened the federal officers, "The best thing you can do to save this city from sack is to surrender. General Mena and General Chamorro are advancing with a heavy column. They sent me ahead. Take me to your commanding officer." It was a bluff. However, the federal officers took the bait and escorted him to their commanding officer. "I'm the commanding officer," said the general.[89] The soldier of fortune, Tracy C. Richardson, told the Nicaraguan general, "'that Managua was surrounded.' Reckoning that the nonchalant American standing before him could not possibly be idiotic enough to make up such a tale, the Nicaraguan commander surrendered on the spot. It was a bluff, and Richardson dispatched a desperate message to Mena to hurry his advance on the capital."[90]

To label Tracy Custer Richardson, *The World's Greatest Machine* Gunner,[91] and a renaissance man might be a stretch. He was certainly more than just a soldier and an aviator who had fought in six wars; he was, to be sure: an adventurer, gold miner, explorer, soldier of fortune, writer, reporter, spy, police detective, accused con man, patriot of England, Canada, and the United States; and a loving husband and brother.

He was born in the city of Broken Bow, deep in central Nebraska on November 21, 1892. His family moved to Lamar, Missouri when he was only a few months old. After high school, he was appointed a corporal in the 2nd Infantry Missouri National Guard when he was only 15 or 16. In 1908, he left his hometown of Lamar and worked for a pipeline construction company until 1909, when at the age of 17, he headed for New Orleans hoping to find his way into the revolutionary wars going on in Nicaragua, Guatemala, and Honduras. He said he did it "for the money and for the hell of it."[92] It was there that he and Sam Dreben formed an allegiance and received tutelage under the guidance of Lee Christmas, one of the western hemisphere's greatest, and craziest, soldiers of fortune.

After perfecting his machine gun skills in a variety of banana republic sieges and single-handily capturing the city of Managua, Richardson, with a bounty of $19,000, headed to San Francisco to begin anew. When his funds ran out, he headed down to El Paso to see if there were any "adventure" prospects. There he ran into a former soldier from the Nicaraguan campaign who told him, "This Francisco Madero is richer than a bank, and he's out to run Porfirio Diaz out of Mexico, we've got a job for you as colonel of machine guns." Richardson said, "It didn't look good to me. I didn't think anybody could run Don Porfirio out of Mexico."[93] Richardson headed for the Honduran rebellion to sell his skills.

Once Richardson and his machine gun buddy, Sam Dreben, reconnected after first meeting during the Boxer Rebellion, they left the South and Central American revolutionary theater, and found their way back to Mexico. They engaged in the "action" that was going on just south of the border from El Paso. Dreben, who frequently resided at the Sheldon Hotel, was notoriously visible in the hotel's bar and lobby with Richardson. Dreben and Richardson were practically inseparable during the Madero and subsequent revolts. Although no direct evidence has surfaced that Richardson resided in the hotel, the various correspondents who shared elbow space at the bar significantly noted his presence among the rotating cadre of soldiers of fortune. Dreben and Richardson frequently fought side-by-side, until near the end of the rebellions; then they found themselves on opposite sides of battle.[94]

Describing his last days in the Mexican Revolution, Richardson wrote:

El Paso, and the whole border, in fact, was alive with Mexican Federal spies. Sam Dreben went to work for them. I didn't know this, and we were together much of the time, working on opposite sides! One day I met General Salazar about forty miles below El Paso. "I'm sorry to tell you," said Salazar, "that your friend Dreben is working for the Federals. Tell him if I ever lay hands on him I'll have to shoot him." Meanwhile Pancho Villa's agents told him I was responsible for Salazar receiving the ammunition that enabled him to stay in the field. Villa posted a reward of ten thousand dollars in gold for me, dead or alive. I had to watch my step. I even slept with a gun. Most of my troubles, strangely enough, were not from Mexicans, but from Americans who wanted to get that reward. Americans came to me with propositions to cross the border to get more buried loot than has been taken in all Mexico's revolutions. Two direct attempts at kidnaping failed when I shot my way out.

Then Pancho Villa came after me himself, to El Paso. Luckily, some of my friends tipped me. The best defense is an attack. I started out looking for Pancho. I ran him down at the bar in the Sheldon.[95] There he was with Fierro, who was known as "Pancho's butcher." I guess it's lucky I had a reputation as a pistol shot. And luckier still that I saw them before they saw me. I was ready.

Before Pancho or Fierro could draw, I had them covered. One of my friends stepped up and took their guns. "I don't want to kill you unless I have to," I told Villa. "I'm letting you off this time. But unless you make a public announcement that the reward is pulled down, and unless you quit messing around me with kidnapers, I'll make it my business to shoot you both on sight."

Pancho looked at me for a minute—and that minute seemed like a year. I didn't want to have to shoot him. Then he smiled. He always smiled with his face, not with his eyes. "Sure," he said. "I'm a sport. That's all right. Have a drink, amigo." We lined up alongside the bar, Pancho Villa, Fierro and I, and we had that drink. We had several, in fact. Then Villa invited me cordially to ride across the border with him as his

> guest. I declined. Many times after that, I met Pancho in El Paso. We had many drinks together. Good-naturedly he talked about his experiences in Mexico.[96]

Few men alive can boast that they held the infamous bandit and revolutionary icon, Pancho Villa, at gunpoint. Let alone; get him to apologize to them.

In 1914, Richardson began to lose interest in the vacillations of power in the Mexican Revolution, and left for Quebec, where he enlisted in the Canadian Light Infantry Regiment, known as the Princess Pats. He fought with the unit in Belgium and was decorated for capturing a machine gun attack at Ypres. Of the 1100 Canadians who served, only 150 survived. He was seriously wounded in the trenches:

> It was getting dark. Our gun barrels were blistering hot from firing hours on hours. Then they [Germans] sent over another wave. We gave them all we had. It was nearly enough to stop them – but not quite. A few of them entered our trench. One big German loomed up over me, where I was crouched by the only remaining machine gun at the bottom of the shallow trench, fighting to get a fresh belt of cartridges into it. I looked up as I saw him rise up above me. We looked into each other's eyes. He laughed hysterically and sprang down at me with his bayonet lunging at my stomach. The butt of his rifle was in his shoulder as he literally dived at me, bayonet first, trying to pin me through the body. I gathered my hands and feet under me faster than I can tell it, and tried to throw myself sideways and backwards. I was too weak to get quite clear. He pinned me to the ground through the inside of my left thigh.
>
> He was laughing hysterically still. I had never carried a rifle that day. My work with the range finder took both hands. But I always carried a .45 Colt automatic pistol. Now as I lay there on my back with that German bayonet through my leg, and that German face laughing down at me, I pulled that pistol and shoved it up into his face. A more surprised man there never was. His expression changed as if a hand had wiped that hysterical laugh off his face. The laugh changed to a scream. His first word was "Kamerad!" But I laughed now. And I pulled the trigger.[97]

In addition to the leg wound, Richardson had been hit with shrapnel in the lower back. He was sent home to Lamar to recuperate. His body bore the scars of six-teen wounds, from bullet, shell, bayonet, and the machete received in Latin America and France. Two weeks later, he received a commission as a first lieutenant in the Ninety-seventh Battalion of the Canadian Army. Before he could be attached to the unit after officer's training, his battalion left for France. He then requested a transfer to the Royal Naval Air Service and became a pilot and flew the North Sea patrol, ferried planes across the English Channel, and began learning aerial machine gunnery. When the United States joined the Allies in 1917, Richardson arranged a released from the British service and transferred over to the American Air Corps as a captain. Wounded again, he was hospitalized in Manchester, England. While he recovered, he completed college work and received a degree from the Royal School of Mines.[98]

During the years that followed WWI, Richardson became an active gold prospector and explorer in Canada and Spanish Honduras and searched for oil in Guatemala. During a row in New Orleans in 1922, Richardson shot and killed a man. No charges were filed as it was determined that Richardson had acted in self-defense. After a short trip back to Mexico, he returned to New Orleans and became a police detective. In 1932, he was arrested on fraud charges stemming from his employment with the Pelican Gold Mining Company. Eventually his name was cleared upon the arrest of the company's president for mail fraud and using Richardson's name without permission. After moving to New York in the 1930s he embarked on a career as a writer and wrote for a number of newspapers and magazines, most notably, Liberty Weekly Magazine and a syndicated column entitled Fighting Under Five Flags.[99]

When the United States entered WWII in 1941, Richardson reenlisted in the army and served until he was discharged in 1947 as a Lieutenant Colonel. He returned to his hometown, Lamar, Missouri, and died from a heart attack at 57 on April 20, 1949, just as he had said about soldiers of fortune, a life full of luck and flat broke.

On second thought, maybe Tracy C. Richardson was a renaissance man.

Emil Holmdahl and Pancho*'s Head*

It seems pretty clear by now that the Sheldon Hotel bar and lobby was a significant conduit for military information being exchanged between the various elements of all phases of the Mexican Revolution. The interactions between the municipal political leaders of both sides of the Rio Grande, the military men, the secret service agents and most importantly, the soldiers of fortune serving both the federals and the rebels, was well documented by not only latter-day historians, but also by the attending news correspondents who witnessed it daily.

Figure 77. Emil L. Holmdahl 1883-1963 Soldier of Fortune.

Emil Holmdahl, born in Fort Dodge, Iowa in 1883, was another of the "wild bunch" of mercenaries who seemed to always be in the middle of the action. Holmdahl's background was not unlike those whose discussions appear above; battles in the Spanish-American War in the Philippines, rebellions in China, South Africa, and the banana republics, and service in WWI. He was particularly visible during the various phases of the Mexican Revolution and the comings and goings in the Sheldon Hotel. He, with typical regularity of the mercenaries, changed his allegiance supporting both the government and the rebel side of the rebellion depending on who was in power and who paid his fees. What set him apart is that biographer Douglas Meed devoted the majority of his book, Soldiers of Fortune, to the adventurers of Holmdahl. In addition, Holmdahl was the central figure in the controversy and folklore surrounding the missing head of Pancho Villa stolen from the cemetery in Parral, Chihuahua. This fascinating piece of the revolution's history plays a role in the writings of well-respected historians, such as Friedrich Katz, as well as a horde of southwest writers who dwell in all facets of conspiracies.

When Villa attacked Columbus, New Mexico in March 1916, Holmdahl joined his former commander from the Philippines, General Pershing, and served as a scout for Pershing's failed Punitive Expeditionary Force. He returned to El Paso when the Army returned to the United States empty-handed as Villa had successfully eluded his pursuer's efforts. Soon after his return, he claimed that he had been contacted by Pershing and Colonel Herbert Slocum and asked to report to Fort Bliss. Holmdahl stated that he was offered $100,000 to return to Mexico and kill Villa. A previous plan to assassinate Villa by poison using two Japanese cooks had failed. The payment would be made by a private donor, Colonel Slocum's millionaire father-in-law, Russell Sage. (Colonel Slocum was the Army commander at the military outpost at Columbus when it was attacked by Villa.) In explaining his rejection of the offer, Holmdahl said, "First, I like Villa personally, even though I fought against him. Second, I am not an assassin. Third, if I killed Villa, I would have never gotten out of Mexico alive."

Holmdahl, like Dreben, was actively involved in gun running and was significantly involved with characters like Victor Ochoa and Felix Sommerfeld. Holmdahl and Ochoa were eventually arrested by American federal agents and charged with violations of the Neutrality Act. In January 1917 the Fifth Circuit Court of Appeals affirmed his conviction and he was sentenced to eighteen months at Leavenworth Federal Prison. He was given a stay of sixty days in order to get his affairs in order. During that time, Holmdahl made exhaustive attempts at obtaining executive clemency. His partner Ochoa was not as lucky. On July 13 President Woodrow Wilson issued Holmdahl a full and unconditional pardon … if he agreed to immediately enlist as a private in the U.S. Army. He served in combat in the 6th Engineer Regiment of the 36th Division in France as part of the Expeditionary Force under General Pershing. He served with distinction fighting alongside the British during the last German offensive and left the army as a captain.[100] Following his active years soldiering he seemed to settle down and concentrate on mining and prospecting.

Nearly eighty years old, Richardson continued to prospect and on April 8, 1963 he suffered a massive stroke and died instantly. He was buried at Forest Lawn Memorial Park in Glendale, California [101] His biographer, Douglas Meed, wrote: "If 'taps' were played at the old soldier's funeral, it sounded not only for the old veteran, but for an age when soldiering could still be an adventure. He was the very last of the swashbuckling soldiers of fortune. It's difficult to come up with a fitting epitaph for a man like Holmdahl. He served his country bravely and honorably in the Philippines as a foot-slogging infantryman, with Pershing and Patton as a daring scout, and as an officer fighting with the American Expeditionary Force in France during WWI. He was respected by honorable men on both sides of the border."[102] However, it must not be forgotten that he was also a spy, machine gunner for hire, arms smuggler, rum runner, con-man, and drifter.

The Missing Head of Pancho Villa

Villa had retired from active military and revolutionary activities in 1920. He lived at his rancho at Canutillo, near the city of Parral, Chihuahua. While on a simple ride into the city of Parral, 45-year-old Villa, traveling in an open car, was assassinated as the car slowed to make a turn by a group of seven men who shot into the 1919 Dodge over 40 times. Villa, who was driving and most of his bodyguards and companions were killed instantly. Villa normally traveled with a large contingent of bodyguards, sometimes as many as 50, but this time chose only to travel with a skeleton crew. Chihuahuan state legislator, Jesus Salas Barraza was among those arrested and convicted of the assassination. He was sentenced to 20 years, but his sentence was almost immediately commuted to three months by the Chihuahuan governor. It has been widely believed that Mexican President Álvaro Obregón and soon-to-be President Plutarco Elías Calles were actually behind the assassination.

On February 6, 1926, three years after Villa's death, it was noticed that the Villa grave had been opened and his head was removed from the body. Emil Holmdahl was in Parral at the time and was immediately arrested. Although the severed head was not found in Holmdahl's possession, he was kept in jail, although released shortly thereafter. It was later rumored that a Colonel Durazo had been ordered by President Obregón to dig up Villa's head and give it to him for use on his desk as a pen holder.[103]

Figure 78. The Assassination of Pancho Villa July 20, 1923 Parral, Mexico.

It wasn't long before another rumor began to circulate. The Los Angeles Times ran an article that quoted a Mrs. Gene Ernest of 103 E. 68th Way, Long Beach, saying that she operated a store in the Sheldon Hotel in 1926 and that, "I became acquainted with Emil Holmdahl, [a resident in the hotel]. I do not know whether he had Villa's head but he had something of great value, which he kept in his room. His Yaqui Indian guide slept in the room and guarded it at all times when Holmdahl was absent."[104]

To add to the mystery of Holmdahl and La Cabeza de Villa, Ben F. Williams, a well-known banker, cattleman, and rancher wrote in his 1926 autobiography, that he was a friend of Holmdahl and had visited him in the Parral jail and that he had told Williams that he had nothing whatsoever to do with the desecration of Villa's body. Taking him at his word, Williams used his influence to get Holmdahl released from jail. Sometime later, when the two of them were having a drink in El Paso, Holmdahl admitted that he had in fact, taken the head of Pancho Villa and that he had been paid $25,000 to acquire the head.[105]

Years later, when in Phoenix visiting a friend, Williams wrote that he met up with Frank Brophy, a graduate of Yale University and a member of the Skull and Bones Society. Brophy told him that the society was a secret honorary club and they have the skulls of prominent people including Pancho Villa's. Williams wrote that Brophy was flabbergasted when he told him about Holmdahl; how he had gotten him out of the Parral jail and about his offer to give me half of the $25,000 he had been paid for taking Villa's head. Brophy said, "By God, that's right! Five of us put up $5,000 apiece. The other members of Skull and Bones covered his expenses."[106] In 1988, the story of the Skull and Bones Society at Yale University and Pancho Villa's head surfaced again. It was repeated in the press that Prescott Bush, a former Senator from Connecticut and the father of newly elected President George H.W. Bush, was somehow involved in the society's acquisition of the bandits head. Bush denied any knowledge of such a thing.[107]

Published in 1960, an article by historian and prolific author Haldeen Braddy reconnects the story of Pancho's missing head and the alleged treasure map drawn upon the skull, and the Sheldon Hotel:

> Bearers of tales from Mexico into Texas report the escapade of Emil Holmdahl as the true and authentic chronicle of the beheading of General Francisco Villa. Most listeners to tales in Mexico believe it, but people in the United States have been rather skeptical.
>
> The yarn most frequently heard in El Paso is a hair-raiser. About 1927, the story goes, Emil Holmdahl brought across the Rio Grande a round object wrapped in used newspapers. He took this package to his room

in the old Sheldon Hotel to show to two of his cronies. [Purported to be L.H. Shadbolt of Denver and a Clyde H. Creighton] He unwrapped the newspapers on the bed, and out rolled Villa's skull.

Though discounted along the Border, the story deserves to be reappraised for one or two matters recently coming to light on Holmdahl and his purported escapade. The first of these is fabulous. A scientific charge of the Mexico ballad writer was that the culprit Holmdahl committed the mutilation because "he would make lots of pesos / Exploiting a vein of gold ore." When Secret Service agents at Los Angeles in 1952 conducted a search for a mysterious hoard of twenty million in gold ingots buried somewhere in the Southwest, the man they arrested was Emil Holmdahl. Did he learn, somehow, the long-guarded secret of Pancho Villa's vast fortune lost in the Sierra Madre? Legend says that Villa's head was shaved and the map to his gold tattooed on his scalp before he went to his grave. Perhaps his hair had already grown sufficiently to hide the map before his assassination. It certainly would continue to grow for a space even after his burial. This means of camouflaging a secret message has been practiced since the days of ancients. Leighton Rudolph, of the University of Arkansas, called my attention to it in a Greek History of the fifth century, B.C., by Herodotus (Book V, Chapter 35). There a Greek shaved the head of his slave, pricked the letters of a message on the skin, and sent him when his hair grew back to his friend Miletus, who easily deciphered the message after shaving the slave's head. Such a method of obtaining concealed information may well have been known to the person who opened Villa's tomb.

The second piece of evidence involving Holmdahl anew is of considerably more import. In 1955 I wrote a book on Pancho Villa entitled Cock of the Walk, which of course mentioned the beheading episode. After reading it L.M. Shadbolt, referred to above, wrote me from Denver, Colorado, on March 14, 1957. His letter, affording pertinent details until now missing, strikes at the heart of the question. In it he said:

> In the early 20's I'd gotten in the oil business at Cisco, Texas, and with my partner, Clyde H. Creighton (since deceased) we'd made some money. Well, shortly before the panic—I'd say about '27 or '28 – we decided, for no other reason than we'd been drinking heavily and it seemed a good idea at the time, to drive to El

> Paso. Well we checked in at the old Sheldon, and the first guy I spotted in the lobby was Emil. It seems Emil was light on funds at the moment, and we were decidedly holding, so he prudently attached—nay, riveted—himself to us; shuttle service to Juarez day and night. This continued for some days, and along about the fifth morning Creighton and I were still padding about in our pajamas and, frankly, not feeling too gay when in strode Holmdahl, a bundle wrapped in newspaper under one arm and a bottle of Don Jose Cuervo under the other. We all took drink, and then Holmdahl said: "Say, I got something to show you guys." And with that, holding one edge of the newspaper wrapping his bundle, he gave a casual flip—and out rolled General Villa's head.
>
> It turned over a couple of times on the bed and came to rest where it seemed to have one eye—that is socket—(if sockets leer) at my partner. I'll never forget the look of frozen horror on his face...
>
> Well, here's Holmdahl's story: The Cassell Institute (whoever and whatever that is), of Chicago, had offered him $5,000 for the skull. He claimed that he was still to make delivery; didn't have the money to get to Chicago. Now this lends some credence to his claim that the skull really was Villa's: He claimed that (in 1923) Villa was riding (as I recall it, driving) a Dodge car and that the firing came from a rise at a point where the road entering Parral came to a dead end—or rather made a sharp turn and then continued and that a car would very much have to slow down. I examined the skull carefully, and the bone at the left temple was shattered and some teeth on the right lower jaw appeared to have been knocked out – which, of course, would perfectly fit were a man shot from the left side from an elevation.[108]

Time magazine, on February 22, 1926, perpetuated the myth with its comments, "In Chicago, federal agents began last week a search for the head of Pancho Villa. The head was stolen recently from Villa's grave at Parral, Mexico. El Universal Grafico (Mexico City) reported that the theft of the head had been financed by a wealthy American; and brain specialists and criminologists were reported as hinting vaguely that the brain might be examined in the interest of science."[109]

There appears to be some evidence that Prescott Bush and some of his secret society members were involved in stealing Apache chief Geronimo's head from its tribal burial grounds and added it to the society's collection, but the inclusion of the Villa skull seems to have been the result of overactive imaginations on the part of the Yalies. The Williams autobiography, Let the Tail Go with the Hide, lacks journalistic documentation, Katz in his Life and Times of

Pancho Villa calls the Skull and Bones claim "the latest story to surface amongst the dozens similar yarns," and the author of the Skull and Bones 2002 exposé, Secrets of the Tomb: The Ivy League, and the Hidden Paths of Power, Alexandra Robbins, completely retracted her statements two years after it was published.

Braddy concluded: "that the head of Pancho Villa, in the absence of proof to the contrary, is still in Mexico. In Mexican folklore Villa's ghost always appears minus the head or with it in his arms. The ghost never materializes before gringos, because they might steal his hidden loot. Long a downtrodden class, the peons believe that his headless bulto continues to guard and protect them. One of the strongest psychological factors in Mexican politics today is the maimed ghost of the revered liberator."[110]

It should also be remembered that Holmdahl spent the last several decades of his life, roaming and prospecting throughout Mexico, ostensibly looking for rich ore or a treasure. Did he have a secret map? To demonstrate the level of ridiculousness that this folk lore has reached, all one has to do is read the Wall Street Journal April 15, 2010 and read of the existence of Villa's trigger finger on display at Dave's Pawn Shop in El Paso, where the owner claims to have the finger, worth $9,500 and he says that not long ago a potential buyer came by saying he already owned Mr. Villa's head.[111]

In 1972, the Mexican government erected a national monument to honor the heroes of the Mexican Revolution in Mexico City. The few remains of Villa were removed from the cemetery in Parral and re-interned in the new monument.

Figure 79. The Monument to the Revolution Mexico City Pancho Villa remains reburied at the monument, 1976.

Oscar Creighton, the Dynamite Devil

Journalist Tim Turner, who was also somewhat of a "soldier of fortune," wrote:

> Federal troops were now arriving at Juárez every few days although Creighton was cutting up the railways to the south and east, stealing freight trains, blowing up bridges. When these were repaired too quickly he would take an engine, fasten strips of track to it by logging chains, and running the engine down the line, roll up the railway, ties and rails and all, twisting the rails out of shape. The young New York broker became the terror of the federal army…Here was a chap named Oscar Creighton, with whom I early made friends with in the lobby of the Sheldon, who was to prove one of the heroes and martyrs of the revolution.[112]

Born in the small town of Danvers, Massachusetts in 1877, Creighton grew up in Somerville, Massachusetts, two miles northwest of Boston. When he was in El Paso, he was inclined to tell people that he was Harvard educated. While his brother Frank did graduate from Harvard and became a physician, Oscar took an entirely different path. His real name was Oscar Merrit Wheelock and used the pseudonym of Creighton to enlist in the rebel forces of the Mexican Revolution in 1910. He was, in fact, a bank robber from San Francisco and was trying to avoid capture. There have been many stories about his being a bookkeeper or stock broker[113] and a husband living in Somerville and that he had joined the revolution as a way to impress his fiancé that he was going to amount to something worthwhile.[114] There is little to verify the romantic tales of his chivalry and where and how he developed his savvy explosive technologies is not well understood.

Creighton, or Wheeler, aided the Madero rebels with his expertise in blowing up trains and locomotives and destroying 250 miles of the Mexican Central Railway throughout the vast region of the rebellion and participated in the failed rebel battle at Casas Grande in March 1911. On April 15, 1911, at the second battle of Bauche, ten miles south of Juárez, he held off a large advancing contingent of federals practically single handedly. Advancing against the enemy, Garibaldi, his commander writes: "Standing fully erect, with his poncho blowing in the wind, he was pumping lead from his Winchester at the advancing federals, when a bullet pierced his heart. The men, seeing him fall, were so enraged that they sprang forward and charged the oncoming enemy. With this action the federal rout began, and we pursued them almost to the town of Juárez."[115]

Creighton's heroic actions were a prelude to the fall of Juárez when he and his men's actions turned an enemy advance into a retreat, the revolution subsequently shifted in favor of the rebels.

Not long after Creighton's death, the San Francisco police chief sent a letter to the El Paso chief of police regarding Oscar Creighton and his mysterious background. The letter revealed the following:

> It seems that one of the San Francisco bank vaults had been opened without setting off the burglar alarm, and the bank was robbed. How it could have been done was a mystery, and the bank, the insurance company, and the police were very anxious to know about it. Finally, a newspaper notice was inserted promising that if the robber who opened the vault without setting off the burglar alarm would show how it was done, his theft of the money would not be punished in any way. A lawyer sent to the bank to investigate came away convinced that the offer was bona fide. Next day, at an appointed hour, the burglar walked into the bank looked around, went to the vault, and opened it without setting off the alarm then he walked out without having spoken a word. [116]

About two weeks after the letter from the San Francisco Police Department arrived; Creighton's wife showed up from New England. Her appearance caused even more concern and considerable embarrassment in the social circles of El Paso. Creighton had indicated that he was single and had gotten engaged to the daughter of one of El Paso's prominent families, Captain John R. Hughes, the local chief of the Texas Rangers and the largest stockholder of the Citizens Industrial Bank in Austin.[117] There was little left to the reputation of one of the revolutions true heroes. When it appeared that nothing more could damage the Creighton name, the Bureau of Investigation (FBI) later determined that Creighton aka Oscar Merrit Wheelock was not even Wheelock, but was in reality James T. Hazzard, an ex-lieutenant in the 7th U.S. Infantry, previously stationed in the Philippines during the Spanish-American War. He had been kicked out of the service in lieu of a court martial in 1908 for "excessive use of intoxicating liquors and for gross immorality."[118]

When the dust finally settled, these new revelations helped explain how Creighton aka Wheeler aka Hazzard was able to not only develop his skill with explosives but it also explained, possibly from his bank jobs, how he was able to uniform and arm his fifty soldiers in his rebel unit with his own funds.

After the battlefield at Bauche was cleared and Garibaldi allowed the prisoners to leave the area and return to their homes, he had Creighton buried next to the railroad tracks at the battle site so that it could be collected at later date for a proper burial.[119] When the war ended, President Madero had the body exhumed and shipped back to Massachusetts and the Mexican government paid for his re-internment at Wadsworth Cemetery in Essex County at the family plot in an unmarked grave next to where his mother would be buried with the headstone of Dearing in 1943. The family had requested a military funeral with honors, but the United States government refused because of his criminal record. On November 15, 1951, forty years after his death, he was posthumously awarded the Mexican Legion of Honor medal.[120]

...and there were others.

Men with honorable intentions, dubious pasts, and questionable futures all made up the profiles of the soldiers of fortune who invaded El Paso during the fermentation and execution of the Mexican Revolution. Some were experienced "worldly" men with military experiences and some were just young teenagers running away from "something." They all lived in, drank at, and/or congregated in the Sheldon Hotel.

There was Captain Ivor Thord-Gray, a 12-year veteran of the Boar Wars, who fought the U.S. Army in the Philippines, served Villa, Carranza, and Obregón in the revolution and then joined the anti-Bolshevik/anti-Communist White Russian Army in 1917. His exploits are chronicled in his memoir Gringo Rebel: Mexico 1913-1914.[121]

Another international mercenary was *Edward "Tex" O'Reilly*. He had some of the same early soldier of fortune experience as did the other mercenaries in the Philippines, the Boxer Rebellion in Asia, and the Central and South American insurrections. He was a common figure in and around the Sheldon Hotel and wrote of his experiences in his book, Roving and Fighting: Adventures Under Four Flags. After he left the battle ground in Northern Mexico, he shifted his career into writing for newspapers and magazines and hosting radio programs. His major accomplishment appears to be the recognition that he received in the highly respected work of Harris and Sadler's, The Secret War in El Paso: Mexican Revolutionary Intrigue, 1906-1920, where the authors write, and quote other sources, that O'Reilly was the, "biggest liar in the legion and whose reputation far exceeded his exploits."[122] There were also General

Benjamin Viljoen, Daniel DeVillers, John R. Madison (aka Dynamite Slim), Alfred Lewis, Frank McCombs, and James C. Bulger. All of them worthy of additional reading and consideration as the core of the American Foreign Legion, that left such a significant impact on the results of the Mexican Revolution from 1910-1920.

Movie star or Mercenary

Soldier, sheriff, deputy U.S. Marshall, Texas Ranger, one of Roosevelt's Rough Riders, hero of the Mexican Revolution, part Cherokee Indian, and a wild west circus performer who was a crack shot and knife-wielding personality equal to Buffalo Bill Cody and Annie Oakley. Tom Mix's name and legend frequently surfaces in the literature regarding the mercenaries attached to the American Foreign Legion that were such a major factor in the Battle of Juárez and the revolution's activities involving the Sheldon Hotel. Mix became the highest paid and greatest western movie star of that time; and is certainly a personality worthy

Figure 80. Western actor, Tom Mix. ca. 1930. Claimed to have been a soldier of fortune in the Mexican Revolution. 1880-1940

Figure 81. One of the earliest of the 300 motion pictures made by Tom Mix.

of note. He appeared in more than 300 motion pictures and earned more than $200,000 per week. Simple calculations with inflation correction, he earned nearly $400 million dollars during his 26-year movie career. If you are under 70 years of age and not a cinephile, you probably have never heard of Tom Mix. Tom Mix and William S. Hart were an earlier version of western actor John

Wayne. In fact, Mix introduced Wayne to the film industry by getting him a job in the prop department at Fox Studios in exchange for football tickets at the University of Southern California where Wayne was a standout player. He claimed to be a native born El Pasoan and more than likely was a frequent visitor at the Sheldon Hotel. But, was he a part of the American Foreign Legion of Madero and did he serve with Garibaldi, Orozco, and Villa? Or did he just believe his own publicity that he and the studios generated? Tom Mix's romantic and adventure-filled life was tailor-made for the pulp novelist. Clifford Irving, the author of the fictional "autobiography" of Howard Hughes in 1972 who confessed that his work was a hoax and spent 17 months in prison for his effort, wrote such a book:, Tom Mix and Pancho Villa.[123]

Mix's third wife, Olive Stokes Mix wrote in her book, The Fabulous Tom Mix, that she had received a letter from Mix's mother regarding his activities in the Mexican Revolution:

> I have always prayed and prayed for Tom, perhaps I was praying for him at the moment he faced that firing squad in Mexico, and maybe that helped. Tom needed money in those days. He was known throughout the West for his great courage. His reputation reached Mexico too, and Francisco Madero heard of him. I guess you remember. He was that famous Mexican bandit who was instrumental in fomenting the Mexican Revolution and who later, starting in 1911, served as Mexico's president until he was assassinated in 1913.[Had she confused Madero and Villa?] Madero sent an offer to Tom. He would give him five hundred dollars if Tom would come to Mexico and capture certain of Madero's enemies who were hiding in the Sierra Madres. Tom accepted the offer. But he weighed the matter carefully before deciding. He knew that Madero was fighting to win the land for the Mexican peons. It was a good moral cause.
>
> So Tom went to Mexico, tracked down Madero's enemies, and delivered them to him. He expected to collect his money and be on his way, but he found a firing squad waiting for him instead. Apparently he had been framed on some trumped-up charge of violating the Mexican military law. Tempers were volatile in those early revolutionary days and trials were short or nonexistent. Tom was saved only by a last-minute confession of treachery by the man who had testified against him.[124]

Mix was one of many southwest cowboys who ventured to El Paso and volunteered for money and adventure at Madero's camp just across the Rio Grande. Because of his beaming personality, he quickly became friends with Villa. The federals eventually captured him for his gun running activities on behalf of the revolution and made arrangements to publicly execute him as a warning to others who might think revolution was a game. When Villa heard of these plans, he and his men held a midnight rescue operation that scattered the federals and returned Mix to camp.[125] Mix reportedly told Villa upon his rescue, "Give me that horse, friend, I've got to get my "gringito" back. I ain't cut out for this fighting business, and I just learned it. There must be something I can do better." [126] And so, he headed to Hollywood.

Thomas Hezekiah Mix was born on January 6, 1880 in the small village of Mix Run, just a few miles north of College Station, Pennsylvania, not in El Paso, Texas. In 1898 he enlisted in the U.S. Army to serve in the Spanish-American War using the name Thomas "Edwin" Mix and lied about his age declaring he was three years older than he was. He never saw combat or left the continental United States. His nephew, Paul Mix, writes in his biography of his uncle:

> Tom was promoted to a first Sergeant on November 13, 1900. The enlisted men under Tom respected him; most of them considered him a natural leader and a nice guy. The Philippine Insurrection ended in March 1901 and he was honorably discharged at Fort Hancock on April 25, 1901. However, the Boer War had started in January 1900 and was still going strong, so Tom immediately reenlisted. He married Grace Allin on July 18, 1902. On October 20, 1902 he took his last furlough. He gave his expected destination as Pittsburgh. It is doubtful that he went there and it is even more doubtful that he ever expected to return to Fort Hancock. On October 25 Tom's furlough expired and he was listed as AWOL. He was officially listed as a deserter. Tom was never apprehended or returned to military control, and therefore he never received a court-martial for that offense or a discharge for his second enlistment. Tom's commanding officer never issued a warrant for his arrest. Tom's desertion had a great impact on his life. First of all, he was never quite sure whether the Army was still looking for him or not. Partly because he had always wanted to go west and partly because he was on the run, he and Grace moved into the southwest in

late 1902 where they settled in Guthrie, Oklahoma, which was then the capital of the Oklahoma Territory.[127]

Mix's marriage to Grace was annulled within the year and he then, in 1905, married Kitty Jewel Perinne and that marriage lasted about a year. Then in 1907, he married Olive Stokes. In 1911, with serious money problems, he left Oklahoma and headed for El Paso. The legend that was to become Tom Mix, movie star was on its way:

> Most of the legendary tales about Tom Mix deal with his birth, boyhood, military service, experience as a law enforcement officer, and early motion picture work. All in all, these stories tended to create an image of Tom comparable with that of the Long Ranger or Renfrew of the Mounties. The reason for the fabrication of these tales is obvious – they created an inspiring, exciting, adventuresome image of a heroic cowboy, something that would tend to lure the public into the old nickelodeon. Also, the stories nicely filled the less romantic gaps in Tom's life, such as when he was a bartender, drum major, inexperienced cowboy, etc. Soon the legend grew to become a ten-headed dragon that was very difficult to slay without killing the man himself. Those who recognized the dragon for what it was kept mum. Why ruin a man's career for the sake of being precise? What the public really wanted was first-class entertainment at a reasonable price, and that's what Tom Mix and the early movie producers gave them. In retrospect, it looks like Tom probably didn't need his ten-headed friend to succeed. Surely, his personality and showmanship would have eventually carried him to the top. But once the legend was established there really wasn't much that he could do, except go along with the "super-sales" pitch.[128]

As for Mix being with Teddy Roosevelt's Rough Riders, he was actually in the Roosevelt Inaugural Parade on March 4, 1905, riding a horse with a group of 50 horsemen behind the Rough Riders.[129] "Previously published stories about Tom Mix indicating that he was a Texas Ranger, a Sheriff in Oklahoma and Kansas, and a Deputy U.S. Marshall from 1905 to 1910 were highly exaggerated," writes his nephew.[130] Mix was never a Texas Ranger, he was however, in 1935 made a "Special" Ranger by the then Texas Governor and the head of the Texas Rangers, William W. Sterling, as a reward for setting up a prison rodeo. Former Texas Governor John Connolly wrote, "Tom Mix was never employed as a Texas Ranger, in fact, he was never a resident of the state of Texas. It is my information, however, that he did hold an Honorary Ranger Commission that was given to him by Governor James Allred." No documentary evidence can be found for a Texas Ranger Certificate issued during this time.[131]

A thorough search of the National Archives revealed that Mix was never a deputy U.S. Marshall. Some evidence was discovered that he was a deputy sheriff in Dewey, Oklahoma where he lived and was a friend of the town's mayor who had asked him to help curb some of the gambling in the town.[132]

Mix had been married a total of five times and had issues with alcohol and gambling. By 1940 his career was on the wane and he spent most of his time making personal appearances and promoting his Wild West and rodeo shows. He had been in Las Cruces, New Mexico, on business and was returning home. On the afternoon of October 12, 1960, the sixty-year old former matinee idol was speeding his yellow 1937 Cord 812 Phaeton down Arizona State Route 79, between Florence and Tucson. Gusts of wind and dust made the drive difficult. Suddenly Mix came upon highway construction workers repairing a bridge that had previously been washed out. Mix was unable to stop in time and the car careened off the highway into a gully. Mix was killed instantly when an aluminum briefcase full of money and jewelry, flew from the back seat into the back of the actor's head, shattering his skull and breaking his neck.

Figure 82. Tom Mix death car. October 12, 1940.

Whether alcohol was a factor in the accident was never formally determined. The gully has been named Tom Mix Wash and a large monument and rest area was dedicated on August 8, 1968 in his honor.[133]

During personal interviews that he had given in the later years of his life, he made every attempt to clear up some of the outlandish claims that he had made about his life, including denial that he was half Cherokee.[134] He was also fond of talking about going into politics, saying that he was going to settle down and "run for dog catcher." Tom Mix is buried at Forest Lawn Memorial Park in Glendale, California.

Figure 83. Tom Mix Memorial near Florence, Arizona on State Route 79. 2016. (Author's Collection)

If the legend of Tom Mix has been debunked, perhaps his spirit may now rest in peace. One sad aspect of the movie and circus legend is that its very existence casts *doubt on those aspects of Tom's life which were in all probability quite true. There is* little doubt that Tom favorably influenced the lives of thousands of young people and that he did his best to publicly represent those virtues which at one time were respected by most Americans.[135]

Notes and References

[1] Thomson, Janice. *Mercenaries, Pirates, and Sovereigns.* (Princeton, NJ: Princeton University Press, 1996.), 26.
[2] Reed, John. *Insurgent Mexico.* (New York: International Publishers, 1969.), 158.
[3] Taylor, Lawrence D. "The Great Adventure: Mercenaries in the Mexican Revolution, 1910-1915." *The Americas.* Vol. 43, no. 1 (July 1986), 26.
[4] Thomson, 31.
[5] Taylor, 41.
[6] Ibid. *El Paso Herald*, May 13, 1911.
[7] *El Paso Herald*, May 13, 1911.
[8] Turner (1935), 81. *El Paso Herald*, November 24, 1959.
[9] Garibaldi (1935).
[10] Smith, Cornelius C., Jr. *Emilio Kosterlitzky: Eagle of Sonora and the Southwest Border.* (Glendale, CA: The Arthur H. Clark Company, 1970.)
[11] Garibaldi, 17-19.
[12] Ibid, 21
[13] "Italy: Garibaldi 's Conversion." *Time*. April 15, 1946, 30.
[14] Garibaldi, 25.
[15] Ibid, 73.
[16] Ibid, 178.
[17] Ibid.
[18] *Time* (April 15, 1946).
[19] Garibaldi, 186-187.
[20] Ibid, 219.
[21] Ibid, 315.
[22] Ibid, 327.
[23] *New York Sun*, January 2, 1915.
[24] The French government refused to allow the Garibaldi Legion to wear their historically famous and influential Red Shirts. The unit was required to wear only the uniform of the *French Foreign Legion*. This was regarded as a pity, as the red shirt has become a talisman, which transforms brave men into heroes. See *NYT*, October 13, 1914.
[25] *New York Times*, July 21, 1915.
[26] *Galveston Daily News*, October 3, 1951.
[27] *Abilene Morning News*, December 2, 1926.
[28] *San Antonio Express*, November 9, 1924. *New York Times*, May 20, 1950. *Frederick News Post* (Maryland), November 20, 1924.

[29] *The Bradford Era* (PA), June 7, 1950.
[30] Jaker, Bill, et.al. *Airwaves of New York: Illustrated Histories of 156 AM Stations in the Metropolitan Area, 1921-1922.* (Jefferson, NC: McFarland Press, 1998.), 52.
[31] *Piqua Daily Call* (Ohio), August 6, 1926. *Portsmouth (Ohio) Daily Times*, April 3, 1929. *Salt Lake Tribune*, June 13, 1929.
[32] Bochiechis, Leonard, and Gen. Giuseppe Garibaldi. *Garibaldi: In the Light of History. (*New York: n. p., 1932.), 8.
[33] Meed (2003), 52.
[34] Ibid, 53.
[35] Haley, J. Evetts. *Jeff Milton: A Good Man with a Gun.* (Norman: University of Oklahoma, 1948.), 287.
[36] Martin, Jack. *Border Boss: Captain John R. Hughes – Texas Ranger*. (Austin: State House Press, 1990.), 200.
[37] Sonnichsen, C.L. *Colonel Greene and the Copper Skyrocket. (*Tucson: University of Arizona Press, 1976.), 202.
[38] Turner, John Kenneth. *Barbarous Mexico*. (Austin: University of Texas, 1969.), 184-185.
[39] Meyer, Michael C., and William L. Sherman. *The Course of Mexican History.* Seventh Edition. (New York: Oxford University Press, 2003.), 469.
[40] Truett, Samuel. "A Mexican Cossack in Southern California." *Huntington Frontiers*. (Huntington Library, Fall/Winter 2005.), 15.
[41] Smith (1970), 189.
[42] Ibid, quoted from the "Kosterlitzky yearns to lead old force," *El Paso Herald*, August 28, 1912, 1.
[43] "Mexican Federals Beaten in Battle." *Logansport Pharos-Tribune*, March 10, 1913.
[44] Captain Smith retained the sword and eventually passed it on to his son, Cornelius Smith, Jr., author of the Kosterlitzky biography. Reported in the *Tucson Daily Citizen*, December 2, 1970, the captain's son returned the sword to Kosterlitzky's son Earnest Kosterlitzky, in a ceremony held at the Pimeria Alta Historical Society, 136 Grand Ave. in Nogales, Arizona.
[45] Ibid, 213.
[46] Ibid.
[47] Ibid, 222.
[48] Agent Webster was an agent for the Bureau of Investigation the predecessor to today's FBI.
[49] Truett, 17.

[50] Smith (1970), 302.
[51] Ibid, 264.
[52] Ibid, 302
[53] *Los Angeles Times*, March 3, 1928.
[54] Turner, (1935), 82-83.
[55] Ibid, 303-304.
[56] Lansford, (1965), 73.
[57] Leibson, Art. *Sam Dreben: "The Fighting Jew."* (Tucson: Westernlore Press, 1996.), 91.
[58] Ibid.
[59] Wilson, Jim. "Sam Dreben and Tracy Richardson: The Professionals." *Shooting Times*. September 23, 2010. Accessed 12 April 2016.
[60] Ibid, 8.
[61] Ibid, 23.
[62] Watson, Elmo S. "Adventurous Americans." *Cambridge City Tribune,* March 2, 1939.
[63] *El Paso Herald-Post*, May 30, 1961.
[64] Rosen, Hymer E. "Sam Dreben: Warrior, Patriot, Hero." *Jews in the Wild West.* (Lathrup Village, MI: Jewish- American History Foundation.), 6. Accessed 7 Nov 2011.
[65] Meister, Gerard. "Fighting Jew—Forgotten Hero." *Doughboy Center: The Story of the America Expeditionary Forces.* (www.worldwar1.com), p.9. Accessed 1 June 2011.
[66] Leibson (1996), 95.
[67] Harris and Sadler (2009), 261-262
[68] San Antonio Light, April 24, 2929.
[69] Harris and Sadler (2009), 262.
[70] Leibson (1996), 120.
[71] Ibid.
[72] *Cambridge City Tribune*, 6.
[73] Ibid, 10.
[74] *El Paso Herald*, November 11, 1934.
[75] Ibid.
[76] Leibson (1996), 112.
[77] Ibid, 148.
[78] *Portsmith Times*. April 12, 1940.
[79] Harris and Sadler (2009.), 262.
[80] Meister, 16.
[81] Ibid, 183.
[82] *Manitowoc Herald News (Times),* March 19, 1925.
[83] *Winnipeg Free Press*, March 19, 1925.

[84] *Oakland Tribune*, June 11, 1925, 3.
[85] Ibid, 190.
[86] Laskin, David. *The Long Way Home: An American Journey from Ellis Island to the Great War.* (New York: HarperCollins Publishers, 2010.), 285.
[87] O'Hea, Patrick. *Reminiscences of the Mexican Revolution. (*Mexico, D.F.: Centro Anglo-Mexicano Del Libro, 1966.), 154.
[88] Leibson(1996), 186-187.
[89] Richardson, Tracy. "A Soldier of Fortune Story: Adventures of the Greatest Adventurer of All the Yanks Who Have Written Fantastic History in
Latin American." *Liberty Magazine*: *A Weekly for Everybody.* October 10, 1925. Vol.2 No. 23 , 10.
[90] Langley, Lester, and T. Schoonover. *The Banana Men: American Mercenaries & Entrepreneurs in Central America, 1880-1930*. (Lexington: The University of Kentucky, 1995.), 111.
[91] Meed, 40.
[92] Ibid, 37.
[93] Richardson, (October 17, 1925.), 35.
[94] Leibson (1996), 48.
[95] Meed, 108-109.
[96] Richardson, (November 21, 1925.), 28-29.
[97] Ibid. (December 5, 1925.), 58.
[98] "Tracy Richardson: Mr. machine gun." *Tomahawks Adventure travel-The official blog of Colonel T.D. Moore. tomahawksadventuretravel.blogspot.com* Accessed 8 February 2015.
[99] *Syracuse Herald*, May 19, July 23, 1929.
[100] Harris and Sadler (2009), 285-286.
[101] Lot 771, space 4.
[102] Meed, 196-197.
[103] Katz (1998), 789.
[104] *Los Angeles Times*, February, 26, 1967.
[105] Irvin, Teresa. *Let the Tail Go with the Hide: The Story of Ben F. Williams.* (El Paso: Mangan Books, 1984.), 78-81.
[106] Ibid, 266.
[107] Meed, 186.
[108] Braddy, Haldeen. "The Head of Pancho Villa. *Western Folklore*. Vol. 19, No. 1 (June 1960. (Grass Valley, CA: Western States Folklore Society, 1960.), 31-32.

[109] *Time*, February 22, 1926.
[110] Ibid, 33.
[111] Casey, Nicholas. *The Wall Street Journal*, April 15, 2010. Accessed 5 May 2016.
[112] Turner, (1935), 24, 43-44.
[113] Ibid, 25.
[114] Harris and Sadler (2009), 41.
[115] Garibaldi, 277.
[116] Bush, Ira J. *Gringo Doctor*. (Caldwell, ID: The Caxton Printers, Ltd., 1939.), 193.
[117] Ibid, 193n.
[118] Harris and Sadler (2009), 41-42.
[119] Garibaldi, 277.
[120] Nagel, Ken. "Oscar Merrit Wheelock." *Find A Grave Memorial*, January 12, 2012. Accessed 6 May 2016.
[121] Thord-Gray, I. *Gringo Rebel: Mexico 1913-1914.* (Coral Gables: University of Miami Press, 1960.)
[122] Harris and Sadler (2009), 40; 235.
[123] Irving, Clifford. *Tom Mix & Pancho Villa* (New York: St. Martin's Press, 1984.)
[124] Mix, Olive Stokes, with Eric Heath. *The Fabulous Tom Mix*. (Englewood Cliffs: Prentice-Hall, 1957), 40-67.
[125] Leibson (1996), 71-72.
[126] Lansford, 85.
[127] Mix, Paul. *The Life and Legend of Tom Mix*. (New York: A.S. Barnes and Co., 1972.), 29.
[128] Ibid, 163.
[129] Ibid, 45.
[130] Ibid, 53-54.
[131] Sterling, William W. Trails and Trials of a Texas Ranger. (Norman: University of Oklahoma, 1969.), 425. Mix (1972), 54.
[132] Mix, (1972), 29
[133] *Tucson Citizen*, October 11, 1990.
[134] Mix, (1972), 171.
[135] Ibid.

Chapter Seventeen

Scavengers of Sensation: War Correspondents

As the battle of newspaper headlines raged with sensationalism, gore, and faked stories, the American public began to clamor for greater exploitation in their newspapers. Joseph Pulitzer (The New York World) and William Randolph Hearst (The New York Journal) were only too willing to accommodate the public's thirst. Pulitzer with his headline, How Babies are Baked to describe the horror of the loss of nearly 400 children in a tenement housing fire and Hearst with his exaggerated and faked stories of the circumstances of the sinking of the Battleship Maine in Havana Harbor that led to the Spanish-American War of 1898. Hearst is remembered for sending reporter Richard Harding Davis and artist Frederic Remington to Cuba in the winter of 1897. When Remington discovered that there wasn't anything substantive going on in Havana and reporting that to Hearst, Hearst reportedly told him, "You furnish the pictures, and I'll furnish the war."[1]

This was the era of yellow journalism; print anything, sensational, morbid, or offensive, but sell newspapers at any cost. "New technologies were raising the cost of doing business, forcing owners and publishers to complete for readers by offering a product that was more entertaining, and more simplified in its approach to the news, than ever before. At the top, the competition was exemplified by the bitter feud between Pulitzer, the eccentric idealist who read Schopenhauer, George Eliot, and Shakespeare for entertainment, and Hearst, the All-American whiz kid whose ignorance of history was exceeded only by his genius for public relations."[2]

The Madero rebellion was drawing international attention, as there wasn't any major war going on at the time. Newspaper men and war correspondents and photographers descended upon El Paso in a swarm with the majority of them taking rooms at the Sheldon Hotel. As the revolution continued, the ranks of correspondents mushroomed, and the Sheldon, in particular, the Sheldon bar, became the centerpiece of newspaper activity. The early correspondents to arrive included William G. Shepherd of the United Press, Alfred Henry Lewis of the Hearst organization, Norman Walker, David Lawrence, Chris Haggerty of the Chicago Tribune, and W.A. Willis of the New York Tribune. Jimmy Hare the most respected news photographer of the time arrived shortly thereafter. Local El Paso Herald reporter, Tim Turner and the El Paso Times' Owen P. White, while their residency in the Sheldon has not been confirmed, were basically "in residence" in the Sheldon's lobby and bar as a constant member of the correspondents contingency.[3] White wrote:

> This being the world's only war at the time, El Paso was soon even more cluttered up with high-power news sleuths than it had been for *Dan Stuart's* Fistic Carnival. These war correspondents, however, were more than mere news getters. They were news makers. They were geniuses who could magnify a friendly gunfight, or a personal cutting affray between Mexicans, into a major engagement of opposing armies, and once they even went so far as to cable columns around the world when three poor peons, who to them were federal spies, were taken in for smuggling mescal.
>
> It was nearly all nonsense, but as every dispatch the boys sent out bore an El Paso date-line, the Chamber of Commerce, out of sheer gratitude to these gentlemen of the Press for the gaudy lies they were telling about the war on the town's doorstep, decided to tender them a banquet [at the Sheldon dining room]. From what I had seen of these fourth-estaters, especially in Tug Wilson's place, where Bill Shepherd and David Lawrence in just one session cooked up a battle and wired descriptions of it to their papers, couldn't understand why they needed a banquet. They already knew how to drink anyhow.[4]
>
> Following this banquet came a few days of peace. Then some real war. From below Juárez came word that a battle was about to take place and along with several hundred other blood-thirsty El Pasoans, and all the news sleuths, I hurried to the front. I arrived early. So early that before

> we knew where we were a friend, Carl Beers, and I found ourselves flat on our stomachs in a shallow ditch with bullets from both sides flying over us.[5]

The onslaught of rumor mongers and scavengers of sensation continued through all phases of the Mexican Revolution, and the Sheldon continued to remain their domicile of choice, even after the sumptuous El Paso del Norte Hotel opened across the plaza. When Pancho Villa invaded Columbus, New Mexico a new type of correspondent was soon to arrive. Among those were Floyd Gibbons of the Chicago Tribune and Damon Runyon of the New York American, men who eventually became icons of American literature.[6]

The lobby and bar of the Sheldon also entertained two other men who became giants of literature. Jack London and John Reed both were in and around the Sheldon during their early years as infantile war correspondents. Jack London, novelist, social activist (White Fang, Call of the Wild, and Sea-Wolf) lived for a time at the Sheldon while he was writing his acclaimed short story The Mexican, before he went south into Mexico and functioned as a reporter.[7] John Reed, journalist and communist activist (Insurgent Mexico, Ten Days that Shook the World, and his first hand reporting of the Russian Revolution of 1917) became a favorite of Pancho Villa and spent four months traveling with him during the early stages of the revolution.[8]

What follows are a seven profiles of Sheldon alumni correspondents, whose lives during and following the revolution, have left their mark on the Who's Who of American journalists and authors. These are the stories of the dean of war correspondents in the first half of the 20th century, who became America's first radio news reporter and commentator; the first female certified war correspondent; newsman-cum-Broadway playwright; the young cowboy want-to-be journalist, who joined the rebel forces and became a spy; and the local news reporter who went deep into Mexico and interviewed most of the major individuals who were involved in the revolution and told their stories to the world press. Also included are the profiles of the world's greatest photojournalist who covered five wars and revolutions, whose record of human suffering and intimidation remains vivid to this day and the prolific local El Paso photographer who chronicled the brutality and scope of the revolutionary days with an almost unending stream of photographs that continues to serve as a foundation for post-revolution historians.

Floyd Gibbons

The globe-trotting war correspondent, who reported on nine major wars and revolutions, who became recognized as the dean of print journalists between 1914 and 1929, who courageously survived the loss of his left eye covering the battle at Belleau Wood in France during WWI, and who also received a star on the Hollywood Walk of Fame for his work in radio (on the west side of 1600 Vine St.); became a central figure in the Sheldon's fabled correspondent's club. Gibbons brought his penchant for hi-jinx, drink, and journalistic exaggeration with him upon his arrival in El Paso; as was highlighted by Owen White in his book, The Autobiography of a Durable Sinner.[9]

In his 2005 book, The Great Reporters, British author, David Randall wrote:

> If you had to nominate one reporter to save your skin by getting into seemingly impossible situations and bringing out the story, then the person to send would be Raphael Floyd Phillips Gibbons...To get his story out first (or impede a rival – in Gibbons' eyes they amounted to two sides of the same task), he had no second's thought about breaking the law, damaging public property, defying a city fire brigade, putting terrorist threats to the test, booking himself on to a ship because it was likely to be torpedoed,[as he did with the sinking of the Laconia by a German U-boat], out-bluffing the leadership of the Soviet Union, and sporting medals from dog shows to impersonate a war hero...Outwardly flinty, trusting almost no one, and with rat-like nose for his own advantage, he seems a man easier to admire at a distance than to know close-up.[10]

Born in 1887 in Washington, D.C., he was the eldest of five children. His father ran a local grocery store and a small community paper and anticipated that his son would join him in the family business enterprise. Gibbons graduated from the Jesuit run Gonzaga College High School and told his father he wanted to go to Georgetown University instead of the grocery business. His academic performance was shallow, but he excelled in playing craps and juvenile hi-jinx. One such prank included the flooding of the entire first floor of a college dormitory. The Jesuit fathers were unimpressed and Gibbons was summarily expelled from Georgetown University. Desperate for a job, he headed to North Dakota for a job in a family friend's coal yard. Several months later, he ended up working for the Minneapolis Daily News.

Under the tutelage of William G. Shepherd, himself a highly respected journalist and soon to become a mainstay at the Sheldon's correspondents club, Gibbons eventually developed a reputation as being adept at covering breaking news for the Minneapolis Tribune. After a few years, he moved on to the Chicago Tribune where he would remain for more than 17 years. In late 1914, after war had broken out in Europe, the Illinois National Guard was mobilized and sent to El Paso to assist in guarding the national border with Mexico and assist in the protection of American lives and property, Gibbons was sent by the Chicago Tribune to report on these activities.[11]

Gibbons seemed to fit right in with the other members of the Sheldon correspondents club. While seemingly satirical, White's vivid description of the gathered newsmen was all too real. Some of the correspondents rose to the occasion and did a superb and accurate job of reporting the borderland activities. Gibbons would soon fit among those few, yet questions about his exaggerations would haunt him throughout his career.[12]

In February, 1915, the Chicago Tribune ordered Gibbons across the border into Juárez to cover the impending Willard-Johnson heavyweight champion boxing fight. The fight had to be held outside of the United States because Johnson was wanted by American authorities on a white-slavery charge. Even though the fight failed to take place until later in Cuba, Gibbons met Hipolito Villa, Pancho Villa's brother who was in charge of smuggling and gun running for the rebel Pancho. As a result of this meeting, Gibbons was able to interview Pancho Villa in the Mexican interior.[13] Many reporters had been denied entry into the country by Mexican authorities, and they stayed in local El Paso hotel rooms, bars, or lobbies and filed whisky-fueled accounts of imaginary battles.[14] Irritated by these exaggerations and fabrications, Villa had issued an ultimatum regarding newspapermen that he would shoot the first American newspaperman he laid his hands on. This made the Villa invitation significant.

Following Gibbons initial meeting with the villainous bandit, Villa expressed his surprised that any newsman would risk his life to meet with him after his earlier ultimatum, and Gibbons was invited to spend several months traveling with the Villa forces.

In fact, Villa was so impressed with Gibbons that he had a railroad boxcar reconstructed and made into a private car for Gibbons, "The inside was partitioned off, one end serving as kitchen and the rest of the car outfitted with bunks and tables. Gibbons then picked up two Chinese cooks, a Mexican photographer, and an interpreter. On the outside of the car was painted in a large circle with white paint and, in Spanish, 'The Chicago Tribune—Special Correspondent.' This special rail car was more elaborate than the one Villa supplied to the movie company that was attempting to document the rebellion under Villa's watchful eye. This car was hooked on to Villa's special train, and Gibbons traveled all over the north of Mexico with the bandit chieftain right at the time he was at the height of his career. Villa's private train was composed of two cars, one containing a kitchen and dining room and the other was a bedroom with a tub and toilet. [15] He was with Villa for four months, until June 1915."[16]

Figure 84. Special correspondent's train car provided by Pancho Villa to Floyd Gibbons. 1916.
(El Paso Public Library, Southwest Collection.)

Gibbons filed his dispatches regularly to his Chicago paper until he was recalled for other assignments.

As rebel fever grew, Gibbons seemed to bounce back and forth between Chicago and El Paso, returning in September for about a month, and then returning back to Chicago by the end of September. He remained on various assignments at the Tribune until March 1916 when Villa attacked the United States at Columbus, New Mexico and the paper sent him back and attached him to Pershing's Punitive Expeditionary Force (PEF). It was reported that Gibbons and fellow journalist, R. Dunn, were the only two news persons permitted to go with the Pershing expedition.[17] Later, the army allowed two additional certified war correspondents to join the search for Villa.[18] Damon Runyon was one of them. By March 12, eighteen other correspondents, including Damon Runyon, returned to El Paso to cover the Columbus story.[19] Some of the stories pertaining to the PEF were so outlandish, so completely false, and sensational that the El Paso mayor, Tom Lea, Sr., had the city council pass an ordinance making the sending of false and alarming reports a misdemeanor.[20] Whether any of the Gibbons' dispatches were part of this was never clearly established. In February 1917, the Tribune sent Gibbons to Europe to cover the ongoing war activity prior to the American declaration of war on April 6, 1917.

The Tribune booked Gibbons' passage on the Fredrick VII because that ship was carrying the German ambassador back to Germany and the paper felt there was little, if any, possibility of the ship being torpedoed. Gibbons immediately rejected the plan and booked passage on the Laconia, bound for Liverpool expressly because it was a potential target of German U-boats. Eight days after leaving New York City, the Laconia was torpedoed 160 miles off the west coast of Ireland and Gibbons wrote a first-hand account of the ensuing melee as the ship was abandoned. Gibbons' account was so riveting that it electrified the country. It was read aloud on the floor of both houses of Congress. Less than two months later, the United States Congress declared war on Germany.[21]

Figure 85. Floyd Gibbons, War correspondent who became one of radio's first news reporters. 1887-1939

In June 1918 Gibbons was imbedded with a U.S. Marine detachment when he was shot in the left eye and nearly died in the military hospital. No longer able to continue as a war correspondent, he returned home and continued his career as a reporter and a fast-talking radio broadcaster. He could speak with clear diction, 217 words per minute, unequaled at that time and had a radio audience of over 30 million.[22] He had returned home as a genuine celebrity.[23] For the next eleven years, Gibbons reported on international crises around the world and began to engage in book writing. He published the well-received The Red

Knight of Germany: The Story of Baron von Richthofen, Germany's Great War Bird; They Thought *We Couldn't Fight*; and the novel, The Red Napoleon.

Part of the mythology of Floyd Gibbons surrounds the nickname Devil Dogs that has surfaced over the years to refer to the U.S. Marines. Like Leathernecks or Jarhead, these universal monikers were accepted by the Marines as terms of utmost respect. Urban legend relates that the term Devil Dogs, the apocryphal use of term Teufel Hunden by the Germans comparing the marines to ferocious Bavarian mountain dogs. The term Devil Dogs, it seems, was used by Gibbons in his newspaper dispatches stimulated by his closeness to the marines when he was imbedded with them; not the German soldiers as is often reported. Whether this has any bases in fact or not, Gibbons appears to have been granted the credit.[24]

Then on September 23, 1939 he suffered, unexpectedly, a fatal heart attack while at his farm near Stroudsburg, Pennsylvania. The Hearst newspapers, the International News Service, and the King Features syndicate ran the following editorial in all the Hearst papers throughout the country:

> The late Floyd Gibbons, war correspondent of extraordinary ability and high personal courage, served the world of newspaper readers as few men have done. He "covered" modern wars in many lands, including the World War I. His professional zeal and his intrepid daring cost him the sight of one eye when a German machine-gun bullet hit him at Belleau Wood, France, in June, 1918. How much the physical strain of his war reporting contributed to the heart ailment which suddenly ended his life at his Pennsylvania farm is a point to consider. The Hearst Newspapers and the International News Service were fortunate in having Floyd Gibbons among their "ace" correspondents in war zones.[25]

Damon Runyon

Of all of the war correspondents to flood the El Paso area during the multi-phase Mexican Revolution, Damon Runyon probably has the greatest name recognition among contemporary society. As the author of Guys and Dolls, a highly successful Broadway musical and Hollywood motion picture, his work is continuously reignited in high schools and on the stages of musical theaters around the country. His thirty-two other books and multiple short stories are favorites of literature classes throughout the world, enhanced by his writing style that has been coined Runyonesque. His fictional characters were based on his real life associations, sometimes humorous, with Brooklyn and Manhattan type gamblers, hustlers, actors, and gangsters, including his friendship with the notorious Al Capone,[26] during the prohibition years. It has been said of Runyon that, "he put a smile into a newspaper, which usually has as much humor as a bus accident."[27]

Figure 86. Damon Runyon 1880-1946 Newspaper Correspondent and playwright.

Runyon was born in Manhattan, Kansas in 1880, to Alfred Lee Runyon, the editor of the local newspaper. The family had to sell their newspaper and moved to Pueblo, Colorado where he attended school until the fourth grade. He eventually found a job with the Pueblo Evening Press while still a teenager. He was a small man, who always looked younger than he was, "A thin man who walked on tiny feet, which took a size 5 ½ B shoe." [28] That led to the legend that he joined the army to serve in the Spanish-American War in the Philippines when he was just fourteen and it was believed that he was the youngest soldier in that war. "As legends usually go, the facts are not as colorful. He was actually eighteen when he enlisted but looked fourteen and that created serious problems with the recruitment officers as they couldn't believe it.

He always took advantage of his young look and let it be believed he was four years younger than he actually was. He served two years in the Philippines and returned without a scratch from musket or mosquito. The most dangerous shots he encountered were those that came at him over a bar."[29] When he returned from the army, he held various jobs with several papers in the West. In 1910 he moved to New York and accepted at job as a sports writer at the Hearst's New York American. Hearst was fond of saying that a man who could write about sports could write about anything. Many a good newspaperman and many a prose stylist started as sports writers.[30]

Runyon arrived in El Paso in 1911 ostensibly to cover some sporting event for his paper. He was at the Sheldon Hotel and witnessed the confrontation between Villa and Garibaldi. Several writers[31] have referenced his presence but indicated that he was staying at the Paso del Norte Hotel. These claims are totally incorrect. The authors, by any reasonable standard, were referring to the Sheldon Hotel as Runyon's residence, since the Paso del Norte Hotel did not open for business until more than a year after the Villa and Garibaldi incident. For the next four years, Runyon covered various aspects of the revolution for the Hearst papers. Following the Villa attack at Columbus in 1916, the American assigned Runyon to the Pershing attempt to catch the villainous outlaw. Once imbedded with the Army as it entered Chihuahua, the publisher had not heard from Runyon for some time.

In response to the inquiry from New York, Runyon sent the following dispatch: "Horses and mules died during first couple of days and were left to the coyotes and the buzzards that trail every column. Cavalrymen rode in saddle sores; infantrymen plodded along and made their camps every night, limpin' a little, but still afoot. Their very souls are steeped in dust during these marches. It is hot overhead. It is powdery soft underfoot. The grind of the wagon wheels and the churn of the horses' hooves have cut the dry roads to chalk. A marching man inhales the dust with every breath. It settles in his clothing, it settles in his eyes, in his throat and in his ears." His biographer writes, "Damon wrote his stories about the men, the crap games played on blankets, and the weather—high winds made it impossible for the men to do anything much but huddle in their tents at night. He let the other correspondents describe the military operations and the skirmishes."[32]

When the Pershing venture ended, Runyon returned to New York for continued assignments. When the United States physically entered WWI, Runyon went to France as a war correspondent for the duration of 1918. He returned as a celebrity and continued with his widely syndicated column, As I See It. The column appeared in hundreds of newspapers and was enjoyed by millions. Hollywood bought many of his books and short stories and Runyon became extremely wealthy.

While he had long ago given up drinking because it had nearly destroyed his relationship with his first wife, Ellen, he continued to gamble and smoke in excess. His marriage to Ellen ended in separation in 1928 over the persistent rumors of his long time affair with a Mexican woman, Patrice, who he had met during the Pershing raid in 1916. After Ellen died, he and Patrice married. That marriage ended when Patrice ran off with a younger man just prior to Runyon's death. In 1944, he had to have his larynx removed as treatment for throat cancer which had developed from his years of unabated cigarette smoking and he continued to communicate using his pen and his typewriter. He died of throat cancer two years later on December 10, 1946 at the age of 66. A week later, on December 18, his ashes were illegally scattered over Broadway in Manhattan from a DC-3 plane with war ace Captain Eddie Rickenbacker at the controls.[33]

Describing Runyon's writing style, one of his biographers wrote, "Runyon translated underworld language and attitude into somewhat believable as well as humorous conflicts between social and antisocial forces. The initial readers may have missed the satire on the larger society as they read Runyon's stories to escape the realities of the Great Depression and WWII."[34]

Jimmy Breslin, Pulitzer Prize-winning journalist and author wrote of Runyon's penchant for using street-speak in his works:

> Damon Runyon heard it with those ears that had listened to people speak in army barracks, in saloons in the West where they still carried guns, on trains and in police stations, in baseball dugouts and fight gymnasiums, at ballparks and racetracks. Heard them speak with twang, brogue, nasal, guttural, heard of Italians called Meyer because they always said "My-a," heard ten thousand Jews lead with the verb, and heard the Germans in New York do the same—"Make the door shut," "Take a haircut"—heard all this speech, and heard well, because Runyon was the great listener. ...He always liked the first person in the present tense and had used it in a couple of stories. But this was all in a warm-up of his later style. It never had the same effect …coming out of the mouths of gangsters. In the ear of the reader, the gangsters seemed to speak in a British accent. So did the narrator, who revealed nothing of himself. The wall remained up, so that neither friend nor reader ever would be allowed to peer at his insides, which were frozen by loneliness. Had he realized that this reluctance to give of himself would prevent him from going past a short story and trying a novel, which requires you to sell your mother and then pull the covering off your soul, he would have said, well, there'll be no novels from this guy? His insides were to live in secrecy. A narrator hiding behind a false voice was the closest he ever would come to allowing his life to be seen and felt by others.[35]

Runyon is best remembered for his distinctive mixture of formal speech and colorful "slanguage" and grammatical structure that avoids contradictions and the use of past-tense:

> Only a rank sucker will think of taking two peeks at Dave the Dude's doll, because Dave may stand for the first peek figuring it was a mistake, it is a sure thing he will get sored up at the second peek, and Dave the Dude is certainly not a man to have sored up at you.
>
> Always try to rub up against money, for if you rub up against money long enough, some of it may rub off on you.
>
> A person who asks questions can get a reputation such of a person who wishes to find things out.
>
> *Damon Runyon*

Peggy Hull Deuell

While she became the first woman war correspondent accredited by the United States War Department and served on four battlefronts, she was also the reporter and columnist with the most names. She was born in 1889 on a farm near Bennington, Kansas about a hundred miles west of Topeka, as Henrietta Eleanor Goodnough. She began her career in the newspaper business as a typesetter for the Junction City Sentinel in Junction City, Kansas. After she married reporter George Hull at the age of 21, she started calling herself Peggy Hull and they moved to Honolulu where she got a job as a cub reporter for the Honolulu Star. She divorced Hull four years later following many major drinking episodes; the last one included him climbing a flag pole in the nude. She returned to the mainland and was working for the Cleveland Plain Dealer when in 1916 she was sent to El Paso along with the Ohio National Guard to join Pershing's punitive expedition to capture Pancho Villa. While in El Paso she resided at the Sheldon Hotel until she was able to arrange for the manager to remodel a room into a studio in which to do her writing at the Paso del Norte Hotel.[36]

Her request to travel with the Ohio National Guard on the Pershing expedition was denied. She chose to stay in El Paso and write piece-meal "letters" back to Ohio about the lives and adventures of the Ohio guard's soldiers and she became a camp "pet" among the various units of the soldiers at the staging area of Camp Furlong near Columbus, New Mexico. It soon became necessary for her to expand her financial base so she began writing a column for the El Paso Herald in late September 1916 entitled "When Peggy Goes A-Shopping." By the end of 1916, she moved her column to the El Paso Times where it became a regular part of the Sunday edition and often appeared in the middle of the week.

With her columns in the Times and Herald, Peggy had become a local celebrity, yet it was her actions on February 6, 1917 and her subsequent reporting that garnered her national recognition. As Pershing, on horseback, was leading his men back to U.S. soil following the failed Villa hunt, newsreel cameras rolled. Suddenly out of nowhere, Peggy appeared, also on horseback, slightly ahead of the general. Newspaper carried the photo and the headline: Peggy Rides at Head of Cavalcade of Distinguished United States Army Officers. There are many versions of how this event happened, Peggy's longtime friend, reporter Irene Corbally Kuhn stated that the event was the result of a trick the men played on Pershing:

> When word came that the General was riding out at the head of the troops. … The newsreel men were tipped off that the best pix were to be had at a certain spot. Peggy was spirited to the rendezvous on her horse, and kept out of sight. At precisely the right moment, as … General Pershing appeared on his charge, and just a moment before the newsreel camera started to grind, the signal was given. Peggy trotted her horse into position, alongside the General, the newsreel camera started whirring, the troops cheered, and the pictures appeared all over the U.S. and the world—"American girl correspondent leads troops out of Mexico with General Pershing."[37]

The General was not amused, "but Peggy's reporting of Pershing's return with his men is considered one of the most accurate accounts of the event. In 1917, Peggy was able to convince the El Paso Times' editor to send her to France to cover World War I. At that time, the War Department did not allow women journalists to become accredited. She sailed for Paris without accreditation, but thanks to her acquaintance with General Pershing, she was able to spend a month and a half at an artillery training camp. Envious male reporters saw to it that she was recalled to Paris, and embittered, she returned to the U.S."[38]

Peggy Hull was continually denied accreditation. The War Department had made it a requirement that all correspondents needed to have the sponsorship of an American newspaper. After more than fifty requests, she was finally able to secure the endorsement of the Scripps-Howard Press Service. Following her accreditation, she was the first woman to receive such recognition and was the only American reporter to go to Russia and cover the American expedition to guard supplies for the White Army in Siberia. Hull spent nine months covering the atrocities and horror along the Siberian railroad, one of the few reporters to do so, but she saw no warfare.[39] Roth writes, "She was in Russia when the armistice was signed ending the war in Europe in 1918 and was in Shanghai in 1932 when the Japanese invaded, and covered campaigns in the Pacific in 1943. Although her stories chronicled GI life... she witnessed her share of violence, including the deaths of Japanese soldiers outside her tent on Guam and baskets of amputated feet on Saipan."[40]

Her writing style captivated her readers, writing about the soldiers' feelings for their loved ones back home, the camp food, the danger; things that really mattered to the troops, the details of military life. She lived among them, in France, Russia, Japan, and Mexico; marching along with them, bivouacking with them in the dankest of places.

Figure 87. Peggy Hull Deuell 1889-1967

She married Captain John Kinley of the British Army in 1921 only to separate in 1925, and then married Harvey Deuell a newspaper editor after her divorce in 1932. Harvey Deuell died in 1939 in an automobile accident. New York Times columnist and reporter, Irene Kuhn wrote of her dear friend, "Hull had a 'will of iron', she was a woman all men loved and no woman ever disliked."[41]

During the last years of Hull's life, she never married again and moved to Carmel-By-the-Sea. She had an on-again-off-again relationship with another writer, Hobert Skidmore, who was heavily beset with personal issues and alcoholism. Her biographers, Smith and Bogart, summarized the life of this Sheldon alumnus:

> The happiest times of her life had been the years she was on the Border and in France during World War I. She was unable to recall, in 1965 where she had been on VJ Day of World War II, while she could remember vividly that at the time of the Armistice in 1918 she was on "a rusty Russian, cockroach filled old steamer on her way to Vladivostok." Her pride was that she had once—a lifetime ago—been a dashing war correspondent.

> To be sure, she had not found happiness in her marriages—well, maybe a little with Harvey, a very little, but a little, and maybe if Harvey had lived—but Harvey had died. She had lived, and now she was, at last, too weak to fight anymore. And she had a new worry, a pain in her left breast that would not go away. She tried to ignore it, no doubt suspecting what it meant. … Always so fiercely independent, so apparently in charge of her own destiny, she began to wonder now if she ever really had been in fact. Perhaps after all, *you don't choose a* life—Life does the choosing for you—*you don't really make a decision* with a capital D—Life is a series of pressures—influences exerting pressures from various directions. You ultimately succumb to the greatest pressure.[42]

On June 18, 1967 Henrietta Eleanor "Peggy" Goodnough Hull Kinley Deuell died from the complications of breast cancer at her home in Carmel, California at the age of 77. She is buried at Woodlawn Cemetery in New Windsor, Orange County, New York.

Jay Monaghan

The inclusion of Jay Monaghan in a profile of significant war correspondents who reported on the Mexican Revolution might, at first glance, appear a bit strange. Born of Quaker parents in Pennsylvania in1891, he attended Swarthmore College, but spent his summers being a cowboy roving from one western cattle roundup after another. In 1911, taking time from his studies, he chose to chase his adventuring spirit all the way to Mexico, something new and different from his cowboy days. As he grew into adulthood, he used his adventures to shape his career, eventually becoming Illinois State Historian and the author of 13 books (Last of the Bad Men: The Legend of Tom Horn, The Man Who Elected Lincoln, and Custer: The Life of General George Armstrong Custer). He editing 11 others, and published more than 60 articles in magazines and professional historical journals.

It is his book, Schoolboy, Cowboy, Mexican Spy[43] he chronicles his adventures in El Paso and his joining Madero's American Legion under the command of Giuseppe Garibaldi. His narrative describing his eyewitness accounts of the men and events of the Battle of Juárez elevates him to the status of a correspondent, even though his accounting wasn't published until 61 years after the fact in 1977. It was his motivation to "scoop" seasoned war correspondent and photojournalist Jimmy Hare out of a story that drew him into

Madero's camp, befriending fellow soldiers of fortune, potentially losing his American citizenship, and being arrested as rebel spy by the Diaz government.

Upon his arrival in El Paso and sensing the uneasiness of the growing potential of the Madero rebellion, he crossed over the international bridge to the beleaguered city of Juárez. Walking about the town, taking photographs at every opportunity of both the town folks, the federal soldiers (many of whom were convicts serving their terms in the army), and the general landscape. He witnessed and photographed federal artillerymen practicing with their cannons and guns. Upon returning to El Paso he went directly to the Sheldon Hotel to write letters to his family about what he had just seen in Juárez:

> A writing room adjoining the lobby was empty, and I sat there at a desk never imagining that a new experience in the revolution was about to occur. I had noticed in the lobby a short man about my father's age who spoke with a British accent. The clerks showed him noticeable deference, and I was told in an awed whisper that he was the war correspondent for *Collier's* and the New York World. Being unacquainted with journalists, I had never heard of the famous Jimmie Hare, and in my letter home I called him "Mr. Herr." I said he was remarkably short-legged and I would plan some way to outrun him getting a better story about the war.
>
> While writing my letter, a United States artillery lieutenant and a man wearing civilian clothes glanced in the door, and then went on, apparently seeking a vacant room. They soon returned and, standing at a table with their backs to me, they spread out oddly cut slips of paper that each had brought separately and now matched together to make what appeared to be a large single sheet. The civilian pointed to spots on the paper and said something so low I could not understand it. The lieutenant replied but all I could hear was numbers that meant nothing to me. Perhaps they noticed my eagerness to overhear, because the lieutenant nudged the civilian and each man hurriedly rolled up his share of the long slips of paper on the table and walked briskly to the doorway. Before going out, the lieutenant paused briefly and looked quickly up and went down the hall. ...Obviously I had interrupted some secret communication between Madero's insurrectos and an officer in the United States army. I, twenty-year-old stranger in town, was not apt to be a dangerous informer, but they were taking no chances and

> hurried away. In their haste one of the long slips of paper had dropped behind the table.[44]

Monaghan picked up the paper and could see that it showed the Diaz gun emplacements on the barricades in Juárez facing the direction of the rebel's camp. He suddenly got the idea that he could beat Jimmy Hare with a story about the double-dealing of the federals with the rebels and get additional war secrets from the insurrectos which Hare would never get. The next morning, Monaghan, with his blanket in tow, headed down to the river to find a way across. There, with a tip from an off-duty American soldier, he found a cheap 10 by 14 foot saloon that had a rickety old foot bridge out back that crossed over to the other side of the Rio Grande. He learned from a marshal who was standing guard near the bridge that it was used constantly by the rebels to go back and forth to the Madero camp site. Monaghan had become acquainted with a stranger in the saloon who had confirmed that he was a member of the American Legion. With his new found friend, the two of them crossed the foot bridge, telling the marshal that they were both members of the American volunteers.

Monaghan entered a dreary camp of some five hundred volunteers and rebels just waiting around, waiting for something significant to happen. Striking up conversations with a variety of men, he learned of the disenchantment that was running wide among the waiting insurrectos and soldiers of fortune. Monaghan wrote:

> Members of Madero's American Legion dressed and looked like the cowboys I had met working for the big outfits in the western United States. Biscuits would have felt at home with them, but none I saw gambled or played cards. A legionnaire told me in blunt-tongued English, 'We got no money, none of us, until we take Juárez. Playin' cards on credit ain't no good. The winner, ever'body owes money to, is sure to get shot in the back come the first fight. Get me? No fight, no loot, When will Madero get goin'? I heard this complaint many times. … Always I heard that complaint about Madero. He was a man of peace who wanted to negotiate for the surrender of Juárez, but his army wanted to fight and prosper on the loot.[45]

Monaghan had learned that the rebels under the control of Orozco and Villa were going to attack without the approval of Madero, who was still in the peace talks. Monaghan wrote, "Here is my opportunity at last. Jimmy Hare would be in the Hotel Sheldon when the battle started. I was going to be in Juárez, watch the insurrectos come in from three sides, write the first authentic account of the battle, and "scoop" the famous war correspondent. I had only one problem. How could I get into Juárez by tomorrow morning?"[46] He reentered the United States without challenge, returned to the Sheldon and prepared to go to Juárez early in the morning on Sunday May 7, 1911.

Things didn't go as planned. Monaghan returned to Juárez that morning and wandered around. He knew where the gun emplacements were and was waiting, with camera in hand, to capture the attack by the rebels. Hours passed and nothing happened. Then, near the end of the day, he was approached by two men who took him off to a government building:

> The room we entered was not brightly lighted, but I saw four uniformed men seated on benches along the inside wall. At the far end an officer sat behind a desk. My captors addressed him as "El Jefe" and, executing a formal about-face with a flash of the scarlet lining of their cloaks, they strode away, leaving me standing alone. El Jefe demanded my camera, wrote something on a slip of paper, put it and the camera in a desk drawer, and told me in English that I would be tried in the morning.
>
> "Tried for what?" I asked him.
>
> "For being a spy." He replied. "Our organization here is good, like in the United States. More better, yes. Our spies in camp of Madero see you there. Today we see you take pictures, yes, of our military positions. Your trial tomorrow will be legitimo, legal, justo, all samc in United States, yes. Buenas noches."[47]

And there he stayed, a prisoner, being moved by his captors from one area to another until almost two days later, when the actual attack began at night, with the rebels burrowing through walls of adobe buildings, firing upon the federals while remaining inside buildings. Eventually, Juárez fell under the onslaught of the actions of the rebels and the American Legion and Monaghan was rescued. Wandering and ducking bullets, he scurried about the town under siege, when suddenly there was a large volley of shots and he and some others had to dodge for cover into a patch of weeds between two houses. A bearded man behind him, with noticeably short legs, was next to him. It was Jimmy Hare, who had evidently been able to cross the bridge from El Paso. In spite of all his plans to "scoop" him, Hare was getting the facts for a firsthand story of the battle. Both Monaghan and Hare were able to witness General Navarro's surrender to Garibaldi. Monaghan wrote, "with a stub pencil I started writing an account of the battle for Juárez – the account that failed to beat Jimmie Hare's, but did bring a sum of money that seemed large to me."[48]

The significance of Monaghan's account of the ground-level view of the Battle of Juárez is extremely relevant, considering the details that were preserved providing a points of view of this historic event that were otherwise not easily available. He died in Santa Barbara, California on October 11, 1980 after a brief illness at the age of 89.[49]

Timothy Turner

Most of the correspondents reported to their newspapers about the Mexican Revolution from a relative safe distance, usually ensconced at the Sheldon Hotel, Paso del Norte Hotel, the Orndorff Hotel, or any number of bars and gaming houses along South El Paso Street. Tim Turner was one of those exceptions who ramrodded his presence directly in the line of fire. As a reward, he was able to witness and interview all of the major characters and events of all phases of the rebellion. He traveled back and forth across the border to file his dispatches from his office at the El Paso Herald or from his unofficial office in the lobby of the Sheldon. Turner described the events along the border as, "Never was there such a colorful, romantic, noble, and foolish period as the first Revolution in northern Mexico."[50] The local Associated Press reporter, David Lawrence, was pulled out of his El Paso/Juárez assignment in late 1912 to report on Woodrow Wilson's presidential campaign and Turner was then given the AP job in addition to his work with the Herald.[51] Turner was often referred to as "Juárez Man" by the press corps.

Figure 88. Tim Turner 1886-1961

Although he maintained his allegiance with the rebels, he moved frequently between both sides of the conflict, gathering insight into the Maderista forces and the Porfiristas of the government. In 1935, Turner published his account of the Mexican Revolution entitled, Bullets, Bottles, and Gardenias. This book is regarded by many historians as the most significant and memorable eye-witness account of the revolution.[52] The only drawback to the Turner book is its availability. While it is held in a large number of rare book and special collections departments of major universities, there are few libraries that have it available for general circulation. Of the hundreds of books about all aspects of the Mexican Revolution read by this author, it is my opinion that Bullets, Bottles, and Gardenias ranks among the top three. There are a few copies of this first edition that are available for sale, but they are exceedingly expensive.

Turner explains the title, Bullets, Bottles, and Gardenias as referring to "his experiences with bullets that didn't have his name on them, some bottles that did, and an overall scent of gardenias which raised the 1910 revolution from a tawdry war to high romance."[53] There have been no biographies published about Turner and the only photograph that was located was the group picture of the El *Paso Adventurer's Club* that Turner co-founded. The profile that follows was gleaned from more than a dozen different sources; many unidentified news clippings and unreferenced documents. Because of the dearth of biographical material, there may be some minor and inadvertent errors.

Turner was born around 1886 and grew up in Grand Rapids, Michigan, son of a local newsman. He knew when he got older that the only smell he liked better than printer's ink was the sawdust and spit of a barroom. With the death of his father, Willis Hall Turner, in March 1906, when he was just a teen, Turner was forced to find work and eventually became a cub-reporter for the Grand Rapids Herald. His early assignments led into some challenging environments of Grand Rapids and he quickly learned to speak Spanish. With his newly acquired language skills, he soon found himself heading to west Texas with the advice: "Mexico? …Keep your mouth shut and your bowels open." He arrived in El Paso and soon had a job at the El Paso Herald and had developed a good relationship with the Mexican federal authorities. This became a major obstacle to him in 1910 as he attempted to gain favor with the growing revolutionary movement. When his writings in the El Paso Herald were picked up by El Diario, El Paso's Spanish language newspaper, he was slowly accepted by the revolutionary junta.

From his unofficial office in the Sheldon, he became friendly with many of the soldiers of fortune, and was soon a favorite of Garibaldi and Creighton.

With those contacts he was able to move freely among the Madero organization and eventually was able scoop his rivals with an exclusive interview with Madero, the first of several. Historian Leon Metz discusses Turner's journalistic zeal, "He gave the Revolution life, color, and zest, introducing characters who might today be unknown were it not for him. But most of all, Timothy Turner provided romance and simplicity to a struggle now known as brutish and complex."[54]

Turner became extremely close to most of the newspapermen that filled the bar and lobby of the Sheldon. Writing in Bullets, Bottles, and Gardenias:

> One day a newspaperman came to El Paso from the East. He never filed a single story for his paper but every week or so he would come up for air, telegraph for funds, which he always got, for they thought a lot of him evidently, and again disappear from sight so far as his office was concerned. This chap, warned to look out for the altitude not to drink too much when he first arrived, but to this he only replied that he was an iron man, and this title, "The Iron Man" stuck to him. One day the word went round that The Iron Man had come down into the Sheldon lobby that morning, cried out in a hysterical manner that he was none other than the one and only legitimate Iron Man and, spinning around, had fallen to the floor. He was taken to the hospital, gibbering. Now it was decided that The Iron Man should be sent back home. This evidently was no environment for him. So somebody telegraphed his paper, making known the situation, and the paper sent several hundred dollars on the understanding that The Iron Man's friends and associates should buy him a ticket and put him on a train headed for home.
>
> This everybody was only too eager to do, and went at it with the comic touch that a lot of drunks have when they are trying to help another drunk. A stateroom on the Golden State Limited was procured, and all went down, after earnestly celebrating the sad occasion, to see The Iron Man off. He was in a daze, but appeared conscious.
>
> Now, in those days about the only time the Golden State Limited was on time was when it was just an even twenty-four hours late. When the crowd of friends arrived with The Iron Man at the station there stood the Limited in the train shed. They rushed the gate man, who, recognizing some reporters he knew, let everybody pass, and carried The Iron Man almost bodily onto the train which was just about to

> leave, and, over the protests of the porter, put him in a stateroom they found empty just as the train pulled out of the station.
>
> The next the Eastern newspaper heard from their wayward correspondent he was telegraphing again for funds to come on, but to their astonishment this telegram was dated at Los Angeles. His friends at El Paso had put The Iron Man on the Golden State Limited going the wrong way.[55]

What Turner was attempting to do was describe the level of integrity and commitment that many of the war correspondents had about covering the bloody and horrendous battles of the Madero rebellion in 1910. The writings of these newspapermen were the only source of information about the Revolution's slaughter that fed the newspapers throughout the nation and around the world. Regarding his own tendency to over-drink, he explained his rationale on his newly acquired abstinence: "Does the pleasure of it outweigh the pain, or the pain the pleasure? If the latter is the case, the man who drinks is simply a fool. He is not getting pleasure at all, but in the sum total, pain. I felt that I had reached that stage, where the worry and headaches, the mental depression had far outbalanced the pleasure of drinking. That was all."[56]

One of the Madero interviews that Turner did was during the peace conference just before the outbreak of hostilities in Juárez led by Villa, Orozco, and Garibaldi. Madero was delaying any Juárez action as the rebel troops were losing their patience. Turner wrote of Madero's indecision: "Madero, I think, was too kind-hearted. … to order a clash of these armed forces, too thorough-going a sentimentalist. His hesitation however, was not from fear. … One of his misgivings about the attack was that fire would kill Americans on the El Paso side and that this might lead to intervention by the United States troops." During the interview, Madero reaffirmed to the American newspaperman that there would be no attack, when word came that the battle began. "Madero lost all self-control," Turner wrote.[57]

Among the passages of Turner's book that takes the reader to the ground, is his description of how the rebels advanced into Juárez and the use of the special home-made cannon that Garibaldi had built in the railway shop:

> It was three o'clock and decided that it was no place for me unless I wanted to lie on the floor of a house for several hours and see nothing, and maybe get killed. So I worked my way back and got out into the

hills again and met Raoul Madero, younger brother of Francisco, who had charge of the big home-made gun which had been set on a hillock near the road that led out along the river from Juárez. He said this hill commanded a good view of the town, but we could see little for there was not a light in Juárez, which was just a blue-black mass against the sky. There was little going on in the town, very occasional rifle shots and still rarer spurts of machine gun fire. We sat up there on the hill and saw the river road swarming with insurrectos moving into Juárez.

They moved in no formation whatsoever, just an irregular stream of them, silhouettes of men and rifles. Thus they were to move in and to move out along that road throughout the battle. They would fight awhile and then come back to rest, sleep and eat, returning, refreshed, to the front. The European-trained soldiers raved at this, tried to turn them back, to make everybody fight at one time. But that was not the way of these chaps from Chihuahua. They knew their business, and they knew it well.

That casual way of fighting, I think, more than any other one thing took Juárez. For by it the insurrectos were always fresh, with high spirits, while the little brown federals with no sleep and little food or water, with their officers behind them ready with their pistols to kill quitters, soon lost their morale.

For the first time I examined the home-made cannon, whose merits were explained to me by the gunner, an American of French extraction named Carpentier, an almost dainty little chap who wore a pair of new kid gloves, I recall. He was as proud as Punch of this curious cannon. It was an extraordinarily long piece with a very small bore, of naval gun proportions. It had a smooth bore, for rifling could not be accomplished with the machinery at Madera. It was breech loading, though, and had home-made shells that threw a solid ball. It was, in short, a sort of mammoth early American squirrel rifle mounted on a pair of small locomotive wheels.

Then I heard a crash in my ear which startled me more than the firing in town. It was the home-made cannon that had gone off, and little Carpentier was dancing about getting in a new shell. That first shot from the Maderistas' only piece of artillery missed Ciudad Juárez altogether. There is no record to show that it hit anywhere, but judging by the length of the piece in ratio to its bore I should not be surprised if

> the shot landed in the desert out near Fabens, forty miles away. But Carpentier and his Mexican helpers had now lowered the muzzle of the long gun and the second time it spoke we felt sure something had happened. It had. Later we learned what it was. Most of the federals were fortified in the town cuartel [barracks], an adobe fortification built around a large patio, used as a drill yard. In the center of that patio there was a water tank, elevated on a framework, and it was plumb through the wooden sides of this tank that the second shaft of solid metal from the rebel gun had gone, making a clean hole as it passed through, and, no doubt, continuing on into the desert. But this lucky hit had something to do with the fall of the town. The poor little federals were showered with the only drinking water they had which contributed greatly to their suffering as the day went on.
>
> Carpentier tried another shot with his big gun. But the sound of it was not the same. Even with my untrained ear I knew that something was amiss. Carpentier started running back up the slope and leaning over, he started to pull something out of the earth. He returned, hugging what proved to be the breech-block of the cannon. Examining it he shook his head dolorously and, sitting down on a large rock, wept bitter tears of grief and exasperation.[58]

Shortly after the collapse of the water tower, General Juan Navarro surrendered Juárez to the rebels and Madero became the victor. Turner's account of the details of the fall of Juárez and the other various events and his interviews with Villa, Orozco, and all of the other significant players makes for fascinating review of the history of the revolution as recorded first hand in Bullets, Bottles, and Gardenias.

Turner left Texas and held a variety of short term assignments at various newspapers, but in 1921 landed in Los Angeles and a new job at the Los Angeles Times. He remained at the Times as a prolific contributor until his retirement in 1954. He wrote another book while at the times, Turn Off the Sunshine: Los Angeles on the Wrong Side of the Tracks, an anthology of short stories about Los Angeles. In 1961, Turner died at the age of 75. An obituary was not located, but a review of it said, "He was a bald, lanky man with glasses, and the unsmiling mug shot with his obituary makes him look serious, cold and, in his signature bowtie, a bit eccentric. However, the story says he took delight in poking fun at all pretensions, lived downtown, and refused to learn how to drive a car.[59]

Jimmy Hare

As the middle of May 1911 approached and the Sheldon bar began to fill with newspapermen in anticipation of the Battle of Juárez, someone said, "Where is Jimmy Hare? This cannot be a war. Jimmy Hare is not here."[60] Not long after that pronouncement, Hare checked into the Sheldon and was seen regularly in and around the Sheldon's lobby by many other writers who included him in their written outtakes of the activities leading up to the decisive battle of the Madero rebellion. [61] Hare was a photojournalist who spent most of his career working for *Collier's Magazine*. With his hand-held camera, leaving most of his fellow journalists standing at the bar, he crossed into Juárez and covered the infamous three-day battle from the front lines, ducking and dodging; he captured the gruesomeness, the heroics, and the aftermath of the most singularly important event of the Mexican Revolution. It was his photographs that bring life to that historic time of more than a hundred years ago.

Figure 89. Jimmy Hare 1856-1946 Photojournalist

By the start of the revolution, Hare's reputation was enormous. He had photographed the aftermath of the sinking of the Maine in Havana harbor, traveled with the Rough Riders up Kettle Hill to the main fortress at San Juan Hill during the Spanish-American War. It was his coverage of the war in Cuba that elevated his status to the top ranks of photojournalists of his day. He snapped the last photograph of President McKinley just seconds before McKinley's assassination in 1901. He photographed the San Francisco earthquake of 1906.

On May 14, 1908, Hare along with reporters: Sulley Stanley, Arthur Ruhl, Byron Newton, and Billy Hoster managed to find the Wright Brothers secret flight test field at Kitty Hawk, North Carolina. Climbing through thickets, scrub timber, and over sand hills, the group, hiding from view:

> ...gazed out across a mile of level beach to a lone shed. To the left of the shed, two black dots, which were men, moved about something set on the sand. This white streak and the skeleton lines beneath it was, in a

way, the center of the world. It was the center of the world because it was the touchable embodiment of an idea, which presently is to make the world something different than it has ever been before. The two little dots working out there in the sun knew more about this idea and carried it further than anybody else. The bedraggled men crouching behind the trees were the first uninvited, as it were, official, jury of the world at large to see the thing in action and judge its success. Really, it was not newspaper reporters; it was the world's curiosity, which was peering across the intervening sands.

The propellers started, the white streak tilted and rose, and the hazy rectangle, with the two dots amidships, bore down across the field. Jimmy Hare rushed out from the cover of the scrub trees and made the first news photo of man in a power driven aeroplane. The flight lasted two minutes and fifty seconds, and covered two miles. The reporters and Jimmy Hare returned to civilization to tell the story to the waiting world: the Wrights can fly; Jimmy Hare had the photo to prove it.[62]

Figure 90. The iconic first photo by a journalist of the Wright Brothers flight, May 14, 1908 taken by Jimmy Hare. Faint outline of plane in the center. (Library of Congress)

The first powered, sustained, controlled, heavier-than-air flights took place at Kill Devil Hills, North Carolina on December 17, 1903. The Wright Brothers photographed and filmed many of their subsequent flights, but kept their photographs and project secret. It was the Hare photograph of the 1905 Flyer III in May 1908 that took their success public when published in *Collier's Weekly* magazine.

As the battle in Juárez unfolded, Jimmy Hare was right in the middle of it, taking pictures at almost every step, particularly without regard for his own safety, acting as if his camera were a bulletproof shield.[63] El Paso newsman, Tim Turner, who was also in the middle of the battle, wrote of Hare's actions:

> Hare had a theory that it was safer to walk up the very center of the street than to keep close to the houses. He explained all this and, while the argument appealed to my sense of logic, my natural instincts were all against it. So I kept hugging the houses while Hare, holding his camera always ready in front of him, went another way. Hare was a little chap and wore a pointed beard, and he made a picture poking about their against a background of blue sky and jagged adobe walls of houses that had been blown up, more like a gentleman amateur photographer taking some snapshots of the ruins of a Spanish mission in California.[64]

During the surrender of General Juan Navarro at the fall of Juárez, Hare was having significant difficulty getting in close enough to photograph the actual surrender. He of course knew Garibaldi well, as they were both living at the Sheldon, and Hare managed to get Garibaldi's attention just as he was accepting the sword of surrender, Garibaldi promptly passed Hare through the crowd just in time for Hare to capture Navarro surrendering himself and his sword to Garibaldi.[65]

After his experience in the Battle of Juárez, he was in the Sheldon at the time of the Villa-Garibaldi confrontation. Hare and Garibaldi had become fairly good friends during the Juárez blood-bath, so when he heard that Villa had entered the Sheldon looking for him; he decided to make every effort to defend his friend and sent word to Garibaldi of the impending danger. Cecil Carnes, Hare's biographer writes:

> With his camera in hand, he confronted Villa in the lobby and asked him if he would come up to the Sheldon roof with him to pose for some pictures and that the pictures "would be published and admired from one side of the United States to the other." Villa shook his head,

"Impossible! I am here for another purpose and have no time to waste. I am going to kill that wretched Garibaldi!"

"He won't mind waiting a bit," said Jimmy.

It was a jest exactly to the monster's taste. He gave a guffaw of laughter. Then the almost childish vanity which was one of his predominant traits turned the scale. He permitted himself to be led to the hotel roof. There, safe from the mischance of a street meeting of the two men. Jimmy went to work with brain and hands. He used every vile and cajolement at his command. He flattered the hideous Pancho into believing himself a perfect Prince Charming. He snapped pose after pose, and, true to the guiding principle of his life, he no sooner snapped one than he asked for another. It was not until a good half-hour had elapsed and he was reasonably certain Peppino Garibaldi must have received his warming and left El Paso, that he allowed the blood thirsty Villa to depart on his already frustrated mission of murder.[66]

James H. "Jimmy" Hare, was born in London in 1856, the son of a successful camera manufacturer. After years as an apprentice in the family business, he chose to leave over a disagreement regarding the value of hand-held cameras. He was convinced that his father's cameras were not keeping up with the new technology and he then went to work for another camera manufacturer. It wasn't long before he lost interest in the manufacturing side of the business and became a photographer.

Again on assignment for *Collier's*, Hare covered the Balkan War in Eastern Europe in 1912 and then returned to Mexico in 1914 to cover the American occupation at Veracruz. With the beginning of WWI, Hare had assumed that he would be going to Europe, but *Collier's* chose to change, under new management, not focus on news and photojournalism, and he ended his lengthy tenure with the magazine and joined the staff of *Leslie's* Weekly and was sent to Europe on August 30, 1914 for about a year, returning to England. After a series of censorship and press restriction he repositioned himself in Belgium to try to cover the war as best as he could. On May 7, 1915, he went to Ireland to record the arrival of the survivors of the Lusitania. In 1918, he returned to Europe and continued his front line photojournalism. Hare ended his war days in 1920 covering the Polish war with Russia. He returned to the United States and finished his final years on the lecture circuit sharing his varied career. He passed away at the age of 90 in Teaneck, New Jersey on June 24, 1946.

The Mexican Revolution was one of the first wars to be documented by legends of photographers. Jimmy Hare was certainly not the only one of significance. Historians of all breeds can be grateful to the large numbers of dedicated photographers who, as did Hare, risked their life and limbs for the "right shot." There was Gerald Brandon, Eva Strauss Lovell, Homer Scott, Fred Feldman, Clara Goodman, Wilford Smithers, and of course, the amateur El Paso photographer, Dr. Herbert Stevenson. Their contributions represent a significant legacy of record for the study of the border at war during the early part of the new century. It was however, Otis Aultman whose photographs of the growth, changes, and record of the change-makers, that is the key to the study of El Paso and its role in the Mexican Revolution.

Otis Aultman

Besides being the only photographer that Pancho Villa trusted, he was admired by historians and newsmen alike as the best known photographer of the Mexican Revolution. He was a fearless adventurer who would go anywhere and dodge bullets and swords to get the right photo.[67] He took photographs of everybody and everything along the border in El Paso and environs, resulting in a photographic record of the beginning of change that came to the area as it entered the Twentieth Century.[68] Aultman was described as, "Wiry, short, and wizened; he was in constant need of a haircut; he was wrinkled and ageless. Like an animated gargoyle he pranced through life, alternately grinning and snarling, hating hypocrisy, and loving the humble. His contempt for people was a delightful thing; and for convention he cared not a whit."[69]

Figure 91. Otis Aultman 1874-1943 El Paso Photographer.
(El Paso Public Library, Aultman Collection)

Born in 1874 in Missouri and raised in Trinidad, Colorado, he grew up in the shadow of his older brother; photographer Oliver Aultman, who became one of the Colorado's most celebrated photographers. After joining his brother in operating a local Trinidad studio and a failed young marriage, Aultman headed west for a new beginning and a life full of adventure. He arrived in El Paso in 1907 at the age of 35 and took a job with the Homer Scott photography studio. As the revolution erupted, he acquired employment with the International News Service and Pathé News to find and photograph the restless and ruthless Pancho Villa… and the rest is history as he accompanied Villa throughout Mexico in a specially built train car similar to Gibbons' Tribune train car. During the 1916 expedition to capture Villa, Aultman photographed the pursuits of Gen. John Pershing.

Following the involvement of the American soldiers of fortune in the Mexican Revolution, Aultman maintained his relationship with the mercenaries, reporters, and military men as they entered and returned from WWI. He was a mainstay of the local Adventurers' Club. Composed of Tracy Richardson, Sam Dreben, Gen. John Pershing, and Tim Turner among others, they would get together, play cards, and socialize whenever two or more of them were in town; and he remained on par with their wild drinking ways when they returned to El Paso.[70] On the March 6, 1943, Aultman died at the age of 69, after falling from a seven-foot platform into an alley adjacent to his studio.

After his death, the Aultman studio was ravaged and ransacked by interlopers who had little regard for the historic nature of his photographs. It was estimated that nearly one half of his entire collection was stolen or destroyed. Fortunately, the El Paso Chamber of Commerce was able to purchase about 6000 negatives for $600 in 1943. The collection was then donated to the El Paso Public Library which, under the guidance of historian C.L. Sonnichsen, in turn shared this significant imprint of Southwest history with the Special Collections Department at the University of Texas at El Paso and the El Paso County Historical Society.

Notes and References

[1] Tuck, Jim. *Pancho Villa and John Reed: Two Faces of Romantic Revolution*. (Tucson: The University of Arizona Press, 1984.), 104.

[2] Milton, Joyce. *The Yellow Kids: Foreign Correspondents in the Heyday of Yellow Journalism.* (New York: Harper & Row, 1989.), xiii.

[3] White, Owen P. *The Autobiography of a Durable Sinner.* (New York: Putnam's Sons, 1942.), 114.

[4] Ibid, 113-114.
[5] Ibid, 115.
[6] Harris and Sadler (2009), 255.
[7] Hendricks, interview.
[8] Tuck, 65.
[9] White (1942), 113-114.
[10] Randall, David. *The Great Reporters*. (London: Pluto Press, 2005.), 159,176.
[11] Gibbons, Edward. *Floyd Gibbons: Your Headline Hunter.* (New York: A Banner Book, 1953.), 53.
[12] Harris and Sadler (2009), 255.
[13] Ibid, 54.
[14] Tuck, 65.
[15] Gibbons, 56-57.
[16] Ibid.
[17] Peterson, Jessie and Thelma C. Knoles (eds.) *Pancho Villa: Intimate Recollections by People Who Knew Him.* (New York: Hastings House Publishers, 1977.), 153.
[18] Weiner, Ed. *The Damon Runyon Story*. (New York: Popular Library, 1949.), 111.
[19] Ibid, 58-59.
[20] Harris and Sadler (2009), 255.
[21] Nelson, Andrew J. *Floyd Gibbons: A Journalistic Force of Nature in Early 20th Century America.* `Unpublished Master's Thesis (University of Nebraska, 2010.), 25.
[22] Gibbons, 12.
[23] Ibid, 26.
[24]www.stripes.com/blogs/the-rumor-doctor/the-rumor-doctor-1.104348/did-marines-not-german-soldiers-coin-the-phrase-devil-dogs-1.130602
[25] Gibbons, 348.
[26] Breslin, Jimmy. *Damon Runyon: A Life*. (Boston: Houghton Mifflin, 1991.), 287.
[27] Ibid, 4.
[28] Ibid, 22.
[29] Runyon, Damon, Jr. *Father's Footsteps: The Story of Damon Runyon by His Son*. (New York: Random House, 1953.), 7.
[30] "The Press: Broadway Columnist." *Time.* September 30, 1940.
[31] Breslin, 127-128.; Hoyt, Edwin P. *A Gentleman of Broadway: The Story of Damon Runyon.* (Boston: Little, Brown, 1964.), 126.
[32] Ibid, 127.
[33] Lewis, W. David. *Eddie Rickenbacker: An American Hero in the Twentieth Century.*

(Baltimore: John Hopkins University Press, 2005.), 506.
[34] D'Itri, Patricia Ward. *Damon Runyon* (Farmington, MI: Cengage Gale, 1982.), 149-150.
[35] Breslin, 278-279.
[36] Smith, Wilda M., and Eleanor A. Bogart. *The Wars of Peggy Hull: The Life and Times of a War Correspondent.* (El Paso: Texas Western Press, 1991.), 128.
[37] Ibid, 62-64.
[38] "Peggy Hull Deuell." *Real People, Real Stories*. (Kansas Historical Society, spring 2008.) Accessed 29 January 2011.
[39] Roth, Mitchel. *Historical Dictionary of War Journalism*. (Westport, CT: Greenwood Press, 1997.), 150.
[40] Ibid.
[41] Kuhn, Irene C. *Assigned to Adventure*. (Philadelphia: Lippincott, 1938.)
[42] Smith and Bogart, 267.
[43] Monaghan (1977).
[44] Ibid, 129.
[45] Ibid, 138-139.
[46] Ibid, 144.
[47] Ibid, 148.
[48] Ibid, 173.
[49] Dilliard, Irving. "Historian in Cowboy Boots: Jay Monaghan 1893-1980." *Journal of the Illinois State Historical Society*. Vol. 74. No. 4 (winter, 1981), 261-278.
[50] Atkin, Ronald. *Revolution! Mexico: 1910-1920.* (New York: J. Day Co., 1969.),63.
[51] Turner (1935), 69.
[52] Metz, Leon. *Borderland: The U.S. Mexico Line*. (El Paso: Mangan Books, 1989.), 202.
[53] *El Paso Herald*, May 6, 1961.
[54] Metz, Leon. *Turning Points in El Paso Texas*. (El Paso: Mangan Books, 1985.), 87.
[55] Turner (1935), 86-87.
[56] Ibid, 221.
[57] Atkin, 66-67.
[58] Turner (1935), 55-58.
[59] Harnisch, Larry. "Rediscovering Los Angeles—Timothy Turner" *Los Angeles Times.* September 17, 2013.
[60] Marion, Mary Warner. *Photography: A Cultural History*. (Englewood Cliffs, NJ: Prentice-Hall, 2006.), 227.
[61] Turner (1935), 55-58; Monagahn, 173.
[62] Faber, John. *Great News Photos and the Stories Behind Them*. (New York: Dover, 1978.), 20.

[63] Romo, 157.
[64] Turner (1935), 55-58, 63.
[65] Carnes, Cecil. *Jimmy Hare News Photographer: Half a Century with a Camera*. (New York: Macmillan Company, 1940.), 212.
[66] Ibid, 214.
[67] Romo, 159.
[68] Sonnichsen (1968), 396.
[69] Harris, Larry A. *Pancho Villa Strong Man of the Revolution.* (Silver City, NM: High-Lonesome Books, 1995.), 11.
[70] Nunez, Aurora, and Amanda Taylor. *Otis A. Aultman Captured Border History in Pictures.* (El Paso Community College: EPPC. libguide, 2002.)

Chapter Eighteen

A Criminal's Lair

Was the Sheldon Hotel a bastion of criminal organizations, which plotted, schemed, and attacked the finances and morality of the community? No, with one notable exception that surfaced near the end of the hotel's life. Did the Sheldon have an assemblage of individuals who had checkered pasts, who were secreting their identities from various law enforcement entities? Absolutely, but certainly no more than were ensconced in the Paso del Norte Hotel, the Orndorff, or any number of other establishments in El Paso, as it underwent transformation from its lawless past to its status as a major business hub and role in valuing respectable mores being brought to town by the new social elite. Were there gamblers, thieves, and political bandits who attempted to control the growth and direction of the future of El Paso? Yes, but their schemes and identities would surface only after significant scrutiny by latter day historians combing through the records of El Paso's turbulent times. Were those branded as criminals convicted ex-cons or just individuals who had escaped prosecution?

In the early days of the Sheldon's existence, local law enforcement was usually the responsibility of former bandits, thieves, and killers who had been given the badge of authority. The integrity of the local justice system was highly suspect. The juries, more commonly than not, freed those accused of crimes out of fear of retaliation or by bribery. Were the revolutionaries and mercenaries criminals? The difficulty of the question of criminality depends on how it is defined.

The perfect example of a criminal patron of the Sheldon Hotel, who had resided in the hotel and who had continued to frequent the hotel even after he had obtained homes away from the downtown district, was a lawyer, businessman, schemer, and politician. He was, according to most historians, allegedly implicated in major crimes that included multiple murders. As a former U.S. Senator and sitting member of President Warren G. Harding's cabinet, he was arrested, tried, convicted, and incarcerated in prison. He was Albert B. Fall. In all fairness, Secretary Fall did leave a long and honorable list of positive contributions to the American people, but most of that faded from history because of the disgrace of his federal conviction for accepting a bribe from oilman Edward Doheny in the heart of the Teapot Dome scandal.

The most disgraceful part of this 1929-1930 scandal and trial was the acquittal of Edward Doheny for giving the bribe in the first place. It doesn't make sense to convict a man of accepting a bribe that another court declared didn't happen. That was a perfect example of the type of justice in the United States and it was particularly commonplace in El Paso during the early history of the Sheldon Hotel. Martha Fall Bethune presents an admirable defense of her grandfather's life and reputation in her book, Race with the Wind: The Personal Life of Albert B. Fall.[1] However, it does little to remove the cloud of suspicion of Fall's alleged participation in the murders of Albert J. Fountain, Fountain's son, and Sheriff Pat Garrett.

Figure 92. Edward L. Doheny 1856-1935

Because the Sheldon Hotel was at the physical center of downtown and the center of social and civic life in El Paso, the hotel's proximity to criminal activity in the surrounding vicinity implicates it in that activity by association. The hotel's location across Oregon Street from the early site of Chinatown and its hidden tunnels, opium dens, and human smuggling; its location a few blocks north of El Paso's bawdy houses and prostitution cribs; and its relative closeness to the international bridge allowing for the Prohibition tourists, who flooded Juárez during America's great social experiment, all add to the Sheldon's identity as a criminal lair.

Figure 93. Remaining prostitution cribs in the *Chihuahuita* section of downtown El Paso, several blocks south of the Sheldon Hotel site in 2009.
(Author's Collection)

Those criminal elements that confronted the community certainly functioned in the guest rooms, the bar, or the lobby of the Sheldon. Schemes planned, deals made, and surely, some of the "women of the night" entertained some of El Paso's elite on the fourth or fifth floor as illegal gaming took place throughout the building, much like what was going on in sister establishments following the outlawing of gambling by the El Paso reformers. The Chihuahuita district, pictured above, has been identified by the National Trust for Historic Preservation, as being one of the eleven most endangered places for 2016.[2]

These criminal activities were not similar to the recently uncovered illegal smuggling ring at El Paso's Gateway Hotel (Est. 1906) in 2011. The owner of that establishment, Song U Chon, received 15 years in federal prison for transporting and harboring illegal aliens in his hotel.[3] The Sheldon Hotel's role in criminal enterprises such as these was significantly more opaque in years past, if at all.

Because of the Sheldon's position in downtown El Paso, adjacent to merchants who were actively involved in the arms business of supplying both sides of revolution, often in violation of federal arms embargos, and because the hotel was the operational center of Mexican Revolution, the American government began to flood the hotel and the surrounding area with agents to locate and arrest those individuals who were violating the U.S. Neutrality Act. The hotel's bar and lobby was a major target and many of the hotel's patrons were arrested on such charges.

The Sheldon's role in El Paso criminal activity appears to be focused on four major areas: Neutrality violations, Human smuggling, Prohibition enforcement, and most regrettably, the incursion of the Klu Klux Klan into the fabric of El Paso's social and civic life.

Criminal activity today has changed the face of both El Paso and its sister city, Ciudad Juárez, currently the most dangerous border city in Mexico and one of the worst in the world. Recently the violence in Juárez has begun to spill over into El Paso, endangering the lives of residents, law enforcement personnel, and other first responders. Juárez has become a battleground for drug-related violence and these gangs show no mercy to Americans. In 2010, stray bullets from a gun battle in Juárez struck El Paso's multi-story city hall (since replaced with a baseball park, co-owned by Paul Foster.) and buildings at the University of Texas at El Paso causing police to shut down a major border highway. The West Texas city of El Paso has been identified as the most dangerous border town in America.[4]

Smuggling

While the smuggling of arms, ammunition, and war materiel during the revolution and alcohol during Prohibition were staggeringly major problems, so it was with human smuggling and trafficking in downtown El Paso in the years leading up to and following the Mexican Revolution and continuing today. Human smuggling and human trafficking are based on three significant components: consent, exploitation, and transportation. Human smuggling centers on the transportation of people into a country involving the deliberate evasion of immigration laws, usually with the individuals consent, and once the destination has been reached, the business transaction is completed. Human trafficking, on the other hand, usually lacks the individual's consent, centering upon exploitation of the victim's labor for the trafficker's material gain.[5] Human trafficking is considered a hidden crime as the victims rarely come forward because of language barriers, fear of the traffickers, and/or fear of law enforcement and potential deportation.

Because Mexican citizens could pass freely into and out of the two border cities, the smuggling in the early years of the Sheldon Hotel concentrated on the movement of Chinese nationals. It was because of that and the passage of Chinese Exclusion Act of 1882, and its renewal, the Geary Act of 1892, that immigration agents, known then as the Immigration Mounted Guard (or Inspectors), roamed the area in and around El Paso.

The Act prevented Chinese laborers, skilled and unskilled and those seeking work in mines, from entering the United States for a period of ten years. The Geary Act extended such prohibition for an additional ten years and required all Chinese to carry "papers" at all times. Those already in the United States could remain, but would have to demonstrate that they had been here previously with their "papers." These requirements were the cause of the establishment and organization of the Chinese smuggling industry spearheaded by the Six Companies (Chinese Consolidated Benevolent Association) that controlled nearly ninety per-cent of the smuggling business. The Six Companies operated an elaborate underground market for the illicit sale of forged and fraudulent merchant, laborers, and naturalization documents.[6]

The Chinese following the passage of these acts often felt the immigration laws to be unjust. They relied upon organizations with elaborate plans to outwit the immigration authorities and smuggle their fellow countrymen into El Paso. Upon arrival in Juárez, they would go to the houses of Chinese friends to wait their chances of illegal entry into El Paso. It was estimated that 150 to 200 unemployed Chinese were in the hideouts of the smuggling firms of Juárez at all times.[7]

Erica Lee, one of the most respected authorities on Chinese smuggling wrote:

> The Chinese of El Paso, Texas, "banded together" with the Chinese company in Juárez, Mexico, illustrates not only the transnational connections between Chinese communities in the United States and those in Mexico but also the permeability of the border region for Chinese immigrants. Indeed, Chinese communities along both sides of the southern border inhabited "a world in motion"—made up of shifting and multiple identities and relationships constructed for the purpose of illegal migration. One of the best examples of how Chinese shifted their identities was their attempts to "pass" as members of another race in order to cross the border undetected. Even though Chinese migration to both Canada and Mexico dated back to the middle of the nineteenth century, Chinese were not viewed as "natural" inhabitants of the northern and southern borderlands, as were Native Americans or Mexicans. Some Chinese immigrants and their guides

> thus learned early on to try to "pass" as members of these two groups as they crossed the border.[8]

Generally speaking, the illegal immigrants would disembark on the Mexican west coast and walk overland to central Mexico, where they would board the Mexican Central Railroad for passage to Juárez and on to El Paso. It was also a common practice for some Chinese, who entered Mexico, to first become Mexican citizens and then attempt to enter El Paso as Mexicans, others would claim that they were U.S. residents but had been visiting friends and family in Mexico and were just returning "home."

The Mounted Guards were part of the Bureau of Immigration in 1885 and were the predecessors of today's U.S. Border Patrol. By the time the Sheldon Hotel opened in 1900, these immigration agents were no strangers to the hotel's lobby and bar. The systematic and somewhat commercial enterprise of smuggling Chinese was a response to the passage of these repressive anti-Chinese bills. Operating out of El Paso, the Mounted Guards, they rarely numbered more than seventy-five agents and were mostly drawn from police departments, Texas Rangers, and Railroad Mail Clerks. They patrolled as far west as California.

When a Chinese immigrant managed to elude the Mounted Guards, there were no other immigrations officers seeking to track them down and they made their way to points west and east. With the outbreak of WWI and the interruption of transpacific shipping and passenger service, growth of the Chinese issue began to dwindle and fade. There were, however, other contributing factors to the decline of El Paso's Chinese colony. American steam laundries drove most of the Chinese hand laundries out of business. Furthermore, gambling was outlawed, putting many Chinese out of business. The El Paso Herald wrote, 'It is undoubtedly a good thing that gambling has been stopped in El Paso. But there is a feature that is to be perhaps regretted, and that is it kept considerable of the Chinese money in town that would have gone to the effete Celestial Empire. Chinese are great gamblers but are so slick in that line that they seldom make any heavy losses."[9]

With the arrival of the railroads in 1881, El Paso began its long and convoluted adventure into the modern age. The arrival of the iron horse was clearly El Paso's seminal event. In its wake, the railroad left behind some 1200 unemployed male Chinese laborers whose labor was essential for the completion of the various railroad projects. Some immediately returned to China; some remained in the employ of the railroad maintenance yards; some set up small businesses to support the small Chinese contingent with stores, lodging, and a social structure that became El Paso's emerging Chinatown; while still others fled El Paso for parts unknown. The Chinese were willing to take on jobs that most Euro-Americans refused to do.

The Chinese colony began to develop in the area around the future site of the Sheldon Building (Hotel). Central to this community was the area around Oregon and St. Louis Streets (Mills) in adobe buildings just west of the original El Paso Times building; and south to Fourth Street, between El Paso and Stanton Streets.[10] The El Paso Herald reported in 1889, "El Paso is the Chinese Mecca of the Southwest. They are liberally patronized, much to the detriment of the Americans. They have a monopoly on the laundry business in El Paso, and realizing this, their prices are rising proportionally."[11]

During most of its lifetime, the Sheldon Hotel sat opposite the Federal Custom House and court building at the corner of St. Louis (Mills) and Oregon Streets. When the existing adobe buildings, dating back to the days of the San Antonio-San Diego Mail Line operated by George Giddings, were razed in order to build the Federal Building, it was discovered that the previous Chinese tenants had burrowed into the dirt floors of the building, creating a subterranean passage that ran from one basement to another; up and down South Oregon Street, literally a honeycomb of underground passages that connected hiding places, storerooms, and opium dens.[12] There is little doubt that the patrons and owners of the various businesses on south Oregon Street, including the Sheldon, knew of the existence of this subterranean maze and community.

Rumors of hidden tunnels and secret underground rooms abound in the folklore of El Paso, including the existence of tunnels at El Paso High School and at the Turtle House at 516 Corto Way in Sunset Heights. It was believed that a tunnel ran under the Rio Grande from the Turtle House to Juárez.[13] Although this legend has never been truly vetted and surely feeds the bevy of conspiracy theorists and amateur history buffs, it is ironic that the house (now an apartment house) is located across the street from the El Paso County Historical Society.

The issue of smuggling Chinese nationals into the United States from Mexico has resurfaced recently. The number of Chinese immigrants illegally crossing the Mexican border into the United States has skyrocketed in the last several years, as the smuggling industry becomes more lucrative, often charging as much as $70,000 per person. In a recent report from the U.S. Customs and Border Protection they apprehended an estimated 663 nationals in the first eight months of 2015, compared with 48 in the entire previous year and only eight the year before that. The Chinese account for the fifth-largest population of illegal immigrants in the country. New smuggling activities involving pregnant Chinese women into special "holding homes" particularly in Southern California, where the women remain until they give birth to what is called "anchor babies."[14]

Prohibition

It is highly unlikely that a bootlegger was operating an illegal distillery out of the basement of the Sheldon Hotel during the fourteen years of this great social experiment. However, there are good odds that booze smugglers were guests from time to time and used their rooms to carefully plan and execute their illegal schemes to bring the illegal contraband into El Paso. But for the most part, the Sheldon Hotel's participation during Prohibition, like the two preceding discussions of human smuggling and neutrality law violations, was more of proximity to easy access to the wild and free-flowing intoxicants that were available a stone's throw across the Rio Grande in Ciudad Juárez. The temperance movement had its early beginning nearly 100 years before Congress passed the Volstead Act. The tenacity and patience of the Women's Christian Temperance Union and the Anti-Saloon League is to be admired.

Both houses of Congress passed resolutions to add the Eighteenth Amendment to the Constitution and on January 16, 1919, the Nebraska legislature became the thirty-sixth state to ratify the amendment making the three-fourths majority necessary for approval. President Woodrow Wilson vetoed the Volstead Act on October 27, 1919 after five months of consideration. The following day, his veto was overridden by both houses of Congress. Under the terms of the statue; processors and sellers of alcoholic beverages were required to cease all activity on January 16, 1920. Eventually all states except Rhode Island and Connecticut ratified the amendment. Many American's viewed this Congressional action as an infringement on their personal rights and freedoms and felt it was unconstitutional. Overnight, the new clandestine adventure began. During these fourteen years, demand for illegal alcohol never diminished. "It was one thing to legislate but another to obtain submission."[15] The limits against alcohol in the Eighteenth Amendment did not include a prohibition against drinking, only the manufacture, transporting, and selling.

The increase of the illegal production and sale of alcohol which was known as "bootlegging"; the proliferation of illegal drinking establishments called "speakeasies"; the rise in dangerous health side-effects from bathtub and moonshine operations; and the accompanying rise in gang violence and other crimes led to waning support for Prohibition by the end of the 1920s. Corrupt and complacent politicians overlooked much of the illegal manufacturing and smuggling that blossomed out of the Volstead Act, as the influence of the likes of Al Capone and the rum-running of Joseph Kennedy became the norm.[16] Under enormous pressure from their constituents, Congress repealed the Eighteenth Amendment with the ratification on December 5, 1933 of the Twenty-first Amendment. This is the only time a constitutional amendment has been repealed. Section 2 of the Twenty-first Amendment granted each state absolute control over alcohol and many states remained "dry" for some time after ratification, often permitting local counties to maintain control over alcohol issues.

While the illegal booze industry grew exponentially, the legal operators faced closure and bankruptcy. However, both Canada and Mexico remained "wet" and had no objections to foreigners investing in and opening up establishments to meet the need of "thirst-stricken Americans."[17] A major exodus of bars, taverns, distillers, brew masters, and allied enterprises crossed the Canadian and Mexican borders. As a result, a tourist boom hit these border towns on both sides of the boundaries. Describing the relationship between El Paso and its sister city Juárez, Langston writes: "Indeed, a commercial boom occurred – but with it came a new series of vexing problems, crime waves, and unfortunate incidents that cast unfavorable light on both nations. The colorful entrepreneurs were not necessarily at fault, but the undesirable human element attracted to the two cities contributed heavily to a disorderly border society. Continual political upheaval in Mexico only aggravated the situation. Actions and pressures brought by one city caused hostile reactions in the other. Ciudad Juárez prospered but at a demanding price that branded it as a 'sin city.' El Paso fared little better."[18]

The Sheldon as well as the other El Paso hotels publicized and encouraged the tourist trade to come to El Paso and "vacation" in Juarez's bounty of "entertainment delights." Besides swelling the financial gain of the hotel operators, it also fostered "disrespect for law and demoralized social and personal manners, customs, and codes of conduct." The tourist trade, while significant, paled to the economy associated with the illegal trade of spirits that flowed across the Rio Grande into the United States, not only in El Paso, but along the entire Texas-Mexico border.

It is hard to imagine, with alcohol so readily available across the river, that alcohol smuggling would develop into such a major enterprise. Nonetheless, the smuggling business would raise its head each and every night. Bootleggers avoided the obvious crossing points and transported their forbidden cargo across the Rio Grande using pack mules and other ingenious means. Cordova Island (Chamizal), slightly over two miles south-east from downtown El Paso, lacked a water barrier and its brush-covered plain became the site-of-choice as the smugglers crossed the imaginary boundary line into El Paso and the gun battles between state and federal agents and the smugglers became a nightly occurrence. In 1963 the treaty that settled the Chamizal dispute transferred 193 acres on Cordova Island to the United States in exchange for an equal area further downstream.

Since the border itself was not a real barrier between the seller and the consumer, it was the various federal agents from the Bureau of Investigation, Treasury Department, the Immigration officers, and Texas Rangers who attempted to hold the smuggling in check. They fought diligently but hopelessly, as the monetary gains available in the smuggling of liquor and other contraband only led to senseless bloodshed. "Prohibition is a hundred percent fiasco…what has not been enforced cannot be enforced…we have made Prohibition the supreme error of our political history."[19]

The smuggling activity was a two-way process, as the smugglers and bootleggers returned to Mexico they often brought with them American food products and consumer goods obtained "in barter" for their alcohol and cash transactions were frequently avoided altogether. The smuggler's objectives were merely to smuggle and make a profit, and "were not primitive rebels or social bandits but circumstantial business persons or opportunists."[20] Yet as the success and profitability of smuggling increased, the enterprise became significantly more violent and Prohibition gangsterism became deeply infused. In addition, liquor smuggling arising from the Volstead Act seemed to become intertwined with border immigration issues. Many of the smugglers, or tequileros, were aliens trying to enter the United States illegally and this drew the fledgling Border Patrol into the policing of prohibition and the anti-smuggling prevention network.[21]

As had occurred during the Mexican Revolution, the Sheldon became a common meeting place for the influx of law enforcement agents, particularly the Texas Rangers, most of whom were well known and well acquainted with the inner workings of El Paso and Juárez. Reflecting upon the new and disappointedly embarrassed role of the once proud Texas Rangers having to become "whiskey cops," Owen White writes in Them Was the Days:

The Texas Ranger is no more! And he has passed away, not gloriously, with his boots on and wrapped in a winding sheet of his own six-shooter smoke but, ignominiously and supinely he has succumbed to the hysteria of a nation and, along with a number of other time-honored and excellent institutions he has become a collateral victim of the operations of the deadly Volstead Act. Such is the gratitude of governments, and so are the mighty fallen!

Just imagine if you can, you who know Texas, and who know how much of its greatness the Lone Star State owes to such men as Jim Gillette, John B. Jones, Dick Ware, George W. Baylor, and a host of others; just imagine any of them going around and patting their fellow citizens on the hip in search of a pint of liquor. They wouldn't have done it! They were real men who had real jobs with traditions behind them, and just considerer for a moment, what a disastrous effect it would have had, not only upon those traditions, but upon the life and happiness of the people as well, if those grand old fellows who fought Apaches, hung horse thieves, captured train robbers, and exterminated cattle rustlers had made it a part of their daily business to snoop and spy and arrest their neighbor just because he was the proud and happy possessor of a bottle of good whiskey.[22]

Naturally, the intense activity of the Rangers could have but one result. It had it. Working industriously and fearlessly over long and strenuous period of years the Rangers have finally succeeded in making Texas as quiet and peaceful as any state in the Union and, at the same time, they have succeeded in working themselves out of a job. Therein lays the secret of their present downfall. For the last ten or fifteen years the Rangers haven't been called upon to fight any Indians, capture any train robbers or hang any cow thieves…under the inspiration of a pious governor, [the Rangers] began to act like prohibition officers—raiding hotels, stopping automobiles, and arresting men who had flasks where they should have had six-shooters (and used them). A howl went up that shook the state from the Panhandle to Brownsville."[23]

It appears almost impossible to pin down the Sheldon's role in these criminal activities because of the lack of registration folio information regarding who was or was not a guest of the Sheldon. The point remains, that through her lifetime, the Sheldon was at the center of most things that went on in El Paso. The very nature of criminal activity implies secrecy, so by historical extrapolation, we can assume with a high degree of accuracy, that if it went on in El Paso, it went on at the Sheldon.

Ku Klux Klan

Unlike the preceding, where the issues of neutrality, smuggling, and prohibition were connected to the Sheldon Hotel by proximity, the establishment of the Klu Klux Klan in El Paso was direct, as it was ensconced within the walls of the Sheldon Hotel. El Paso was primed for the penetration of this evil in 1921. El Pasoans had grown weary of the negative impact of the multi-year turmoil of the Mexican Revolution, angered over the lack of support of America's WWI effort by El Paso's Mexicans,[24] and frustrated by the onslaught of the gangsterism and violence of Prohibition. This left El Paso's social and political essences in disquietude. As a consequence, civic life began to focus on 100 percent "Americanism" and there began a repression in the local society of anyone and anything that did not appear to be fully in tune with this Americanism. The Anglo community in El Paso "became increasingly convinced that Mexicans were a cruel mercurial people inherently prone toward social disorganization. Such sentiment particularly prevailed among El Paso's newer residents, many of whom were natives of east Texas and the Deep South and had never had the opportunity to be socialized into the Pass's tradition of cultural tolerance."[25]

In May 1921, Klansman C.C. Kellogg, the Klan's King Eagle of New Mexico came to El Paso and set up residency in the Sheldon Hotel. Soon after his arrival, he opened a Klan recruiting office also in the Sheldon and by July, Kellogg along with Klan organizers C.L Ferman and Clifford Sirmans, established Frontier Klan No. 100. Sonnichsen reports, "Crosses began to burn on Mount Franklin. Lawyers, doctors, preachers, and business leaders joined and it was estimated that the aggregate worth of the membership by July was sixteen million dollars."[26] Cross burning dates back to medieval times, particularly to Scottish clans setting crosses on fire in the foothills as symbols of defiance against an advancing enemy. The Klan held that era in esteem because most of Europe and Scotland were racially homogenous.[27]

In March of 1922, more than a thousand hooded Klansmen, with their car license plates covered, passed over closely guarded roads to the western foothills, near today's Kern Place (just opposite the University of Texas at El Paso

Figure 94. Newspaper photograph of KKK in *El Paso Herald,* Mar. 13, 1922.
(Courtesy Trish Long, *El Paso Times.*)

campus.), gathered in ceremonial bonfires to tout their "anti" rhetoric and begin a systematic plan to take over the local schools and civic government.[28]

Kellogg, from his perch in the Sheldon Hotel clearly was the Invisible *Empire's* advance man, according to the leading authority on Klan activity in El Paso, Shawn Lay.[29] This new incarnation of the KKK had little in common with the organization that grew out of the Civil War Reconstruction era except the name. Its goals and rhetoric was native, white, Protestant supremacy and its targets were Catholics, anti-Prohibitionists, Jews, and any person of liberal or radical views.[30]

The Klan was fervently anti-Hispanic and anti any race but white. It would seem that El Paso would be an unlikely place to set roots because at least fifty percent of the population was Catholic and the El Paso real estate, manufacturing, and retail business were mostly Jewish owned.

Part of the energy that established the Klan's presence in El Paso came from incendiary "enlightenment" spewed from the local pulpits of the local Protestant churches, including the Baptists and Methodists. A visiting Baptist evangelist pastor declared from the largest El Paso congregation: "If the Ku Klux Klan stands for 100 percent Americanism and for clean living, and is opposed to immorality, I'm for it." Reverend Knickerbocker, reputed to be the highest paid Methodist pastor in the South, proclaimed from his brother's pulpit at the Trinity Methodist Church that: "Justice may sometimes be rightfully administered outside the law. Jesus Christ did this when He took the cat o'nine tails and drove the thieves and money changers from the Temple…In this respect He was the first Ku Klux Klansman."[31] From other Protestant churches emanated threatening admonitions that "the world was going to the devil," that "the automobile was replacing the red light district," that dance halls and movie theaters were "cesspools of El Paso," and that those who used tobacco "by example and influence were sending others to hell."

The city became divided into two camps, those under the leadership of the anti-Klan El Paso Times editor James Black who called the Klan, "anarchists and public enemies who seize the purpose of the state."[32] The El Paso Herald tended to be supportive of the Klan. Of the 12 members of the editorial staff at the Herald, 11 were active members of the Klan.[33] This newspaper access was a great advantage to the Klan as it provided it with a highly visible platform upon which to espouse its beliefs.

During his anti-Klan activity, Black had been assaulted by a local policeman, apparently a Klan member, for a story he was preparing. After the assault, Black's wife reported that she had received a threatening phone call:

> We know all about the Times and we would have gotten its editor long ago, but instead of going to his business alone and unafraid, he chose to nightly ride from his work in a city auto at city expense, escorted by two of El Paso's finest officers. But we will get him yet, for he does not know that he often rides home with two policemen who are active members of Frontier Klan No. 100.[34]

The pro-Klan group of local business and government leaders, included the high profile and very vocal "Mama De", Mrs. Charles De Groff, the matriarch of the company which previously owned the Sheldon Hotel.[35] Whether Mrs. De Groff's son, Seth Orndorff who was the local sheriff, was a Klan supporter has not been documented. However, author Lay suggests that he was in fact anti-Klan as shown by his actions.[36] The dissension between the two groups appeared in most of the city's civic clubs and associations. The League of Women's Voters, El Paso Bar Association, the American Legion, and the various masonic and shrine organizations were rife with pro and anti-Klan issues resulting in major community upheaval and unpleasantness. Tension and conflict was the dark cloud that hung over El Paso during the early twenties.

In 1922, all members of the El Paso grand jury except two were active members of the Klan; three members of the school board were affiliated with the Klan and dominated school affairs over the opposition of the two anti-Klan members. The sealer of weights and measures, coerced business people who used scales to join the organization or else. Just about all city positions were heavily dominated by Klansmen. Under the strength and determination of the District Attorney for El Paso County, Charles L. Vowell, Klan opponents were able to force exposure of the Klan's membership lists and from that, the Klan's influence began to ebb. The hoods were off and the secret was out.[37]

The power and influence of the Klan over El Paso collapsed when anti-Klan State Senator Richard M. Dudley handily defeated the Klan candidate, P. Gardner for mayor of El Paso on February 24, 1923.[38] The school board elections also turned against the Klan in their election in April. Many of the pro-Klan Protestant ministers resigned, and with the influx of new blood, pastors who sensed that the cultural pro-Klan attitude was changing, seemed to modify their Klan support, if they had any, and moved on to extol religious tolerance.

In the school board election of April 4, 1923, four anti-Klan candidates swept the ballot and all pledged "to end Klan domination in school affairs." The hope of gaining domination in local government affairs faded as did the Klan as a central issue in El Paso. The El Paso Times editorial of April 4, 1923 stated:

> It is exceedingly pleasant...to come across references in newspapers and other periodicals to the Ku Klux Klan-ridden state of Texas, coupled with the favorable exception of El Paso. It shows that El Paso is already beginning to gain in the country's respect as a result of the blow which her citizens delivered six-weeks ago to the pretensions of the masked and white-robed, self-asserters of their peculiarly vicious form of self-styled virtue.[39]

During the Klan era in El Paso, the Sheldon Hotel was owned by Albert Mathias, local real estate magnate and businessman, and a well-respected member of the Jewish community. His personal feelings regarding the Klan's residency in the Sheldon are not clearly known. But, he was a very successful businessman and may have just allowed the Klan's presence because it was good business.

After the opening of the Hotel Paso del Norte in 1912, the Sheldon became the second most coveted hotel in town. It and the del Norte were side by side in the heart of downtown and were equally connected by proximity to the criminal element, but it appears that the Sheldon served as a hub for the influx of the various law enforcement organizations that arrived to combat these issues, many of them prior to the building of the del Norte Hotel.

The Red Flannel Raid and the Spencer-Crawford Murder

One of the most interesting headline grabbing instances involving the Sheldon Hotel began 800 miles west in the City of Angles, and was referred to as the Red Flannel Raid. During the roaring twenties there were two crime bosses in Los Angeles, one above ground and out in the open whose activities' were, at the very least, quasi-legal and the other one who ran the seedy underground network of criminal enterprises. Edward L. Doheny and his scandal ridden family, along with the Chandler family of the Los Angeles Times, were the most powerful and ruling aristocratic families Los Angeles had ever known. Doheny's early life read like a cheap "Western dime novel, but his power reached throughout the realm, rivaling that of J.P. Morgan and John D. Rockefeller. He was a legend and by 1925 was wealthier than Rockefeller."[40] Success had earned him $300 million by the early 1920s as the first to extract the black gold from beneath LA's serene landscape and bestowed upon him the reputation as the Napoleon of Los Angeles.[41] He brought in the first oil well in Los Angeles on November 4, 1892 and within a couple of years, had more than 2,000 producing wells within the city limits.[42] Doheny had spent his early years as a prospecting partner with the disgraced Senator Albert B. Fall and no doubt, was a poker partner at the gaming tables at the Sheldon of early El Paso.

Doheny eventually became one of the central characters of the Teapot Dome Scandal, but survived with an acquittal of bribing Fall as Fall was found guilty of accepting the bribe. During the Mexican Revolution, Doheny was unrivaled in his bribery of Mexican officials to protect his vast Mexican holdings. He was the president of the Mexican Petroleum Company based at Tampico, and he controlled most of Mexico's oil production. Frustrated by the American government's reluctance to protect his Mexican oil properties, he created and funded a private army of nearly 6,000 soldiers for the expressed purpose of protecting the Mexican oil empire.[43]

Doheny, it was reported, had been involved in plots, uprisings, and attempted coups d'état and was, according to contemporary documents and historical studies, believed to be the financier behind the assassination of Mexican President Venustiano Carranza in 1920.[44] Doheny's tainted wealth would eventually find its way to serve and benefit society through his generous donations to the University of Southern California and the Catholic Church. The 2007 academy award winning motion picture, There Will Be Blood, inspired by Upton Sinclair's novel, Oil, is loosely based on 's life and his oil empire. Doheny died on September 8, 1935. His crypt is located in a special family niche, adjacent to the altar in the main mausoleum, just up the hill from the grave of Col. Kosterlitzky at Calvary Cemetery in East Los Angeles.

The underground leader of Los Angeles was the notoriously treacherous crime boss Charles H. Crawford.[45] Crawford had been a crime lord in Seattle and controlled dance halls, gambling, prostitution, and saloons thus became the "Vice-lord of Seattle's Tenderloin, "a bottomless cauldron of sin."[46] He controlled the local vice until 1911, when local reformers took the city back, recalled the mayor, and arrested the police chief who had been one of Crawford's lackeys. With this change in fortune, Crawford headed south to Los Angeles and set up an operation at the Maple Bar at 230 East Fifth Street. Prohibition did little to dissuade Crawford's control, as he had captured the city's politics and police department, which had "mixed seamlessly with crime through the simple expedient of money."[47]

Crawford, who disliked public attention and constantly stayed in the shadows, had other visible souls, like Albert Marco, his enforcer, and Jerry Giesler, the lawyer whose resumé would include defenses for actors Errol Flynn and Charlie Chaplin, mobster Bugsy Siegel, and stripper Lili St. Cyr. He was adept at grabbing headlines and keeping Crawford's profile "below the fold."[48] Crawford was often called the 'Gray Wolf of Spring Street," and had developed such influence with local politicians and police department officials, that his organization became known as the City Hall Gang. Under his power and influence, he managed public corruption to a new level in Los Angeles. Responding to a comment that he wasn't really a bad man, Crawford is quoted as responding, "No, I'm not bad, not like they've painted me. They say I'm the head of the underworld, but I don't know what that is. The only underworld I know anything about are the sewers and I reckon they can't mean those."[49]

By the late 1920s, criticism of Crawford's control of the city began to surface, much of it spearheaded by a reform-minded Los Angeles City Councilman named Carl I. Jacobson. As the heat expanded under Jacobson's relentless efforts, Crawford set in motion a plot to "get Jacobson" and turned the plan over to Albert Marco (aka Marco Albori). Crawford had assumed that Jacobson was as corruptible as the other local politicians and, through Marco, offered him a $25,000 bribe to quiet down. Jacobson refused.[50] From the halls of one of Crawford's brothels, a young blond widow, Callie Grimes (aka Mrs. Helen Ferguson), managed to befriend Councilman Jacobson and eventually was able to invite him to "her" home at the 4372 Beagle Street in the El Sereno section of LA. Marco had arranged with Grimes to pay her $2,500 and the promise of a $100-per-month payment for the rest of her life.[51]

Grimes went to Jacobson's city hall office to discuss a proposed street assessment on her property. On the evening of August 5, 1927, driven by the tears of the impending assessment, Grimes convinced Jacobson to stop by her house to discuss the matter further, when at the perfect moment, five cops and several reporters and photographers burst in the door to photograph Jacobson and Grimes in a compromising position. Whether Jacobson was actually dressed in only his red flannel underwear or whether the cops forcefully disrobed him, then

Figure 95. Charles H. Crawford 1879-1931
(*Los Angeles Times* Collection UCLA Special Collections.)

Figure 96. Carrie Grimes
(*Los Angeles Times* Collection UCLA Special Collections)

Grimes disrobed and the photographs were taken of the two of them next to a bottle of whisky. Jacobson and Grimes were arrested and charged with lewd conduct.[52] Jacobson claimed that he had been framed and refused to sign a confession. Interestingly, Grimes was defended by Marco's and Crawford's personal attorney. Jacobson continued his steadfast effort at reform and demanded a jury trial. When the jury of 11 women and one man declared that they were hopelessly deadlocked, charges of jury tampering surfaced. Before the second trial began the charges were suddenly dropped.

About a year later, Grimes had a change of heart, primarily because Marco, who had been arrested for a shooting, had failed to keep up on his $100-a-month payments. Grimes, for a fee, was willing to tell the story to a local newspaper and signed an affidavit implicating Crawford and Marco in the Red Flannel conspiracy. As a result, Crawford and Marco were indicted on conspiracy charges. The prosecutor, David H. Clark, filed for a trial date with Callie Grimes as his chief witness and Crawford posted his bail and Marco remained in jail on other charges. Grimes failed to appear for various pre-trail hearings as she had simply vanished. Wire taps were placed on Grimes' mother's telephone and when contacted by her daughter, authorities were able to trace her to the Sheldon Hotel in El Paso, where Crawford had stashed her. When she was returned to Los Angeles to appear in court, stolen Sheldon silverware and towels were found in her procession, and she refused to back up the accusations she had made in her affidavit and the case was dismissed.

In October 1930, Crawford was indicted for bribery in a securities scandal, but the charges were ultimately dismissed as the chief witness for the government wouldn't testify. Big surprise!

Jacobson's political career was over; the several policemen involved in the frame-up were released after a hung jury in their trial; and Crawford returned to his City Hall gang where he continued to polish his skills as the evil boss man of Los Angeles' underworld. On May 20, 1931, Crawford and a local journalist, Herbert Spencer, were assassinated by David H. Clark, the former deputy district attorney and judicial candidate at Crawford's Hollywood office at 6665 (now 6671) Sunset Blvd. During his trial for the Spencer-Crawford murders, Clark admitted the shooting, but declared that it was self-defense because the two men had tried to get him to frame his friend, Police Chief Roy E. Steckel.[53] Clark's first trial was deadlocked and he was acquitted in the second trial with only one juror voting guilty. According to the Los Angeles Times, that lone juror found a bomb on his front lawn the next day.[54] In 1954, after pleading guilty to the second-degree murder of the wife of his former law partner, Clark died of a stroke at Chino state prison near San Bernardino, California.[55]

Following Crawford's death, his wife took control of the former 2.7 acre site of the Hollywood office where Crawford was shot, and in 1936 built one of the first outdoor shopping malls in the country. Called the Crossroads of the World, the mall is designed to resemble an ocean liner surrounded by a small village of cottage looking bungalows. The corruption that Clark and Jacobson had fought against didn't really come together until the election of Mayor Fletcher Bowron in 1938.

There is little doubt that the Sheldon Hotel's location at the American border with Mexico served it well in attracting patrons from all over the United States, particularly those individuals who needed quick and often surreptitious access to the international boundary. The Sheldon was just steps from rail lines that converged on El Paso from almost everywhere and just a couple of blocks from the international bridge that could provide people with refuge from whatever they were running from. It also afforded easy access to the "quickie divorce and marriage" business that would soon flourish beyond expectation. The Sheldon Hotel provided a distant and out-of-the-way locale in which to stash witnesses that would otherwise prove embarrassing to certain social elements who were facing legal and questionable challenges. The Sheldon became a place de choix for the criminal syndicates of Chicago and New York as well as Los Angeles during the roaring twenties.

Figure 97. Crossroads of the World, site of the Spencer-Crawford murder. ca. 1940.

Figure 98. Rear view of ship styled outdoor shopping mall with European village surrounding. 2014
(Author's Collection)

Notes and References

---

[1] Bethune, Martha Fall. *Race with the Wind: The Personal Life of Albert B. Fall.* El Paso: Novio Book, 1989.
[2] "America's Most Endangered Historic Places, 2016." *National Trust for Historic Places.* (savingplaces.org) Accessed 6 November 2016.
[3] "El Paso hotel owner sentenced to 15 years for smuggling and harboring illegal aliens." *ICE Report Crimes. 2011*. Accessed 26 May 2016.
[4] "The 8 Most Dangerous Border Towns in America." *Criminal Justice Degree Guide*. Accessed 10 April 2016.
[5] Neumann, Vanessa. "Never mind the metrics: disrupting human trafficking by other means." *Journal of International Affairs*. Vol. 68, No. 2. (Spring/Summer 2015), 39-53.
[6] Carey, Elaine, and Andrae M. Marak. *Smugglers, Brothels, and Twine: Historical Perspectives on Contraband and Vice in North America's Borderlands* (Tucson: The University of Arizona Press, 2011.), 22.
[7] Farrar, Nancy. *The Chinese in El Paso*. (El Paso: University of Texas at El Paso, 1972.), 19.
[8] Lee, Erica. *At America's Gate: Chinese Immigration During the Exclusion Era 1882-1943.* (Chapel Hill: The University of North Carolina Press, 2003.), 161.
[9] Farrar, 34-35.
[10] Ibid. 4
[11] *El Paso Herald*, February 5-6, 1889.
[12] Fahy, Anna L. "Chinese borderland community development: A case study of El Paso, 1881--1909" (January 1, 2001). *ETD Collection for University of Texas at El Paso.* Paper AAIEP05521.
[13] *El Paso Times*, April 27, 2012.
[14] *Los Angeles Times*, June 7, 2016.
[15] Langston, Edward L. *The Impact of Prohibition on the Mexican-United States Border: The El Paso-Ciudad Juárez Case*. Unpublished Dissertation (PhD in History) (Lubbock: Texas Tech University.1974.), 4.
[16] There are countless references that support the contention that Joseph P. Kennedy was directly involved in illicit activities during Prohibition that included rum running and operating speakeasies, particularly in New England and Canada. Author Robert K. Hudnall in his book, *No Safe Haven: Homeland Insecurity* (2004) goes further on page 113 where he claims that Kennedy brought alcohol into the United States thru El Paso. The problems with his writings is that he offers no documentation to his comments to make it anything but an anecdotal remark.

[17] Langston.
[18] Ibid, 5.
[19] *El Paso Times*, December 4, 1927.
[20] Carey, 67.
[21].Ettinger, Patrick. *Imaginary Lines: Border Enforcement and the Origins of Undocumented Immigration, 1882-1930.* (Austin: University of Texas Press, 2009.), 153.
[22] White, Owen P. *Them Was the Days: From El Paso to Prohibition* (New York: Minton, Balch & Company, 1925.)
[23] Ibid, 125-126.
[24] Lay, Shawn. (Ed.) *The Invisible Empire in the West: Toward a New Historical Appraisal of the Ku Klux Klan of the 1920s*. (Urbana: The University of Illinois, 2004.), 69.
[25] Ibid.
[26] Sonnichsen, C. L. and M.G. McKinney. *The State National Since 1881: The Pioneer Bank of El Paso.* (El Paso: Texas Western Press, 1971.), 83.
[27] Holden, 107.
[28] Miller, Carol P. "Resisting the Ku Klux Klan in El Paso." *Password* Vol. 54, No. 1(Spring 2009), 19.
[29] Lay (2004), 73.
[30] Middagh, John. *Frontier Newspaper: The El Paso Times.* (El Paso: Texas Western Press, 1958.), 194.
[31] Lay, Shawn. War, Revolution, and the Ku Klux Klan: A Study of Intolerance in a Border City. (El Paso: Texas Western Press, 1983.), 105.
[32] Mendoza, Vanessa, et. al. "Ku Klux Klan Had Short Life in El Paso." *Borderlands/21.* (2002-2003), 6.
[33] Romo, David D. *Ringside Seat to a Revolution: An Underground Cultural History of El Paso and Juárez 1893-1913.* (El Paso: Cinco Puntos Press, 2005.), 148.
[34] Lay (1985), 130.
[35] Ibid, 145.
[36] Ibid, 107.
[37] Sonnichsen (1971), 368.
[38] Chapman, Bob. "Dudley beats K.K.K. by 2,120." *El Paso Times*, February 25, 1923.
[39] Middagh, 213.
[40] Rayner, Richard. *A Bright and Guilty Place: Murder, Corruption, and L.A.'s Scandalous Coming of Age*. (New York: Doubleday, 2009.), 56.
[41] Ibid, 55.

[42] La Botz, Dan. *Edward L. Doheny Petroleum, Power, and Politics in the United States and Mexico.* (New York: Praeger Publishers, 1991.), 10.
[43] Davis, Margaret L. *Dark Side of Fortune: Triumph and Scandal in the Life of Oil Tycoon Edward L. Doheny* (Berkeley: University of California Press, 1998.), 111. Marshall, Norman. "The Forgotten Bagman of Teapot Dome Edward 'Ned' Doheny Jr." *Californians and the Military*. www.militarymuseum.org/.html Accessed 27 June 2016.
[44] Ibid, 99. See also: *The Nation*. Vol. 109, September 13, 1919, 358.
[45] Rasmussen, Cecilia. *L. A. Unconventional: the men and women who did LA their way.* (Los Angeles: The Los Angeles Times Co., 1998.), 66.
[46] Ibid, 79.
[47] Ibid, 81.
[48] "Below the Fold" refers to the bottom half of the front page of a broadsheet newspaper that is not very visible when the paper is folded.
[49] Rayner, 118.
[50] Ibid, 86.
[51] "A Real-Life Film Noir, Except for the Ending. *Los Angeles Times*, January 31, 1999.
[52] Ibid.
[53] Rayner, 183-192.
[54] "Mall is legacy of '20s crime and corruption." *Los Angeles Times*, October 3, 1999.
[55] Ibid.

Chapter Nineteen

Behind the Badge

Given its placement in time; at the end of the era of the Wild West; the Mexican Revolution, Prohibition and the roaring twenties; it is no wonder that the Sheldon Hotel was also the center of law enforcement and immigration control action. There can be little doubt that any law enforcement agency that was stationed in or temporarily assigned to El Paso, Texas during the first three decades of the Twentieth Century had some official activity that involved the Sheldon Hotel. Whether it was protecting heads of state, investigating criminal activity, or spying on the suspicious behaviors of the enormously varied characters that lived at or lingered around the Sheldon Hotel; law agents of every imaginable kind seemed to always be there. The local police, the sheriff, and the Texas Rangers seemed to be omnipresent. There is ample evidence that the Mexican secret service agencies were equally present.

Three specific federal law enforcement agencies and their specific functions are uniquely connected to the Sheldon Hotel. (See figure 123) The Secret Service, the FBI, and the Border Patrol have such a relationship. Information about the United States government's intelligence activities during this time was declassified in the early 1970's and historians have, upon examining those records, stated that in response to the Mexican Revolution of 1910 and the activities that swirled around the Sheldon Hotel, an American intelligence community was established.[1]

The Secret Service

When researching the intelligence activity of the Federal Government, it is common to come upon the use of the term "secret service," in lower case. This is because the term "secret service agent" was used by various governmental agencies, including the Army, the Post Office, the Immigration Service, the

Department of Justice, and the Department of the Interior. As the various secret service agents in residence at the Sheldon co-mingled with the Mexican Secret Service agents, who also were constantly found in and around the Sheldon, their interaction was the first time in United States history that a foreign intelligence service was allowed to operate within American territory as blatantly as during the early phases of the Mexican Revolution.[2] The Mexican Secret Service was present in the Sheldon primarily to keep an eye on the Madero family. The Mexican Secret Service provided the Díaz regime with general intelligence gathering, surveillance, espionage, counterespionage, and propaganda activity.[3]

None of those other federal agencies could compare in the number of agents, magnitude of work, or extensive ramifications with the Department of Treasury's agents, hereafter referred to as the United States Secret Service. Historians have described the Secret Service, which had performed its espionage duties particularly well in the area of counterintelligence, as the "pivotal intelligence agency of its day."[4] Yet, because of political and bureaucratic rivalries, this intelligence gathering function of the Secret Service became sidetracked with a new mission and that void was quickly and capably filled by the growth of the Bureau of Investigation (BOI) and its successor, the FBI.

The use of spies and counterespionage agents has long been part of our military dating back to the days of the Revolutionary War. The use of well-organized private detective agencies to gather intelligence against an enemy was a common tactic practiced by Union General George B. McClellan during the Civil War. McClellan hired Allan Pinkerton and his Chicago based detective agency to develop an intelligence gathering network and to infiltrate the Confederate forces. Pinkerton called his Civil War private action group, the U.S. Secret Service, sometimes referred to as the National Detective Agency. In 1861, while working on a criminal case in Baltimore, Pinkerton learned of a plan to assassinate President-elect Lincoln and was able to convince the President to change his itinerary and thus avoid the plot. "Impressed with Pinkerton's skills at intelligence gathering and intrigued by his reputation as a sleuth, Pinkerton persuaded Lincoln that he could create and run a spy agency, dispatching agents to penetrate the Confederate armies and government, gathering intelligence, and planting disinformation."[5]

Pinkerton's company was assigned to General McClellan's command. President Lincoln was not particularly impressed with General McClellan's successes during the war, but tolerated it by saying, "he would hold McClellan's horse if it would win the war."[6] Shortly thereafter, Lincoln relieved McClellan of his command. McClellan would, with a disastrous effect, run for president against Lincoln in 1864 and later he was elected governor of New Jersey in 1878. General Ulysses S. Grant, following the war said, "McClellan is to me one of the mysteries of the war."[7] Unhappy with the level of success produced by the use of the privatized agents, the President relied increasingly on military operators. The Pinkerton operation soon collapsed.

President Lincoln did not totally rely on McClellan's spy network and he employed his own secret agents to gather information and report it back to the White House to assist the President in the prosecution of the Union cause. A major national issue during the Civil War was the counterfeiting of paper money issued by many different states and municipalities, the sheer presence of "funny money" made Lincoln's war effort even more difficult. Lincoln was able to convince Congress to pass the National Banking Acts of 1863 and 1864 which asserted federal control over the country's banking and established a uniform national currency, which indirectly helped the Federal Government finance the Civil War.

Five days after Confederate General Robert E. Lee surrendered at the Appomattox Court House, Treasury Secretary Hugh McCulloch convinced Lincoln on April 14, 1865 to establish a permanent enforcement and investigative force to put "counterfeiters out of business," and Lincoln drafted such an order and left it on his desk as he left that fateful evening to attend the play, Our American Cousin at Ford's Theater. After months of chaos following the Lincoln assassination, the United States Secret Service was formally established on July 5, 1865 to investigate and combat counterfeiting of United States Currency. Secretary McCulloch appointed William P. Wood, former superintendent of the Old Brick Capitol Prison, as the first chief of the new agency.

The Old Brick Capitol in Washington, D.C., now the site of the U.S. Supreme Court, served as temporary Capitol of the United States from 1815 to 1819. The building was a private school, then a boarding house, and finally a prison during the Civil War. Colonel Lafayette Baker, who ran the War Department's National Detective Service and was known as the Union's Spy Chief joined William Wood in developing the anti-counterfeiting mission of the new agency.[8] The irony of Lincoln's actions can't be missed as the new agency did not add presidential protection to its mission until 1901, thirty-six years after the formation of the agency, following the assassination of two additional Presidents, Garfield (September 10, 1881) and William McKinley (September 14, 1901).

At the time of the creation of the Secret Service, there were only a few federal law enforcement agencies; the U.S. Park Police, U.S. Postal Service, and the U.S. Marshal Service. These agencies lacked major manpower for investigation and enforcement of federal laws, so the Secret Service frequently had to assist these other federal agencies and became involved in crimes ranging from murder, bank robbery, and illegal gambling. The Secret Service became the first domestic intelligence and counterintelligence agency, even investigating the early activities of the Ku Klux Klan in the late 1860s.[9] As other federal law enforcement agencies came on line, the mission of the Secret Service became more defined to deal with financial and currency crimes and Presidential protection that included the vice-president, their families, and eventually presidential candidates and visiting foreign dignitaries. The Sundry Civil Expenses Act of 1907 legalized the support for the protection of the person of the President of the United States.[10] It didn't become a federal crime to murder the president and other federal officers until 1965 following the Kennedy assassination in 1963.

Congress had restricted the functions of the Secret Service to counterfeiting crimes, and the Secret Service Chief, William Hazen, was demoted because he had assigned several agents to guard Presidents Cleveland and McKinley. In 1898 John Wilkie, a former journalist, replaced Hazen and became the chief of the Secret Service.[11] The selection of a newspaperman from the Chicago Times and later the Chicago Tribune at first might appear odd. However, Wilkie's "nose for news," his experience as a police reporter, his telegraph experience, and his executive ability, made him the perfect candidate. Over the years, with the ever changing mission of the agency, including investigation of all types of financial schemes, land fraud, and assisting in controlling arms smuggling. The secret police agents of the Customs Service were reorganized with the Secret Service and retained their separate existence, but were placed under Wilkie's supervision.[12] The Customs agents were eventually relocated to another department.

Wilkie was a frequent visitor to the Sheldon Hotel in his official capacity. Specifically during the McKinley presidential visit in 1901 and the Taft-Diaz meeting in 1909, Wilkie maintained a relatively high profile as he stood guard as the presidential parties moved between the St. Regis Hotel, the Sheldon Hotel, and Chamber of Commerce building during the Taft-Diaz event.[13] By 1910, the Justice Department's Bureau of Investigation and the Treasury Department's Secret Service both posted at least two agents each to El Paso to interact with approximately twenty-five Mexican Secret Service agents operating in and around the Sheldon Hotel as the Mexican Revolution activity began to escalate.[14]

Following the September 11, 2001 terrorist attack and the formation of the Department of Homeland Security, the United States Secret Service was transferred from the Department of the Treasury to the newly formed agency in March of 2003. Today, the United States Secret Service has expanded its investigatory realm beyond counterfeiting and financial crimes to include, identity theft, computer fraud, and computer-based attacks on the nation's financial and telecommunications infrastructure. The Uniform Division of the Secret Service protects the facilities related to the Presidential Protection function of the Secret Service, including the residence of the vice-president and 170 foreign embassies located in Washington, D.C. Until 1930, the division was known as the White House Police.

Neutrality Laws

Since the early nineteenth century, International Law has established the right of a nation to abstain from participation in a war between other states, including internal strife. This meant that a neutral state cannot provide assistance to the belligerents or to their allies, who cooperate and assist them. Those legal positions were modified and later codified in the Hague Conferences V of 1907. Once a nation decides on a position of neutrality, it must take significant steps to prevent its territory from becoming a base for military operations of a belligerent.

During the revolution on the frontier along the United States-Mexican border, American troops were sent to prevent hostilities from crossing the boundary line. This was done primarily to enforce the observance of the neutrality of the United States. El Paso became the loci in the arms and ammunition trading right from the beginning of the Madero movement in 1910. Men, women, and even children, came from Juárez and surrounding areas to purchase arms from the United States and return them freely back to Mexico. As the revolution continued through its various phases and its response to the American arms embargo, arms and ammunition smuggling became a major activity.[15] Mexican merchant firms, many owned by El Pasoans, were in sympathy with the rebels and imported materiel from their state-side subsidiaries and partners. El Paso thus became a base of supplies for the rebel forces, and created a major challenge to American neutrality.[16]

Congress passed the Neutrality Act of April 20, 1818 and subsequently used it as a base template for succeeding neutrality acts and proclamations:

> SEC. 5281. Every citizen of the United States who, within the territory or jurisdiction thereof, accepts and exercises a commission to serve a foreign prince, state, colony, district, or people in war by land or by sea, against any prince, state, colony, district, or people, with whom the United States are at peace, shall be deemed guilty of a high misdemeanor, and shall be fined not more than two thousand dollars, and imprisoned not more than three years. The law is limited in its application to citizens of the United States and does not apply to all persons indiscriminately. A foreigner not owing allegiance to the United States could accept a commission in the service of his own country or any other country without being liable to prosecution.
>
> SEC 5282. Every person who, within the territory or jurisdiction of the United States, enlists or enters himself, or hires or retains another person to enlist or enter himself, or to go beyond the limits or jurisdiction of the United States with intent to be enlisted or entered in the service of any foreign prince, state, colony, district, or people, as a soldier, or as a marine or seaman, on board of any vessel of war, letter of marque, or privateer shall be deemed guilty of a high misdemeanor, and shall be fined not more than one thousand dollars, and imprisoned not more than three years.[17]

Following acts of guerilla warfare of varying success, the rebel forces of Madero were able to dispose of Diaz's dictatorship on May 25, 1911. Less than three months after Madero was elected president in October 1912, a second revolution broke out under the control of Pascual Orozco, Madero's former commander. Juárez again fell into the new rebel's hands and El Paso, once again, became the center of arms and ammunition sales and smuggling. On March 2, 1912 President Taft issued a proclamation against the action of the neutrality violations regarding an arms embargo, but made exceptions on shipments to the Mexican government during Madero's presidential term thereby showing American favoritism toward the Madero government.[18]

It became immediately apparent to Congress that additional action needed to be taken with regards to the emergence of arms problems in El Paso. Accordingly, on March 14, 1912, Congress passed the following joint resolution:

Resolved by the Senate and House of Representatives of the United States of America in Congress assembled, That the joint resolution to prohibit the export of coal or other material used in war from any seaport of the United States, approved April twenty-second, eighteen hundred and ninety-eight, be, and hereby is amended to read as follows:

That whenever the President shall find that in any American country conditions of domestic violence exist which are promoted by the use of arms or munitions of war procured from the United States, and shall make proclamation— thereof, it shall be unlawful to export except under such limitations and exceptions as the President shall prescribe any arms or munitions of war from any place in the United States to such country until otherwise ordered by the President or by Congress.

Sec. 1. That any shipment of material herby declared unlawful after such a proclamation shall be punishable by fine not exceeding ten thousand dollars, or imprisonment not exceeding two years or both.[19]

The joint resolution thus empowered the President of the United States to recognize the existence of conditions under which the act makes it unlawful to export any arms or munitions of war to the country designated. It is a distinct advance over the Joint Resolution of 1898, that was previously established just prior to the Spanish-American War, but "because it [the 1912 Resolution] imposes a specific penalty upon offenders; it thus takes its place as a permanent amendment to the Neutrality Act of 1818. In pursuance of the power conferred upon him, President Taft issued, on the same day, a proclamation announcing the existence in Mexico of the conditions described in the joint resolution of Congress, and the consequent applicability of the terms of the resolution." [20]

Under this resolution arms and munitions were defined by the Department of Justice as "articles primarily and ordinarily used for military purposes in time of war such as weapons of every species used for the destruction of life, and projectiles, cartridges, ammunition of all sorts and other supplies used or useful in connection therewith, including parts used for the repair or manufacture of such arms, and raw materials employed in the manufacture of such ammunition, also dynamite, nitroglycerin or other explosive substances."

The flourishing sales and bartering of arms, ammunition, and battle supplies by El Paso firms as: Krahauer, Zork and Moye; Ketelsen & Degetau Hardware; and Shelton-Payne Arms Company, became the impetus to the American government flooding the El Paso community with federal agents in search of neutrality law violations. The laws clearly stated that any American citizen, who became involved in the violation of the United States' position of neutrality regarding the internal insurrection against the sitting and officially recognized Mexican government, would be subject to arrest, fine, and or imprisonment. Since the Sheldon Hotel was the home of the revolution's planning and execution; and the scene of the greatest activity of the soldiers of fortune, most of whom were American citizens and thus subject to arrest under the neutrality laws, the Sheldon Hotel became the primary focus of the federal agents.

Since violations of neutrality laws were now a federal criminal offense, it became the jurisdiction of the Justice Department to enforce such laws. The Justice Department had previously established, on July 26, 1908, a Special Agent Force to become its investigative squad. Despite being referred to as secret service, "black cabinets," spies, or federal detectives, the squad was enhanced by ten Secret Service agents from the Treasury Department and together with twenty-five other Justice Department investigators formed the backbone of the staff that became responsible for, among other things, the enforcement of neutrality laws. On March 16, 1909 the unit became known as the Bureau of Investigation (BOI) until it was formally renamed the Federal Bureau of Investigation (FBI) on July 1, 1935.[21]

The BOI had significant success in enforcing Neutrality Act cases beginning with the actions surrounding revolutionary activities in and around the Sheldon Hotel beginning in late 1910. In 1916 alone, "the Bureau had gathered evidence leading to more than 200 prosecutions for neutrality and antitrust violations. Neutrality Act provisions were even used with some success against saboteurs, but the attorney general said that additional legislation was needed to address the problem of Germany's domestic spying." [22] When the BOI hired 100 new agents in 1915 to address the neutrality issues, the Treasury Department saw that increase as a threat to their Secret Service function, and the seeds of inter-agency hostility, competition, and lack of cooperation were sown until changes were brought about in the post-911 era. The federal efforts to enforce Neutrality Law violations were occasionally assisted by the Texas Rangers, often under the command of Captain John Hughes, a frequent guest and high-profile visitor at the Sheldon Hotel. In their book, The Texas Rangers and the Mexican Revolution Harris and Sadler state:

> Enforcement of the neutrality laws was anything but a cut-and-dried affair. The statutes provided an effective way to settle old scores...Another aspect of neutrality law enforcement was that on occasion someone arrested as a member of a revolutionary group

> turned out to be an undercover agent of the Mexican government. But in a larger sense, the Mexican Revolution itself provided a vast umbrella for the settling of political and personal accounts, in Texas as well as in Mexico. ...'it is not so much the desire to enforce the laws, as it is trying to get even with some fellow on this side, who (sic) is antagonistic or unfriendly.'[23]

The FBI

Personal jealousy, regional rivalries, and battles over "turf" were the common themes of the ever changing phases of the Mexican Revolution, and they all seemed to center around El Paso, Texas. The task of keeping a close eye on these anti-government insurgents, the Mexican Government placed many of their secret agents in El Paso not only gather intelligence on the insurgents, but also on the American Government's position and intentions on dealing with the border emergency. The Mexican Secret Service was not an independent intelligence agency of the Mexico City regimes until after 1916, but rather was a function of the various Mexican Consulates scattered throughout the country.[24] Particularly obvious was El Paso Consul's efforts at recruiting and handling their own agents, informants, operatives, and the hiring of international private detectives to identify and "resolve" the revolutionaries and their intentions. These Mexican secret service agents were especially adept at code breaking, intercepting postal communications, and suborning public officials and journalists.

It was relatively easy for these Mexican Secret Service agents to gather information on the American military, as one of the local newspapers, the El Paso Times reported daily on the Army's activity at Fort Bliss. Eventually, two Mexican "spies" were arrested by El Paso city police at the front door of the Sheldon Hotel, taking notes on the military units that were passing through the plaza on parade.[25] In an effort to keep closer tabs on the Mexican intelligence operation, the Department of Justice's Bureau of Investigation began sending their agents to El Paso and the Sheldon Hotel. This action resulted in not only monitoring the Mexican agents, but in developing a cooperative and sharing relationship that at first assisted both the American Government's action on the neutrality law issues but also in keeping a close watch on the full intent of the Mexican agents' activity.

The Bureau of Investigation objective was severely hampered by the fact that its first agents in the area did not speak Spanish, and were "largely ineffective in their attempts to penetrate exile groups, stem the flow of smuggled arms and ammunition, or check the barrage of inflammatory propaganda that exacerbated anti-Mexican passions."[26] This soon changed when the Bureau required that its agents in El Paso had to be fluent in Spanish and English and have a working knowledge of Mexican and United States laws.[27] With this new level of cooperation, the Mexican Secret Service "was to investigate and expose anyone who was suspected of violating the laws of the United States in an attempt to subvert the social and political institutions of Mexico. Because Mexican agents lacked authority to arrest suspects, their principal task was to secure and present evidence to United States law enforcement officials, who would apprehend and punish offenders."[28]

The Mexican Secret Service became the eyes and ears of the Bureau of Investigation and the U.S. Secret Service.[29] This level of cooperation began to weaken as the Diaz regime crumbled and the American administration showed some support for the rebels. It was here, in and around the Sheldon Hotel and its bars and lobby that the Bureau of Investigation began to focus its actions on American citizens who were violating the federal laws of the United States. Many of the escapades involved Mexican spies, including, Felix Summerfeld and Mexican Consul, Enrique Llorente—and the dishonored Bureau of Investigation El Paso's resident agent, Louis E. Ross. Their arms smuggling activities in the Sheldon Hotel and the local activities of the BOI are detailed in the Harris and Sadler book, The Secret War in El Paso: Mexican Revolutionary Intrigue, 1906-1920 and is worthy of review. The authors introduced their book with:

> El Paso was the base of operations for constant intrigue involving U.S. and Mexican authorities, Mexican revolutionists, and others. The population of El Paso was only sporadically aware of this struggle, usually when some incident got into the newspapers. But in this secret war it was often difficult for the players to keep secrets secret from each other. Heretofore no work has focused on this struggle. El Paso may be visualized as a kaleidoscope in which constantly changing combinations and permutations occurred among a cast of characters that included many larger-than-life figures. The city was inundated with refugees and was a magnet attracting revolutionists, adventurers, smugglers, gunrunners, counterfeiters, propagandists, secret agents, double agents, criminals, and confidence men of every stripe, but as one Bureaus agent put it, "Valuable information is sometimes obtained

> from very shady sources. The revolution also became big business, and some of the city's most respectable citizens were quite profitably involved. And it was the Mexican Revolution that produced a huge military buildup in El Paso and transformed it permanently into the "army town" that it is today [30]

It is no wonder that the Department of Justice sent special agents from their fledgling law enforcement division, the Bureau of Investigation, to El Paso to stretch their wings and flex their muscles. Under political pressure from President Roosevelt to deal with the growing crime problems, Congressional hearings were held in 1908 that resulted in the Justice Department borrowing Secret Service agents from the Treasury Department to carry out its investigative activities. The result of which discovered some questionable and illegal activities of members of Congress.[31] As a result, Congress attached to the appropriations bill for the Treasury Department on May 27, 1908 a rider, in retaliation, that prohibited the Treasury Department from loaning its agents to the Justice Department and this in turn significantly diminished the Justice Department's Bureau of Investigation from doing its investigating job. On July 26, 1908, under orders from the President, Attorney General Charles Bonaparte created a squad of "spies and federal detectives" composed of ten Secret Service agents transferred from the Treasury Department, thirteen Justice investigators who were employed on peonage cases and twelve examiners provided by statute, to become the new federal enforcement unit.

On May 16, 1909, the secret unit was named the Bureau of Investigation and would continue under that title until 1935, when the agency was renamed the Federal Bureau of Investigation. The Justice Department had previously used private detectives, such as Pinkerton Agents, but that had become increasingly unpopular and was discontinued after the passage of a statue in 1893 (Pinkerton Act 1893) that prohibited the government from employing Pinkerton or any other private detectives.[32] The Bureau became the cutting edge of neutrality enforcement and surveillance of persons of interest as well as investigating white collar crimes that involved national banking, bankruptcy, naturalization, antitrust, and land fraud laws.

With the passage of the Mann Act, (White Slave Traffic Act) in 1910, an early attempt to halt interstate prostitution and human trafficking, and subsequent passage of both the Espionage Act of 1917 and the Sedition Act of 1918 (Repealed December 13, 1920.), the Bureau thus began investigating "enemy aliens" and individuals who opposed military conscription, sowed dissension within the armed forces, or willfully aided foreign adversaries. The range of responsibilities for the Bureau was greatly expanded. Private contractors with special qualifications were "handled" by the Bureau such as the previously discussed Col. Kosterlitzky in 1922. By 1915, the Bureau had grown from its original 34 agents to over 360 special agents and support staff. (The FBI today has more than 35,000 agents and support staff.) The Bureau opened a number of field offices around the country to facilitate their investigations in smuggling and neutrality violations. Southwest Texas became the focus of the Bureau's efforts at investigating neutrality law issues. A field office was opened in El Paso and played, "a central role in ensuring threatened revolutionary schemes against foreign governments would not be supported from American soil."[33]

The Sheldon Hotel was the center of spy activity involving the Bureau and its effort to curtail arms smuggling into Mexico in violation of several arms embargoes.[34] The Bureau often resorted to tactics beyond surveillance, sometimes carrying out "black bag" operations to gather evidence as well as having access to Western Union and Post Office records. During the investigation of arms smuggling, the El Paso Bureau office was under the control of resident agent, Louis E. Ross who maintained close affiliation with the Mexican Consul Llorente. In October, 1912, it was discovered that Agent Ross, another Bureau agent, and one of Llorente's associates, Abraham Molina, were running a side business out of the Sheldon Hotel. They were selling the ammunition that they had seized as evidence in smuggling investigations back to the Mexican revolutionaries. Molina was described as a "man of little education, very shrewd…having little conscience. He has no political allegiance nor does he care about politics, having no other aim than that of serving whomever pays him best, whether as a smuggler, a recruiter, or as secret agent."[35] After Ross was fired from the Bureau, he reappeared as a Mexican Secret Agent working for Llorente.

The Bureau's national security responsibility increased significantly as the war fever in Europe grew. Because of El Paso's geographic location, the U.S.-Mexican border was becoming a major launching point for Germany's intelligence operations against the United States. Agents of the Bureau of Investigation usually didn't carry firearms and did not have the power of arrest until 1934 and that only increased the danger of their efforts during this time frame in the border region. The El Paso Bureau office was closed in 1932 as a cost cutting effort resulting from the economic downturn cause by the Great

Depression. This was also the time where the Bureau's profile rose as a response to its involvement in dealing with violent criminals of the like of John Dillinger and the El Paso area became a major focus of many of those investigations. The El Paso office was reopened in February 1934 and today remains one of the Federal Bureau of Investigation's major investigative centers.

The U.S. Border Patrol

One of the major differences between the U.S. Secret Service, the Bureau of Investigation, and the U.S. Border Patrol is that the genesis of the Border Patrol came directly out of El Paso, while the other two federal agencies were spawned in Washington, D.C. and realigned their focus and mission once they arrived in El Paso. In response to the Chinese Exclusion Act, Congress established the Bureau of Immigration in 1885 and in 1903 transferred its operation to the Department of Commerce and Labor and established strategically placed Immigration Stations along the border. The U.S. Immigration service organized in 1904 was a small band of lawmen with varying experiences, known as the Mounted Watchmen, to patrol the border area between the immigration stations to prevent the illegal border crossing of Chinese immigrants. Based out of El Paso, the Watchmen's success was tied directly to the ebb and flow of available resources and therefore was extremely irregular in both its actions and success.

These mounted inspectors underwent routine name changes that included Mounted Guards and Chinese Immigration Agents. Because of El Paso's unique location at the center of the Chinese smuggling operation, the majority of the Mounted Guards were a familiar site around El Paso in general and the Sheldon Hotel specifically. The early group of inspectors was led by Jeff D. Milton, a former Texas Ranger, railroad agent, U.S. Marshal, Deputy Sheriff, and Chief of Police of El Paso. Milton also was a Customs Mounted Inspector in the late 1880s who spent practically every day on horseback with his rifle and pistol attempting to keep out thieves, drug smugglers, and illegal immigrants; and doing it in the most inhospitable of regions.[36] Milton had served as El Paso police chief in 1904 and attempted to clean up the wildness of early El Paso. He was fired in 1906 when the gambling interests in El Paso re-took the city government from the "reformers."

Milton was appointed a Mounted Chinese Inspector by President Theodore Roosevelt and has been referred to as the "first Immigration Border

Patrolman." His reputation as an honest and successful lawman far outreaches his experience with the Immigration Service during the heyday of taming the Wild West when El Paso was a gambler's paradise, filled with booze, bunco, and bordellos. There he captured some of the most notorious outlaws of the turn of the century.[37] Even though Milton had lost the use of one arm in a shooting while he was working as a railroad agent, he was frequently called the "one-man Border Patrol."

As a Border Patrol agent trying to prevent the smuggling of Chinese immigrants, he would often be side-tracked into a variety of dangerous situations. Milton once attempted to catch three train robbers by himself and his fellow patrolmen didn't hear from him after a long time had elapsed and they feared that he had been killed. When his friends had given up all hope of his safe return, they received a telegram from him, "HQ: Send two coffins and a doctor."[38] He remained an active agent until the age of 70. When he expressed his intention to retire, the Border Patrol administrators in Washington asked him to remain an additional two years. He finally retired in 1932 and died at his home in Tombstone, Arizona in 1947 at the age of 86.

In March 1915, Congress authorized the establishment of a separate group of Mounted Guards or Inspectors to be based in El Paso, but with significantly more reliable resource funding than the previous attempt. With the passage of the Eighteenth Amendment and the limitations placed on immigration, border enforcement became a major political issue. With the onset of Prohibition, our borders became significant routes for smugglers to bring illegal alcoholic products into the country and as a response to this, Congress officially established the U.S. Border Patrol.[39]

Regarding the effect of Prohibition on El Paso, Sonnichsen wrote:

> Some of the bad effects of Prohibition were unknown in El Paso, largely as a result of the facility with which liquor could cross the border. Since bonafide whiskey and gin could be obtained easily and more or less cheaply, the poisonous concoctions evolved in cellars and bathrooms throughout the rest of the nation, were almost unknown in El Paso. As result the incidence of blindness, paralysis, and death from drinking weird potions was very low indeed. Juárez was always a thorn in the flesh to the reformers—a target for sermons and editorials and public speeches. In their long and futile campaign to make us good by legislation, these men were constantly looking for ways to separate the imbiber from his bottle. One obvious method was to keep him from

> crossing the river, especially at night. In 1926 a long-drawn-out campaign was initiated to close the bridge at six o'clock. It never came close to succeeding, but it was revived during prohibition.[40]

A young sickly nineteen-year-old from Sharon, Wisconsin, Clifford Alan Perkins arrived in El Paso in 1908 to find the cure for his suspected tuberculosis. The dry climate improved his health, and he needed a job and was having a rough time finding one in El Paso. He was staying at the Sheldon Hotel,[41] when someone suggested that he apply for a job at the Post Office that was across the street from the hotel in the Federal Building. Shortly after applying, he got a desk job in the registered mail department. He then moved to a rooming house at 709 Magoffin Ave. where he lived until he married and had a family.[42]

Frustrated by the monotony of the job, he complained to one of his customers who suggested that he apply for a position at the Immigration Office and on January 4, 1911 he was appointed a Mounted Chinese Inspector.[43] The El Paso District office of the Immigration Service was contacted by Congressmen Claude Hudspeth, who intended to introduce an amendment to an appropriation bill that would establish the Border Patrol. Perkins was assigned the duty to assist Congressmen Hudspeth in developing the organizational plan of action, the uniforms, and all the details that would encompass the creation of the new law enforcement agency.[44]

On May 28, 1924, Congress passed the Labor Appropriation Act of 1924 which officially established the U.S. Border Patrol to maintain security of the border between the official immigration stations, eventually expanding its reach to the coast. The uniformed agency started in El Paso with funding of one-million dollars and 450 officers.[45] The El Paso Patrol District began its operation on July 1, 1924 with Perkins as its chief and in December 1934 graduated its first class of Border Patrol Agents from the new Border Patrol Academy in El Paso. On March 1, 2003 the U.S. Border Patrol became part of the U.S. Customs and Border Protection, a component of the Department of Homeland Security.[46]

Today, the U.S. Border Patrol is the largest uniformed federal law enforcement agency. It functions to detect and prevent illegal aliens, terrorists, and terrorists weapons from entering the United States, and to prevent illegal trafficking of people and contraband. U.S. Customs and Border Protection maintain unlimited power of search and seizures through the border search exception which is a doctrine of the United States criminal law and does not violate the Fourth Amendment as long as the search is conducted at the border. It is interesting to note, that as long as the action of the search is not visually broken in surveillance, the border can be extended beyond the actual U.S. borderline, even from coast to coast.[47]

Historian Patrick Ettinger, in addressing the current social and political border issue, wrote in his 2009 book, Imaginary Lines:

> The vision of the border as, at best, a deterrent to illicit entry (rather than a guarantee against it) seemed a bitter pill for many ardent restrictionists to swallow in 1920. But border officials understood that promises beyond that were impossible to keep and foolish to make. At mid-decade, the Secretary of Labor discouraged notions that any Immigration Service patrol could close the border to the determined immigrant: "If we had the Army on the Canadian border and on the Mexican border, we couldn't stop them; if we had the Navy on the water-front we couldn't stop them...Not even a Chinese wall, nine thousand miles in length and built over rivers and deserts and mountains and along the seashores, would seem to permit a permanent solution.... An unrealistic border has created unrealistic expectations for an unrealistic and ever more expensive program of border enforcement.[48]

El Paso continues to be the nexus of border security and the operation of the U.S. Border Patrol, as the migration of illegal aliens continues to be a major social, cultural, and political "hot button" issue. To say that the Sheldon Hotel played a direct role in the establishment and transformation of the Border Patrol would be far beyond literary license, but the role that El Paso played cannot be dismissed, and if it went on in El Paso from 1900 to 1929, the Sheldon Hotel was in the middle of it all.

Notes and References

---

[1] Hurst, James W. *Pancho Villa and Blackjack Pershing: The Punitive Expedition in Mexico.* (Westport, CT: Praeger, 2008.), 55.

[2] Harris, Charles L., and Louis Sadler. *The Border and the Revolution: Clandestine Activities of the Mexican Revolution 1910-1920.* (Silver City, NM: High-Lonesome Books, 1988.), 56.

[3] Smith, Michael M. "The Mexican Secret Service in the United States." *The Americas:*

Quarterly Review of Inter-American Cultural History. (Academy of American Franciscan History). Vol. 59, No.1 (July 2002), 65-85.

[4] Melanson, Philip H. *The Secret Service: The Hidden History of an Enigmatic Agency.* (New York: Carroll & Graf, 2005.), 28.

[5] Ibid, 4.

[6] Packard, Jerrold. *The Lincolns in the White House: Four Years that Shattered a Family.* (New York: St. Martin's Press, 2013.), 110.

[7] Rafuse, Ethan S. *McClellan's War: The Failure of Moderation in the Struggle for the Union.* (Bloomington: Indiana University Press, 2011.), 384.

[8] Lafayette Baker's notorious career is worthy of further pursuit by serious historians, but is beyond the scope of this book's mission. As the Army's chief spymaster, he carried a silver badge with the mantra "Death to Traitors." He had developed a reputation for arresting and punishing suspects without warrant, or the semblance of law or justice. He was the War Department intelligence chief during the American Civil War, a spy, and a colonel in the cavalry. He was put in charge of the investigation of the assassination of Abraham Lincoln, was at the capture and death of John Wilkes Booth, and brought away the items in Booth's pockets...including Booth's diary. See his book, the *Secret Service in the Civil War* and Melanson's *The Secret Service: The Hidden History of an Enigmatic Agency.*

[9] "United States Secret Service Secret History. U.S. Department of Homeland Security, U.S. Secret Service. Accessed 14 May 2014.

[10] Melanson, 32.

[11] Ibid, 22.

[12] *New York Times*, November 19, 1910.

[13] Crawford, Charlotte. "The Border Meeting of Presidents Taft and Díaz." *Password* (1958) Vol. 3, 88.

[14] Carman, Michael D. *United States Customs and the Madero Revolution*. Southwestern Studies Monograph No. 48. (El Paso: Texas Western Press, 1976.), 59.

[15] Harris, Charles, and Louis R. Sadler. *The Texas Rangers and the Mexican Revolution: 1910-1920*. (Albuquerque: University of New Mexico Press, 2004.), 103.

[16] Fenwick, Charles G. *The Neutrality Laws of the United States*. (Washington: The Endowment, 1913.), 57-59.

[17] Ibid.

[18] Calvert, Peter. *The Mexican Revolution 1910-1914: Diplomacy of the Anglo-American Conflict.* (New York: Cambridge University Press, 1968.), 121-122.

[19] Fenwick, 57-59.

[20] Ibid.

[21] Holden, Henry M. *FBI 100 Years: An Unofficial History*. (Minneapolis: Zenith Press, 2008.), 12-13.
[22] Ibid, 19.
[23] Harris and Sadler (2009.), 83.
[24] Smith, Michael M. "The Mexican Secret Service in the United States." *The Americas: Quarterly Review of Inter-American Cultural History.* (Academy of American Franciscan History). Vol. 59, No.1 (July 2002), 66.
[25] Harris and Sadler (2009), 265.
[26] Smith, M. (2002), 75.
[27] Ibid, 73.
[28] Ibid.
[29] Harris and Sadler (2009), 83.
[30] Ibid, x.
[31] In 1904 Secret Service agents on loan to the Justice Department obtained evidence that led to the conviction of land fraudsters that included U.S. Senator John H. Mitchell. See Jeffreys-Jones' book *The FBI: A History* (2007), 39.
[32] Ibid.
[33] "The Nation Calls, 1908-1923." *A Centennial History, 1908-2008*. (Washington, D.C.: The Federal Bureau of Investigation) Accessed 12 June 2014.
[34] Harris and Sadler (2009), 35.
[35] Ibid, 59.
[36] www.thevillagesteaparty.org/border-patrol-history.html accessed 25 January 2016.
[37] See Haley, J. Evetts. *Jeff Milton: A Good Man with a Gun.* (Norman: University of Oklahoma, 1948.)
[38] Rak, Mary Kidder. *Border Patrol* (New York: Houghton-Mifflin, 1938.), 6-7.
[39] http://immigrationtounitedstates.org/borders/ Accessed 26 January 2016
[40] Sonnichsen C.L., and M.G. McKinney. "El Paso—from War to Depression." *The Southwest Historical Quarterly*. Vol. 74, No. 3. (January 1971), 365.
[41] Clifford Alan Perkins who became a high profile Immigration agent in El Paso, resided at the Sheldon Hotel in 1909 before he established his own residence in town with his wife and two children. Perkins' residency in the Sheldon was confirmed by C.M. Hendricks, MD., the tubercular specialist at the Baldwin Sanatorium in El Paso. Perkins was among a group of historically well-known patients and close friends of Dr. Hendricks that included General John Pershing, General George Patton, Pat Garrett, Senator Albert Fall Jeff Milton and Pancho Villa. Perkins died on December 21, 1977 in Chula Vista, California at the age of 88. Dr. Hendricks was interviewed by the author in December

1952. Follow up conversations regarding Dr. Hendricks' circle of acquaintances was conducted with Mrs. Hendricks in 1960.

[42] *El Paso City Directory, 1910*, 375.

[43] Hernández, Kelly Lytle. *Migra!: A History of the U.S. Border Patrol* (Berkeley: University of California Press, 2010.), 36.

[44] Perkins Clifford Alan, and C. L. Sonnichsen *Border Patrol: With the U.S. Immigration Service on the Mexican Boundary 1910-1954.* (El Paso: Texas Western Press, 1978.), 90.

[45] *Handbook of Texas Online*, Leon C. Metz, "United States Border Patrol" Accessed 13 June 2016.

[46] Cbp.gov/border-security. accessed 28 May 2016

[47] U.S. v Ramsey 431 US 606. (1977)

[48].Ettinger, Patrick. *Imaginary Lines: Border Enforcement and the Origins of Undocumented Immigration, 1882-1930.* (Austin: University of Texas Press, 2009.), 157; 176.

Chapter Twenty

Flames and Ashes

As the Sheldon entered the third decade of the 20th Century, she appeared a bit diminished from her halcyon days as the most glorious hotel in the southwest. With the arrival of the Paso del Norte Hotel, a grand edifice of marble, teak, and Tiffany glass across the plaza in 1912, the Sheldon had to accept her second place position among El Paso's hostelry. Gone were the days when, as an office building, the Sheldon was home to all the local doctors, dentists, and lawyers. Her occupancy remained high, as tenants turned their offices and rooms into housekeeping quarters, with cook stove pipes stuck out of the windows and gossip spread throughout El Paso that young women of ill repute were occupying some of the rooms. She fell into disrepute until, the building's owner, Lucius M. Sheldon, stepped up and remodeled, adding a fifth floor, and reopened the building as a first-class, opulent for its day, "the best hotel in the southwest," at the dawning of the new century.[1]

There were many wealthy and highly successful businessmen who remained loyal to the Sheldon as her luster began to fade. It wasn't unusual for visiting ranchers and cattlemen to have their wives and children nestled in either the Paso del Norte or some other local hotel, while they themselves would register at the Sheldon as they would refuse to give up the hostelry that had been their home away from home for so many decades. It continued to be a rancher's, businessman's, and newspaperman's harborage and refuge.[2]

Bell boy, Jesus Loya, on his way back to the lobby noticed smoke coming from the fifth floor. It was 12:00 p.m. hour on April 9, 1929, the hotel was packed, every guest room occupied. Jesus hurried to the office to report the incident to P.C. Steel, the hotel's manager and proprietor. As the Sheldon burns Steel immediately turned in a general alarm to the El Paso City Fire Department. The Sheldon building and land were owned by local businessman Albert

Mathias, but the hotel's operation was under the control of Steel. The fire department was on scene within three minutes. Steel, the bell boys, and other hotel employees and city police officers rushed from room to room, helping the guests evacuate the building. Most left all their personal belongings as the fled to the streets. The building was cleared in about 15 minutes.

It was first reported that the fire started in room 323 on the fourth floor on the southwest wing of the building and may have been the result of a burning cigarette. Within seven minutes of noticing the presence of smoke, the roof and fourth and fifth floor were a solid mass of flames. The winds sent smoldering embers onto adjacent buildings. The hotel's telephone operator, Mrs. Wood, remained at her board as long as she could, to call rooms and warn guests of the fire. Jesus and Ramon Loya and several other employees remained in the building to turn off the oil, gas, and electricity and they ran for their lives as they fled the roaring fire.

The exact cause and site of the start of the fire remained somewhat confusing. Besides the rumor that it started from a cigarette on the fourth floor, it was also reported that the fire was ignited by a hotel maid who had left a candle burning in a linen closet, but the most plausible explanation was expressed by fire officials who indicated that the fire started between the ceiling and the roof as a result of defective wiring and that the fire had been most likely smoldering for some time before it burst through windows of the wooden fifth floor.

Thousands of spectators gathered in both plazas to watch the fire by 2:30 p.m. The fire tore through the fourth and fifth floor, working its way down to the third floor. Hook and ladder companies poured steady streams of water from the roof, but the firemen soon had to abandon their positions on the fifth and fourth floor, as the roof began to collapse. Finally, the third floor had to be abandoned as well. The firemen were left with fighting the fire from the outside through the windows of the burning hotel. Five firemen were reported to have been overcome by the smoke, one was rushed to the hospital, and another was sent home, the remaining three returned after a brief respite to fight the inferno. Many of the hotel guests appeared in various states of dress and were attempting to get their personal belongings to safety. With the building engulfed, firemen fighting the blaze, and guests rushing to the streets; local thieves took advantage of the ongoing confusion to steal several pieces of baggage and personal effects from the lobby of the burning building.

The occupants and businesses on the ground floor suffered major smoke and water damage. Those whose businesses were in various states of ruin were:

Joel Friedkin Tailor, Elite Millinery shop; Sheldon Jewelry, Texas and Southwest Cattle Raiser's Association, the Bluebonnet café, several real estate offices, and the barber and beauty shops.

Figure 99. April 9, 1929, the Sheldon Hotel burns.
(El Paso Public Library, Aultman Collection)

Sheldon Hotel fire, April 9, 1929.

Figure 100. Close-up of fire and damage to the Sheldon Hotel upper floors.
(El Paso Fire Department)

The Renfro-Cordell Drug store, the successor to former Mayor Kelly's drug company, suffered the heaviest loss of any of the stores in the building.[3]

The tailor shop of Joel Friedkin had just opened several days before the fire after being completely remodeled with new fixtures and stain glass. Joseph Friedkin, Joel's son, reported years later, that he was trying to be helpful to his father in getting as much merchandise and fixtures out of the shop on the day of the fire, only to find that he had saved so much that his father was unable to recover from an insurance claim.[4] After the loss of the shop in the Sheldon fire, Joel Friedkin moved to Hollywood and became an actor with more than a 100 film credits including *It's a Wonderful Life* with Jimmy Stewart and Bedtime for Bonzo with Ronald Reagan.[5]

The El Paso fire chief, John T. Sullivan, identified a significant piece of irony regarding the Sheldon Hotel fire on Tuesday April 9, 1929. The day of the fire was also local Election Day and the voters overwhelmingly approved a bond issue containing seventeen specific provisions, with the provision for new fire stations and firefighting apparatus receiving the highest voter approval. What role the Sheldon fire had in affecting the vote was never determined.[6] In the mid-1950s another hotel took the name Sheldon Hotel, located in the Shamaley Building at 310-318 S. El Paso Street. This other Sheldon also suffered a disastrous fire in November 1954. This hotel had absolutely no relationship to the iconic Sheldon Hotel at Block 5 Lot 28.[7]

The determination of the financial loss as a result of the fire fluctuated, including the structure, its furnishings and the losses suffered by the tenants, but was estimated to be about $250,000. However, Ed Krohn, owner Mathias' son-in-law and business manager stated that the loss was nearer to 1.5 million dollars. Krohn had indicated that the Mathias Company had turned down an offer for purchase of 1.5 million dollars from a Dallas firm prior to the fire. City fire officials were unable to accurately identify a dollar amount but did state that not a single store in the building escaped major damage and that the structure was a total loss and remained a shell of its former self. Following the fire, rumors began to flow that Mathias was planning on selling his property. He immediately responded by saying: "Reports that I have been planning on selling my property are absurd. As for plans to erect a new office building, no such a thing has been discussed, and inasmuch as I am the owner of the property, I am the only one who can make such plans."[8] Mathias purchased the property in 1920 for $500,000 from a holding company that was controlled by Joe Goodell and banker Sam Young along with a Dallas hotel man by the name of Conrad Hilton.[9]

Less than two weeks after the fire, the city council told Mathias that his burned-out property was a menace to public safety and needed to be torn down immediately, as a high wind might cause bricks and other debris to fall. Mathias had applied for a building permit immediately after the fire to rebuild the Sheldon to look as it did before the fire. After consulting with the city building inspector, the city council denied the permit. And on May 1, 1929 the city council ordered the building demolished. Mathias demanded that the mayor appoint a board of appeal and threatened to go to court over the issue.[10]

On June 25, the El Paso Herald had a front-page cartoon labeled "El Paso's structural beauty" the sky scrapers forming the background to the burned and broken Sheldon Hotel. Mayor E. Thomason was shown looking at the Sheldon's burned out structure in the cartoon and saying, "It's got to be torn down." Aldermen Robertson, Poe, Allen, and Sherman were chanting in chorus, "It's got to be torn down." Mr. Mathias and his son-in-law Ed. Krohn; walking away from the officials, saying I have nothing to say." On July 11, the council ordered the Sheldon torn down.

Figure 101. From *The El Paso Herald* June 25, 1929.

On August 16, when the city council let the contract to the R.E. McKee Company for the demolition of the Sheldon Hotel remains, the council received a letter from Mathias:

> Referring to any action which you have taken or may take concerning the condemnation or wrecking of Sheldon Hotel building, please be advised that all such action is without authority from me, without my consent, is protested by me and therefore at your own risk. If it is your desire to communicate with me further concerning said matter, please make such communication in writing directed to E.H. Krohn or Jones, Goldstein, Hardie, and Grambling, my attorneys.[11]

The R.E. McKee construction firm agreed to demolish the building and pay the city $350 and the company would keep the salvage.[12] Sometime during the next several weeks, out of the ashes of the old Sheldon, negotiations between Mathias and the city improved. In addition, a Dallas hotel man had expressed interest in the old Sheldon site. Conrad Hilton entered El Paso with the thought of building his first ground-up high-rise hotel. Hilton wrote:

> El Paso is the gateway to Mexico. It has all the color of the rugged Old West plus the romantic flavor engraved on it by the Spanish dons. It was smaller than Dallas but it was a big Texas city even then, with a tradition and traffic all its own. In the middle of town, facing on the historic Pioneer Plaza, was a piece of ground where an old hotel had burned down. I wanted to build a new one there, something special, with buildings and décor embracing the best of the town's Spanish and western legacy.[13]

In his book, Be My Guest, Hilton gives the impression that he stumbled on the suddenly available property and wanted to take advantage of its potential, never mentioning the Sheldon Hotel or Albert Mathias by name. The truth of the matter is that Hilton was very much aware of both. During the period of ownership of the Sheldon under Joe Goodell and prior to its sale to Mathias, Hilton was the vice-president of the Sheldon Operating Company.[14]

This becomes a bit of a red flag regarding when he actually became interested in the prime Sheldon site and what may have been behind the motivation of the mayor and city council to recite "It's got to be torn down." and their denial of Mathias' request for a building permit.

WALDORF HOTEL
DALLAS, TEXAS

TERMINAL HOTEL
FORT WORTH, TEXAS

MOBLEY HOTEL
CISCO, TEXAS

Sunday Nov 24

Hotel Sheldon
IN THE HEART OF EL PASO

J. E. GOODELL,
PRESIDENT

C. N. HILTON,
VICE PRESIDENT

EL PASO, TEXAS

Figure 102. Letterhead of the Sheldon during the period of ownership by Goodell and Hilton prior to the fire in 1929. (Courtesy: Albert Fall Papers, New Mexico State University.)

In the negotiations with the city, Mathias agreed to retain ownership of the land and deed-away some of the frontage of the property to the city whereby Sheldon[15], Mills, and Oregon streets would be widened. In exchange, the city would give up about a fourth of Pioneer Plaza to add to the Sheldon site and thus increase its attractiveness as a future hotel site. This quadrilateral strip of the plaza would add more than 1300 square feet of ground more than what Mathias gave to the city.[16] The city did establish stipulations to the trade transaction, any new hotel on the site must be pretentious, as planned, no three or four story building will be acceptable, Mathias shall bear all expense for paving the additional street surface resulting from the change, and he shall pay damages to water mains that may be disturbed by the alterations.[17]

In August of 1929, Mathias was meeting with Robert McKee regarding the demolition of the Sheldon site at the summer resort at Cloudcroft, New Mexico, McKee told Mathias that Conrad Hilton was interested in a long-term lease of the Sheldon property for the purpose of building a 17 or 19 story high-rise hotel. Mathias was unaware that Hilton had retained McKee as the potential contractor of a Trost and Trost designed building. Additional meetings were held and a final agreement on a ninety-nine-year lease was reached. In addition, agreement was reached for Mathias to mortgage the title of the property for $600,000 to assist in the financing of the 1.7 million dollar building budget. Mathias would receive a lien on the building and its contents as security for the arrangements with The Pacific Mutual Life Insurance Company of California.

Figure 103. Albert Mathias
1862-1946
(El Paso County Historical Society)

Figure 104. Conrad N. Hilton
1887-1979

Figure 105. From Pioneer Plaza, the remains of the ruins of the Sheldon Hotel fire.
(El Paso Public Library, Aultman Collection)

Figure 106. Construction of the El Paso Hilton on the former site of the Sheldon Hotel, 1929-1930. The Federal Building is seen in the background of the excavation site. On the right the nearly completed Hilton Hotel.
(El Paso County Historical Society)

Mathias could immediately take possession of the building and contents should Hilton default on any aspect of the mortgage or municipal and state taxes.[18]

Notes and References

---

[1] *El Paso Herald*, August 28, 1929.
[2] *El Paso Times*, April 10, 1929.
[3] The details of the Sheldon Hotel fire included here were culled from several different sources, but included: *The El Paso Herald* April 9, 1929 and *The El Paso Times*, April 10 and 11, 1929.
[4] *El Paso Herald*, November 20, 1972.
[5] See IMDb for the actor's profile.
[6] *El Paso Fire Department Yearbook. :* 36. Reviewed by the author at Fire Department Headquarters in August 2007.
[7] *El Paso Herald*, November 25, 1954 and November 26, 1956.
[8] *El Paso Times*, April 10, 1929.
[9] *El Paso Herald*, May 5, 1920.
[10] *El Paso Herald*, April 29, 1929.
[11] *El Paso Herald*, August 16, 1929.
[12] Ibid.
[13] Hilton, Conrad. *Be My Guest* (Englewood Clifts: Printice Hall, 1957.), 147-148.
[14] Letter from Mrs. A.B. Fall November 26, no yr. to Mr. Thorman. Sheldon Hotel letterhead. A.B. Family Paper, (MS0008), New Mexico State University.
[15] The narrow one block long alleyway behind the Sheldon Hotel was for more than 30 years called the Sheldon Alley. Then the city council changed its name to Sheldon Court. The word alley means "a narrow, backstreet, while the word court, means "a short street." After the Hilton Hotel was built, the street became the Sheldon Alley once again. In 2011, the name was changed back to Sheldon Court as the alleyway was extended to the first part of San Francisco Ave. to front the El Paso Museum of Art, now making it "a short street." See E.M. Pooley's comments in the *El Paso Herald*, August 8, 1962.
[16] *El Paso Herald*, October 10, 1929; *El Paso Times*, October 18, 1929.
[17] *El Paso Times*, October 13, 1929.
[18] Mathias, Albert. Written Declaration, May 31, 1934.

Chapter Twenty-One

The Silver Spade

On September 1, 1929 a lease agreement was reached between Mathias and Hilton to rent the ground of Block 5 Lot 28. The agreement required Hilton to pay $50,000 per year, in monthly installments on a graduated scale for ninety-nine years, expiring in 2028.[1] The payments would begin on September 1, 1930 at $30,000 for the first five years, rising to $42,000 for the next five years, to $48,000 for the next fifteen years and $55,000 for the remaining sixty-three years. Hilton would be responsible for utilities, improvements, maintenance, and taxes.[2] The agreement was signed on October 9, 1929 and construction began immediately. Less than three weeks later, on Thursday, October 24, 1929, the stock market began a week-long crash which resulted in the Great Depression of 1929. Wall Street crashed, stocks lost $24 million in paper value in a single day—more than $25 billion, or $319 billion in today's dollars was lost in the crash of 1929. A year later, November 30, 1930, Hilton opened his 350 room 19-story Art Deco styled hotel with its 60 foot long, 24 foot wide, and 40 foot ceiling lobby, with an open mezzanine that surrounding the entire lobby. The hotel opened to great fanfare as the major impact of the Depression had not quite reached the southwest. The building was designed by Trost and Trost, using a style similar to and influenced by Frank Lloyd Wright, particularly on the interior. The exterior of the steel-framed concrete building was faced with brown brick and had a copper-sheathed pyramid sitting on top of two bungalow-styled four-room penthouses. The exterior of the hotel remains largely unaltered from its appearance on opening day.

It wasn't long after the opening that Hilton, who by then owned eight hotels and was more than a million dollars in debt, could see the extended wave of the Depression descending upon the southwest, and El Paso in particular. His awareness that he was going broke caused him to write:

> The panic that paralyzed the East in 1929 and sent men leaping from windows did not immediately engulf the southwest. It swept toward us slowly but inevitably. It was not like a sudden plunge off a steep precipice but like slipping out of control down a rocky hillside, bump, bump, bump, getting sorer and weaker all the time. We had only started to slide when, on November 5, 1930, I managed to complete the El Paso Hilton.[3]
>
> After the El Paso opening I went broke by inches. There was no thought now of more hotels, or new hotels. The constant struggle was to keep the ones I had, to hang onto a few, or finally, even one. My plans to be more attentive to my family were eventually swept away beneath a frenzied effort to keep them fed, clothed, and housed. What happened first was that hotel occupancy fell off. People weren't traveling. Salesmen weren't selling. The rolls of unemployed mounted steadily. I would sit late at night in my office at the Dallas Hilton and go over the ailing books. ...Week by week the income was a little less than before. Yet each week the operating costs remained constant. I would dash from one to the other to cut those costs. ...I would close off a floor to save light and heat. I would take the room phones out and save fifteen cents on each. It took a good deal of talking to bolster the flagging esprit de corps of our personnel and teach them to smile while reducing menus, serving half pats of butter, turning off every possible light bulb. "Clean beds, towels, fresh soap, always," I said over and over. "We will not economize on linen. But guard the luxuries—even the pen points, stationary, ink." And still the revenues fell—and kept falling. And still the land leases, interest on loans, taxes, had to be met. These land leases, which had not tied up valuable capital, and the fact that I had always done business with conservative banks, helped prolong, the inevitable, but that was all.[4]

In May 1933, Hilton was behind in his ground rent and had failed to pay city, county, and state taxes on Block 5 Lot 28. Mathias had no recourse but to foreclose on the lease agreement. In conversations between Hilton and Mathias, Hilton confirmed that he and his company were not going to be able to meet the demand. Mathias then began to act on the default and take possession of the hotel and its contents.[5]

Mathias wanted the $30,000 in arrears and he took the building, sort of dangled it over Hilton, to press him into action. Hilton describes his meeting with Mathias:

> "You get me some money and I'll give the hotel back to you." Mathias demanded.
>
> "I'll get it," Hilton responded, "You aren't going to keep my hotel or anything else I have built by sweat and work."
>
> "Brave talk, come back in exactly six weeks and we'll see how it stands up." Mathias responded.[6]

It took Hilton five weeks and three days to raise the urgent $30,000. He managed to get $5,000 each from a beer distributor, a local dairyman, and from the owner of a large commercial laundry. He arranged a quid pro quo agreement to exclusively use these gentlemen and their products in the operation of the regained hotel. Still short, he managed $5,000 from Sam Young, the local banker that he had been associated with when he was involved in the Sheldon Operating Company years earlier, and the remainder of the money came from his mother.[7]

Shortly after paying off his debt to Mathias and regaining control of his hotel, Hilton began, with his improving fortunes, to set his sights on the Hotel Paso del Norte and in short time, had acquired the hotel lease. With the help of two of his "benefactors" from the El Paso Hilton Hotel rescue, he signed a ten-year $500,000 lease to operate the Paso del Norte Hotel owned by long time El Paso businessman Zack White.[8] Once in control of the two grand hotels in El Paso, Hilton turned his attention to the acquisition of the Sir Francis Drake Hotel in San Francisco. [9] From his experience with the Hotel Paso del Norte and the Sir Francis Drake, Hilton realized that because of the damage incurred by the Depression, he could acquire fine, well-built, established hotels for a fraction of their true value, sometimes for as little as ten cents on the dollar.[10] Things began a slow and painful turnaround, but in the end, well, the rest is hotel history.

Albert Mathias died from myocarditis at his El Paso home at 607 W. Yandell on February 9, 1946. Following his death at the age of 84, control of the lease and ground property was transferred to the Mathias Trust Estate that was controlled by E.H. Krohn, Mathias' son-in-law.

Because of the role that Conrad Hilton played in the last years of the Sheldon Hotel and Block 5 Lot 28, it is significant to review some facets of

Hilton the man. During the successful years following the Great Depression, the EL Paso Hilton, particularly the penthouse, became home to Hilton's mother and his daughter-in-law, actress Elizabeth Taylor during her short marriage to Hilton's son Nicky. Hilton remained a constant visitor to El Paso and ingratiated himself to all the right people, both social and political. Hilton, expressed, most eloquently in his "autobiography," Be My Guest much of his personal philosophy that he claims led him from rags of the Depression to multimillionaire, if not billionaire status.

Hilton's motto was "Never try to outsmart a bank," and his philosophy revolved around, "Belief in God; I believe that the way to God and His love is through prayer. I believe in my country; I believe that its destinies are great and noble. And finally, I believe in truth; I believe that the man who willfully tells a lie is a man willfully crippling himself." This philosophy comes from the forward that he penned for Whitney Bolton's biography, The Silver Spade: The Conrad Hilton Story. Hilton contracted actor, reporter, and writer, Whitney Bolton, who Hilton had met during his fanciful days in Hollywood. Hilton wanted a biographical book to be placed in every room of every Hilton Hotel around the world.[11]

After The Silver Spade was released and placed in all Hilton rooms, a writer from The New Yorker magazine, E.J. Kahn [12], picked up a copy and read it while staying in a Hilton Hotel. He felt that it was a "Kiss-ass" puff piece to serve Hilton's massive ego. As a result, the writer wrote an article regarding his experience reading the book which was published in the magazine and hurt Hilton's feelings. Because of that, Hilton had all the copies removed and destroyed. (Some copies of The Silver Spade have survived.) Using a ghost writer, he had the book re-written to be published as an autobiography.[13] The new book, Be My Guest was published en masse and placed next to the Gideon Bible in all Hilton rooms.

This newly written "autobiography" of 1957 is virtually the same book as the Bolton book of 1954, with the addition of some color to events and perceptions, but the books remain 95 percent the same, in most cases, word for word and nowhere is Bolton given any credit whatsoever. Heavily discussed in both books is Hilton's basic principle of honesty as highlighted in one of Hilton's presumed philosophical statements, "I believe in truth; I believe that the man who willfully tells a lie is a man willfully cripples himself." This raises some serious questions regarding Hilton's veracity and integrity. The books are like twins, not identical twins, but clearly look almost identical. Hilton died on January 3, 1979 at the age of 91.

There is little doubt that he built a massive financial empire which he later converted into a series of most honorable and valued charities. But, he was a man, a man who managed to suppress much of the negative aspects of his life, specifically the charge of the rape of one of his wives, Zsa Zsa Gabor that resulted in the birth of his daughter Francesca,[14] and an extended family filled with chaotic experiences and life styles. Nonetheless, he was a major factor in the story of the Sheldon Hotel's transition into Hilton Plaza Hotel, on Block 5 Lot 28, that still casts a mighty shadow on the city of El Paso.

Until the hotel was sold in 1963, most likely because of aging mechanical systems and high utility operating costs and facing changing times and demand for more modern facilities, it had been the keystone of the burgeoning Hilton Hotel system worldwide. The Hilton Corporation opened a new Hilton Hotel, called the Hilton Inn, at the newly expanded El Paso International Airport, and was not involved in the sale of the El Paso Hilton. The Hilton Inn would remain part of the Hilton chain. The Hilton Corporation had acquired the land (Block 5 Lot 28) from the Mathias Trust Estate on January 2, 1959 and thus, for the first time, owned the entire property.[15]

The new operator/leasee of the El Paso Hilton was Allen B. Kramer, who operated the Kramer Hotel Organization which had multiple hotels in New England and the historic 800-room Tuller Hotel in Detroit. Kramer got his start in the hotel industry when he was 15 years old, when he worked the ice machine in the basement of the Statler Hotel near his home.[16] (The Statler hotel chain eventually was acquired by Hilton.) Kramer took control of the El Paso Hilton on October 1, 1963 with a 10-year lease with an option to buy before expiration of the first year of the lease.[17]

Kramer brought in Harold Wheeler, who had managed Kramer's Vermont hotel, as the new manager of the El Paso Hilton. One of the first things Wheeler did was to establish a "Change Our Name Contest." As soon as a name was selected, the Kramer Organization would begin extensive remodeling, redecorating, and modernizing. The winner of the contest would receive an all-expense paid Champagne weekend at the re-opened hotel.[18] The new name for the hotel was the Plaza Motor Hotel. Kramer operated the hotel for about a year, when the option to buy clause expired. The Plaza Hotel management stated: "Rumors that another leasee will operate the Plaza Motor Hotel are completely false. Hilton executives met several months ago and gave us an extension of the option to purchase, though not the extension we requested. I think that is how the rumors started. We did not take up the option to purchase and it expired Jan. 1. But we have a 10-year lease and we will continue to operate the Plaza hotel undisturbed. No changes are planned at present."[19]

Apparently the optimism expressed by the Kramer people was short lived, because the Plaza Hotel lease was retrieved by the Hilton Corporation and the building and land was sold to the late Mike Dipp, Sr. in April 1969 for $550,000.[20] In an interview with Mike Dipp, Jr. in 2016, he stated, "that his father met with Hilton and banker, Sam Young, and purchased the Plaza Hotel including the land. This indicated that Hilton assumed ground ownership from the Mathias' sometime in the 1940s or 1950s, when Hilton had excellent cash flow from the El Paso property because of the large Juárez-based quickie divorce business."[21] Dipp, was a Lebanese immigrant who first migrated to Mexico and then to El Paso in 1933. He became a very successful grocer with his discount food operation known as Economy Cash & Carry. Ever the clever entrepreneur, he turned his retail operation into a farming business in Anthony, New Mexico and amassed a large portfolio of downtown El Paso real estate, which in time included the Cortez Hotel (built by the DeGroff/Orndorff family) and the magnificent Plaza Theater which he purchased to prevent it from being torn down.[22] Dipp saw the Plaza Hotel as a good investment and also acquired multiple adjacent properties for parking lots.

Mike Dipp Sr. had four children, son George managed the Cortez Hotel and son Mike Jr., became the manager of the Plaza Hotel in 1970. Their sister, Mary Jean, was active in the management of the other property holdings that included several shopping centers. Paul Dipp became an El Paso realtor and operates Plaza Properties with his brother Mike, Jr.[23] George R. Dipp owns the Cortez Building which was recently remodeled by the Franklin Land Company, a subsidiary of the El Paso Electric Company.[24] In 1980, the Plaza Hotel was placed on the National Register of Historic Places. (80004110).

In 2001, the Dipp family finally shut down the Plaza Motor Hotel. Mike Dipp Jr. explains:

> With the urban sprawl and development of major malls and shopping centers, the Downtown area was having difficulty in competing...But I had to do it because about 10 years ago new handicap regulations became law, and there was no way we could adjust for that. The hotel

> was built in 1930 and the bathrooms and the rooms themselves weren't wheelchair accessible. All the doorways have an old-style marble ridge on the floor. The only way we could have met the new rules would have been to convert three rooms into one, which wouldn't have been profitable. And all of the elevators would have had to be redone.[25]

After sitting abandoned since the hotel's closure by the Dipp family, The Plaza Hotel was sold to billionaire Paul L. Foster's Mills Plaza Properties on February 15, 2008, adding to his downtown renovation project, and he commenced a major gutting of the iconic 19-story local treasure that looks down upon both of El Paso's historic plazas.

When Mike Dipp, Sr. made the effort to save the historic Plaza Theater from the wrecking ball, he appears to have set in motion interest in local pride and historic preservation that seemed to generate interest and action in saving the few historic buildings that were left in the downtown district. Many history-laden buildings had been leveled to make room for modern structures, parking lots, fast food drive-ins, or left to crumble under the intense stress from Mother Nature. There were many significant buildings available that needed to be saved and eventually restored. That was going to take someone with vision and a lot of money. Mentioned earlier was the Dipp Family's Cortez Building on the east side of San Jacinto Plaza, the Plaza Hotel, The Blue Flame Building (the former headquarters of the El Paso Natural Gas Company but currently owned by the El Paso Independent School District), The Centre Building (the old White House Department store and McCoy Hotel), and of course, the 100-year-old Mills Building (former headquarters of the El Paso Electric Company since 1997).

The historical savior appeared to be local El Paso businessman Bob Jones. He had stepped forward with the purchase of two downtown buildings with the hope to spur Downtown redevelopment. The El Paso Times quoted Jones as saying, "Downtown El Paso can be the hub it once was and much more, one key to doing that is to have more people occupying office buildings there."[26] Jones purchased the 16-story Blue Flame Building for $1.6 million and the 12-story Mills Building for approximately $1 million from the National Western Life Insurance Co. of Austin, as well as the Luther Building at 218 N. Campbell St. (now part of the City Hall complex). Over the more than 20 years that Jones had been in El Paso, there had been many attempts to accomplish the redevelopment concept, but he obviously felt that he could pull it off.[27]

Jones was the CEO of the National Center for Employment of the Disabled, a not-for-profit corporation. Jones was also actively involved in various real estate deals and was a partner in the East Side's Physicians Hospital. It was an interesting source of financial stability to engage in such high-stakes redevelopment plans. Jones was perceived by most El Paso business men and investors as being an experienced real-estate developer and a very significant force in the community.[28]

The Jones controlled National Center for Employment of the Disabled, later named Ready One Industries, employed disabled individuals in the manufacturing of military garments, especially chemical-warfare suits for soldiers. The organization had received over $800 million in government contracts that required that at least 75 percent of the manufacturing was done by blind or severely disabled employees.

In March 2006, Jones' great ambitions for the redevelopment of downtown El Paso came to a screeching halt with his arrest in a public corruption scandal, that included tax evasion; embezzlement; bribing public officials, dating back to 1998; and violating the tenents of the Jarvis-Wagner-*O'Day Program*, a federal program that helps blind and other severely disabled people. One of Jones' vehicles of deception and fraud was Access Administrators, a health-plan administration company that had contracts with city, county, and various school districts to administer their self-funded health benefits plans that covered more than 65,000 public employees and their dependents.

After some legal maneuvering, Jones pled guilty on July 2, 2009[29], and was sentenced to a 10-year term in prison and a restitution of over $65 million. Jones was incarcerated at the La Tuna Federal Prison, just a few miles west of El Paso until just recently, when he was relocated to another Federal Prison because of health issues. During the year prior to his guilty plea, he began to sell off his properties, including the Luther Building, the Mills Building, and the Plaza Hotel property. These properties were purchased, most likely at a fire-sale price, by billionaire Paul L. Foster, the founder and Co-Executive CEO of Western Refinery, a major El Paso and southwest entity. With Jones out of the picture, Foster has taken up the mantle of renovating some of El Paso's most iconic structures including the complete restoration of the Centre Building and the Mills Building as well as building a new baseball stadium and bringing an AAA (minor league) baseball team to downtown. He also appears to be part of the driving force behind returning a trolley or streetcar system to El Paso.[30]

Paul L. Foster is a gracious, affable, unassuming, clever, and astute business entrepreneur who has a track record of taking failing businesses and turning them into enormously successful enterprises. Foster took the near bankrupt refinery operations in El Paso belonging to Chevron and its neighbor, the Texaco refinery, and created the Western Refinery Company, considered by some, with its operations in New Mexico and Minnesota, as being three of the four most profitable oil refineries in the country.[31]

Foster's investing portfolio extends well beyond the oil business, with interests in retail shopping malls, sports and entertainment, aviation, land development, construction, and the hospitality industry. He is the benefactor of the Paul L. Foster Success Center, the Paul L. Foster Campus for Business and Innovation, and McLane Stadium at his Alma mater, Baylor University. He also gave $50 million to the Texas Tech University Health Sciences Center in El Paso for the Paul L. Foster School of Medicine and is the chairman of the University Of Texas Board Of Regents.

Figure 107. Paul L. Foster
(Western Refinery Inc.)

Even though the Borderland Princess is long gone, the Plaza Hotel, currently sits empty, its future is real and in Foster's hands. Paul Foster's impact on downtown El Paso and his ownership of the Plaza Hotel makes his inclusion in this tome essential. His acquisition and renovation of the Centre Building and the Mills Building; and his conversion of the parking lot where the old St. Regis Hotel stood adjacent to the Mills Building, into a multilevel parking structure with its appearance to resemble the old St. Regis Hotel, clearly demonstrates his commitment to bringing El Paso's history back to the 21st Century.

On April 22, 2015, Foster was interviewed for this book at his offices in the Mills-Centre building complex. He indicated that he had no idea of the history surrounding the Plaza Hotel that he had recently purchased from the Dipp family. Foster indicated that he really doesn't want to horde his wealth, but wanted to return it back to the community that he now considers his hometown. Foster was born in Loving, New Mexico and got calluses on his hands working as a pipe welder in the oil fields of Texas. He eventually headed to Waco to attend Baylor University to study medicine, but soon changed directions and majored in accounting, becoming a CPA shortly thereafter. From a middle management position in the oil refining industry, he ventured forward and soon took over the refineries.

Today the Plaza Hotel has been completely gutted and its future remains somewhat in limbo. (See figure 125)

Foster indicated that when the time is right, he was thinking that he might turn it into a 4-star hotel or a boutique type hotel with associated condominiums. Foster was very firm in his perception that downtown El Paso could sustain two top-tier hotels, including the Camino Real Hotel, formerly the Hotel Paso del Norte, across the plaza from both the Centre-Mills Building complex and the Plaza Hotel. He intimated that the Camino Real Hotel was not well managed or maintained by the Mexican-based corporation that owns it. That what is needed is a new owner that would restore it as he had done with his other downtown buildings. Foster stated that what he does to the Plaza Hotel rests solely on what develops with the Camino Real Hotel.[32] (See figure 124)

Figure 108. Camino del Norte Hotel, (formerly Hotel Paso del Norte) soon to be remodeled and restored to its original name. 2016 (Author's Collection)

On July 12, 2016, it was announced that the hotel operations of the Camino Real Hotel had been purchased by the Myers Group of Miami and El Paso. The developer plans a $70 million renovation of the stately grand hotel, returning it to its former glory and name, Hotel Paso del Norte. The Myers family is connected to El Paso history through the family's matriarch; she is the widow of El Paso entrepreneur, the acclaimed boot maker Tony Lama.[33]

While the future of Block 5 Lot 28 remains somewhat in limbo, its history has been, to say the least, varied, from its earliest days as part of the Ponce de Leon rancho to a stage station for the San Antonio-San Diego mail route, to the Mexican Revolution, to the days of military and federal agency intervention in Prohibition and smuggling; the old hotel remained unflappably sturdy, taking it all in.

The criminals, the spies, the soldiers of fortune, the secret agents, and the presidents; all rubbing shoulders, sharing drinks, and swapping stories and telling lies of the way the old west used to be. ... Oh if the walls could talk.

Notes and References

[1] *El Paso Herald*, October 5, 1929.

[2] Mathias Hilton Lease Agreement, 216.

[3] Hilton, Conrad. *Be My Guest* (Englewood Clifts: Printice Hall, 1957.), 150-151.

[4] Ibid, 153.

[5] Mathias-Hilton.

[6] Bolton, Whitney. *The Silver Spade:The Conrad HiltonStory*. (New York: Farrar, Straus and Giroux, 1954.), 63.

[7] Hilton, 168.

[8] *El Paso Herald*, April 14, 1937.

[9] Bolton (1954), 64.

[10] Ibid, 65.

[11] *Bolton, W.F.* Telephone interview. North Granby, CT, 17 March 2011.

[12] Kahn, E.J. "The Silver Spade a book review." *The New Yorker*, November 24, 1956.
[13] Ibid.
[14] Mayoras, Danielle, and Andy Mayoras. "The Tragedy of Francesca Hilton, Daughter of Zsa Zsa Gabor and Hilton Founder." *Forbes* Accessed 10 June 2016.
[15] Book 1140/Page 583, El Paso County Clerk's office.
[16] www.historicdetroit.org/building/tuller-hotel/ Accessed 16 June 2016.
[17] *El Paso Herald*, September 26, 1963.
[18] *El Paso Herald*, October 18, 1963.
[19] *El Paso Herald*, January 8, 1965.
[20] Book 248/Page 571, El Paso County Clerk's office.
[21] Mike Dipp, Jr., Telephone interview, June 20, 2016.
[22] *El Paso Inc.*, September 2, 2011. Accessed 26 April 2015.
[23] Ibid.
[24] *Lubbock Avalanche-Journal*, April 17, 2011.
[25] El Paso Inc., 2011.
[26] Kolenc, Vic. "Bob Jones buys Blue Flame Building." *El Paso Times*, June 12, 2004.
[27] Ibid.
[28] Ibid.
[29] By pleading guilty, Jones admitted that he conspired with others to use ill-gotten cash and campaign contributions to pay for votes of members of the El Paso County Commissioners Court and trustees of the El Paso, Ysleta, and Socorro school districts. One of Jones' vehicles of deception and fraud was Access Administrators a health-plan administration company that had contracts with city, county, and various school districts to administer their self-funded health benefits plans, which covered more than 65,000 public employees and their dependents.
[30] *El Paso Times*, March 30, 2016
[31] "Western Refining wants to buy Northern Tier Energy: What it means for investors." *The Motley Fool*. November 22, 2015. Accessed 20 June 2016.
[32] Paul L. Foster interview, April 22, 2015, El Paso, Texas.
[33] *El Paso Times*, July 13, 2016; *El Paso Development News*, July 13, 2016; and KVIA. com Accessed July 13, 2016.

Appendix 1

The History of El Camino Real

Rising from the topography of North America, mountain ranges tend to traverse the continent from north to south with wide valleys and plains separating the ranges. These open plains generally provided unobstructed passage, yet the ranges created huge obstacles for passage from east to west as the history of the westward migration of North America has recorded. Topography governs the migration of man and beast as well as the flow of rivers and streams. A great natural pass exists through the Rocky Mountains as the range descends into the great Chihuahuan Desert to become the Sierra Madres. These paths and trails were first followed by wild animals and savage men.[1] Evidence supports that man has occupied the El Paso del Norte region, in quest of food, water, and shelter for the past 11,000 years.[2]

When the Spanish explorers arrived in the 16th century, they found the great river, the Rio Grande, emerging from the arroyo between the two ranges. They named the site El Paso del Norte (the Pass of the North). As the Rio Grande streamed south from its headwaters in the Colorado Mountains, it rounded the bend below the pass and began to flow eastward. This formed a natural ford, where travelers, adventurers, merchants, cowboys, outlaws, gold-seekers, and the gaming crowd all collided over the ensuing four hundred years to become Ciudad Juárez on the west bank in Mexico and El Paso, Texas on the east bank. Today the passage has evolved into a major thoroughfare of man, machine, and commerce, the I-10.

Following eight hundred years of warfare, Spain finally cast-off the Moors' hold on her sovereignty at the end of the fifteenth century. Spain soon represented the image of "unity, wealth, and power."[3] With pride and independence, men of substance left their homeland and traveled the world from the West Indies and the City of Mexico, into the lands of Florida, and New

Mexico to plant not only Spain's flag and the cross of Roman Catholicism, but to find the rumored cities of gold and other riches.

To these armored knights, "hardship, peril, death, had no terrors for this soldier knight. If he was pitiless towards others, so was he pitiless toward himself. He saw his mission enveloped with romantic glory. Such were the conquistadors, who, after the capture of the Aztec capital in the summer of 1521, carried the Spanish banner northward."[4] Expeditions under the leadership of Ponce de León, Hernán Cortés, Coronado, de Soto, Rodriguez, Narváez, Cabeza de Vaca, and Oñate left such an indelible mark of destruction of cultures and customs as they plundered the peoples of the southwest in search of riches and converts for their king and cross.

In 1536, Álvar Núñez Cabeza de Vaca, with the Spanish king's financial support, wandered throughout the Southwest, often acting as mercantile trader and shaman to the many of the native tribes he encountered. Cabeza de Vaca was a junior member of a failed expedition wandered into Texas from the Mississippi River, passing through New Mexico, before he eventually was rescued by Spaniards and lived to report on his wanderings, including the lost cities of Cibola, which were actually pueblos in northern New Mexico. Reviews of his narratives (meant to provide the Spanish Crown with information of the area) indicate that he was the first European to pass through the El Paso region of New Mexico.[5] Information gathered from Cabeza de Vaca eventually lead the Spanish Crown to send Francisco Coronado to march across what is now Arizona into New Mexico and conquer the Pueblo tribes and head towards the golden agricultural treasures of Kansas. The true effect of the Coronado expedition did not surface for more than a hundred years when the Indian descendants sought revenge against the immigrating Europeans.[6]

In July 1588, the Spanish Armada was defeated off the coast of France by the British navy under the command of Sir Francis Drake. Following this devastating loss, King Phillip II of Spain (one of the Hapsburg ruling cousins of Europe) began a valiant attempt to rebuild Spain's prestige by pursuing further conquests and activity in Mexico and secure his power in the New World.

In 1595, wealthy scion of a Spanish-Basque silver baron, Don Juan Oñate, whose wife, Isabel, was the great-granddaughter of the Aztec Emperor Montezuma, lobbied extensively his friend, the Spanish viceroy, Luis Velasco. Having repeatedly heard of the tales of the Seven Cities of Cibola and the Kingdom of Quivira,[7] he remained persistent until he received the commission from King Phillip II for permission to explore the region of New Mexico. In

1597, Oñate left Santa Barbara, Mexico with an expedition consisting of 130 soldier-settlers, and their families, a band of Franciscans, a large procession of Negro and Indian slaves, seven thousand head of stock, and eighty-three wagons and carts for woman and children.[8]

On April 30, 1598, as his caravan headed towards El Paso, Onate took formal possession declared, "In the name of King Philip II, all the kingdoms and provinces of New Mexico" at a location a few miles from the current city of El Paso.[9]

Leaving the El Paso area, Oñate continued north along the Rio Grande towards what we now know as Santa Fe, New Mexico. Oñate arrived in July and set up his community at the pueblo of Okeh and then a year later relocated his Spanish colony and the first European capital of New Mexico. at San Gabriel del Yungue (San Juan Pueblo near Espanola, NM). The capital was eventually moved about 20 miles south to Santa Fe in 1610 [possibly as early as 1607] by then Governor Don Pedro Peralta.[10]

Historians have described Oñate as, "understanding and sympathetic, yet arbitrary and dogmatic. Committed to looking after the livelihoods of his settlers, he used his mailed fist of authority against those who opposed his policies…extraordinary pressures often transformed Oñate into an oppressor rather than a leader."[11]

Oñate chose to travel up to the Rio Grande on a new route and travel northward through the Chihuahuan Desert and connect with the river in the area of today's El Paso on April 20, 1598. This route established the southern portion of the Camino Real and the trail would be used for the next 250 years to supply trains, traders, missionaries, and government activities. El Camino Real had become a functional highway, of sorts. The entire trail is called El Camino Real de Tierra Adentro (the Royal Road of the Interior Lands) and remains historically the oldest route between Mexico City and San Juan Pueblo (Ohkay Owengeh, twenty miles north of Santa Fe, NM). The commercial corridor is 1500 miles in length.[12] (Today a portion of Oñate's Trail is New Mexico Highway 28 that runs through the rich Mesilla valley orchards and farms that is also designated as part of the Butterfield Stage route. Another portion of the trail has become Interstate Highway 25 from Las Cruces to Santa Fe, NM)

For the purpose of clarity, the term New Mexico (Nuevo México) refers to the entire area claimed by Spain that encompass today's California, Arizona and the current state of New Mexico. It is interesting to note that Spanish leaders, both in Mexico and Spain, believed that New Mexico (Nuevo México) stretched as far as Newfoundland bordering the North Sea. It has been reported that Oñate had requested of the Spanish King, "two ships annually to the new colony unaware that the closest arm of the ocean was hundreds of miles away."[13] The contemporary boundaries of the state of New Mexico show little similarities to that of Nuevo México, but reflect those that were created following the Mexican-American War (1846-1848) and highlighted in the Treaty of Guadalupe-Hildalgo of 1848 and the Gadsden Purchase in 1853.

Over the years and under Spanish rule, the villages and agricultural areas along the Oñate Trail flourished; soon there were other well established settlements in addition to El Paso del Norte. Ysleta, San Elizario, Socorro, and Senecú, [The latter was a pueblo originally established by the Piro Indians and was the first settlement discovered by Oñate upon entering New Mexico.]

Following Oñate's establishment of the Spanish colony, the conflicts between the Spanish "benefactors" and the local Pueblo Peoples rarely improved. There were approximately 40,000 Indians inhabiting the region of the Spanish colonies. Insurrection followed insurrection, with the Spanish colonists killing or enslaving hundreds of the Indians. In one revolt, with the Acoma Pueblo, Oñate ordered severe punishment be meted out following his victory after the three-day battle:

> Twenty-four males over age twenty-five to have one foot cut off and condemned to twenty years of personal servitude.
>
> Males twelve to twenty-five years old condemned to twenty years of personal servitude.
>
> Women over twelve years of age condemned to twenty years of personal servitude.
>
> Two Moquis captured in the Acoma fight to have the right hand cut off and to be set free to take home news of their punishment.
>
> Children under twelve, whom Oñate ruled free of guilt, to be handed over to Father Martínez and Zaldívar for a Christian upbringing. (Sixty of the small girls were afterward sent to Mexico City for parceling among the convents there. None ever saw their homeland or relatives again.).[14]

He declared that this act would instill fear of the Spanish among the Indians. Through this all, the Franciscan missionaries continued to "Christianize" the natives.

Following the Pueblo Revolt of 1680, led by the Indian shaman Popé (Po-pay), all the Spanish colonies had been destroyed and the Spanish colonial capital at Santa Fe was under violent attack. In August of that year, New Mexico Governor de Otermin led the Spaniards out of Santa Fe without contest and retreated southward along the Rio Grande to settle at the village that had been established at El Paso del Norte. En route to safety, the Spanish refugees added to the tiny populations of the various communities along their escape route, the villages at Ysleta, Senecú, and Socorro. The Spanish government established a presidio at Paso del Norte to afford some level of protection for the colonies. As the 17th century ended, the tiny village at the Pass grew as its mercantile entrepreneurs thrived, as did the growing of corn, beans, and grapes, spurred on by the abundance of water.[15] For the next eighteen years there was not a single Spaniard living north of El Paso del Norte. The Indians held New Mexico with a tight reign. Then in 1692, Don Diego de Vargas, the Spanish governor of the New Spain territory of New Mexico led the reconquest of Nuevo México. Vargas succeeded his conquest with very little bloodshed as most of the pueblos were captured by surprise. The following year, Vargas was able to take control of the northern towns and had full control by 1694.[16]

For the next 125 years, New Mexico remained under Spanish control as an isolated and sluggish Spanish outpost, very unlike the mining and political centers further to the south in New Spain.[17]

Mexico gained its independence from Spain on September 27, 1821. The river valleys of New Mexico became richly productive with wheat, corn, and cotton farming. The raising of cattle, sheep, and horses led to the establishment of many large haciendas and the hills of both New Mexico and Chihuahua erupted with huge caches of copper, gold, silver, and other metals of value. These successes spurred the population and economy of El Paso del Norte, the crossroads and portal into the route to Mexico City via El Camino Real de Tierra Adentro.

Appendix II

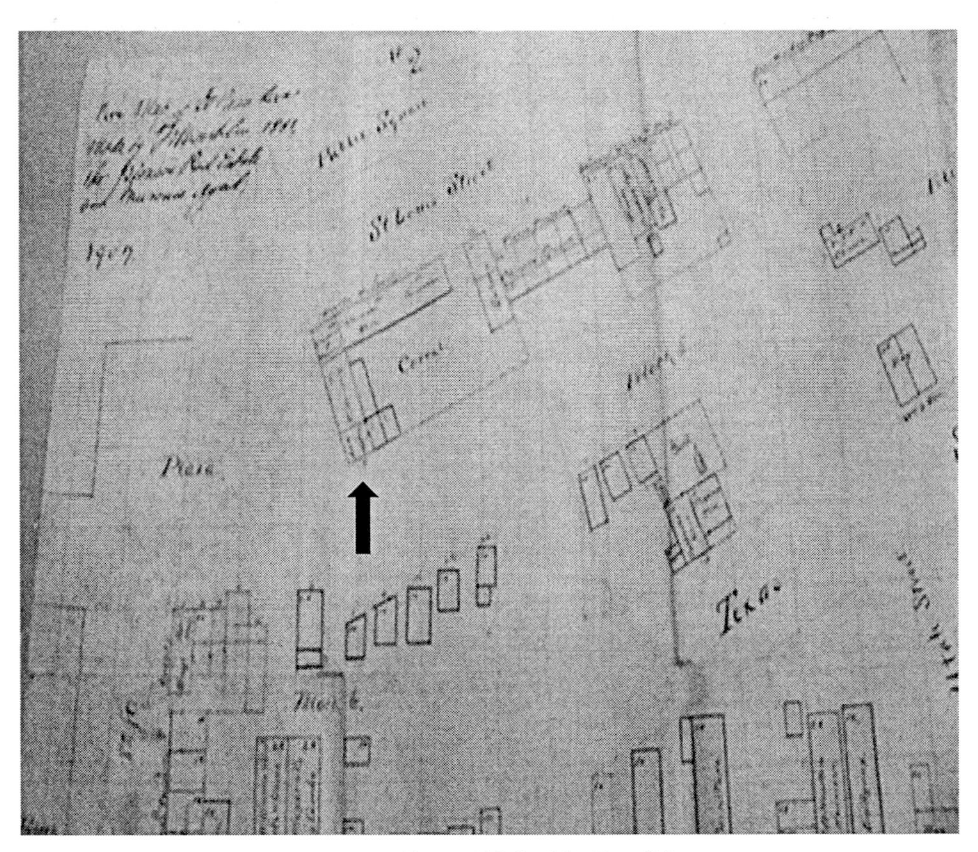

Figure 109 Conklin Map # 1

Original hand drawn 1881 Conklin fire insurance map showing the future site of the Sheldon Hotel, and the Giddings San Antonio-San Diego Mail route (arrow). The Central Hotel and the Grand Central were located where the numbers "1907 are located.

(Courtesy: Special Collections Department, University of Texas at El Paso.)

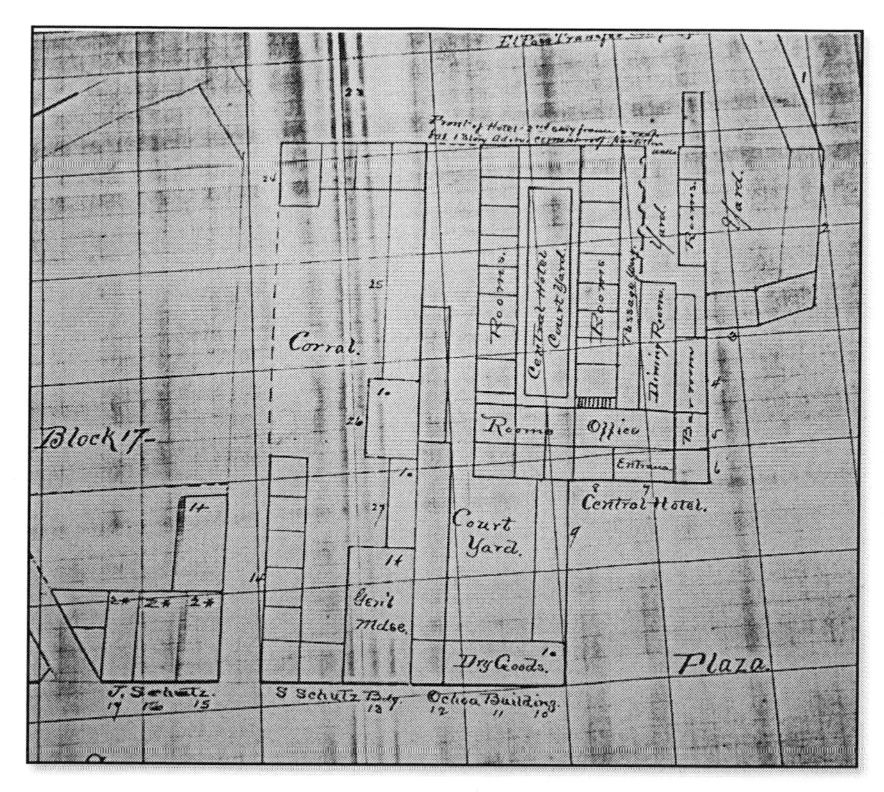

Figure 110. Conklin Map # 2

Original hand drawn 1881 Conklin fire insurance map showing building plan of the Central Hotel at the head of El Paso Street at the Little Plaza. Vacant yard would become Grand Central Hotel.

(Courtesy: Special Collections Department, University of Texas at El Paso.)

Notes and References

---

[1] *El Paso Times*. December15, 1944.

[2] Timmons, W.H. *Four Centuries at the Pass: A new history of El Paso on its 400th Birthday.* (El Paso: City of El Paso Arts Resources Department, 1980.), 1.

[3] Bolton, Herbert E. *The Spanish Borderlands*. (1920). (North Charleston, NC: CreatSpace: 2014.), 9.

[4] Ibid, 10.

[5] White, Owen P. *Out of the Desert: The Historical Romance of El Paso*. (El Paso: The McMath Company, 1923.), 6.

[6] Ibid.

[7] Quiveria is thought to be the current location of Wichita, Kansas.

[8] Bolton (1920), 71. In Riley (1995), 247, are presented the details of the components of the expedition. *There were 129 soldiers and an unrecorded number of women, children, servants, and slaves. The Governor [Oñate] provided more than 3000 sheep and goats precursors of the great herds that would be built up over the next eighty years. He also brought some 200 horses, mares, and colts. There were about 800 head of cattle plus 500 calves, in addition to pigs, mules, and donkeys. The many carts were pulled primarily by oxen. Supplies were plentiful: iron tools, equipment for horses, cooking ware, sewing paraphernalia, foodstuffs including wine, oil, and sugar, writing paper, medicines, blacksmithing tools, horseshoes and nails, weapons, gunpowder and lead, quicksilver (for mining purposes), and more. The governor also took a great variety of trade items, including perhaps 80,000 glass beads of various kinds, rosaries, sacred images of tin, amulets and medals, clay whistles, knives, mirrors, needles, thread, thimbles, rings, glass earrings, and hawks bells, among other things. Clearly, Oñate expected great profit from trade. In addition to what Governor Oñate contributed, the individual colonists had their own mounts and equipment, household goods, carts and wagons, weapons, cattle, mules and donkeys, and large numbers of extra horses. It was a well-equipped expedition and obviously one that came intending to stay. The Franciscan contingent of ten was led by Fray Alonso Martinez.*

[9] Riley, Carroll L. *Rio del Norte: People of the Upper Rio Grande from Earliest Times to the Pueblo Revolt.* (Salt Lake City: University of Utah, 1995.), 247.

[10] Ibid, 253.

[11] Etulain, Richard W. (ed.) (in Marc Simmons' *The Last Conquistador: Juan de Oñate and the Settling of the Far Southwest.* Norman: University of Oklahoma Press, 1991.), xi.

[12] CARTA Camino Real de Tierra Adentro Trail Association.

[13] Simmons, Marc. *The Last Conquistador: Juan de Oñate and the Settling of the Far Southwest.* Norman: University of Oklahoma Press, 1991.), xiii.
[14] Ibid, 145.
[15] Martinez, Oscar. *Border Boom Town. Ciudad Juárez since 1848I.*(Austin: University of Texas, 1978.), 9.
[16] Bolton (1920), 74.
[17] Ibid.

Maps, Legacy Monuments, and Vintage Postcards

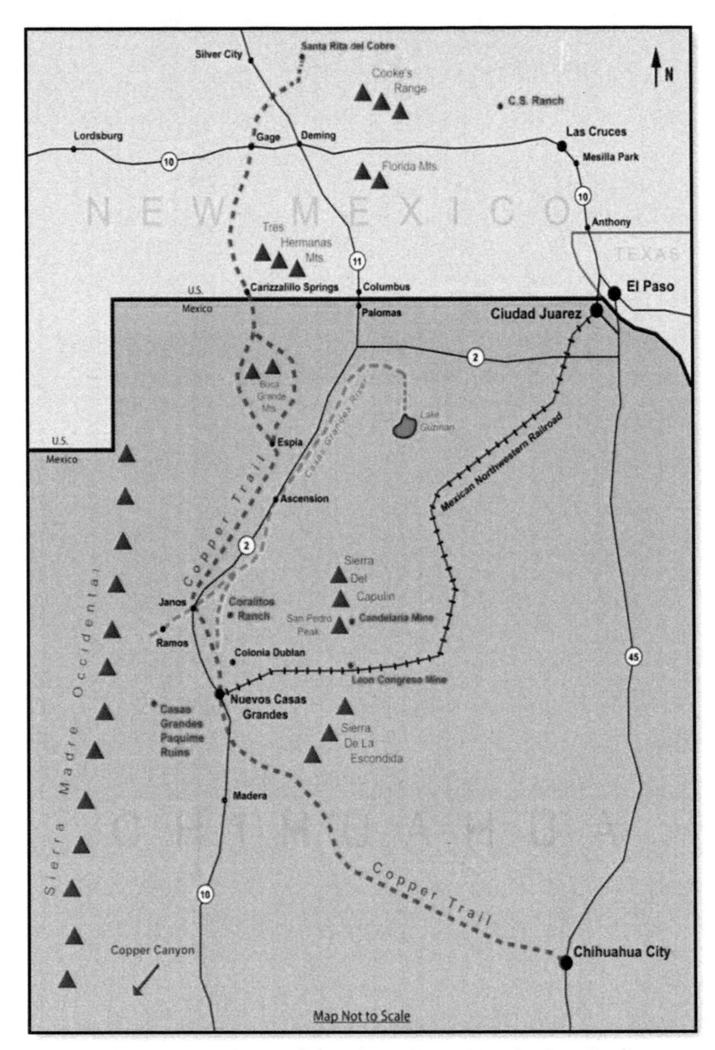

Figure 111. Map of the Corralitos Ranch, San Pedro Mining Region, and the Copper Trail of the 1850s. The Casas Grande River and Lake Guzman are frequently dry beds. (Author's Collection)

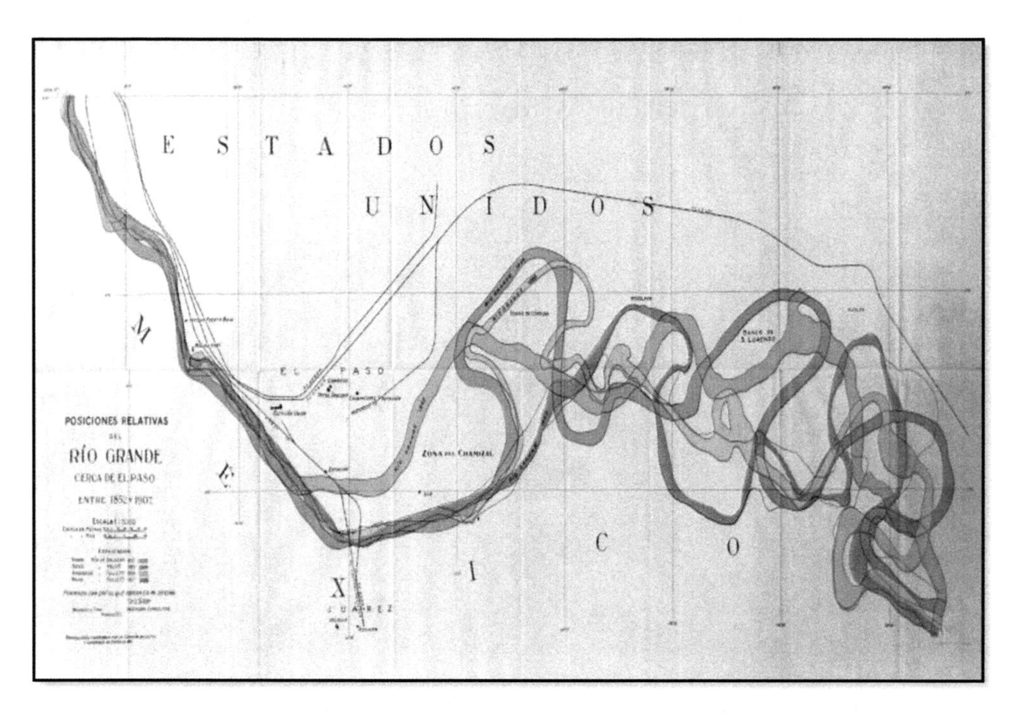

Figure 112. The meandering Rio Grande and the constantly changing United States-Mexico Boundary. Key: Green – 1832, Blue – 1889, Yellow – 1899, Red – 1907. International Boundary Commission – 1911

(From Vol. III, Memoria Documentada del juicio de arbitraje del Chamizal celebrado en virtud de la convencion de junio 24 de 1910. Tomo II. Apenice. Documentos y Planos. Anexos a los Alegatos. Páginas 1 a 810. Tomo III. Apendice. Documentos y Planos. Anexos a los Ale.)

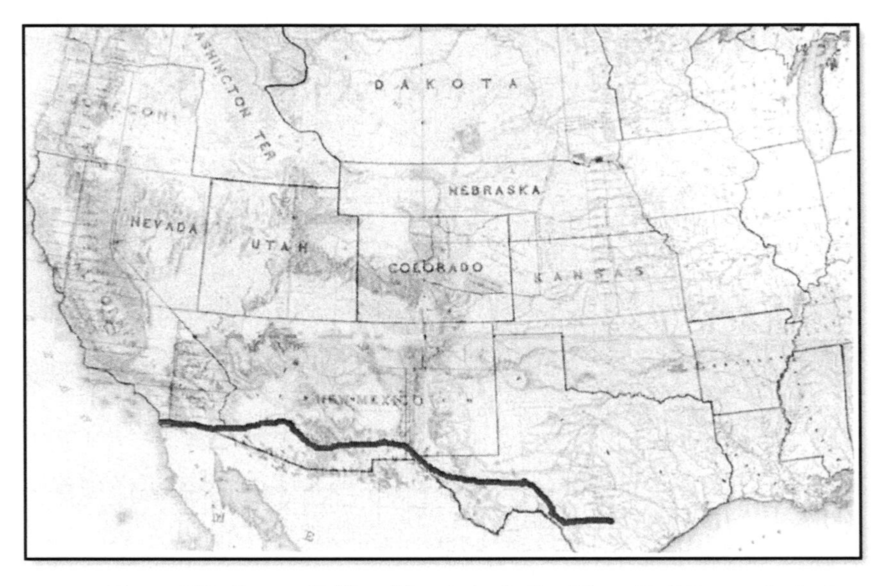

Figure 113. George Giddings' San Antonio-San Diego Mail Line route. Latter to be operated as the Butterfield Overland Mail Company and then the Overland Mail Corporation.

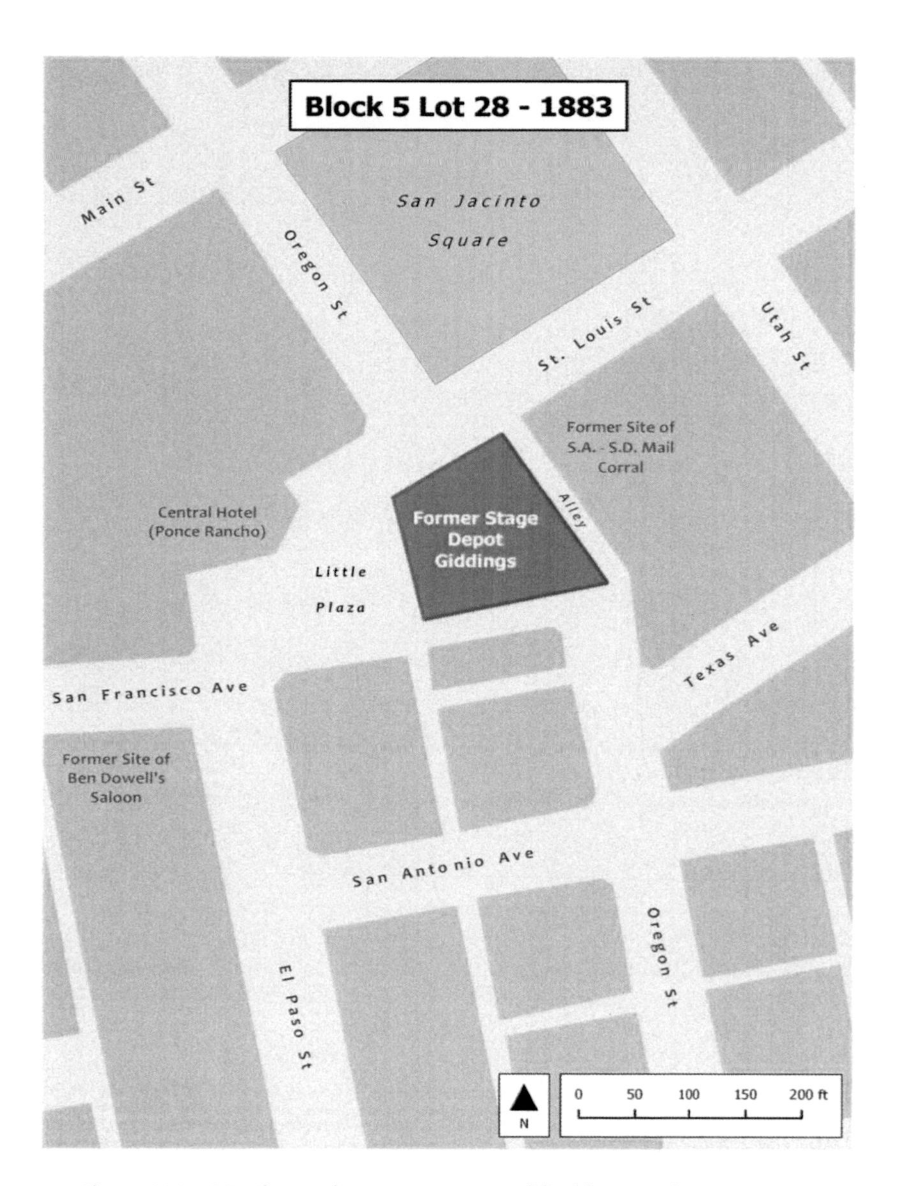

Figure 114. 1883 El Paso downtown map modified from Sanborn Fire Maps.
(Author's Collection.)

Figure 115. The Sheldon Memorial Tiffany Widow on the north wall in the sanctuary of the First Presbyterian Church at 124 Henry St., Brooklyn; donated by Henry and Lucius Sheldon in 1882 in memory of their parents. The window is titled *The Fisherman*. The church was originally founded in 1822 and moved to its present location in 1847 when residents of Brooklyn were warned to "extricate yourself from the narrow, dirty and disagreeable streets of the City of Brooklyn with all possible dispatch." (Courtesy of Charlie Russell)

Figure 116. Sheldon Knoll, Green-Wood Cemetery, Brooklyn. The obelisk is a memorial to Henry K. Sheldon. The headstones are the rest of his and his brothers' families. 2016.
(Courtesy of Charlie Russell)

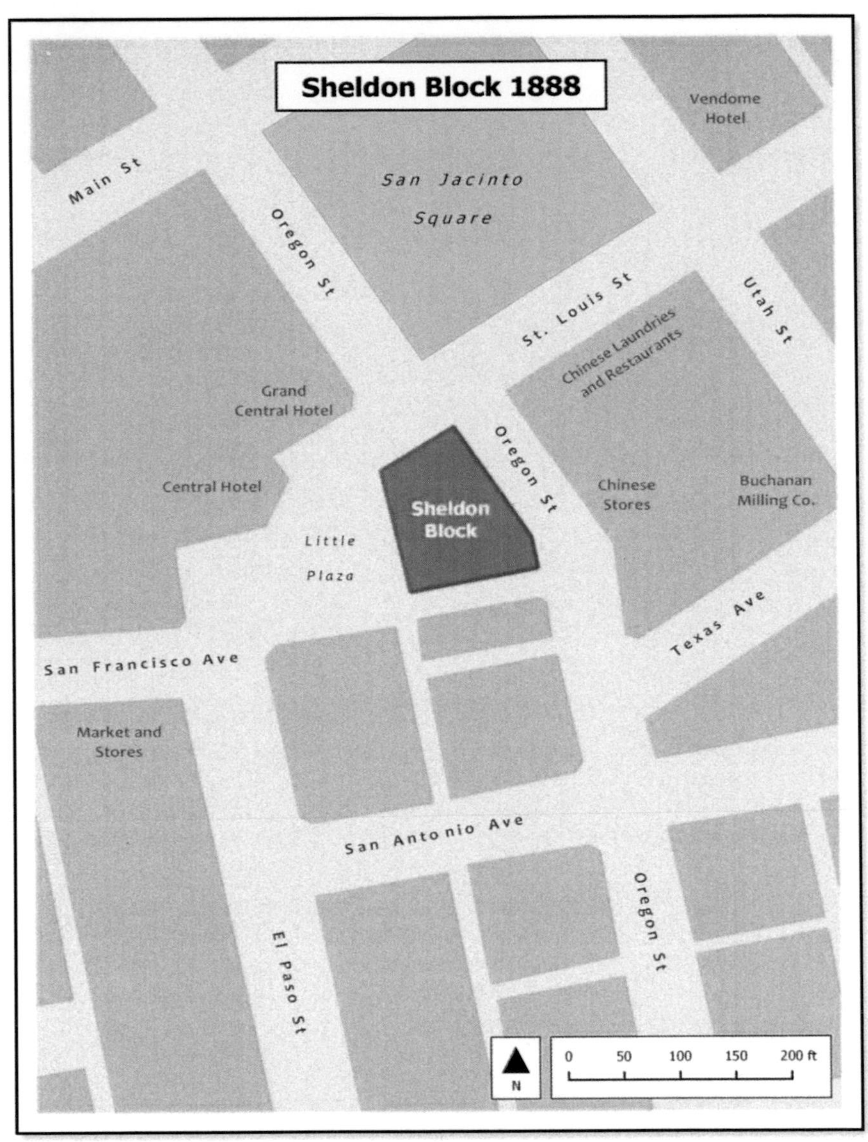

Figure 117. Downtown El Paso 1888.
(Author's Collection)

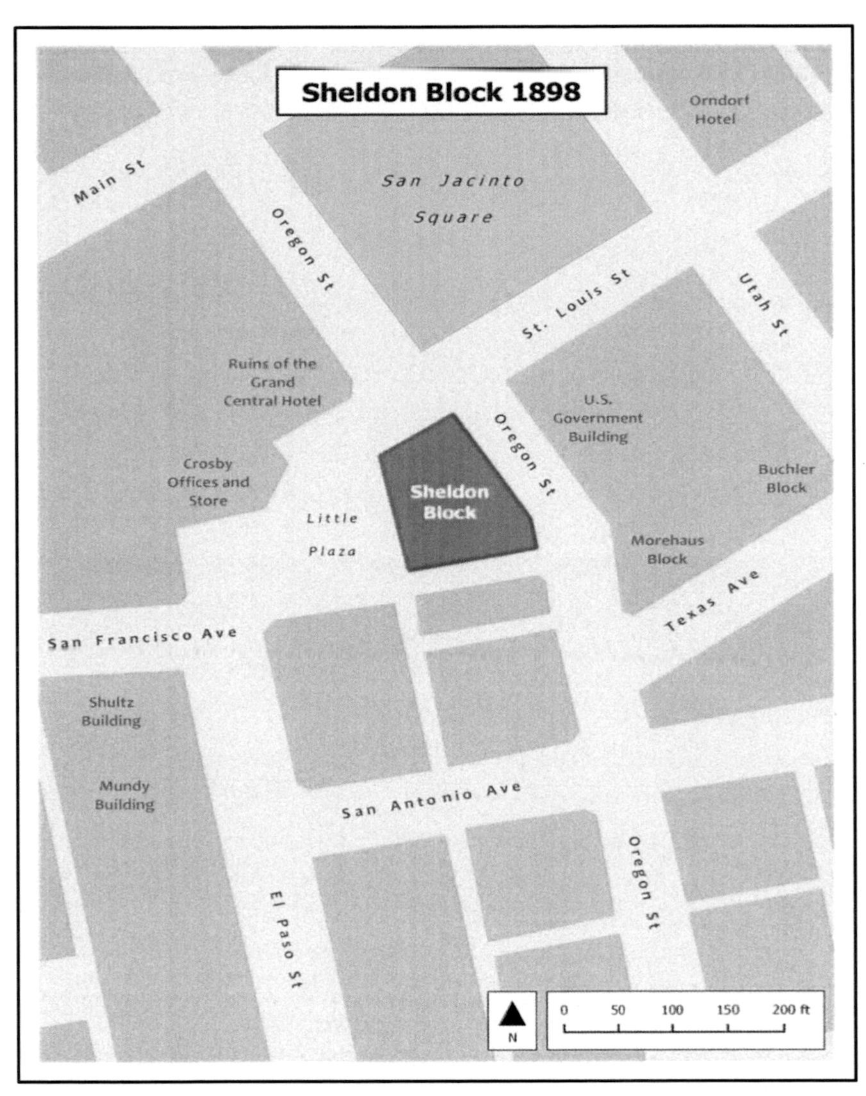

Figure 118. 1898 El Paso downtown map modified from Sanborn Fire Map.

Figure 119. A pair of widely circulated vintage postcards of the Sheldon Hotel.
(Author's Collection)

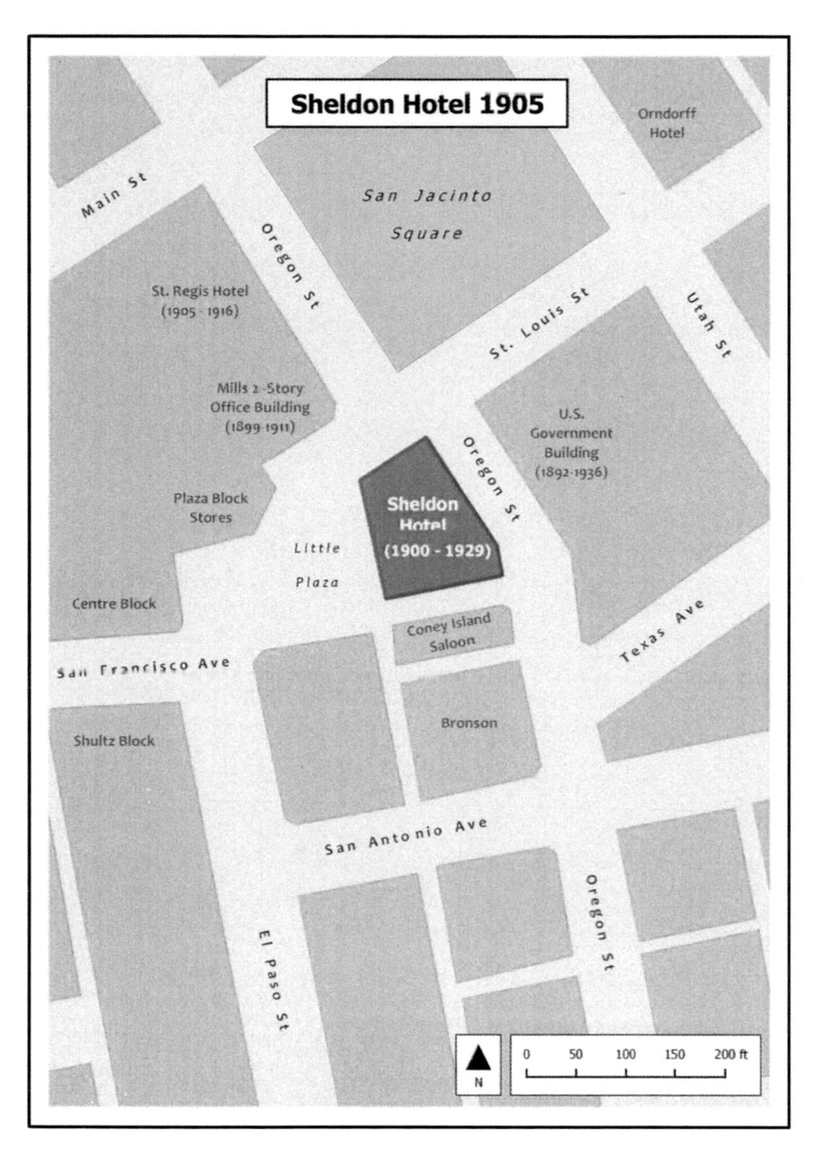

Figure 120. Downtown El Paso in 1905.
(Author's Collection)

Figure 121. Vintage postcard of the lobby of the Sheldon Hotel, 1912.
(Author's Collection)

Figure 122. Vintage postcard of the formal dining room at the Sheldon Hotel.
(Author's Collection)

Figure 123. Behind the Badges

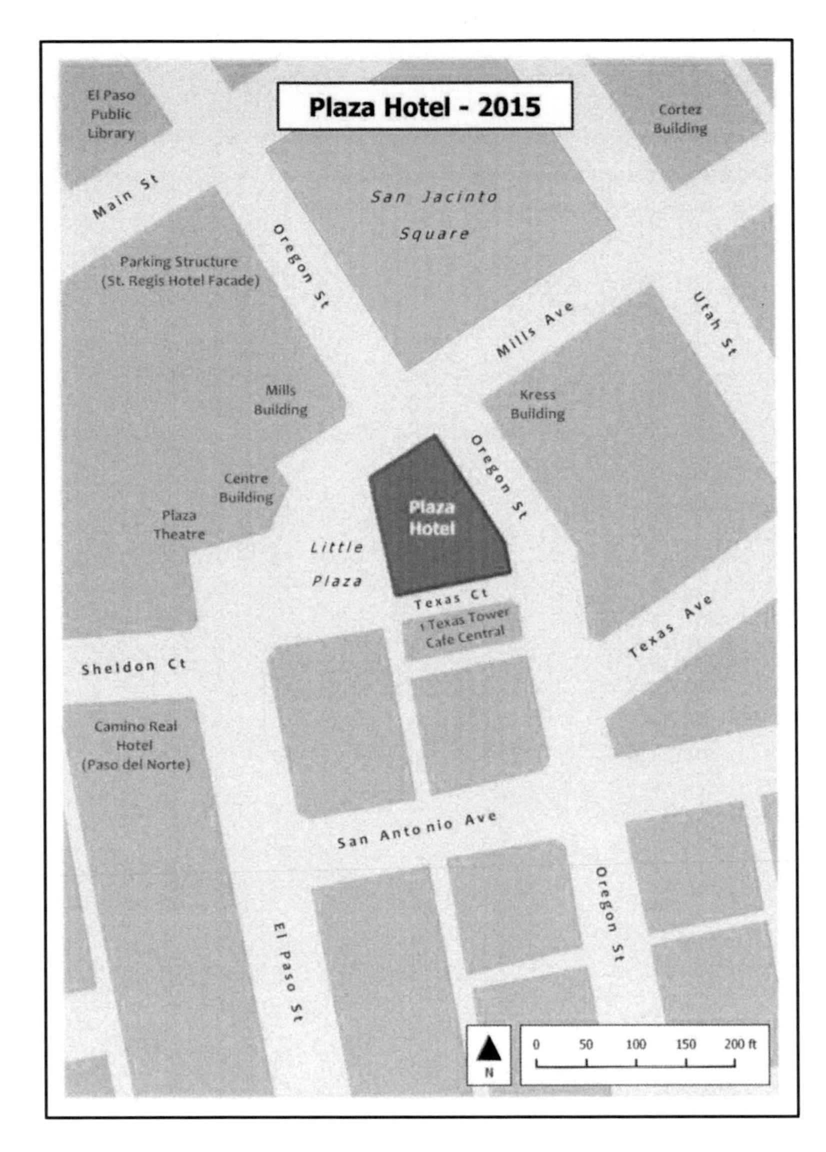

Figure 124. Downtown El Paso 2015
(Author's Collection)

Figure 125. The Plaza Hotel 2016
(Courtesy of Landon Berg)

The Borderland Princess

BIBLIOGRAPHY

(P = Print W= Web.)

"Asarco: A History Timeline of the Smokestack in El Paso!" Nov. 2015. (W)

Adams, John A., Jr. *Conflict and Commerce on the Rio Grande: Laredo, 1755-1955.* College Station: Texas A & M University Press, 2008. (P)

Aker, Andrea. "The Story of Sarah Bowman: Yuma's First Citizen Left a Lasting Impression." *Arizona Oddities*. January 21, 2011. 9 September 2015. (W)

Anderson, Greta. *More Than Petticoats: Remarkable Texas Women*. Guilford, CT: Morris Book Publishing, 2013. (P)

Anderson, Judith. *William Howard Taft: An Intimate History*. New York: W.W. Norton, 1981. (P)

Arredondo, Jaime M. et.al.(eds.) *Open Borders to a Revolution: Culture, Politics, and Migration.* Washington, D.C., Smithsonian Institution Scholarly Press, 2013. (P)

Atkin, Ronald. *Revolution! Mexico: 1910-1920.* London: Macmillan, 1969. (P)

Austerman, Wayne R. *Sharps Rifles and Spanish Mules: The San Antonio – El Paso Mail, 1851-1881.* College Station: Texas A & M University Press, 1985. (P)

______. "San Antonio-El Paso Mail." *Handbook of Texas Online (2010).* 27 August 2015. (W)

Baack, Stephen. "State National becomes Compass." *El Paso Inc*. 21 June 2009. (W)

Bailey, Kenneth K. "Three blocks of Federal Avenue: a treasure trove of history." *Password*. Vol. XXXVI. pp. 77-78. (P)

Banning, William and George H. Banning. *Six Horses.* New York: The Century Company, 1930. (P)

Bartlett, John Russell. *Personal Narrative of Explorations and Incidents in Texas, New Mexico, California, Sonora, and Chihuahua, Connected with the United States and Mexican Boundary Commission, during the years 1850, 51, 52, and 53.* Vol. I and II. New York: D. Appleton & Company, 1854. Web. 19 December 2013. (W)

Belford, David. "Kohlberg, Krupp, Zielonka became business and civic leaders." *Borderlands*. El Paso: El Paso Community College/20. 1 June 2009. (W)

Bethune, Martha Fall. *Race with the Wind: The Personal Life of Albert B. Fall*. El

Paso: Novio Book, 1989. (P)

Blevins, Don. *A Priest, a Prostitute, and Some Other Early Texans*. Guilford, CT: Globe Pequot, 2008. (P)

Boardman, Mark. "The Curious Murder of Manny Clements." *True West Magazine*. April 22, 2014.(w)

Bochiechis, Leonard, and Gen. Giuseppe Garibaldi. *Garibaldi: In the Light of History*. New York: n. p., 1932. (P)

Bolton, Herbert E. *Spanish Exploration in the Southwest 1542-1706.* New York: C. Scribner's Son, 1916. (P)

_____, *The Spanish Borderlands*. (1920) N. Charleston, S.C.: CreatSpace, 2014. (P)

Bolton, Whitney. *The Silver Spade: The Conrad Hilton Story*. New York: Farrar, Straus and Giroux, 1954. (P)

Bowden, J.J. *Spanish and Mexican Land Grants in the Chihuahuan Acquisition*. El Paso: Texas Western Press, 1971. (P)

Braddy, Haldeen. "The Head of Pancho Villa." *Western Folklore*. Vol. 19, No. 1 (June 1960. Grass Valley, CA: Western States Folklore Society, 1960. (P)

Brands, H.W. *The Age of Gold: the California Gold Rush and the New American Dream.* New York: Anchor, 2003. (P)

Brenner, Anita. *The Wind That Swept Mexico: The History of the Mexican Revolution of 1910 – 1942*. Austin: University of Texas, 1971. (P)

Breslin, Jimmy. *Damon Runyon: A Life*. Boston: Houghton Mifflin, 1991. (P)

Brockmoller, Janet. "An interview with Mrs. Enriqueta Rubio Lopez." *Password*. Vol. XXVII. Pp. 34-40. (P)

Brown, Bryan W. "Boyhood in early El Paso–1903." *Password.* Vol. XV. Pp49-52. (P)

Bush, Ira J. *Gringo Doctor*. Caldwell, ID: The Caxton Printers, Ltd., 1939. (P)

______, "Dr. Bush recalls days of 25 years ago in El Paso." *Password*. Vol. XLII, 190-194. (P)

Calhoun, Frederick S. *The Lawmen: United States Marshals and Their Deputies, 1789 – 1989.* Washington: The Smithsonian Institution Press, 1989. (P)

Calleros, Cleofas. *El Paso....Then and Now.* Vol. VII. El Paso: American Printing Company, 1954. (P)

Calvert, Peter. *The Mexican Revolution, 1910-1914: Diplomacy of the Anglo-American Conflict.* New York: Cambridge University Press, 1968. (P)

Campbell, C.E. *Going the Extra Yard: An Army Doctor's Odyssey*. (Burbank: Endangered History Project, 2013. (P)

_____, *Mines, Cattle, and Rebellion: The History of the Corralitos Ranch*. Sunset Beach, CA.: Green Street Publications, 2014. (P)

Carey, Elaine, and Andrae M. Marak. *Smugglers, Brothels, and Twine: Historical Perspectives on Contraband and Vice in North America's Borderlands* (Tucson: The University of Arizona Press, 2011. (P)

Carman, Michael D. *United States Customs and the Madero Revolution*. (Southwestern Studies Monograph No. 48.) El Paso: Texas Western Press, 1976. (P)

Carnes, Cecil. *Jimmy Hare News Photographer: Half a Century with a Camera*. New York: Macmillan Company, 1940. (P)

CARTA El Camino Real de Tierra Adentro Trail Association. Las Lunas, NM. 3 August 2013. (P)

Chambers, Kathy. "A man without a country." *Password* Vol. XIV pp.84-85. (P)

Chapman, Bob. (1946, August 25) "Sheldon was the center of civic life." *El Paso Times*. (P)

_____, (1952, June 22) "Elaborate Toltec Club Society's gathering place in early days." *El Paso Times*. p.32. (P)

Cioc-Ortega, Mark, and Evelina Ortega. "The Leech Trial of 1910: The Hardest Fought Legal Battle in the History of the El Paso Courts." *El Paso Bar Journal*. Part I Dec. 2011-Jan.2012. Part II Feb. - Mar. 2012. (W)

Cioc-Ortega, M. "Anson Mills and the Platting of El Paso, 1858-1859." (*Password*. Vol. 58. (2014). (P)

_______,"What's in a name? An homage to the original Newspaper Tree." *newspapertree.com* July 4, 2007. 27 March 2015. (W)

Cleland, Robert G. A History of Phelps Dodge 1834 - 1950. New York: Alfred A. Knopf, 1952. (P)

Clendenen, Clarence C. *Blood on the Border: The United States Army and the Mexican Irregulars.* Toronto: The Macmillan Company, 1969. (P)

Collins, Sandra L., and Lea Fatuch. *Under the Dome: Footsteps Through History* (Paso del Norte Hotel). El Paso: El Paso Electric Company, 1989. (P)

Conkling, Roscoe F. and Margaret B. *The Butterfield Overland Mail: 1857-1869: Its Organization and Operation Over the Southern Route to 1861; Subsequently over the Central Route to 1866; and under Wells, Fargo and Company in 1869.* Volume I and II. Glendale, CA: The Author H. Clark Company, 1947. (P)

Cool, Paul. "J.A. Tays: The Frontier Battalion's Forgotten Officer." *The Texas Ranger Dispatch Magazine.* Issue 7, Summer 2002. Waco, TX: The Texas Ranger Hall of Fame and Museum, 2002. 8 September 2015. (W)

____. *Salt Warriors: Insurgency on the Rio Grande*. College Station: Texas A&M University Press, 2008. (P)

Corcoran, Lillian H. "He brought the railroad to El Paso – The Story of Judge James P. Hague." *Password*. Vol. 1, No. 2 May 1956. (P)

Cox, C.C. "From Texas to California in 1849: The Diary of C.C. Cox." *Southwestern Historical Quarterly*. Vol. 29 No.2. (October, 1925) . (P)

Crawford, Charlotte. "The Border Meeting of Presidents Taft and Díaz." *Password* (1958) Vol. 3 (P)

Creelman, James. "President Díaz: Hero of the Americas." *Pearson's Magazine*. Vol. XIX No. 3 (March 1908) (P)

Crichton, Kyle S. *Law and Order Ltd.: The Rousing Life of Elfego Baca of New Mexico.* Santa Fe: New Mexican Publishing Corporation, 1928. (P)

Crippen, Robert B. "Celebration on the Border." Password (Fall 1984) (P)

Cumberland, Charles C. *Mexican Revolution: Genesis Under Madero.* Austin: University of Texas, 1952. (P)

Cunningham, Mary S. *The Woman's Club of El Paso: Its First Thirty Years*. El Paso: Texas Western Press, 1978. (P)

Cutter, William R. *New England Families: Genealogical and Memorial; A Record of the Achievements of Her People in the Making of Commonwealths and the Founding of a Nation. Vol. III.* New York: Lewis Historical Publishing Company, 1913. (W)

Davis, Margaret L. *Dark Side of Fortune: Triumph and Scandal in the Life of Oil Tycoon Edward L. Doheny*. Berkeley: University of California Press, 1998. (P)

Dawson, Ronald E. *Streetcars at the Past*: *The Story of the Mule Cars of El Paso*.
Vol. 1. Lincoln, NE: iUniverse, Inc., 2003. (P)

Devine, Dave. "Respect and Esteem: A Look back at Henry O. Flipper, A Tucsonan and West Point's first African American graduate." *Tucson Weekly.* February 16, 2006. (P)

de Wetter, Mardee B. *Watchtower on the Rio Grande: St. Clement's Church, El Paso, Texas 1870- 2008.* Mesilla Park, NM: The Institute of Historical Survey Foundation, 2012. (P)

______ "Revolutionary El Paso:1910-1917." *Password.* Vol. III. pp. 46-119. (P)

Deutsch, Hermann R. *The Incredible Yanqui: The Career of Lee Christmas.* Gretna, LA: Pelican Publishing Company, 2012. (P)

Dickey, Gretchen. "Downtown Opium Dens Attracted Many." *Borderlands*. (EPPC Libraries.) Vol. 21, 2002. Accessed 11 Dec. 2010. (W)

Dilliard, Irving. "Historian in Cowboy Boots: Jay Monaghan, 1893-1980." *Journal of the Illinois State Historical Society*. Vol. 74. No. 4 (Winter, 1981).

Dillon, Richard H. *Texas Argonauts: Isaac H. Duval and the California Gold Rush.* San Francisco: Book Club of California, 1987. (P)

D'Itri, Patricia Ward. *Damon Runyon.* Farmington, MI: Cengage Gale, 1982. (P)

Dobie, J. Frank. *Babicora.* Kansas City: American Hereford Journal, January 1, 1954. (P)

Eckhardt, E.C. "The Lost Epic: Henry O. Flipper, 10th Cavalry." *Texas Escapes.* Feb. 7, 2010. (W)

"El Paso." *The New International Encyclopaedia* Editors: Gilman, Daniel, et.al. Vol. VII. (New York: Dodd, Mead and Company, 1905.) Google Books. (W)

"El Paso". *Monthly Business Review.* Vol.36, No. 7.(Dallas: Federal Reserve Bank of Dallas, 1931.). (P)

"El Paso history is never dead." (2010, May 12). *El Paso Times*. 28 May 2010. (P)

Ely, Glen S. "What to Do About Texas?" *New Mexico Historical Review*. Vol. 85, No. 4. Fall 2010. (P)

Emery, William H. P. "The Jackass Mail Route of 1857-1858." *The American Philatelist.* May, 1983. (P)

Emerson, Edwin. *Madero of Mexico.* New Outlook (Alfred E. Smith, ed.) New York, 1911. Google books. (W)

Eppinga, Jane. *Henry Ossian Flipper: West Point's First Black Graduate*. Plano, TX: Republic of Texas Press, 1996. (P)

______. "Henry O. Flipper in the Court of Private Land Claims: The Arizona Career of West Pont's First Black Graduate." *The Journal of Arizona History*. vol. 36, Spring 1995. (P)

Ettinger, Patrick. *Imaginary Lines: Border Enforcement and the Origins of Undocumented Immigration, 1882-1930.* Austin: University of Texas Press, 2009. (P)

Faber, John. *Great News Photos and the Stories Behind Them*. New York: Dover, 1978. (P)

Farrar, Nancy. *The Chinese in El Paso*. El Paso: University of Texas at El Paso, 1972. (Southwestern Studies). (P)

Fenwick, Charles G. *The Neutrality Laws of the United States*. Washington: The Endowment, 1913. (P)

Flipper, Henry O. *Black Frontiersman: The Memoirs of Henry OL Flipper.* Compiled and edited by Theodore D. Harris. (Fort Worth: Texas Christian University Press, 1997. (P)

_______,*The Colored Cadet at West Point: Autobiography of Lieutenant Henry O. Flipper, U.S.A.* (Introduction by Quintard Taylor Jr.) Lincoln: University of Nebraska Press, 1998. (P)

Frantz, Edward. "A March of Triumph? Benjamin Harrison's Southern Tour and the Limits of Racial and Regional Reconciliation." *Indiana Magazine of History*. Vol. 100 No. 4.(2004), (P)

Freudenthal, Samuel. *El Paso Merchant and Civic Leader from 1880s Through the Mexican Revolution*. Southwestern Studies Monograph No. 11. El Paso,TX: Texas Western Press, 1965. (P)

Frost, H. Gordon. The Gentlemen's Club: The Story of Prostitution in El Paso. El Paso: Mangan Books, 1983. (P)

Fry, Sandra. *Remembering El Paso*. Nashville: Turner Publishing Company, 2010. (P)

Funkhouser, Barbara. *The Caregivers: El Paso's Medical History, 1898 – 1998.* El Paso Sundance Press, 1999. (P)

García, Mario T. *Desert Immigrants: The Mexicans of El Paso, 1880 – 1920.* (Yale Western Americana Series, 32.) New Haven: Yale University Press, 1981. (P)

García, Neftalí. *The Mexican Revolution: Legacy of Courage*. Bloomington, IN: Xlibris Corp., 2010. (P)

Gallucci, Alfred D. *James E. Birch: His Empire on Wheels - Volume I California Stage Company.* Yakima, WA: by author, 1989. (P)

Gardner, Mark L. *To Hell on Fast Horse: Billy the Kid, Pat Garrett, and the Epic Chase To Justice in the Old West.* New York: William Morrow, 2010. (P)

Garibaldi, Giuseppe. *A Toast to Rebellion*. New York: Bobbs-Merrill Company, 1935. (P)

Garrett, Pat F. *The Authentic Life of Billy the Kid: The Noted Desperado of the Southwest, A Faithful and Interesting Narrative.* Santa Fe: New Mexico Printing and Publishing Company, 1882. Available from gutenberg.net.au. (W)

Garnsey, Clarke H. " The Heralding the Union Depot." Password. Vol. XXXI. pp.103-110. (P)

Gia, Gilbert. "Presidential Visits to Bakersfield, 1880 and 1891." *Historic Bakersfield and Kern County.* (W)

Gibbons, Edward. *Floyd Gibbons: Your Headline Hunter.* New York: A Banner Book, 1953. (P)

Giddings, Emily Chase and Emmie Wheatley Mahon. "The Jackass Trail." *Password*. Vol. II, No. 3 (August 1957) (P)

Giddings, George H. *The Case of George H. Giddings, Contractor on the Overland Mail Route from San Antonio to San Diego.*(Washington, D.C.: H. Polkinhorn Publishers, 1860. (P)

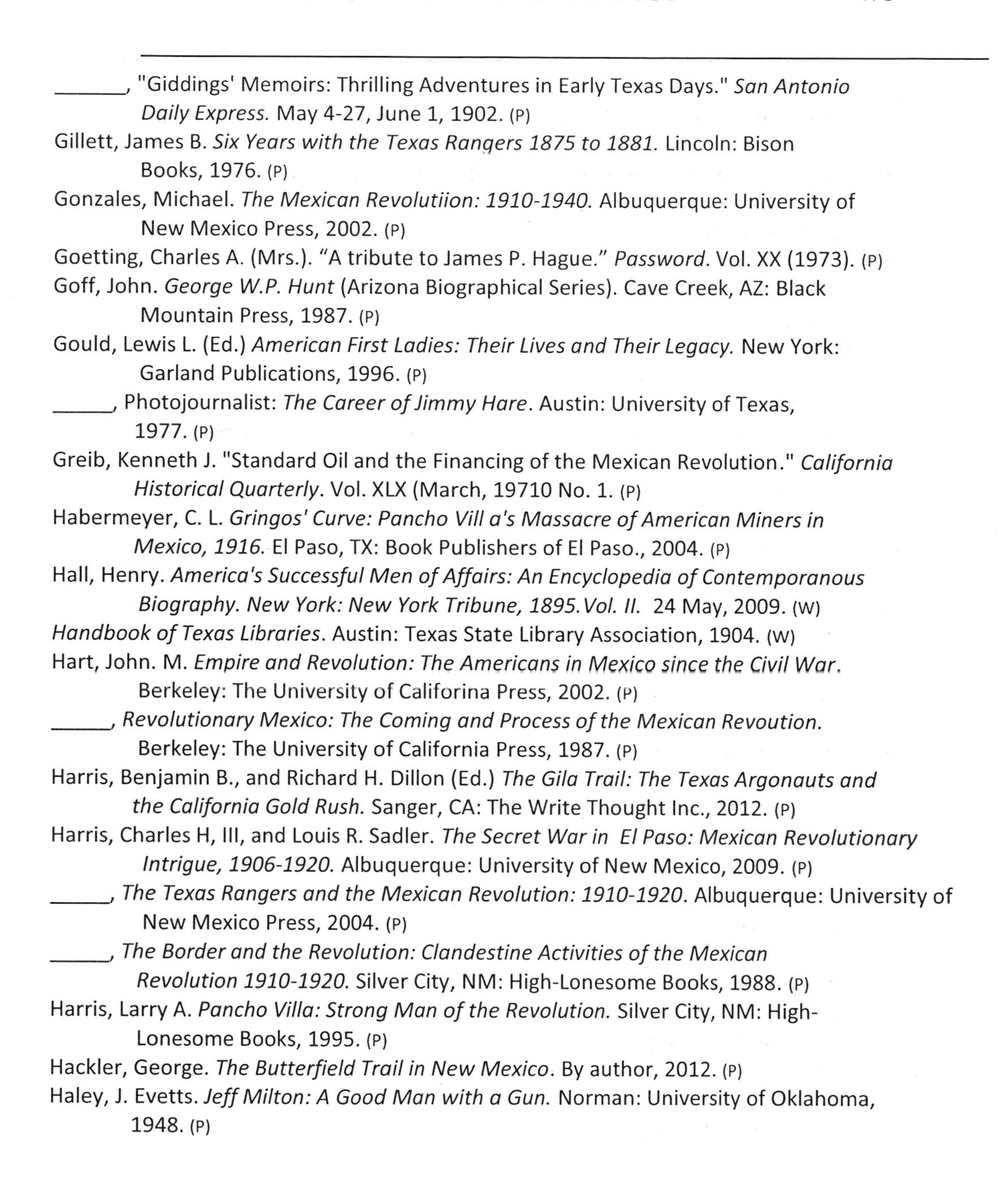

______, "Giddings' Memoirs: Thrilling Adventures in Early Texas Days." *San Antonio Daily Express.* May 4-27, June 1, 1902. (P)

Gillett, James B. *Six Years with the Texas Rangers 1875 to 1881.* Lincoln: Bison Books, 1976. (P)

Gonzales, Michael. *The Mexican Revolutiion: 1910-1940.* Albuquerque: University of New Mexico Press, 2002. (P)

Goetting, Charles A. (Mrs.). "A tribute to James P. Hague." *Password.* Vol. XX (1973). (P)

Goff, John. *George W.P. Hunt* (Arizona Biographical Series). Cave Creek, AZ: Black Mountain Press, 1987. (P)

Gould, Lewis L. (Ed.) *American First Ladies: Their Lives and Their Legacy.* New York: Garland Publications, 1996. (P)

_____, Photojournalist: *The Career of Jimmy Hare*. Austin: University of Texas, 1977. (P)

Greib, Kenneth J. "Standard Oil and the Financing of the Mexican Revolution." *California Historical Quarterly*. Vol. XLX (March, 19710 No. 1. (P)

Habermeyer, C. L. *Gringos' Curve: Pancho Vill a's Massacre of American Miners in Mexico, 1916.* El Paso, TX: Book Publishers of El Paso., 2004. (P)

Hall, Henry. *America's Successful Men of Affairs: An Encyclopedia of Contemporanous Biography. New York: New York Tribune, 1895.Vol. II.* 24 May, 2009. (W)

Handbook of Texas Libraries. Austin: Texas State Library Association, 1904. (W)

Hart, John. M. *Empire and Revolution: The Americans in Mexico since the Civil War.* Berkeley: The University of Califorina Press, 2002. (P)

_____, *Revolutionary Mexico: The Coming and Process of the Mexican Revoution.* Berkeley: The University of California Press, 1987. (P)

Harris, Benjamin B., and Richard H. Dillon (Ed.) *The Gila Trail: The Texas Argonauts and the California Gold Rush.* Sanger, CA: The Write Thought Inc., 2012. (P)

Harris, Charles H, III, and Louis R. Sadler. *The Secret War in El Paso: Mexican Revolutionary Intrigue, 1906-1920.* Albuquerque: University of New Mexico, 2009. (P)

_____, *The Texas Rangers and the Mexican Revolution: 1910-1920*. Albuquerque: University of New Mexico Press, 2004. (P)

_____, *The Border and the Revolution: Clandestine Activities of the Mexican Revolution 1910-1920.* Silver City, NM: High-Lonesome Books, 1988. (P)

Harris, Larry A. *Pancho Villa: Strong Man of the Revolution.* Silver City, NM: High-Lonesome Books, 1995. (P)

Hackler, George. *The Butterfield Trail in New Mexico*. By author, 2012. (P)

Haley, J. Evetts. *Jeff Milton: A Good Man with a Gun.* Norman: University of Oklahoma, 1948. (P)

Hamilton, Nancy. "Tribute to Ben Dowell." *Password.* Vol. XXXVIII. pp.16-20. (P)

______, *Ben Dowell: El Paso's First Mayor.* (Southwestern Studies No. 49) El Paso: Texas Western Press, 1976. (P)

Haverstock, Nathan A. *Fifty Years at the Front: The Life of War Correspondent Frederick Palmer*. Washington, DC: Brassey's, 1996. (P)

Hedges, Charles. *Speeches of Benjamin Harrison: Twenty-third President of the United States.* New York: John Lovell Company, 1892. (P) Currently available as a reprint from Gray Rabbit Publishing, Brooklyn, New York. (2014)

Helmich, Mary. "The Butterfield Overland Mail Company." (California Department of Parks) 16 September 2012. (W)

Henderson, Peter V. *In the Absence of Don Porfirio: Francisco León de la Barra*. Wilmington, DE: 2000. (P)

Henn, Nora. "The House on Golden Hill Terrace." *Password.* Vol. XXXVII. pp.127-136. (P)

Hernández, Kelly Lytle. *Migra!: A History of the U.S. Border Patro*l. Berkeley: University of California Press, 2010. (P)

Hervey, James M. "The Assassination of Pat Garrett." *True West Magazine*. March-April 1961. (P)

"Henry K. Sheldon." *Biographical Record of Northeastern Pennsylvania including the counties of Susquehanna, Wayne, Pike and Monroe.* Chicago: J.H. Beers & Co., 1900. Google Books. (W)

Hilton, Conrad. *Be My Guest*. Englewood Clifts: Printice Hall, 1957. (P)

Holden, Henry M. *FBI 100 Years: An Unofficial History.* Minneapolis: Zenith Press, 2008. (P)

Hooten, W.J. (1944, December 16.) "Everyday Events." El Paso Times. (P)

Hoyt, Edwin P. *A Gentleman of Broadway: The Story of Damon Runyon.* Boston: Little, Brown, 1964.

Hudnall, Robert K. *No Safe Haven: Homeland Insecurity.* El Paso: Omega Press, 2004. (P)

Humphrey, David C. "Prostitution." *Handbook of Texas Online*. August 2008. (W)

Hunt, Frazier. *Cap Mossman: Last of the Great Cowmen.* New York: Hastings House, 1951. (P)

Hurst, James W. "The Death of Pat Garrett." *Southernnewmexico.com* July 17, 2003. (W)

______. *Pancho Villa and Blackjack Pershing: The Punitive Expedition in Mexico.* Westport, CT: Praeger, 2008. (P)

Irvin, Teresa. *Let the Tail Go with the Hide: The Story of Ben F. Williams.* Bloomington, IN: UL Publishing, 2001. (P)

Isaacks, S.J. (1938, March 3) "Saloon on skyscraper site of El Paso 25 years ago." El Paso Herald Post, p.16. (P)

"Italy: Garibaldi's Conversion." *Time.* April 15, 1940 (Vol. 35, No. 16): 30. (P)

Jackson, Ken. "Joe Brown's murder trial." *El Paso Bar Journal*. October/November 2012.
Jaker, Bill, et.al. *Airwaves of New York: Illustrated Histories of 156 AM Stations in the Metropolitan Area, 1921-1922*. Jefferson, NC: McFarland Press, 1998. (P)
Jandura, Greg. "The Pan-American Exposition 1901. Chapter 1, McKinley and Prosperity" http://trainweb.org/wnyrhs/panam1901.htm (W)
Jeffreys-Jones, Rhodri. *The FBI: A History*. New Haven: Yale University Press, 2007. (P)
Johannsen, Robert W. *To The Halls of the Montezuma: The Mexican War in the American Imagination.* New York: Oxford University Press, 1985. (P)
Johnson, Barry C. *Flipper's Dismissal: The Ruin OF Lt. Henry O. Flipper, U.S.A. First Coloured Graduate of West Point.* Privately printed, 1980. (P)
Johnson, David N. *Madero in Texas.* San Antonio: Corona Publishing Company, 2001. (P)
Johnson, William W. *Heroic Mexico: The Violent Emergence of a Modern Nation*. Garden City, NY: Doubleday and Company, 1968. (P)
Jones, Harriot H. (Ed.) *El Paso: A Centennial Portrait. A Project of the El Paso County Historical Society 1973 Centennial.* El Paso: Superior Printing, 1972. (P)
Jowett, P., and A. de Quesada. *The Mexican Revolution 1910-20*. New York: Osprey Publishing, 2006. (P)
Kahn, E.J. "The Silver Spade: a book review." *The New Yorker*, November 24, 1956. (P)
Katz, Friedrich. *The Life and Times of Pancho Villa.* Palo Alto: Stanford University Press, 1998. (P)
______, *The Secret War in Mexico: Europe, The United States and the Mexican Revolution.* Chicago: The University of Chicago Press, 1981. (P)
Kelly, Bill. "Pat Garrett: The West's Unluckiest Lawman." *Desert USA*. 2009. (W)
Kemper, Steve. *A Splendid Savage: The Restless Life of Frederick Russell Burnham.* New York: W.W. Norton, 2016. (P)
Kessler, Ronald. *The Bureau: The Secret History of the FBI*. New York: St. Martin's Press, 2012. (P)
Knight, Oliver. *Life and Manners in the Frontier Army.* Norman: University of Oklahoma, 1978. (P)
Krauze, Enrique. *Mexico: Biography of Power, A History of Modern Mexico, 1810-1996.* Translated by Hank Heifetz. New York: Harper-Collins, 1997. (P)
Krauss, Erich, and Alex Pacheco. *On The Line: Inside the U.S. Border Patrol*. New York: Citadel Press, 2004. (P)
Kohout, Martin. "Ponce de León, Juan Maria." *Handbook of Texas Online*. 5 March 2015. (W)
Kuhn, Irene C. *Assigned to Adventure*. Philadelphia: Lippincott, 1938. (P)

La Boz, Dan. *Edward L. Doheny: Petroleum, Power, and Politics in the United States and Mexico.* New York: Praeger Publishers, 1991. (P)

Lansford, William Douglas. *Pancho Villa*. Los Angeles: Sherbourne Press, 1965. (P)

Lay, Shawn. (Ed.) *The Invisible Empire in the West: Toward a New Historical Appraisal of the Ku Klux Klan of the 1920s*. Urbana: The University of Illinois, 2004. (P)

_____, *War, Revolution and the Ku Klux Klan: A Study of the Intolerance in a Border City.* El Paso: Texas Western Press, 1985. (P)

Langley, Lester D. and T. Schoonover. *The Banana Men: American Mercenaries & Entrepreneurs in Central America, 1880-1930*. Lexington: The University of Kentucky, 1995. (P)

Laskin, David. The Long Way Home: An American Journey from Ellis Island to the Great War. New York: HarperCollins Publishers, 2010. (P)

Latham, William I. "Early El Paso Churches." *Password* Vol. XXVII. pp. 99-114. (P)

______ "Remarks." *Password*. Vol. XXII, p. 182. (P)

Lea, James D. "President McKinley's visit to El Paso." *Password.* Vol. XLI. pp. 128-134. (P)

Leach, Joseph. *Sun Country Banke: The Life and the Bank of Samuel Doak Young. El Paso: Mangan Books,* 1989. (P)

Ledbetter, Suzann. *Shady Ladies: Nineteen Surprising and Rebellious American Women.* New York: Forge Books, 2006. (P)

Lee, Erika. *At America's Gate: Chinese Immigration During the Exclusion Era, 1892-1943.* Chapel Hill, NC, 2003. (P)

Leibson, Art.(1959, July 26). " 'Uncle Henry' Kelly ruled El Paso politics 30 years." *El Paso Times*. (P)

______, (1989, April 23). "If you think this mayor strong, C.E. Kelly ruled with iron fist." *El Paso Times*. (P)

______, *Sam Dreben: "The Fighting Jew."* Tucson: Westernlore Press, 1996. (P)

Lewis, W. David. *Eddie Rickenbacker: An American Hero in the Twentieth Century.* Baltimore: John Hopkins University Press, 2005. (P)

Krauze, Enrique. *Mexico: Biography of Power. A History of Modern Mexico, 1810-1996.* New York: Harper-Collins Publishers., 1997. (P)

MacCallum, Esther D. *The History of St. Clement's Church, El Paso: 1870-1925*. El Paso: The McMath Company, 1925. (P)

McClure, Alexander K. *The Authentic Life of William McKinley: Our Third Martyr President together with a Life Sketch of Theodore Roosevelt*. Washington, D.C.: W.E. Scull, 1901. (P)

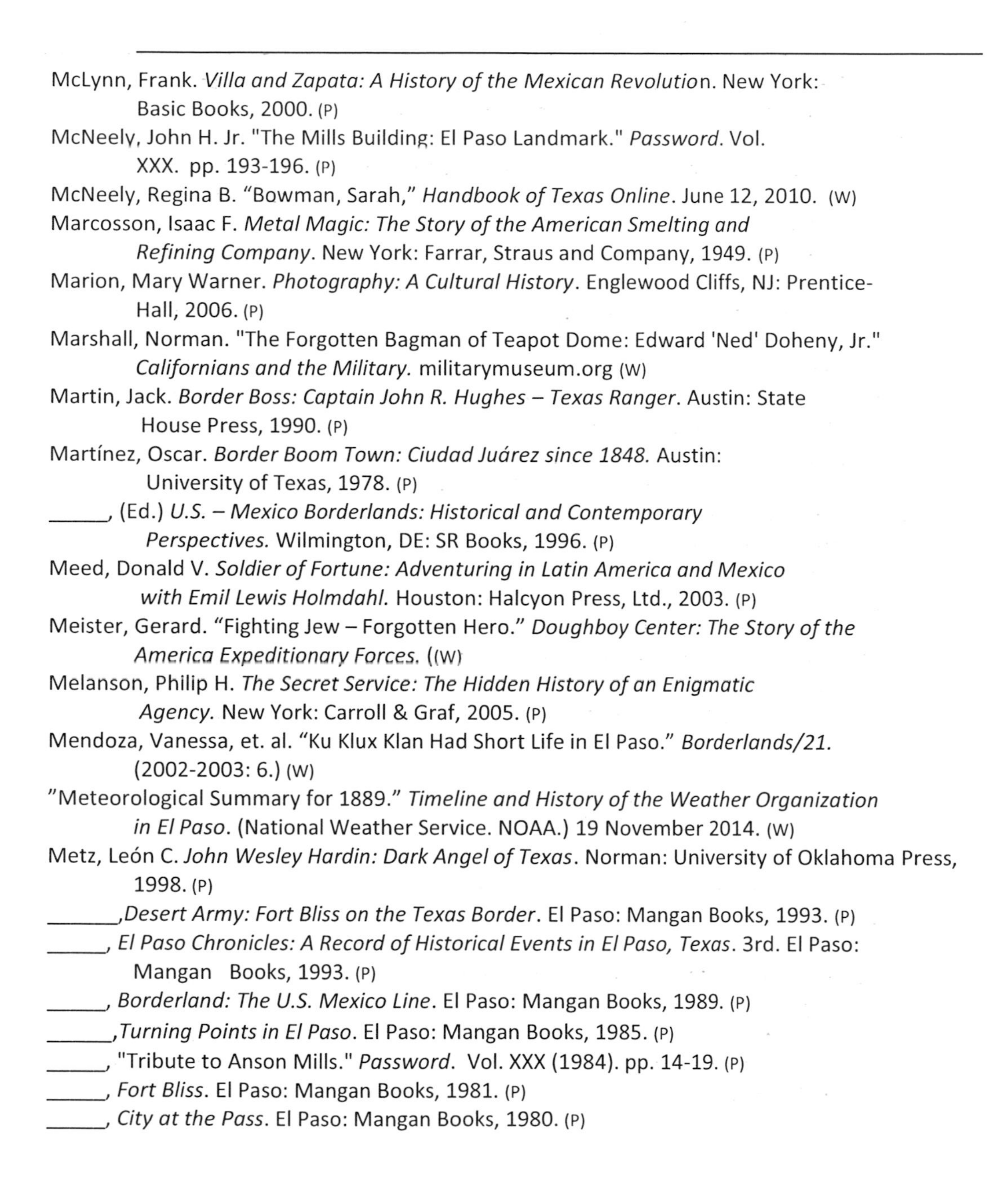

McLynn, Frank. *Villa and Zapata: A History of the Mexican Revolution*. New York: Basic Books, 2000. (P)

McNeely, John H. Jr. "The Mills Building: El Paso Landmark." *Password*. Vol. XXX. pp. 193-196. (P)

McNeely, Regina B. "Bowman, Sarah," *Handbook of Texas Online*. June 12, 2010. (W)

Marcosson, Isaac F. *Metal Magic: The Story of the American Smelting and Refining Company*. New York: Farrar, Straus and Company, 1949. (P)

Marion, Mary Warner. *Photography: A Cultural History*. Englewood Cliffs, NJ: Prentice-Hall, 2006. (P)

Marshall, Norman. "The Forgotten Bagman of Teapot Dome: Edward 'Ned' Doheny, Jr." *Californians and the Military.* militarymuseum.org (W)

Martin, Jack. *Border Boss: Captain John R. Hughes – Texas Ranger*. Austin: State House Press, 1990. (P)

Martínez, Oscar. *Border Boom Town: Ciudad Juárez since 1848.* Austin: University of Texas, 1978. (P)

_____, (Ed.) *U.S. – Mexico Borderlands: Historical and Contemporary Perspectives.* Wilmington, DE: SR Books, 1996. (P)

Meed, Donald V. *Soldier of Fortune: Adventuring in Latin America and Mexico with Emil Lewis Holmdahl.* Houston: Halcyon Press, Ltd., 2003. (P)

Meister, Gerard. "Fighting Jew – Forgotten Hero." *Doughboy Center: The Story of the America Expeditionary Forces.* ((W)

Melanson, Philip H. *The Secret Service: The Hidden History of an Enigmatic Agency.* New York: Carroll & Graf, 2005. (P)

Mendoza, Vanessa, et. al. "Ku Klux Klan Had Short Life in El Paso." *Borderlands/21.* (2002-2003: 6.) (W)

"Meteorological Summary for 1889." *Timeline and History of the Weather Organization in El Paso*. (National Weather Service. NOAA.) 19 November 2014. (W)

Metz, León C. *John Wesley Hardin: Dark Angel of Texas*. Norman: University of Oklahoma Press, 1998. (P)

______,*Desert Army: Fort Bliss on the Texas Border*. El Paso: Mangan Books, 1993. (P)

_____, *El Paso Chronicles: A Record of Historical Events in El Paso, Texas*. 3rd. El Paso: Mangan Books, 1993. (P)

_____, *Borderland: The U.S. Mexico Line*. El Paso: Mangan Books, 1989. (P)

______,*Turning Points in El Paso*. El Paso: Mangan Books, 1985. (P)

_____, "Tribute to Anson Mills." *Password*. Vol. XXX (1984). pp. 14-19. (P)

_____, *Fort Bliss*. El Paso: Mangan Books, 1981. (P)

_____, *City at the Pass*. El Paso: Mangan Books, 1980. (P)

______, *The Shooters*. El Paso: Mangan Books, 1976. (P)
______, *Pat Garrett: The Story of a Western Lawman*. Norman: University of Oklahoma Press. 1974. (P)
______, *Dallas Stoudenmire: El Paso Marshal*. El Paso: Mangan Books, 1969. (P)
______, *John Selman: Texas Gunfighter*. El Paso: Mangan Books, 1966. (P)
Meyer, Michael C. *Mexican Rebel: Pascual Orozco and the Mexican Revolution 1910-1915.* Lincoln: University of Nebraska Press, 1967. (P)
Meyer, Michael C., and William L. Sherman. *The Course of Mexican History.* Seventh Edition. New York: Oxford University Press, 2003. (P)
Middagh, John. *Frontier Newspaper: The El Paso Times.* El Paso: Texas Western Press, 1958. (P)
Milholland, David. "John Reed in Mexico & Latin America." *Oregon Cultural Heritage Commission.* 12 April 2016. (W)
Miller, Carol P. "Resisting the Ku Klux Klan in El Paso." *Password* Vol. 54, No.1 (Spring 2009). (P)
Miles, Susan, and Mary Bain Spence, "Ficklin, Benjamin Franklin," *Handbook of Texas on Line.* June 12, 2010. 15 September 2015. (W)
Mills, Anson. *Plat of the Town of El Paso*. El Paso: Anson Mills, 1859. (P)
______, *My Story*. Washington: Press of Byron S. Adams, 1918. (P)
Mills, W.W. *Forty Years at El Paso 1858 - 1898: Recollections of War, Politics, Adventure, Events, Narratives, Sketches, Etc*. Washington: Library of Congress, 1901. (P).
Milton, Joyce. *The Yellow Kids: Foreign Correspondents in the Heyday of Yellow Journalism.* New York: Harper & Row, 1989. (P)
Mix, Olive Stokes, with Eric Heath. *The Fabulous Tom Mix*. Englewood Cliffs: Prentice-Hall, 1957. (P)
Mix, Paul E. *The Life and Legend of Tom Mix*. New York: A.S. Barnes and Company, 1972. (P)
Monaghan, Jay. *Schoolboy, Cowboy, Mexican Spy.* Berkeley: University of California Press, 1977. (P)
Morgenthaler, Jefferson. *The River Has Never Divided Us: A Border History of La Junta de los Rios.* Austin: University of Texas, 2004. (P)
Morris, J.A. *Deadline Every Minute: The Story of the the United Press.* Garden City, New York: Doubleday and Company, 1957. (P)
Morris, Montrose. . "Walkabout: The Parfitt Brothers, part 2. *Brownstoner: Brooklyn Inside and Out.* 28 Oct. 2010. 14 Feb. 2011. (W)
Morris, Ray, Jr. *Ambrose Bierce: Alone in Bad Company*. New York: Oxford University Press, 1995. (P)

Mullin, Robert N. (ed.) *Maurice Garland Fulton's History of the Lincoln County War.* Tucson: University of Arizona Press, 1968. (P)

. *Stagecoach Pioneers of the Southwest*. (Southwestern Studies Monograph No. 71.) El Paso: Texas Western Press, 1976. (P)

Murphy, James R. *Images of America: El Paso 1850-1950.* San Francisco: Arcadia Publishing Co., 2009. (P)

Neal, Dorothy J. *The Lodge, 1899-1969, Cloudcroft, New Mexico*. Alamogordo Printing Company, 1969. (P)

Newfield, Jack, and Mark Jacobson. (Eds.) *American Monsters: 44 Rats, Blackhats, and Plutocrats*. New York: Thunder's Mouth Press, 2004. (P)

"Norman M. Walker, Correspondent." 1 July 2009. (W)

Nugent, Daniel. *Spent Cartridges of Revolution: An Anthropological History of Namiquipa, Chihuahua.* Chicago: The University of Chicago, 1993. (P)

Nuñez, Aurora and Amanda Taylor. "Otis A. Aultman captured border history in pictures." *Borderlands/21.* 1 October 2009. (W)

Obituary Record of Graduates of Yale University. New Haven, CT: Yale University, June 1895. (P)

O'Hea, Patrick. *Reminiscences of the Mexican Revolution.* Mexico, D.F.: Centro Anglo-Mexicano Del Libro, 1966. (P)

O'Neal, Bill. *Encyclopedia of Western Gunfighters*. Norman: University of Oklahoma, 1979. (P)

O'Reilly, Edward "Tex" S. *Roving and Fighting: Adventure Under Four Flags*. New York: The Century Company, 1918. (P)

Orozco, Nora. "Tom Lea, Jr.: El Paso Lawyer and Mayor." *El Paso Bar Journal*. April 2008. pp. 13-15. (P)

Owen, Gordon R. *The Two Alberts: Fountain and Fall*. Las Cruces, NM: Yucca Tree Press, 1996. (P)

Packard, Jerrold. *The Lincolns in the White House: Four Years that Shattered a Family.* New York: St. Martin's Press, 2013. (P)

Perales, Monica. *Smeltertown: Making and Remembering a Southwest Border Community*. Chapel Hill: The University of North Carolina Press, 2010. (P)

Perkins, Clifford Alan, and C. L. Sonnichsen. *Border Patrol: With the U.S. Immigration Service on the Mexican Boundary 1910-1954.* El Paso: Texas Western Press, 1978. (P)

Perry, John. *Pershing: Commander of the Great War*. Nashville: Thomas Nelson, 2011 (P)

______. *Jack London: An American Myth*. Chicago: Nelson-Hall, 1981. (P)

Percy, Frederick A., " El Sabio Sembrador, Vol. 1 No. 3." In Rex W. Strickland's *El Paso in 1854.* 1968. (P)

Peterson, Jessie, and Thelma C. Knoles (eds.) *Pancho Villa: Intimate Recollections by People Who Knew Him.* New York: Hastings House Publishers, 1977. (P)

Petro, Joseph. *Standing Next to History: An Agent's Life Inside the Secret Service.* New York: Thomas Dunne Books, 2005. (P)

Phelps, Oliver S., and A.T. Servin. *The Phelps Family of America and their English Ancestors, with Copies of Wills, Deeds, Letters, and other Interesting Papers, Coats of Arms and Valuable Records.* Nabu Public Domain Reprints, n.d. (P)

Pierce, Burtram Orndorff and Alzina Orndorff Gay. "Mama De: Tower Builder." *Password*, Vol. XVIII (1973). (P)

Plat of the Town of El Paso. Anson Mills, Surveyor. Jan-Feb. 1859. Special Collections, University of Texas at El Paso. (P)

Porter, Eugene O. "From Austin to El Paso in 1873: A Saga of the Coldwell Family." *Password.* Vol. IX, No. 2. (P)

______. Lord Beresford and Lady Flo. Southwestern Studies Monograph No. 25. El Paso: Texas Western Press, 1970. (P)

Portrait and Biographical Record of Arizona: Commemorating the Achievements of Citizens Who Have Contributed to the Progress of Arizona and the Development of its Resources. Chicago: Chapman Publishing Company, 1901. (P)

Prendergast, Simon. "Personnel of El Banco Commercial." *Paper Money of Chihuahua* (W)

Prestwood, Nadine H. "Life in the 1880's in El Paso." *Password* Vol. XI (1966), 162-169. (P)

Rafuse, Ethan S. *McClellan's War: The Failure of Moderation in the Struggle for the Union.* (Bloomington: Indiana University Press, 2011. (P)

Rak, Mary Kidder. *Border Patrol*. New York: Houghton-Mifflin, 1938. (P)

Randall, David. *The Great Reporters*. London: Pluto Press, 2005. (P)

Randall, Charles and Debra Adleman. *Reminiscences: The Russell Estate at Silver Lake*. By author, 2007. (P)

Rasmussen, Cecilia. *L A Unconventional: the men and women who did LA their way.* Los Angeles: The Los Angeles Times Co., 1998. (P)

Rayner, Richard. *A Bright and Guilty Place: Murder, Corruption, and L.A.'s Scandalous Coming of Age*. New York: Doubleday, 2009. (P)

Reed, John. *Insurgent Mexico.* New York: International Publishers, 1969. (P)

Reyes, Daniel et al. "Frontera Settlement." *Historical Markers Project*. (El Paso: EPCC Libraries, 2003.) 3 March 2014. (W)

Richardson, Tracy. (as told to Meigs Frost) "A Soldier of Fortune Story: Adventures of the Greatest Adventurer of All the Yanks Who Have Written Fantastic History in Latin American." *Liberty Magazine*: *A Weekly for Everybody* Vol. 2 No. 23, 24, 26, 29, 31. October 10, 17,31. Nov. 21, Dec 5, 1925. (P)

Riley, Carroll L. *Rio del Norte: People of the Upper Rio Grande from Earliest Times to the Pueblo Revolt.* Salt Lake City: University of Utah Press, 1995. (P)

Robinson, Charles M. III. *The Fall of a Black Army Officer: The Racism and the Myth of Henry O. Flipper.* Norman, OK: University of Oklahoma Press, 2008. (P)

______, *The Court Martial of Lieutenant Henry Flipper.* Southwestern Studies No. 100. El Paso: Texas Western Press, 1994. (P)

Romo, David D. *Ringside Seat to a Revolution: An Underground Cultural History of El Paso and Juárez 1893-1913.* El Paso: Cinco Puntos Press, 2005. (P)

Rosales, F. Arturo. *¡Pobre Raza!: Violence, Justice, and Mobilization Among Mexico Lindo Immigrants, 1900-1938.* Austin: University of Texas, 1999. (P)

Rose, Temi. "Change over time: El Paso, Texas through the window of Sanborn Maps and City Directories 1883-1920." 16 August 2009. (W)

Rosen, Hymer E. "Sam Dreben – Warrior, Patriot, Hero." *Jews in the Wild West.* (Lathrup Village, MI: Jewish- American History Foundation.) (W)

Ross, Ishbel. *An American Family: The Tafts, 1678 to 1964*. Cleveland: World Publishing Company, 1964. (P)

Ross, Peter and William Smith Pelletreau. *History of Long Island: from its earliest settlement to the present time.* New York: Lewis Publishing Company, 1903. Google Books. (W)

Ross, Stanley R. *Francisco I. Madero: Apostle of Mexican Democracy*. New York: Columbia University Press, 1955. (P)

Roth, Mitchel. *Historical Dictionary of War Journalism*. Westport, CT:Greenwood Press, 1997. (P)

Ruíz, Ramón E. *Triumphs and Tragedy: A History of the Mexican People.* New York: W.W. Norton, 1992. (P)

_____, *The Great Rebellion: Mexico 1905-1924.* New York: W.W. Norton, 1980. (P)

Runyon, Damon, Jr. *Father's Footsteps: The Story of Damon Runyon By His Son*. New York: Random House, 1953. (P)

Sanborn Maps of Texas. Austin: University of Texas, Perry-Castañeda Library Map Collection, El Paso. (W)

Sandwich, Brian. *The Great Western: Legendary Lady of the Southwest.* Southwestern Studies No. 94, El Paso: Texas Western Press, 1991. (P)

Scheina, Robert L. *Villa: Soldier of the Mexican Revolution*. Dulles, VA: Brassey's Inc., 2004. (P)

Schell, William, Jr. *Integral Outsiders: The American Colony in Mexico City, 1876 – 1911*. Wilmington, DE: SR Books, 2001. (P)

Schooris, Earl. *The Life and Times of Mexico*. New York: W.W. Norton, 2004. (P)

Schneider, Beth. "Giddings, George Henry." *Handbook of Texas Online*. 28 April, 2011. (W)

Schwantes, Carlos A. *Vision & Enterprise: Exploring the History of Phelps Dodge Corporation.* Tucson: The University of Arizona Press, 2000. (P)

Scott, Hugh L. *Some Memories of a Soldier.* New York: The Century Co. , 1928. (P)

Selcer, Richard. (Ed.) *Legendary Watering Holes: The Saloons That Made Texas Famous.* College Station: Texas A & M University Press, 2004. (P).

Shandorf, Peter. "Violent days in old El Paso." *Password* Vol. XV (1970). 73-74. (P)

Shannon, Mary K. "Joseph Magoffin: El Paso Pioneer." *Password.* Vol. XLIV (1944). 158-172. (P)

Shapleigh, Ballard C. "¡Viva Los Licenciados!" *El Paso Bar Journal*. October/November 2010. Part I. (W)

Shaw, Henry W. *Everybody's Friend, or Josh Billings's Encyclopedia and Proverbial Philosophy of Wit and Humor.* Hartford, CT: American Publishing Company, 1874. (P)

Sheldon & Co.'s. Business or Advertising Directory; Containing the Cards, Circulars, and Advertisements of the Principal firm of the cities of New York, Boston, Philadelphia, Baltimore, etc. etc. A book of Reference. New York: John F. Trow & Company, 1845. 9 September 2009. Google Books. (W)

Shepherd, William G. *Confessions of a War Correspondent.* New York: Harper & Brothers Publishers, 1917. (P)

Shirley, Glenn. *Shotgun for Hire: The Story of "Deacon" Jim Miller, Killer of Pat Garrett*. Norman: University of Oklahoma Press, 1970. (P)

Simmons, Marc. *The Last Conquistador: Juan de Oñate and the Settling of the Far Southwest.* Norman: University of Oklahoma Press, 1991. (P)

Smith, Gene. *Until the last Trumpet Sounds: The Life of General of Armies, John J. Pershing* New York: Wiley and Sons, 1998. (P)

Smith, Cornelius C., Jr. *Emilio Kosterlitzky: Eagle of Sonora and the Southwest Border.* Glendale, CA: The Arthur H. Clark Company, 1970. (P)

Smith, Michael M. "The Mexican Secret Service in the United States." *The Americas: A Quarterly Review of Inter-American Cultural History.* (Academy of American Franciscan History). Vol. 59, No.1 (July 2002), pp.65-85. (P)

Smith, Wilda M., and Eleanor A. Bogart. *The Wars of Peggy Hull: The Life and Times of a War Correspondent.* El Paso: Texas Western Press, 1991. (P)

Smythe, Donald. *Pershing: General of the Armies*. Bloomington, IN: Indiana University Press, 1986. (P)

Sonnichsen, C. L. *Tularosa: Last of the Frontier West.* Albuquerque: The University of New Mexico, 1980. (P)

_____, *Colonel Greene and the Copper Skyrocket.* Tucson: University of ArizonaPress, 1976. (P)

_____, and M.G. McKinney. *The State National Since 1881: The Pioneer Bank of El Paso.* El Paso: Texas Western Press, 1971. (P)

_____, and M.G. McKinney. "El Paso – from War to Depression." *The Southwest Historical Quarterly*. Vol. 74, No. 3.(January 1971). (P)

_____, *Pass of the North: Four Centuries on the Rio Grande.* El Paso: Texas Western Press, 1968. (P)

_____,*The Southwest in Life and Literature.* New York: The Devin-Adair Company, 1962(P)

Spellen, Suzanne. "Walkabout: Parfitt Brothers, Architects." *Brownstoner: Brooklyn Inside and Out.* (26 Oct. 2010.) 12 Dec 2012. (W)

Spellman, Paul N. *Captain John H. Rogers, Texas Rangers*. Denton: The University of North Texas Press, 2003. (P)

Spier, Wener et. al. "Tuberculosis: The biginnings of El Paso as a medical center." *Password.* XLII (1997). pp. 107-119. (P)

Starr, Kevin and Richard Orsi (eds.) *Rooted in Barbarous Soil: People, Culture, and Community in Gold Rush California*. Berkeley: University of Califiorina Press, 2000. (P)

Sterling, William W. *Trails and Trials of a Texas Ranger*. Norman: University of Oklahoma Press, 1969. (P)

Stratton, David H. *Tempest over Teapot Dome: The Story of Albert B. Fall.* Norman: University of Oklahoma, 1998. (P)

Strickland, Rex W. *Six Who Came to El Paso: Pioneers of the 1840's.* El Paso: Texas Western Press, 1963. (P)

_____, *El Paso in 1854*. El Paso: Texas Western Press, 1969. (P)

Suhler, R.A. "Ben Williams, Lawman." *Password.* Vol.XXVII (1992). pp. 19-25. (P)

Sweet, Ellen L., and Lynne Newell. *Historic Stage Routes of San Diego County*. Charleston, SC: Arcadia Publishing, 2011. (P)

Tarleton, John. "The Mexican Revolution." *John Tarleton's Brief, Irreverent History of Mexico* (1997). 20 Feb 2007. (W)

Taylor, Lawrence D. "The Great Adventure: Mercenaries in the Mexican Revolution, 1910-1915." *The Americas.* Vol. 43, no. 1 (July 1986) (P)

Thiel, J. Homer. "In Search of *El Presidio de Tucson*" Official Website of the City of Tucson. Accessed 11 Mar. 2016. (W)

"The Jackass Mail and Butterfield Line." *The Southern California Rancher*. January, 1957. (P)

Timmons, W.H. *James Wiley Magoffin: Don Santiago – El Paso Pioneer.* (Southwestern Studies Monograph No. 106.) El Paso: Texas Western Press, 1999. (P)

_____, *El Paso: A Borderlands History*. El Paso: Texas Western Press, 1990. (P)

_____, (Ed.) *Four Centuries at the Pass: A New History of El Paso on its 400th Birthday*. El Paso: The City of El Paso Arts Resources Department, 1980. (P)

Thord-Gray, I. *Gringo Rebel: Mexico 1913-1914.* Coral Gables: University of Miami Press, 1960. (P)

Thomson, Janice. *Mercenaries, Pirates, and Sovereigns.* Princeton, NJ: Princeton University Press, 1996. (P)

Tompkins, Frank. *Chasing Villa: The Last Campaign of the U.S. Cavalry*. Harrisburg, PA: Military Service Publishing Company, 1934. (P)

Torok, George. "Historical Narrative: Caples Building Site." *National Endowment for the Humanities Historical Markers Project.* El Paso: El Paso Community College/20. 12 September 2008. (W)

Trevizo, Jacqueline."1880s Brought First Theaters to Town." *Borderlands*. (EPPC Libraries.) Vol. 19, 2000. (W)

Tuck, Jim. *Pancho Villa and John Reed: Two Faces of Romantic Revolution.* Tucson: The University of Arizona Press, 1984. (P)

Truett, Samuel. "A Mexican Cossack in Southern California." *Huntington Frontiers*. (Huntington Library), Fall/Winter 2005. (P)

Turner, John Kenneth. *Barbarous Mexico*. Austin: University of Texas, 1969. (P)

Turner, Timothy G. *Bullets, Bottles and Gardenias.* Dallas: South-West Press, 1935. (P)

Tweedie, E.A., and Dolores Butterfield. "The Downfall of Díaz: Mexico Plunges into Revolution" (1911). *The Great Events by Famous Historians* (Charles F. Horne, ed.) Vol. XXI. London: The National Alumni, 1919. (P)

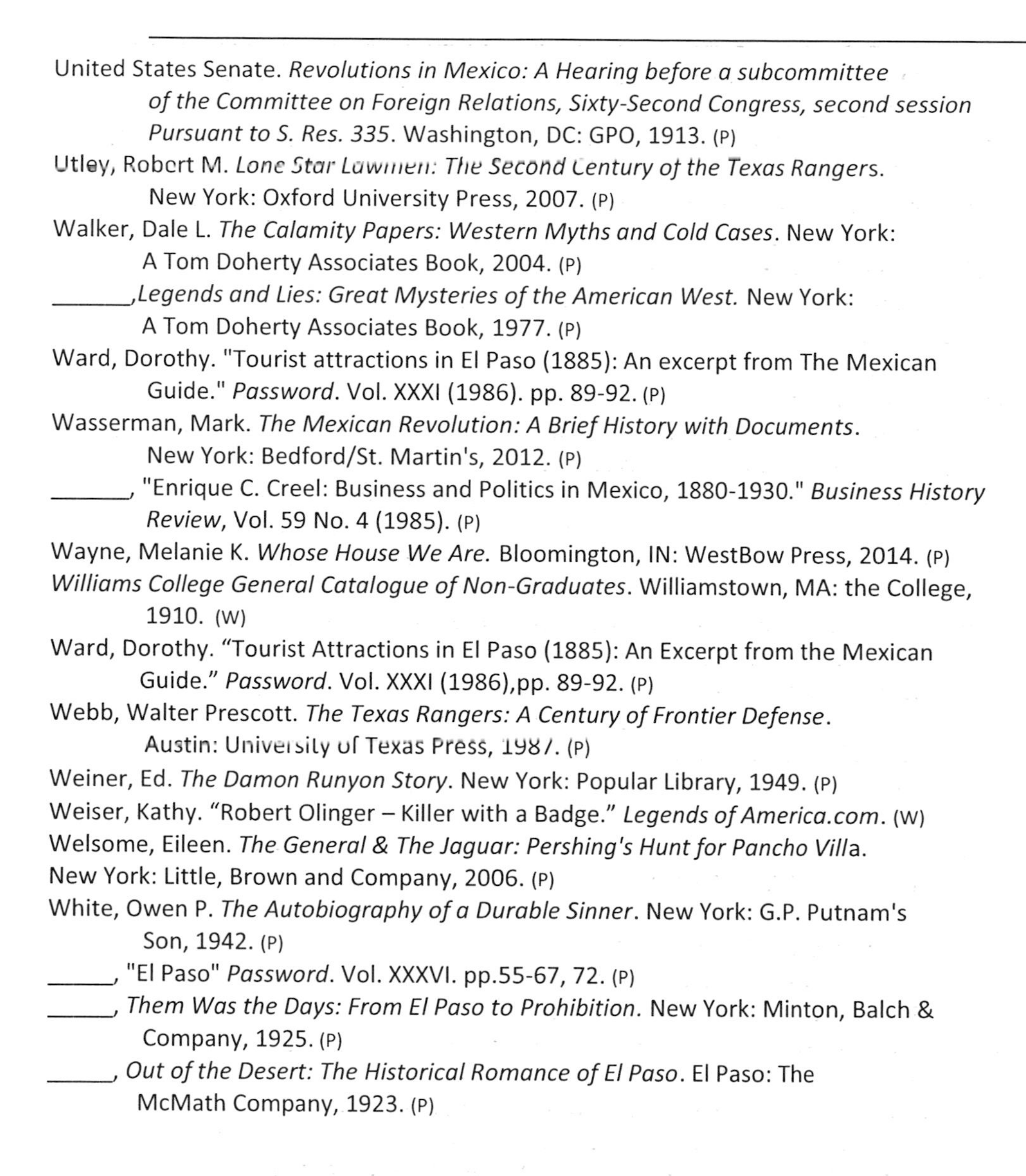

United States Senate. *Revolutions in Mexico: A Hearing before a subcommittee of the Committee on Foreign Relations, Sixty-Second Congress, second session Pursuant to S. Res. 335*. Washington, DC: GPO, 1913. (P)

Utley, Robert M. *Lone Star Lawmen: The Second Century of the Texas Rangers*. New York: Oxford University Press, 2007. (P)

Walker, Dale L. *The Calamity Papers: Western Myths and Cold Cases*. New York: A Tom Doherty Associates Book, 2004. (P)

_______,*Legends and Lies: Great Mysteries of the American West.* New York: A Tom Doherty Associates Book, 1977. (P)

Ward, Dorothy. "Tourist attractions in El Paso (1885): An excerpt from The Mexican Guide." *Password*. Vol. XXXI (1986). pp. 89-92. (P)

Wasserman, Mark. *The Mexican Revolution: A Brief History with Documents*. New York: Bedford/St. Martin's, 2012. (P)

_______, "Enrique C. Creel: Business and Politics in Mexico, 1880-1930." *Business History Review*, Vol. 59 No. 4 (1985). (P)

Wayne, Melanie K. *Whose House We Are.* Bloomington, IN: WestBow Press, 2014. (P)

Williams College General Catalogue of Non-Graduates. Williamstown, MA: the College, 1910. (W)

Ward, Dorothy. "Tourist Attractions in El Paso (1885): An Excerpt from the Mexican Guide." *Password*. Vol. XXXI (1986),pp. 89-92. (P)

Webb, Walter Prescott. *The Texas Rangers: A Century of Frontier Defense*. Austin: University of Texas Press, 1987. (P)

Weiner, Ed. *The Damon Runyon Story*. New York: Popular Library, 1949. (P)

Weiser, Kathy. "Robert Olinger – Killer with a Badge." *Legends of America.com*. (W)

Welsome, Eileen. *The General & The Jaguar: Pershing's Hunt for Pancho Villa*.
New York: Little, Brown and Company, 2006. (P)

White, Owen P. *The Autobiography of a Durable Sinner*. New York: G.P. Putnam's Son, 1942. (P)

_____, "El Paso" *Password*. Vol. XXXVI. pp.55-67, 72. (P)

_____, *Them Was the Days: From El Paso to Prohibition.* New York: Minton, Balch & Company, 1925. (P)

_____, *Out of the Desert: The Historical Romance of El Paso*. El Paso: The McMath Company, 1923. (P)

Newspapers

Abilene Daily Reporter
Abilene Morning News
Brooklyn Eagle
Cambridge City Tribune (Indiana)
Chicago Journal (1909)
El Paso Herald (AKA: El Paso Post, El Paso Herald Post.)
El Paso International Daily Times (1899)
El Paso Times (AKA: *El Paso Morning Times*.)
Frederick News Post (Maryland)
Galveston Daily News
Geneva Gazette (New York)
Hereford Texas Reporter (1901)
La Opinión (Los Angeles)
Logansport Pharos-Tribune (Indiana)
Logansport Semi-weekly Reporter (Indiana)
Lone Star Newspaper (El Paso)
Los Angeles Herald
Lubbock Avalanche-Journal
Manitowoc Herald News (Wisconsin)
Milwaukee Journal
New York Sun
New York Times
New York World
Oakland Tribune
Piqua Daily Call (Ohio)
Portsmouth Daily Times (Ohio)
Salt Lake Tribune
San Antonio Express
San Francisco Call (1901)
The Daily Journal (Telluride ,CO)
Syracuse Herald
The Oregonian (Portland)
The Tombstone Epitaph

Tucson Daily Citizen
Wall Street Journal
Washington Times (1911)
Winnipeg Free Press
Tucson Daily Citizen

Special Collections

Albert B. Fall Family Papers. (MS 0008)
Archives and Special Collections
Branson Library
New Mexico State University
Las Cruces, New Mexico
Burges-Perrenot Papers (MS 262)
Special Collections
University Library
University of Texas at El Paso
Horace B. Stevens Papers. (MS 153)
Special Collections
University Library
University of Texas at El Paso
Kohlberg Family Papers 1575-1895 (MS 369)
Special Collections
University Library
University of Texas at El Paso
Papers of Albert B. Fall 1887 – 1941 (FA boxes 1-109)
Manuscripts Department
Huntington Library
San Marino, California
Sheldon Family Papers, 1854-1899. (M-3116.7, 1995)
Manuscript Division
William L. Clements Library
University of Michigan

Sheldon Family Papers, 1880-1899. (MS 402)
Special Collections
University Library
University of Texas at El Paso
Thomas Wentworth Peirce, Jr. Papers, 1900-1923.
Benson Latin American Collection
University of Texas at Austin

Interviews

Avila, Guillermo (Memo) E. Personal interview. El Paso, TX, 5 August 2011.
Bolton, W.F. Telephone interview. North Granby, CT, 17 March 2011.
Bowden, Celia. Telephone interview. Bronte, TX, 16 November 2013.
Bussell, Richard. Personal interview, El Paso, TX, 20 August 2010.
Cole, Martha. Telephone interview. Richmond, VA, 9 June 2011.
Dawson, Ronald E. Personal interview. El Paso, TX, 9 August 2011.
Dent, Barbara. Telephone interview. El Paso, TX, 24 February 2011.
De La Cruz, Tony. Personal interview. El Paso, TX. 12 April, 2012.
de Wetter, Mardee B. Personal interview. El Paso, TX, multiple dates from 2011 to 2014.
Dipp, Mike, Jr. Telephone interview, El Paso, TX, 20 June 2016.
Eckhardt, Charles F. Telephone interview. Sequin (San Antonio), TX, 26 September 2012.
Foster, Paul L. Personal interview. El Paso, TX, 22 April 2015.
Goodell, Phillip C. Telephone interview. El Paso, TX, 14 March 2011.
Goodell, Grace and Phillip Goodell. Personal interview. El Paso, TX, 5 August 2011.
Harris, Theodore D. Personal interview. Seal Beach, CA, 29 August 2012.
Hendricks, C.M. Personal interview. El Paso, TX, 20 December 1952.
Houghton, E.C. (Ted), IV. Personal interview. El Paso, TX, 26 June 2011
Kligman, Sidney. Personal interview. El Paso 26 July 2006.
McKenzie, Prince C. Personal interview. El Paso, TX, 2 January 2011.
Meed, Michael. Telephone interview. Austin, TX, 5 July 2011.
Metz, Leon C. Personal interview. El Paso, 16 Aug 2008.
Orndorff, Seth, III. Telephone interview. Austin, TX, 7 July 2011.
Owen, Henrietta R. Telephone interview. El Paso, TX, 27 January 2011.

Peirce, Jay. Telephone interview. Topsfield, MA, 13 March 2014.
Posey, Evelyn. Telephone interview. El Paso, TX, 25 February 2011.
Proud, Gay. Personal interview. Newport Beach, CA, 22 July 2011.
Randall, Charles. Telephone interview. Brackney, PA, 22 December 2010.
Rivers, Claudia. Personal interview, El Paso, TX, 15 July 2015.
Russell, Anthony. Telephone and email interviews. 13-15 January 2011, November 13, 2015, February 17, 2016.
Radmacher, Jason. Pastor, Telephone interview. John St. Methodist Church, New York City 13 February 2013.
Wallace, William W., II. Personal interviews: 29 December 2010, El Paso; 24-30 November 2013, Corralitos, Chihuahua, Mexico.
Wallace, William W., III. Personal interviews: El Paso, TX, 17 May, 14 July, 29 December 2010, El Paso; 21 July 2011 El Paso; 18 April, 21 June 2012 El Paso; 25 June 2013 El Paso, ; and 24-30 November 2013, Corralitos, Chihuahua, Mexico.
Williams, Carl C. Telephone interview. Midland, TX, 28 August 2008.
Wittrup, Bert. Telephone interview. Elk Horn, IA, 9 June 2011.

Institute of Oral Histories

DigitalCommons@University of Texas at El Paso:

Burges, Richard. Interview by unknown, May 26, 1934. Contained within MS262 Burgess-Perrenot Papers, Box 25. Special Collections.
Chope, Chester interview by Wilma Cleveland, 1968 "Interview no. 27."
Day, James M. interview by Lori D. Lester, 1978 "Interview no. 639."
Greet, Eleanor interview with Wilma Cleveland, 1968 "Interview no. 35."
Harper, Clarence interview by Wilma Cleveland, 1968 "Interview no. 38."
Kelly, Anne , Elizabeth Kelly, and Mary Kelly Quinn. interview by David Salazar, 1973, "Interview no. 87.1."
Metz, León C. interview by unknown, 1970, "Interview no. 87.2."
Porras, Charles V. interview by Oscar J. Martinez, 1975, "Interview no. 212."
Stamper, Tommy Powers (Mrs.) interview by León Metz, 1968, "Interview no. 44."

Dissertations, thesis, and unpublished documents

Bowden, Jocelyn J. (1952) *The Ascárate Grant.* Unpublished Master's Thesis (History). University of Texas at El Paso.

De Wetter, Mardee B. (1946) *Revolutionary El Paso, 1910-1917.* Unpublished Master's Thesis (History). University of Texas at El Paso.

Dunn, Mary E. *The Jackass Mail Line: From San Antonio to San Diego*. Unpublished paper. n.d. San Diego Historical Society. Accessed 18 August 2015.

Fahy, Anna Louise "Chinese borderland community development: A case study of El Paso, 1881—1909" (January 1, 2001). *ETD Collection for University of Texas, El Paso*

Higdon, Theresa. *The Federal Building: 1892-1936.* Seminar paper, May 20, 1952. Special Collections, University of Texas at El Paso.

Johnson, M.M. (1938) *The San Antonio-San Diego Mail Line.* Unpublished Master's Thesis (History). University of Southern California.

Klaess, William. (2015) *The President of the Whole People: William McKinley's Visit to Texas in 1901.* Unpublished thesis, Department of History. Fort Worth: Texas Christian University.

Langston, Edward L. *The Impact of Prohibition on the Mexican-United States Border: The El Paso-Ciudad Juárez Case*. Unpublished Dissertation (PhD in History) Texas Tech University. May 1974.

Martin, M.J. (1956) *C.E. Kelly: Mayor of El Paso, 1910-1915*. Unpublished seminar paper.(Microfilm 283, Roll 6). University of Texas at El Paso.

Mahon, Emmie Wheaton. (1955) *George H. Giddings and The San Antonio-San Diego Stage Coach Line.* Unpublished paper. Special Collections Department, University of Texas at El Paso.

Mathias, Albert. (1934) *A written declaration of the events surrounding the lease of the Hilton Hotel property.* (formerly the Sheldon Hotel property) to Conrad N. Hilton and the resulting default of said lease. Executed on May 31, 1934. Document

Mathias – Hilton Lease Agreement. El Paso County Clerk's Office. (DR Vol. 00520 Page 215) September 1, 1929.

Nelson, Andrew J. (2010) *Floyd Gibbons: A Journalistic Force of Nature in Early 20th Century America.* Unpublished Master's Thesis (Journalism and Mass Communications), University of Nebraska.

Orndorff, H. (1956) *A History of Hotel Cortez*. Unpublished seminar paper.(Microfilm 283, Roll 6). University of Texas at El Paso.

Tanner, E. C. (1970). *The Texas Border and the Mexican Revolution.* Unpublished Master's Thesis (History). (pdf file 31295004727318, University Library). Texas Tech University.

Taylor, Maj. John J. *Does Anyone Care? Henry O. Flipper and the United States Army.* Unpublished Master's Thesis. Army Command and General Staff College. Fort Leavenworth, KY., 1995.

Thorn, Steven Giddings. (1994) *Col. George H. Giddings: The San Antonio–San Diego Stagecoach Line and other adventures in the great southwest.* Unpublished Master's Thesis (History). University of San Diego.

Index

A

B

C

D

E

F

G

H

I

J

K

L

M

N

O

P

R

S

T

U

V

W

Y

Z

Additional Works by the Author

Non-fiction

The Last Shaman of the Desert: Disillusion, Danger, and Evangelism at ZZYZX.
Mines, Cattle, and Rebellion: The 275-Year History of the Corralitos Ranch.
Going the Extra Yard: An Army Doctor's Odyssey.
The Price Paid for Victory: A Photographic Diary of an Army Doctor in WWI.
It's the Journey: My Life and Unlearned Lessons.

Academic

Dimensions of Human Sexuality: A Comprehensive College Text.
Human Sexuality: A College Student's Guide to Controversial Issues.
Drugs in Society: A Public Health Disaster.
Child Abuse and Neglect: A Handbook for Educators.
Child Abuse and Neglect: Education for Nurses.
Defenses Against Quackery: Consumer Health Protection.
Understanding Venereal Disease: A Programmed Approach.

Documentaries

Undercover Angel: Alan O'Day and the Role of Popular Music in Sexuality.
Nobody Wants to Talk About It: Immunization Against STD.